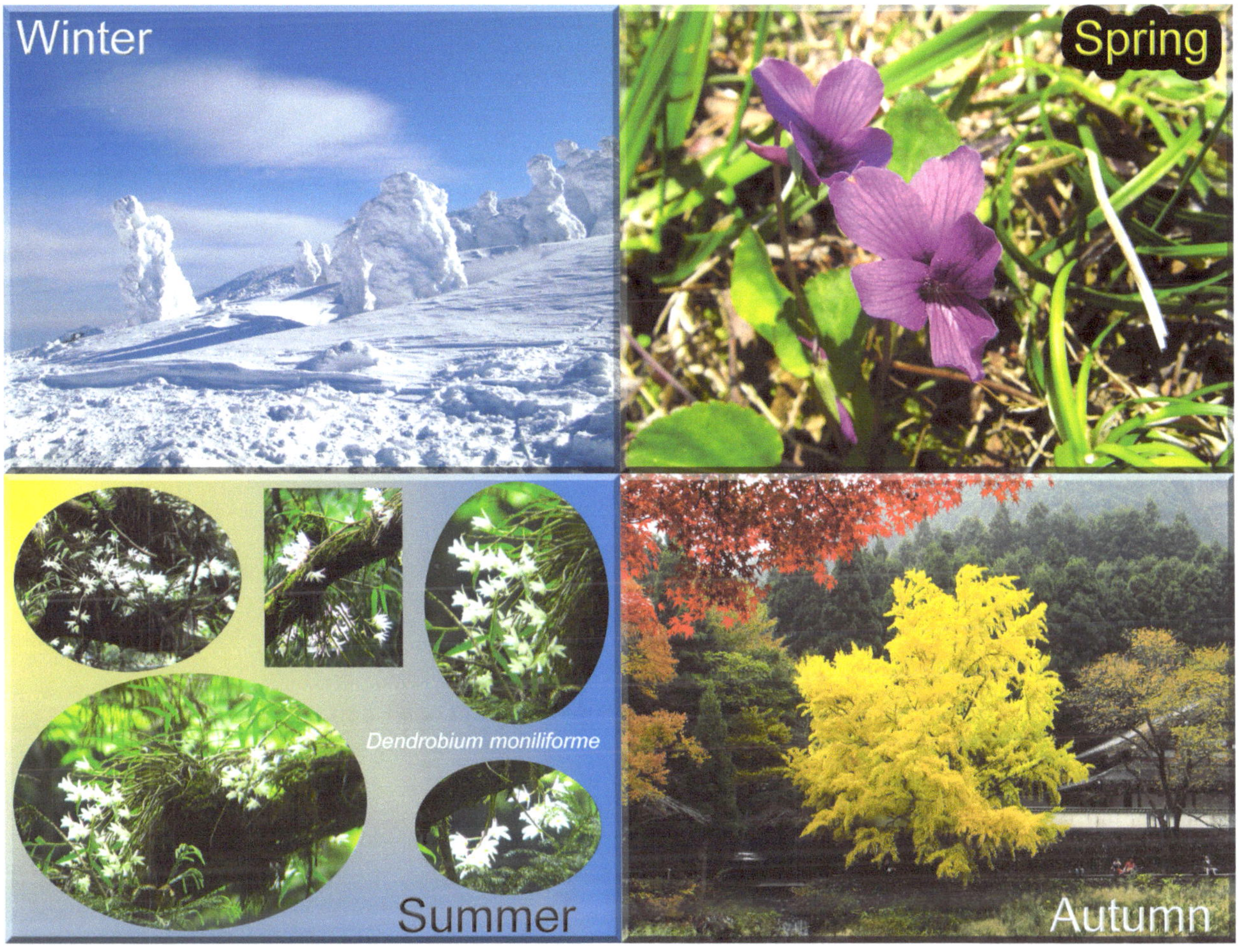

Outdoor Photography of Japan:

Through the Seasons

Daniel & Kazuya Outdoor Photographers

Daniel H. Wieczorek and Kazuya Numazawa

Outdoor Photography of Japan:

Through the Seasons

ISBN-13: 978-0-9962161-0-4
ISBN-10: 0-9962161-0-3

DEDICATION:

This work is dedicated, first of all, to my partner, Kazuya Numazawa. He always keeps my interest in photography up and makes me keep striving for the perfect photo. He also often makes me think of the expression "when the going gets tough, the tough keep going".

Next, I want to dedicate this, and offer a special thank you, to Chad in New York, for his invaluable suggestion about using black backgrounds and white text for pages which start each month.

After that I want to say thank you to Steve and Tim in Oregon and Mike in Australia. They all gave encouragement to us and they all said – many times through the years, that we should create a book of photos of Japan.

Finally, it is dedicated to my mother and father, bless them, for tolerating and even encouraging my photography hobby from the time I was 12 years old, paying for film and processing back in those days and then looking at and commenting on those photos as well as offering suggestions.

Some other books by Daniel H. Wieczorek and Kazuya Numazawa

"English - Ilokano and Ilokano - English Dictionary"; ISBN/EAN13: 1456599720 / 978-1456599720; 100 Pages; March 4, 2011

"English - Ilokano and Ilokano - English Dictionary - With Some Notes on Ilokano Culture"; ISBN/EAN13: 147752276X / 978-1477522769; 150 Pages; May 22, 2012

"A Book of Anagrams - An Ancient Word Game"; ISBN/EAN13: 1468180878 / 978-1468180879; 116 Pages; January 6, 2012

"A Book of Anagrams - An Ancient Word Game - Volume #2"; ISBN/EAN13: 1470015528 / 978-1470015527; 152 Pages; February 2, 2012

"Forest Resource & Allowable Cut - Fairbanks Working Circle (Alaska)"; ISBN/EAN13: 1475056834 / 978-1475056839; 122 Pages; March 23, 2012

"Some Violets of Eastern Japan - 2nd Edition"; ISBN/EAN13: 1499262809 / 9781499262803; 118 Pages; April 26, 2014

"Climbing a Few of Japan's 100 Famous Mountains - Volume 1: Mt. Daisetsu (Mt. Asahidake)"; ISBN/EAN13: 1493777203 / 9781493777204; 66 Pages; December 5, 2013

"Climbing a Few of Japan's 100 Famous Mountains - Volume 2: Mt. Chokai (Choukai)"; ISBN/EAN13: 1494368404 / 9781494368401; 72 Pages; December 8, 2013

"Climbing a Few of Japan's 100 Famous Mountains - Volume 3: Mt. Gassan"; ISBN/EAN13: 149487217X / 9781494872175; 70 Pages; January 4, 2014

"Climbing a Few of Japan's 100 Famous Mountains - Volume 4: Mt. Hakkoda & Mt. Zao"; ISBN/EAN13: 1495396568 / 9781495396564; 88 Pages; January 31, 2014

"Climbing a Few of Japan's 100 Famous Mountains - Volume 5: Mt. Kumotori"; ISBN/EAN13: 1495980529 / 9781495980527; 84 Pages; February 17, 2014

"A Pocket-Size Version of Climbing a Few of Japan's 100 Famous Mountains - Volume 5: Mt. Kumotori"; ISBN/EAN13: 1497444942 / 9781497444942; 90 Pages; March 25, 2014

"Climbing a Few of Japan's 100 Famous Mountains - Volume 6: Mt. Shirane (Kusatsu)"; ISBN/EAN13: 1497303230 / 9781497303232; 80 Pages; March 11, 2014

"Climbing a Few of Japan's 100 Famous Mountains - Volume 7: Mt. Shibutsu"; ISBN/EAN13: 1497539277 / 9781497539273; 80 Pages; April 4, 2014

"Climbing a Few of Japan's 100 Famous Mountains - Volume 8: Mt. Kiso-Komagatake"; ISBN/EAN13: 1499178638 / 9781499178630; 72 Pages; April 18, 2014

"Climbing a Few of Japan's 100 Famous Mountains - Volume 9: Mt. Kitadake"; ISBN/EAN13: 1499786085 / 9781499786088; 62 Pages; June 4, 2014

"Climbing a Few of Japan's 100 Famous Mountains - Volume 10: Mt. Mizugaki"; ISBN/EAN13: 1500235288 / 9781500235284; 70 Pages; June 18, 2014

"Climbing a Few of Japan's 100 Famous Mountains - Volume 11: Mt. Shiroumadake (includes Mt. Shakushidake & Mt. Yarigatake)"; ISBN/EAN13: 1500463884 / 9781500463885; 178 Pages; July 9, 2014

"Climbing a Few of Japan's 100 Famous Mountains - Volume 12: Mt. Tate (Tateyama)"; ISBN/EAN13: 150094632X / 9781500946326; 176 Pages; August 26, 2014

"Climbing a Few of Japan's 100 Famous Mountains - Volume 13: Mt. Yatsugatake (Mt. Akadake)"; ISBN/EAN13: 1502877589 / 9781502877581; 208 Pages; October 22, 2014

Note Well: All above are also available as Kindle Editions.

FOREWORD

The purpose of this book is to show you some places where you can go and see some wonderfully picturesque flowers and scenes during the four seasons of the year in Japan. We shall start with winter and work our way through spring, summer and finally autumn. Many of the photos to be found in this book were taken in Tokyo. You have to understand that Tokyo, Japan is much more than a city. Governmentally it is treated as a separate Prefecture (a state in the USA). Tokyo is 2,187 sq. km (844 sq. mi). The east to west length of Tokyo is about 83 km (52 mi) and the north to south width is about 20 km (12 mi). The elevation ranges from sea level to 2,017 meters (6,617 feet) and this book shall take you to both extremes – nearly sea level to 2,017 meters.

This book will take you as far north as you can go on Hokkaido, the Northern Island, as well as to Akita, Aomori, Fukushima, Gifu, Gunma, Kanagawa, Nagano, Niigata, Saitama, Shizuoka, Tochigi, Toyama, Yamagata and Yamanashi Prefectures.

In some cases a particular place has been photographed in more than one season and in some of those cases we will try to place the multi-season photos on the same or the following page.

All of the photos were taken by us – Daniel Wieczorek and Kazuya Numazawa. If you ever see any of these photographs on display with claims under a different name, please let us know.

We try to get out virtually every weekend, although sometimes we are hampered by poor weather, poor health or some other problem and we end up staying at home.

We hope that you will find some photographs herein which will excite your imagination and make you want to come to Japan and tour around to some of the places you see here.

In some cases we are purposefully vague as to the precise locations where a flower was found. Plant theft is a very real problem in Japan and we are afraid to tell you where we find some of the less common flowers.

By the way, I (Daniel) did all of the writing and Kazuya did a fair percentage of the photography. So, do not be surprised from time to time when you see references such as "Kazuya" and "that's me…".

Table of Contents

Regions & Prefectures of Japan

Hokkaido		Kansai	
Tohoku		Chugoku	
Chubu		Shikoku	
Kanto		Kyushu	

Regions visited in this book are:
Hokkaido, Tohoku, Chubu and Kanto

Prefectures by Region:

Hokkaido: 1. Hokkaido

Tohoku: 2. Aomori, 3. Iwate, 4. Miyagi, 5. Akita, 6. Yamagata & 7. Fukushima

Chubu: 8. Niigata, 9. Toyama, 10. Ishikawa, 11. Fukui, 12. Yamanashi, 13. Nagano, 14. Gifu, 15. Shizuoka & 16. Aichi

Kanto: 17. Ibaraki, 18. Tochigi, 19. Gunma, 20. Saitama, 21. Chiba, 22. Tokyo & 23. Kanagawa

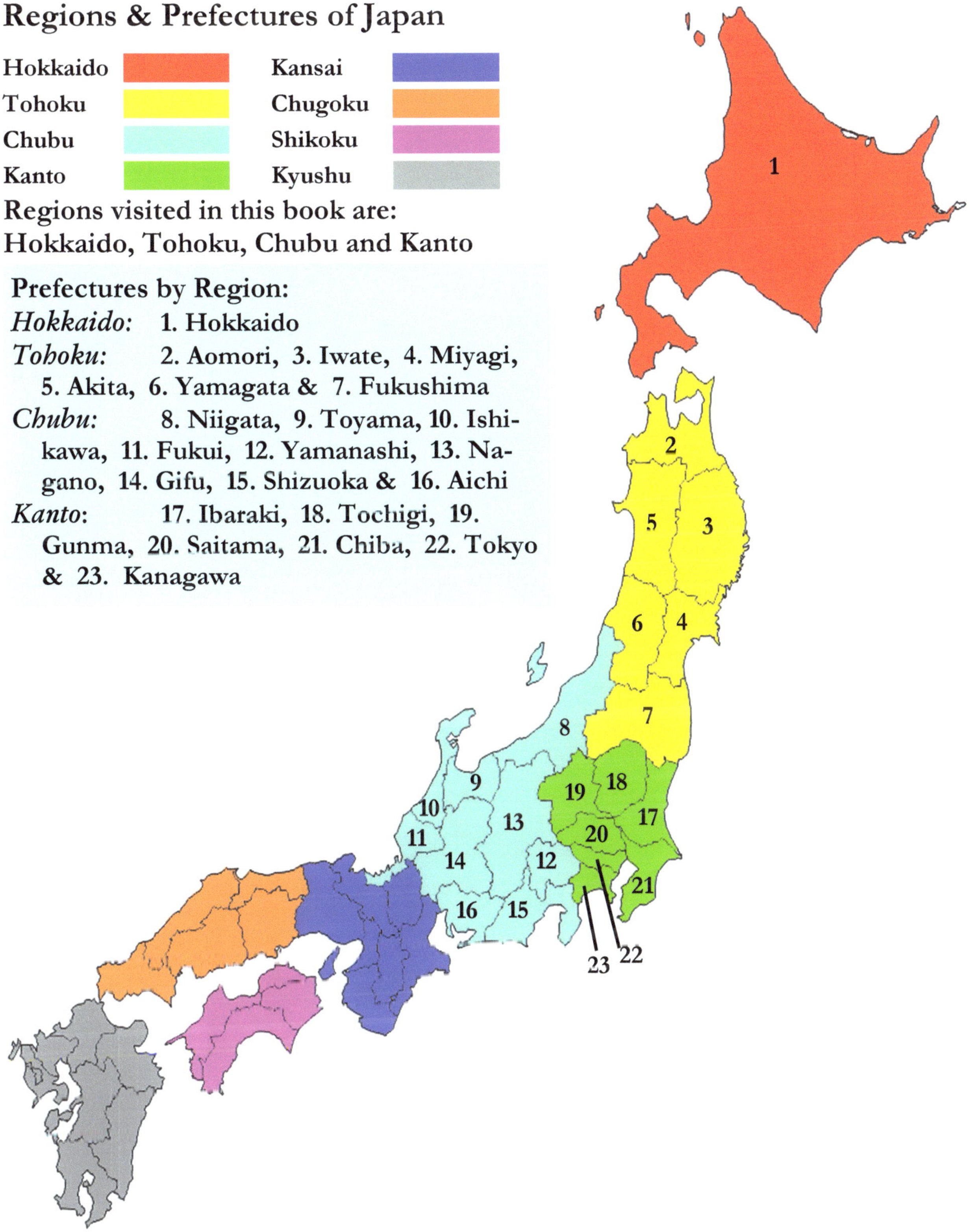

PART 1: WINTER

These photos of **Frost Flowers** were taken at **Mt. Takao** (**Takao-san**) (599 meters = 1,965 feet) on or about December 21st – the first day of winter. These incredible things occur on the stems of ***Keiskea japonica*** (***Shimobashira*** in Japanese) (no English common name). You may ask how they form. It appears that water, or perhaps the sap, within the stem may freeze, which causes the stem tissue to burst like a frozen water pipe, and this allows the water or the ice to extrude outward. As the moisture within the stem freezes, it pushes outward like toothpaste from the tube, thus forming the ribbon-like pattern common to many of these formations. As it extrudes, the ribbon may curl and loop as gravity and other forces affect the process.

Note the amazing shapes to be found.

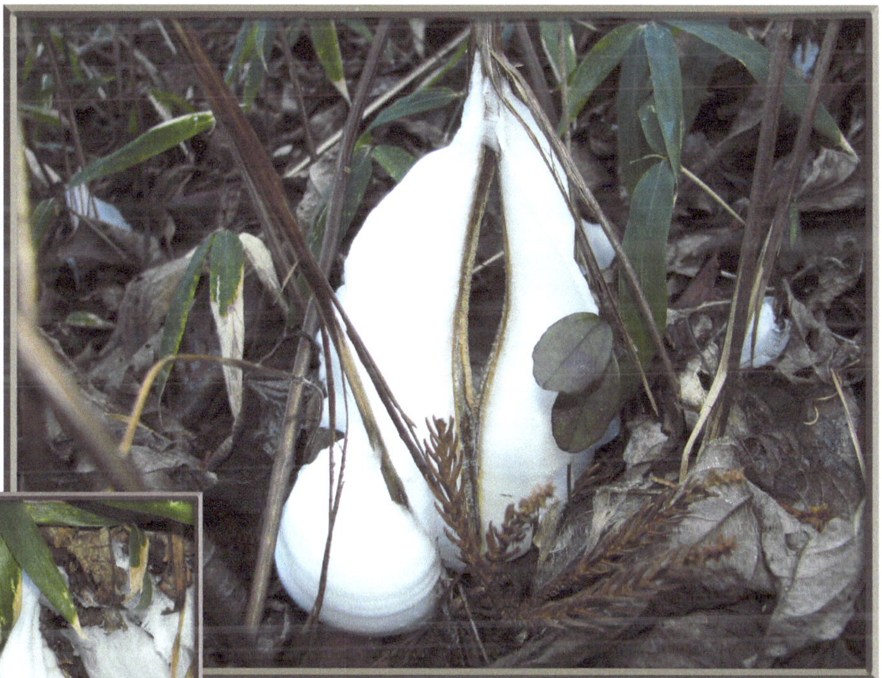

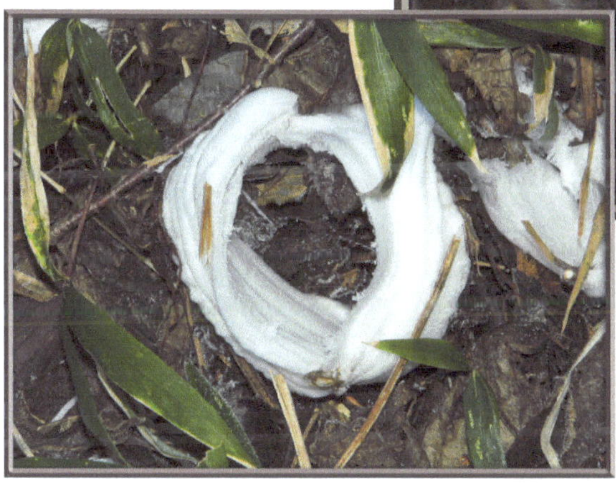

Overleaf: Two more **Frost Flowers**. The height of the one on page 3 is about 45 centimeters (18 inches) in height.

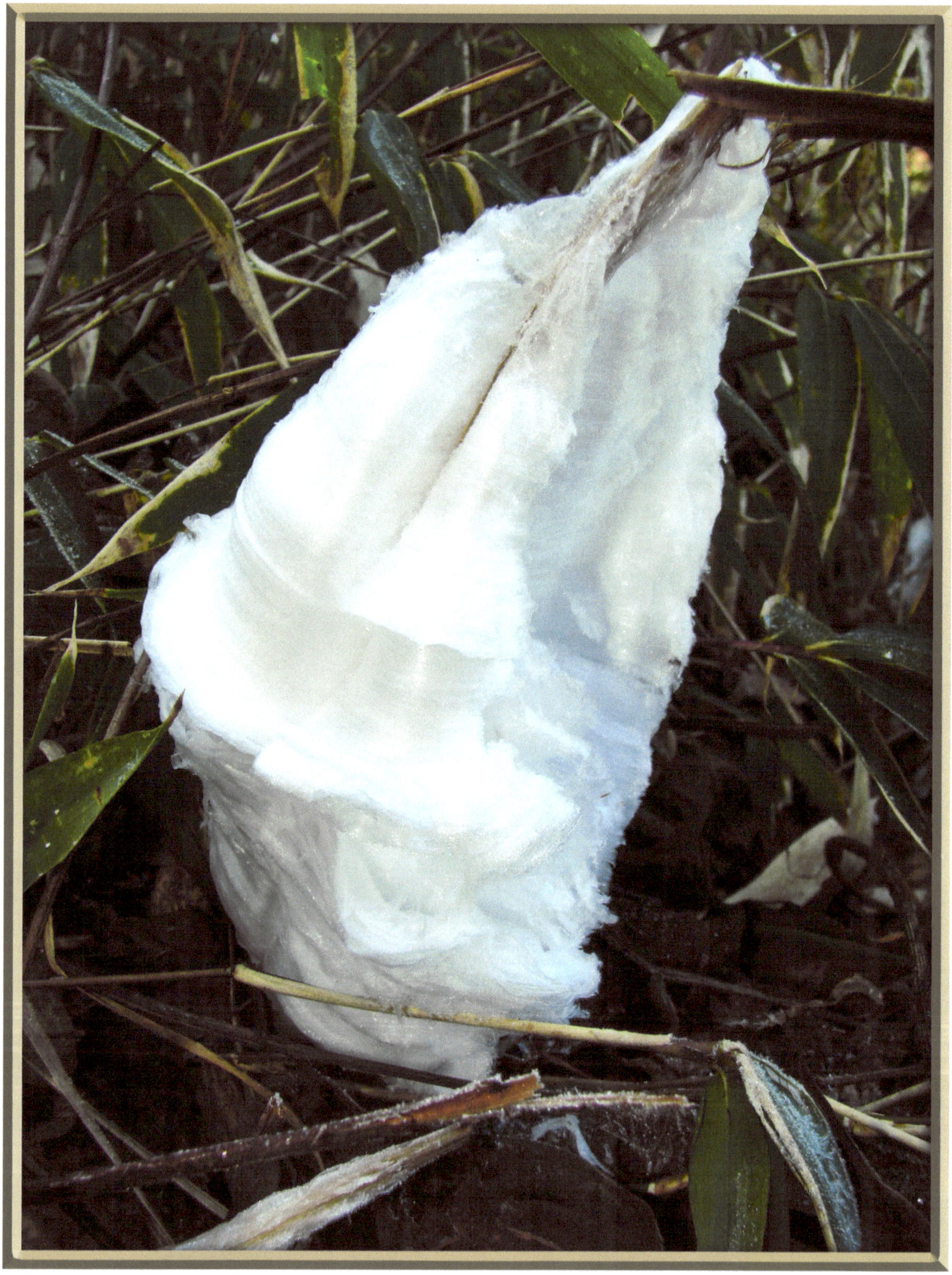

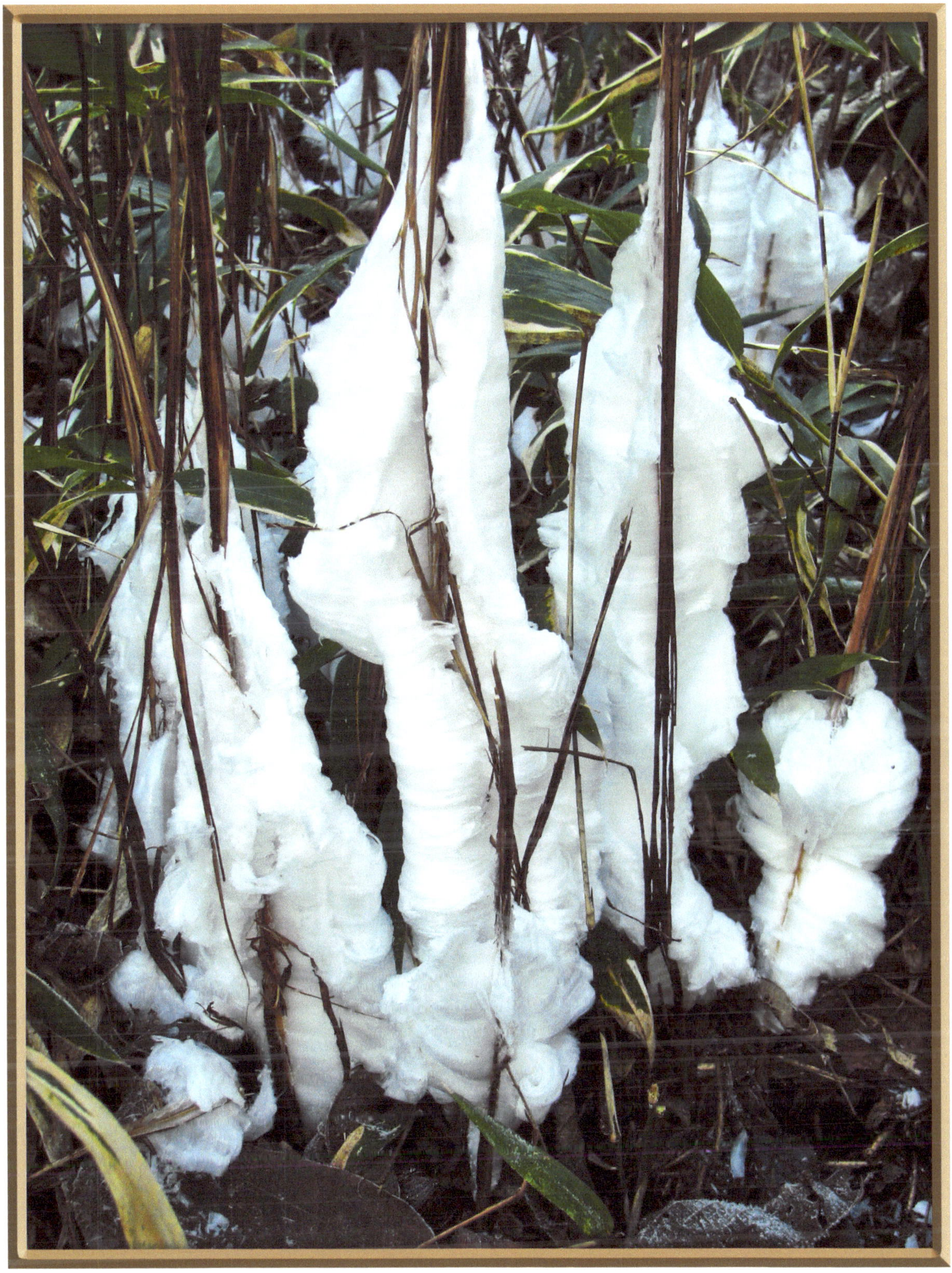

On the same day that we find frost flowers at **Mt. Takao (Takao-san)** we also can usually see a phenomenon called ***"Diamond Fuji"***. This is the day when the sun sets directly behind **Mt. Fuji** from this location. It usually happens very close to the winter solstice.

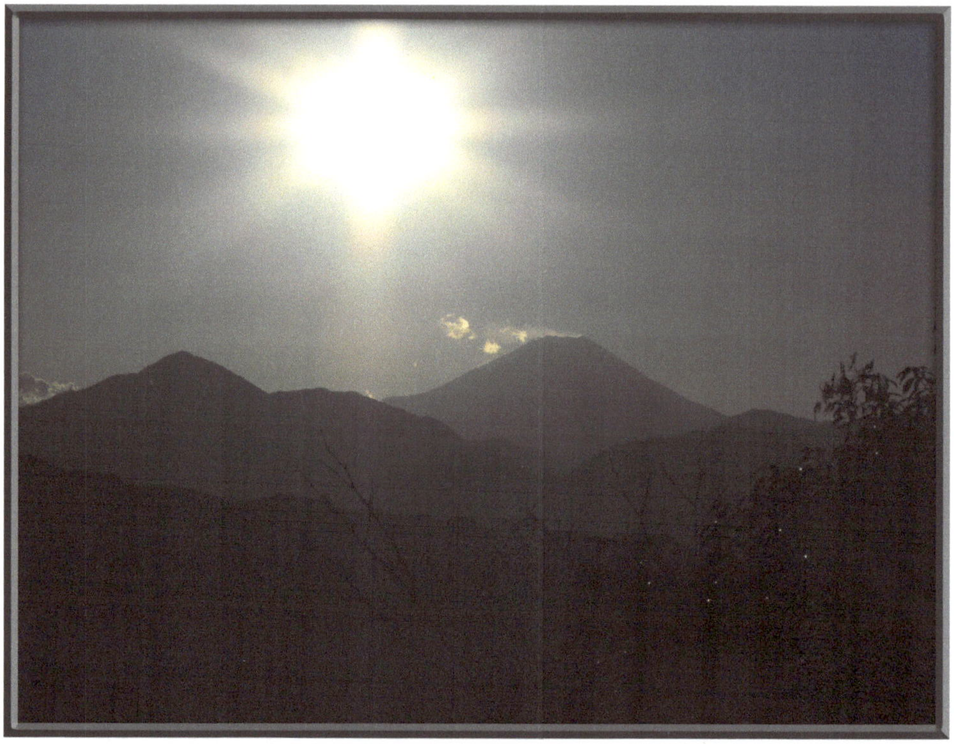

Note how far to the left of **Mt. Fuji** the sun is in the upper photo. It is amazing that the second photo was taken just twenty-four minutes later – on the same day.

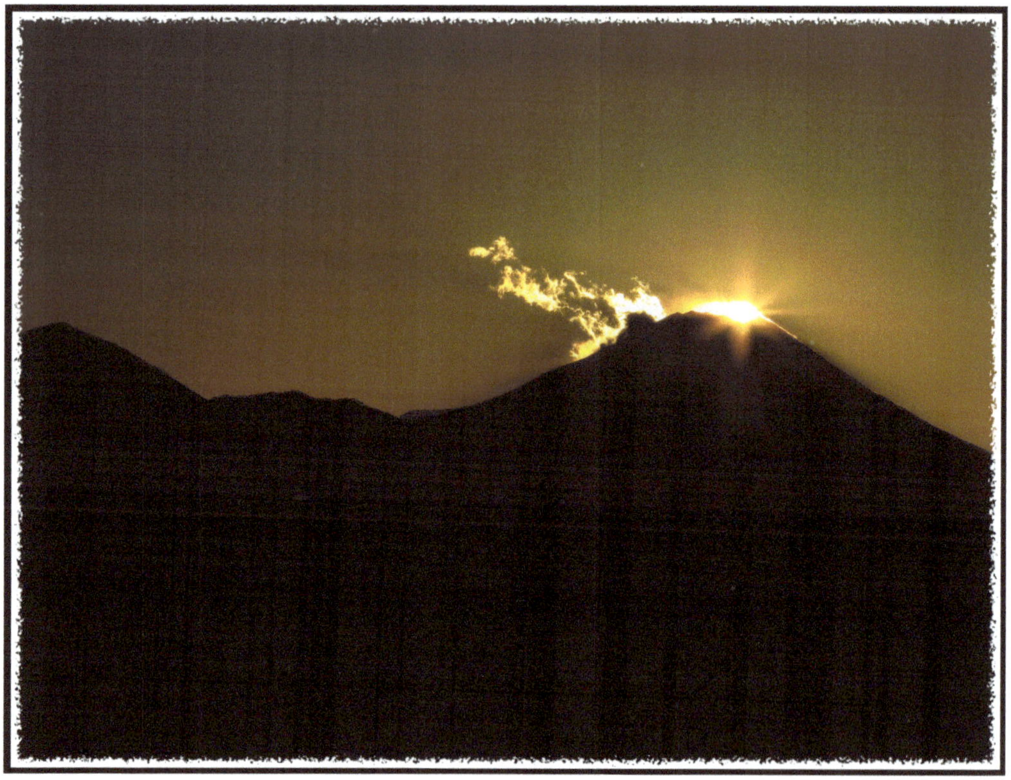

Here are two very snowy shots taken at **Tsuru-no-yu** (**Hot Spring of the Crane**) in **Akita Prefecture**. This is a very wonderful place to go for a winter holiday. There are several hot springs here. The one shown here is the largest one and the only one which is outdoors. The photo below shows some of the hot spring buildings.

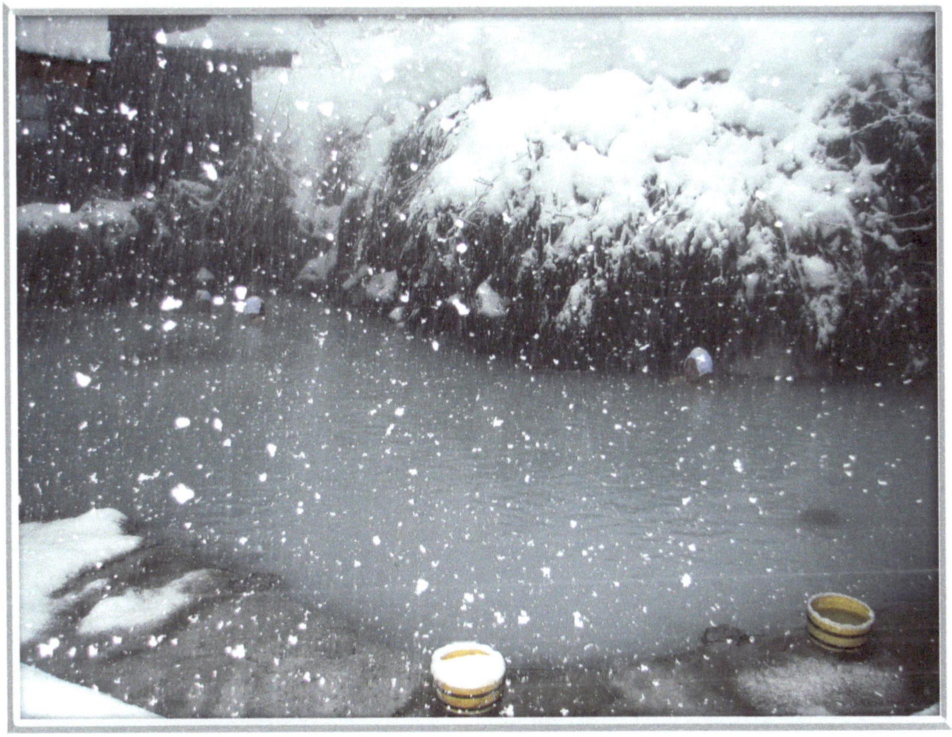

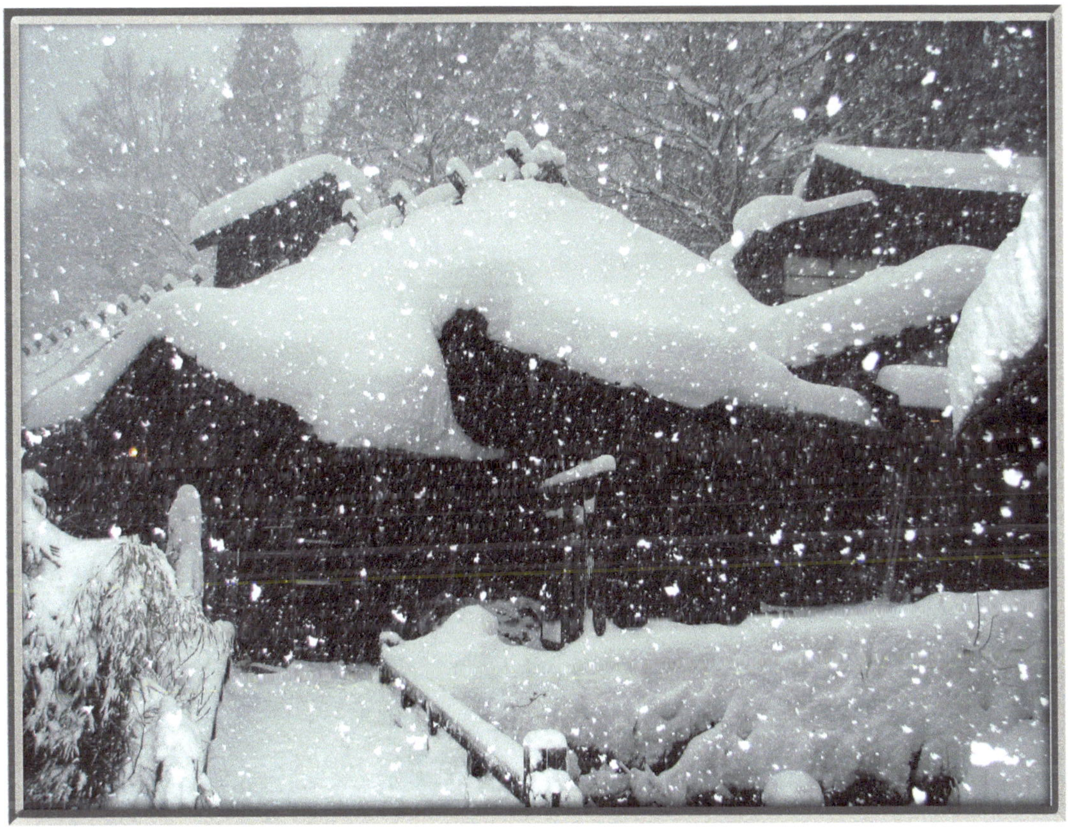

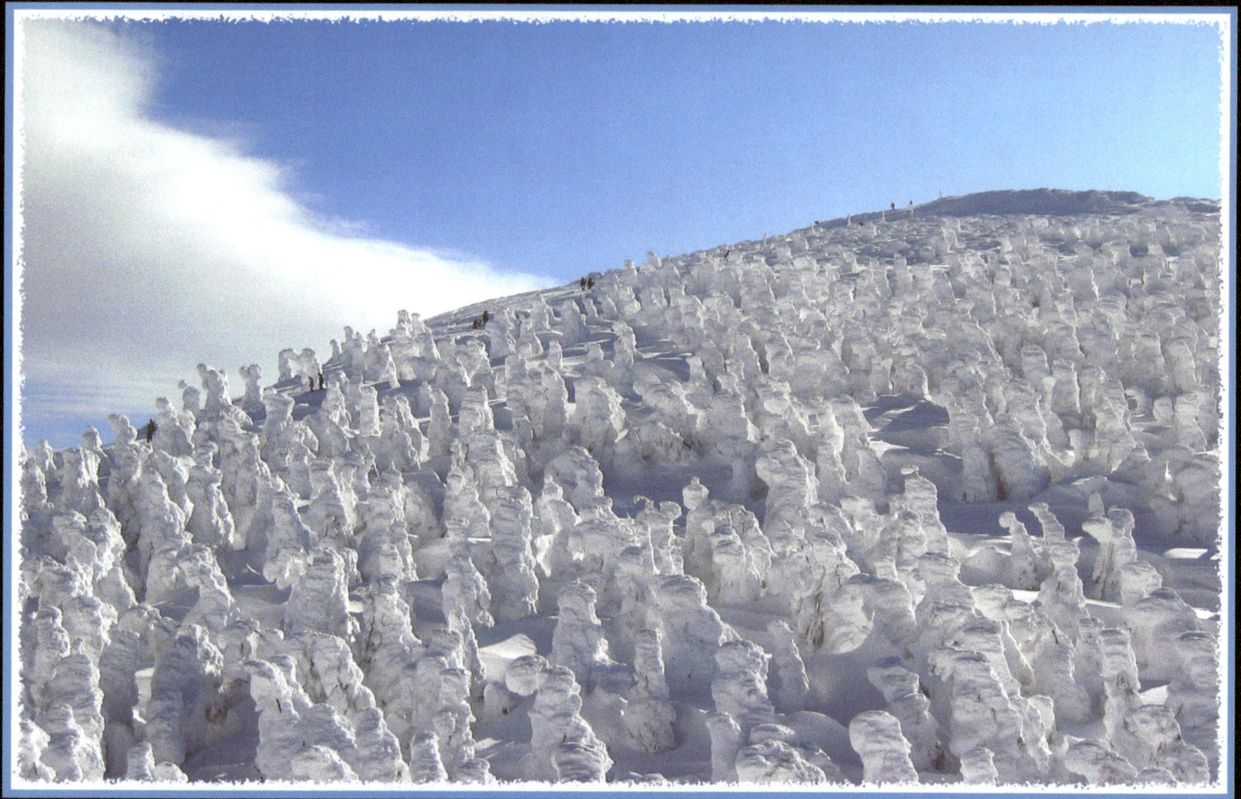

January Photos and Story

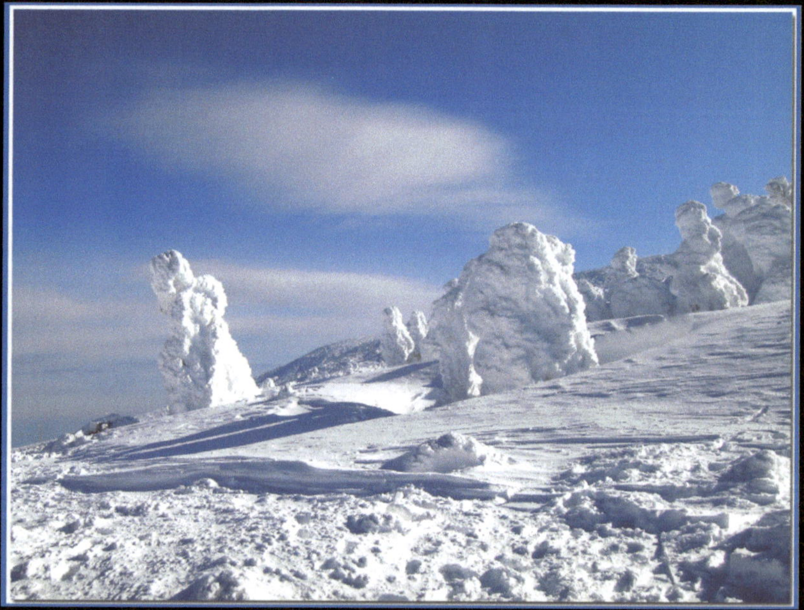

These photos were taken at **Mt. Zao** (1,841 meters = 6,040 feet) in **Yamagata Prefecture**. **Mt. Zao** is famous as a ski resort and also famous for the scenic "snow monsters" which occur on the trees when winter weather conditions are proper. These "snow monsters" are a rime and hoarfrost phenomenon and they can accumulate to three or more feet (= 1+ meter) thick on the trees. In the picture above you should notice the skiers for scale.

If you are a skier then this is a great place to go for a ski adventure with a little extra – not every ski area has these scenic "snow monsters". The Japanese term for "snow monster" is ***"Ju Hyou"***.

Facing page: A final "snow monster" photo.

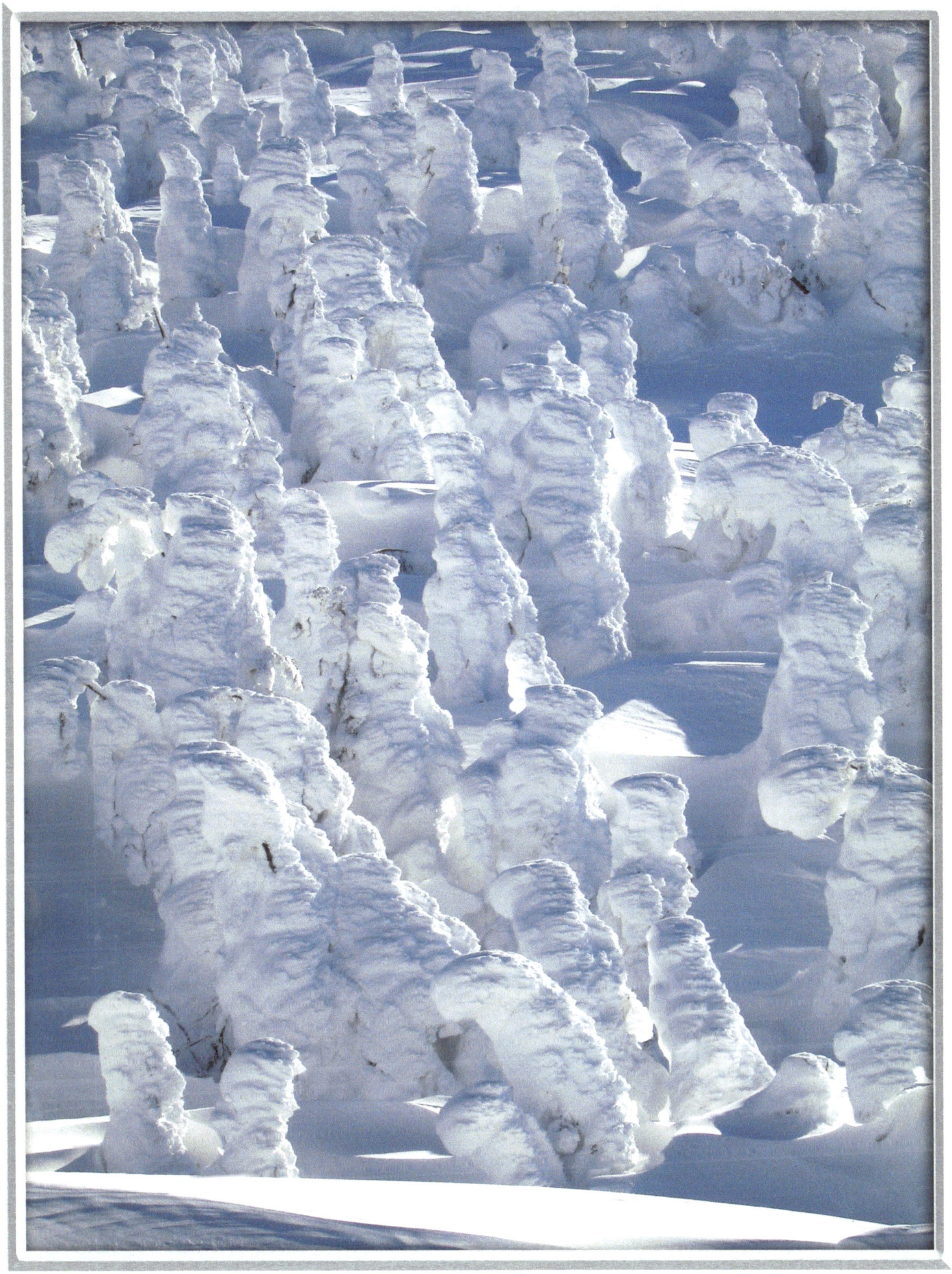

Ginzan Onsen is an **Onsen (Hot Spring)** area in **Obanazawa, Yamagata Prefecture**.

Just below is a black and white photo of **Ginzan (Silver Mountain) Onsen**. The name originates from a silver discovery in this area around 500 years ago. Very graceful and picturesque three and four-story wooden inns line the banks of the **Ginzan-gawa**, or **Ginzan River**. The promenade here is lit by gas lamps and it presents a stunning view as the lamps reflect off the river at sunset and at night.

There are several therapeutic Hot Springs here. The water is milky-white, and is supposedly particularly effective for curing exhaustion and relieving stress. The **Ginzan Hot Springs** are hotter than most, reaching temperatures over 55° C (131° F). These hot springs will warm you to the very core and keep you warm after you get out, so they're especially great for people who have trouble with cold temperatures.

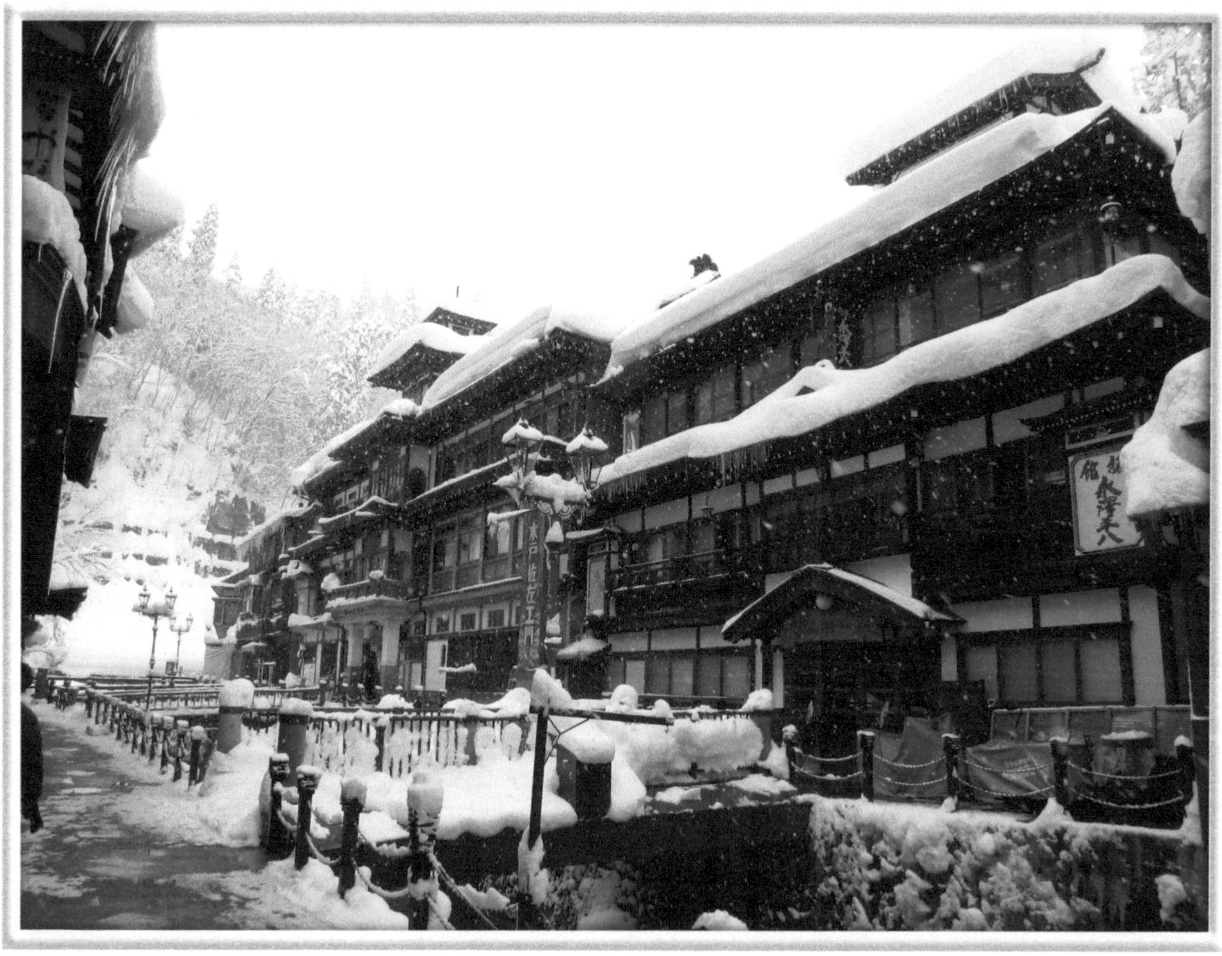

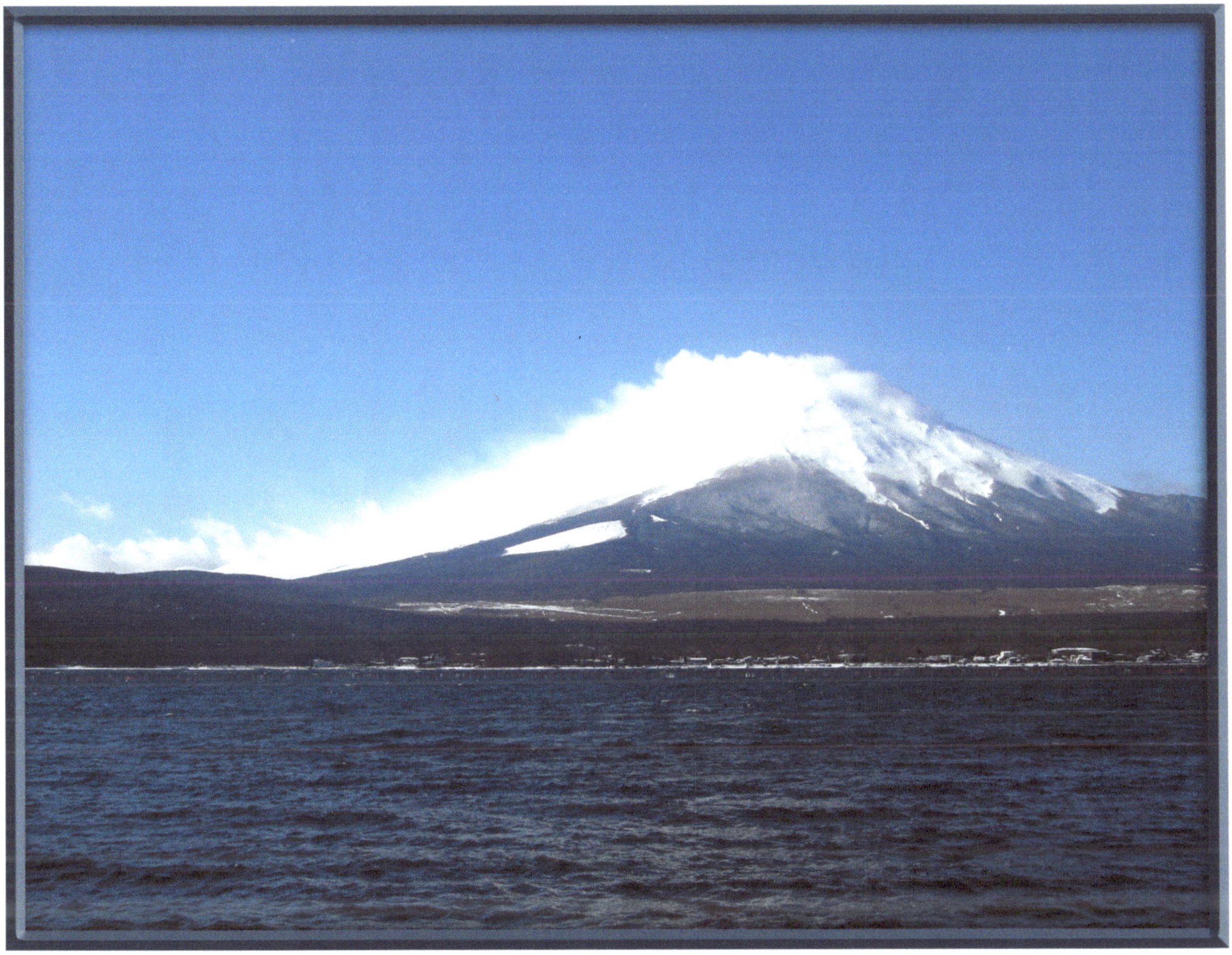

The photo above is one of **Yamanaka Lake** – one of the group of the "Mt. Fuji 5 Lakes". The 5 Lakes include Lake Kawaguchi – the most famous of the group – Lake Motosu, Western Lake (Saiko), Lake Shoji and of course – Yamanaka Lake.

This photo was taken on January 7th. It was a bright sunny day, but the wind was howling around **Mt. Fuji** and it was also blowing pretty terribly right here where we were standing. It was cold and we were a bit miserable. This is the north side of **Yamanaka Lake**. Early in the morning it is fun to witness the sunrise from here. At that time of the day the lake is generally mirror calm and of course Mt. Fuji is perfectly reflected in the lake.

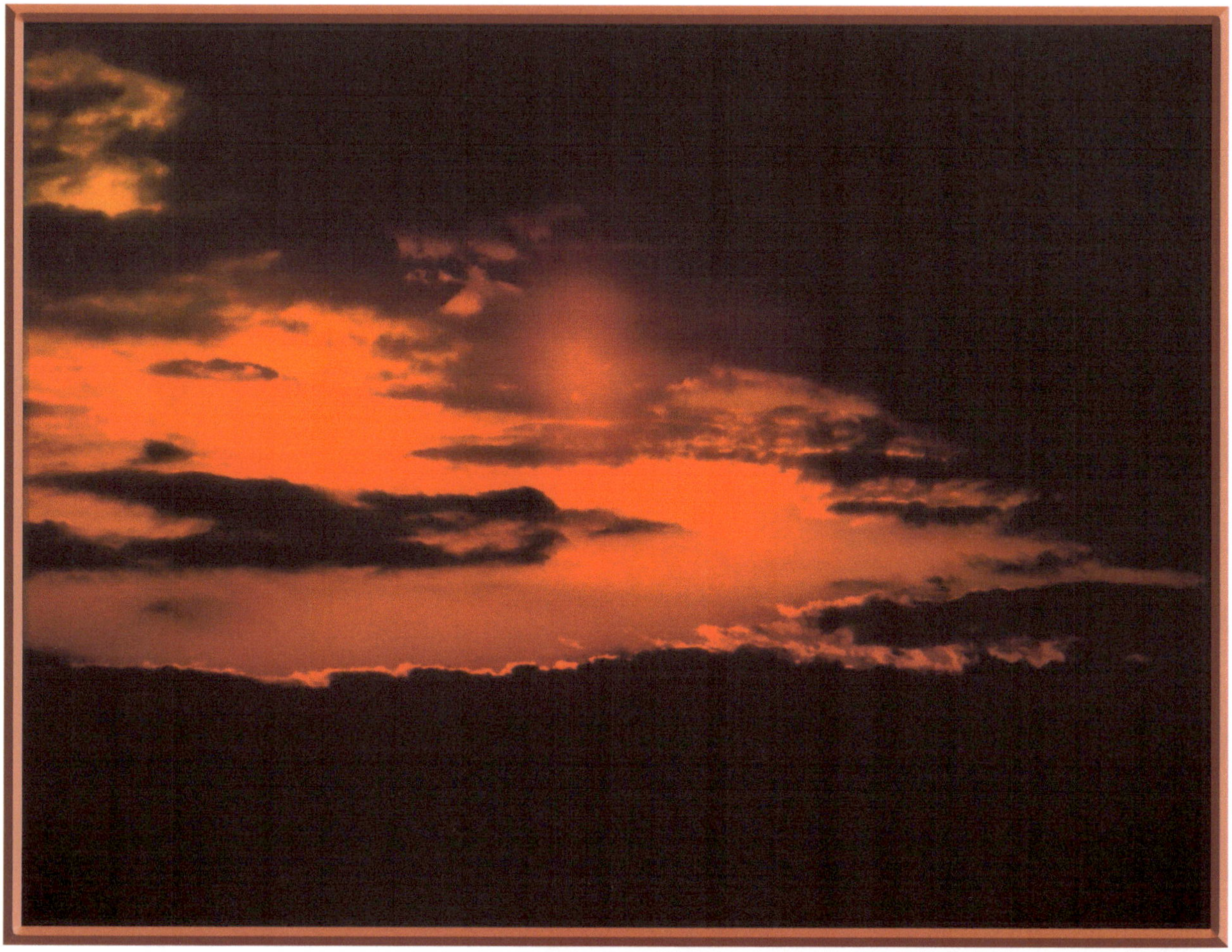

Here is something which you don't see every day. The bright red spot in the above photo is a partial ***"sun pillar"***, as is the column of red above the sun in the photo to the right.

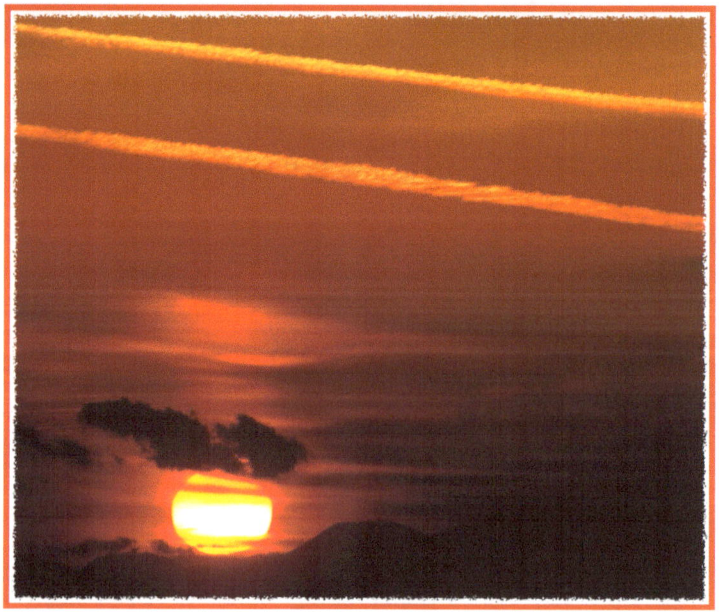

Sun pillars are a phenomenon created by sunlight reflecting off of distant falling ice crystals. The ice crystals have near horizontal parallel planar surfaces.

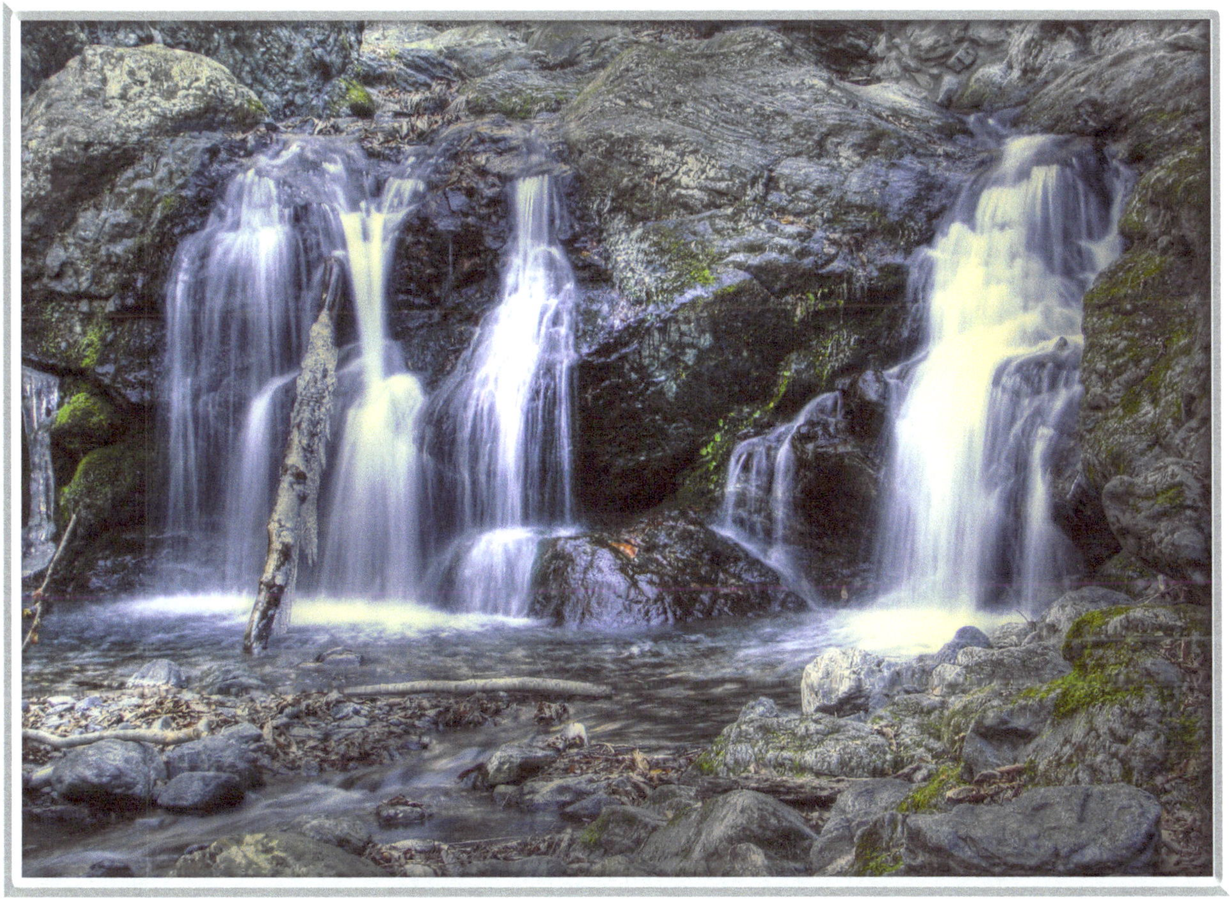

The photo shown above was taken on a trail which leads to **Mt. Kawanori**, a 1,364 meter (= 4,474 feet) mountain in Western Tokyo. There are several small and medium sized waterfalls along this trail. This photo was taken on a cloudy winter day as we were hiking this trail up to the largest waterfall – **Hyakuhiro Waterfall**.

The photos on the next two pages show you **Hyakuhiro Waterfall** in winter and in summer. This waterfall is 30 – 40 meters in height; there is no definitive height information published.

Both the winter photo and the summer photo show a person for scale. In the winter photo you will surely notice the large ice cone at the bottom of the falls. Also, notice the large rock near the person. This rock fell from the cliff sometime after the summer photo was taken.

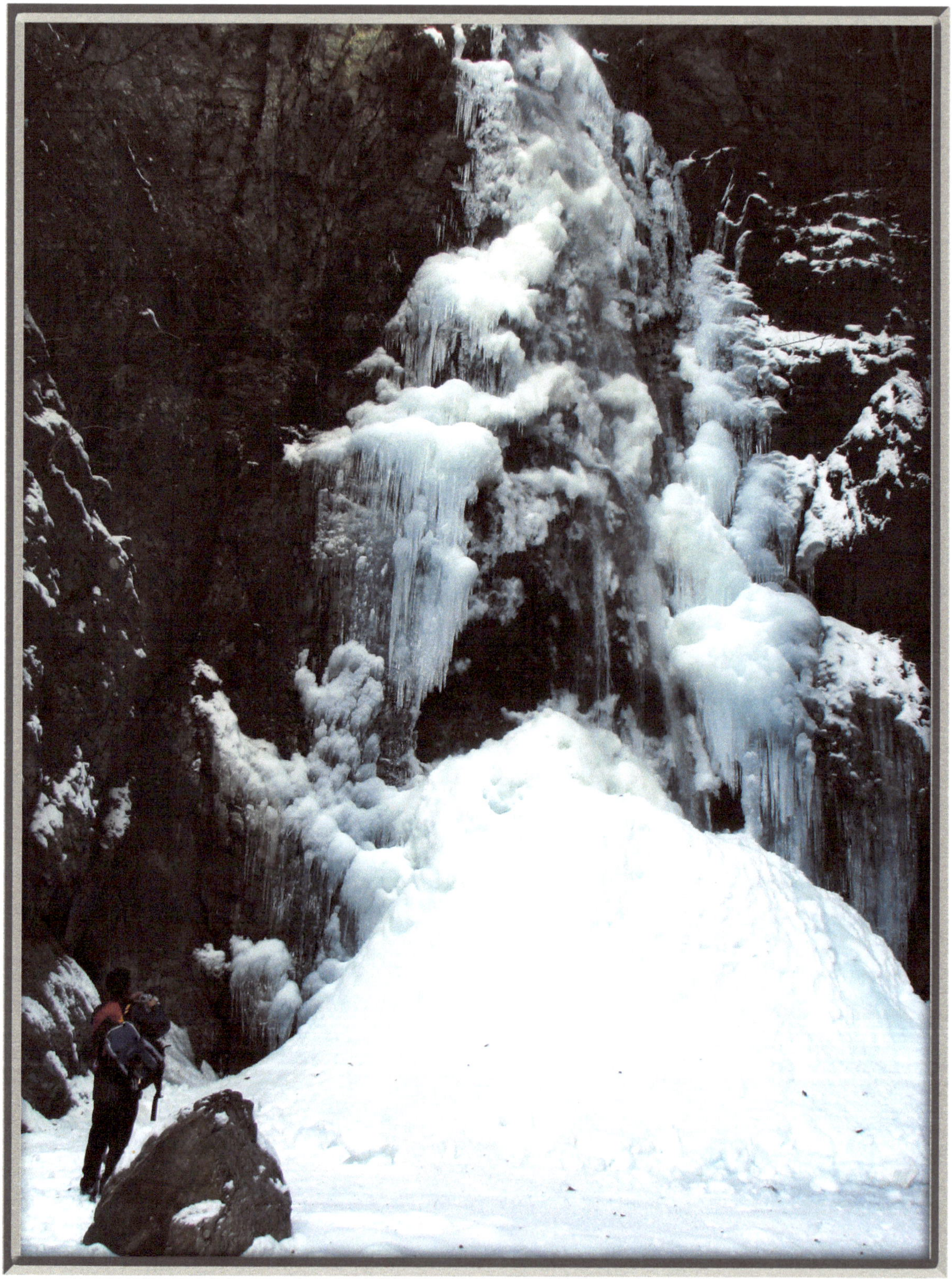

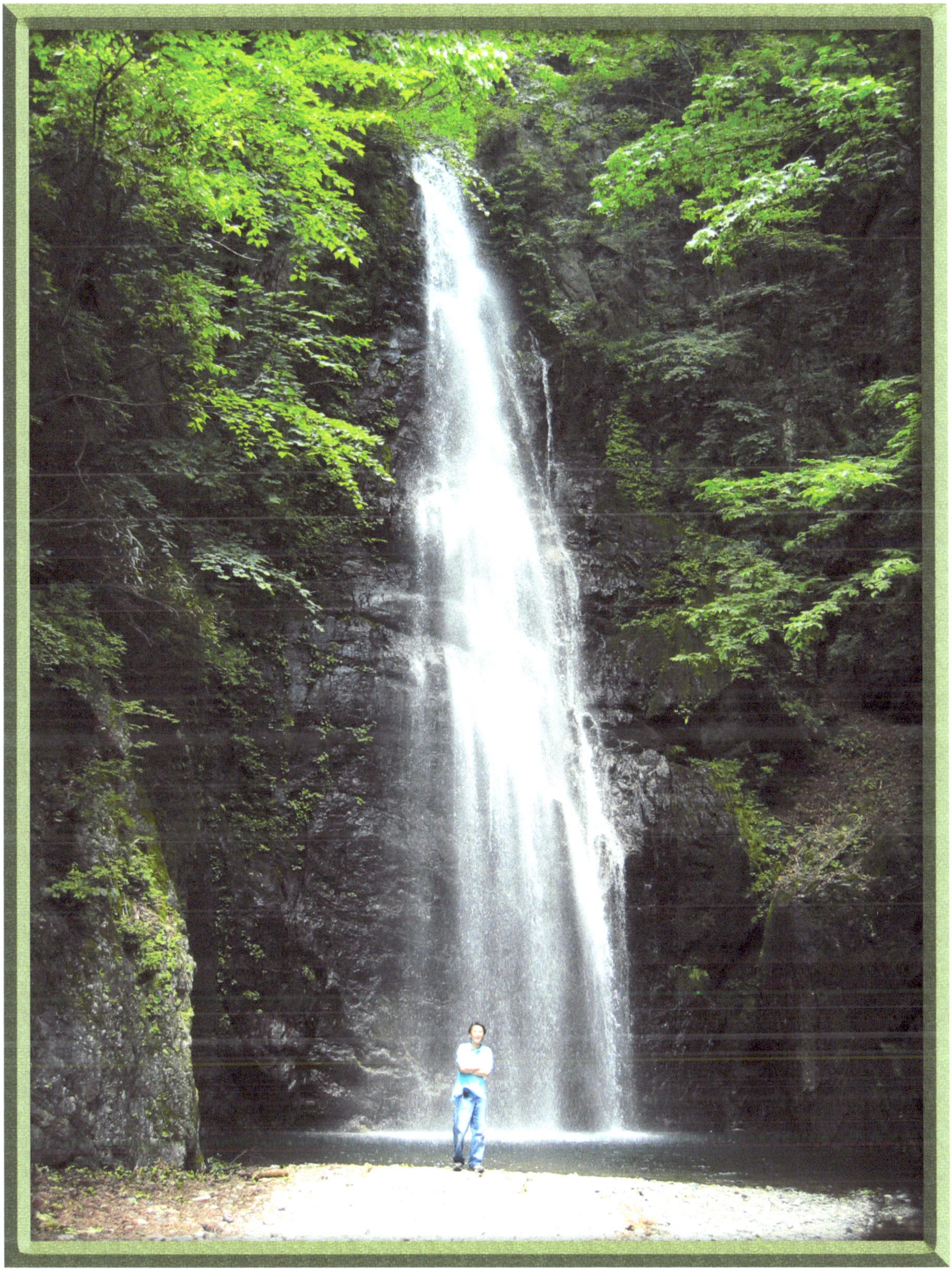

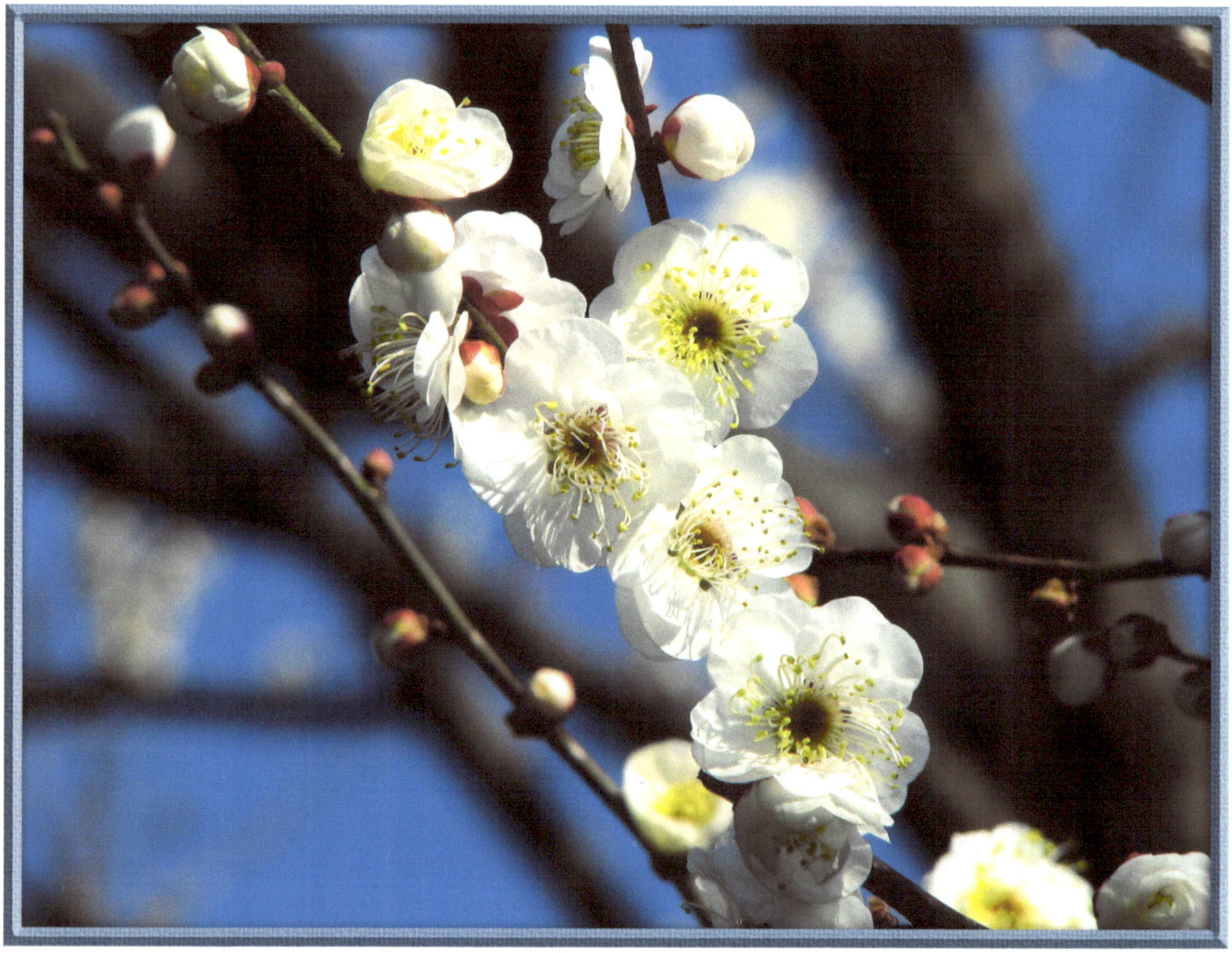

The above photo is a beautiful white **Plum Blossom** (***Prunus* sp.**). Plum blossoms can be found around the Tokyo area from about mid-January through mid-March or thereabouts. This photo was taken at **Jindai Botanical Garden**.

The facing page photo exhibits a beautiful pink Plum Blossom, also at **Jindai Botanical Garden**.

The photo on page 16 shows the pond at **Jindai Botanical Garden**. The coniferous trees have their snow protectors on them. The purpose of these ropes is, as the name implies, to protect the trees from heavy snowfalls. The heavy snows would break the branches. Of course the ropes do not catch all of the snow, but they catch enough so that the branches do not break. In the Tokyo area snow is not common and when it falls it is very wet and heavy and generally melts in a day or two.

And that ends the photos which we want to show you from January.

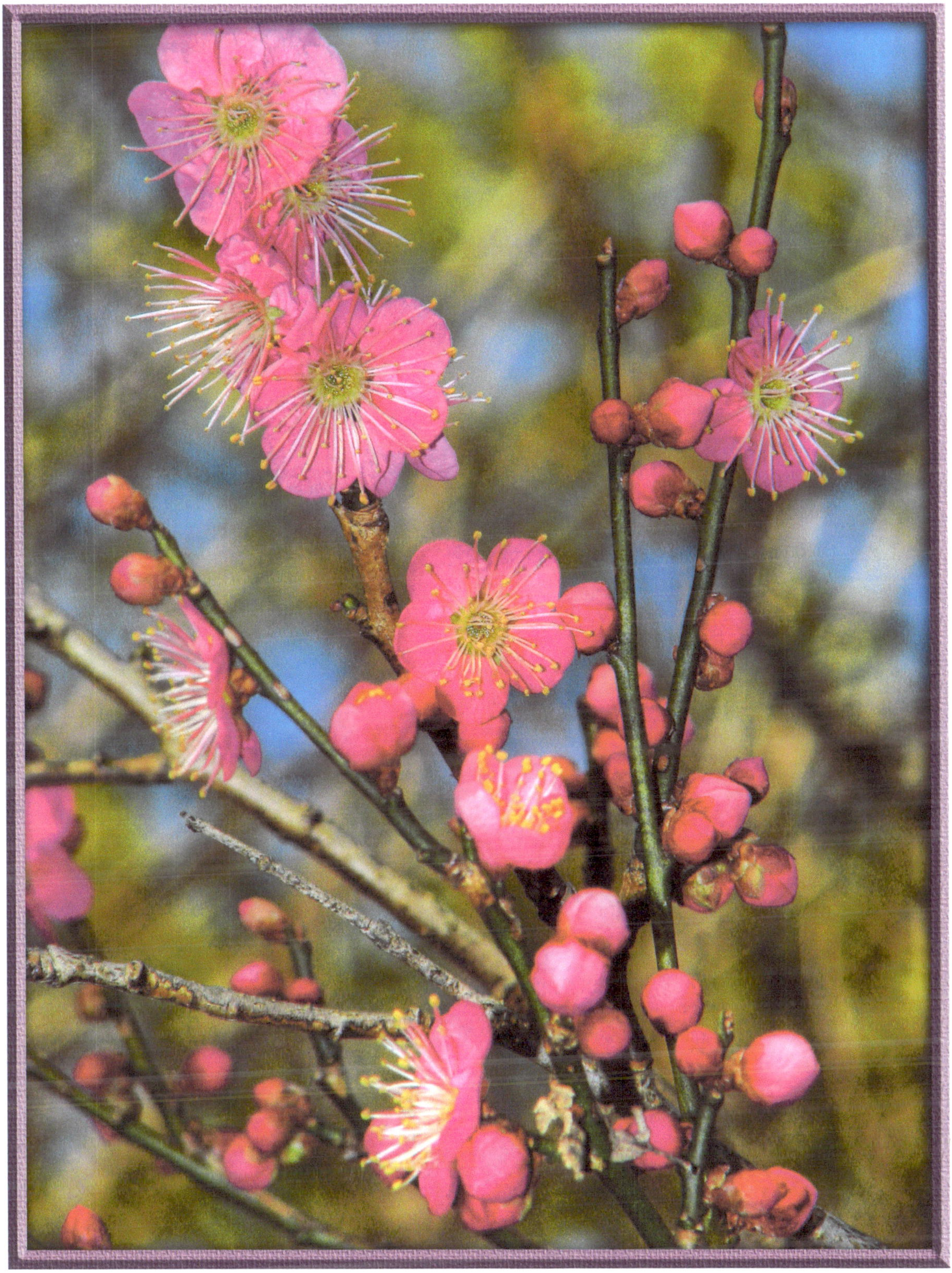

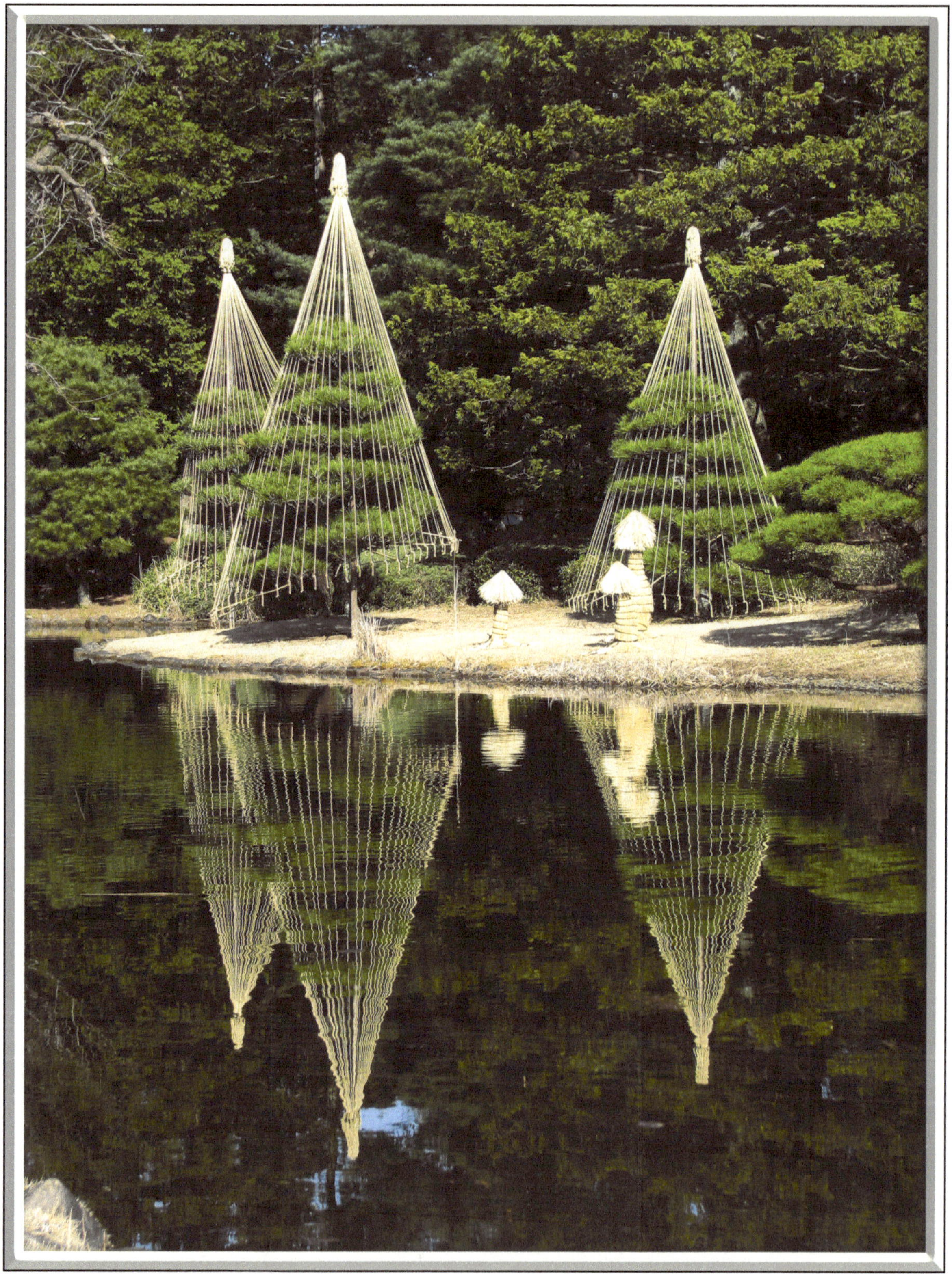

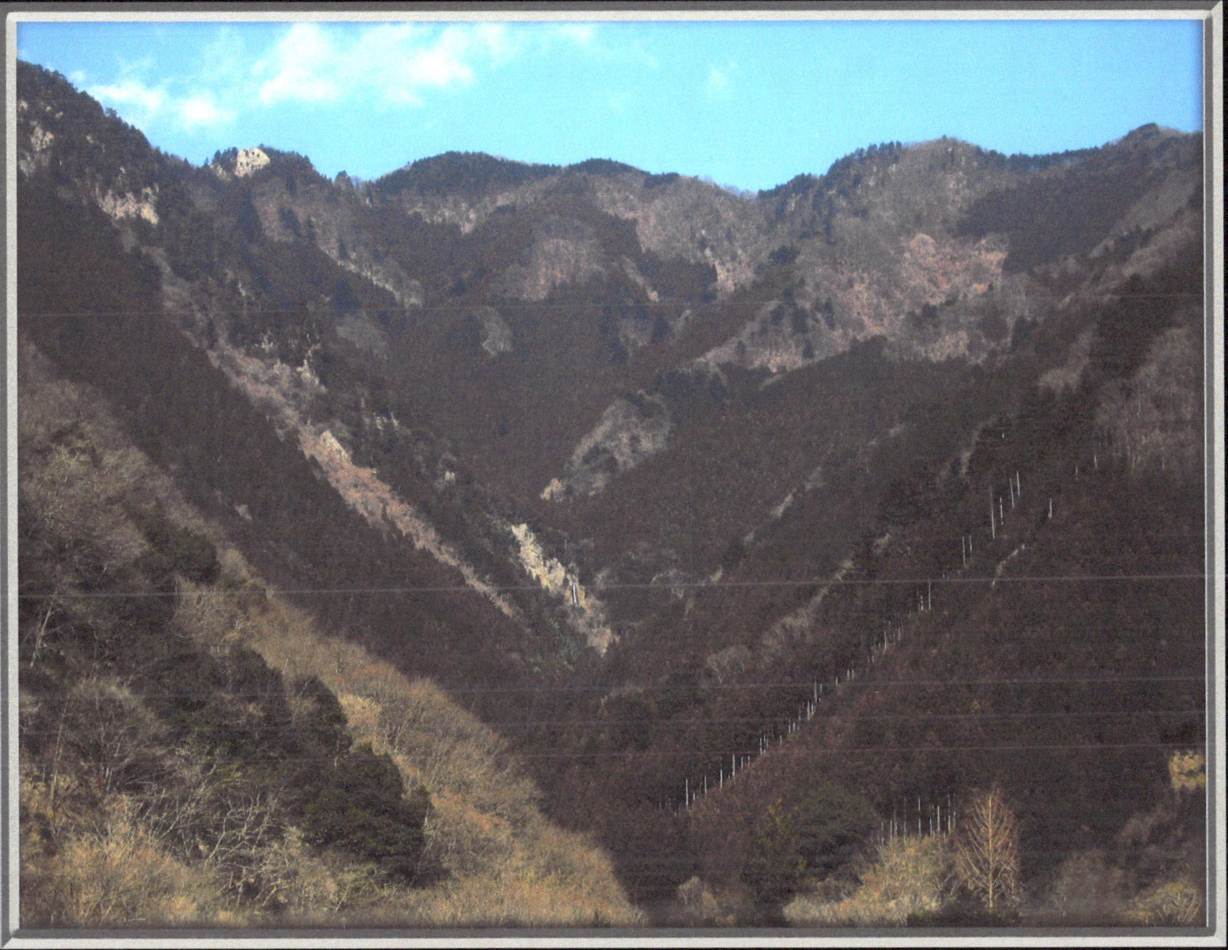

February Photos and Story

Here is a photo which was taken in early February near **Hinohara**, in **Far Western Tokyo**. Isn't this just the prettiest small valley you can imagine? It is to us. Can you find the waterfall up there just a little bit below the center of the photo? That is **Tengu Waterfall**. We hiked up this valley later in the season on a search for spring flowers and we will show you a photo of the waterfall from up close at that time.

If you are going to spend the next hour searching for the waterfall then we'll show you where it is. It shows up quite well through binoculars.

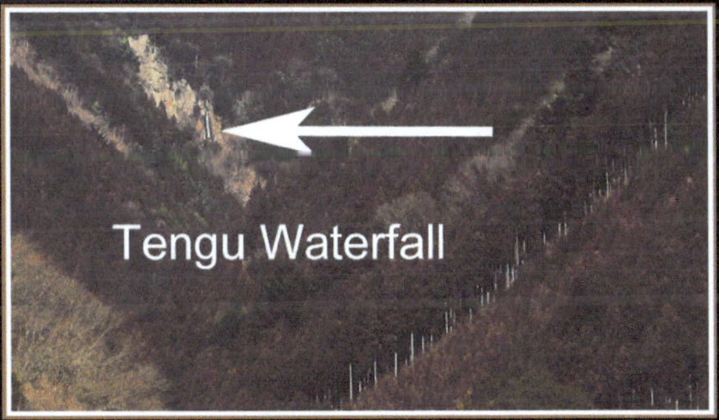

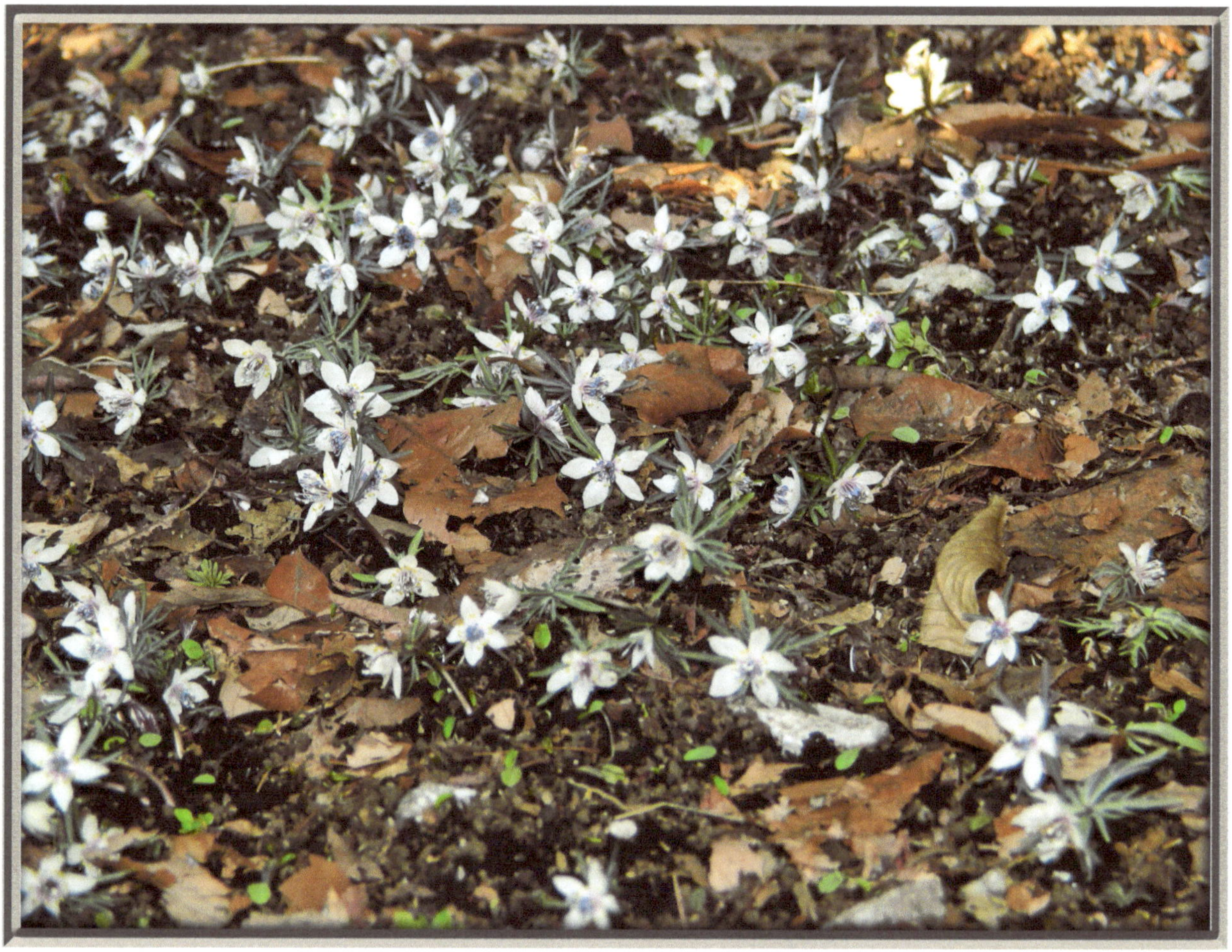

The photo above and the two photos on the facing page, taken in **Nogawa Park**, are ***Shibateranthis pinnatifida*** (***Setsubun-sou*** in Japanese). This is the very first small ground flower which we find around the Tokyo Area. We sometimes find the first flowers as early as the second week of January, but they do not peak around the Tokyo Area until later on in February. In the mountains they do not peak until late March. When we find this flower it is always a rather exciting day because it indicates that spring will be coming again one of these days relatively soon.

The above photo shows quite a large patch of this plant. The upper photo on the facing page shows a nice accumulation in a small space. The lower photo on the facing page is the most perfect specimen we have ever seen. The yellow objects are the nectaries – note the perfect circle in which they are arranged.

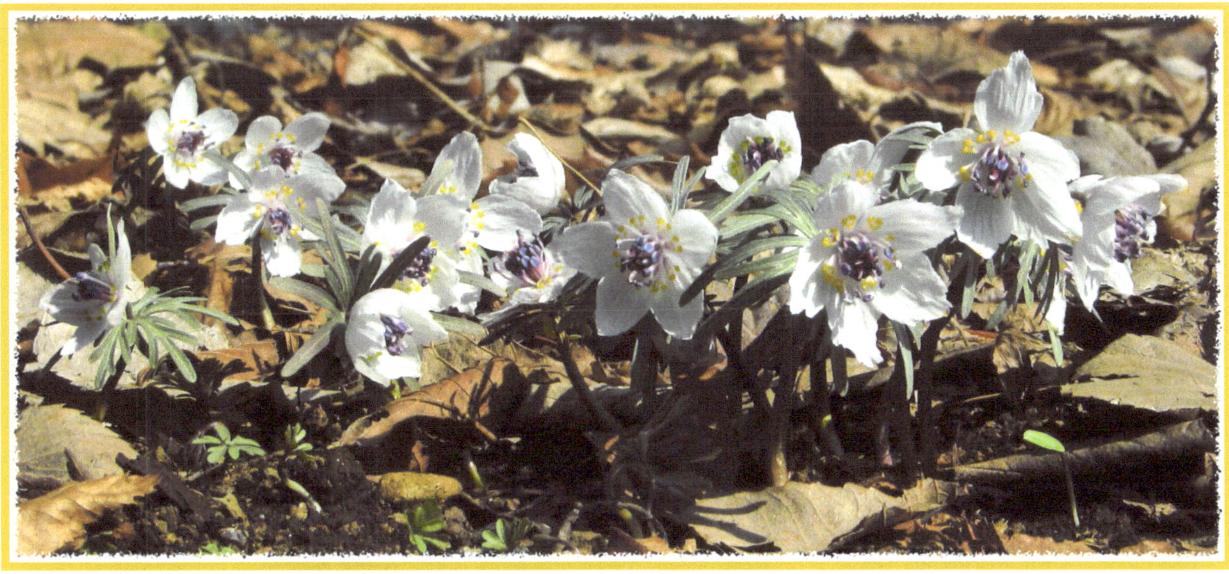

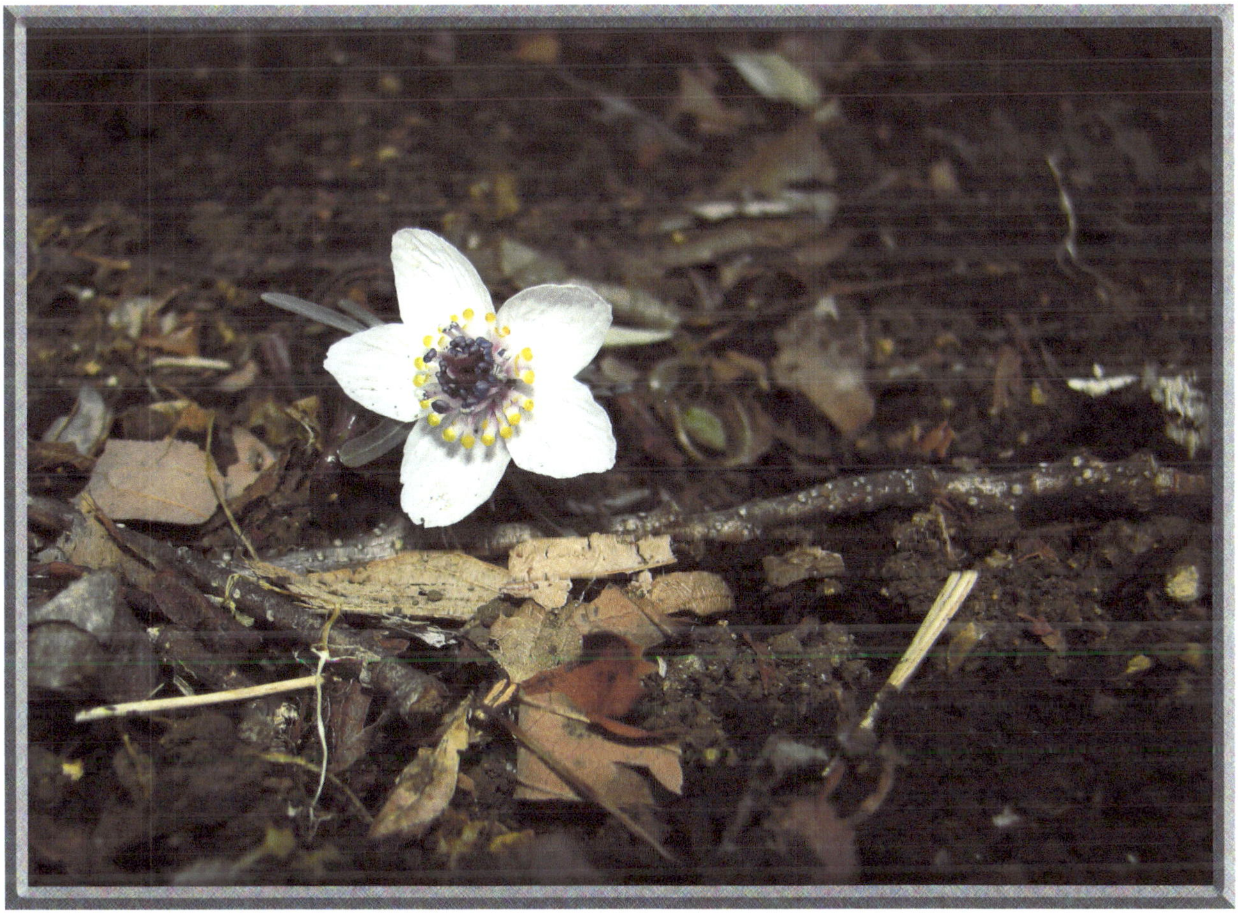

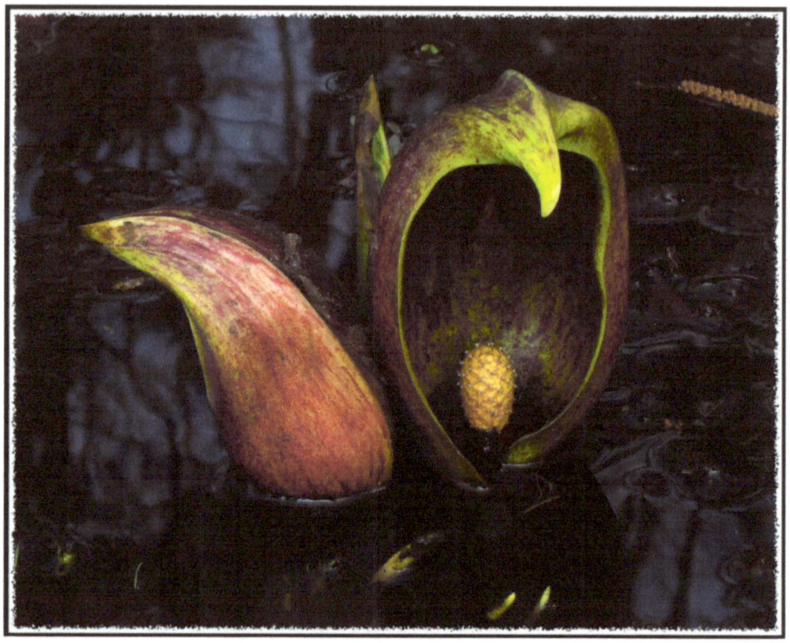

The flowers on this page, also taken in **Nogawa Park**, are **Skunk Cabbage** (*Symplocarpus foetidus*) (***Zazen-sou*** in Japanese). The top image was taken in mid-February and the lower image was not taken until the middle of March. In the upper photograph the flowers are still perfectly shaped and quite colorful whereas they are becoming faded and losing their shape in the lower photo.

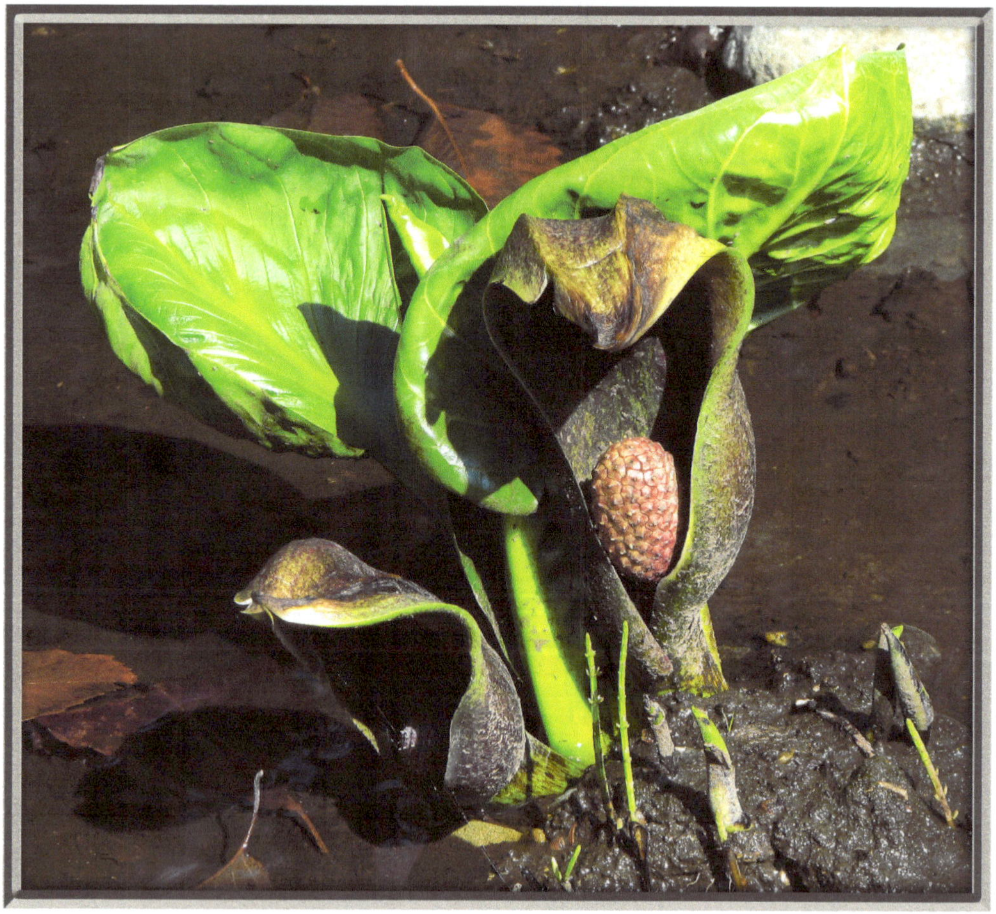

There are at least two kinds of Skunk Cabbage in Japan. This type is the earlier type. The other type does not occur until later in the season. We will show you a photo of it later on.

After those photos of spring flowers on the previous few pages, can you believe that you're seeing this photo of very heavy snow? Well, obviously these were not taken in Tokyo. These two photos, were in fact, taken in **Fukushima Prefecture** in mid-February. They were also both taken from the windows of the **Tadami Line Train**. It's very difficult to take photos from a train window when it's moving, if you don't believe it, then you should try it. There are often electrical wires in the way, in addition to markers and other items alongside the railroad tracks. Good luck with your own efforts.

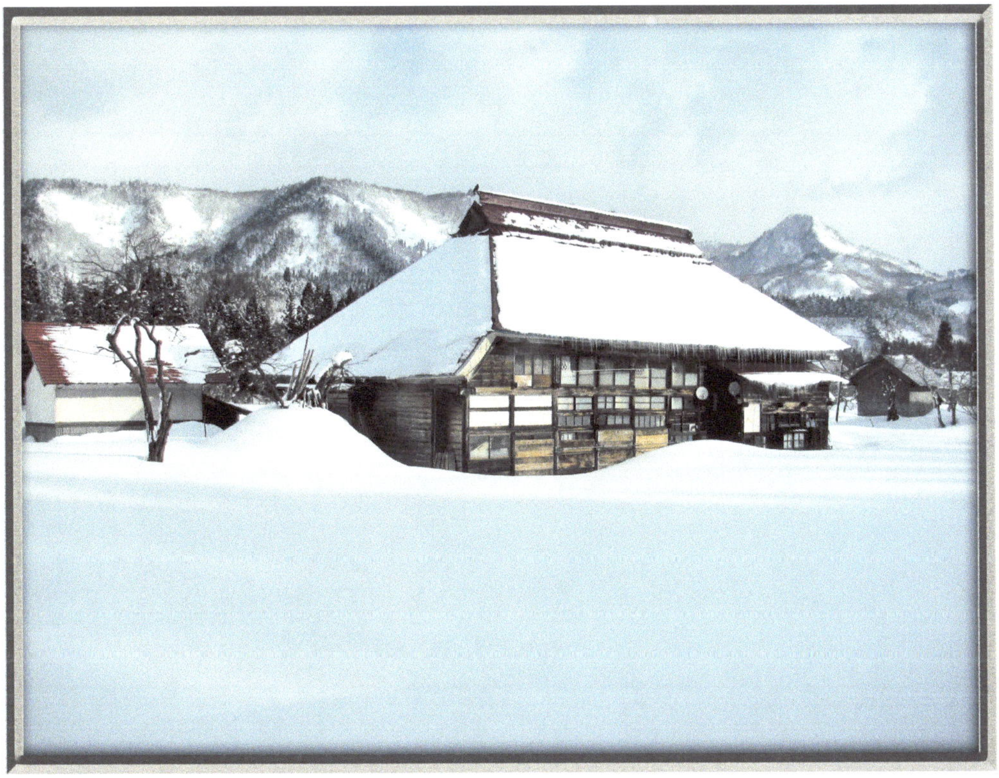

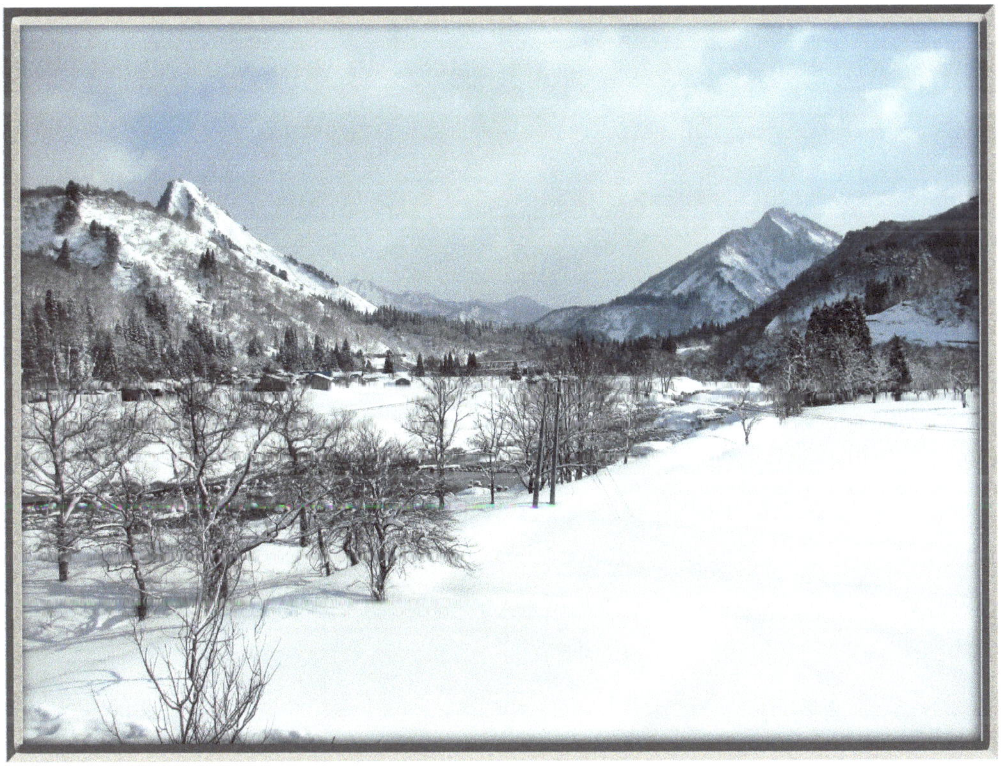

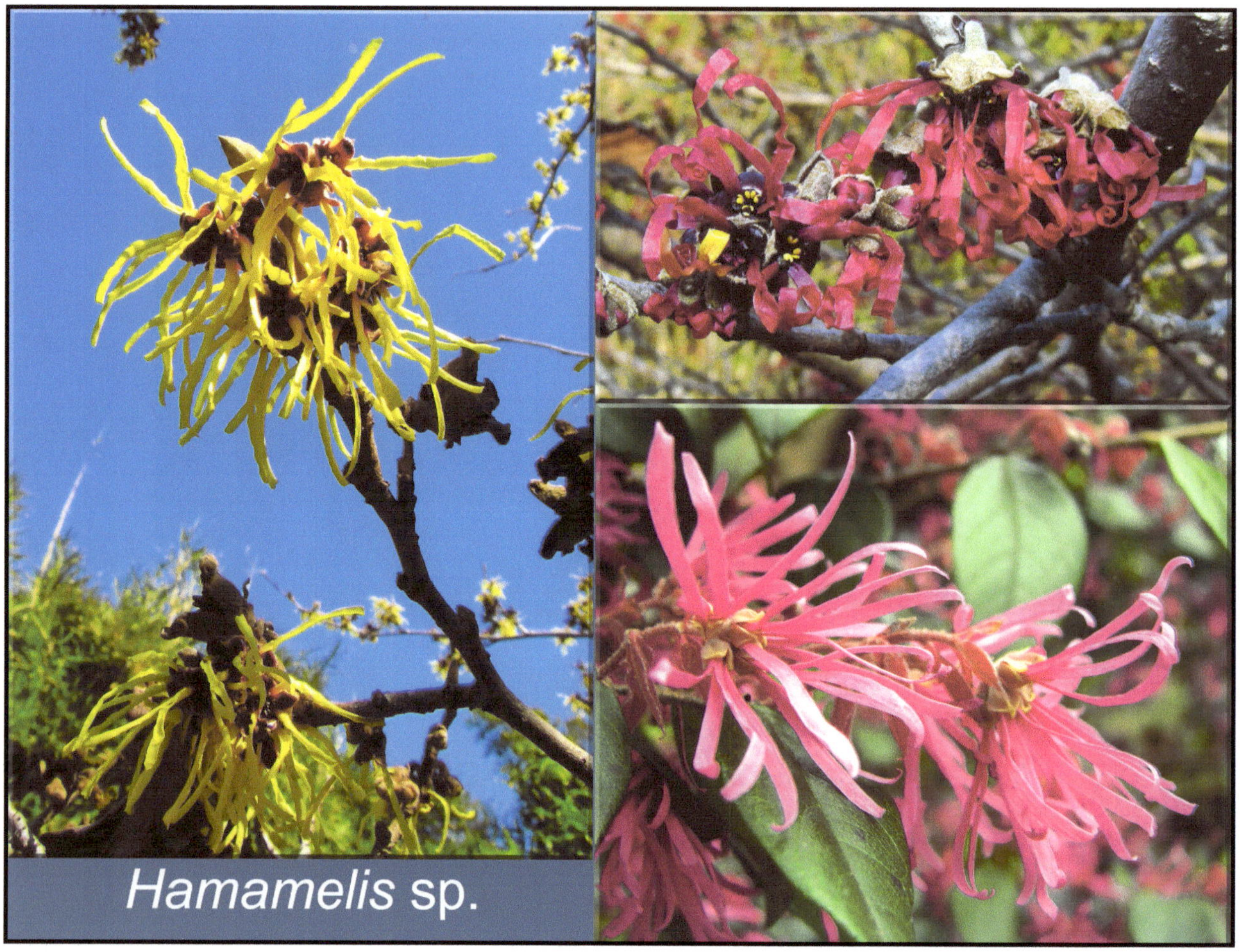

Here is another spring flower for you to enjoy. This photo collage shows three cultivars of **Witch Hazel** (***Hamamelis* sp.**). We find this flower later on in February and in early to mid-March in the Tokyo Area. These three photos were all taken in or near **Jindai Botanical Garden** on the west side of Tokyo. We often go to Jindai Botanical Garden and also to a special natural plants area of **Nogawa Park**. Both of these places are near enough to our apartment so that we can easily bicycle to them.

Entrance into the natural plants area of Nogawa Park is free and entrance into Jindai Botanical Garden is reasonable considering the size of it. We generally buy a one year pass – it pays for itself in merely four visits.

And that's the final February image.

March Photos and Story

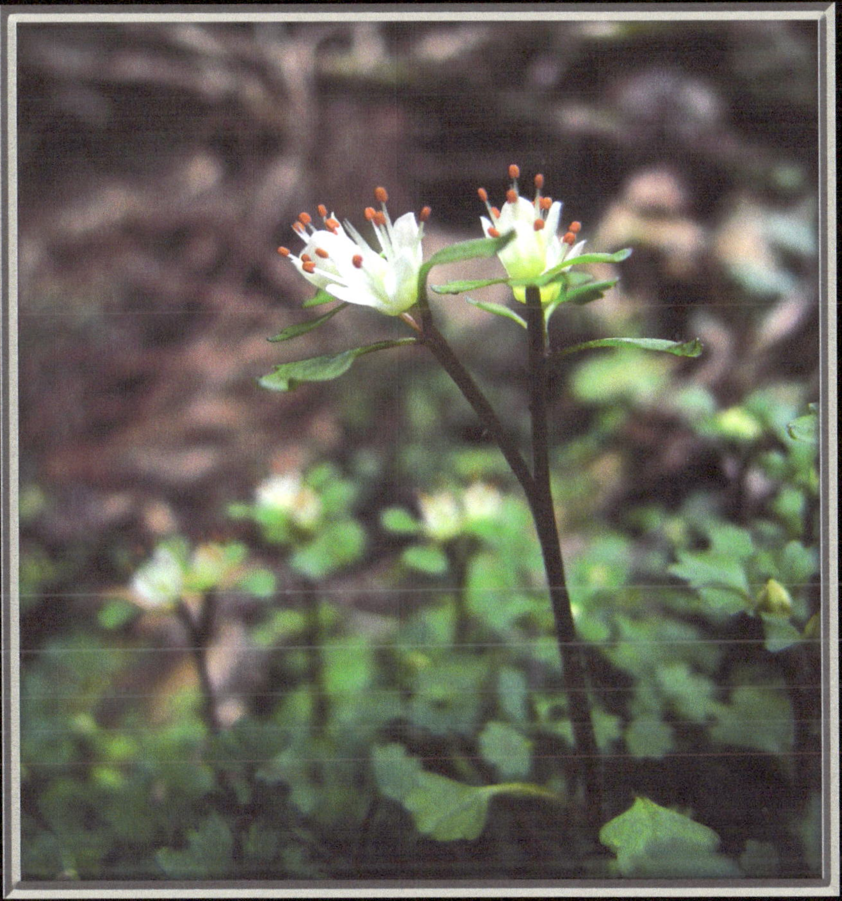

This cute little plant is ***Chrysosplenium album*** **var.** ***stamineum***. It can be found as one of the earlier tiny flowers in damp to wet areas along mountain trails. It likes to grow on rocks and rock outcroppings. The flower is about 5 millimeters (0.25 inch) in diameter, so it is a challenge to photograph. It is also found in areas which get very little direct sunlight, another reason it is difficult to photograph. We always look for it on **Mt. Takao** (**Takao-san**) in late winter to early spring.

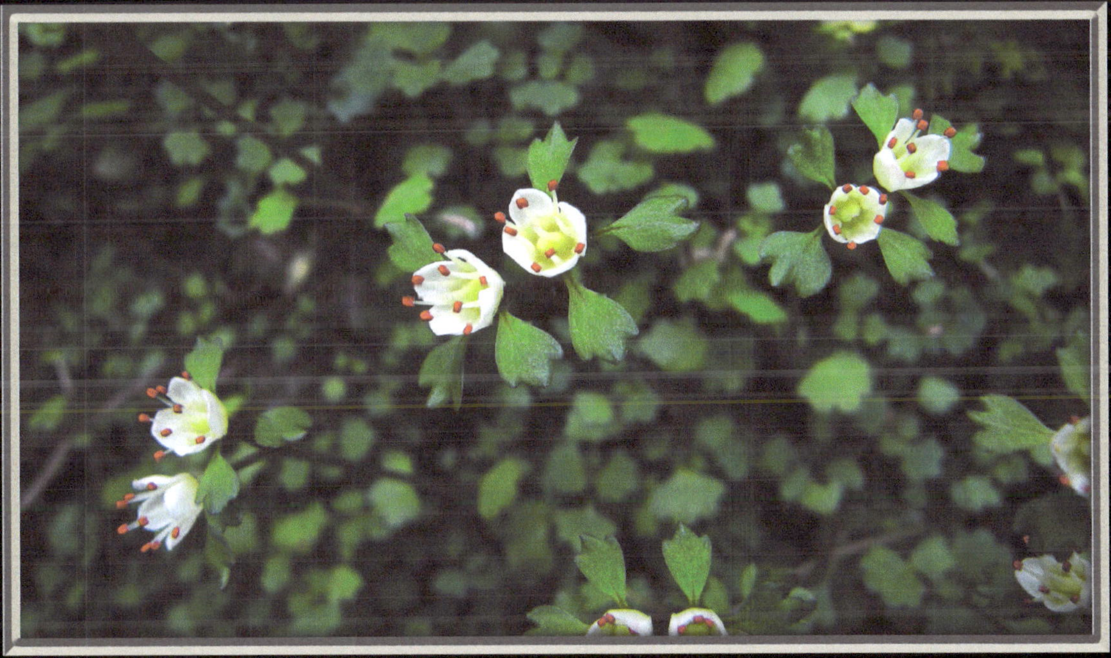

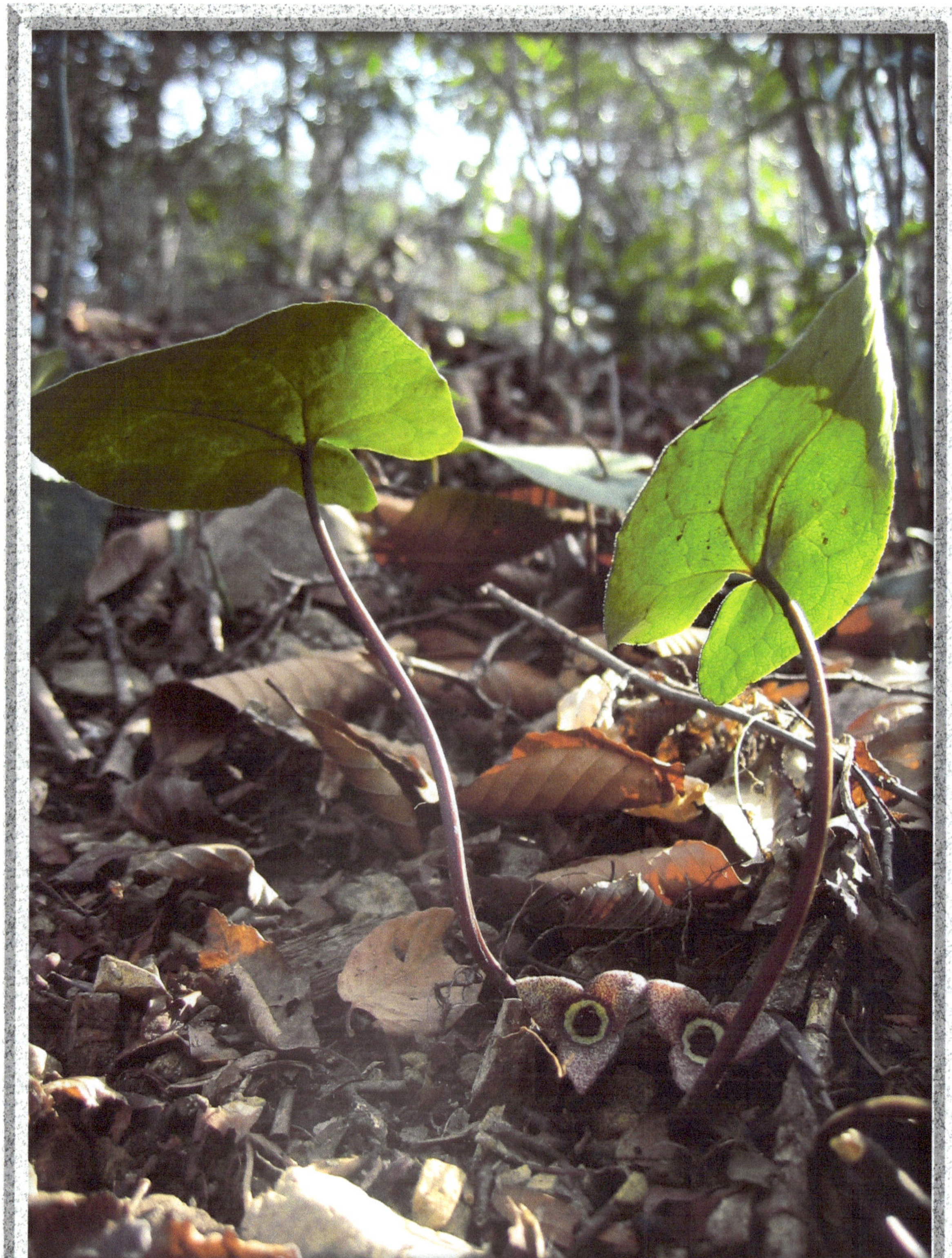

On the facing page you can see a photo of ***Asarum nipponicum***. This is also known as ***Heterotropa nipponica*** and also as ***Heterotropa kooyana* var. *nipponica***. The flowers of ***Asarum*** are often buried under the leaves and other forest litter and generally you have to do a bit of digging to expose the flower. The flowers develop during the winter, which is probably the reason they develop under the forest litter. This photo exhibits a particularly interesting lighting effect. The specimen shown here was found on one of the slopes of **Mt. Takao**.

The weird little plant and flower just below is ***Mitella pauciflora***. The left photo shows the entire plant and the right photo shows a close-up of the flowers. This is another plant of very damp areas and can often be found right on the banks of small streams and on small islands in those streams. It grows only where the water is clean and cold. The ***Mitella*** genus is native to temperate and arctic North America and Asia. It can also be found on somc of the slopes of **Mt. Takao**.

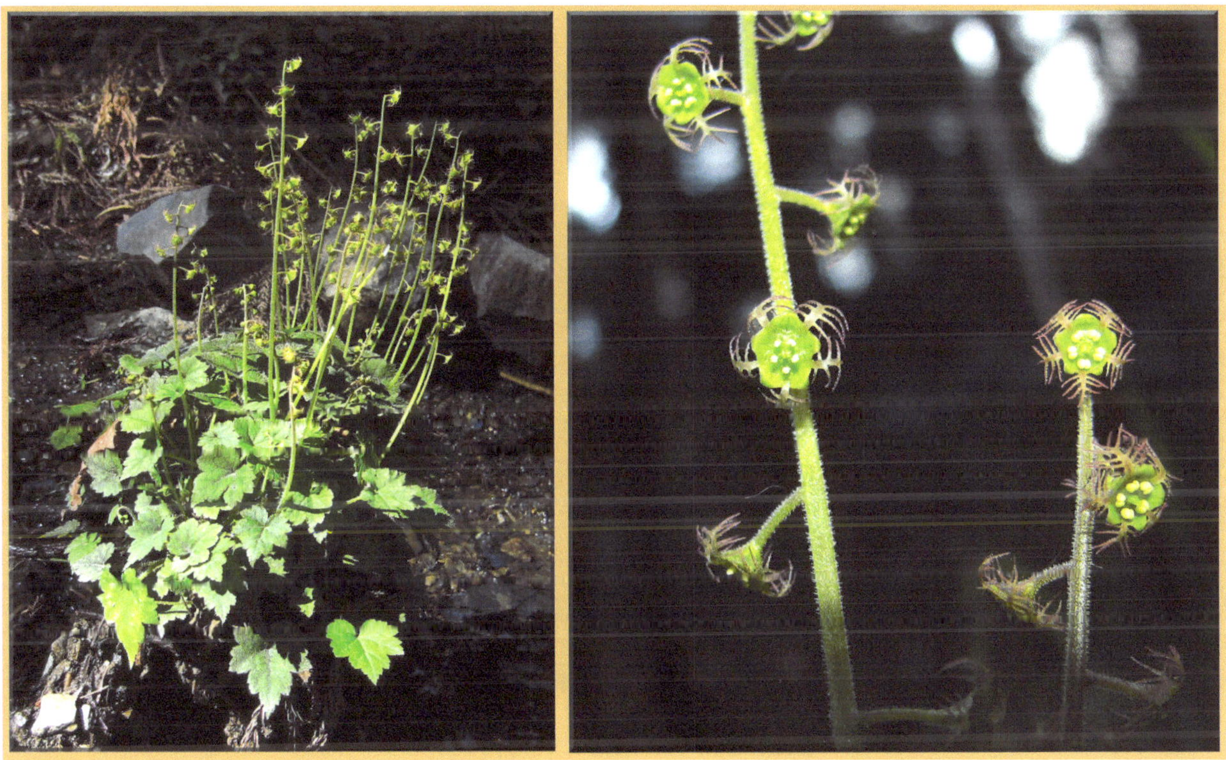

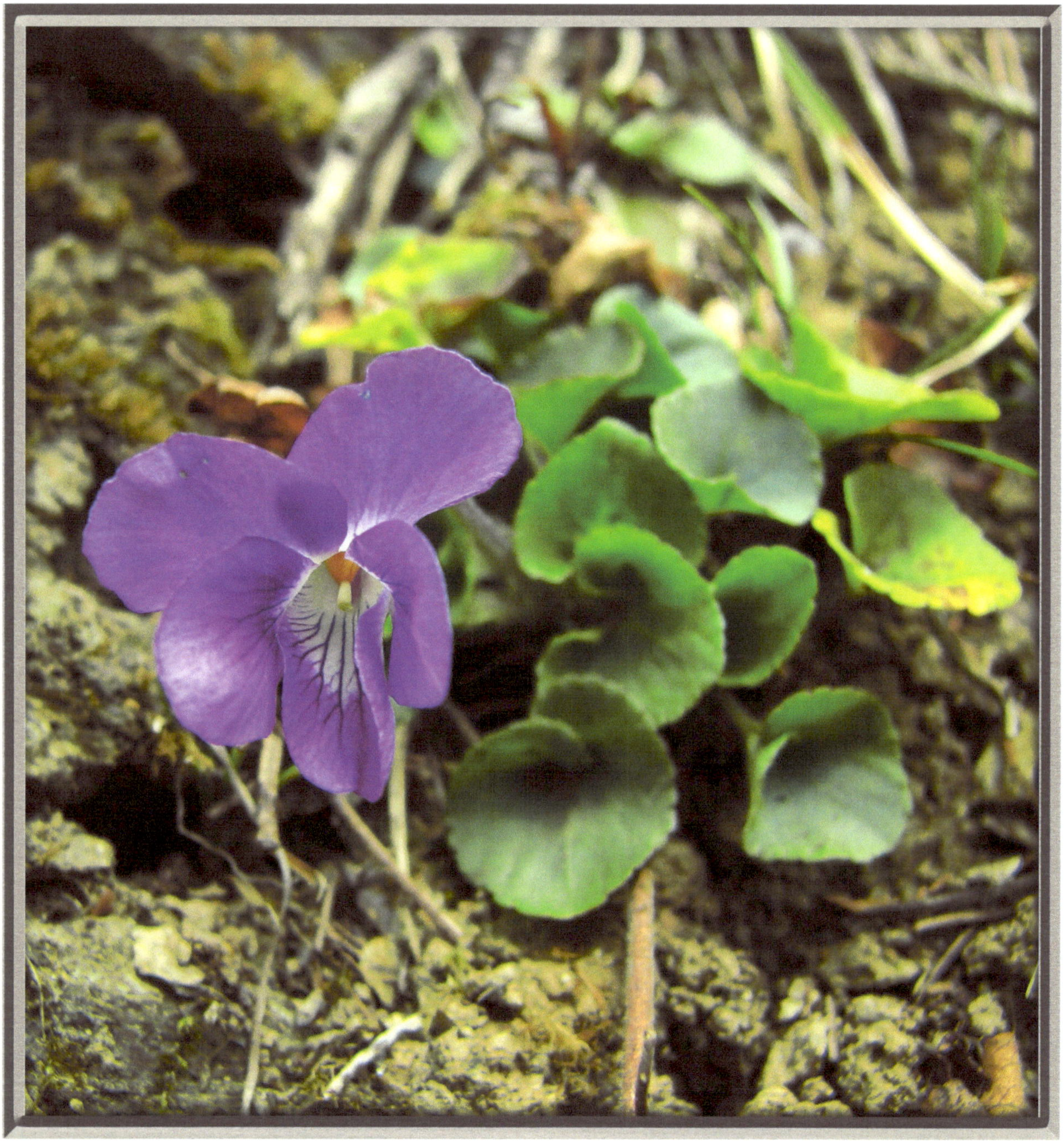

Here is a beautiful specimen of ***Viola obtusa***, one of several violets which can be found near **Mt. Takao** (**Takao-san**) beginning around mid-March. We have taken many photos of violets – we might even be considered violets maniacs by some people. We'll be showing you some more selected photos of violets as we enter the Spring season, just a few pages from here. Before that though – we are going to go to another snowy place.

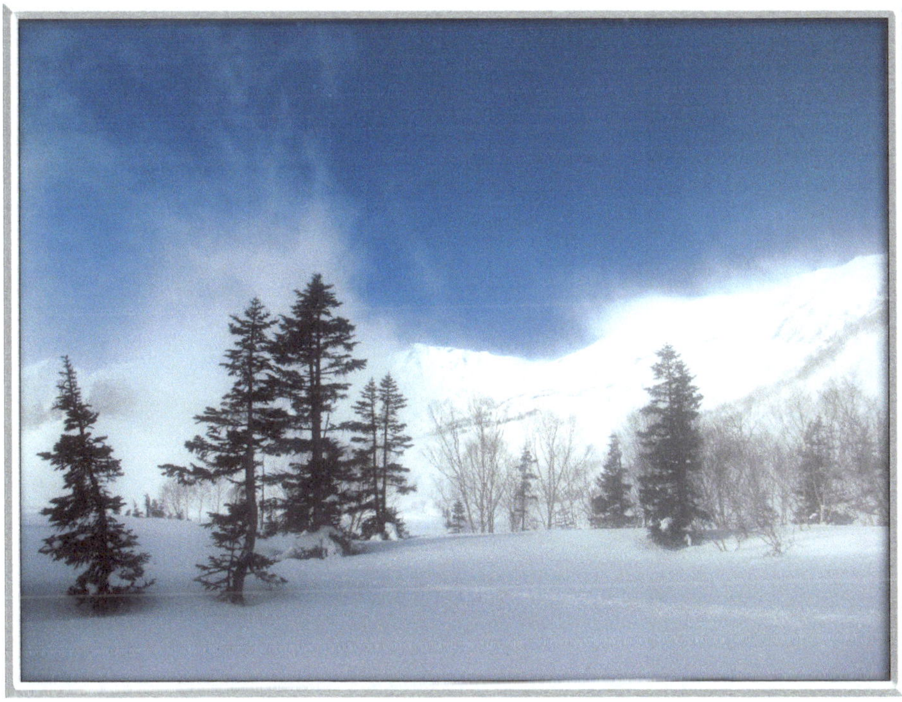

Let's take a trip to the **Hakuba Mountains** of **Nagano Prefecture**. They are part of the **Hida Mountains** – also known as the **Japanese Northern Alps Mountain Range**. When we visited this area, on March 14th, it began as a very cloudy day up at this elevation. We did not expect to be able to see anything except clouds all day long. The photo to the right shows a scene that surprised us greatly when the clouds parted. We were not expecting anything nearly as beautiful as this. Clouds came and went for the next hour or so, but when there were no clouds the scenery was beyond belief.

Upper photo:
10:22 AM

10:27 AM

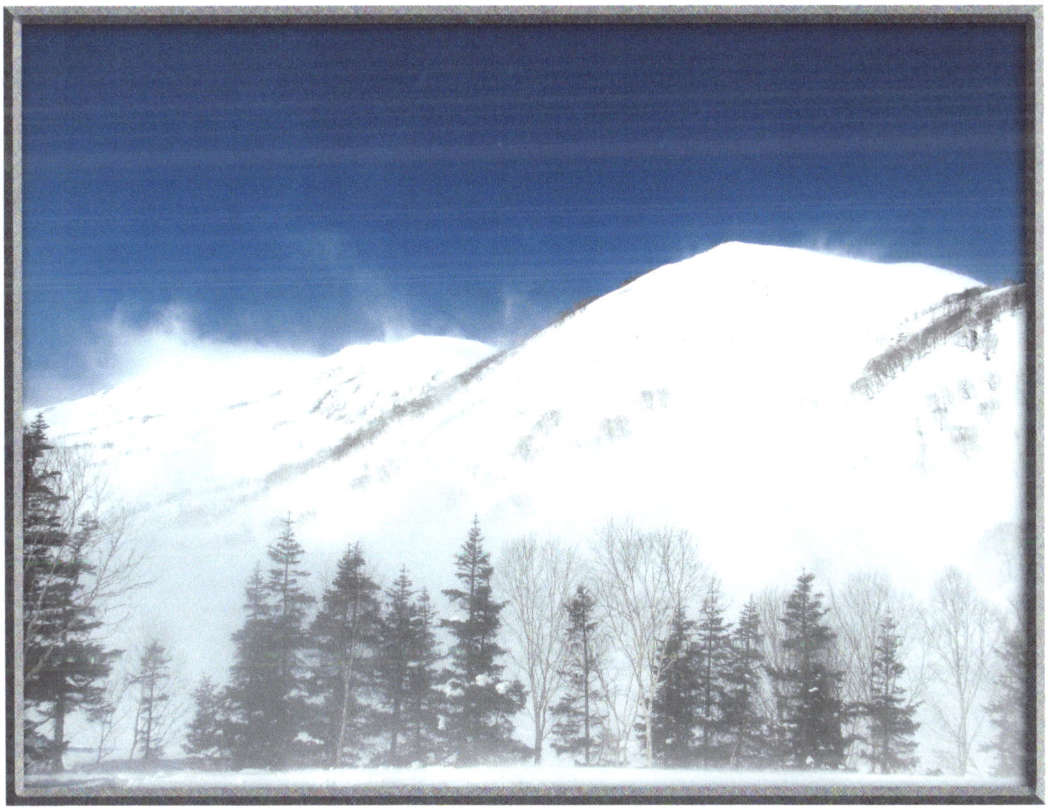

10:30 AM

These photos were all taken at **Tsugaike Kogen**. This is not very far from the top of the highest ropeway on the mountain. The elevation here is about 1,850 meters or 6,070 feet. As you can see, we are quite far below the summits of the surrounding **Hakuba Mountains**.

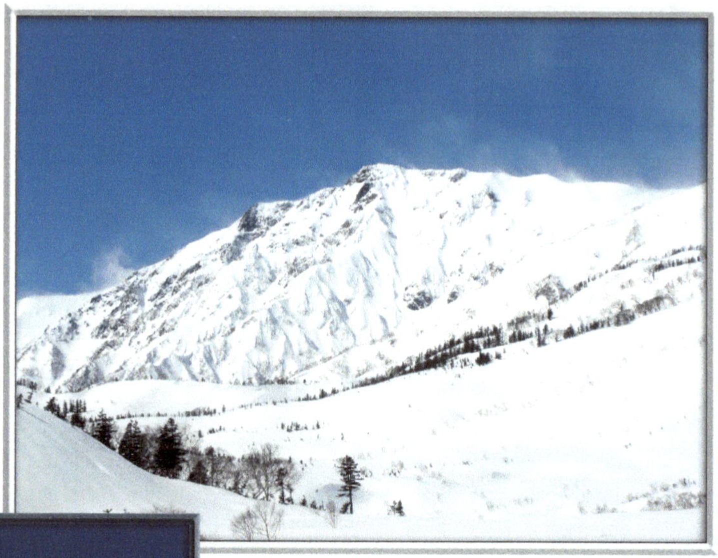

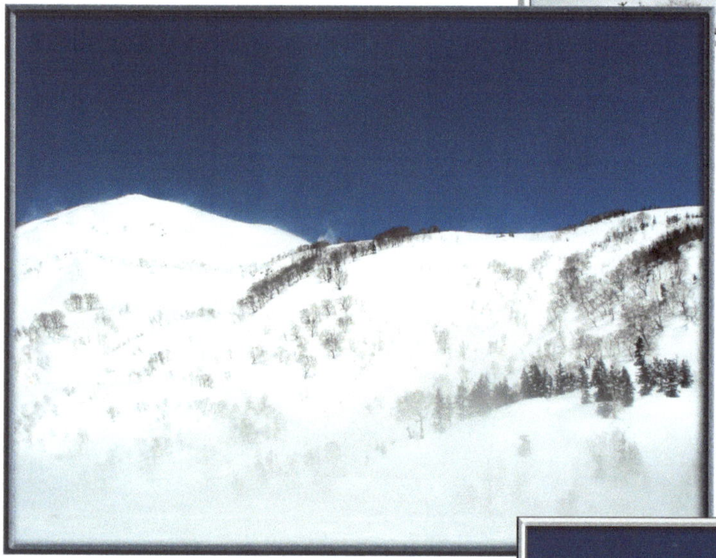

10:31 AM

We will return to this area again in July, and show you additional photos of these mountains which were taken in the summer months.

10:35 AM

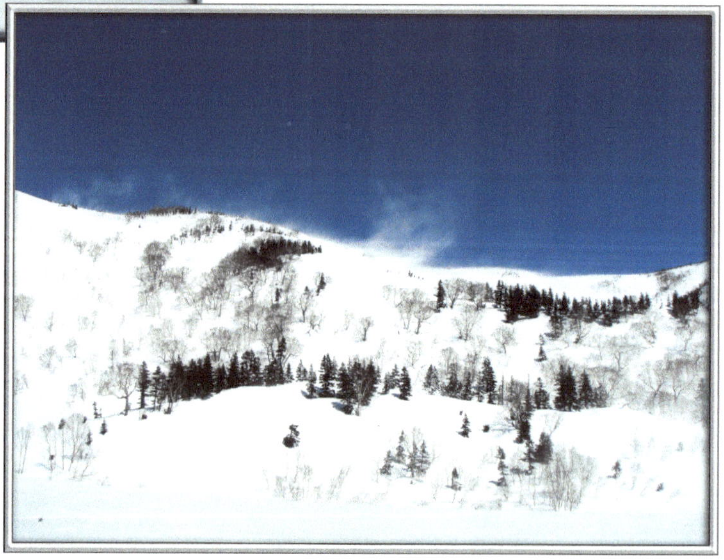

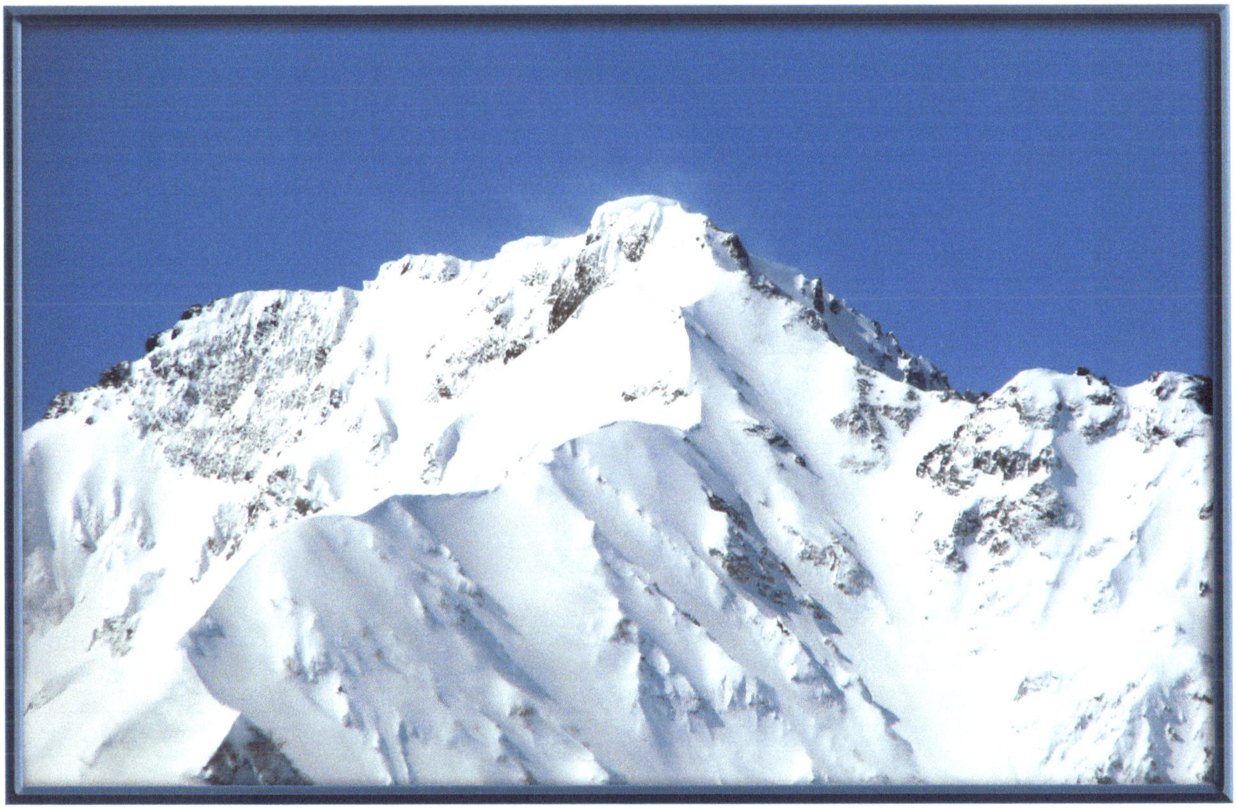

Upper Photo:
10:45 AM

Right:
10:47 AM

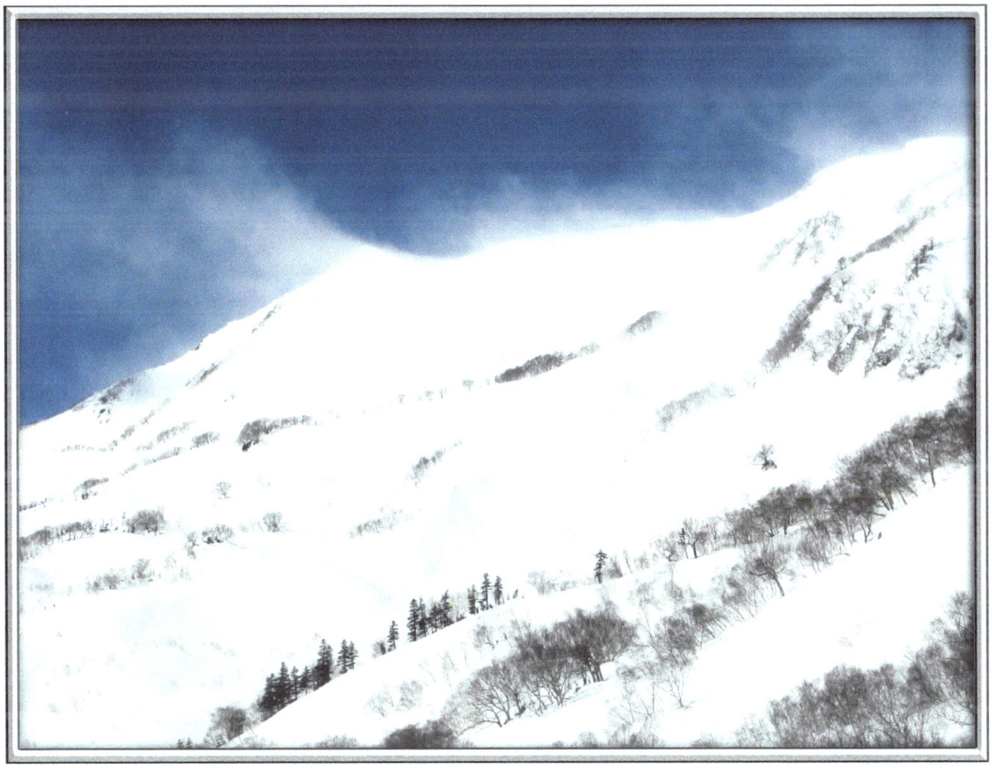

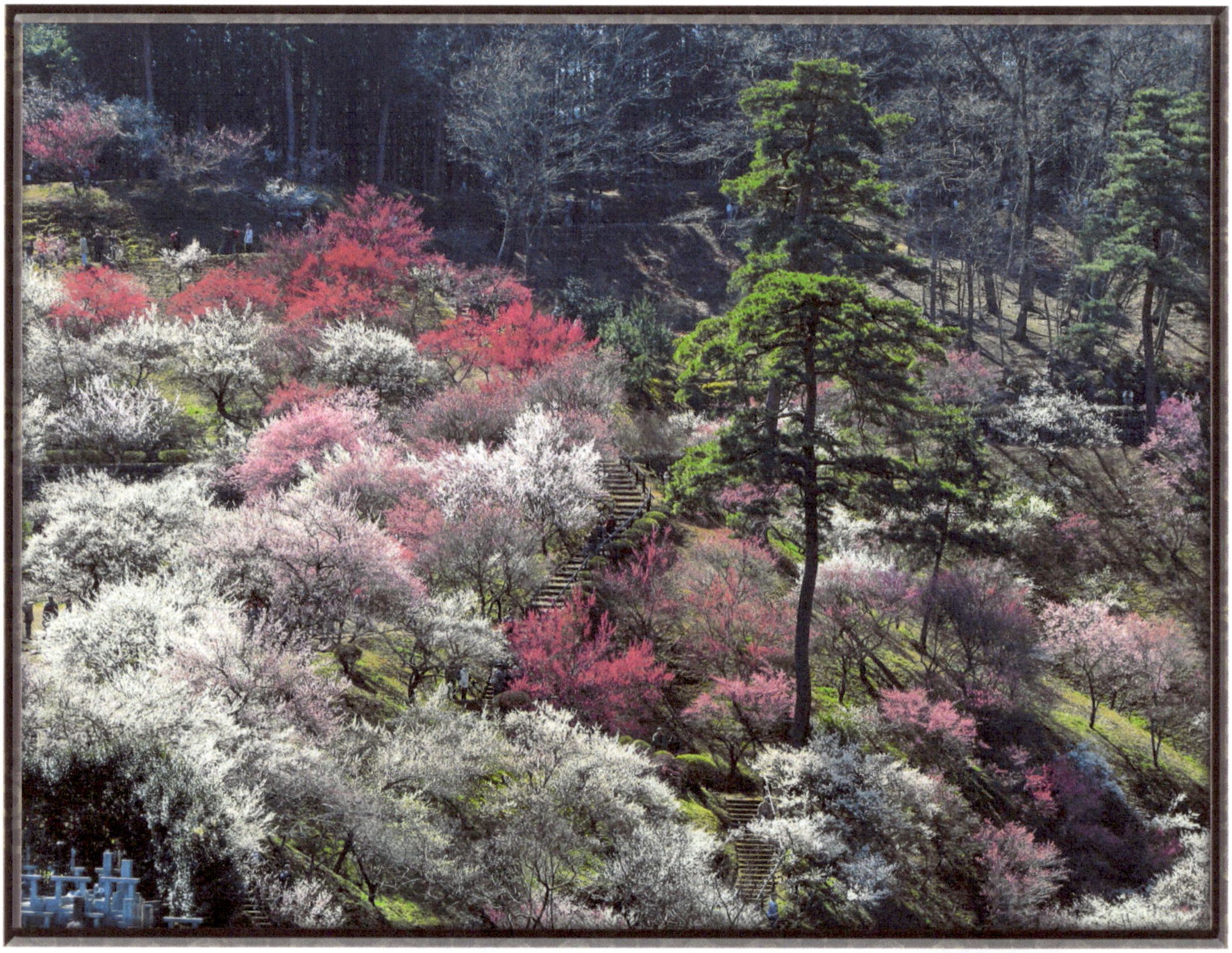

These two photos, and the one on the facing page, were taken on or about March 15th in various years. They are all of a place named **Yoshino Baigo**. This is in **Hinatawada**, a part of **Ome City**. It is served by the **East Japan Railway – Chuo Line**. It is in Western Tokyo.

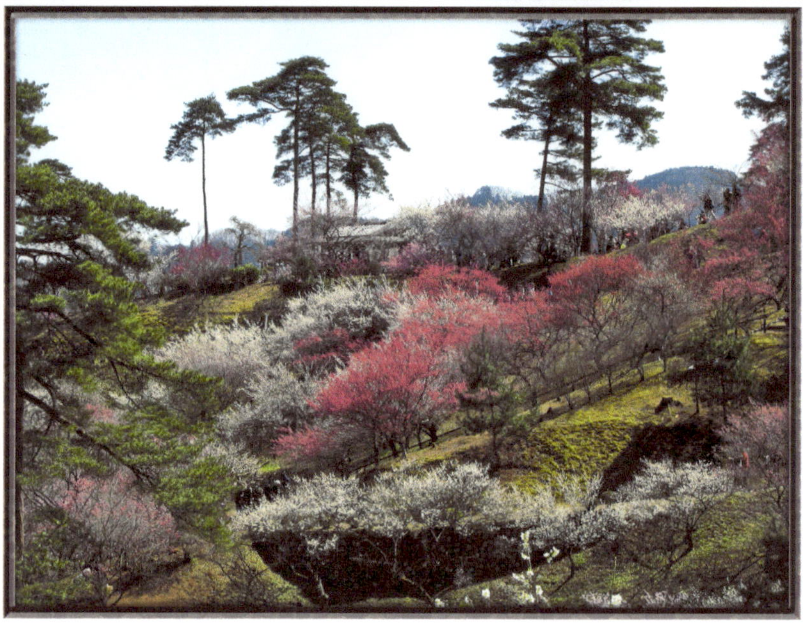

We have visited this place several times and we can warn you that, at this time of the year it can rain, so be careful when picking the day that you want to make a trip to this place. It can also be quite crowded if you choose a beautiful weather Saturday or Sunday to visit. Don't get discouraged, just do your best to ignore the other people and enjoy yourselves.

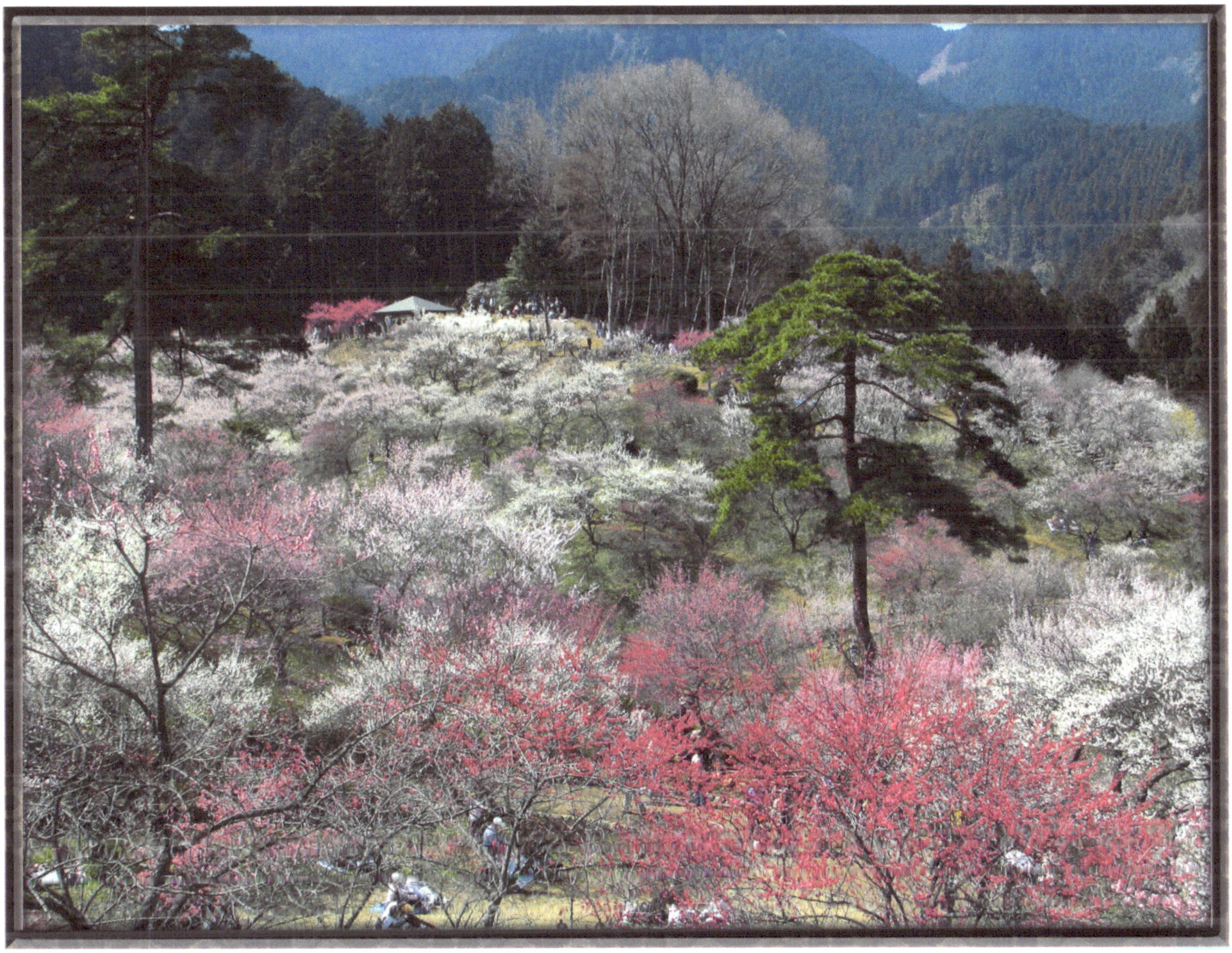

You can pick up a map of the **Hinatawada Area** at the train station before you start walking. There are a lot of plum trees in this area and you can very easily spend an entire day hiking around the area enjoying the beautiful plum blossoms.

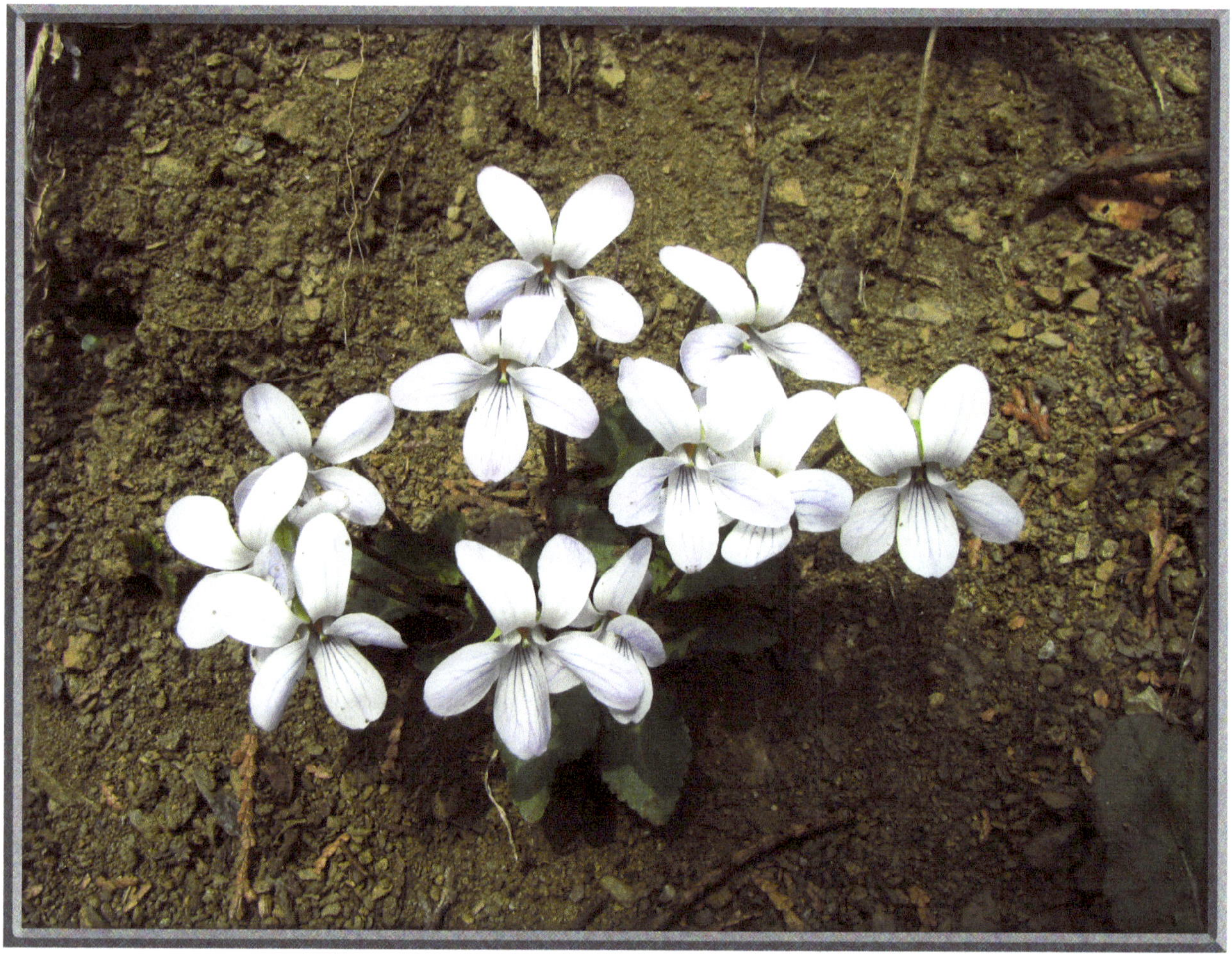

This is, quite obviously, another violet – this one is ***Viola japonica***. We're not going to tell you the specific location where we find this plant every year other than to say that it is somewhere on **Mt. Takao (Takao-san)**. This is such a beautiful plant. Apparently it is quite happy with this site because it always has a large number of flowers and it never fails to amaze us. This species, ***V. japonica***, comes in at least two colors – this white one and also a very beautiful purplish-blue colored one.

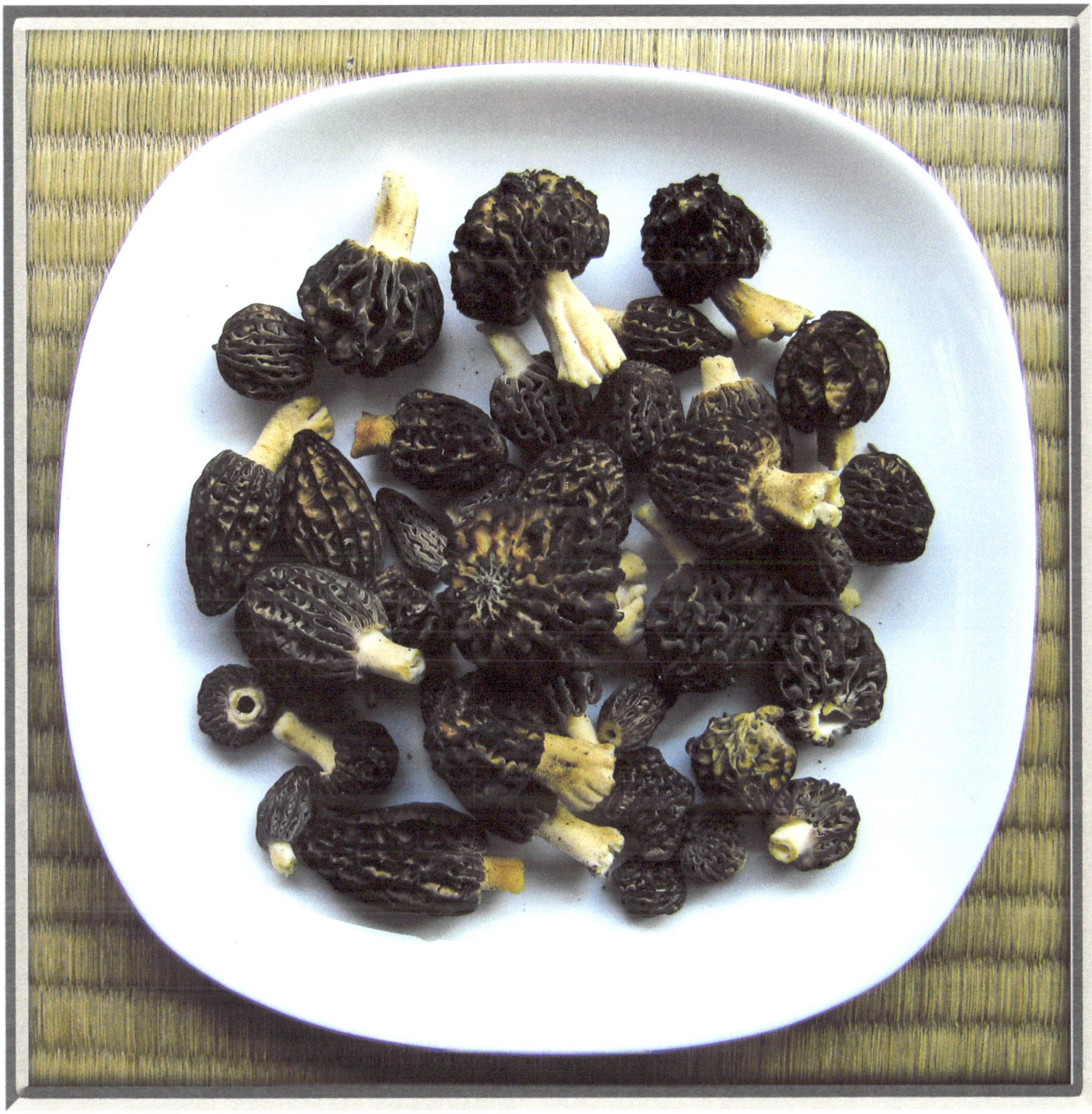

Have you ever eaten **Morel Mushrooms** (***Morchella esculenta***) with a fine Japanese steak? We can tell you that the taste is the most amazing thing this side of heaven! We can generally find these mushrooms just a few days before the spring equinox near our house. It is fortunate that most Japanese people do not realize that this is an edible mushroom, and therefore there is no competition for it.

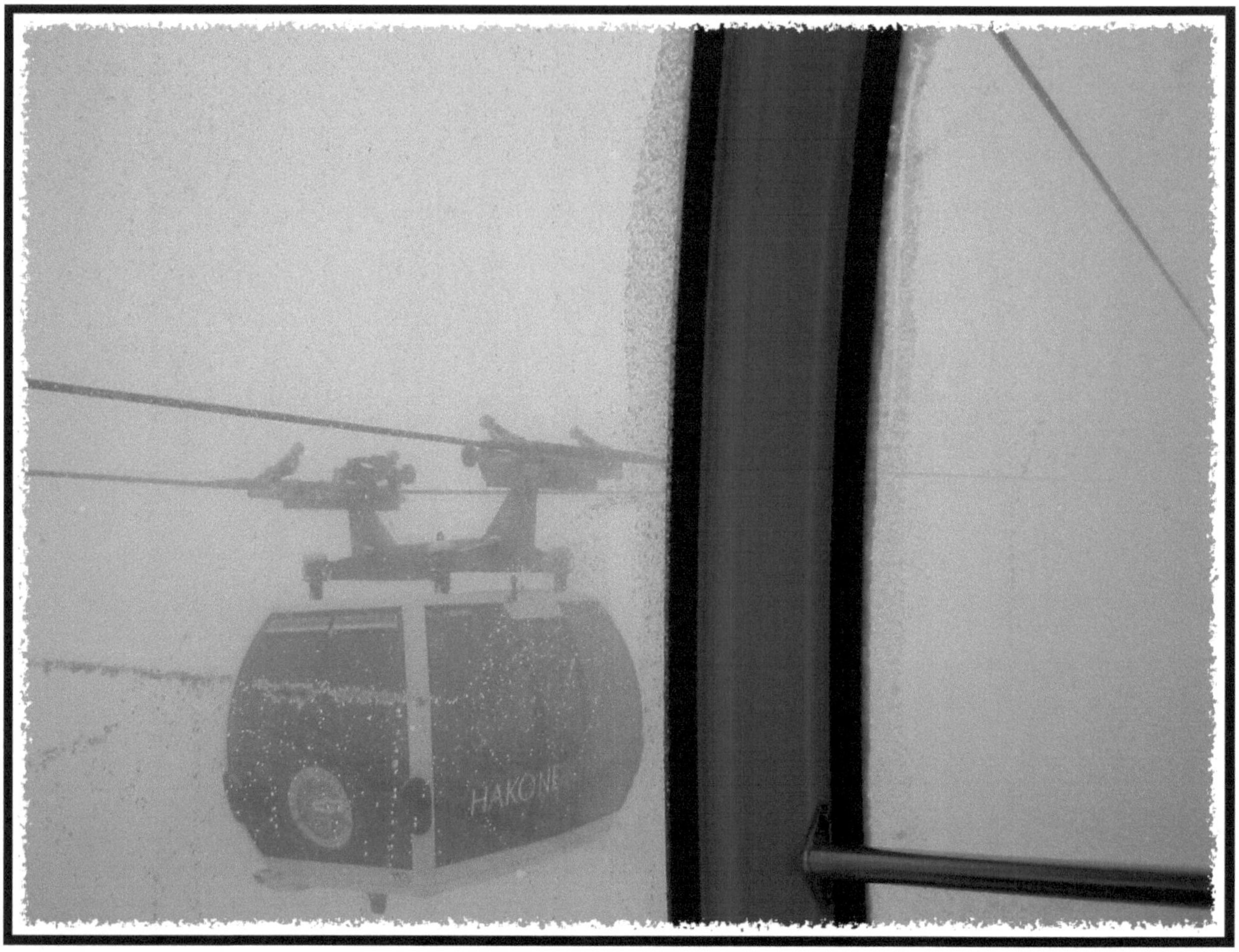

The above photo was taken from the **Owakudani Ropeway** in **Kanagawa Prefecture** on March 20th one year. It was snowing and blowing and we wondered if we would be blown off the cable. There were not many people at Owakudani on this trip. The Owakudani Ropeway is one of the routes you can take to travel to **Hakone** and **Lake Ashi** (***Ashinoko*** in Japanese) (also in Kanagawa Prefecture). The view from the summit of Owakudani is amazing on a clear day – you can see Mt. Fuji very wonderfully.

This is a volcanic area and the photo on the facing page shows eggs which have been hard-boiled in the hot volcanic water. These **"Black Eggs"** are a popular attraction for tourists visiting the area. Legend has it that each egg you eat will lengthen your life by seven years. If the legend is true, we will both live to be VERY OLD MEN!

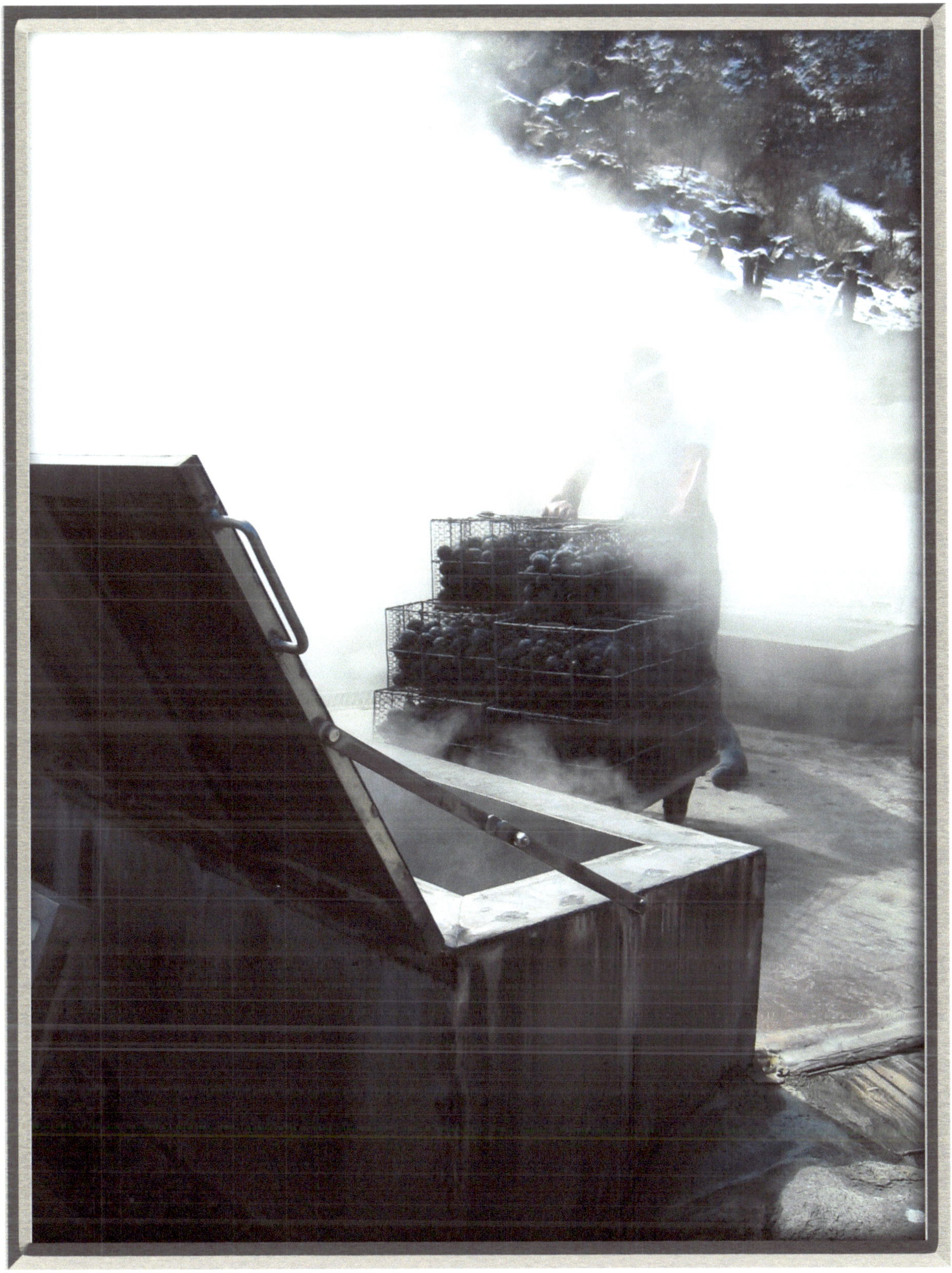

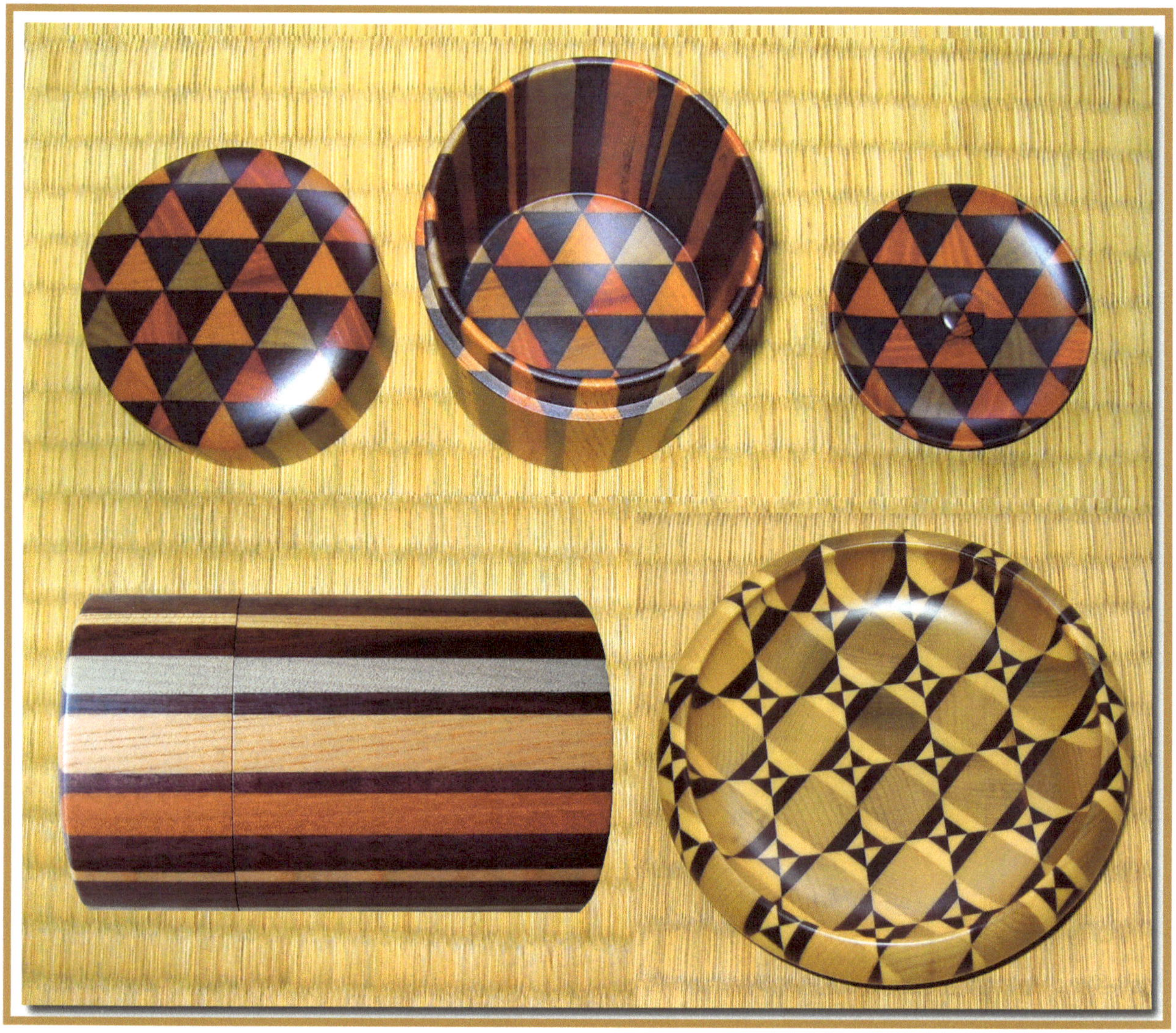

This is the final photo of winter, on the facing page we will begin spring. This is **"Yoseki"**. It is an elaborate wood mosaic and has been treasured in Japan since olden times. The top three pieces in the above collage are the parts of the bottom left image of a very beautiful tea box. The bottom right image is an accessory bowl or candy bowl. Different woods are used for the different colors. Rods of the different woods are glued together and then the glued together rods are turned on a wood lathe to create the objects which you see in this photo. Supposedly this **Yoseki** is made only in the **Hakone** area.

PART 2: SPRING

As we enter the spring season we start to find an abundance of flowers and we start getting out a great deal more than we do during the winter. As we mentioned previously, some people would consider us to be violets maniacs – be mentally prepared for several violets photos! Below is a ***Viola phalacrocarpa***. This violet flower has a very hairy center and the flower is VERY purple. It is a beautiful violet which we generally do not see many specimens of in the short violet season.

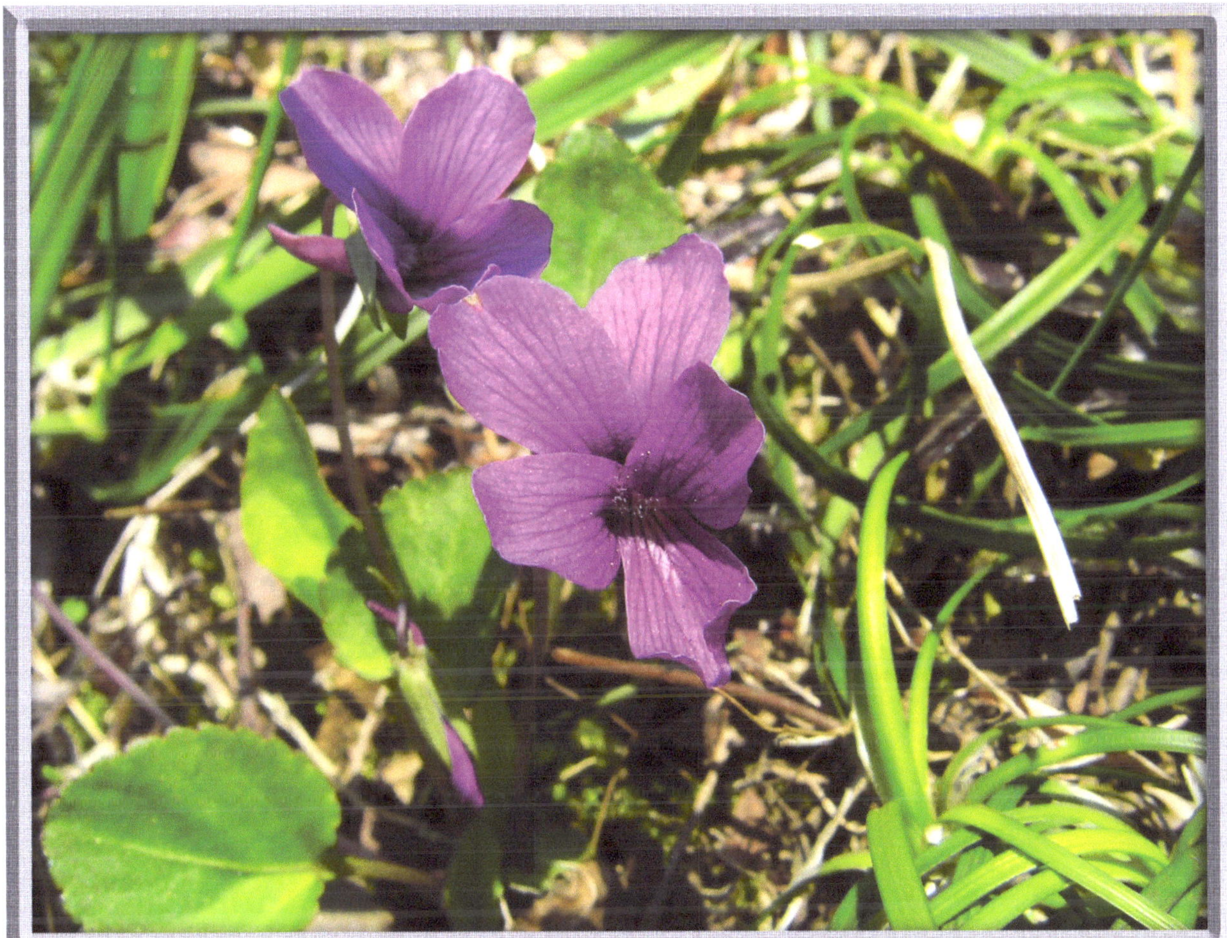

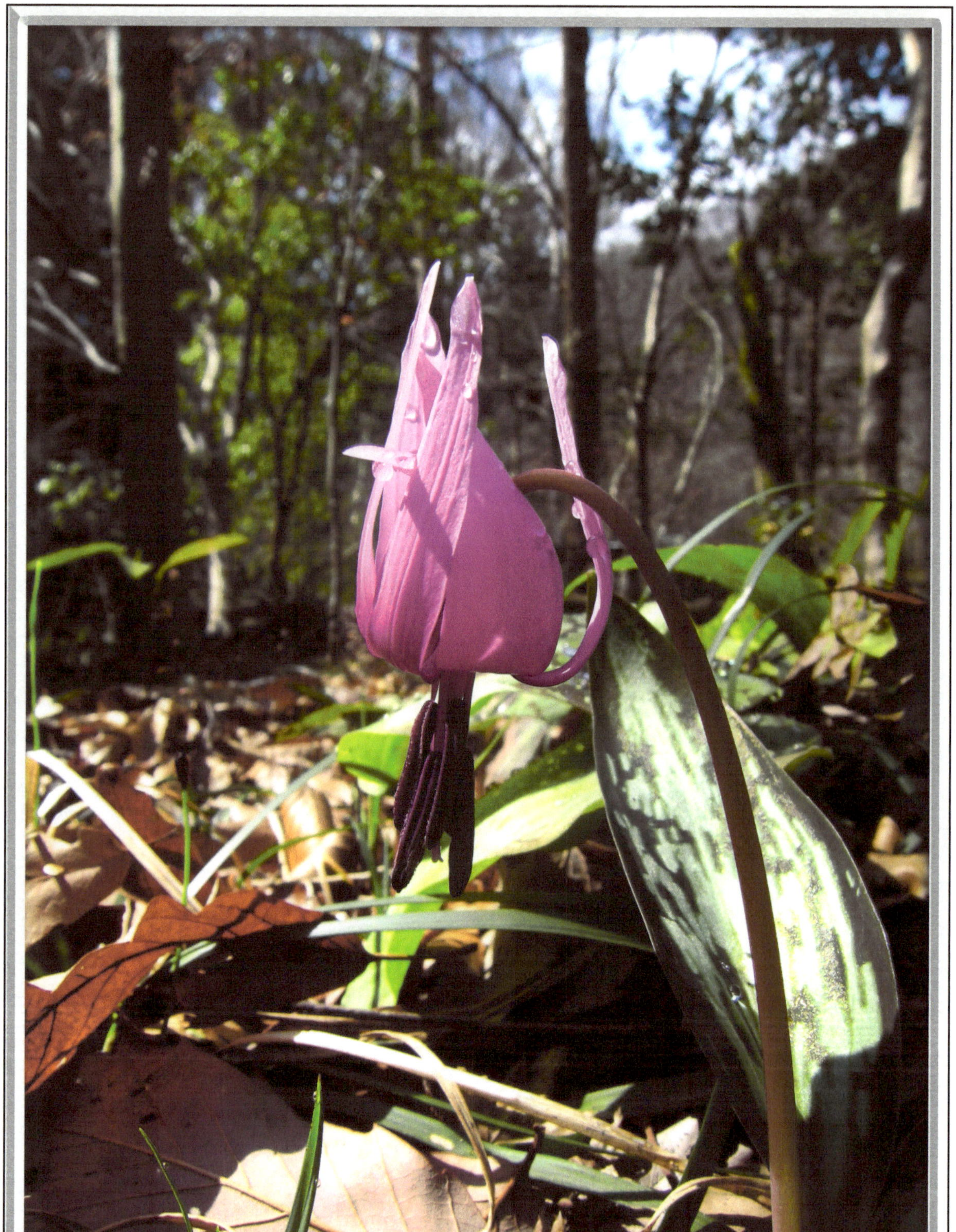

The photo on the facing page is a **Trout Lily** – an ***Erythronium japonicum***. It is a very beautiful flower and can be found from late March until mid-April and even into May, depending on where you search for it. Notice the mottling of the leaves. It is a protected species here in Japan, although it does not seem rare. This photo was taken at **Jindai Botanical Garden**.

The photo below is an orchid. This is ***Cymbidium goeringii***. It is getting more rare every year due to its popularity as a lawn and yard flower. When we first started searching for this species it was fairly common in some of our regular mountain haunts. A few years later it had virtually disappeared in some of the areas where we had previously found it in abundance, with the only indications that it had been there being a series of holes in the ground. This action on the part of humanity is so very disappointing to see. This particular photo was taken in **Nogawa Park**.

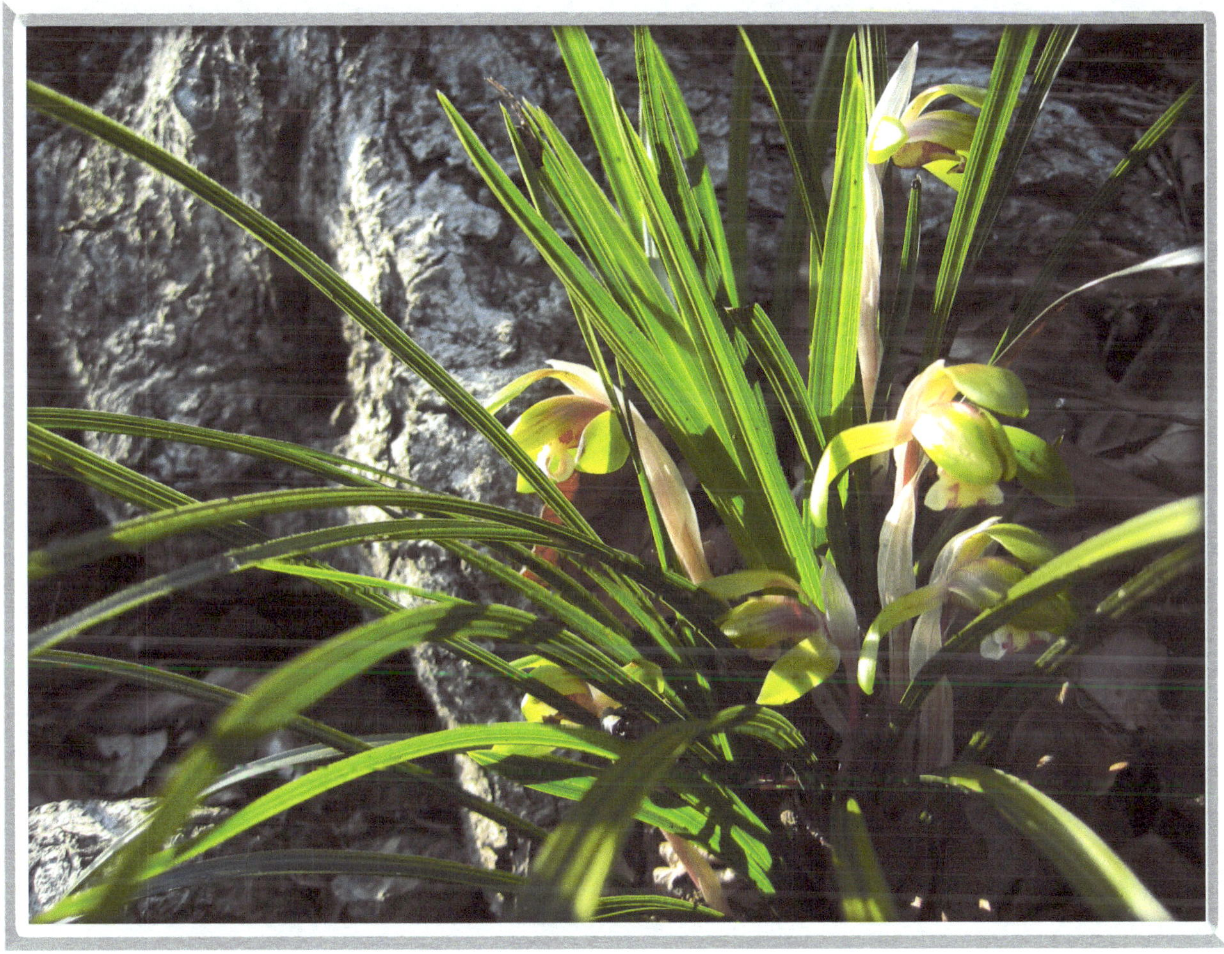

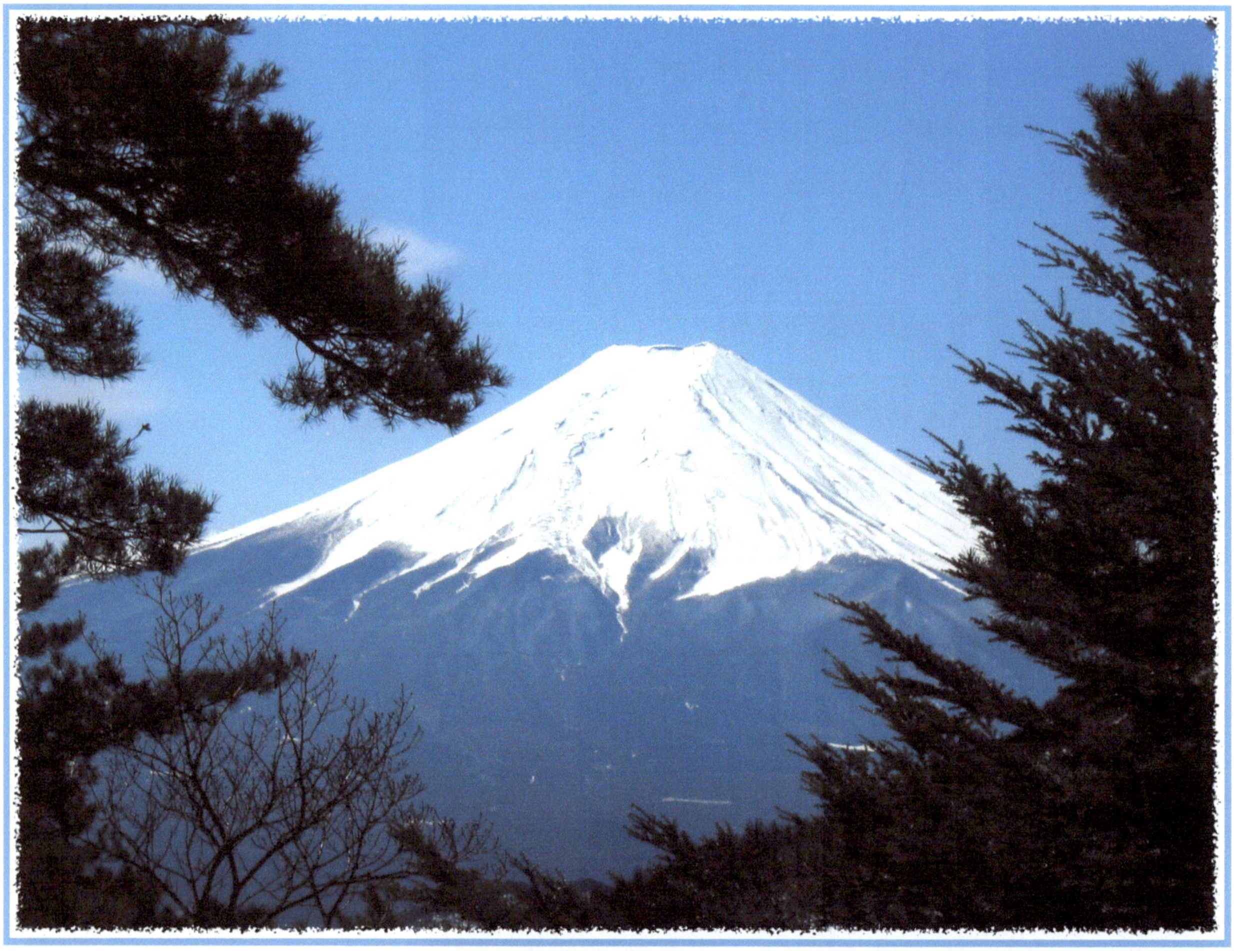

The above photo is **Mt. Fuji**. It was taken from along the trail hiking to the summit of **Mt. Mitsutouge** (1,785 m = 5,857 ft). The triple peak of Mt. Mitsutouge is shown in the photo to the right. Mt. Mitsutouge is a steep mountain to climb. It can be climbed either from Kawaguchi Lake or from **Mitsutouge Train Station**. The route from Mitsutouge Station is the steep way. If you choose this route be mentally prepared for the steepness.

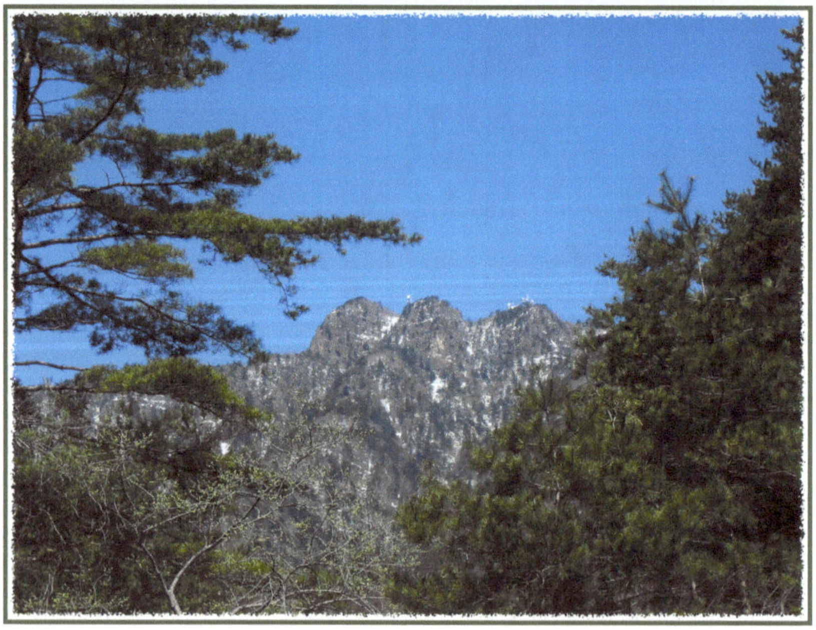

April Photos and Story

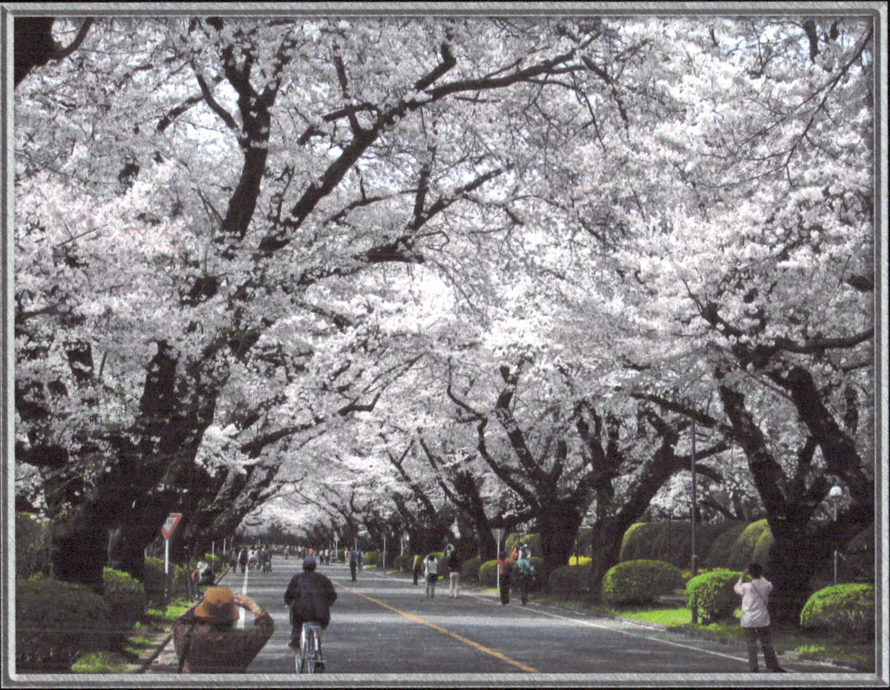

The two photos on this page were taken near the beginning of April in different years. They are, of course, cherry blossoms. The upper photo was taken on the **International Christian University** (**ICU**) entry road in **Mitaka**, on the west side of Tokyo. The lower photo was taken at the **Imperial Palace – Chidorigafuchi Moat**. What an amazing scene! You can just about set your clock by the appearance of the Cherry Blossoms. They always appear at just about the 1st of April.

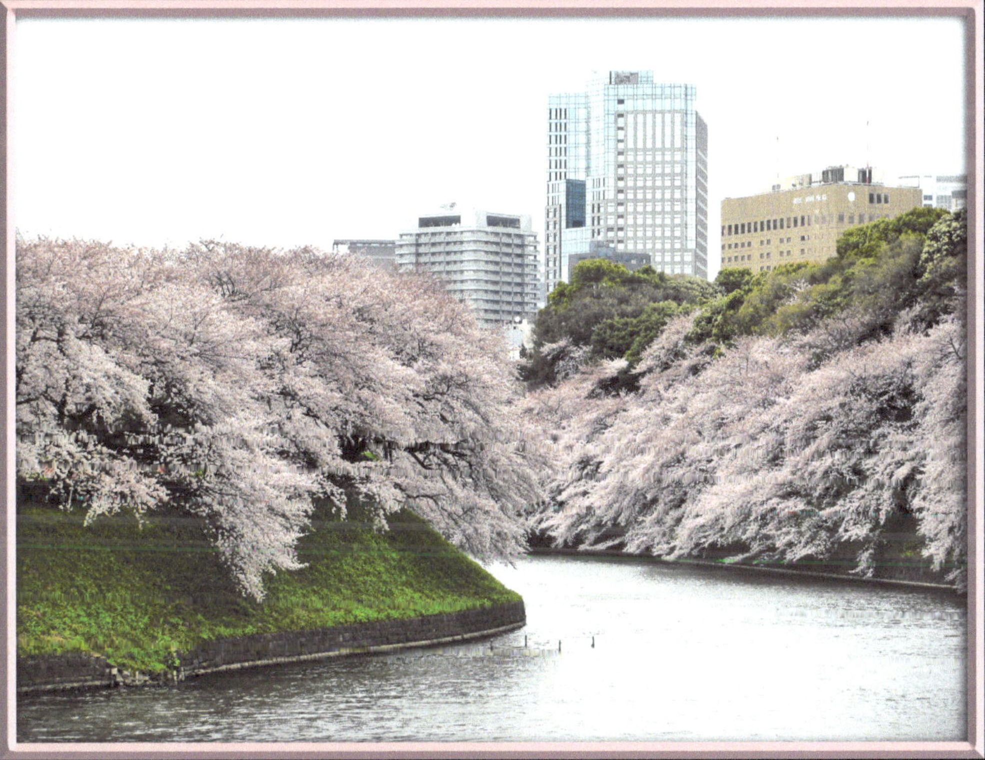

Cherry Blossom viewing is called **"Hanami"** and it is a nice thing to do with a bento (lunch box) and a bottle of high quality Saké. You will find many people out enjoying the cherry blossoms. They are only at their peak for about three days, so don't miss this occasion.

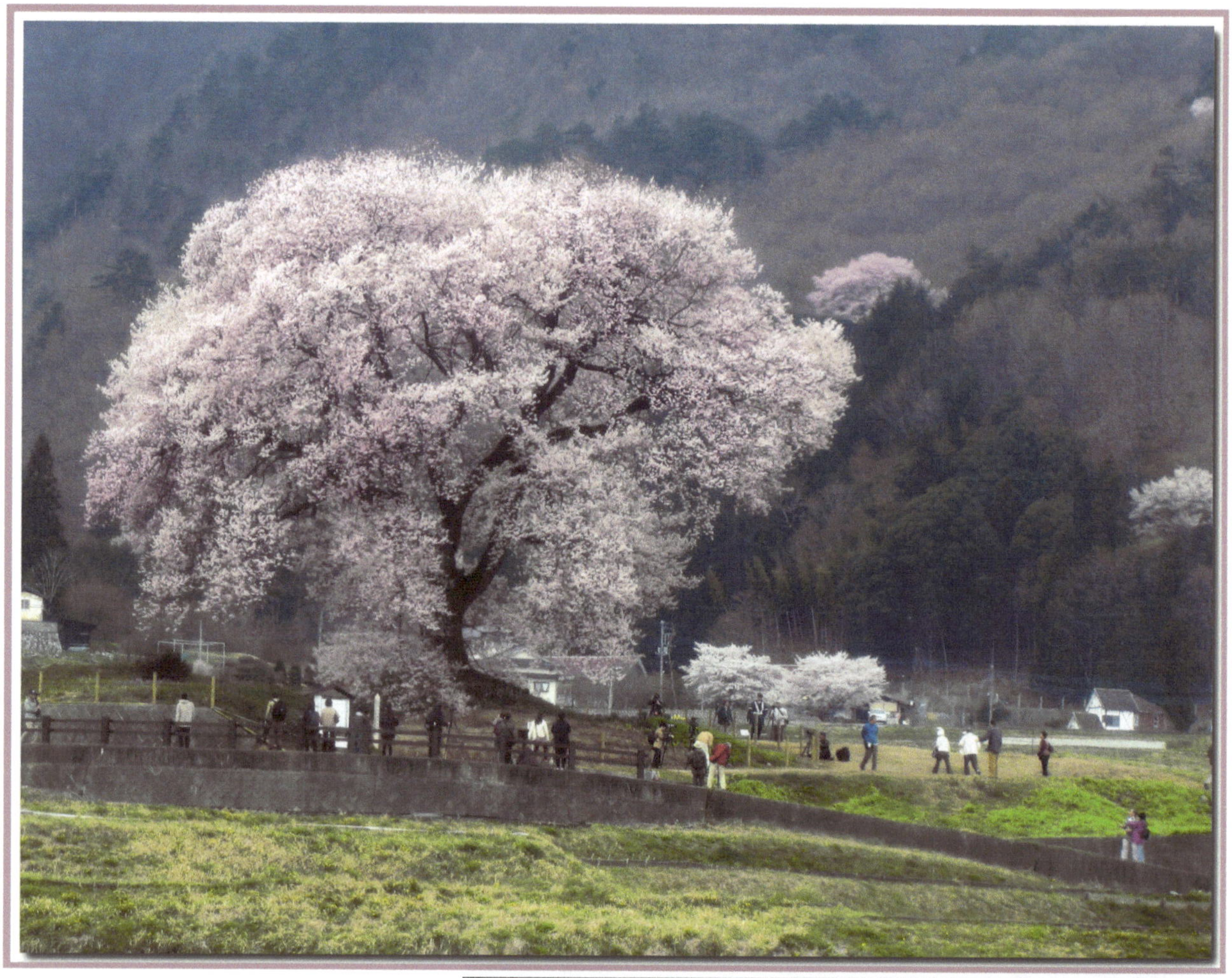

Here are two additional Cherry Blossom photos. The one above is out in the countryside and is so beautiful as to just about be shocking. The one to the right was taken at night with a flash. The full moon stands out nicely in the clear sky.

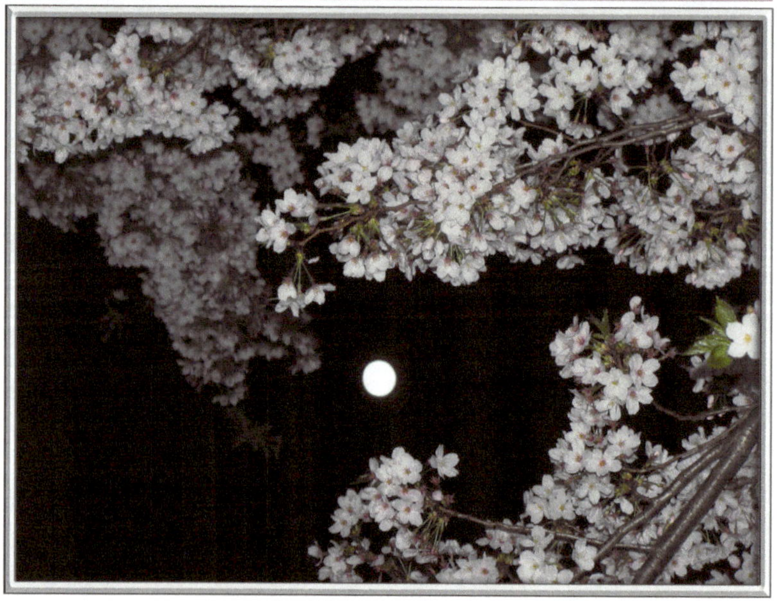

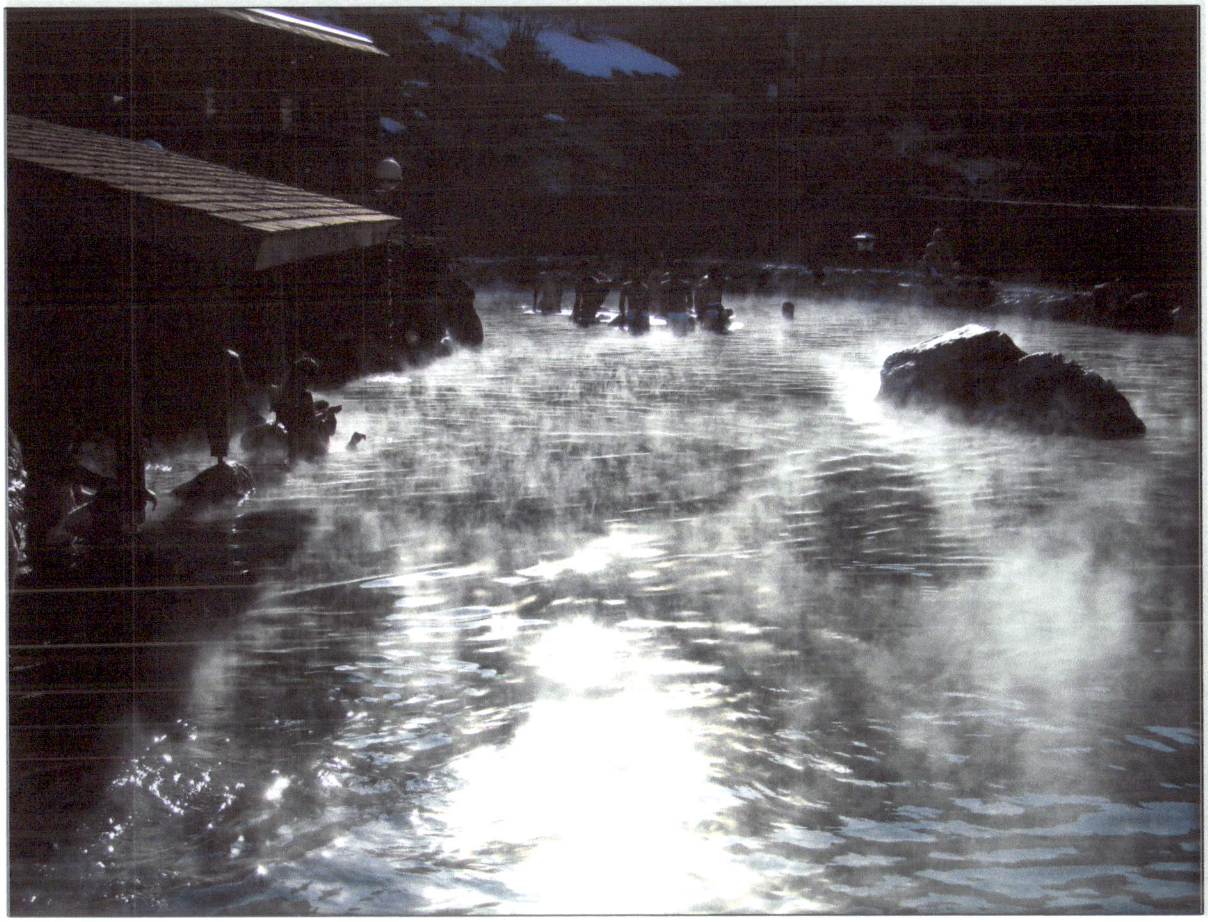

The photo above was taken at **Kusatsu**, in **Gunma Prefecture**. It was just about sunset and the sun was reflecting off the waters of the Outdoor Hot Spring, or Rotenboro, in **Sainokawara Park**. The weather was typically cool and in the mountains of Gunma Prefecture there was still more snow than a person wanted to think about. In fact, when we went hiking the following day, we found that there was still enough snow so that people were skiing and snowboarding. Needless to say, it was still going to be a while before cherry blossom season arrived here.

Kusatsu Onsen is accessible from Tokyo via a bus ride of three to four hours, depending on traffic conditions. The scenery along the way is nice to see. There are plenty of hotels in Kusatsu, as well as a Youth Hostel and several Pensions and other types of Inns.

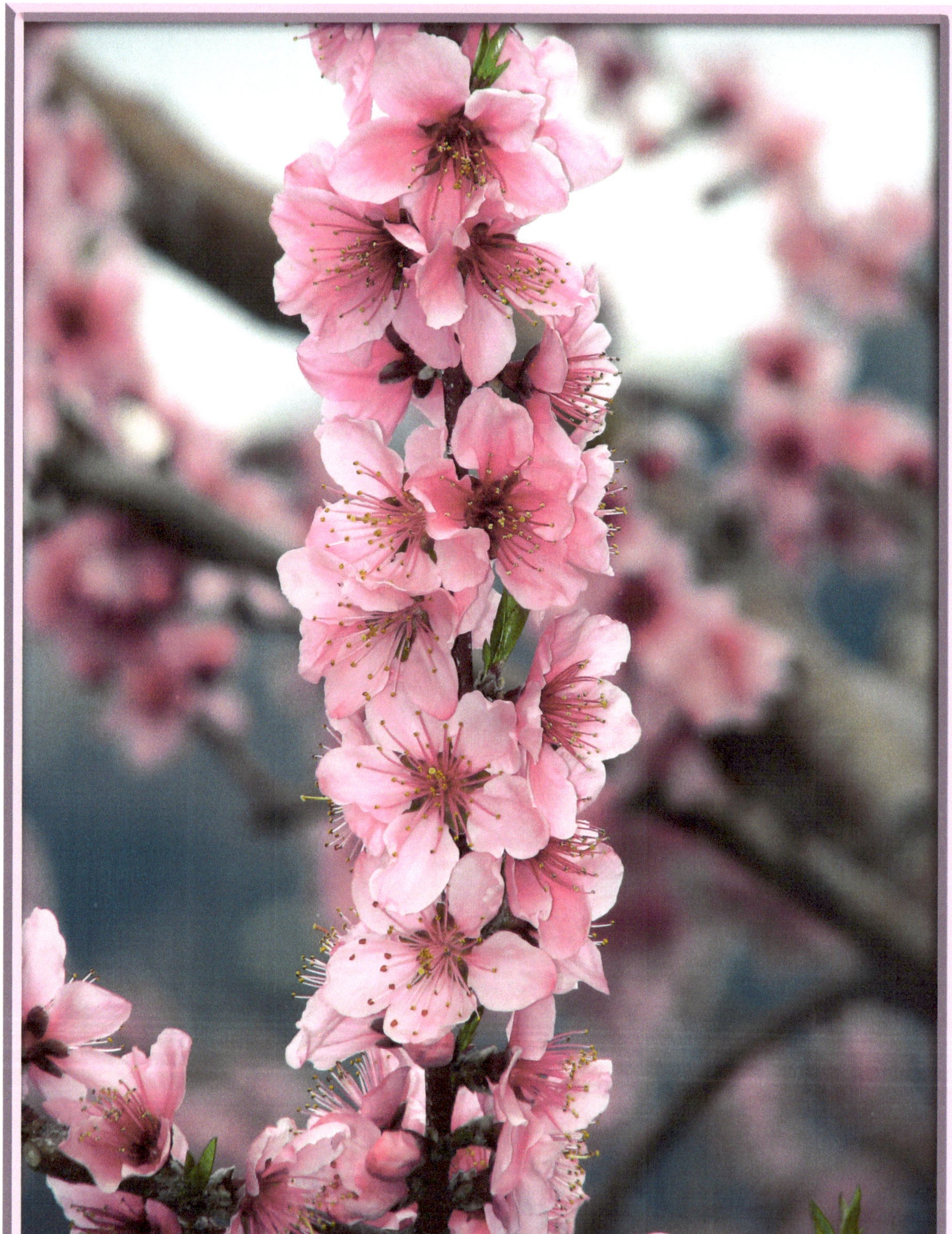

The photo on the facing page is a shot of **Peach Blossoms**. It was taken near **Yamanashi City** in **Yamanashi Prefecture**. The Yamanashi City area is a great place to go for both Cherry Blossoms and also Peach Blossoms. The blooms are a bit later there than they are in the Tokyo Area.

Below is an additional shot of Trout Lily (***Erythronium japonicum***). The previous photo, on page 38, was taken at **Jindai Botanical Garden**, on the west side of Tokyo. The photo below was taken in **Niigata Prefecture** on one of the slopes of Mt. Kakuda. On the Mt. Kakuda trails there are so many thousands or millions of Trout Lilies that you cannot believe your eyes. If you ever find yourself in Niigata Prefecture in Trout Lily season it would definitely be worth your time and effort to climb Mt. Kakuda – especially as it is only 482 meters (= 1,580 feet) in elevation.

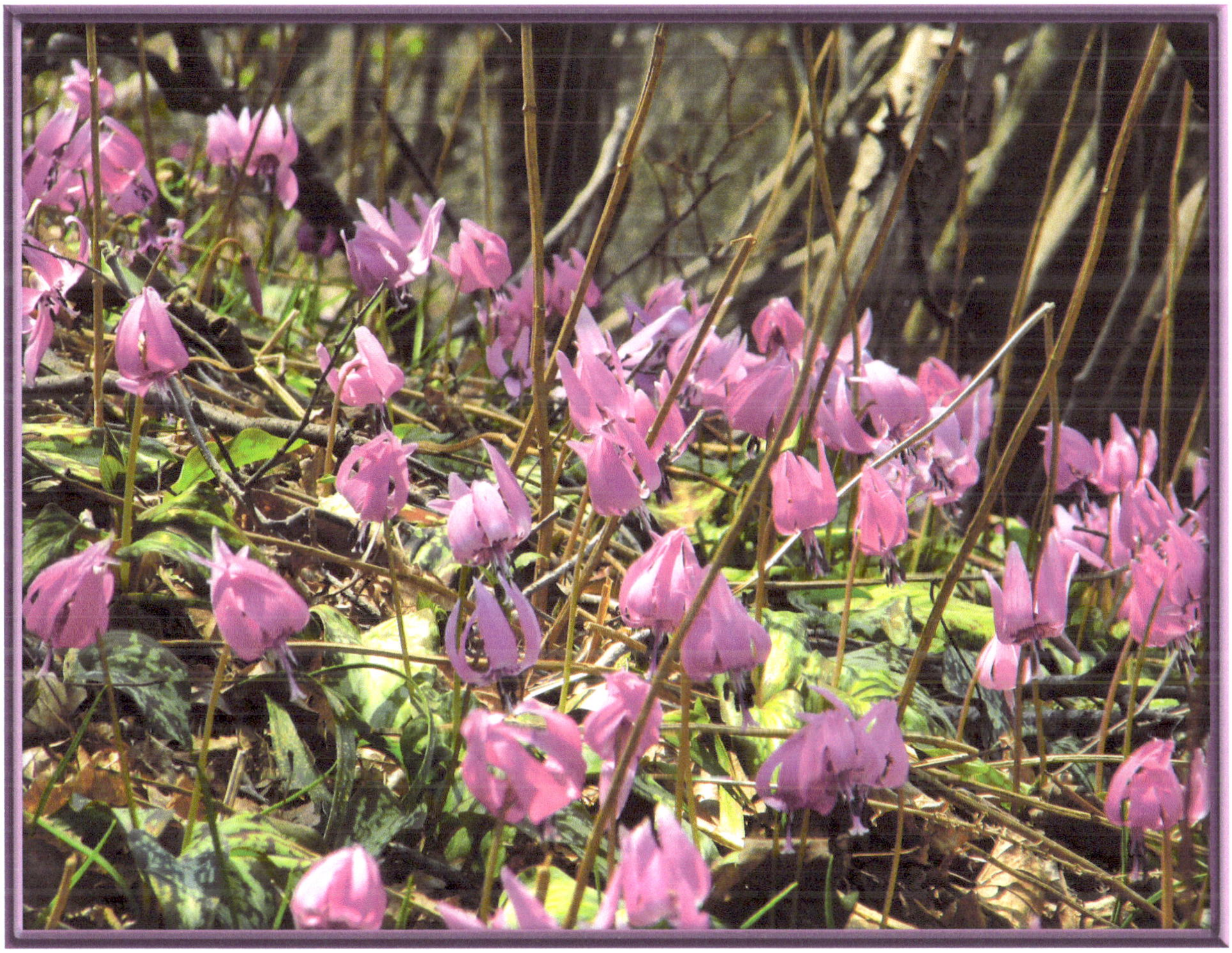

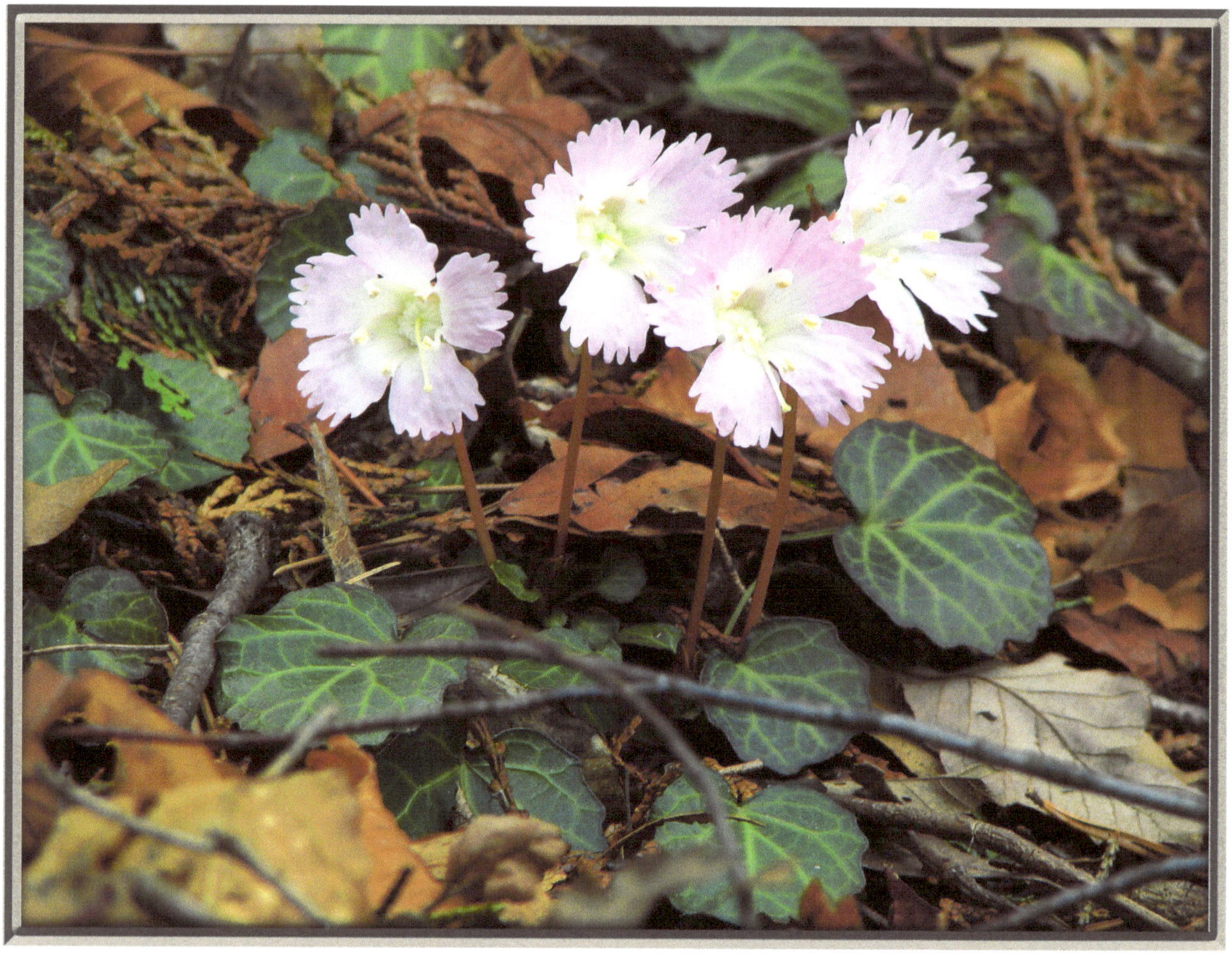

The above flower is ***Shortia uniflora***. We have always found it only on very steep and rocky slopes and it is therefore always dangerous to try and get near enough to it to take any decent photos. This specimen was found in the mountains near **Mitake** in far Western Tokyo. The flower is a very delicate pink in color. The colors have never shown up true to life in any of the many photos of this flower which we have.

The photo on the facing page shows you the waterfall which you previously saw a hint of way back on page 17. This is **Tengu Waterfall** in far Western Tokyo near **Hinohara**. We like to hike up this valley in early spring in search of violets and other spring flowers.

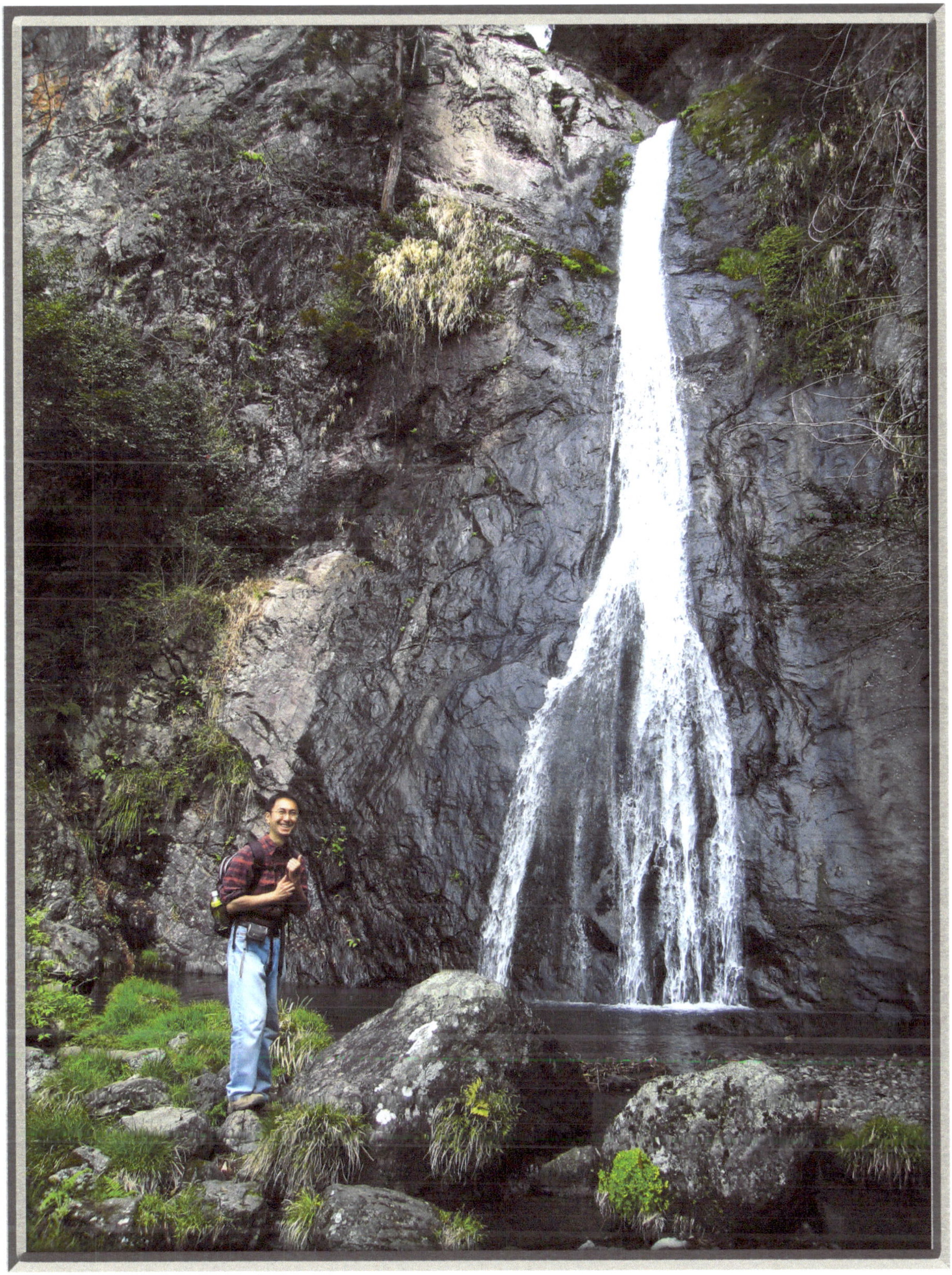

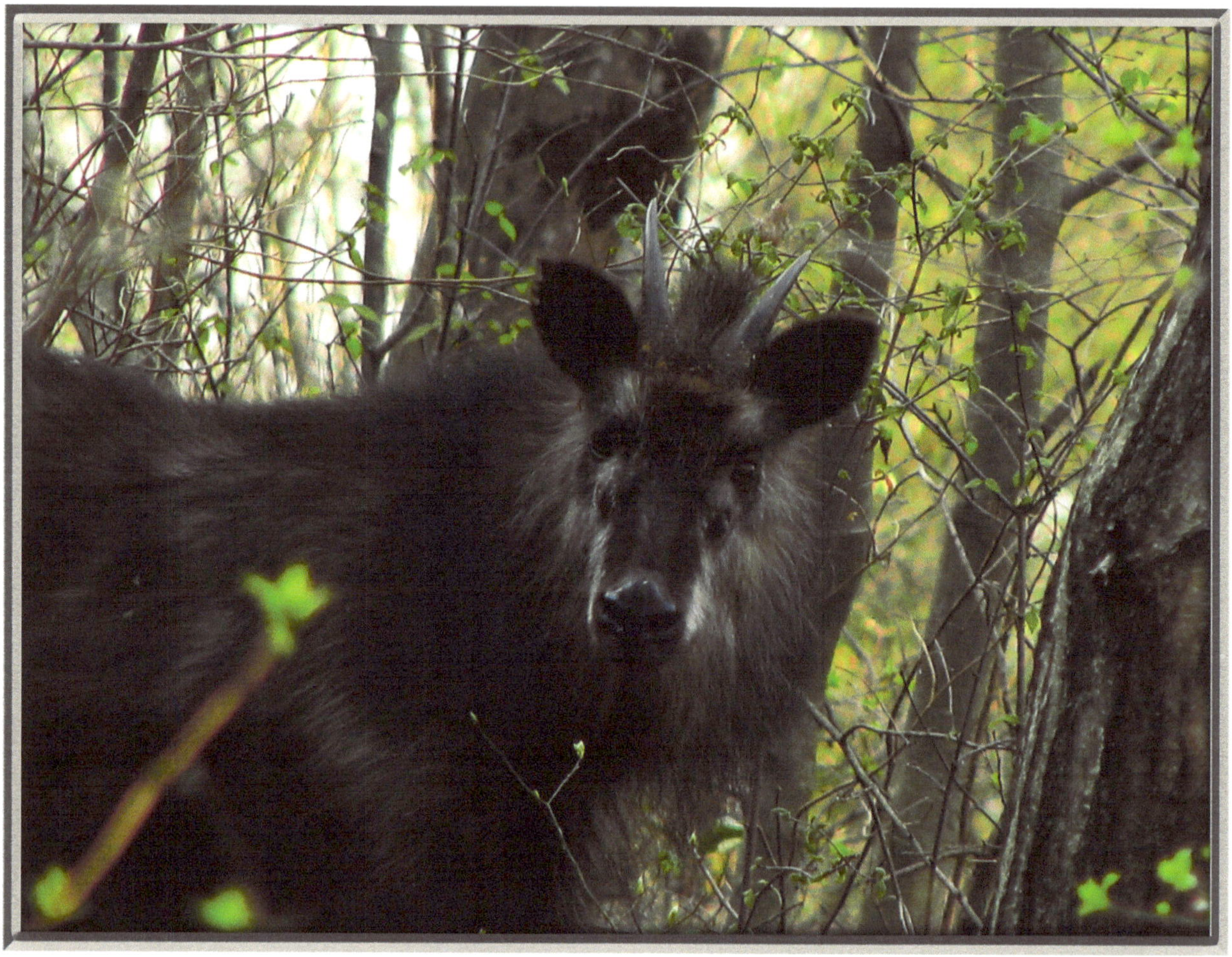

The above photo is a ***Capricornis crispus***, a **Japanese Serow** (***Kamoshika*** in Japanese). Although not rare, we have only seen this animal in the wild about six or seven times. It likes the deep forests and high mountains and is quite shy. This specimen is the most beautiful one we have seen due to it being very early spring and it still having its long winter hair in place. This animal marks its range with a substance similar to vinegar, which is secreted from the pre-orbital glands, which can be seen just in front of the eyes in this photo.

The photo on the facing page is a ***Viola eizanensis*** – an **Eizan Violet**. This is an exceptional specimen due to the pinkish flower color. This species generally has pure white flowers. we'll show you one additional photo of this species later on, one which is a mutant and also pure white.

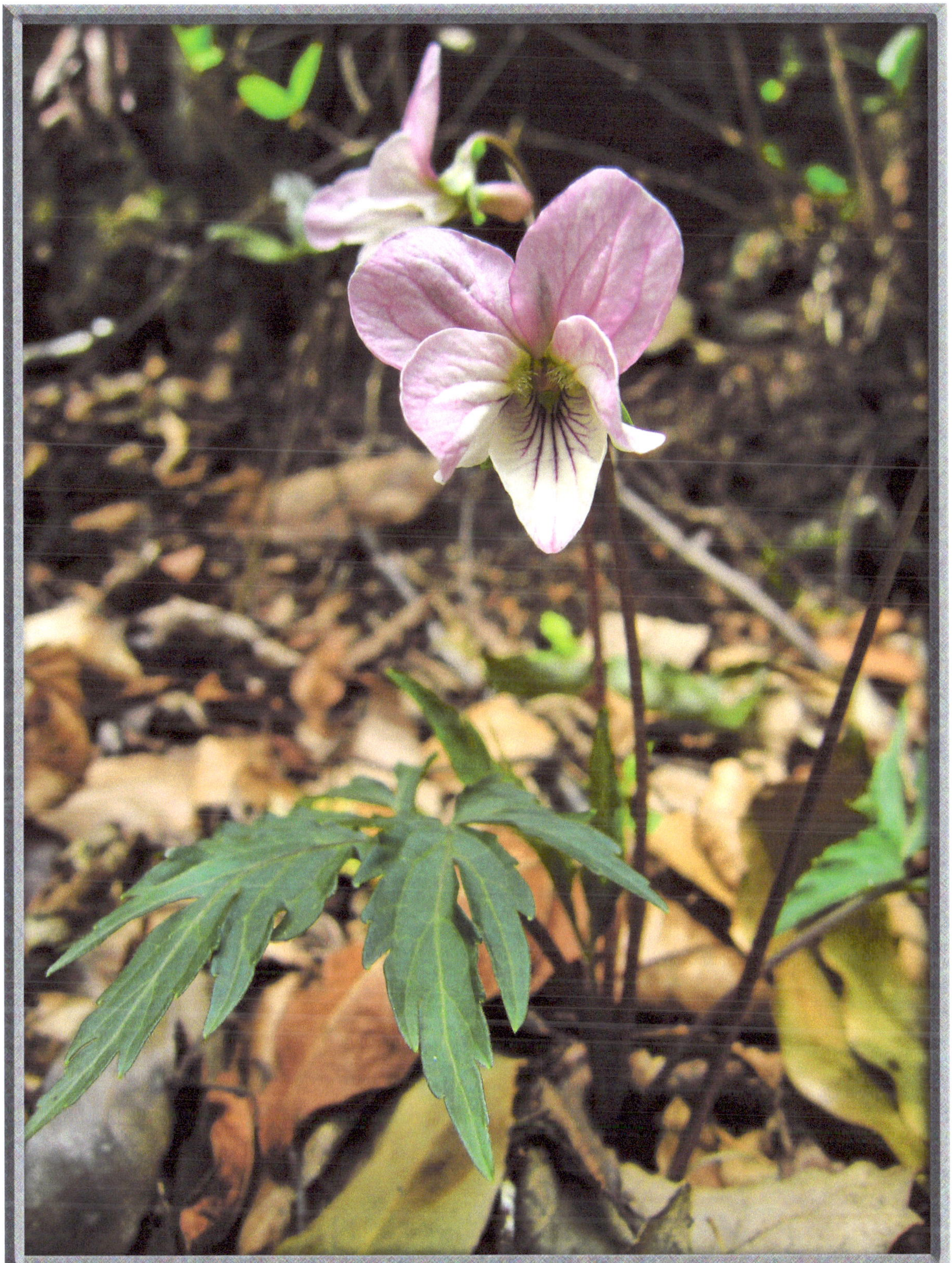

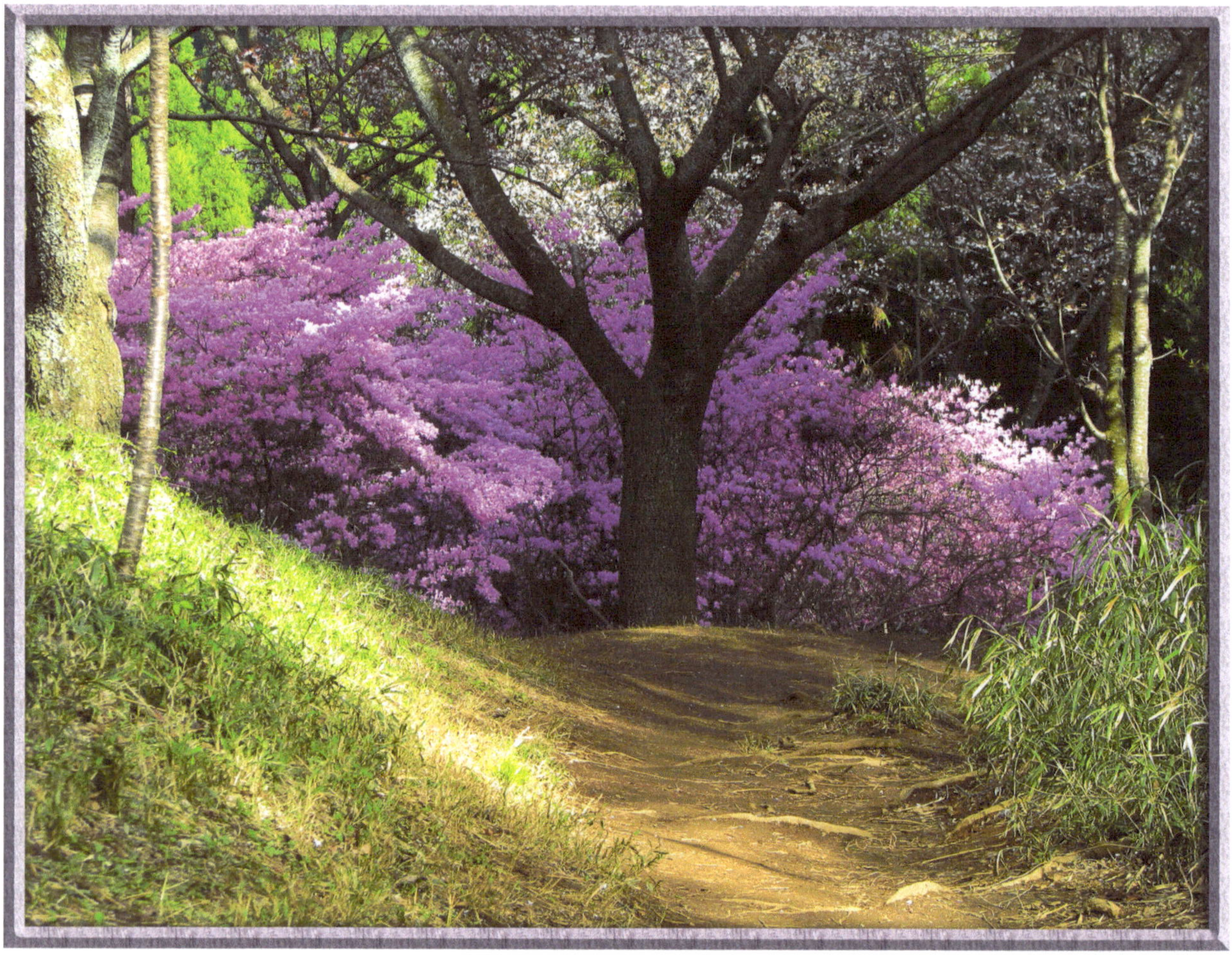

The above photo was taken on April 15th along one of the several **Mt. Takao** (**Takao-san**) trails. It is a stunning shot of a **Mountain Azalea** bush in full bloom.

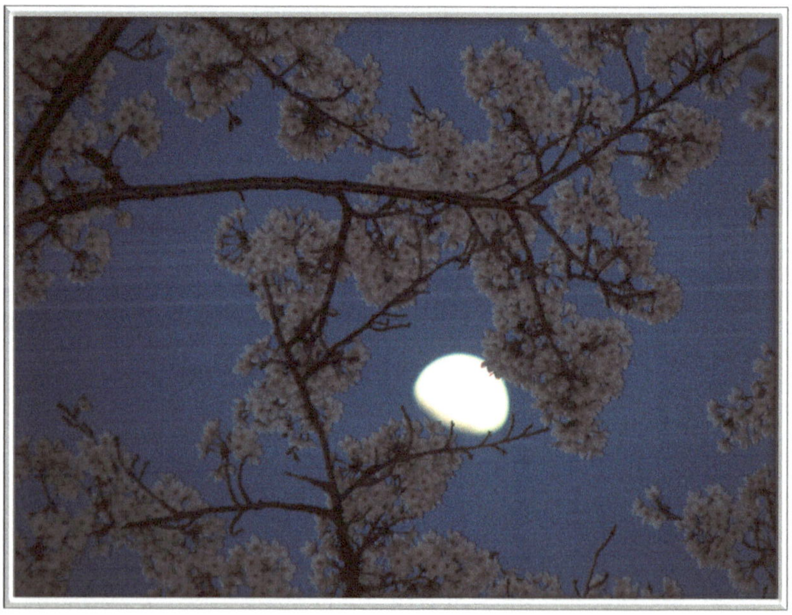

The photo to the right was taken just after sunset on the same day at **I-Ccho-Daira**, near **Mt. Takao**. This is a **Mountain Cherry** (***Yama-Zakura*** in Japanese) tree with a ¾ moon.

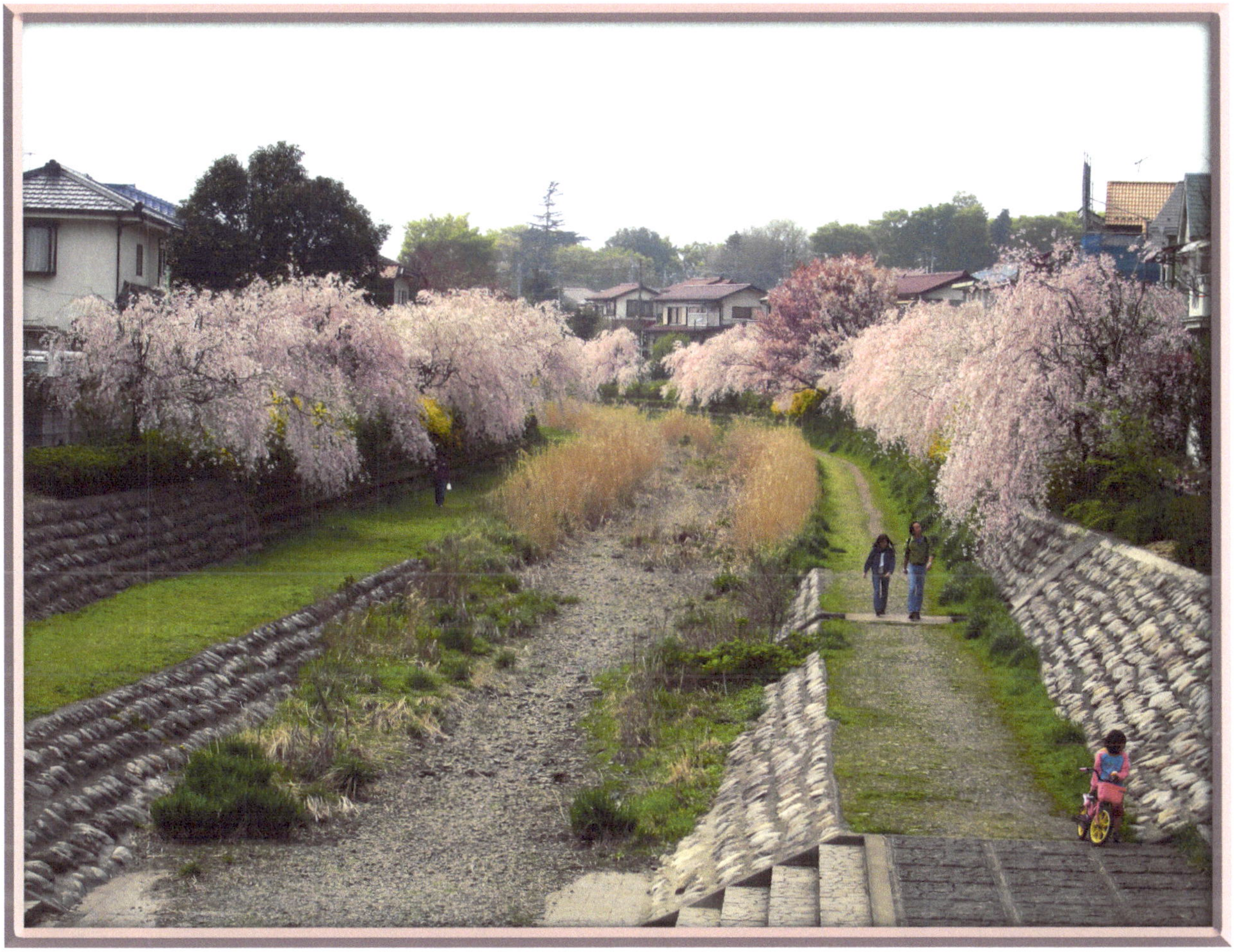

The photo inserted immediately above is of the **Nogawa** (**No River = 野川 = Field River**) with an abundance of late blooming Cherry Trees along the upper banks of the river. This photo was taken near mid-April one year when the cherry blossoms were later than normal. These are growing in people's yards, so they are most likely one of the many cultivated varieties and not merely plain and simple cherry trees.

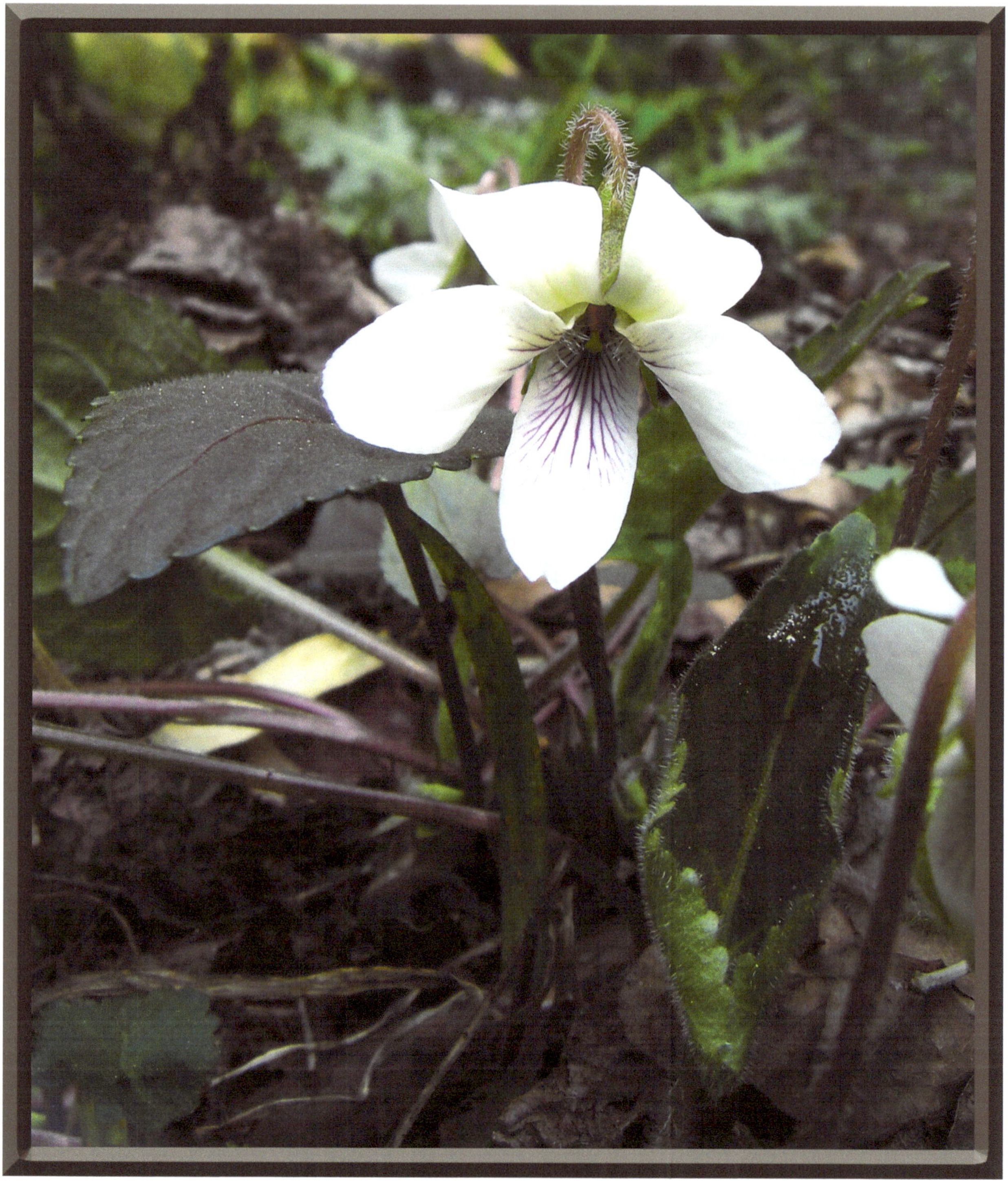

This photo above is of a **Takao Violet** (***Viola yezoensis* f. *discolor***). The **forma *discolor*** denotes the purplish colored leaves. This is a famous violet and is, of course, found around **Mt. Takao** (**Takao-san**), as well as in other places.

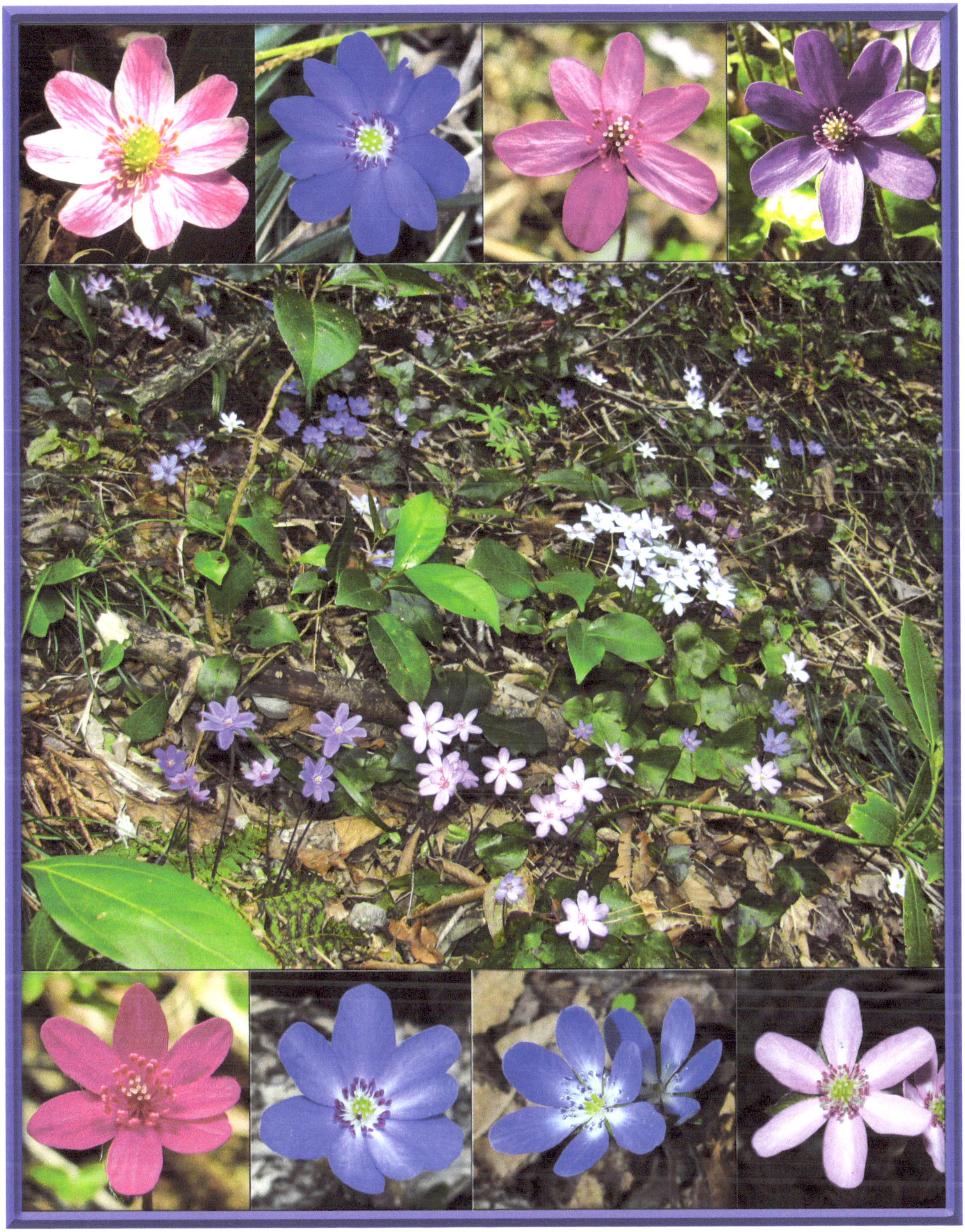

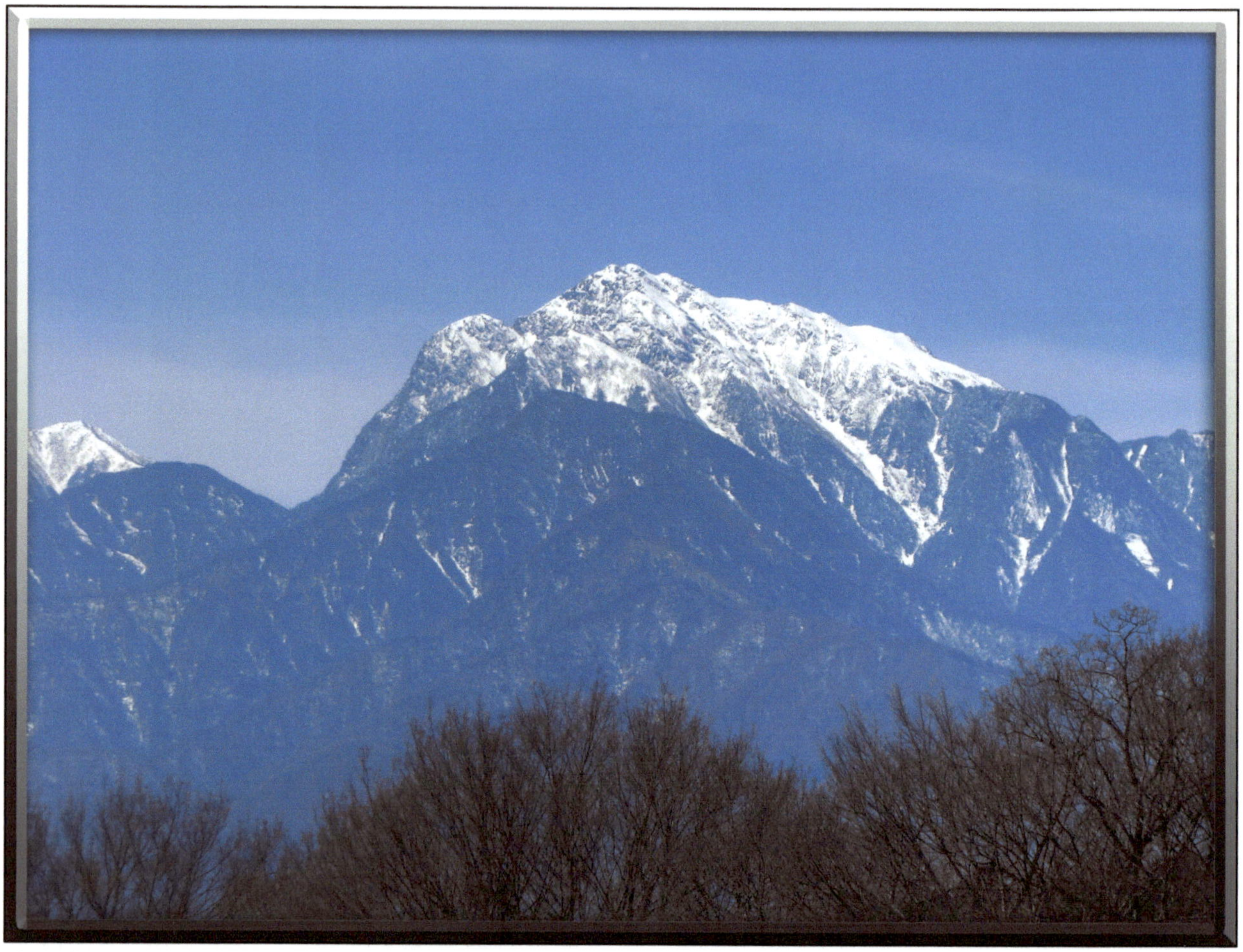

On the previous page is a photo collage of several plants and several colors of ***Hepatica nobilis* var. *japonica* f. *magna***. These photos were taken on **Mt. Kakuda**, in **Niigata Prefecture**. Mt. Kakuda is famous for its Hepatica flowers in the spring of the year. We were very fortunate to find a place that looked like this. On the more traveled slopes of Mt. Kakuda the Hepatica is becoming harder to find due to plant thieves. This is an amazing collage showing so many colors.

In the above photo we are not sure what the name of this mountain is, but it was near **Nagasaka Station**, in **Yamanashi Prefecture**. We hiked a ten kilometer trail there one time in search of some specific violets. We found the violets we were in search of, but this photo of the nearby mountains was probably the most impressive photo taken on that day.

The facing page shows another species of ***Asarum***. You saw a photo of a different species of ***Asarum*** back on page 24. The one you saw there was ***Asarum nipponicum***. The one shown to the right is ***Asarum caulescens***. As you will note, this species has more delicate blossoms and they are above the ground. This species blooms later than the previously shown one and the flowers of this species are much shorter lived.

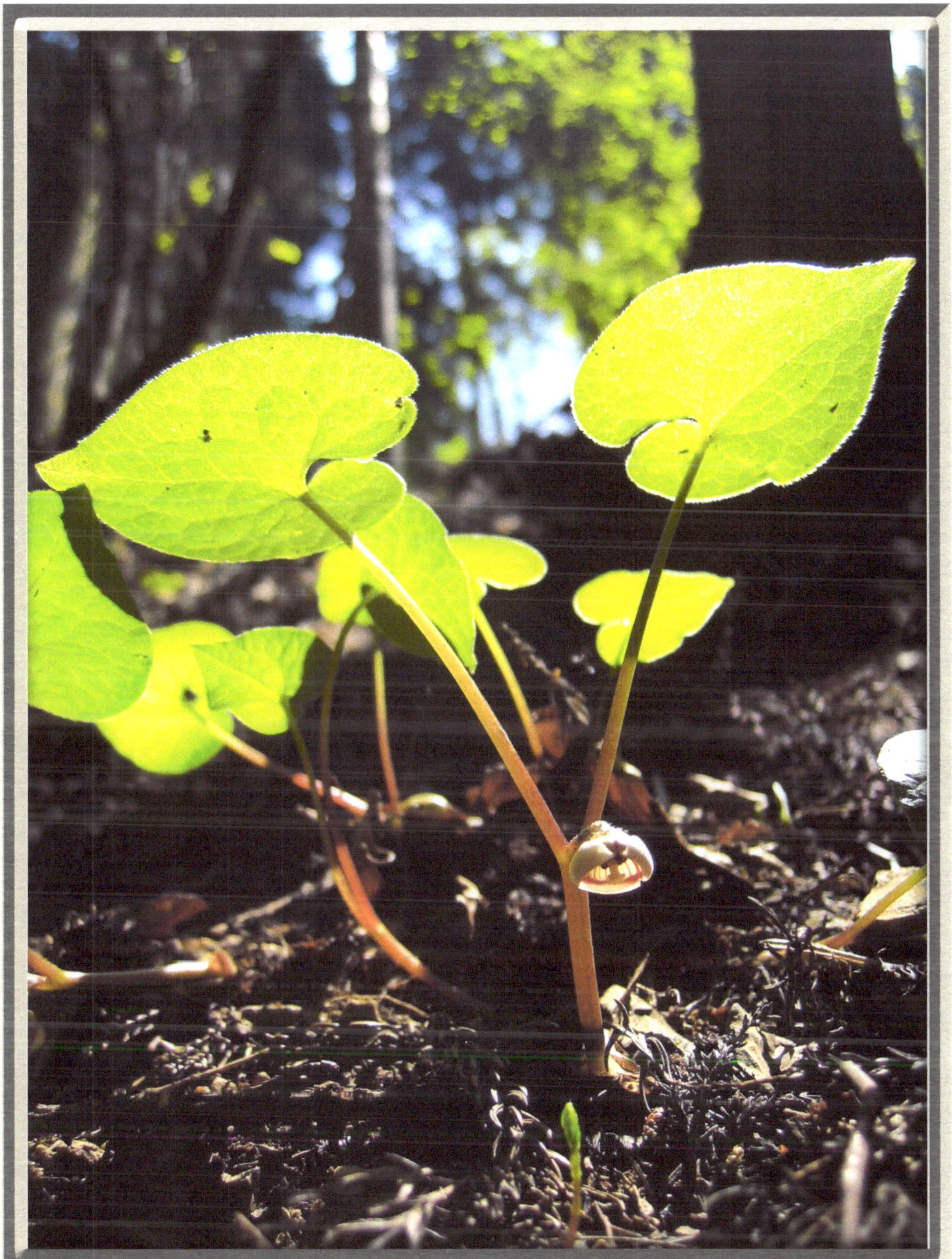

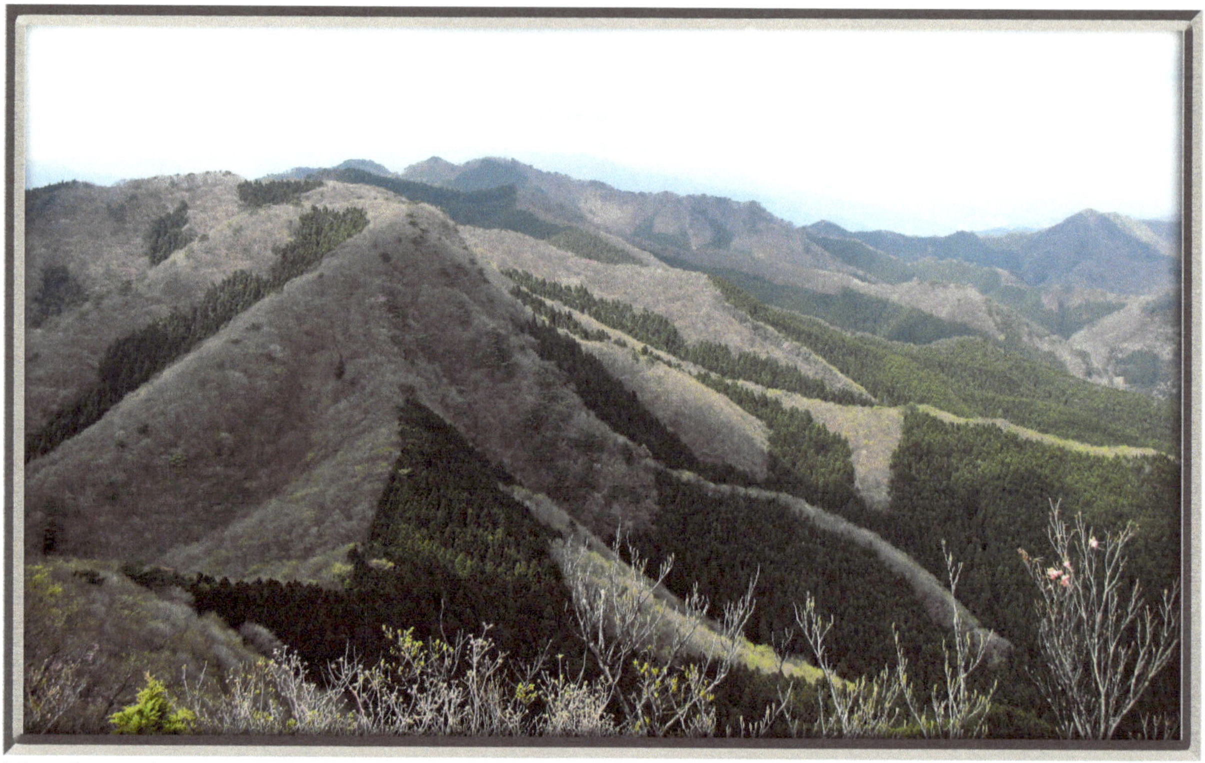

The above photo was taken from the summit of **Mt. Narukami** in **Gunma Prefecture**. Note that it was not yet spring in the mountains.

The below photo – **Mt. Fuji** – was taken from **Asagiri Kogen** in **Shizuoka Prefecture**. This was another violet hunting expedition.

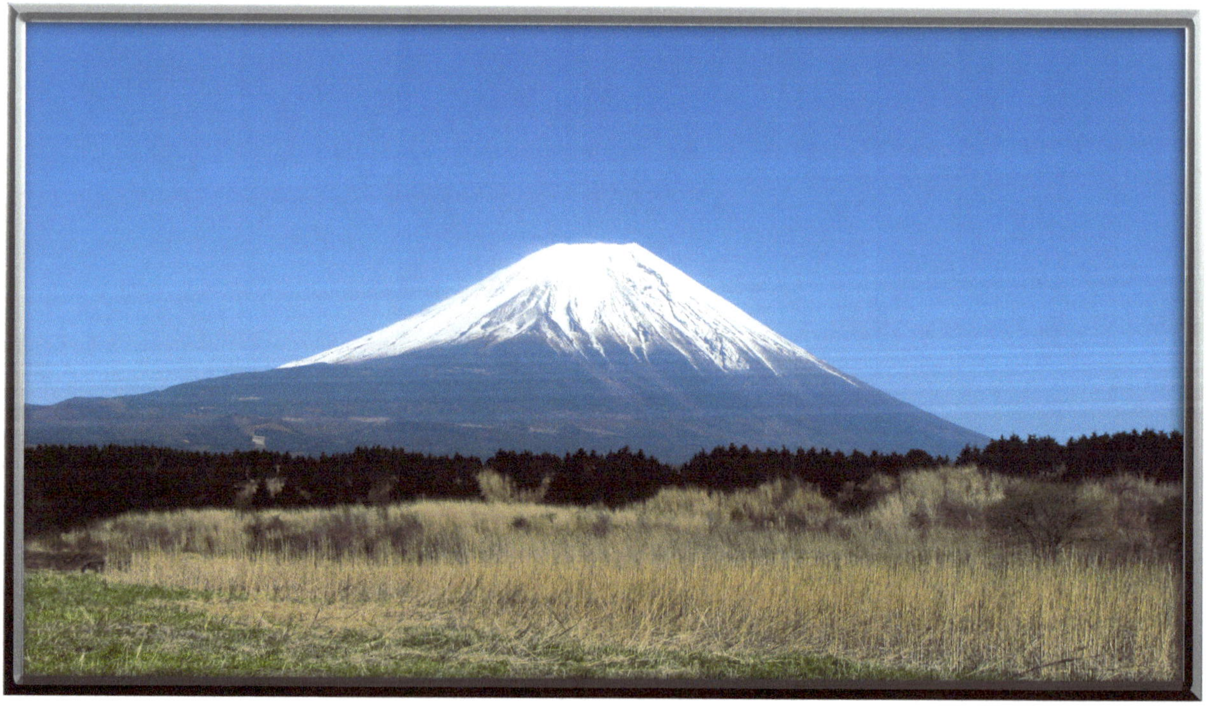

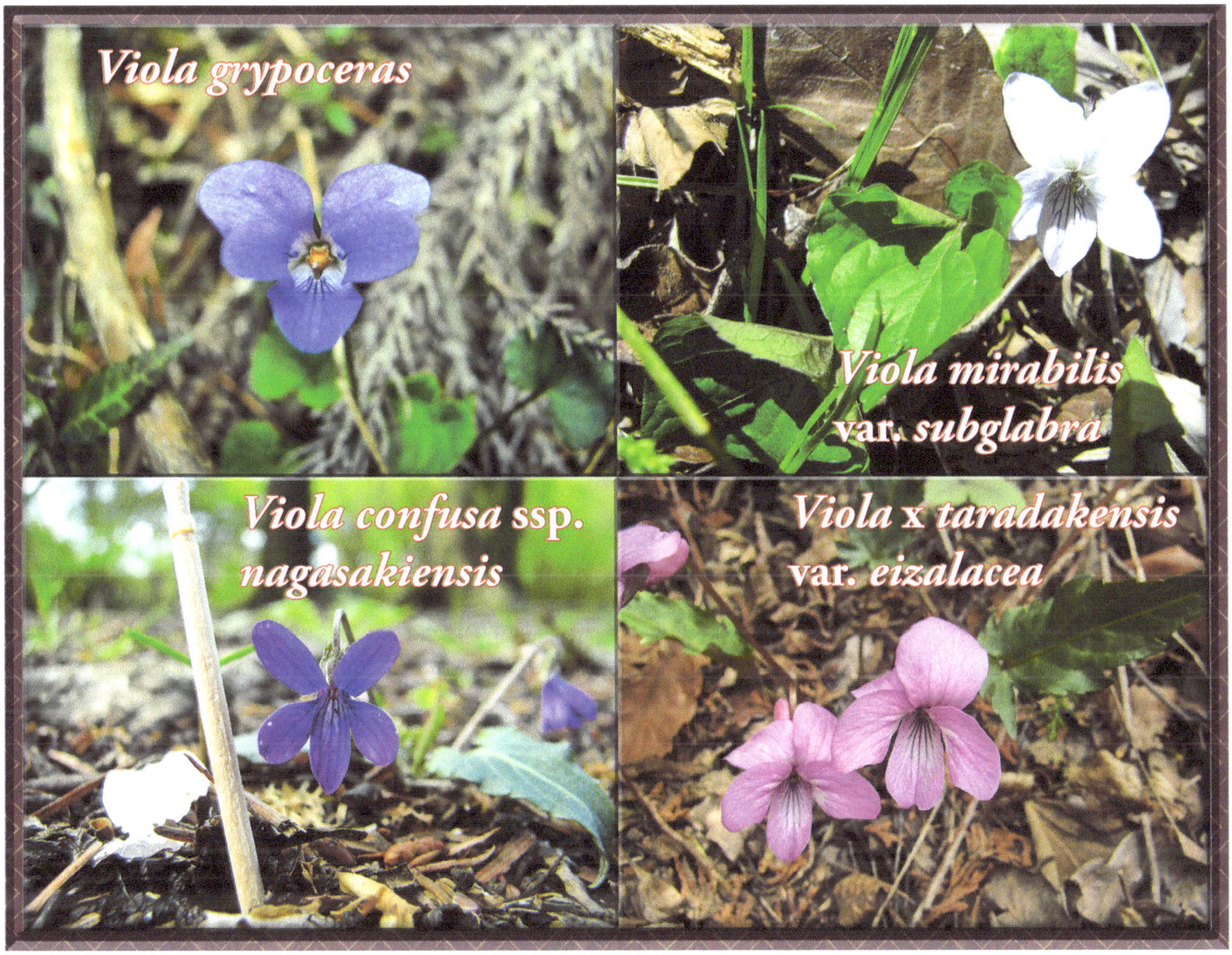

The photo just above is the final one of April. It shows four violets which we often find (or hope to find) in April which we have not shown separate photos of. ***Viola grypoceras*** is one of our most common violets around the Tokyo Area. ***Viola mirabilis* var. *subglabra*** is one which is quite special and rare for us. We have only found it in two places in our years of violet hunting. ***Viola confusa* ssp. *nagasakiensis*** is another one which is quite rare for us, in fact we have never seen it in the wild, only in parks and Botanical Gardens. The final one – ***Viola* x *taradakensis* var. *eizalacea*** is extremely rare – we only know of one place to find it.

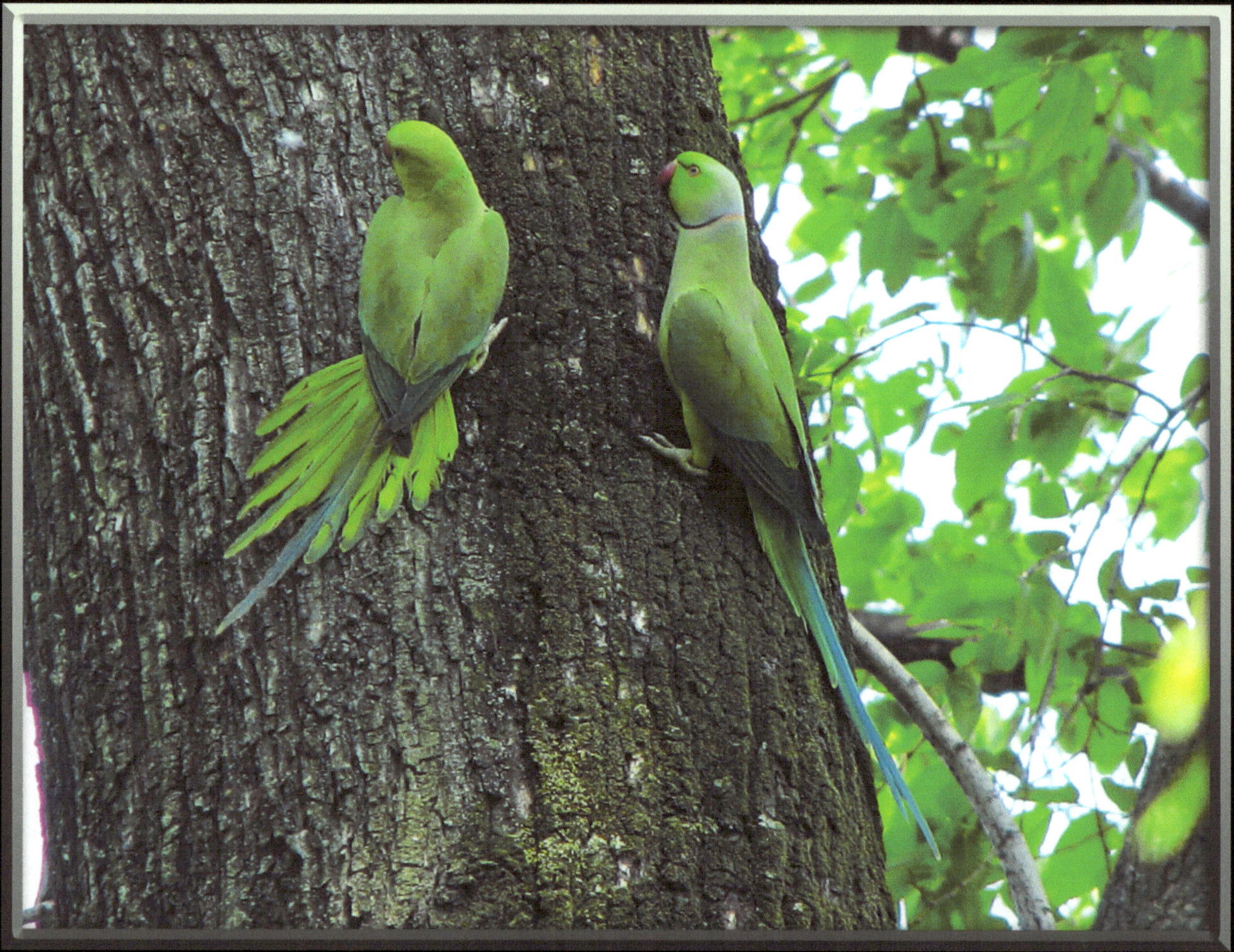

May Photos and Story

Above is a photo of two **Feral Parakeets** going through their annual mating ritual. Parakeets like this are not native to the Tokyo Area. This bird is actually ***Psittacula krameri manillensis***, a parakeet that is native to southern India and Sri Lanka. Its common name in English is the **Rose-Ringed Parakeet**; in Japanese, it's called ***Wakake Honsei Inko***. Apparently there was a pet boom in the 1960's and many Japanese became pet owner's for the first time. Large numbers of tropical birds were imported and many were either released or escaped. There is not much known about these birds, the researchers do not even seem to know their diet, let alone their effects on local native bird populations. By the way, the male is the one with the ring around its neck (right side).

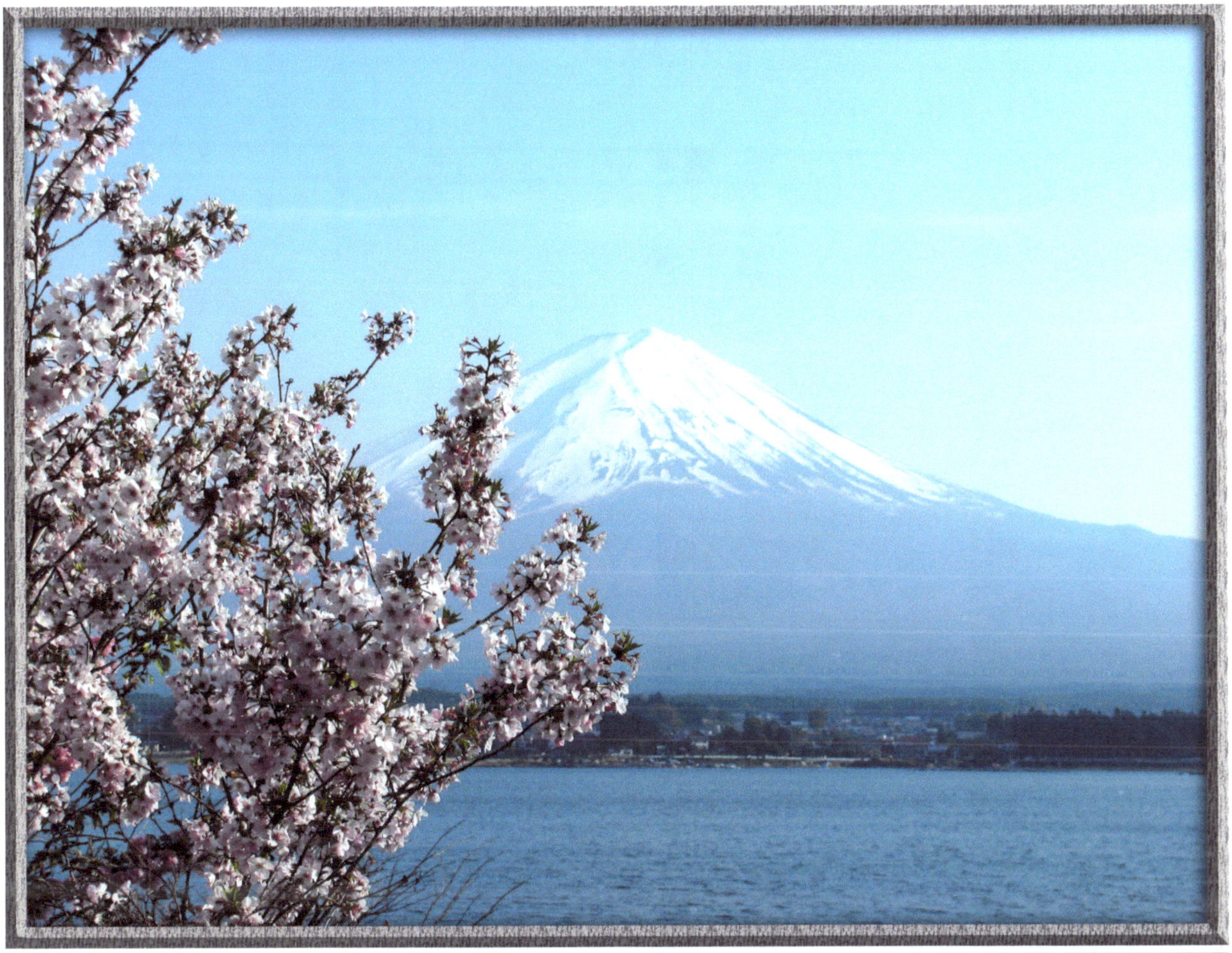

Above is a photo of **Mt. Fuji** with a Cherry Tree adding a very interesting effect to the photo. The lake is **Lake Kawaguchi**.

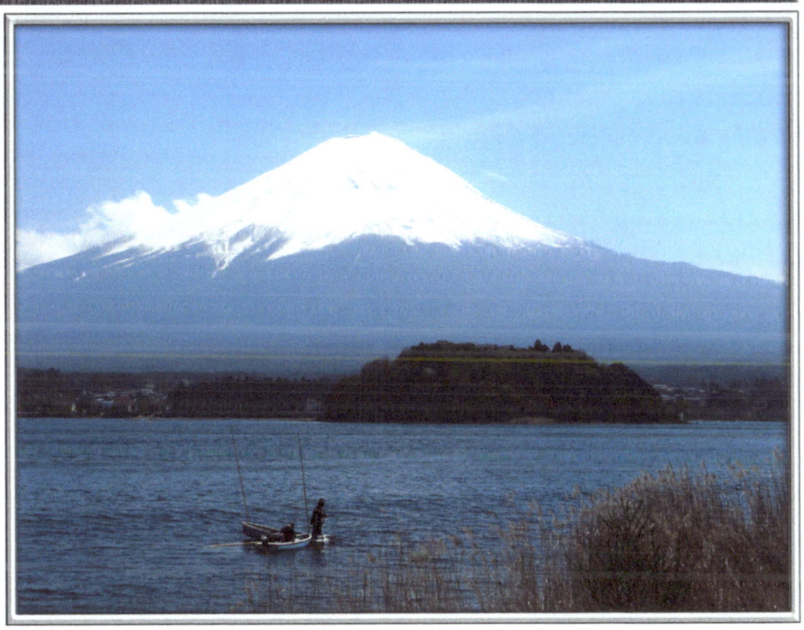

The photo to the right is Mt. Fuji and Lake Kawaguchi with no cherry tree. Both of these photos were taken on May 1st, but in different years.

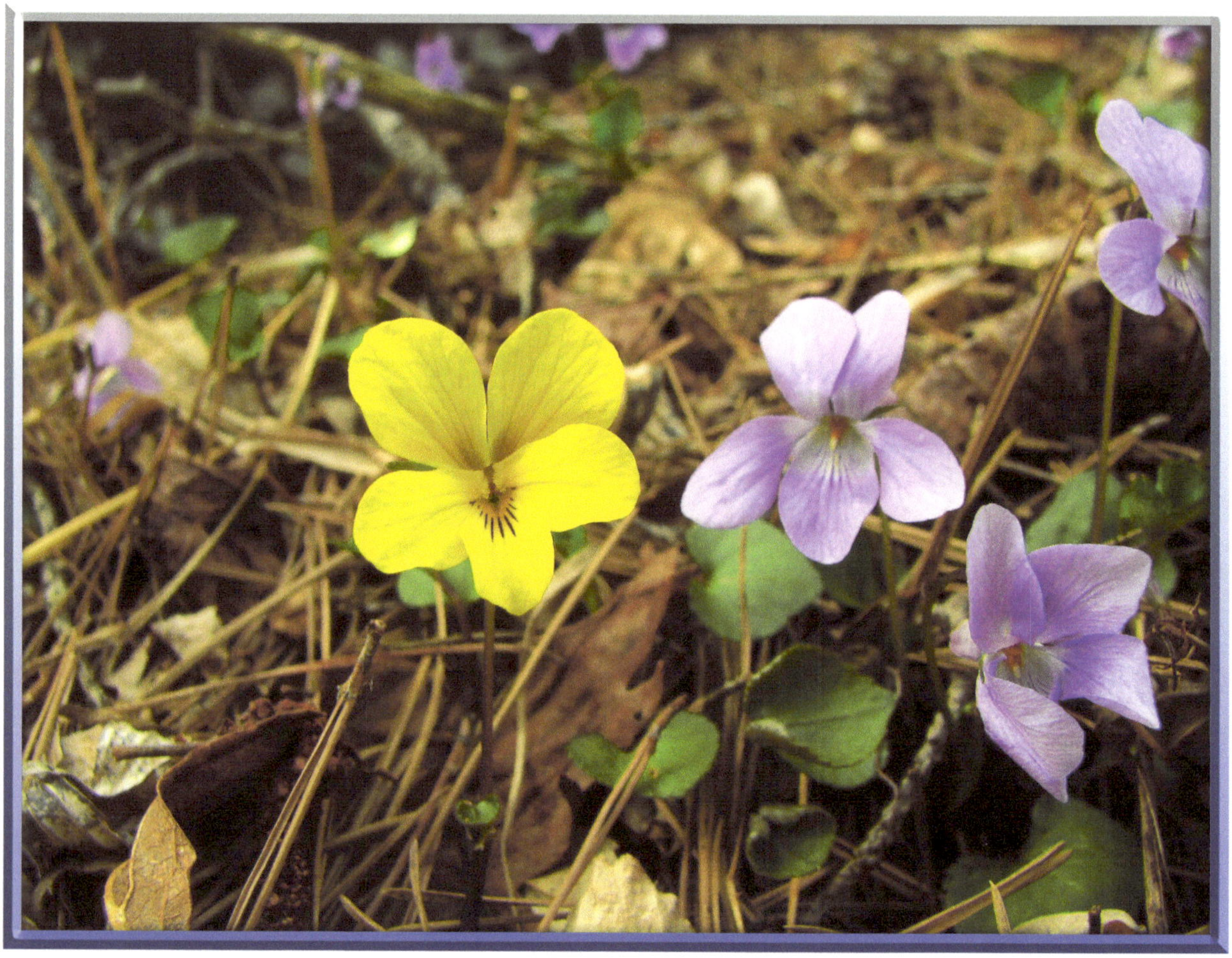

The above photo shows you a contrast between ***Viola orientalis*** (the yellow one) and ***Viola grypoceras*** (the purple one). This is a fairly rare sight to see and even more rare to be able to take a photo with both of these violets in it. This was near **Kawaguchi Lake**. We often take a trip to Kawaguchi Lake and hike around the area quite extensively at around April 30th or May 1st. We generally stay for two or three days and hike many of the mountain trails on the north side of the lake. It is a good time of the year to find violets which are not very common in other areas and also to see some great mountain scenery.

On the facing page you can find an additional photo of **Trout Lily** (***Erythronium japonicum***). This is a very beautiful shot – looks like an American Indian painting!

On page 49 we showed you a photo of ***Viola eizanensis*** with a promise to show you a photo of a pure white one which is a mutant. This final photo of the mutated form of ***Viola eizanensis*** is also on the facing page. The mutation, by the way, is the shape of the two upper petals.

Erythronium japonicum (Trout Lily)

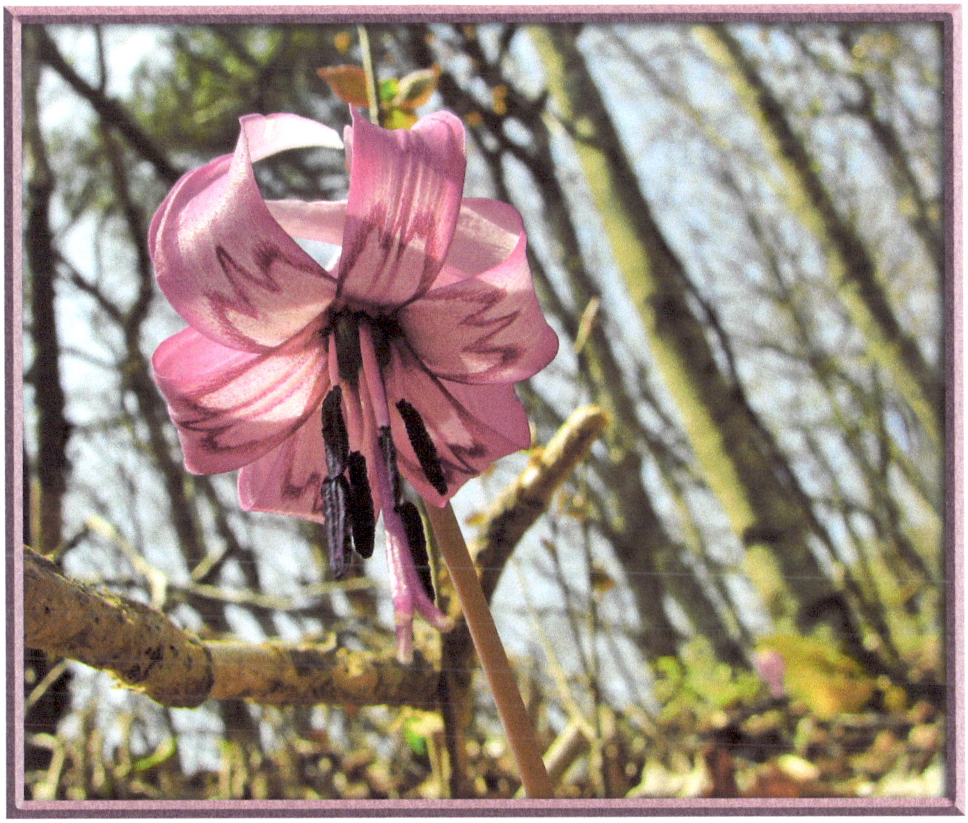

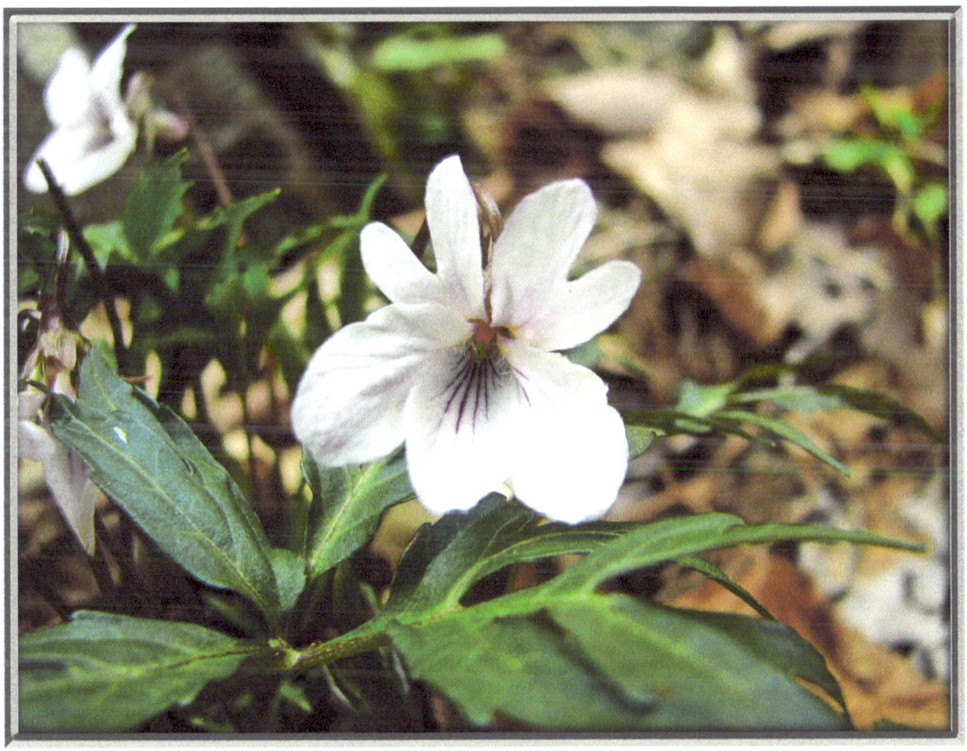

Viola eizanensis (Eizan Violet) (mutant flower)

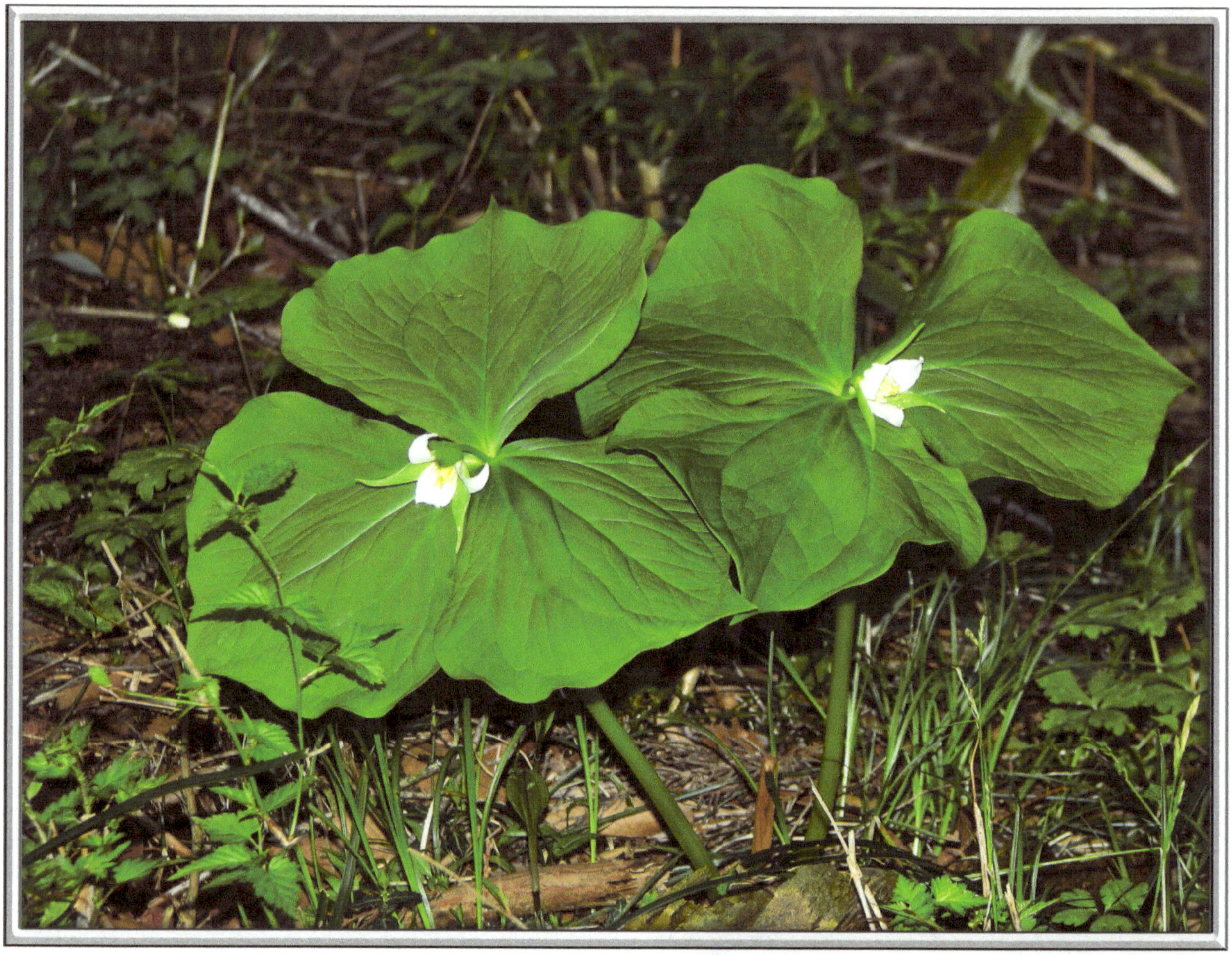

The plant shown above is a ***Trillium tschonoskii*** – a relatively rare ***Trillium***. The leaves are whorled and the plant is very beautiful to see. There is another ***Trillium*** in Japan – ***Trillium smallii***. This species is shown to the right. As you can see, the flower is brown in color on the ***Trillium smallii***.

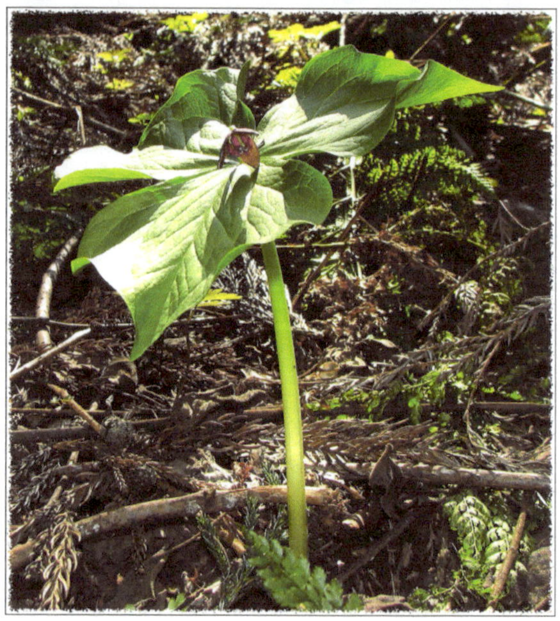

On the facing page is a photo of **Hahanoshira Waterfall** near **Kawaguchi Lake**. This waterfall is very photogenic, but it is in a very shady place and is therefore difficult to get good photos of.

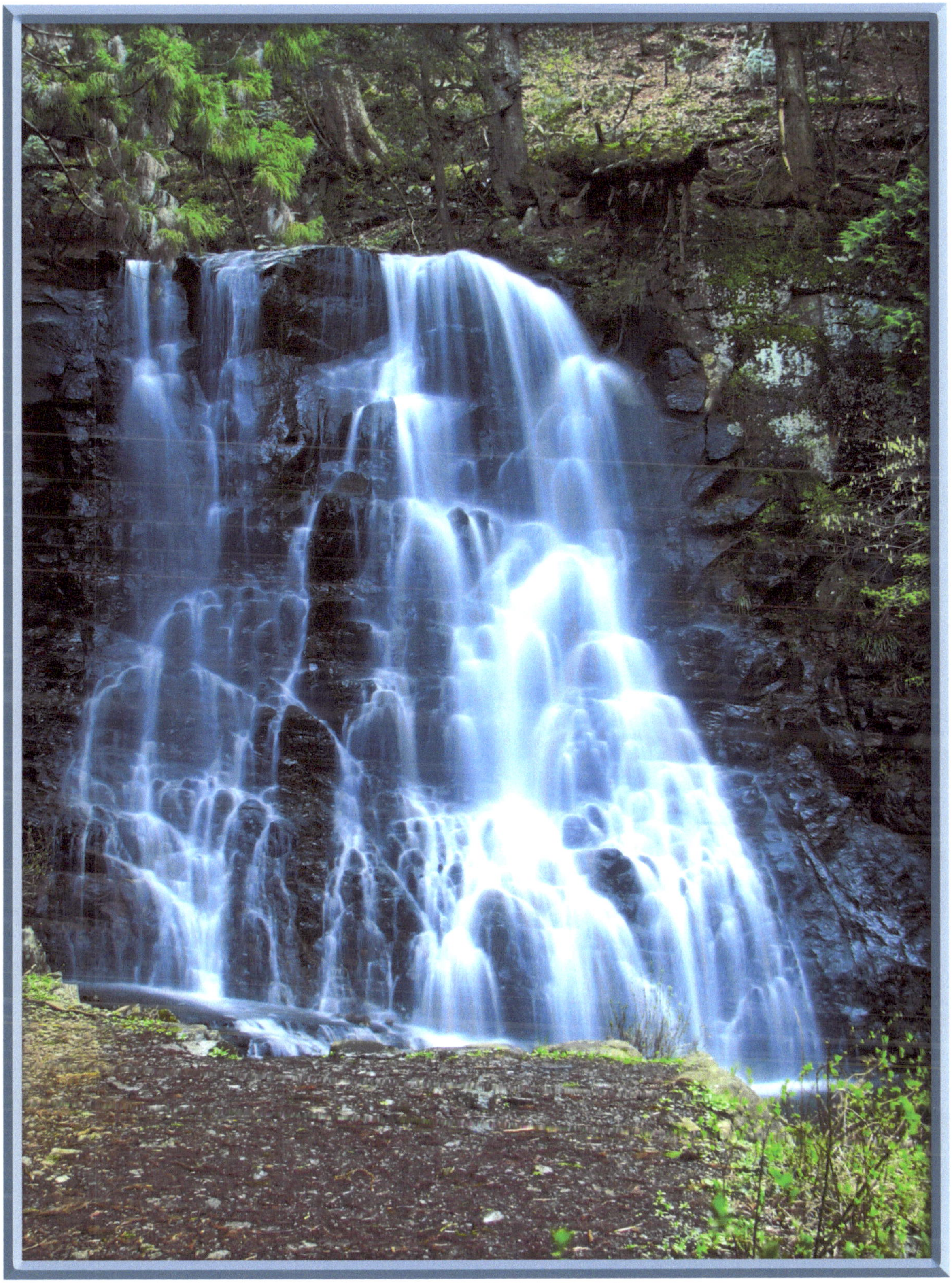

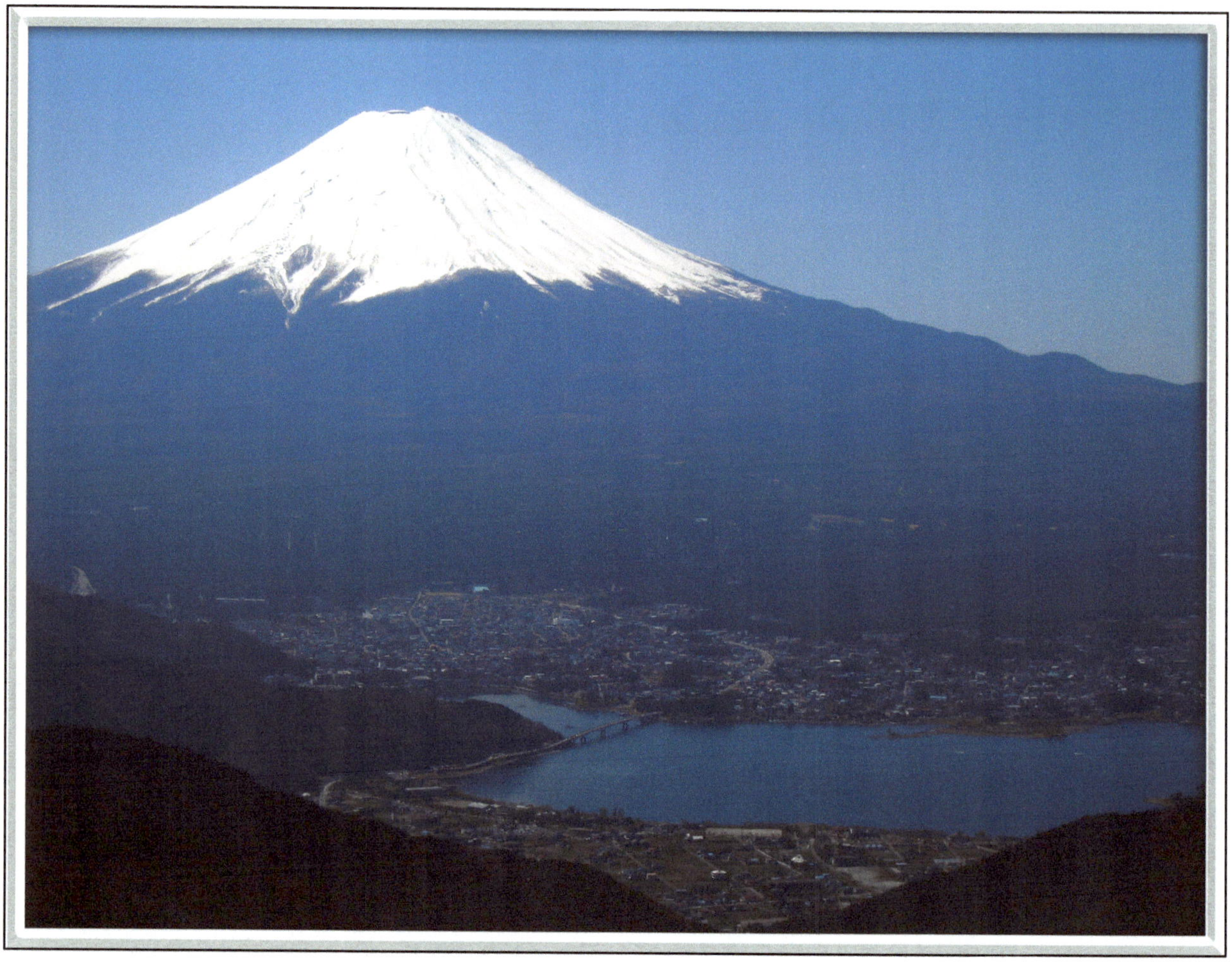

The photo above is a very beautiful shot of **Mt. Fuji** from the ridge on the north side of **Kawaguchi Lake**. The weather was so amazingly clear on this particular day – we had been here a few times before this and we have been a few times since we took this photo, but we have never experienced a day which was so beautifully clear and free of haze as this one was.

On the facing page is a photo of a tree snag on Mt. Kumotori. **Mt. Kumotori** is the highest point in Tokyo, at 2017.6 meters (= 6,619 feet). This photo is rather intriguing with its nice sunset colors. This photo was actually taken in 2004 and to our surprise this dead tree is still standing – or at least it was when we last visited Mt. Kumotori on September 3, 2010.

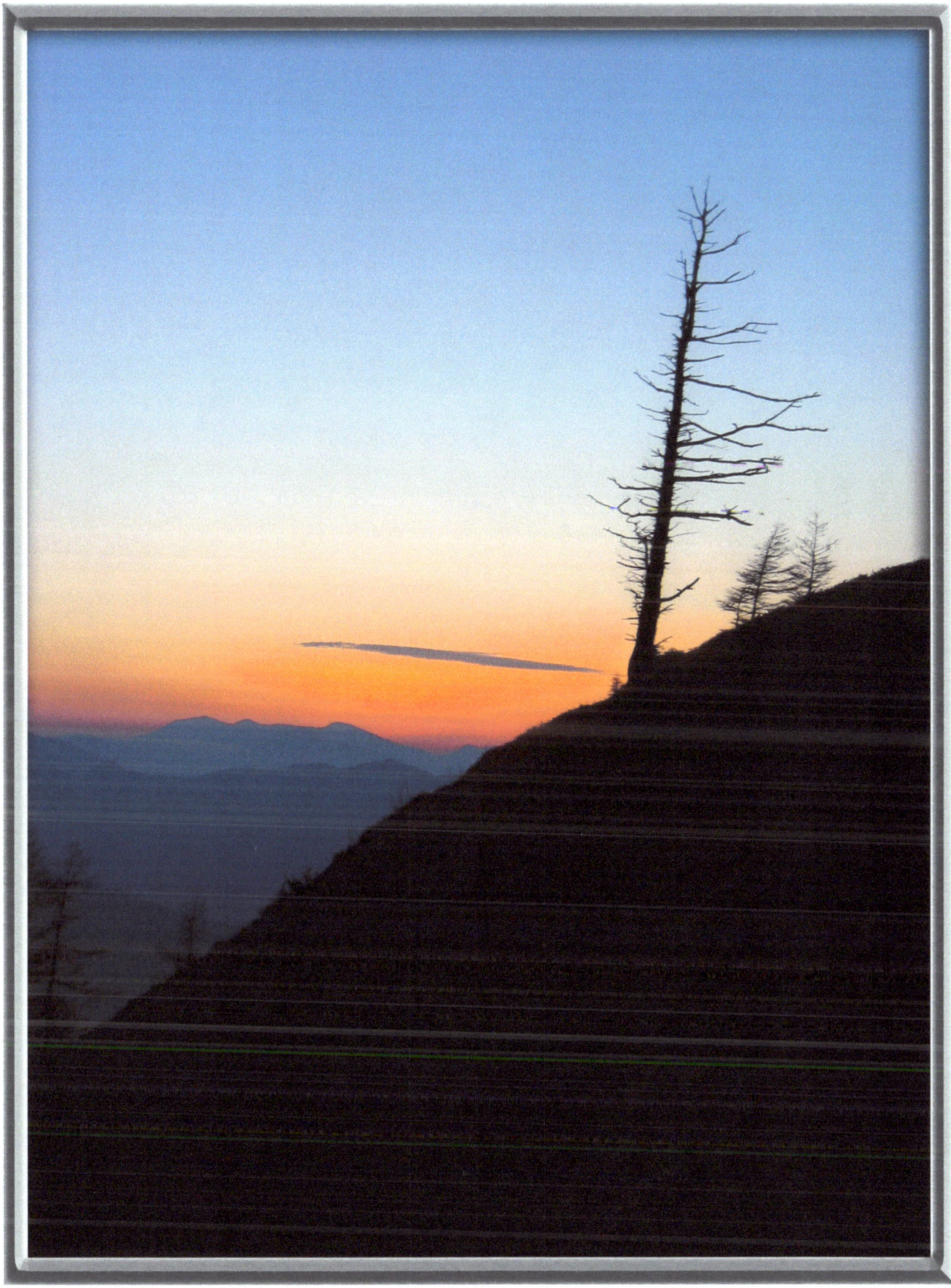

These two photos show just about the most beautiful sunset we have ever seen in our lives. This was the most amazing day. These shots were taken from the summit of **Mt. Kumotori**. The brightness and contrast have been adjusted a bit in both of these photos, but not very much, to enhance the beauty and make the photos closer to what we believe we saw when we were standing there. We like to return to **Mt. Kumotori** whenever we can in hopes of seeing another sunset like this one.

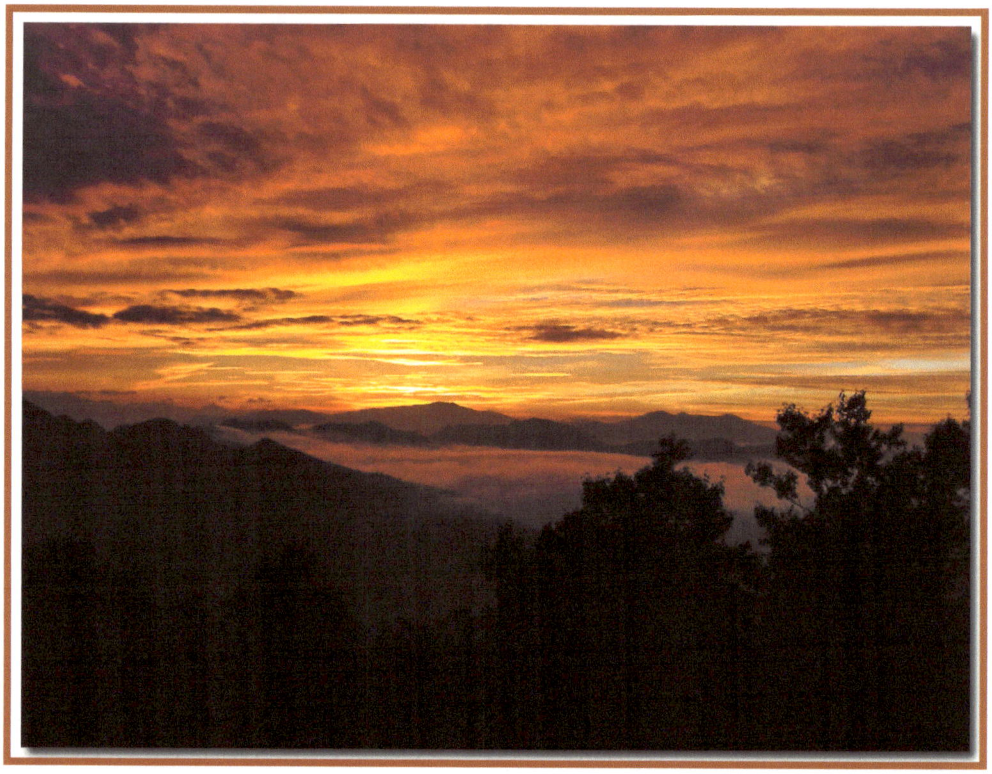

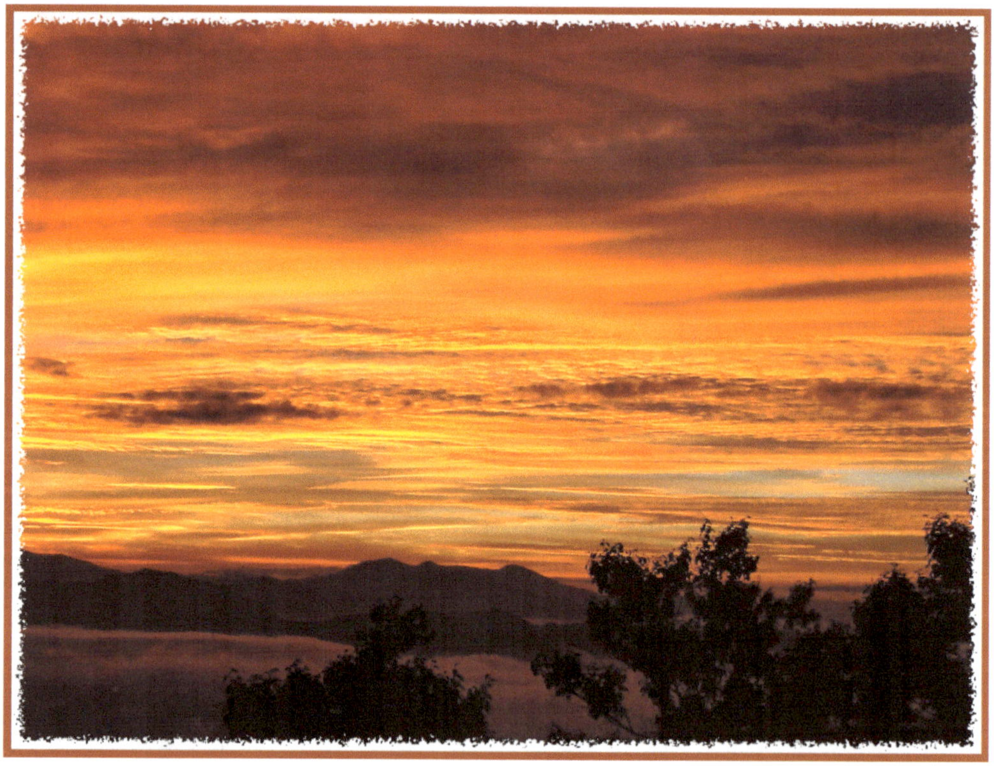

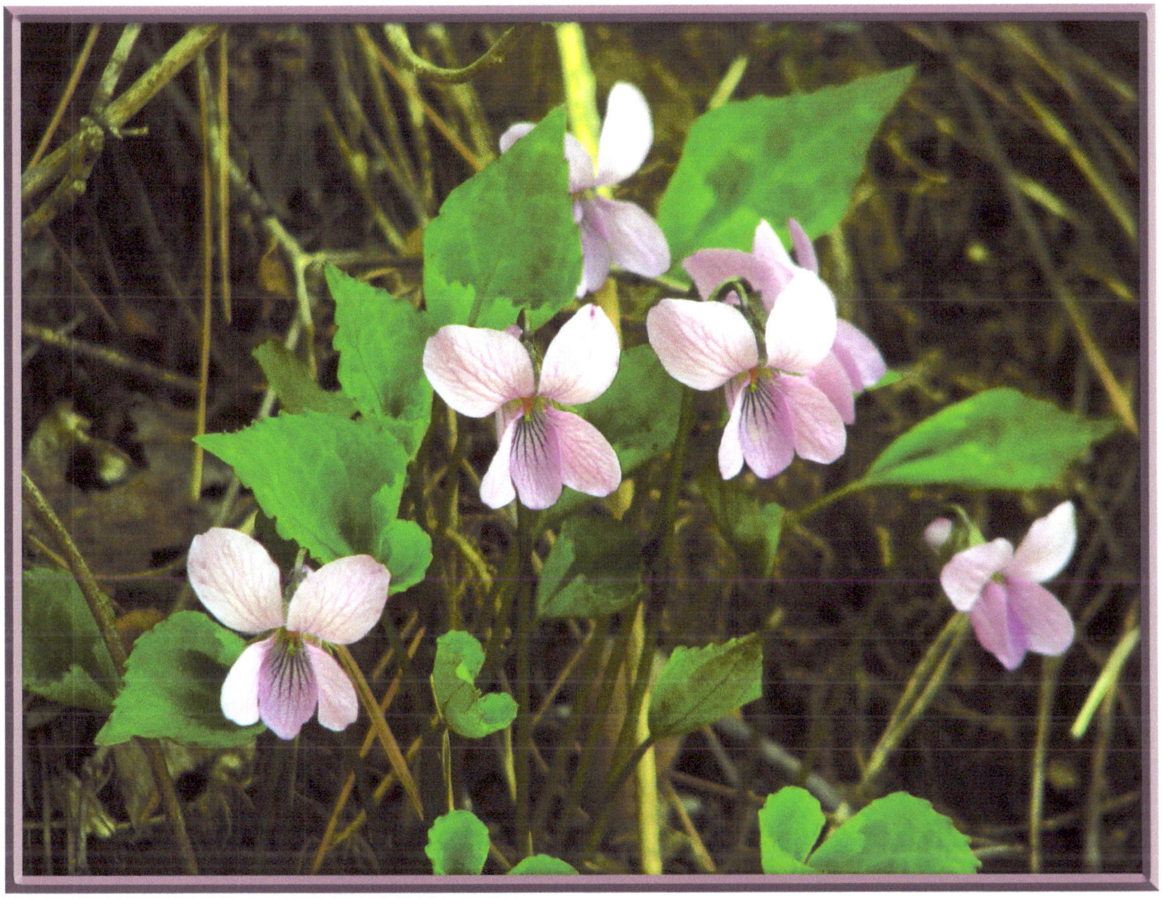

Above is a very beautiful ***Viola rossii*** (aka ***rossi***) plant with many flowers. We had never seen a single plant with as many flowers as were on this one. Note how the leaves are still curled up. Sometimes we find flowers on this species while the leaves are only emerging from the ground.

To the right is a ***Viola violacea* var. *makinoi***. Note that this one does not even have any leaves visible yet.

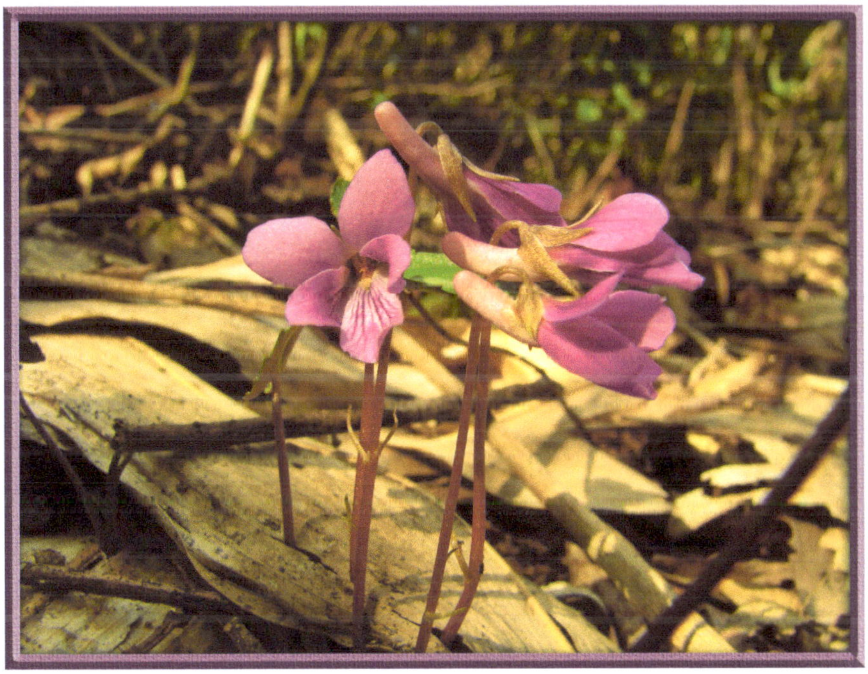

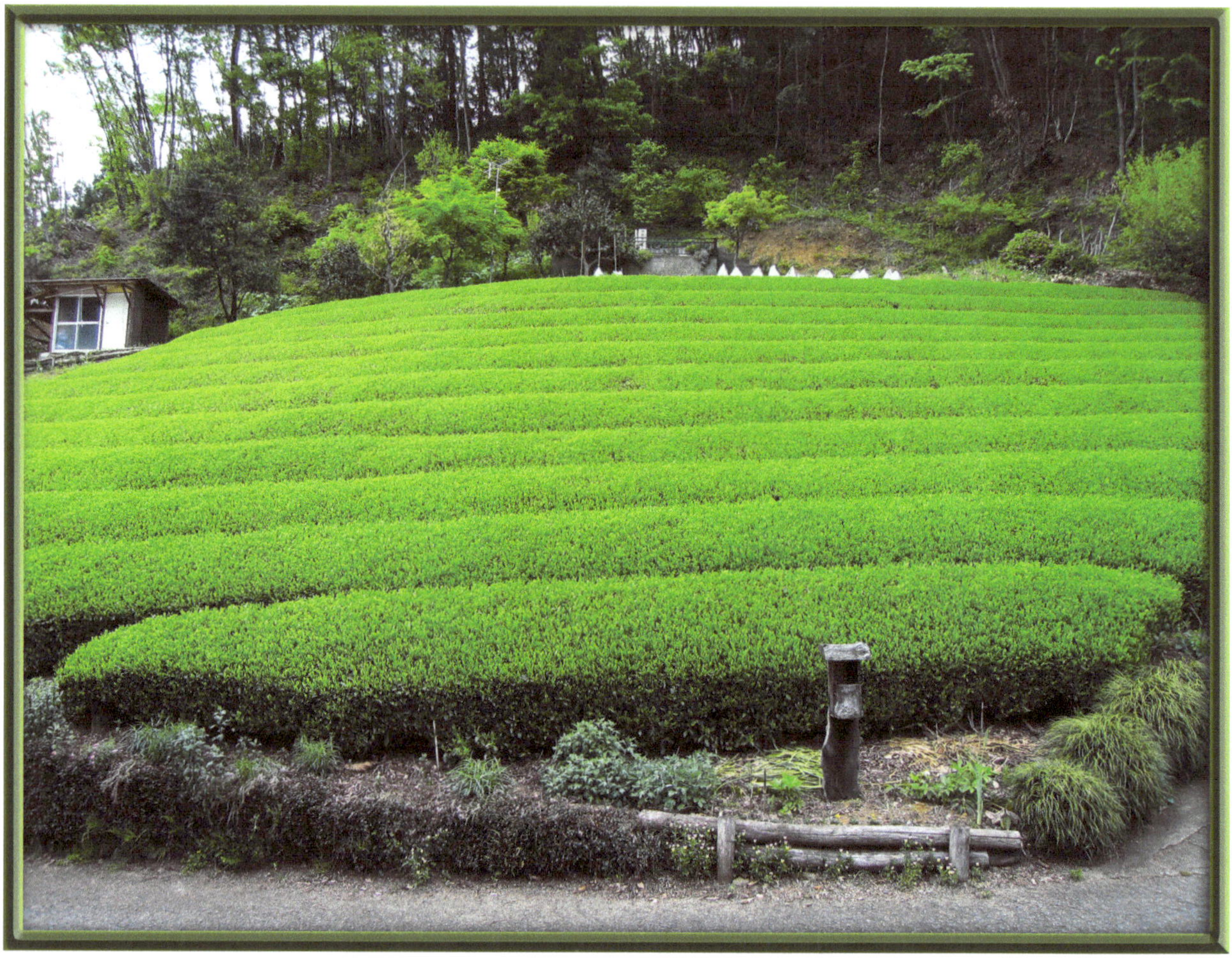

Can you guess what this plant in the above photo is? No? It is a very small tea field, yes, that's correct – the kind of tea which you drink – **green tea**. It takes between four and eight years for tea seedlings to come into full production, depending on the specific location. Usually, from the second year the bushes are trained into the desired shape. By careful pruning, the height of the main trunk is curbed and lateral growth is encouraged. We are not authorities on tea growth, but it appears that this field is about at its prime.

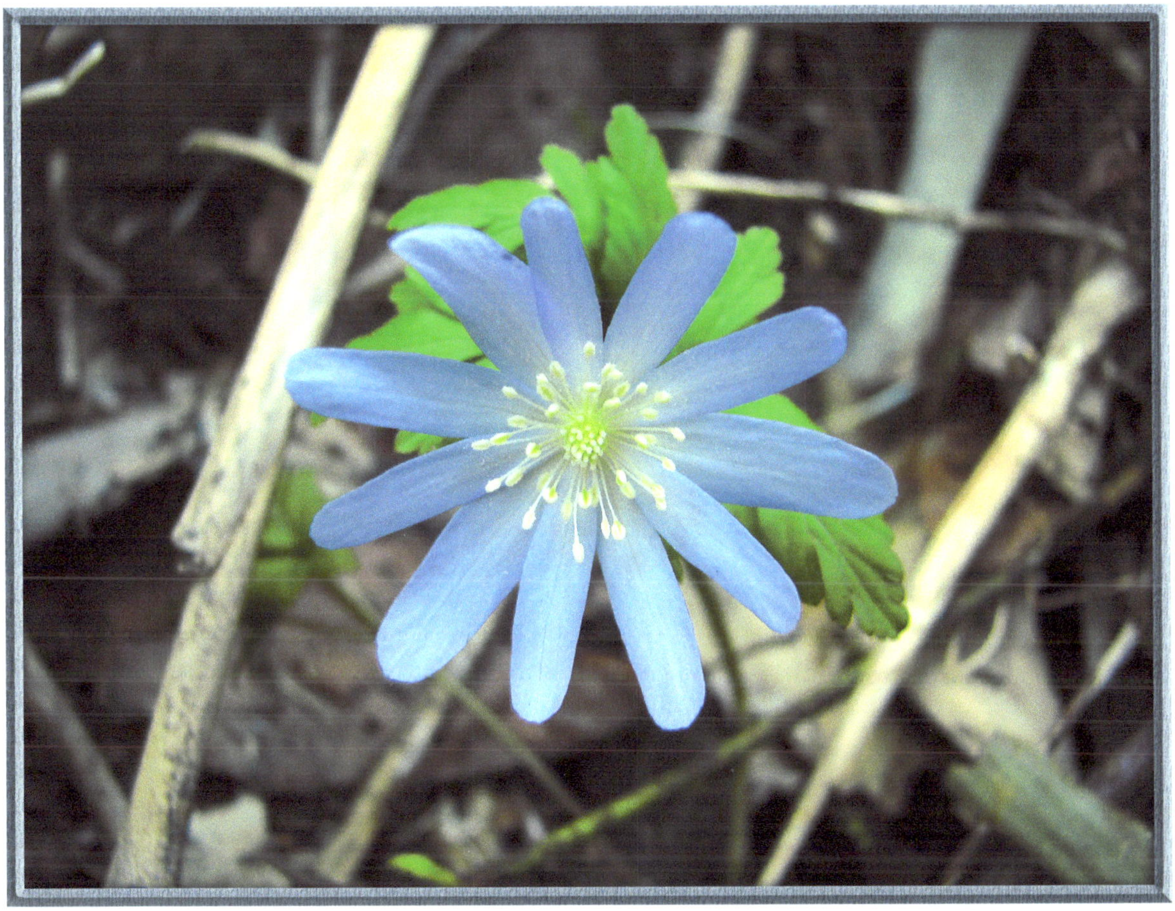

Above is a blue anemone, an ***Anemone pseudoaltaica***. This plant sometimes has a bluish/purplish flower and sometimes a pure white flower. The bluish flowered ones are certainly more photogenic.

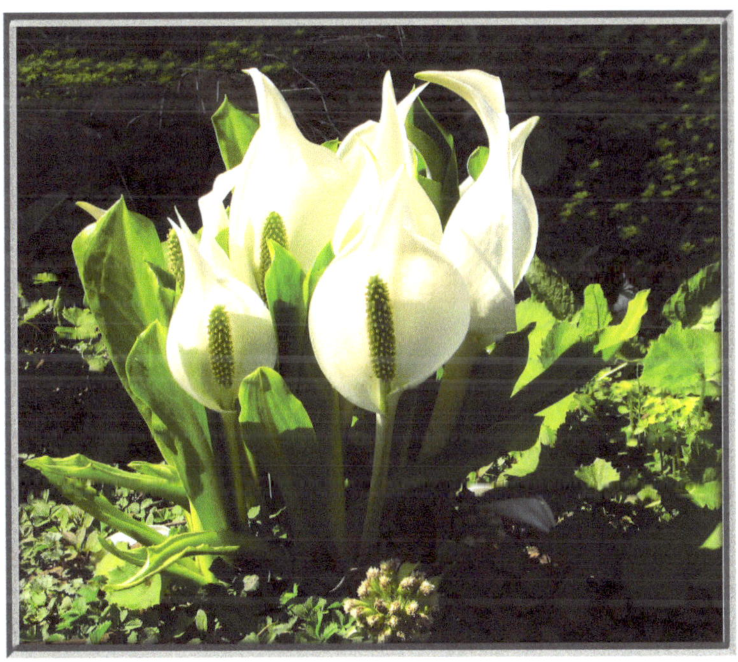

To the right is ***Lysichiton camtschatcense***, or **Skunk Cabbage**. You saw a different genus and species of Skunk Cabbage way back in the winter (page 20). The one shown here flowers somewhat later and is much more beautiful. This one is called ***Mizubashou*** in Japanese.

Both of these photos were taken in **Yamagata Prefecture**.

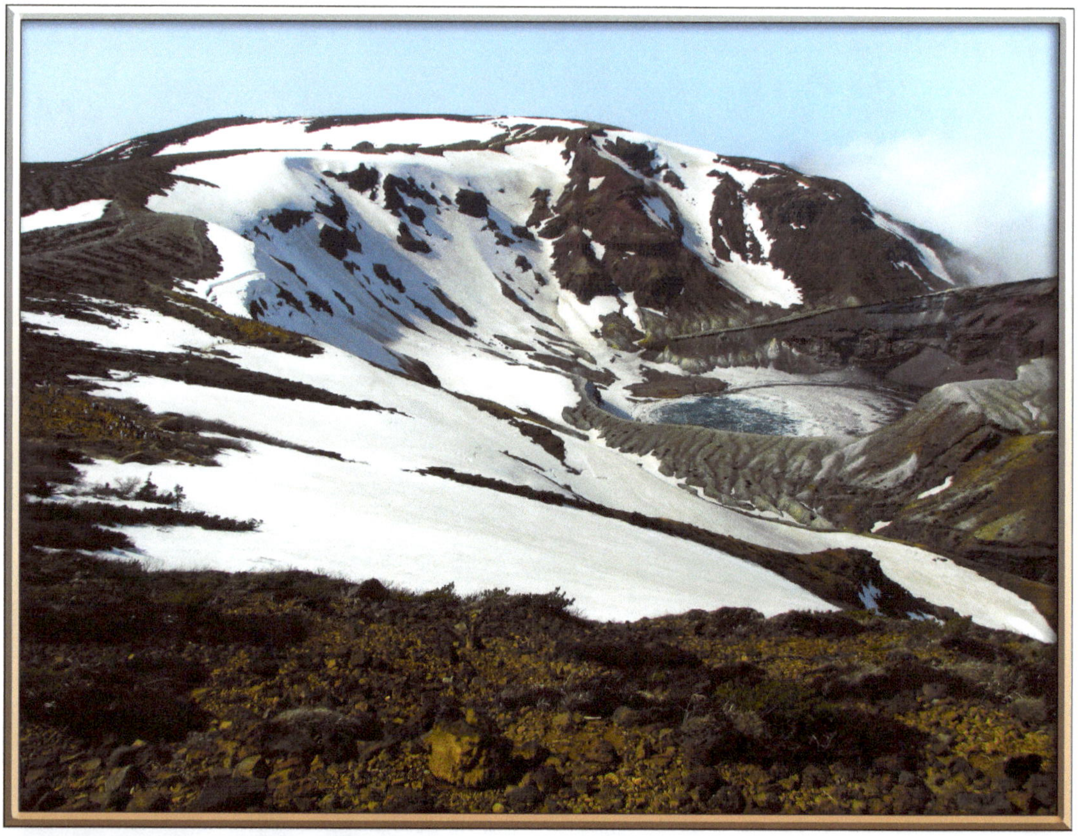

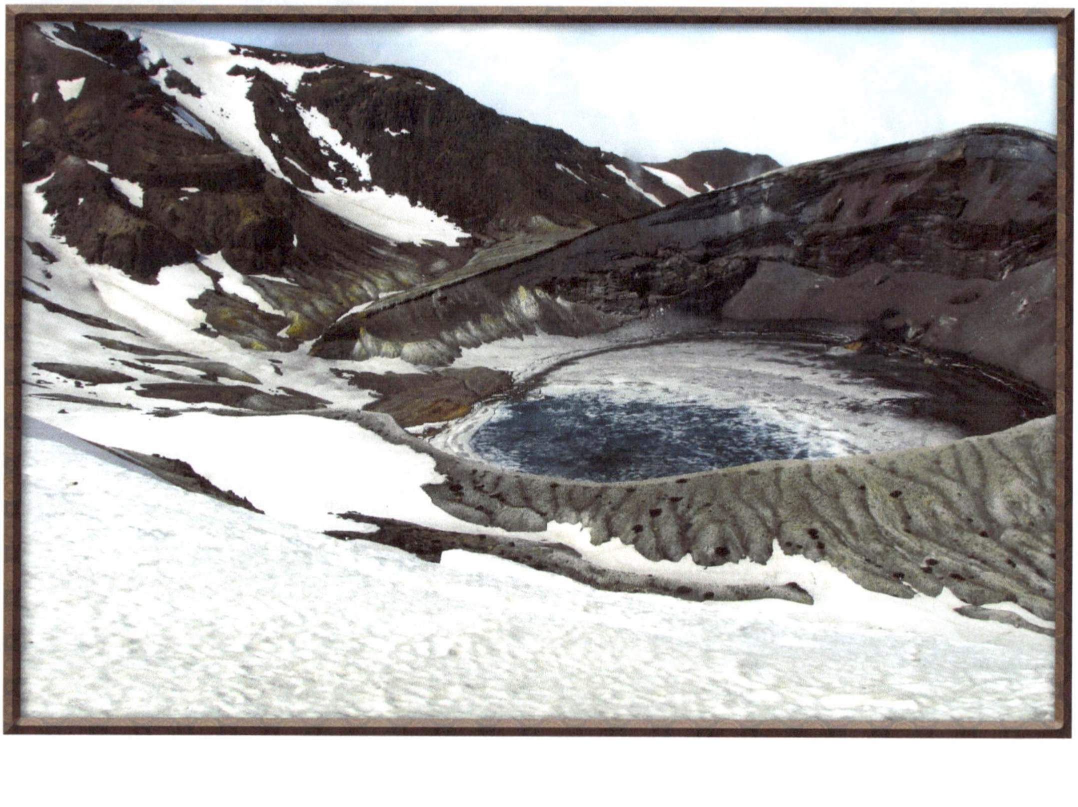

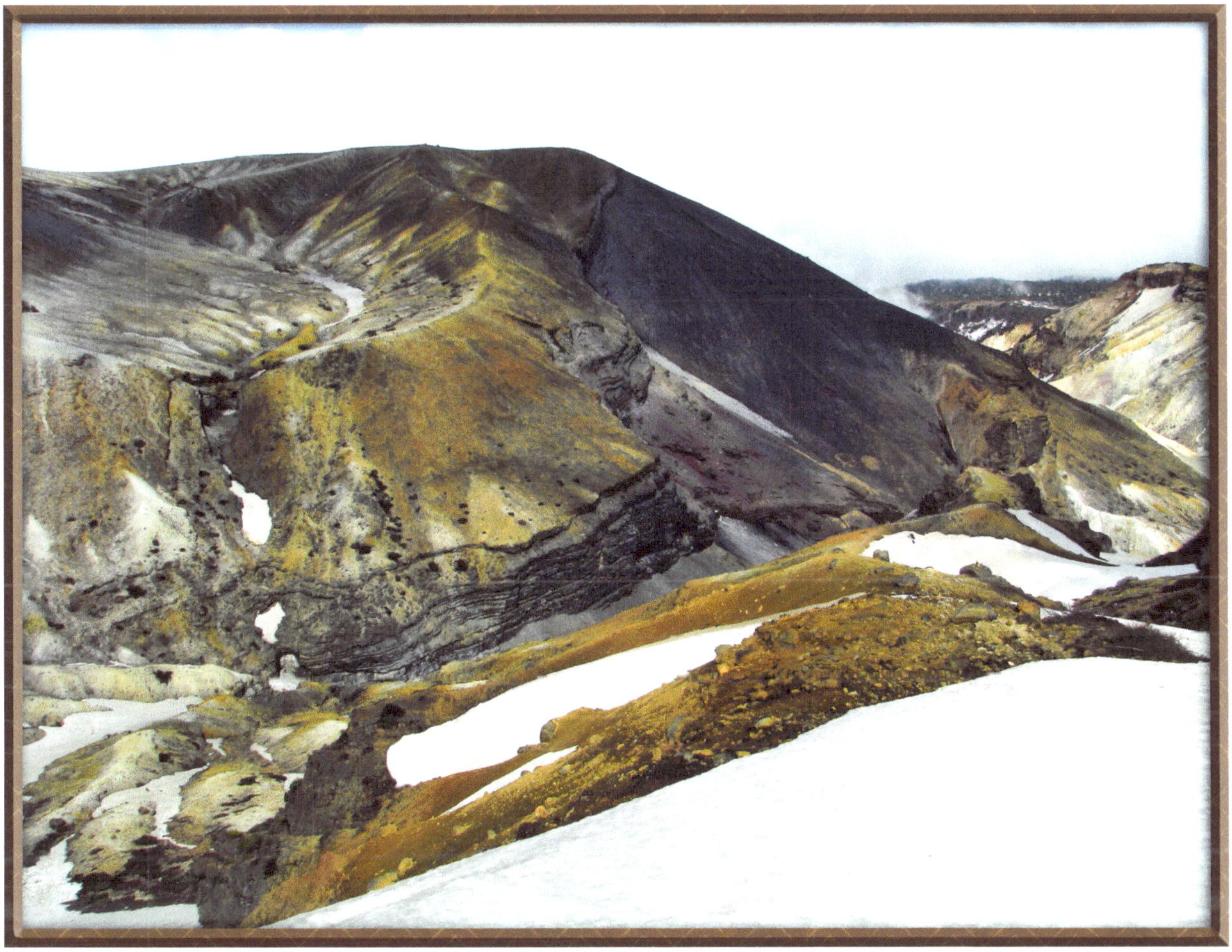

All three photos on these two pages were taken at and around **Okama Caldera** on **Mt. Zao in Yamagata Prefecture**. This was early in the month of May, but the elevation is quite high, probably around 1,700 meters from what we can learn through research on the internet, and that is the reason there is still a good deal of snow and also why the lake is still covered with ice. Supposedly this crater lake changes through five distinct colors depending on the weather. We would like to see this area in different seasons of the year.

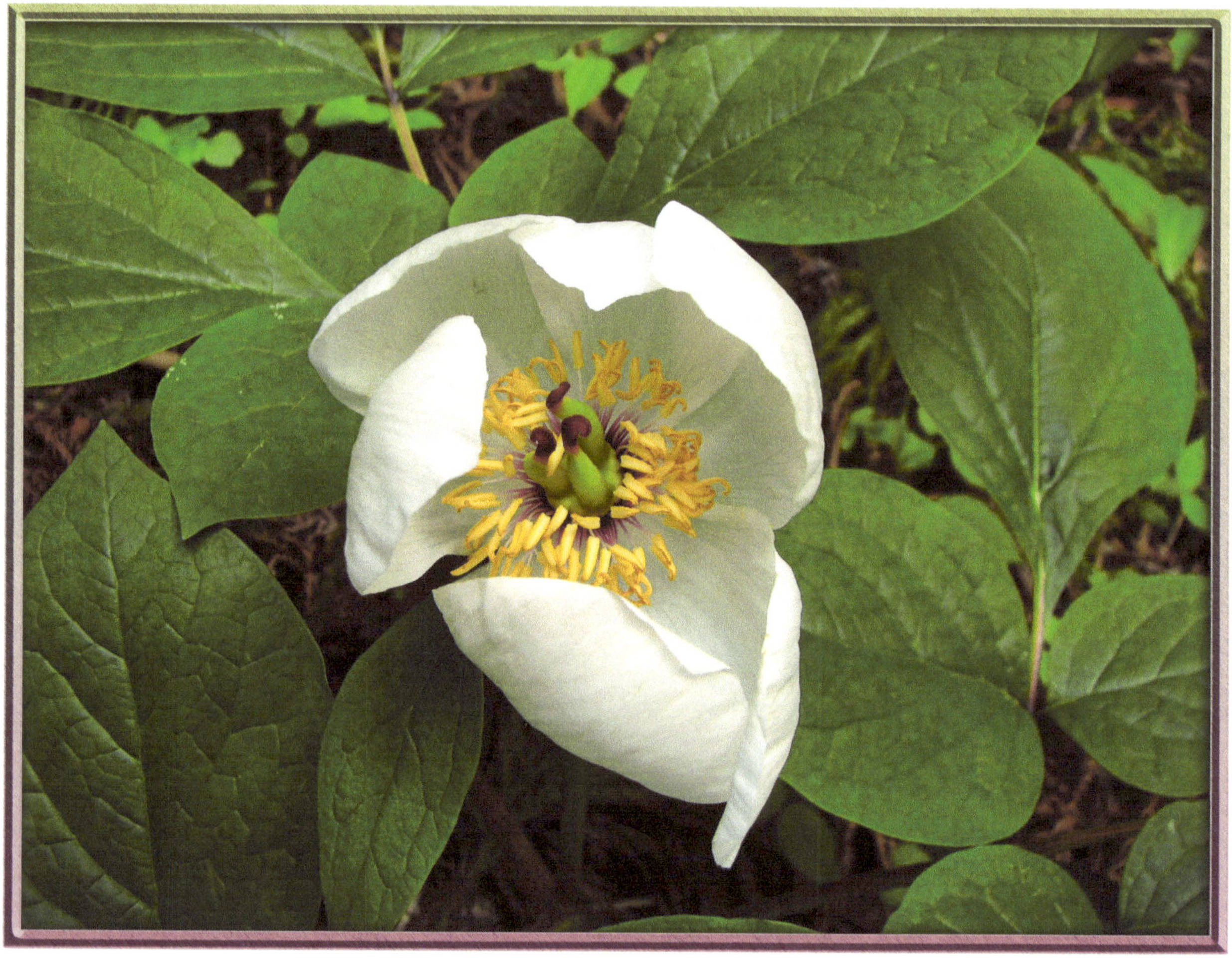

The photos on these two pages show you a very rare sight. This is the flower of the ***Paeonia japonica*** plant (**Japanese Peony**). In ten years of mountain hiking in the spring months we have only found this plant about five times and have only found it in bloom three times. It is a threatened species due to over-zealous collectors who believe it will look better in their yards than it looks in the wild. For this reason we never say where we find it. If you are ever fortunate enough to find this flower in your wanderings in the forest, please leave it where you find it so that other people might be able to come and experience the thrill of finding it too.

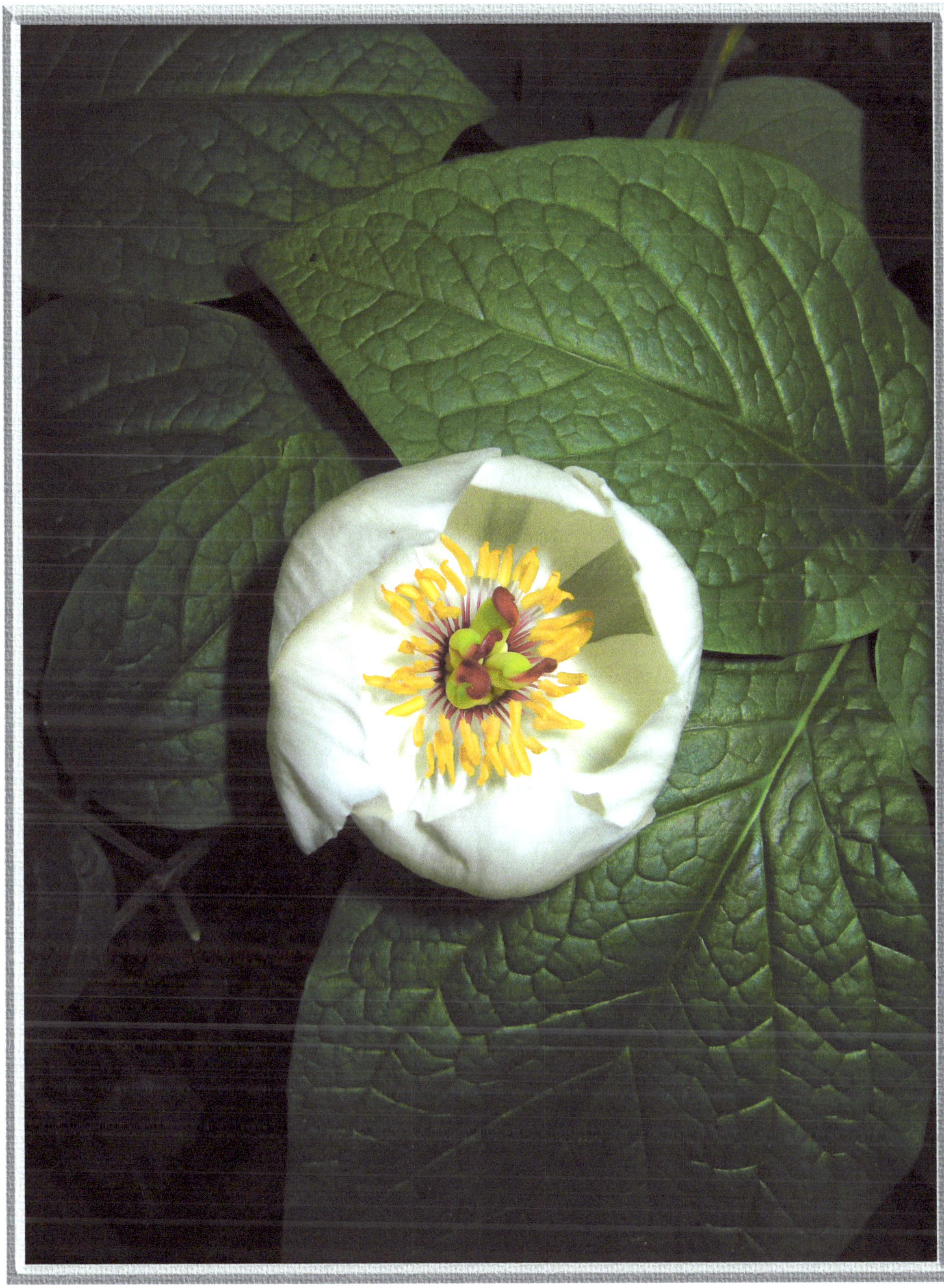

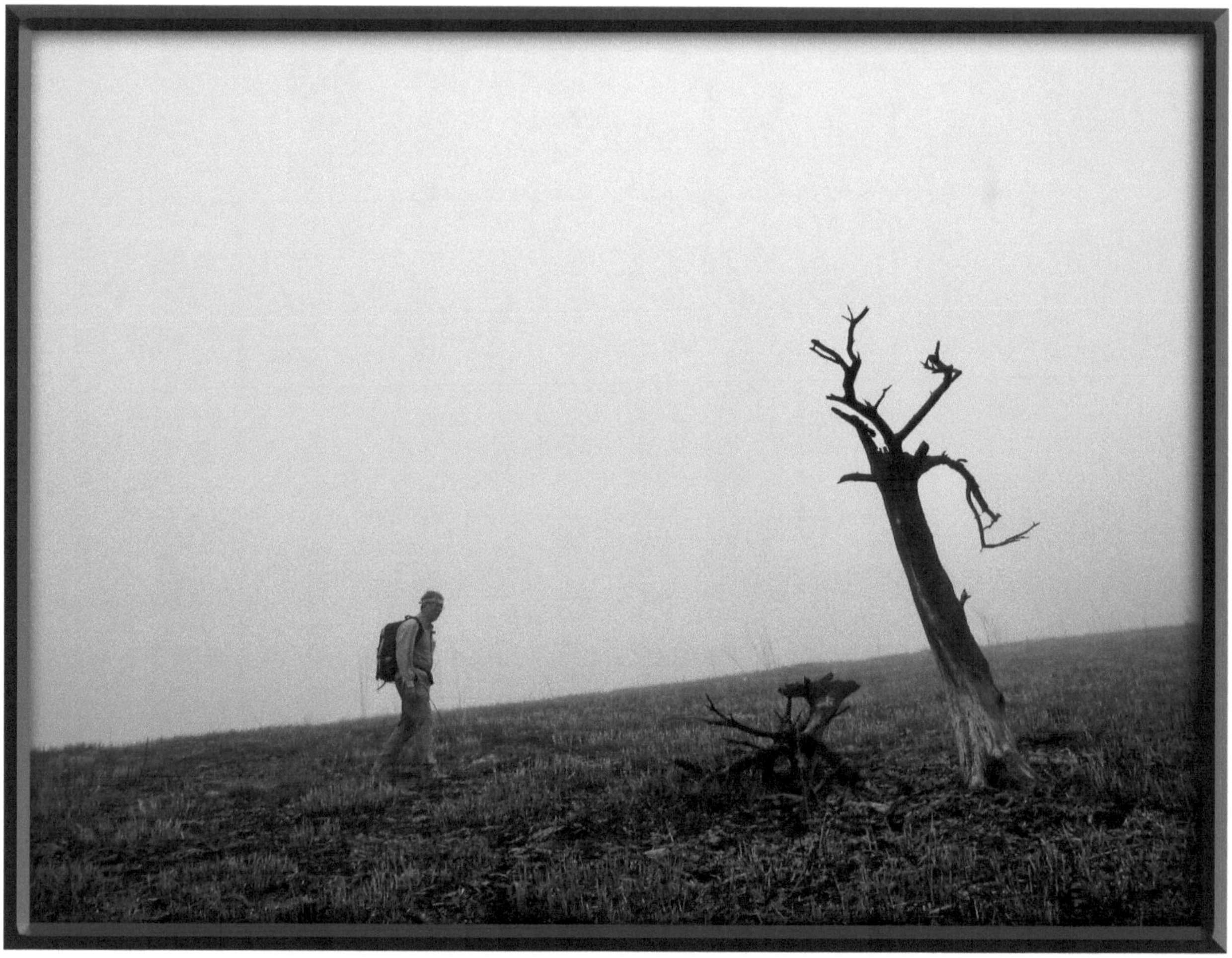

Now let's visit **Yamanaka Lake** again (see page 9 for the previous visit) during this month of May. Sometime during May they schedule a burn of the dry grass on **Mt. Myoujin**. We are not sure why they do this, possibly it is to make sure that it gets burned when there is a relative lack of danger of the fire escaping and burning down some houses. Maybe it is to be sure it gets burned when there are fire fighters available to watch it and control it, because the grass gets so dry that it would be dangerous if somebody tossed a burning cigarette from their car. Whatever the reason, this photo makes for an eerie appearance as I walk across the landscape.

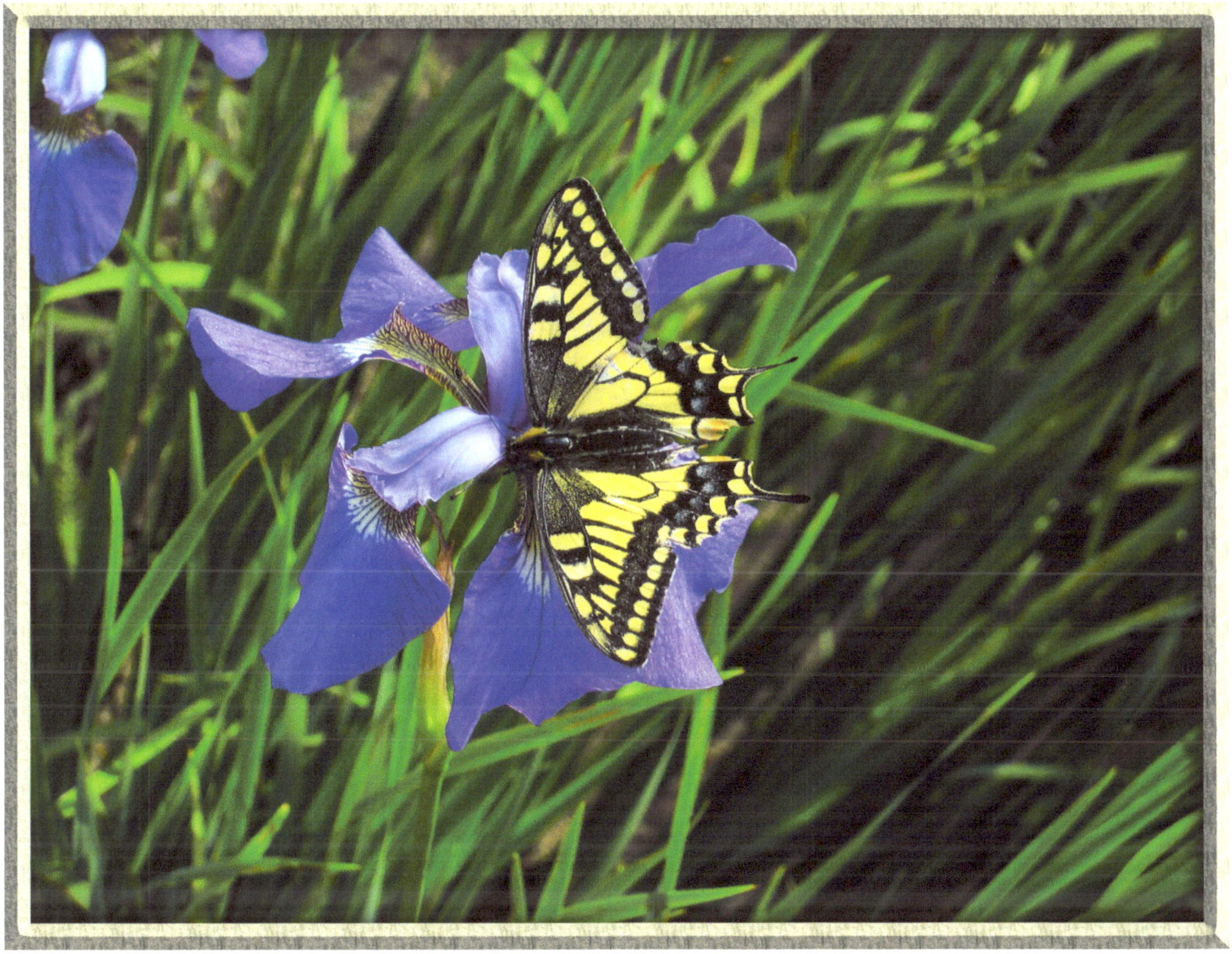

Above is a beautiful early **Iris Bloom** with a **Swallowtail Butterfly** sitting on it. This photo was taken at **Jindai Botanical Garden** in early May. The combination of the green, blue, yellow and black makes for quite a stunning photo. Butterflies seldom stay in one spot long enough to catch a shot like this.

There are many swallowtail butterflies in Japan and we see them quite often. We have several plants growing in pots on our porch, one of them being a mountain pepper tree (***Zanthoxylum piperitum*** or ***Japanese Prickly Ash***). The swallowtail butterfly especially likes to lay eggs on this tree.

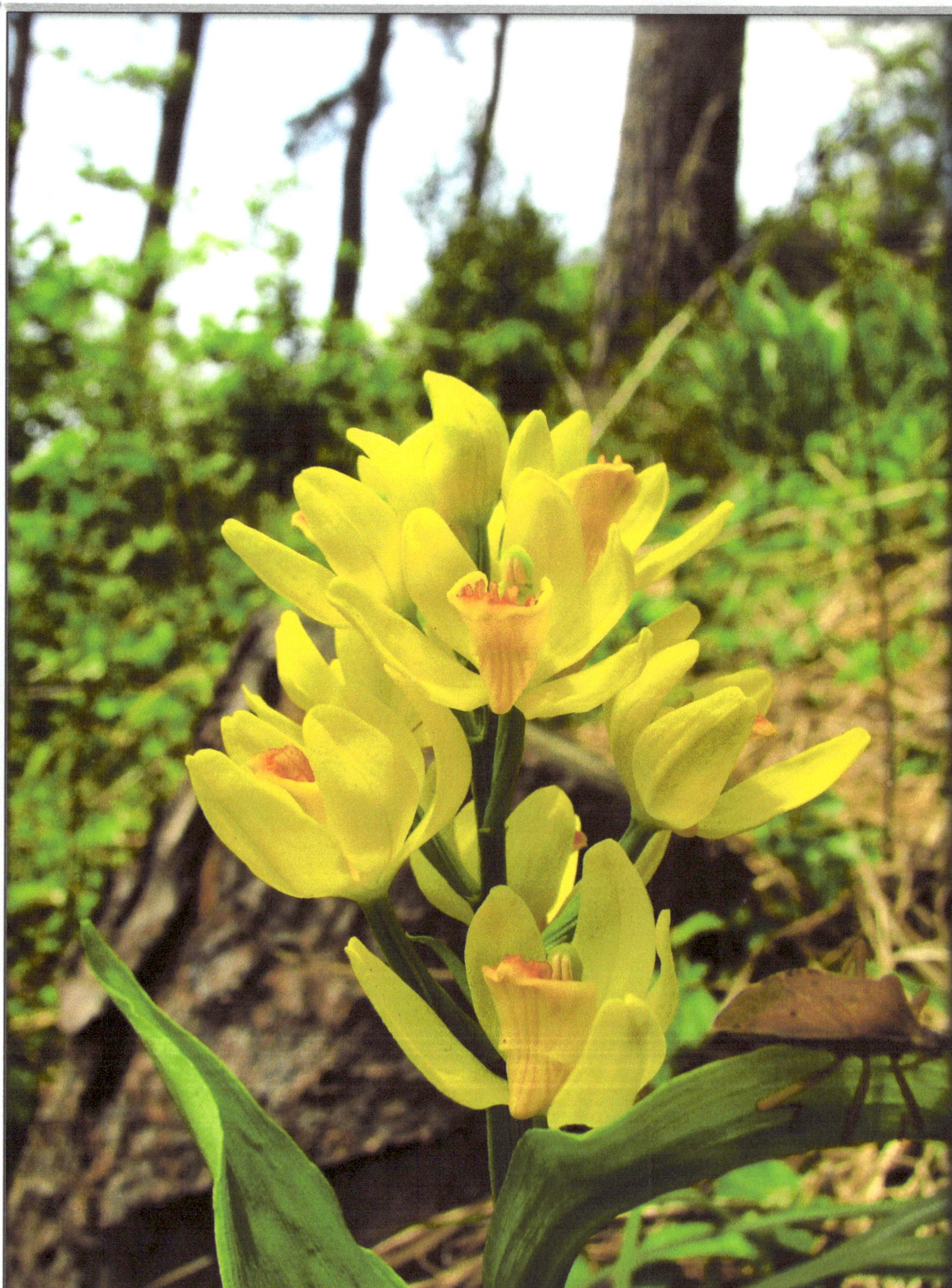

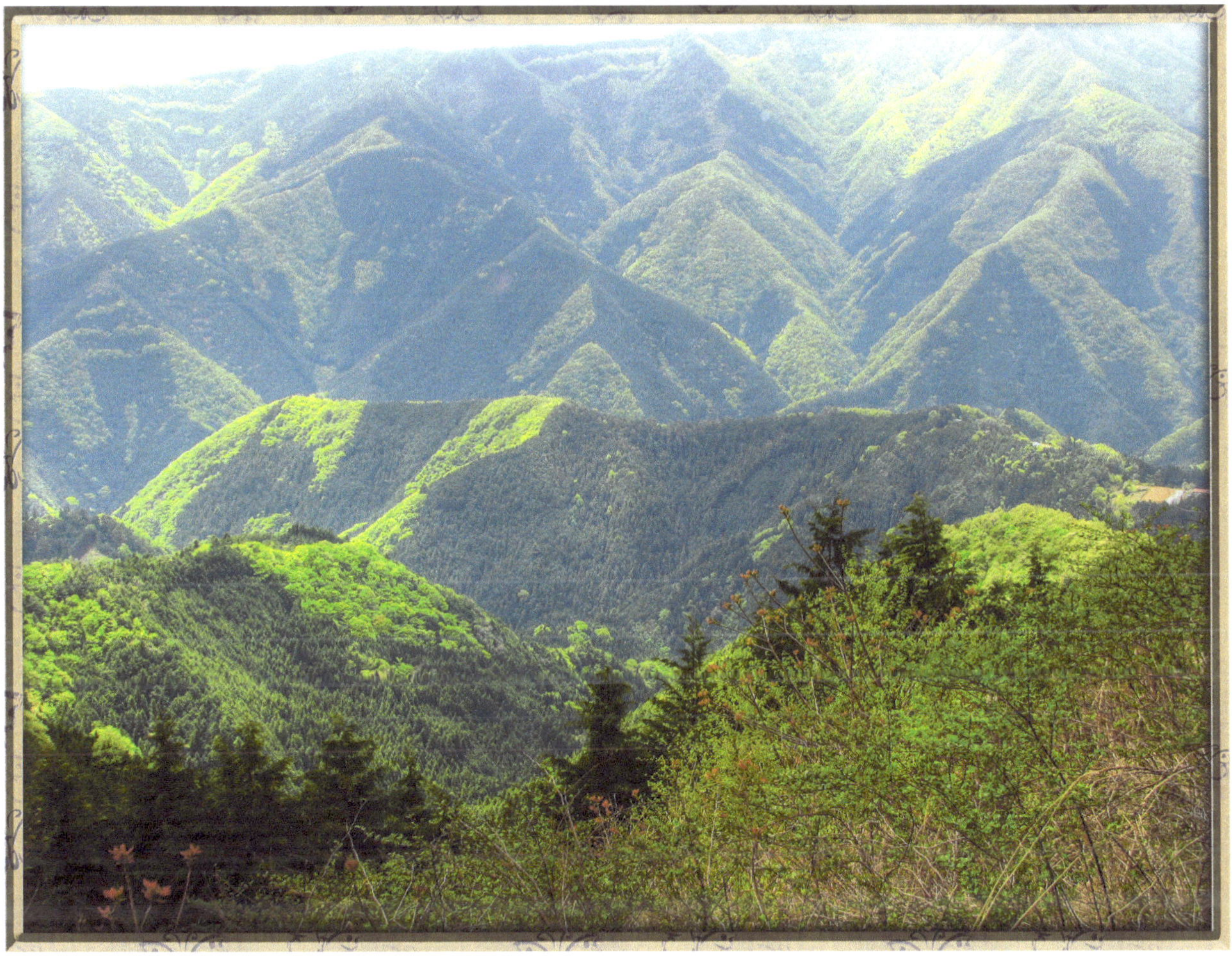

On the facing page is a ***Cephalanthera falcata***, a **Golden Orchid**. This photo was taken on one of the slopes of **Mt. Takao** just a few days before mid-May. This flower possesses rare beauty and when you find one of these flowers there are generally a few photographers standing around it waiting their turn to get in and photograph it.

The photo on this page is very similar to the one shown on page 56 in the top position. The two photos were shot in different areas and in different months and therefore the difference in the progression of the emergence of the early leaves of spring is quite marked. Please go back to page 56 and compare these two photos.

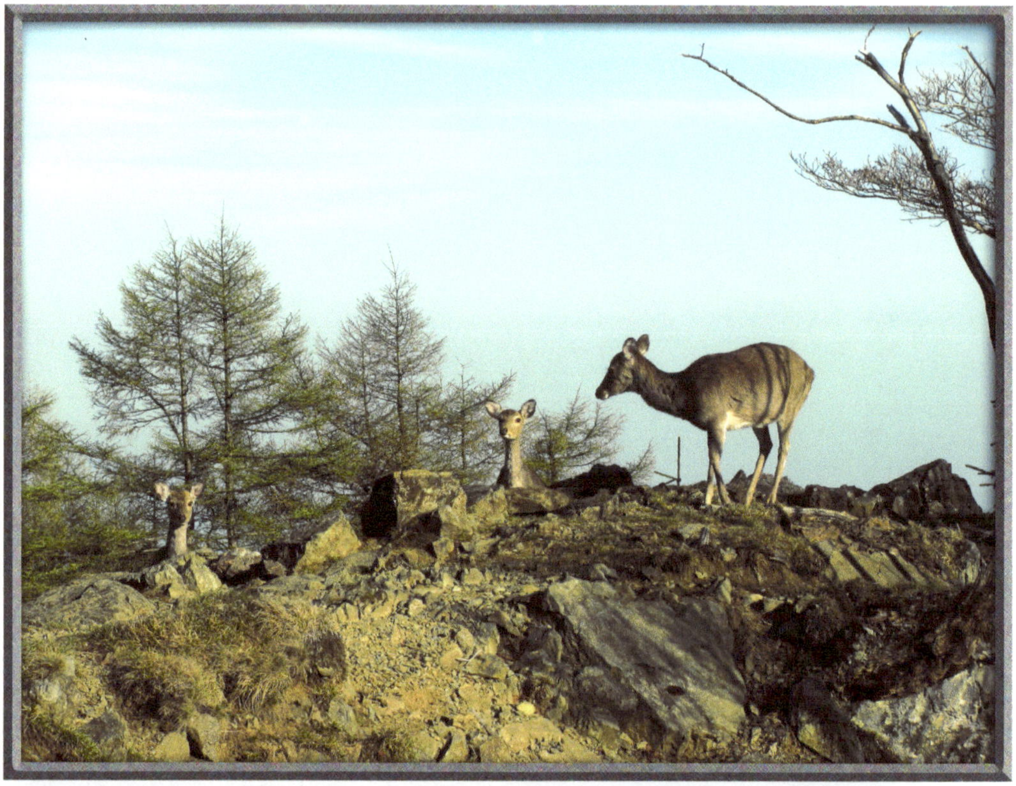

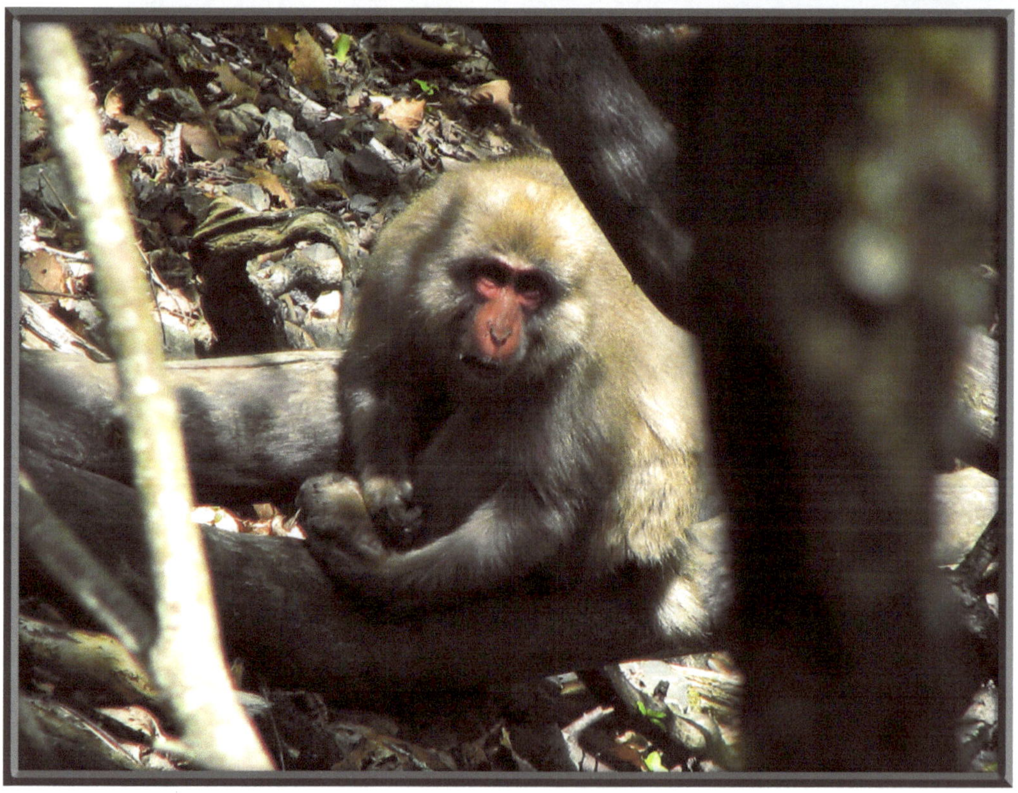

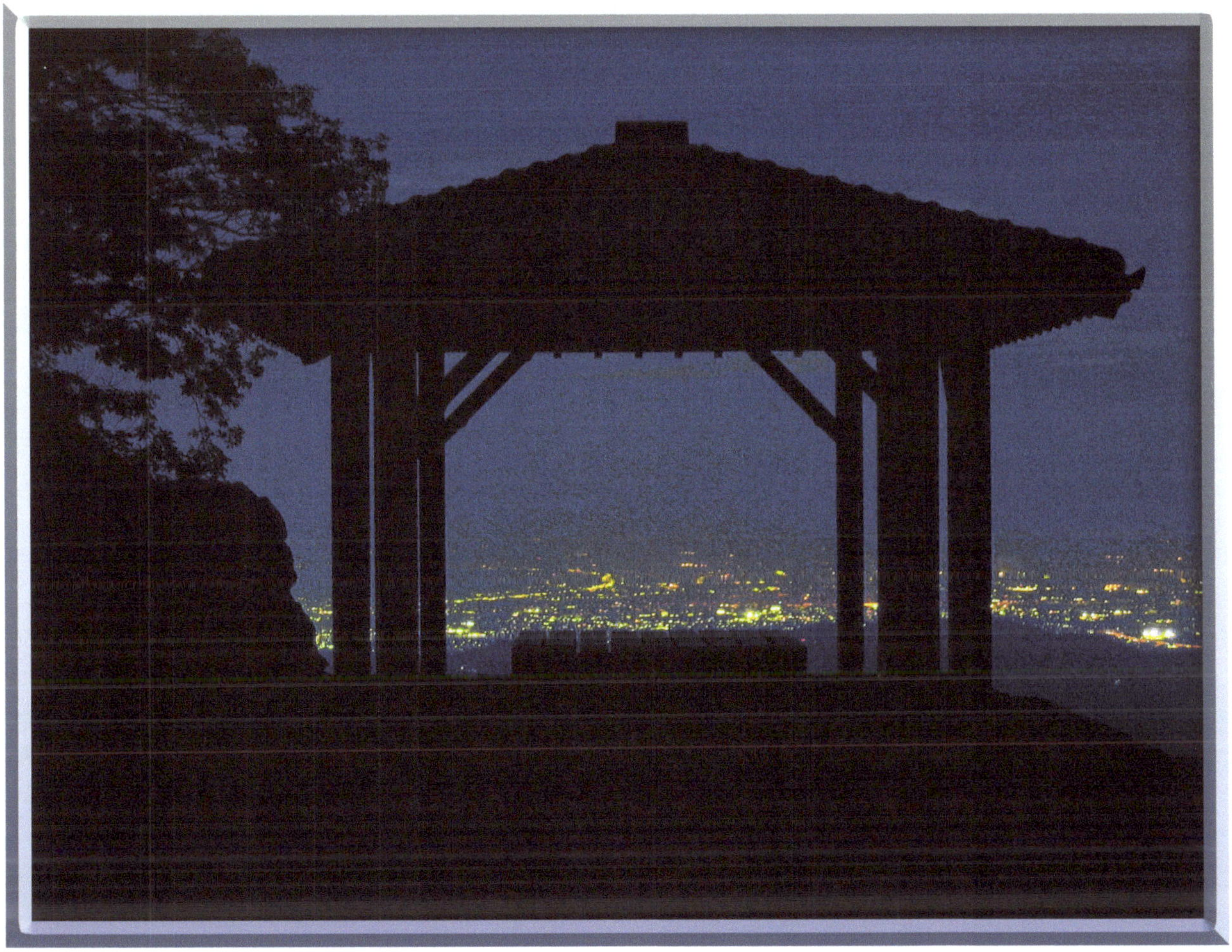

On the facing page are photos taken on the **Mt. Kumotori** trail. You may recall that Mt. Kumotori is the highest point in Tokyo (2017.6 meters = 6,619 feet). The top photo is an interesting one with three deer. It appears that they are looking at us and asking "*Huh, when did you come up here?*" The bottom photo is a Japanese Monkey.

The photo just above is the summit shelter at **Mt. Hinode**. Mt Hinode is near Mt. Mitake and it is 902 meters (= 2,959 feet). Mt. Mitake is 929 meters (= 3,048 feet). There is a cable car which takes you nearly to the summit of Mt. Mitake. Mt. Hinode is about a one-hour hike from the top of the cable car. We generally visit here two or three times a year. This photo was taken one night when we camped out here in our tent. All of those lights down there are Western Tokyo. We'll be showing you an additional photo of this shelter in summer, which was taken at sunrise.

And that ends the photos for May.

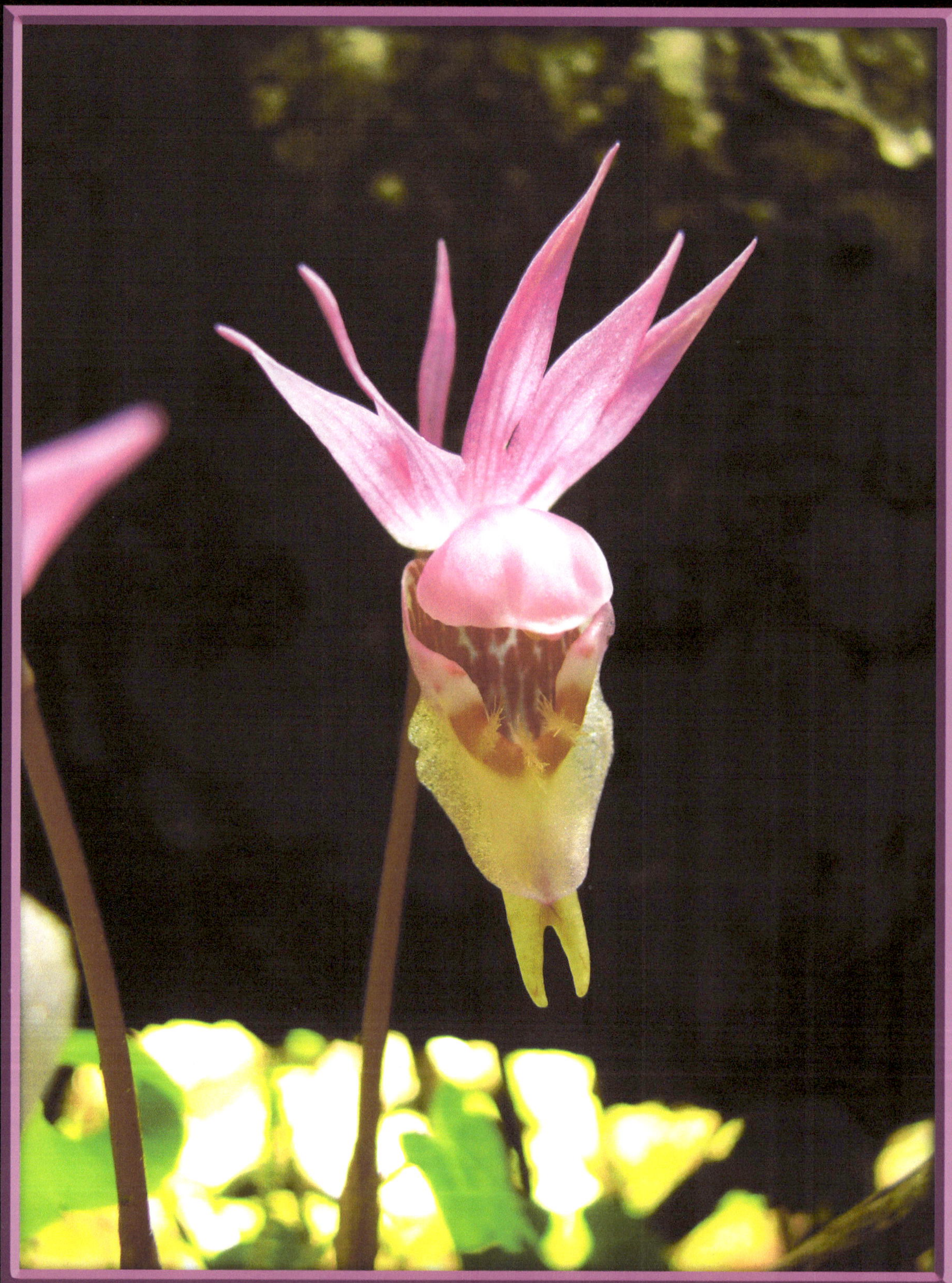

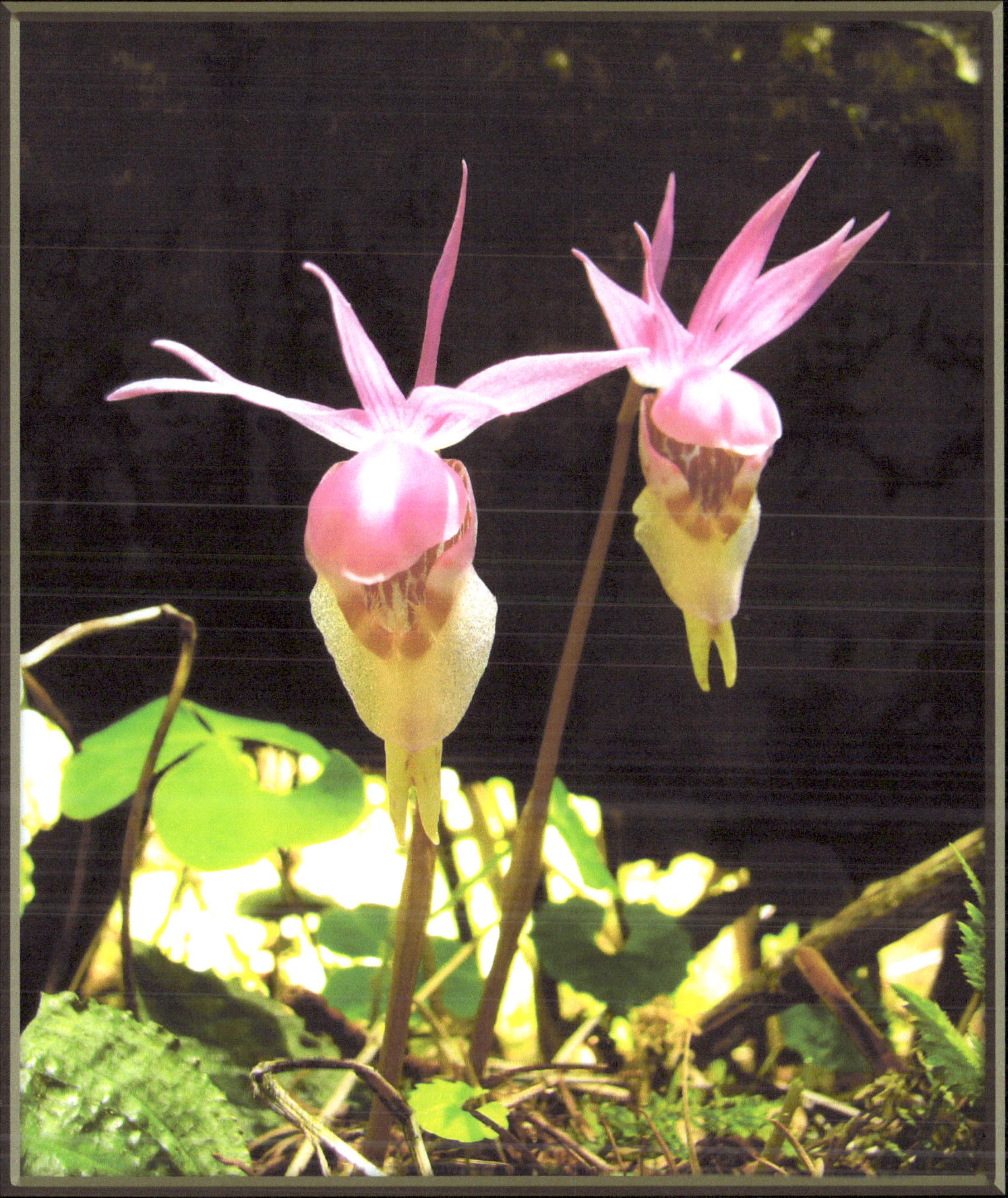

June Photos and Story

The photos on this page and on the facing page are of ***Calypso bulbosa* var. *speciosa***, the **Calypso Orchid**. This is such a magnificent flower as to be unbelievable. We're not going to tell you where we found it other than to say along one of the Mt. Yatsugatake trails. This species is much too rare and endangered to tell people where to find it. We think you will agree with the statement that it is amazingly beautiful.

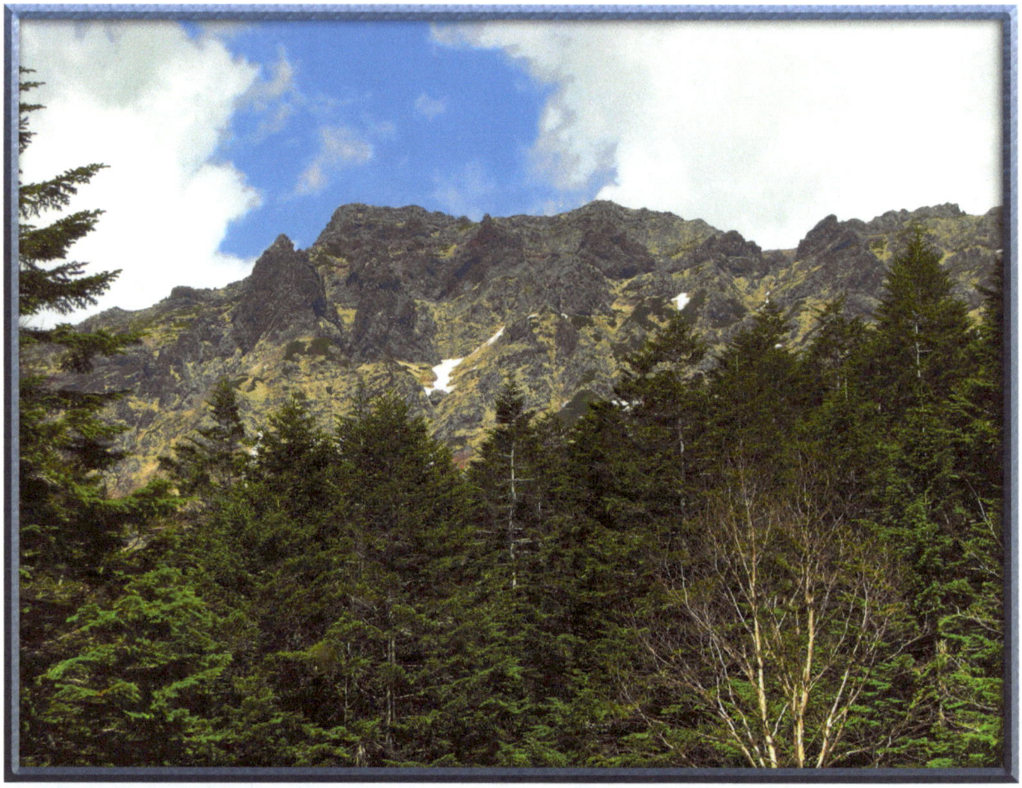

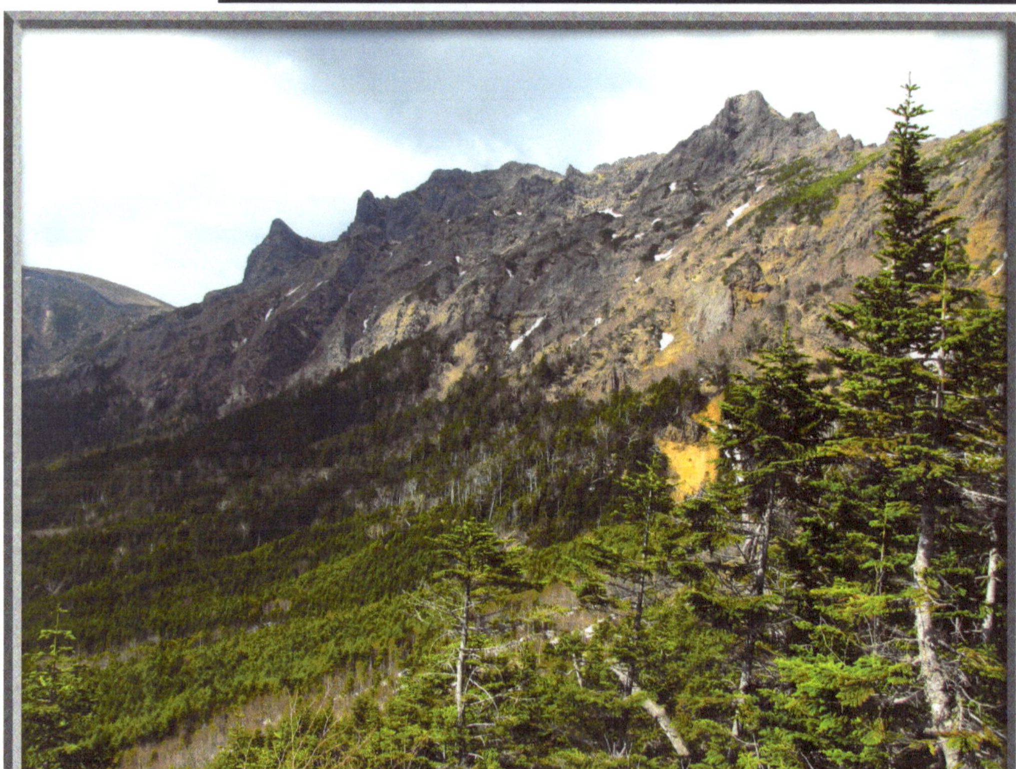

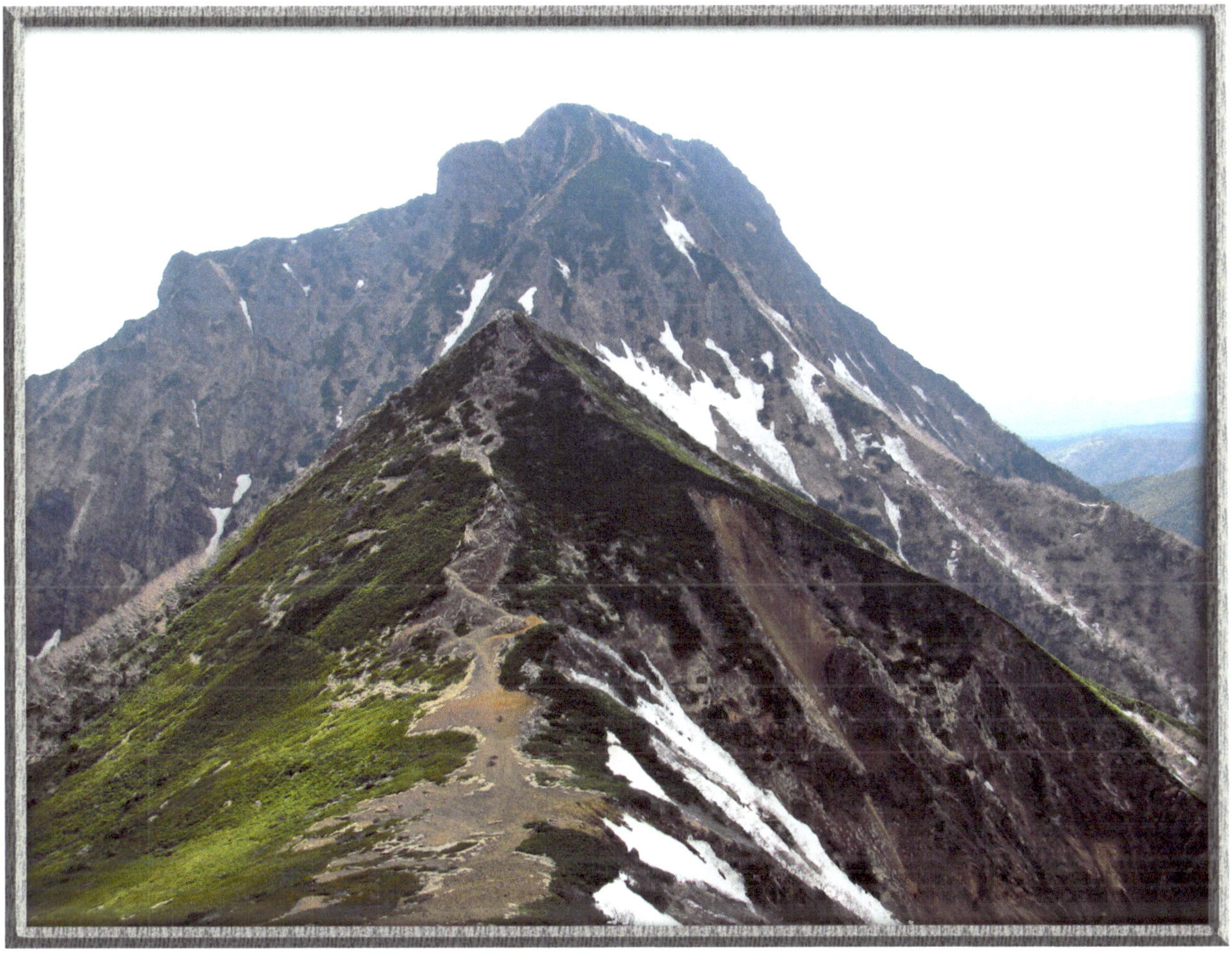

All three photos on these two pages were taken on the southern end of the **Yatsugatake Range** of Mountains. The Yatsugatake Mountains are a volcanic mountain range on the border between **Nagano Prefecture** and **Yamanashi Prefecture**. We have climbed these mountains twice. The first time was in July 2009 and the second time was in June 2010. That means that you will see additional photos of this range of mountains with the July photos. The first photo, on page 82, was taken as we hiked along the trail on the way to the summit of **Mt. Akadake** (2,899 meters = 9,511 feet). The second photo shows **Bunzaburou Ridge** and the photo on this page shows **Mt. Nakadake** in the foreground and **Mt. Amidadake** directly behind it – we did not climb either of these peaks.

Our goal for today was Mt. Akadake.

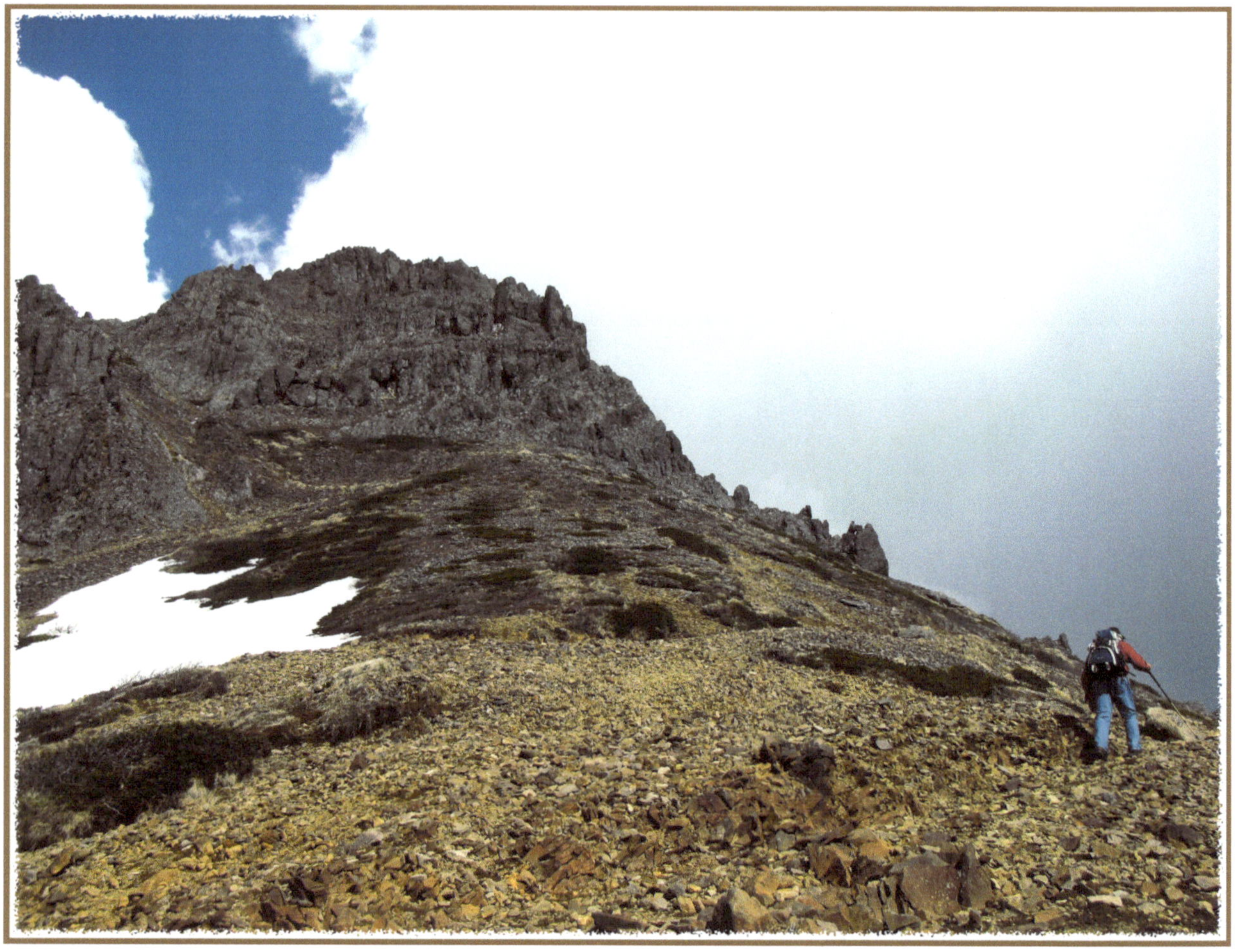

This photo shows Mt. Akadake – the actual summit is behind and to the left of the furthest left point in this photo, but you can get an idea of the area we are climbing in, as well as the steepness. The person on the trail is me. At this point we were about fifty minutes below the summit of Mt. Akadake. As you may note, there are some clouds moving in now.

About an hour after we arrived at the summit hut, and while we were eating the supper which they prepared for us at the hut, it hailed for about forty-five minutes. The hail stones were about 2 mm in diameter (maybe 1/8 inch) and the hail accumulated to about 7 – 10 millimeters in depth (about 3/8 inch). There was still some on the ground the following morning when we left.

Here is a photo of a small and relatively rare plant on Mt. Yatsugatake – it is a ***Pulsatilla nipponica***. The below photo shows **Mt. Yokodake** on the left (2,829 meters = 9,281 feet) and all the way back to **Mt. Akadake** (on the right side of the photo).

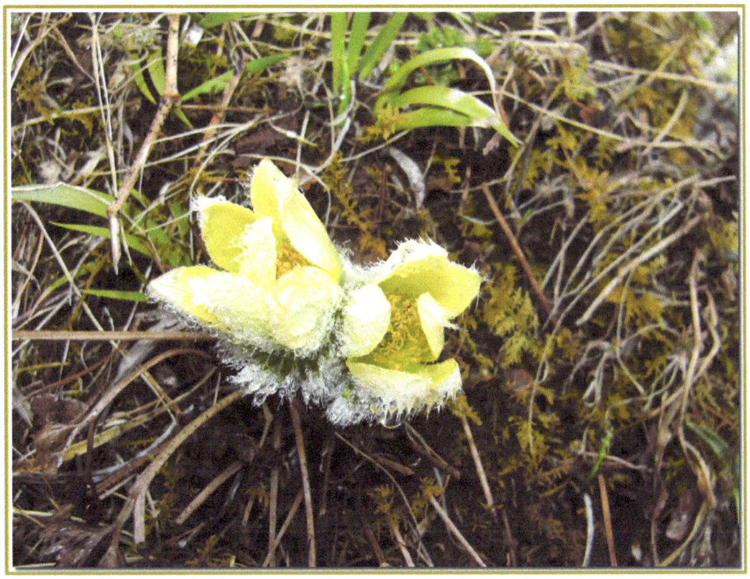

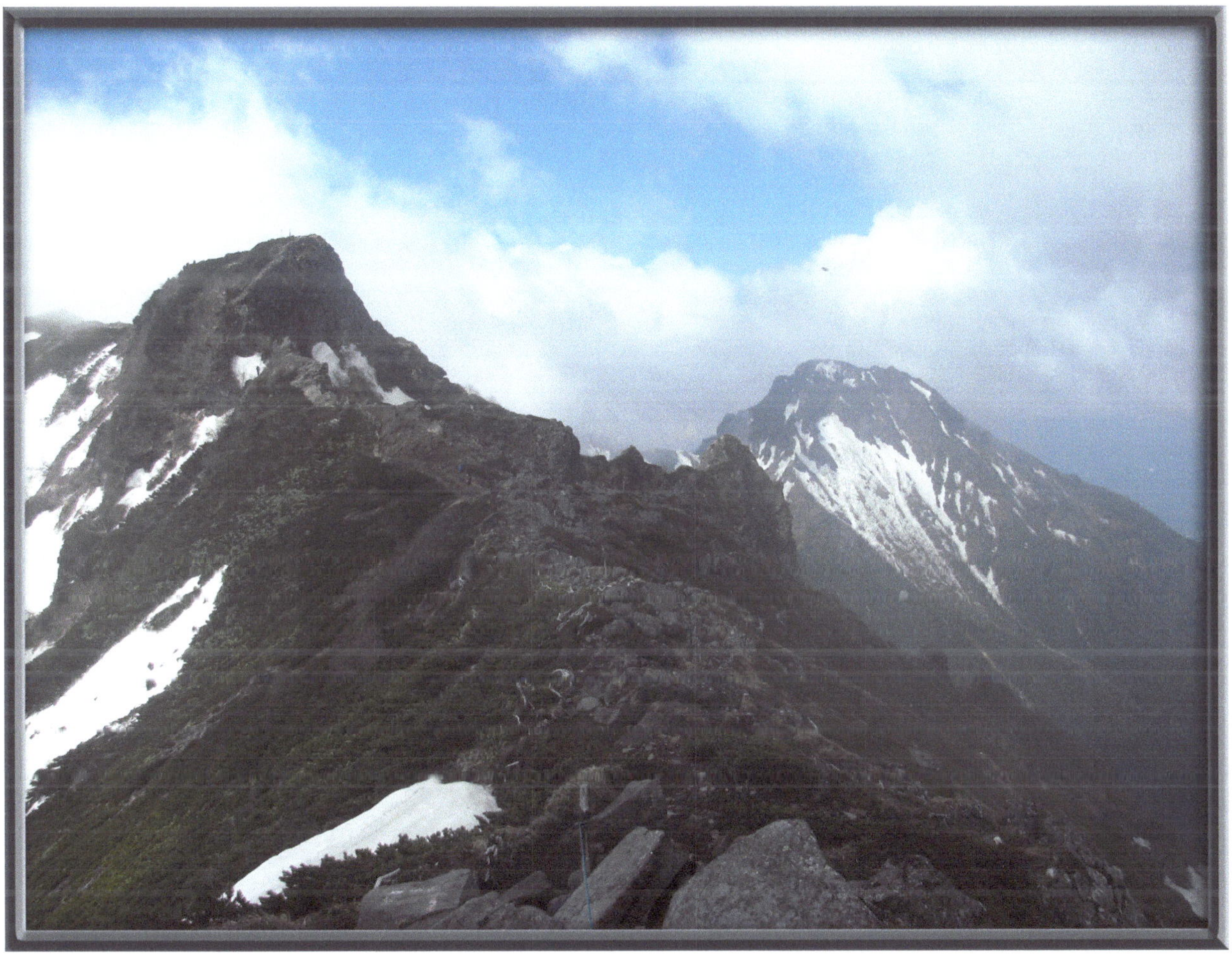

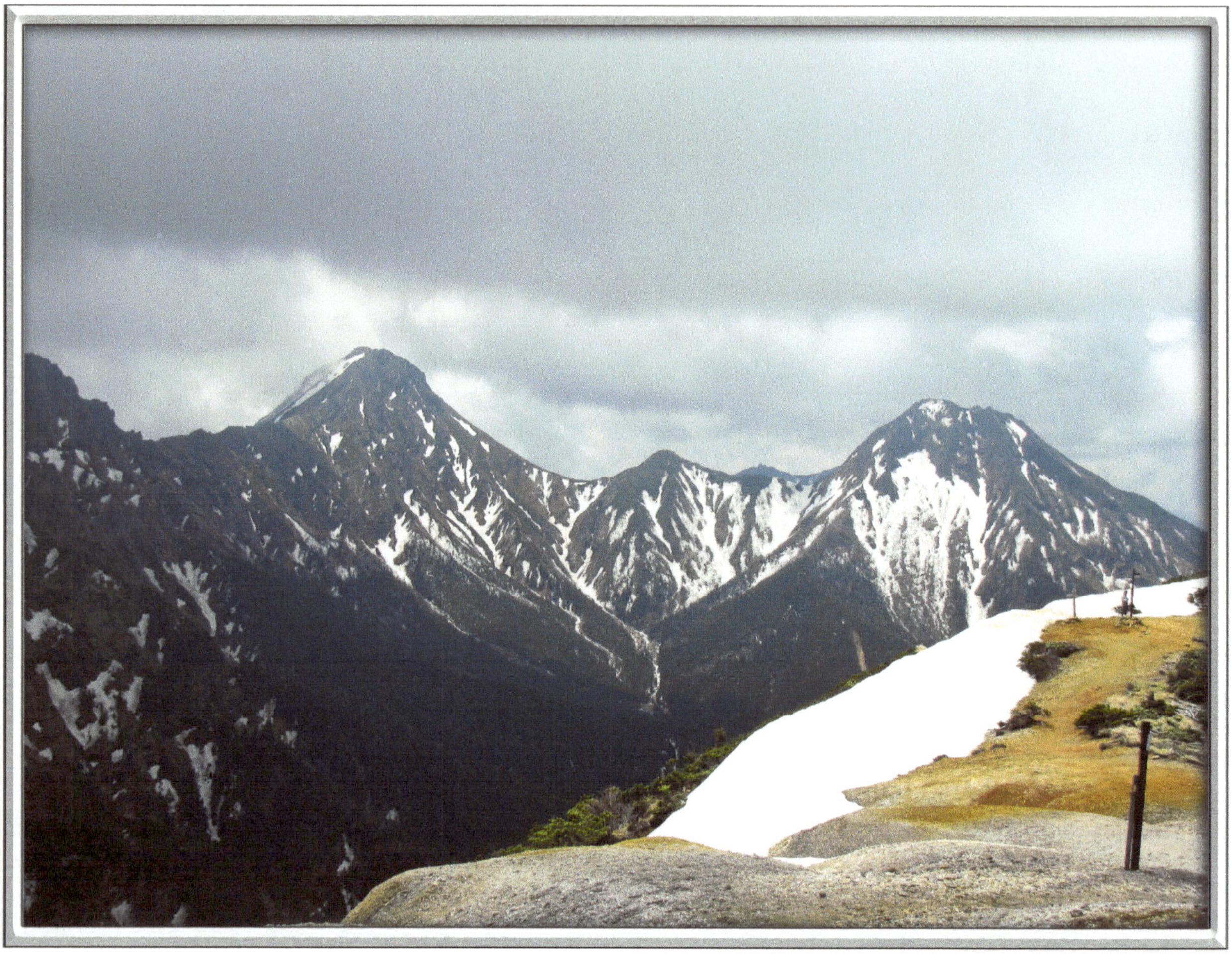

The above photo was taken at **Akaiwa No Kashira** – a fork in the trail below Mt. Iodake. This photo shows (from right to left) **Mt. Amidadake**, **Mt. Nakadake** and then **Mt. Akadake**. Mt. Akadake is the one where we spent the night last night.

The facing page photo is the final one of Mt. Yatsugatake and the immediate area which we want to show you that was taken during the month of June – it is a nice collage showing some photos you have seen and some photos you have not seen.

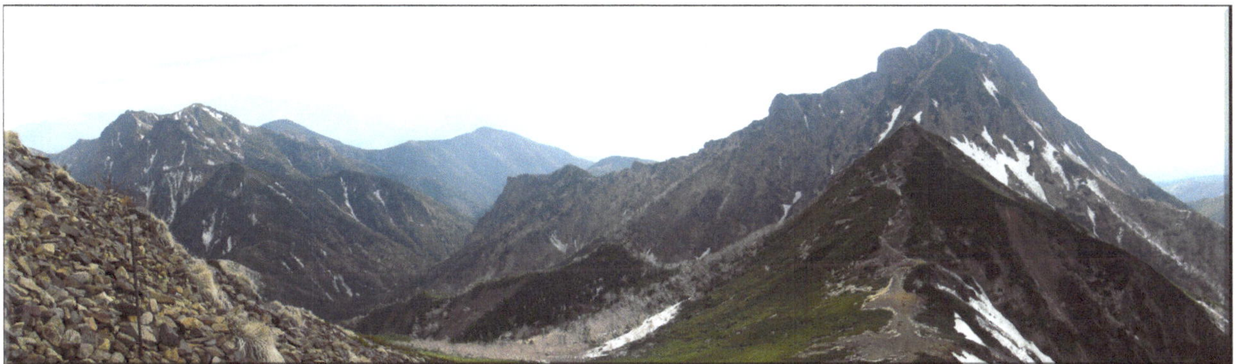

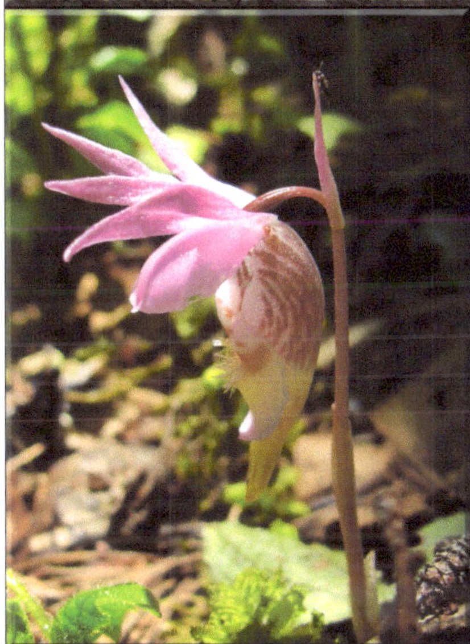

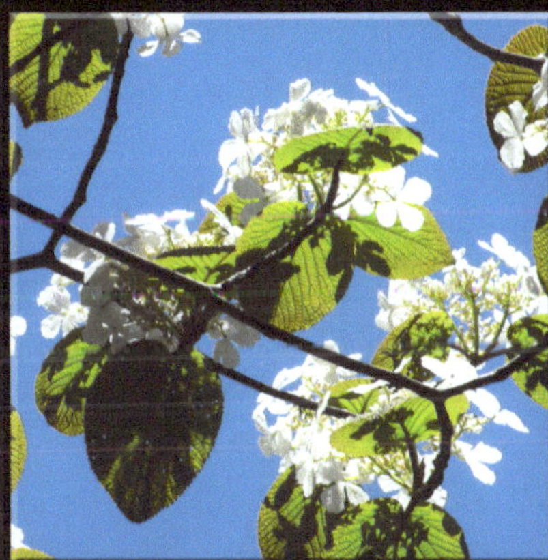

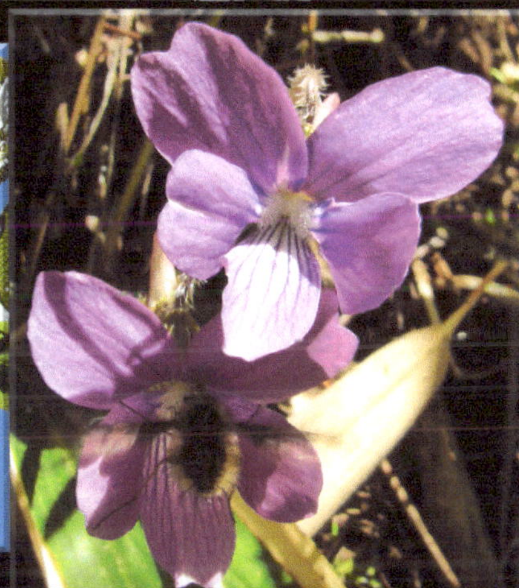

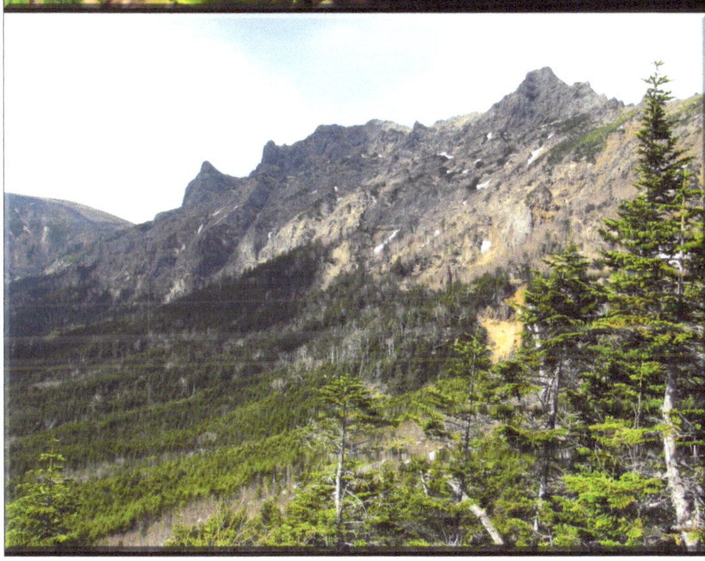

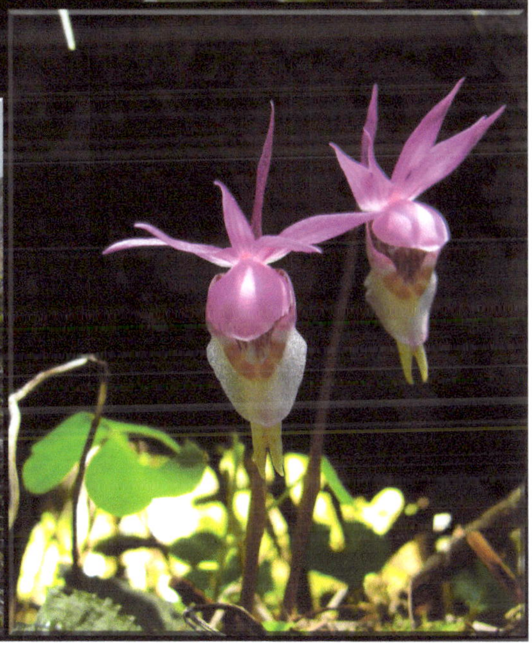

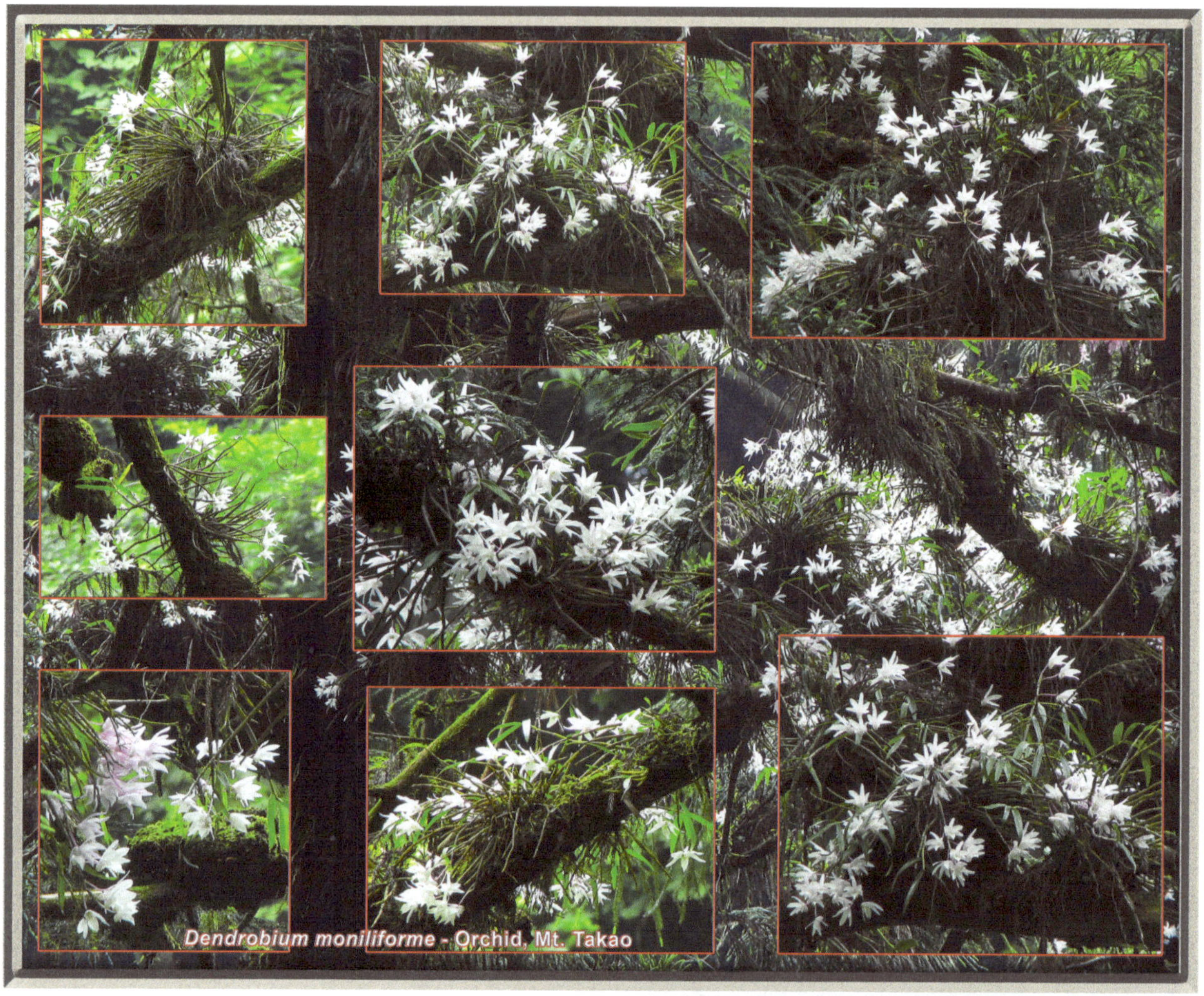

Dendrobium moniliforme - Orchid. Mt. Takao

Coming back closer to home, in about mid-June is when the ***Dendrobium moniliforme*** Orchids (**Sekkoku** in Japanese) flourish on **Mt. Takao** (**Takao-san**). These orchids bloom in the tallest and oldest Cedar Trees. The above photo shows a collage of photos superimposed on the photo shown to the right.

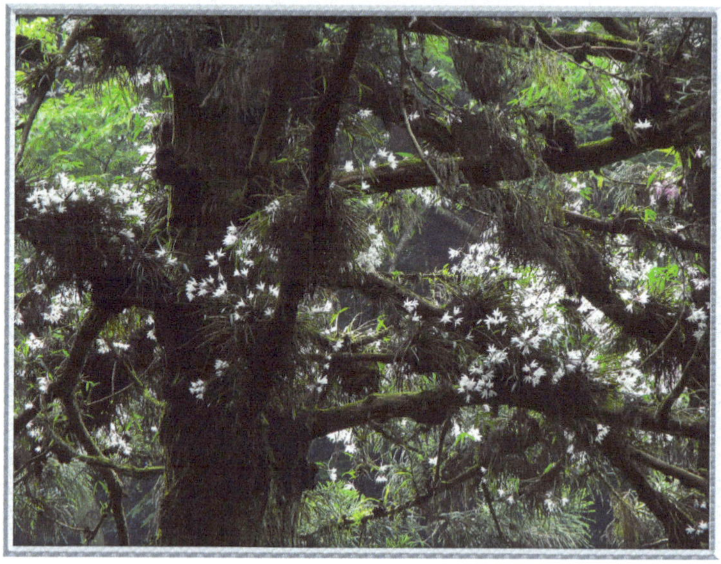

On the facing page is another Orchid – ***Cremastra appendiculata***. This is found on some slopes of Mt. Takao at the same time as the Sekkoku.

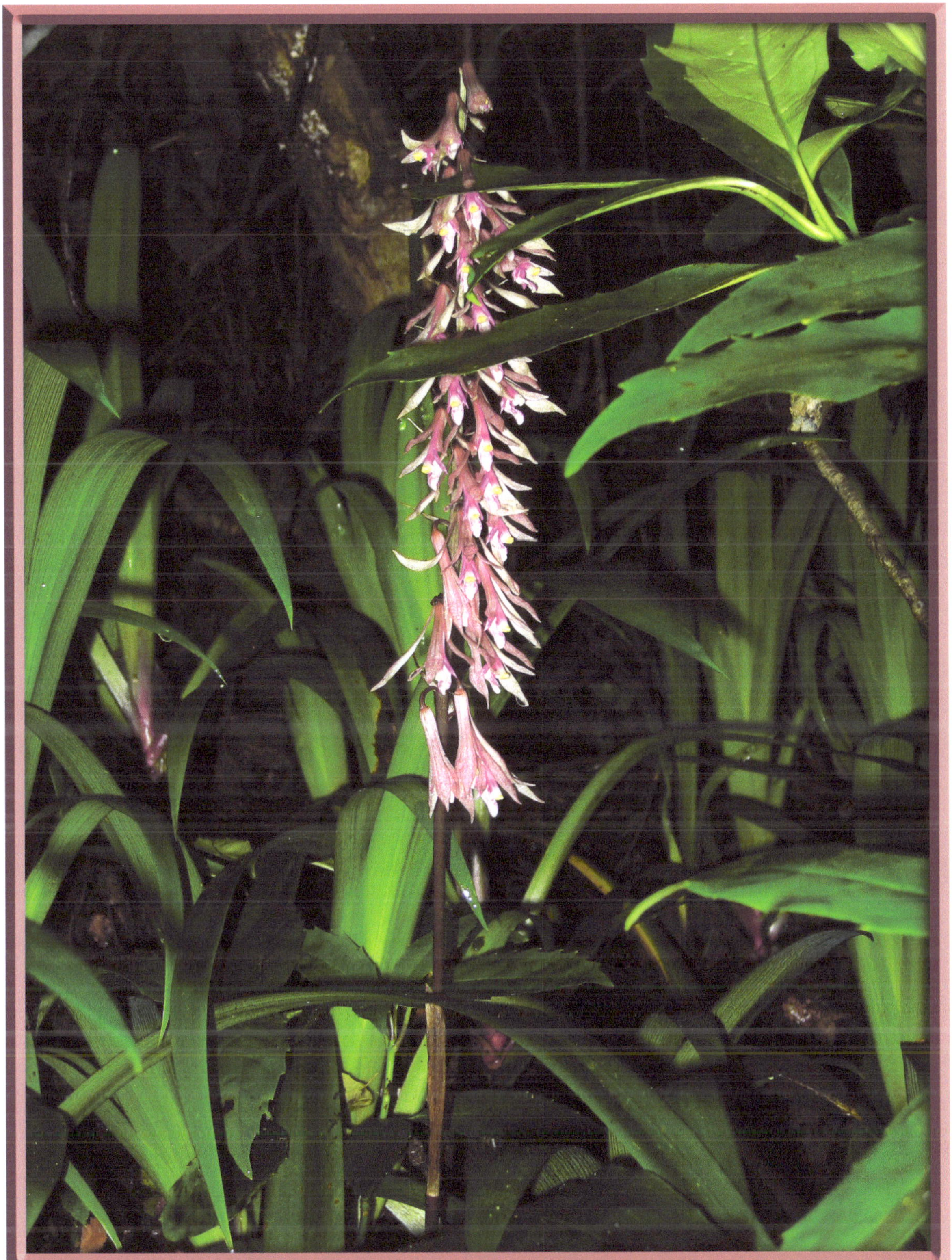

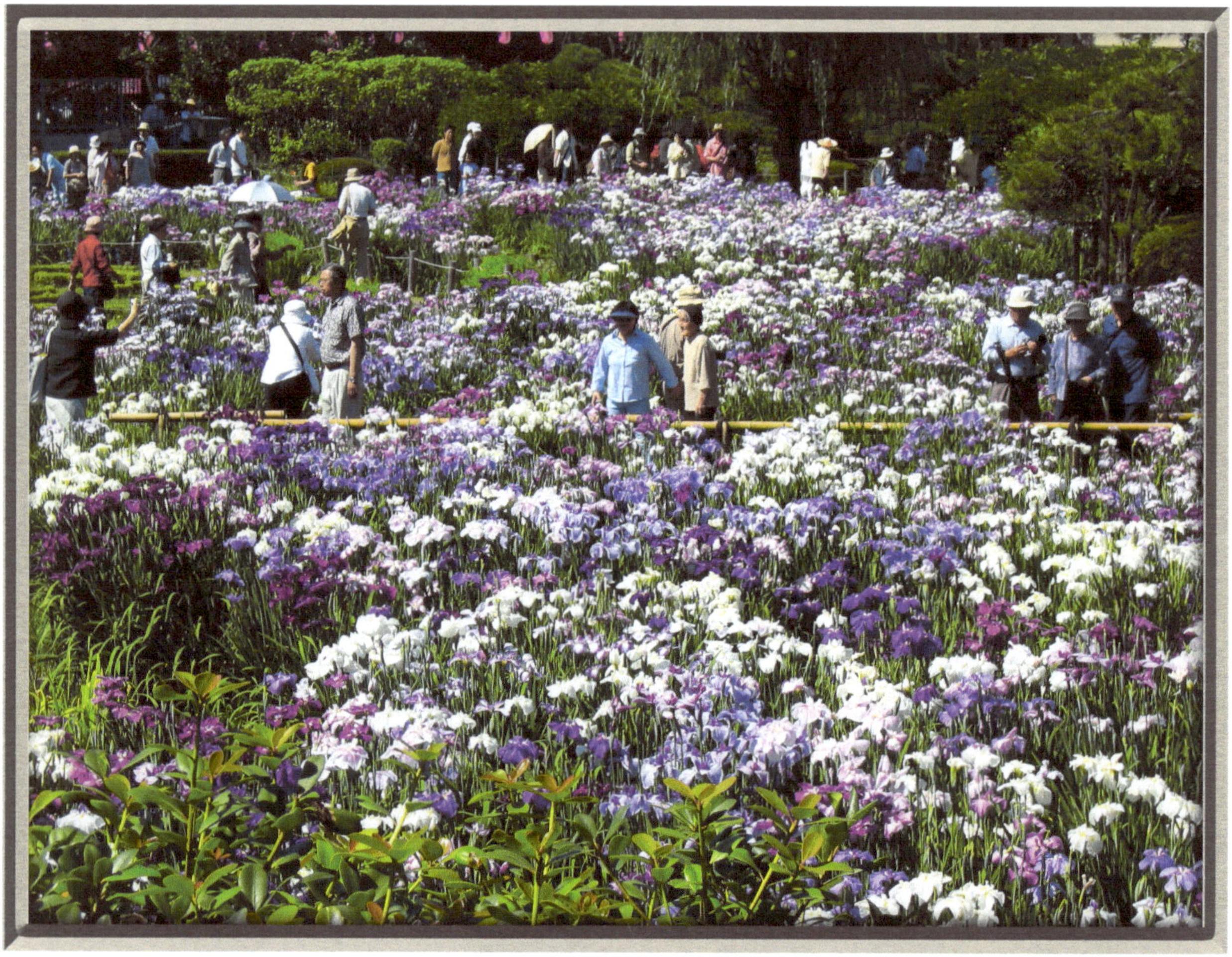

In mid-June you can also find many **Iris Gardens** in full bloom in and around Tokyo. These gardens grow the type of **Irises** which thrive in standing water. The two photos on this page show **Horikiri Iris Garden** in Tokyo. The two photo collage on the facing page shows two types of beautiful Irises at **Fukiage Iris Garden** in **Ome City** – in Western Tokyo.

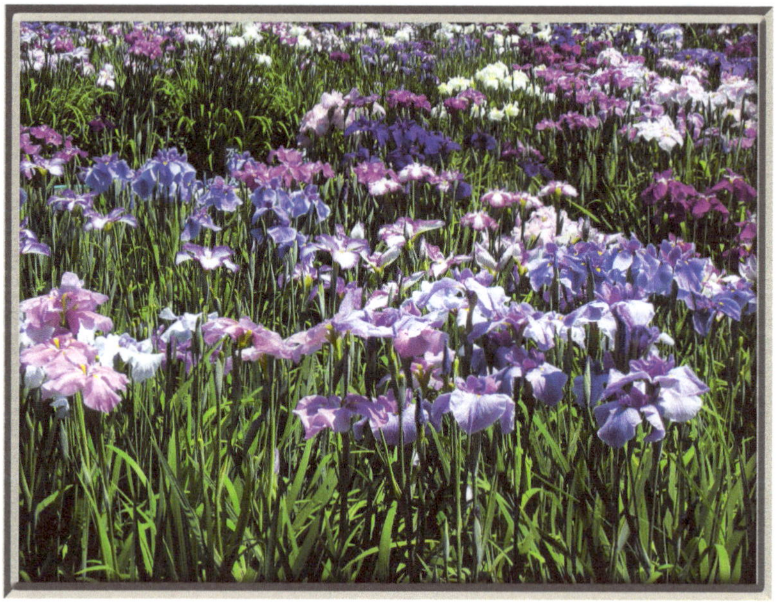

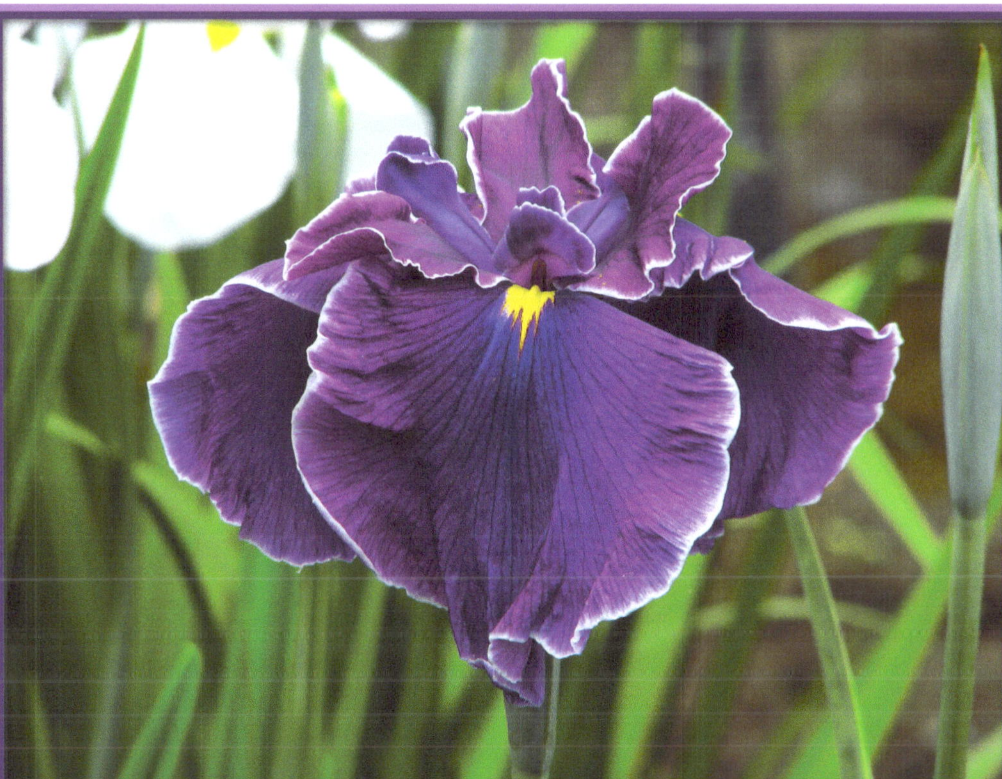

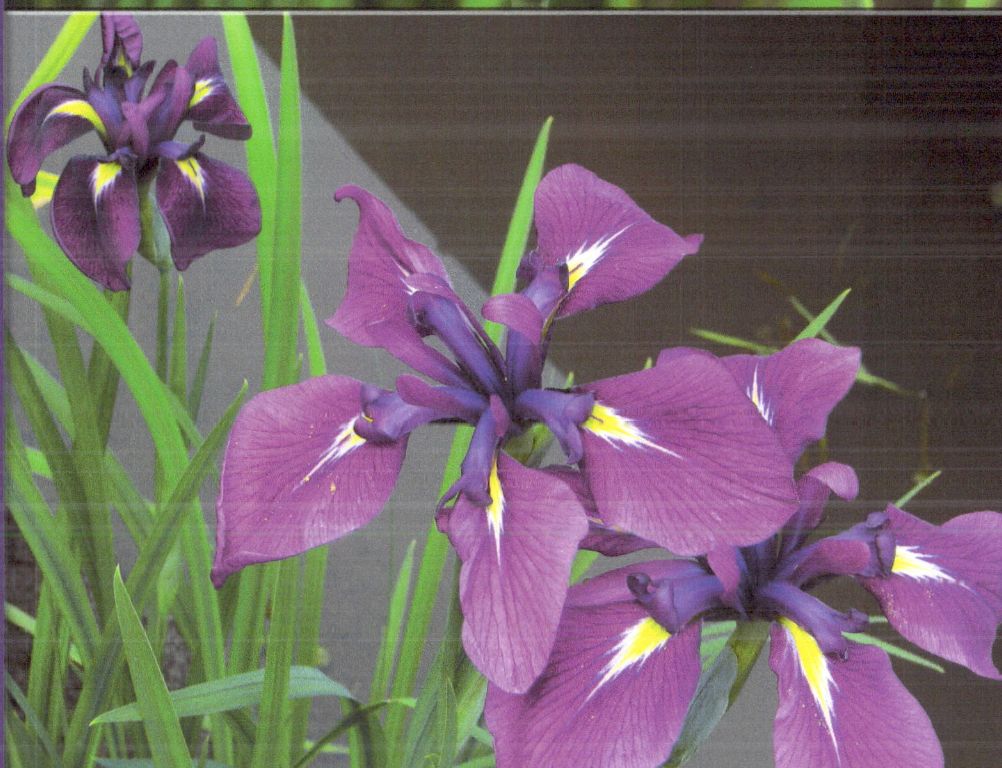

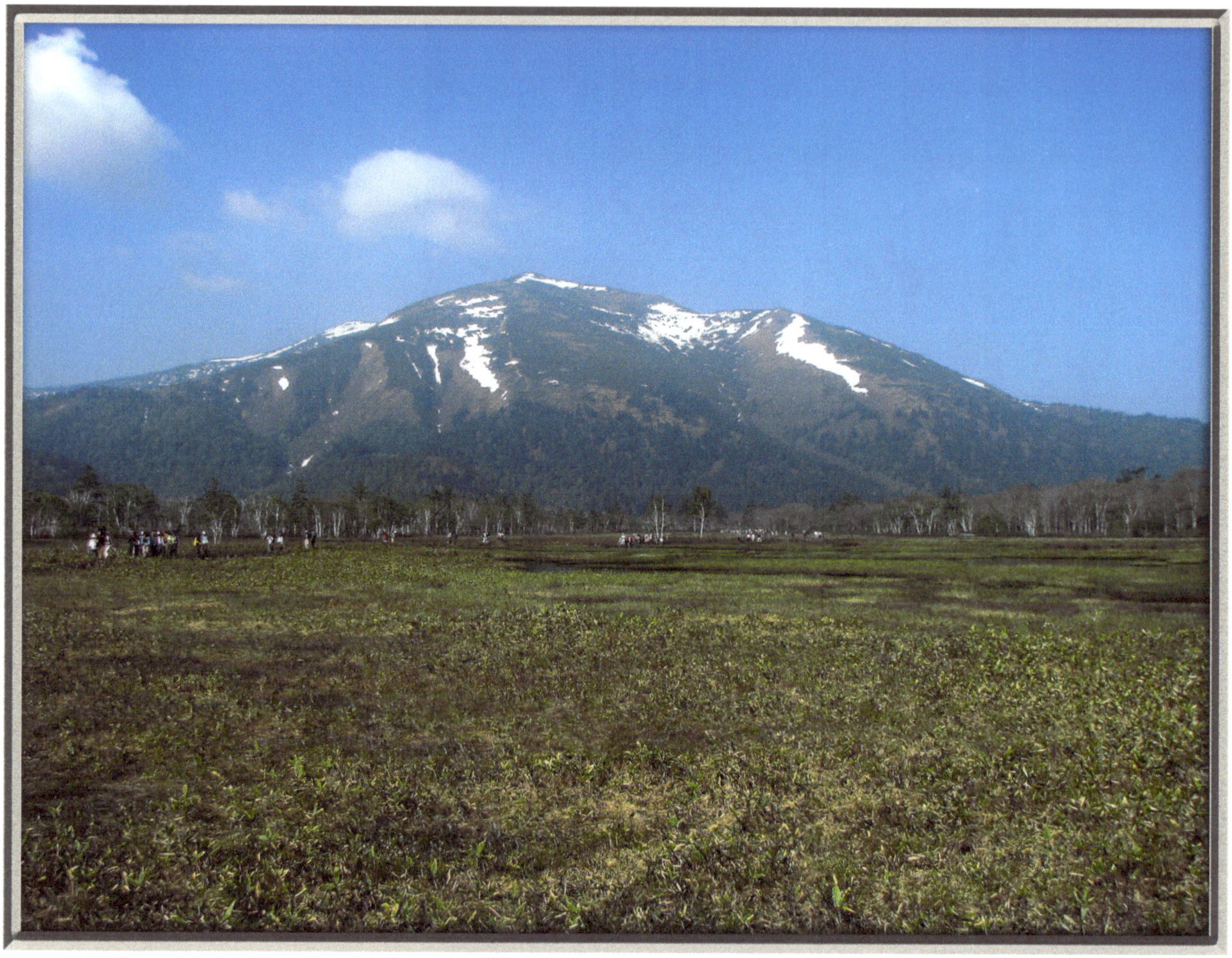

These two photos were taken at **Oze National Park** in **Fukushima, Tochigi, Gunma** and **Niigata Prefectures**. It is a marshland. It is packed with people during the peak of the season and you can only walk on the boardwalks – as you can see, it is wet! The mountain back there is **Mt. Shibutsu** – we will climb it later in the season.

The photo on the facing page is a *Viola kamtschadalorum* – one of the flowers we came here to find.

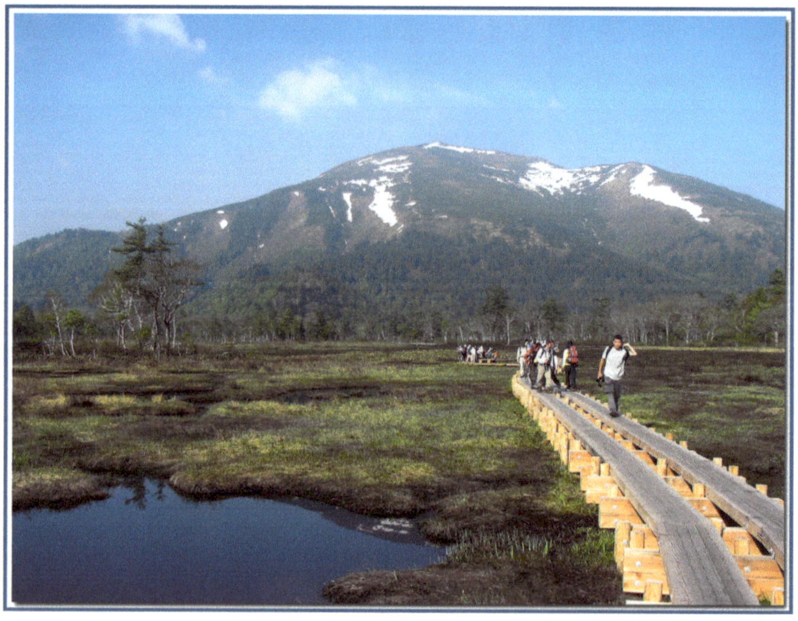

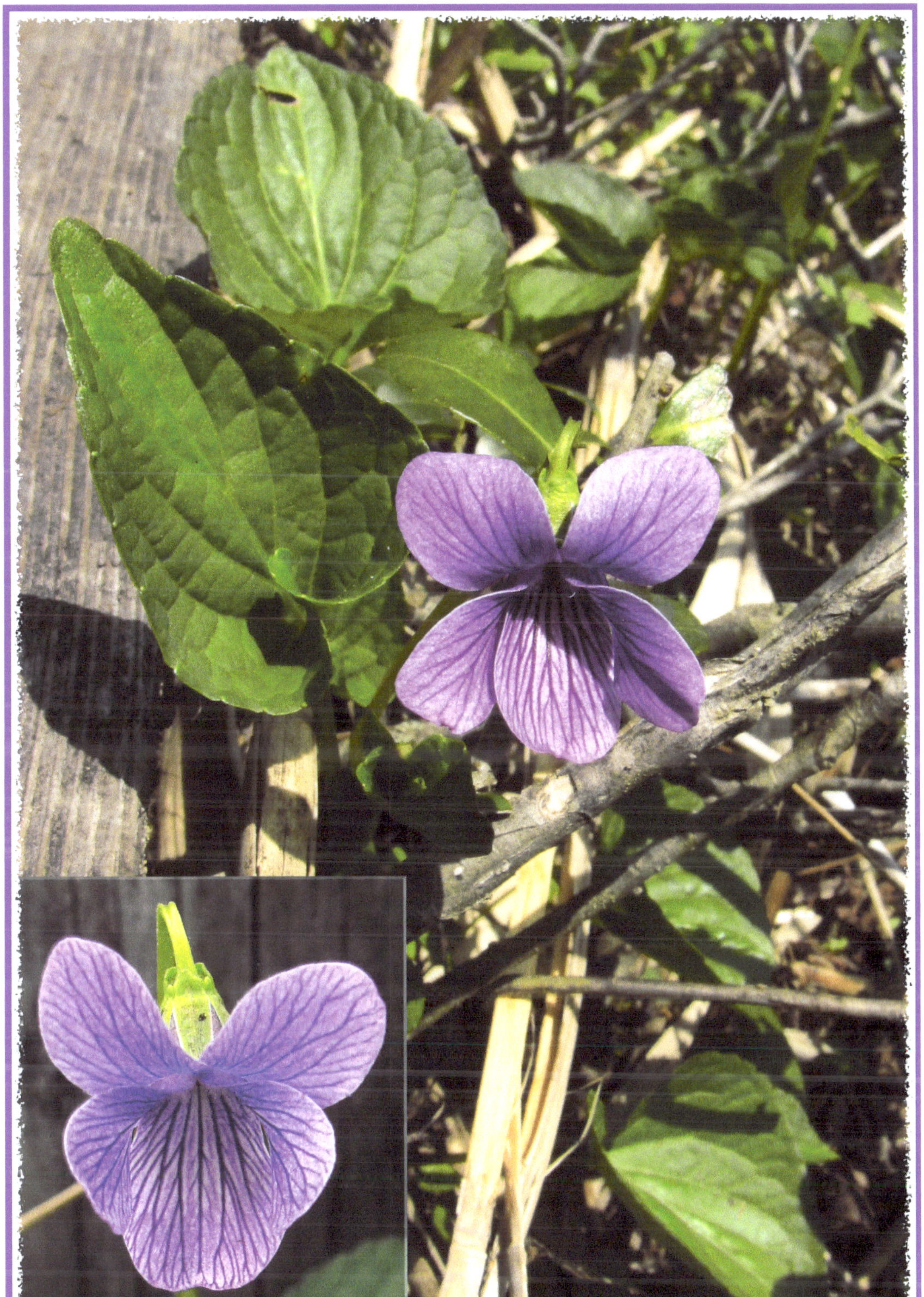

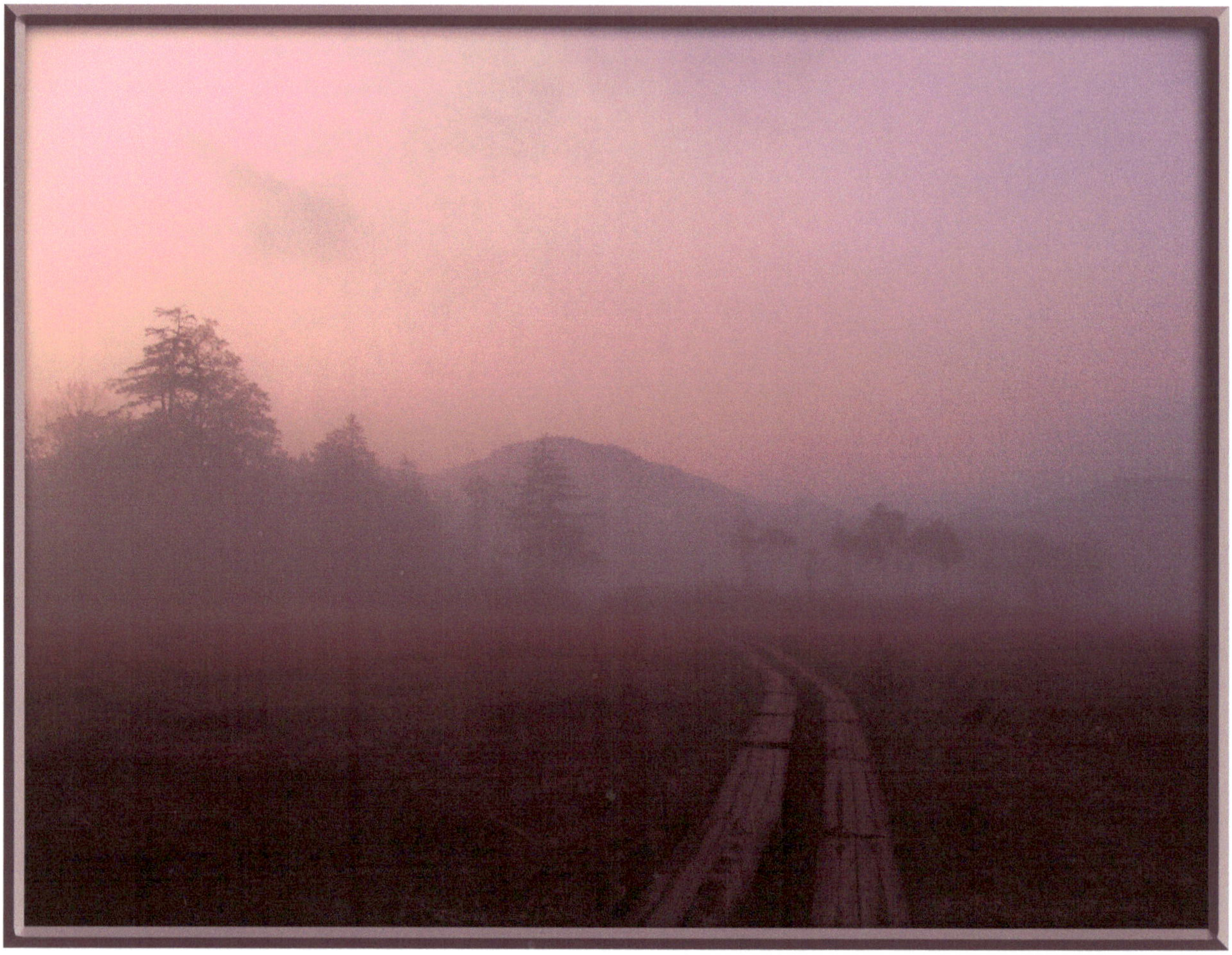

Let us say something more about the ***Viola kamtschadalorum*** on the previous page. It is a very tall violet and also has a very large flower. It is actually rather amazing to see this violet.

The above photo is a sunrise shot taken in **Oze National Park**. The sky was a very eerie pink color for just a few moments before the sun actually rose. It was very strange. In this photo you can also see the boardwalk.

There are several inns in this National Park and there are two campgrounds for those people who would like to bring their tents and other camping gear with them. We chose to camp in our tent both times that we came here.

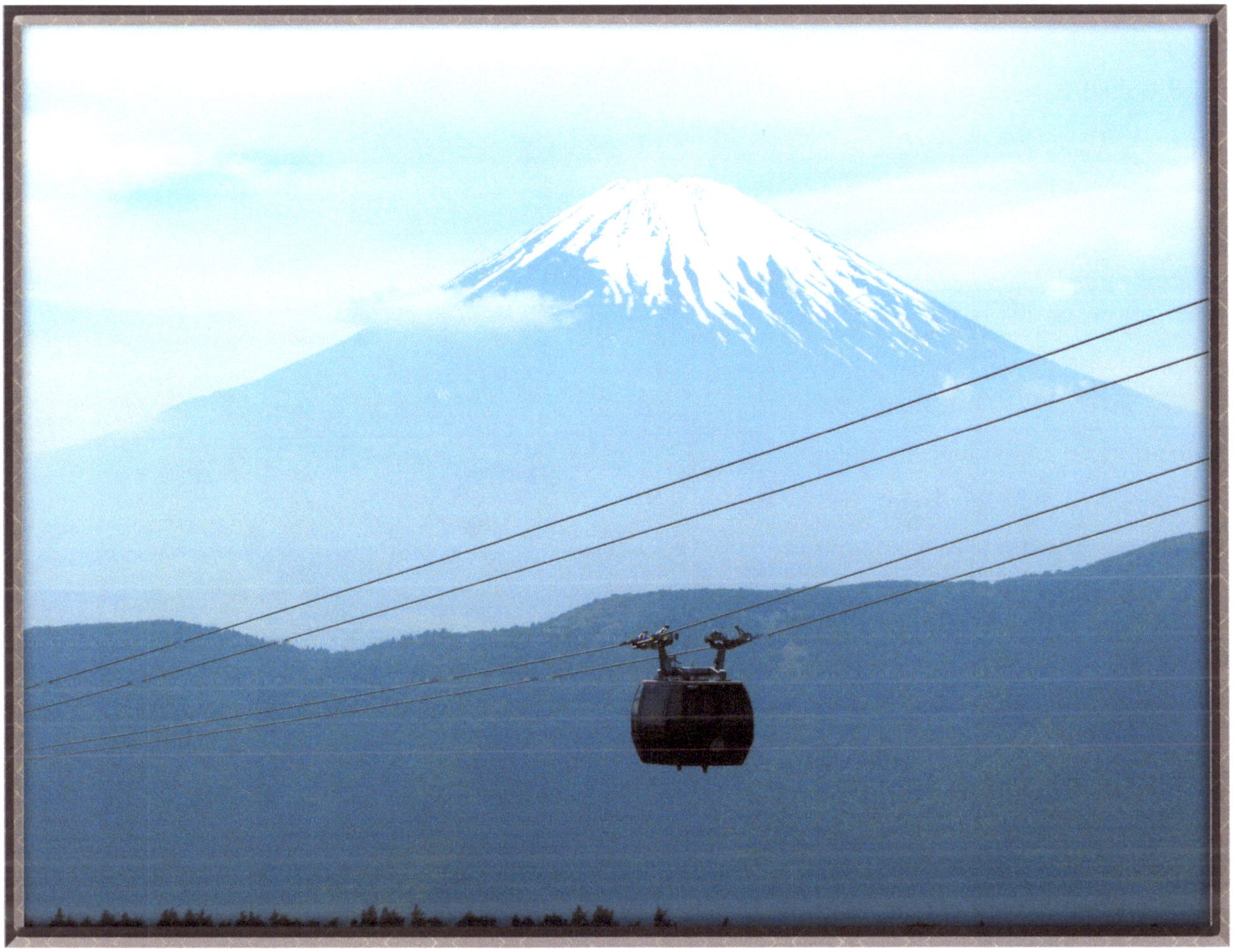

Back on page 34 we took a trip to **Owakudani** and we mentioned that you can see **Mt. Fuji** on a clear day. Here is another trip to **Owakudani** and the Ropeway with **Mt. Fuji** as the background.

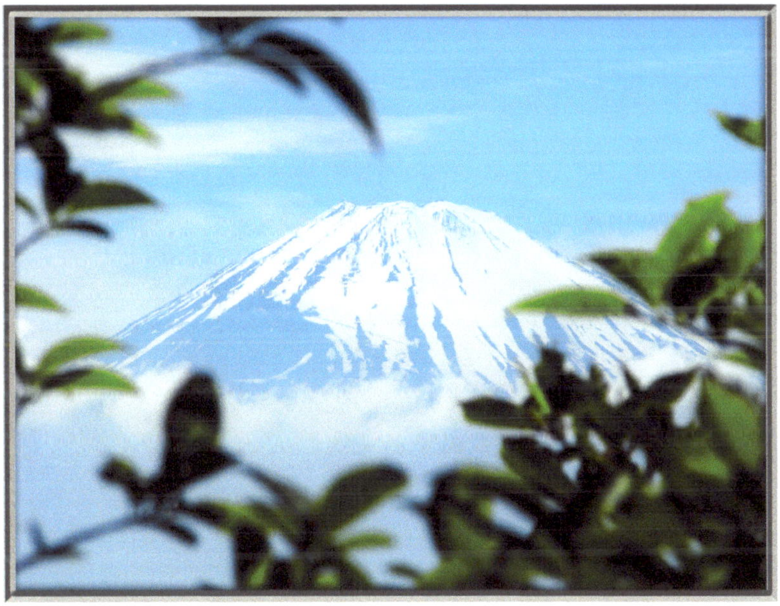

Both of these photos were taken from the Owakudani parking lot.

On page 34 we also mentioned the hard-boiled eggs which are cooked in the hot volcanic water. Here is how these eggs are sold in little paper bags containing five eggs.

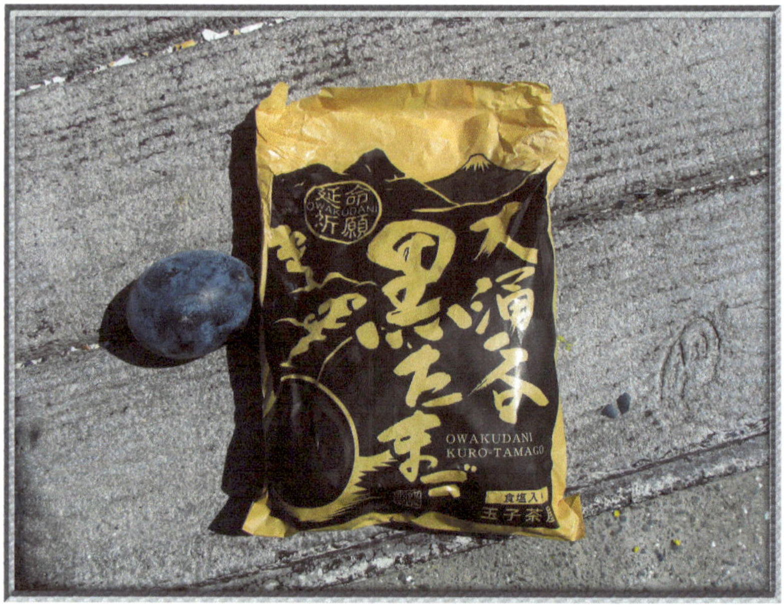

The below photo is the shrine at the summit of **Mt. Komagatake** (1,357 meters = 4,451 feet). **Mt. Komagatake** is the high mountain on the east side of **Lake Ashi** (**Hakone**) and there is a ropeway to the summit.

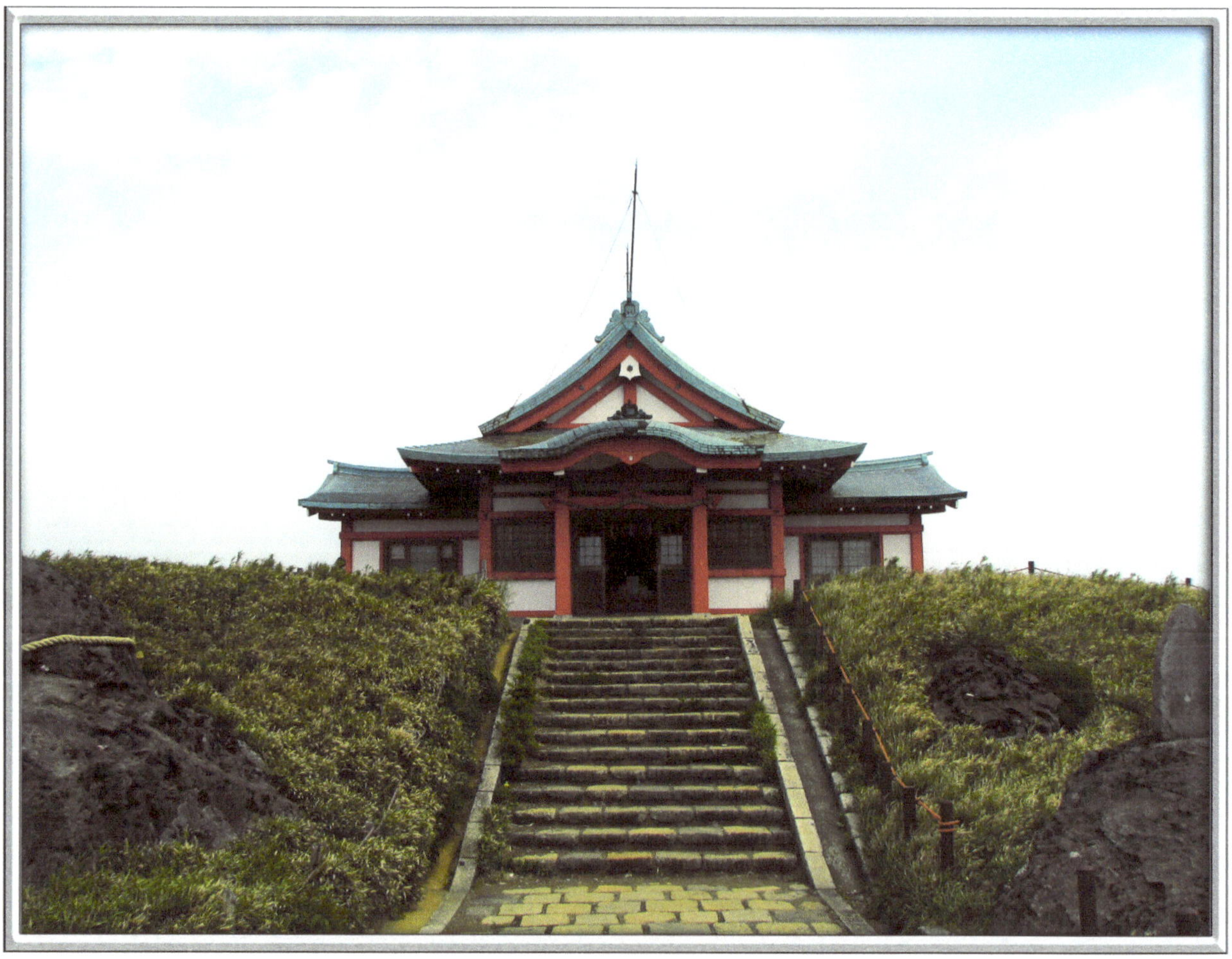

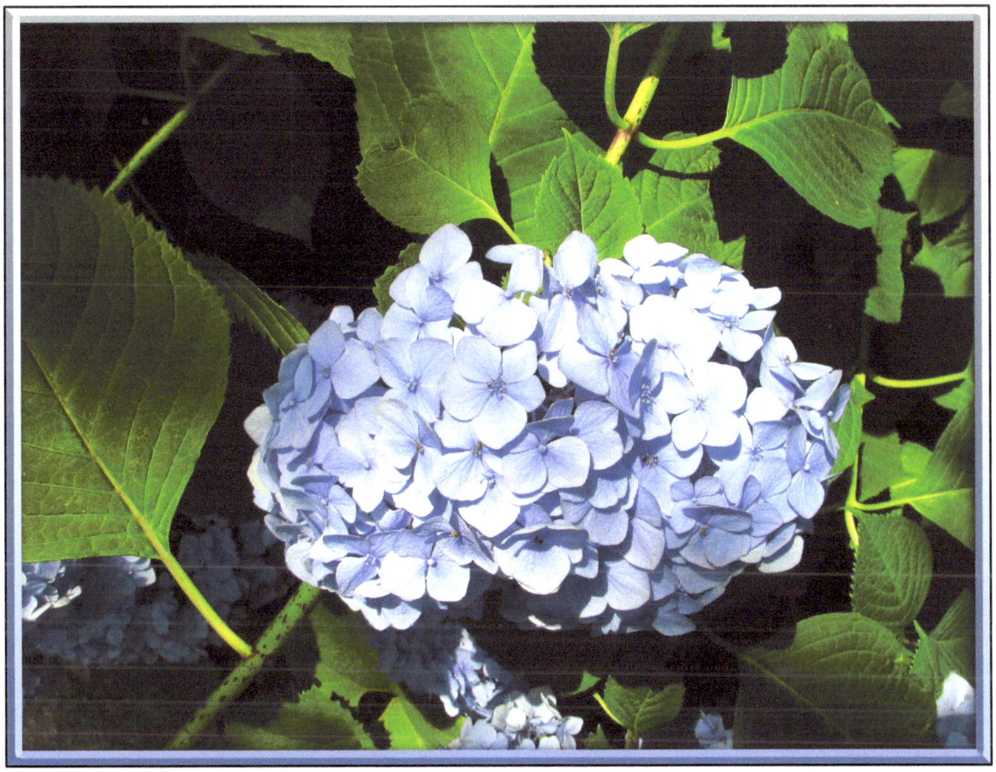

This page features **Hydrangea** flowers. Around the middle of June the **Hydrangea** flowers really come out around Tokyo. There are several **Hydrangea Gardens** where you can go to see them. Here (above right) is a blue flowered bush. Blue colors come from aluminum in the soil and a pH of about 5.2 to 5.5. To the right is a pink flowered **Hydrangea**. Pink comes from a lack of aluminum in the soil and a pH of about 6.0 to 6.2.

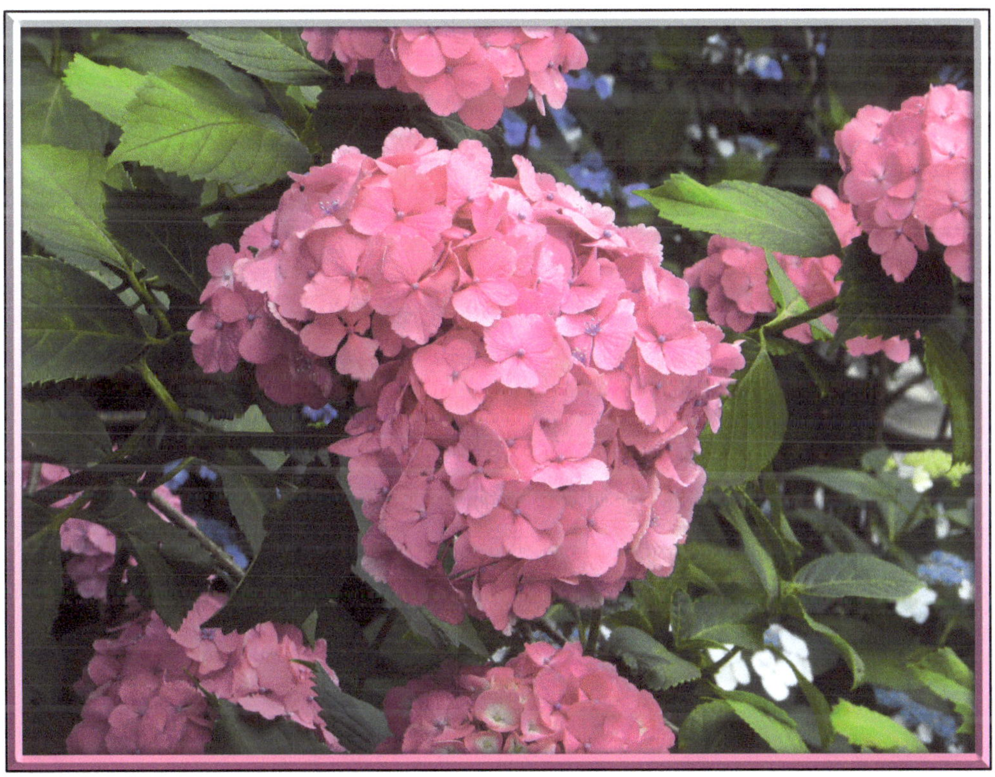

PART 3: SUMMER

We have now finished with the spring photos and we enter summer at this point. It can be very hot in Tokyo in the summer – up to 40° – 42° C (= 104° – 108° F), which is really difficult to endure. For that reason we go to the mountains whenever we possibly can to escape the heat. There are not as many flowers in the summer, but you will still find a few flower photos, mostly high mountain flowers.

The below photo is once again the summit shelter at **Mt. Hinode** (we showed you a somewhat similar photo on page 79). This time it is just after sunrise, while last time it was a short while after sunset. The photos on the following two pages show four shots of the sun as it rose on this date. The fourth shot – at 4:30 AM – shows a nice series of **crepuscular rays**.

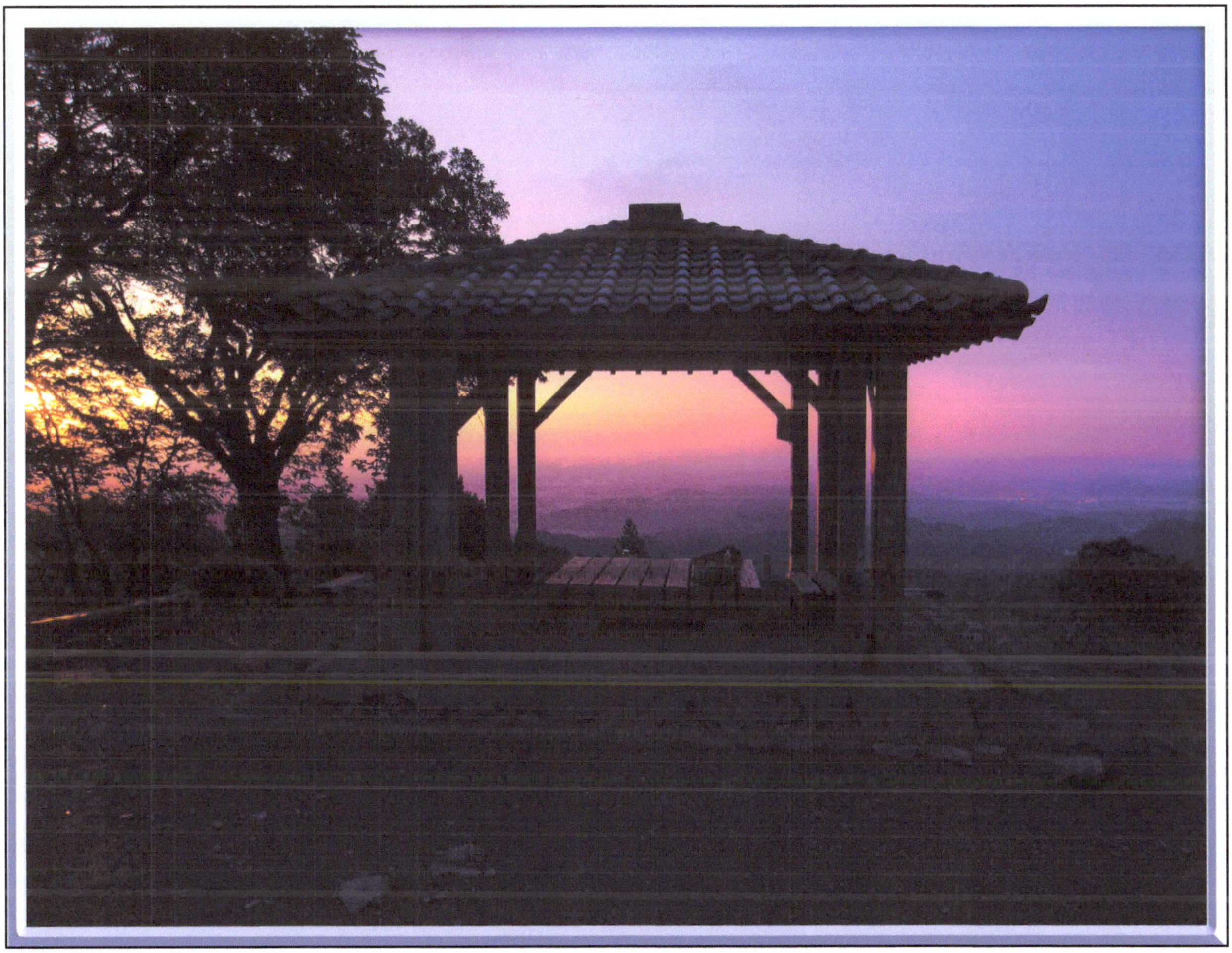

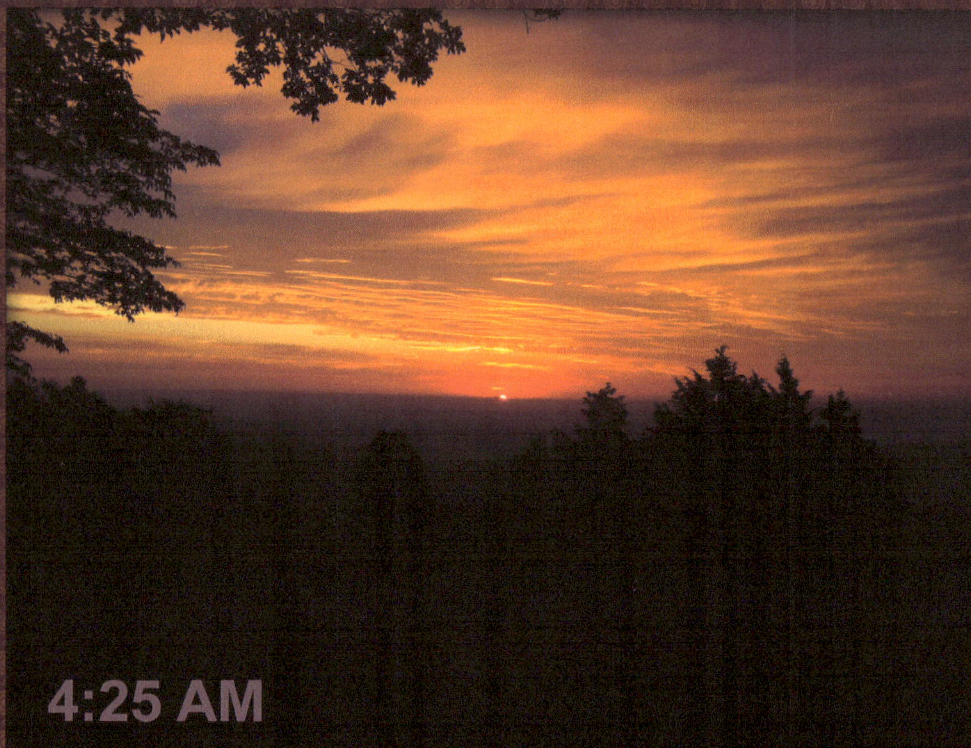
4:25 AM

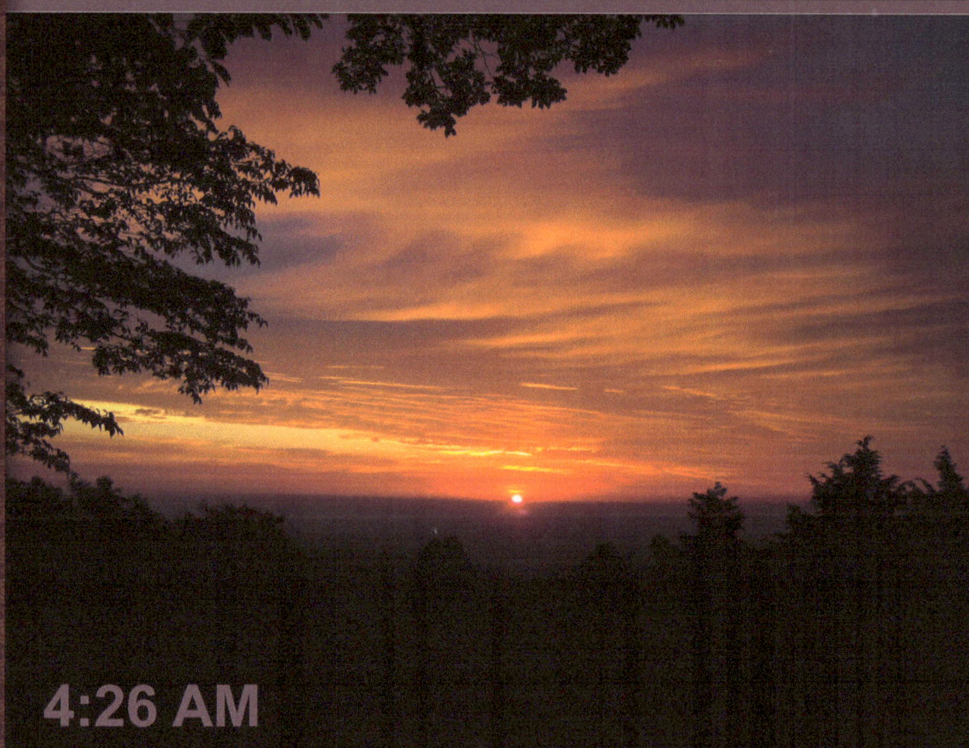
4:26 AM

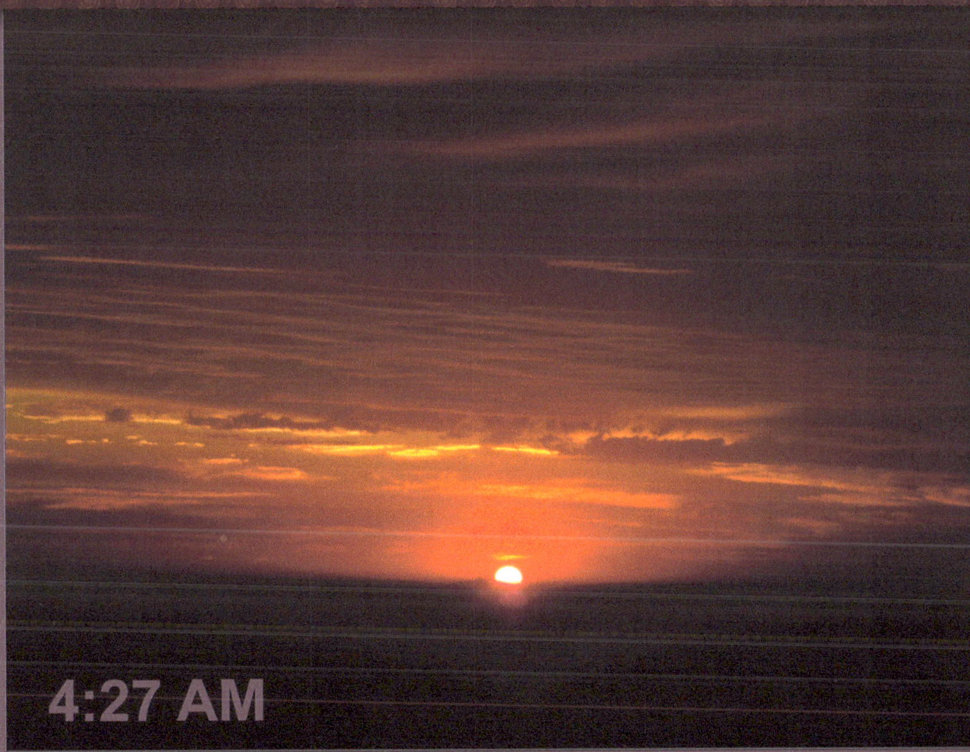
4:27 AM

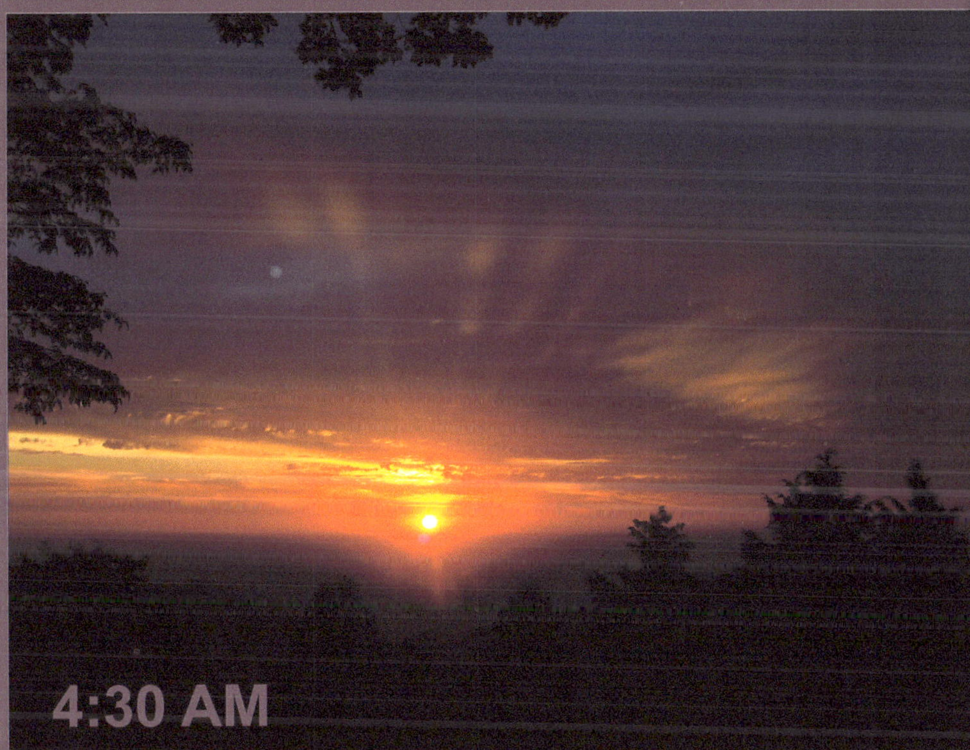
4:30 AM

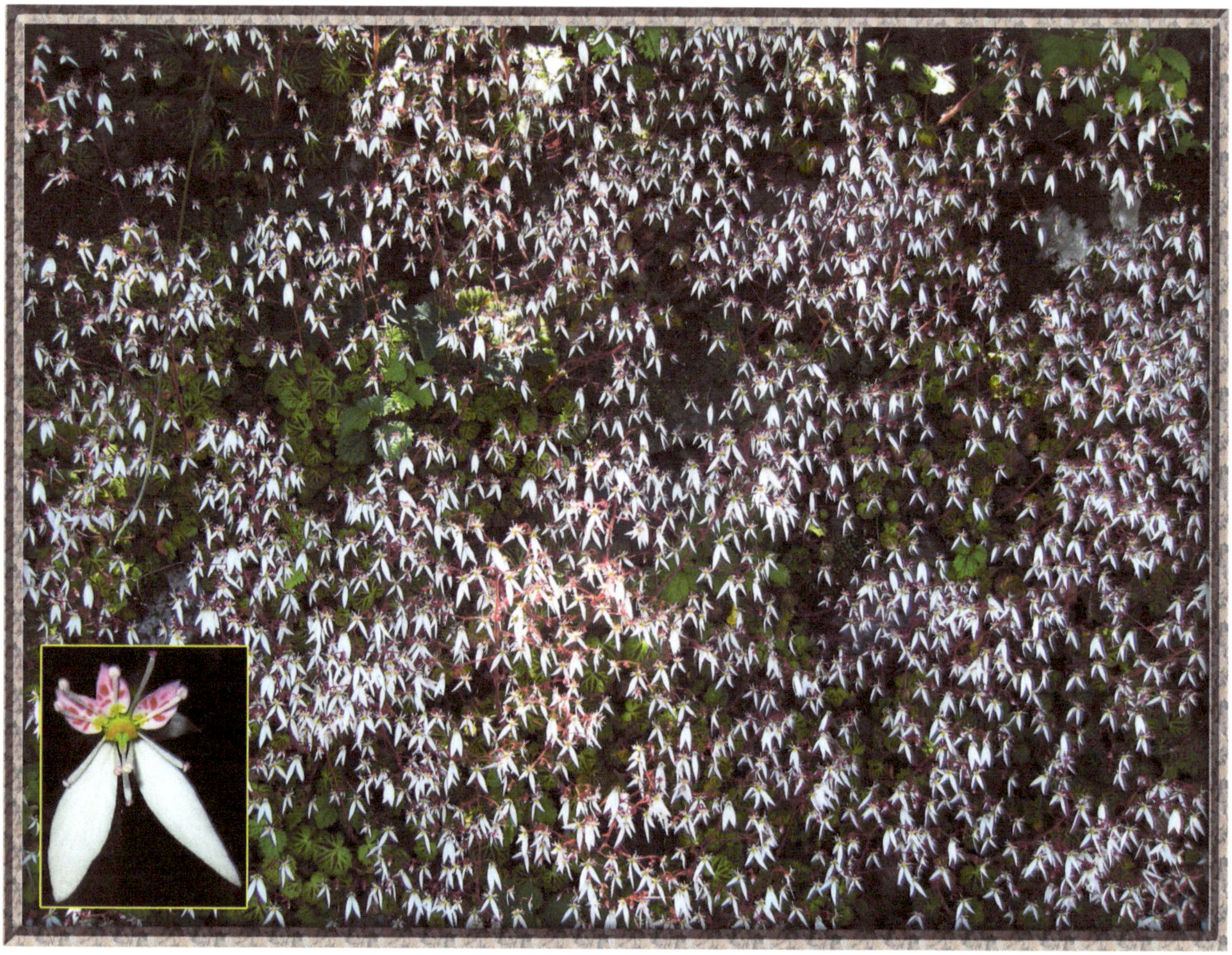

This photo is ***Saxifraga stolonifera***. In Japanese this flower is called the ***"Dai"*** flower as it assumes the shape of the kanji character Dai (**大**). We have inserted a single flower photo to show you a close up. It is an interesting flower which is found on rocky areas near streams and other wet places. We found this patch along the stream on our descent of **Mt. Hinode**.

On the facing page is a **"Screw Flower"** – a ***Spiranthes sinensis*** – an **Orchid**. It should be obvious why it is called a "Screw Flower. It comes in "right-hand" and "left-hand" threads too.

And then on the following two pages (104 – 105) is a waterfall which can be found along one of the several trails which one can select as the descent route from **Mt. Hinode**. This is **White Rock Waterfall**. The first photo shows it in its full summer costume of green. The second photo shows it in its winter costume of brown.

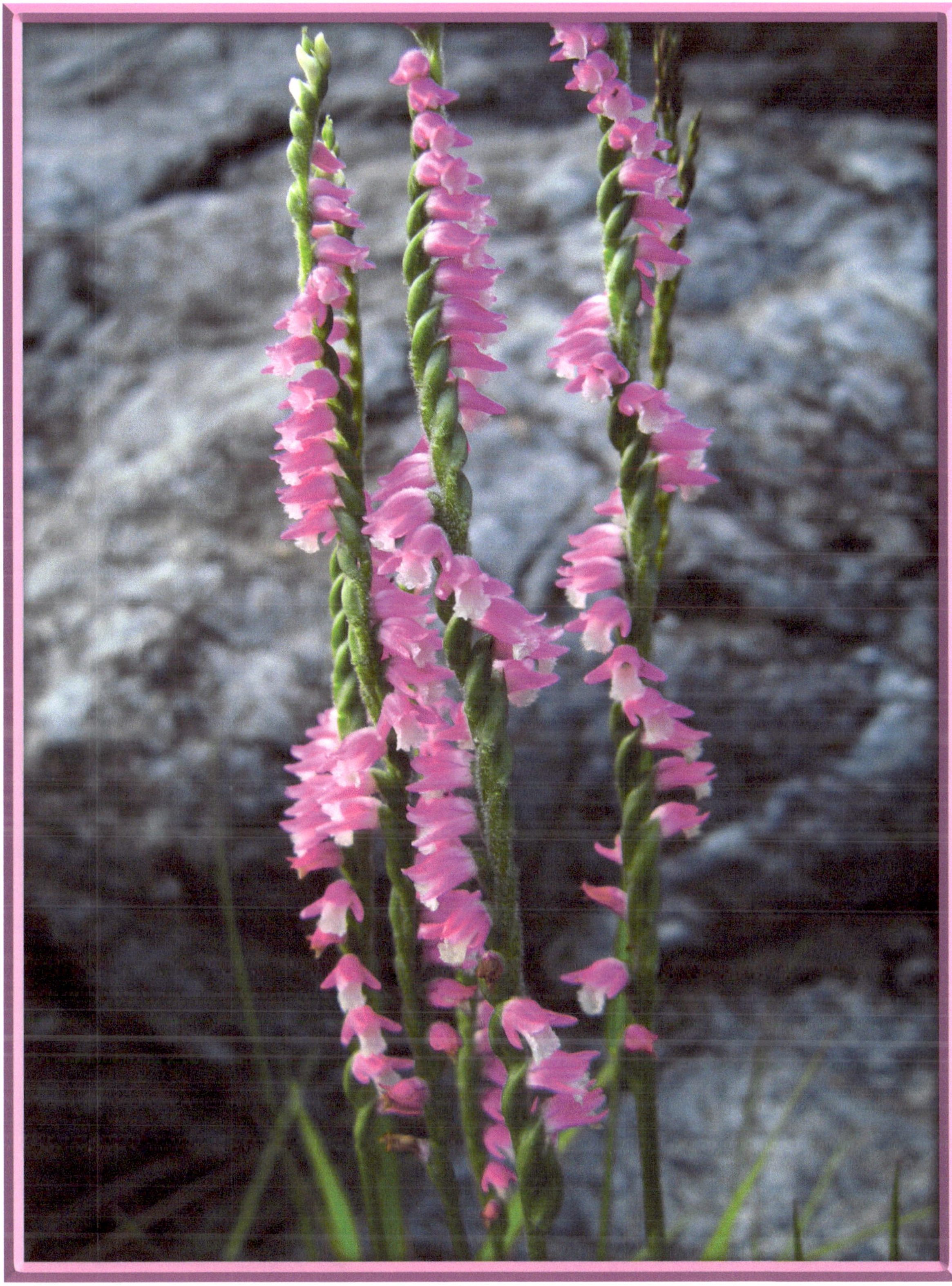

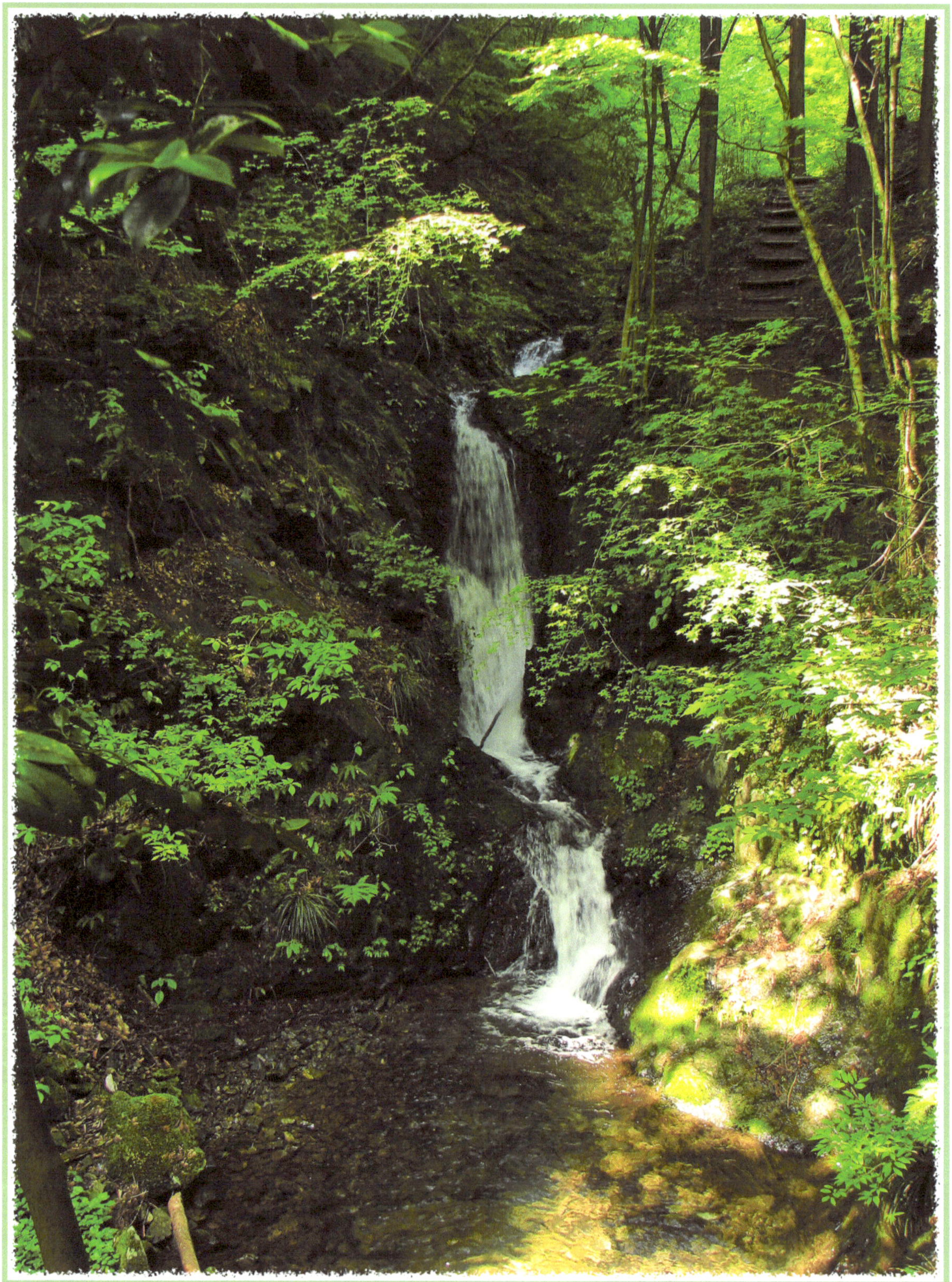

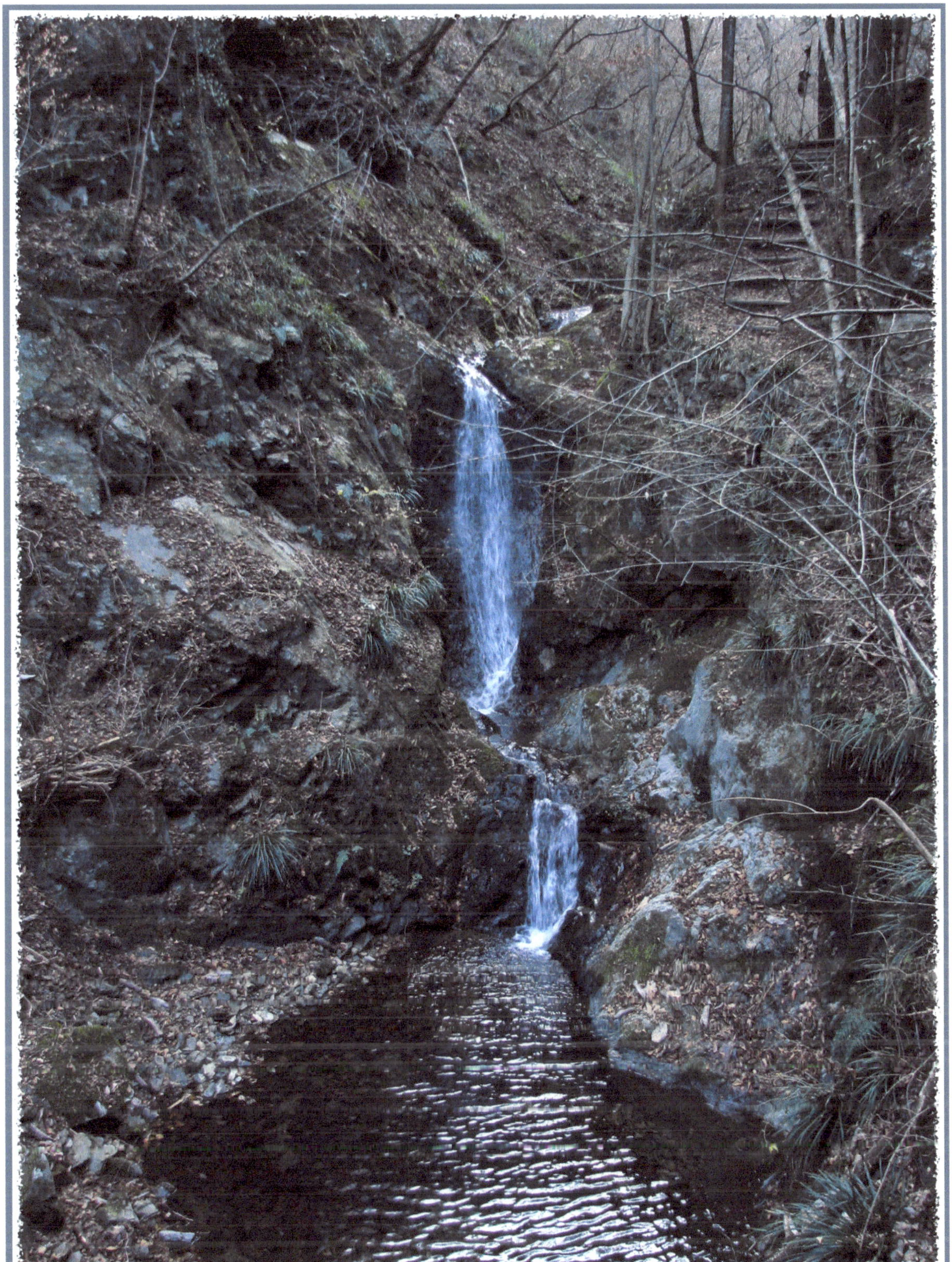

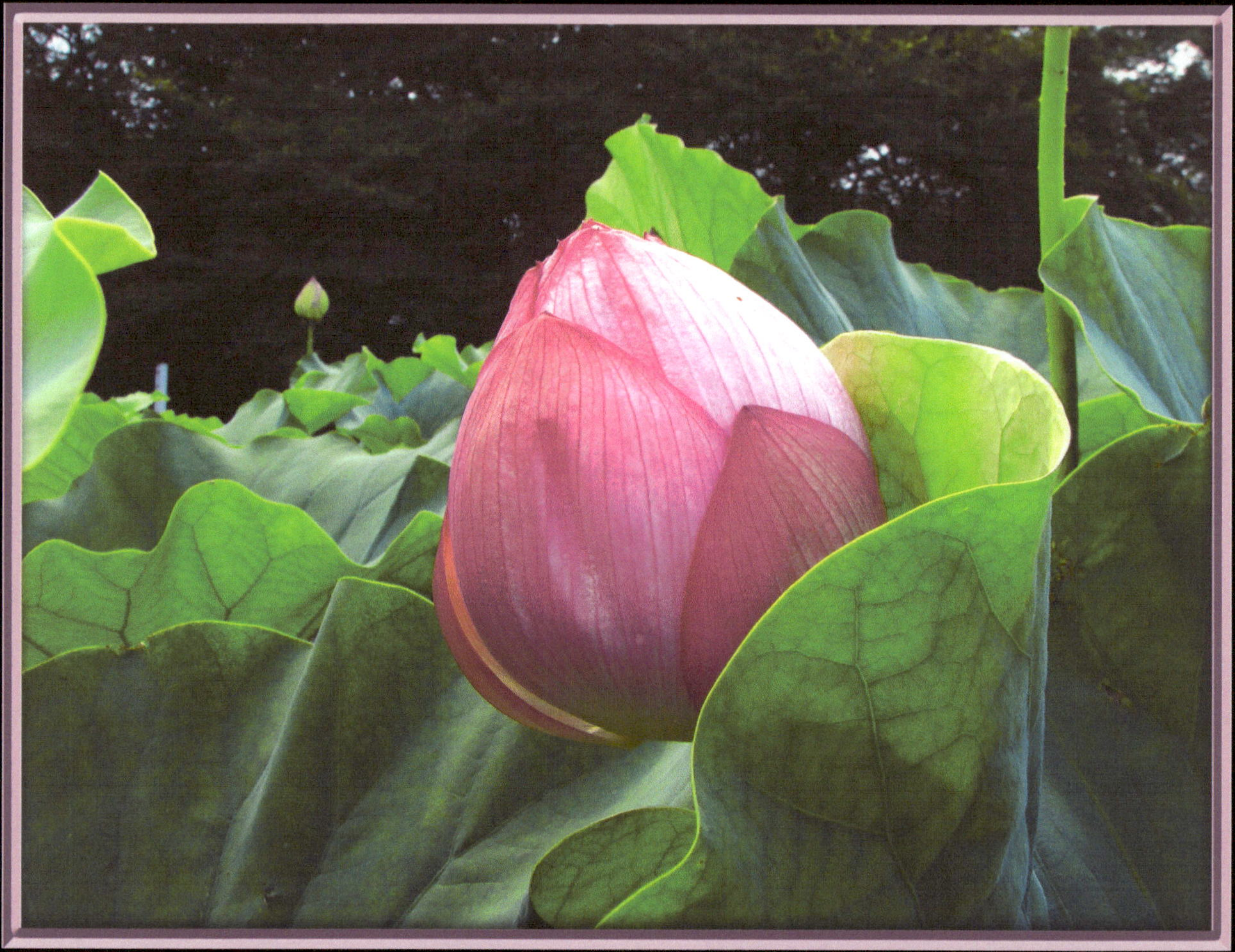

July Photos and Story

Now it's July and the **Lotus** (***Nelumbo nucifera***) starts to bloom. It is very hard to catch a flower which is fully open and undamaged, not falling apart already or imperfect in some other way. So, here is a bud which is nearly ready to open. These flowers can be about 15 cm. (6 in.) in diameter and are very beautiful. This plant grows in standing water, and therefore you need a water garden to grow it. Later on, in the autumn, we'll show you a photo or two of the seedheads of this plant. Oh, by the way, the roots can be eaten, and they are quite delicious and rather crunchy. The lotus flower is very important in the Buddhist religion and is often used as an example of divine beauty. This photo was taken in **Jindai Botanical Garden**.

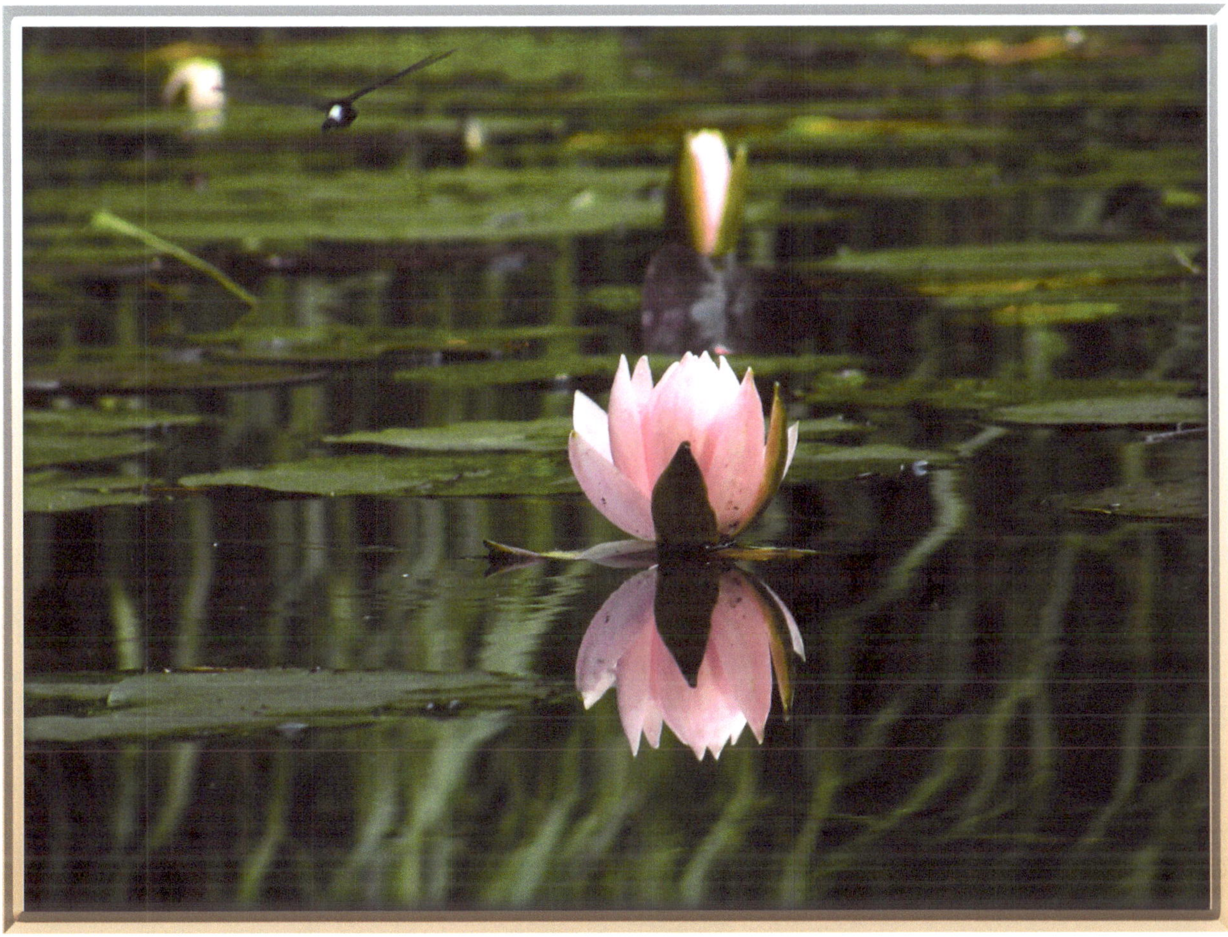

Above is a beautiful **Water Lily** and its perfect reflection at **Jindai Botanical Garden**. If you look a little closer you'll note a white-tailed dragonfly in the upper left portion of the photo.

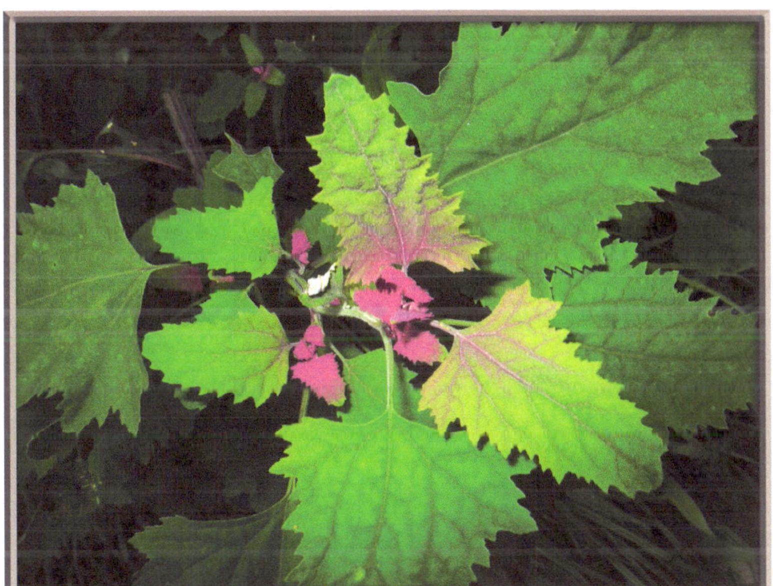

To the right, in **Nogawa Park**, is a strange plant, but it occurs naturally this way. It is a ***Chenopodium album* var. *centrorubrum***. We never see many of this plant. ***Chenopodium album*** is a relatively common plant, but not the **var. *centrorubrum***.

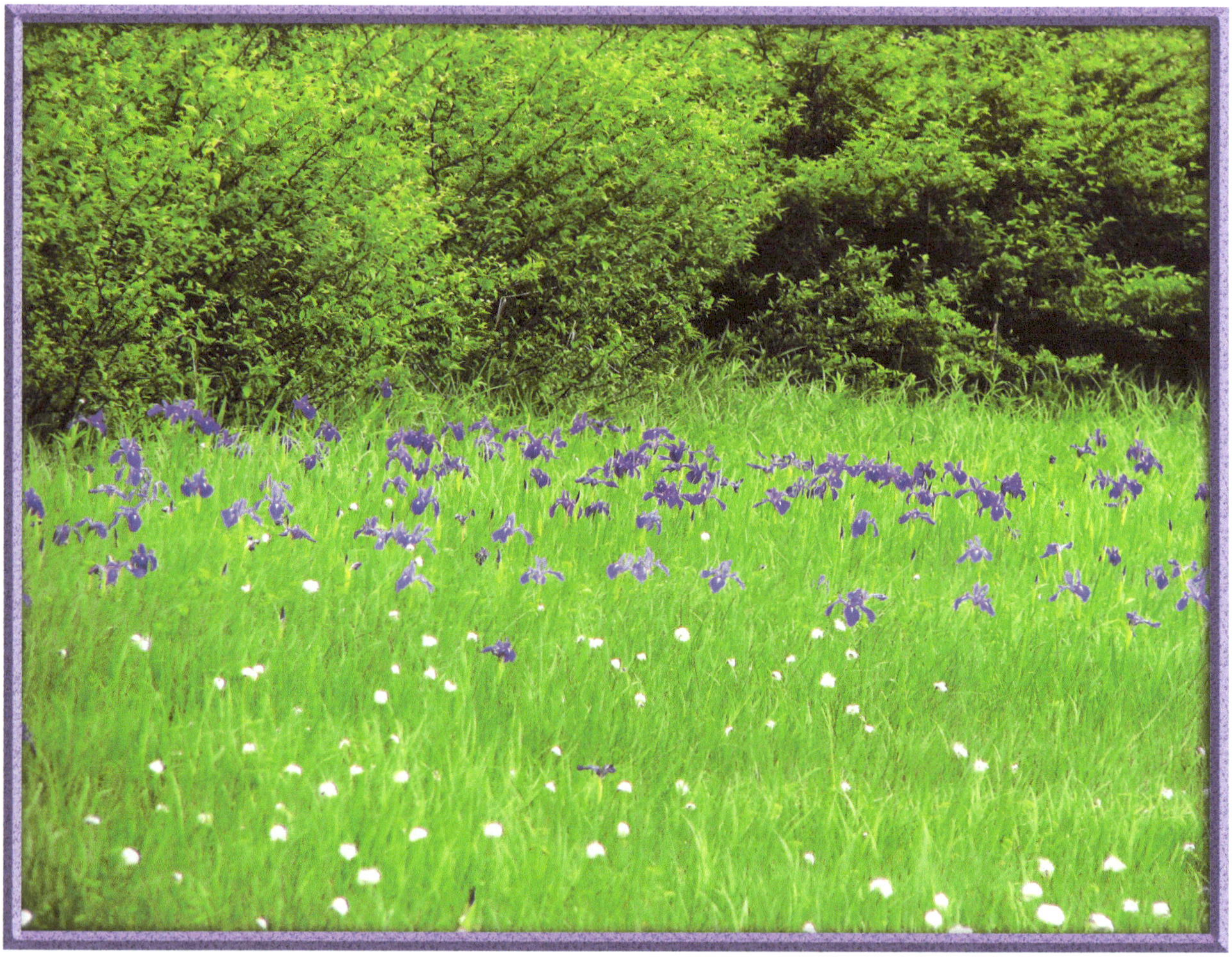

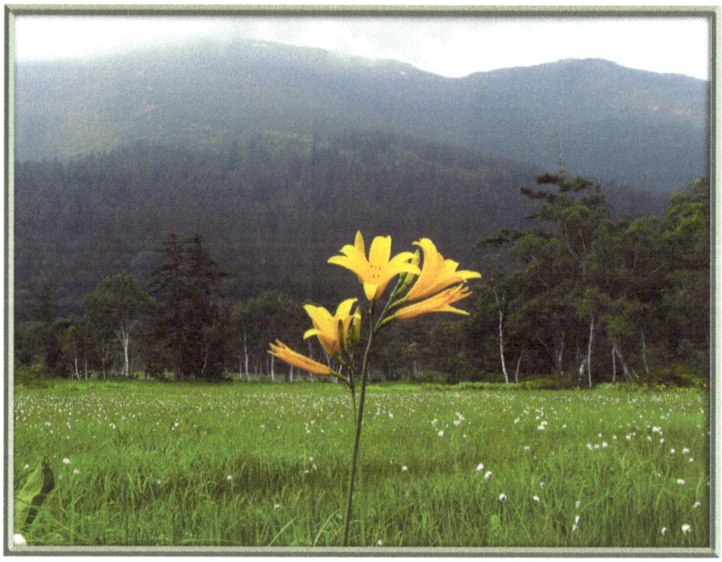

Now let's return to **Oze National Park**. Oze N.P. was last seen back in the spring. We showed you only four photos from that trip. On this trip, in the summer, we have found several photos which we think are worthy of being seen. The first one, above, shows you **Cottongrass** (***Eriophorum vaginatum***) and ***Iris laevigata***. It was so amazing to see so many wild flowers, and due to it being a wet marshland there were no people walking around and trampling things down. To the right is a ***Hemerocallis dumortieri* var. *esculenta*** a.k.a. ***Hemerocallis middendorffii* var. *esculenta***.

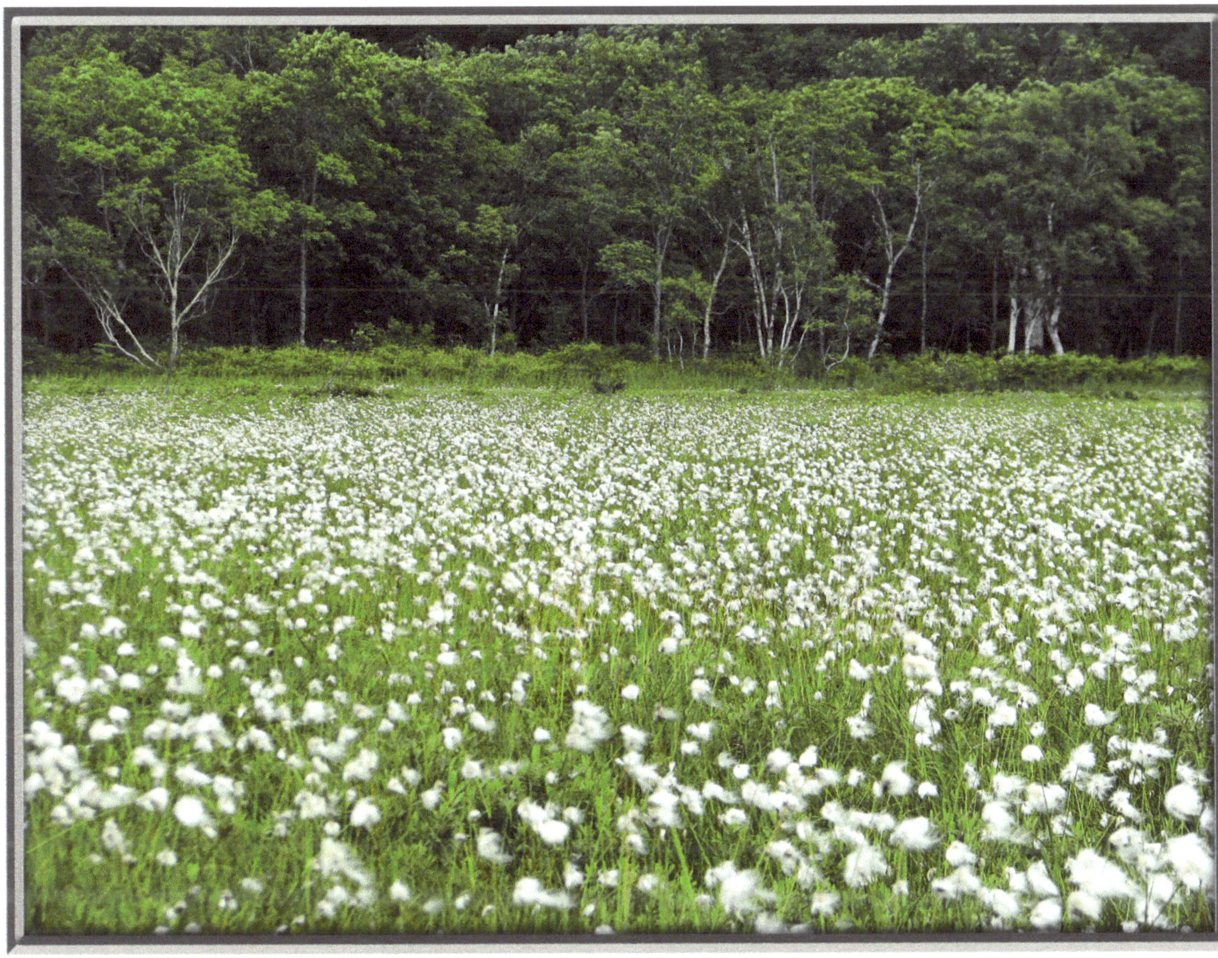

Above, is a shot of only Cottongrass (***Eriophorum vaginatum***). Can you believe that it can be in such abundance? Pretty amazing isn't it?

On the following day in Oze N. P. we climbed **Mt. Shibutsu** (2,228 meters = 7,310 feet). The two photos on the subsequent page show you what the trail looked like early in the morning as we climbed. It rained all night and the flowing water on the trail was the result of all of that rain. Fortunately it stopped raining a little while before dawn. By midday it was actually a nice day.

The second photo on the next page gives you an idea of what we saw as we climbed Mt. Shibutsu. It was slowly clearing up and the sun shining through the holes in the clouds gave the impression of a spotlight on the marsh. The campground is near those buildings which you can see in the lower right of the photo. You can also see the boardwalk snaking across the marsh.

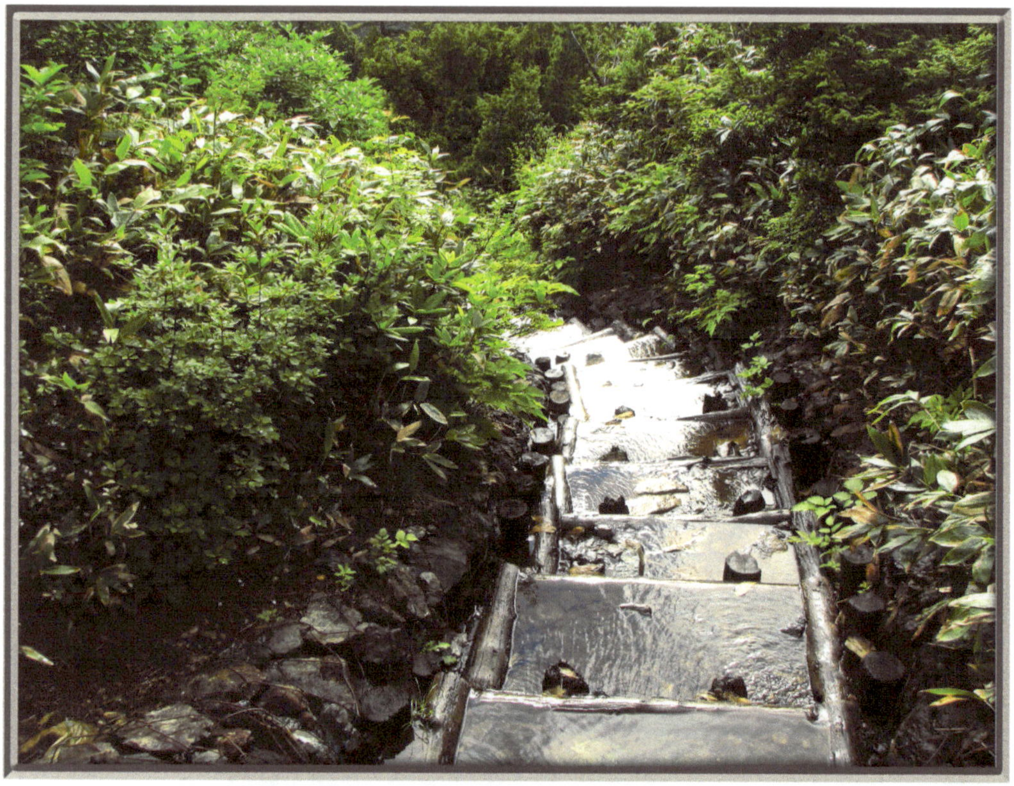

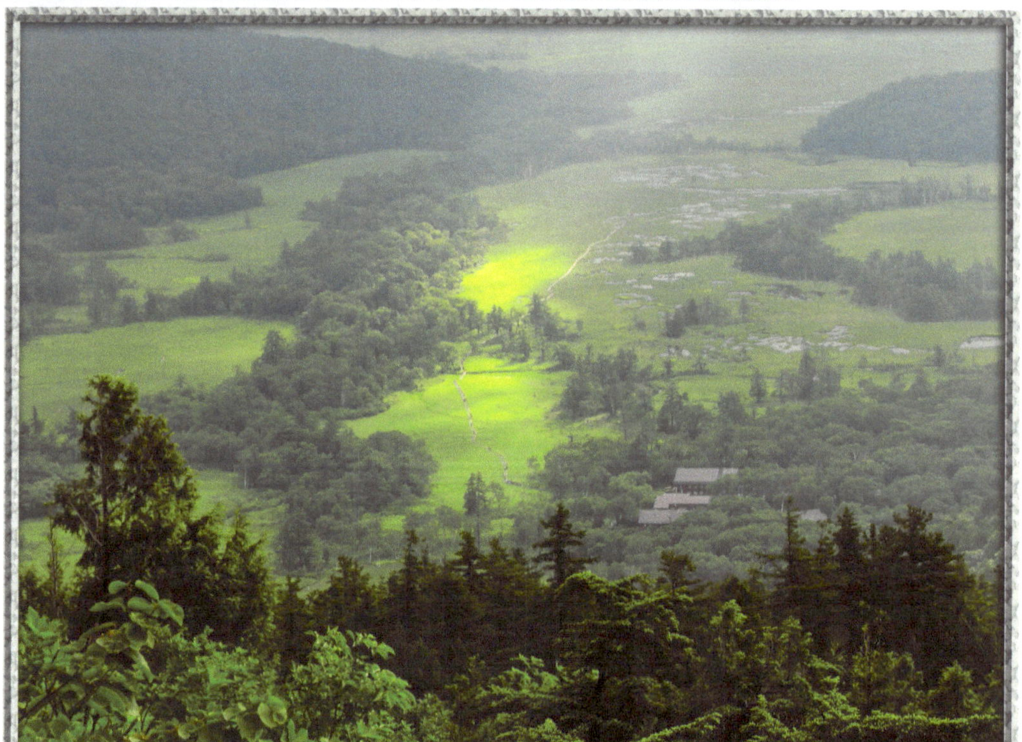

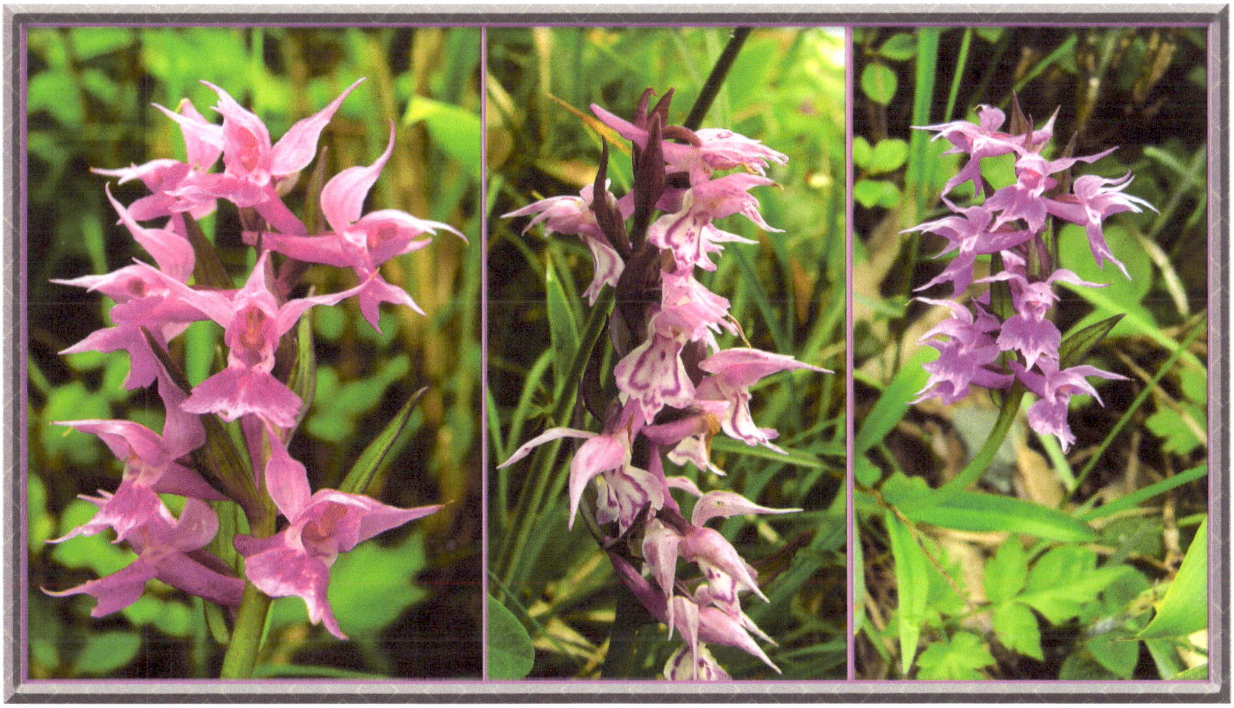

At the top of this page are three shots of ***Dactylorhiza aristata*** – another Orchid. This orchid came in many colors and with many different patterns inside of the flowers.

The lower photo shows **Mt. Shibutsu** – this was taken after we crossed the summit, so this is looking back at it. You can also see the marsh down there (to the right).

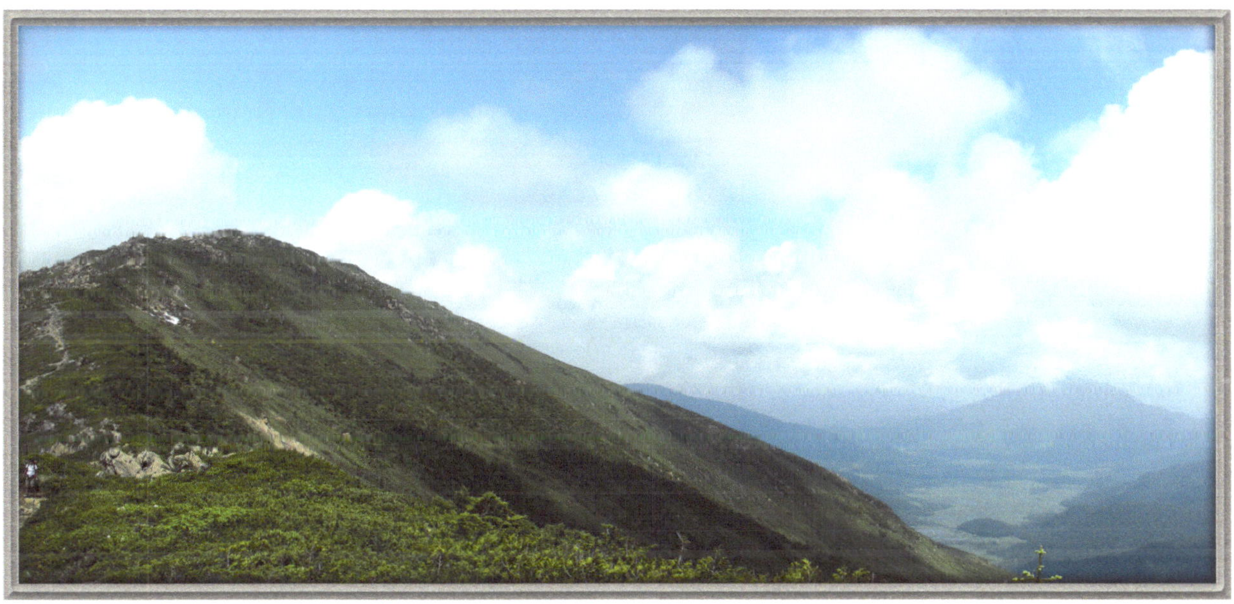

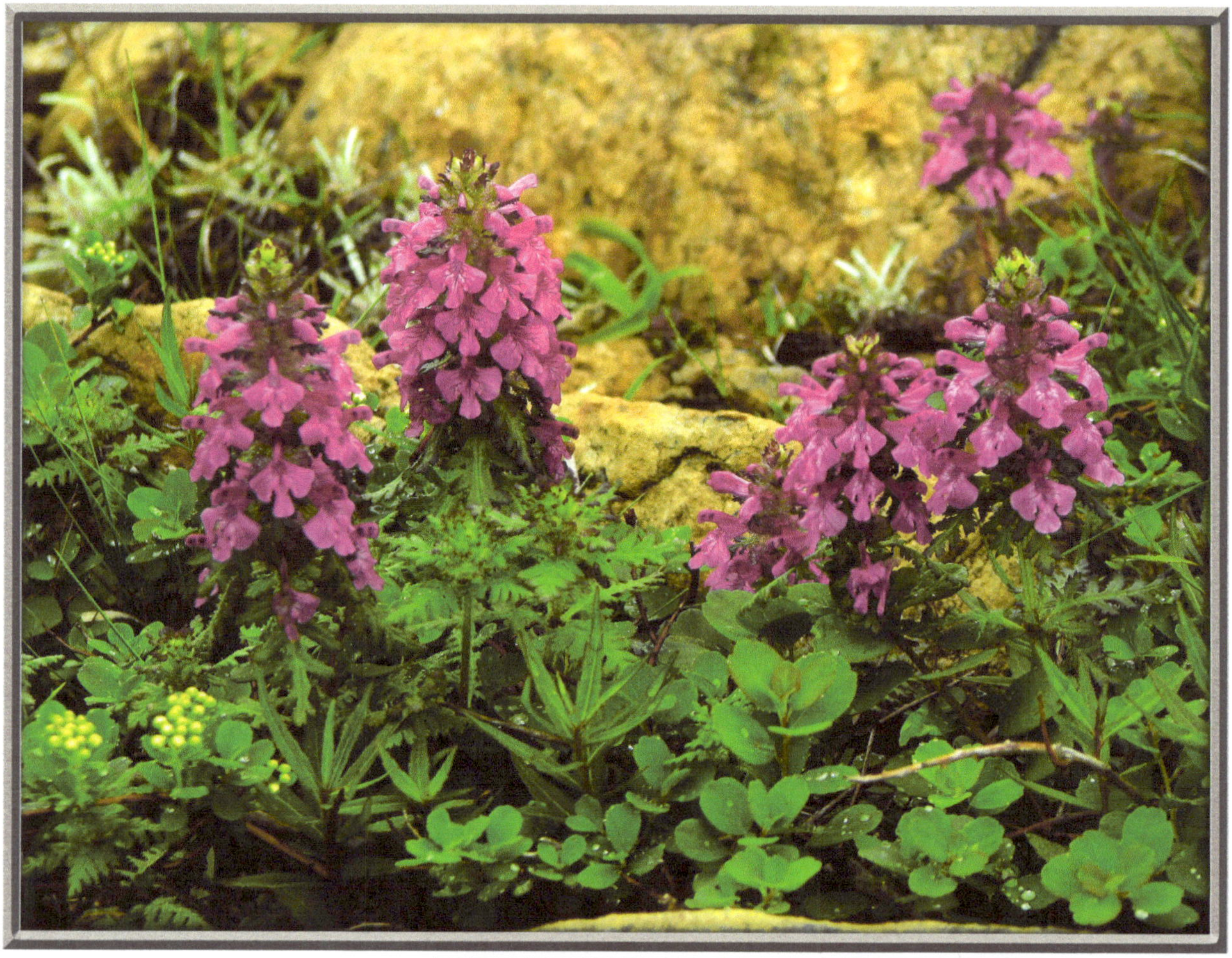

Above is a photo of ***Pedicularis verticillata*** in Oze National Park. This is not a rare plant on the mountain, but it's very beautiful.

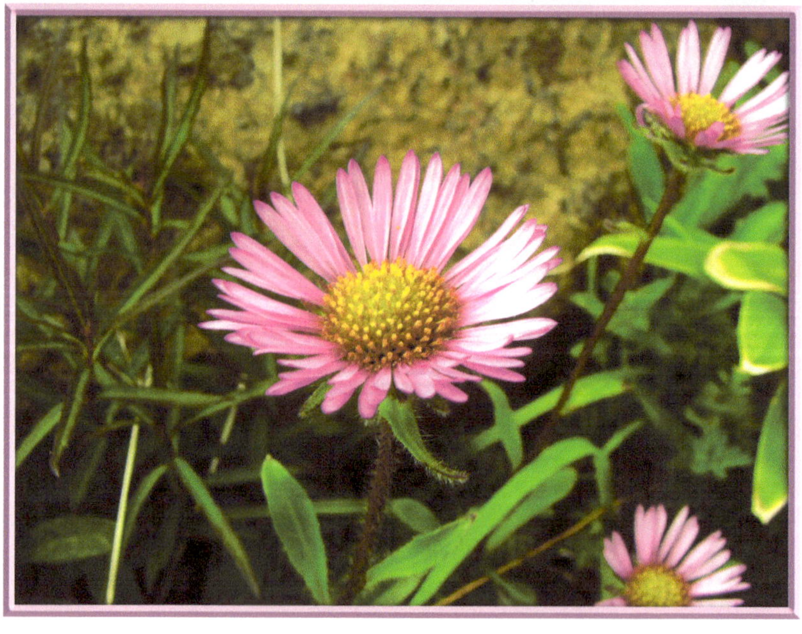

To the right is an ***Erigeron thunbergii* subsp. *glabratus* var. *heterotrichus*** – a member of the Aster, Sunflower or Daisy family. This species was uncommon and a pleasure to see. We took many photos of it. This is the final photo on Mt. Shibutsu.

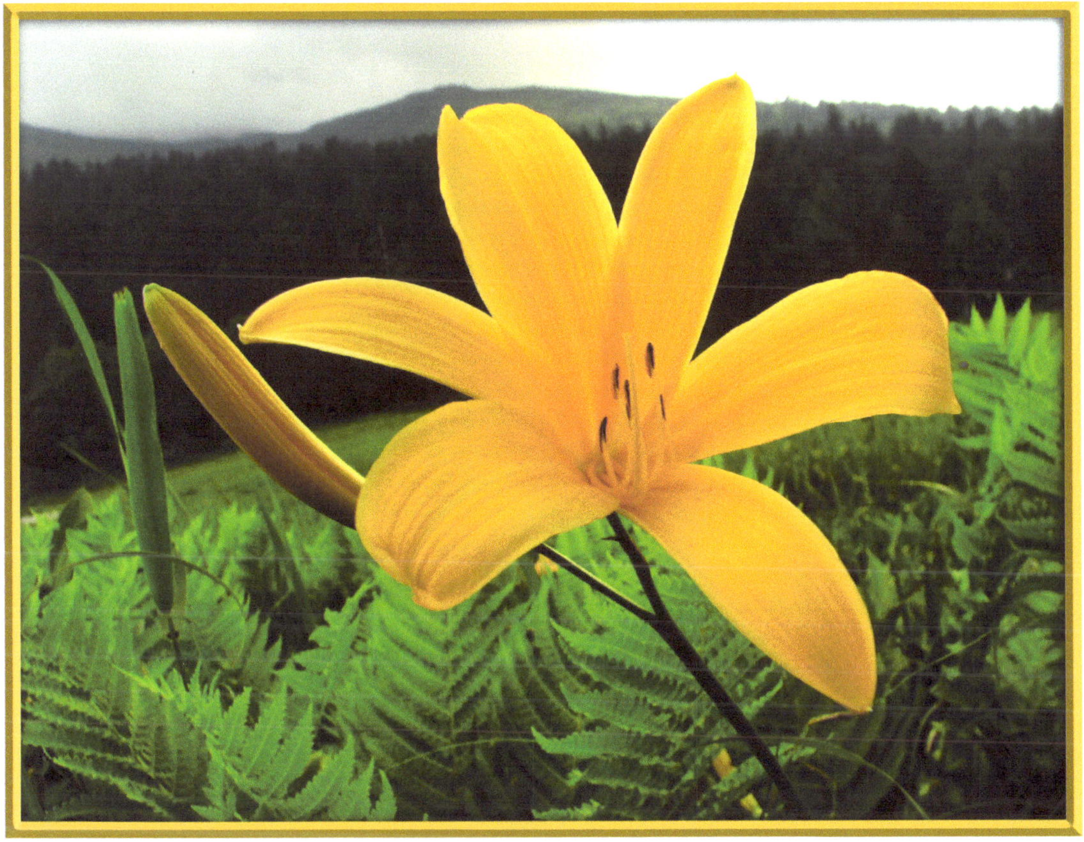

Here are two shots of ***Hemerocallis dumortieri* var. *esculenta*** a.k.a. ***Hemerocallis middendorffii* var. *esculenta***. This was such an amazingly beautiful Day Lily that we could not resist taking many photos of it. This flower was not on the mountain, it was restricted to the marsh.

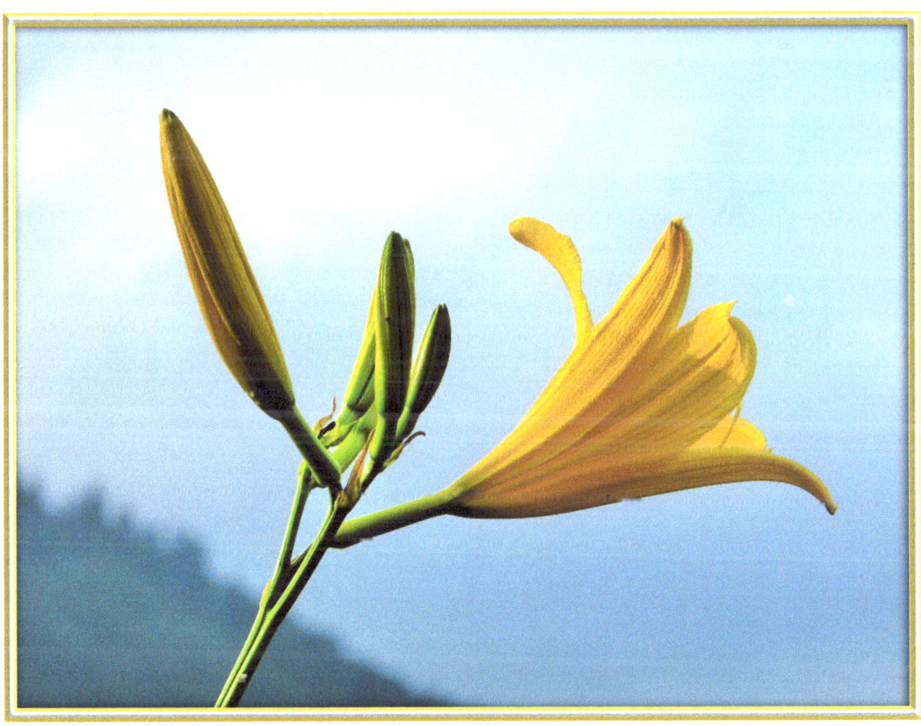

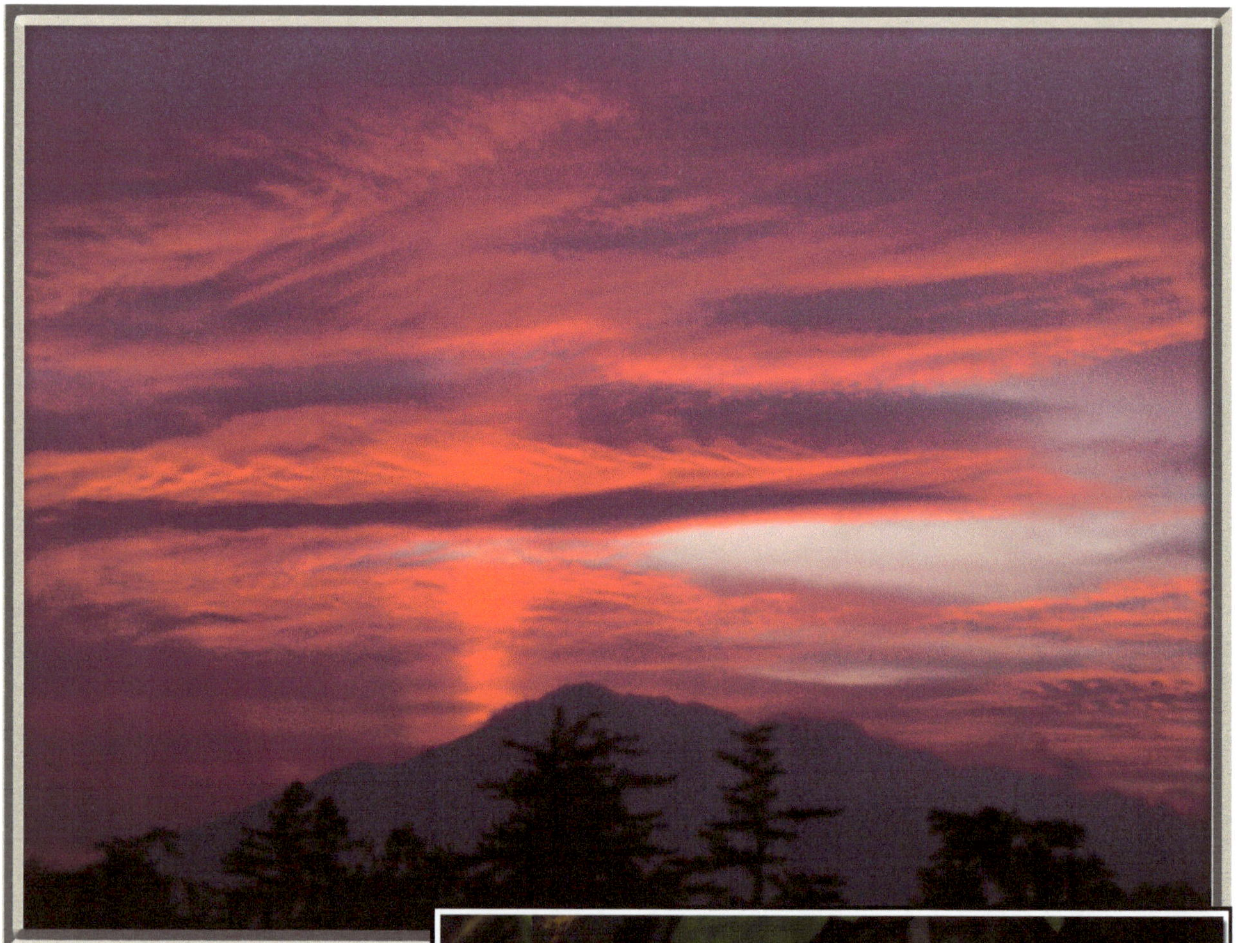

The following dawn we were given the special treat of some good early morning sunrise colors in **Oze National Park**. They only lasted a very few minutes. This was the day we had to head for home. On the trail hiking back to the bus we found the amazingly shiny **Indian Pipe** (*Monotropa* **sp.**) shown to the right.

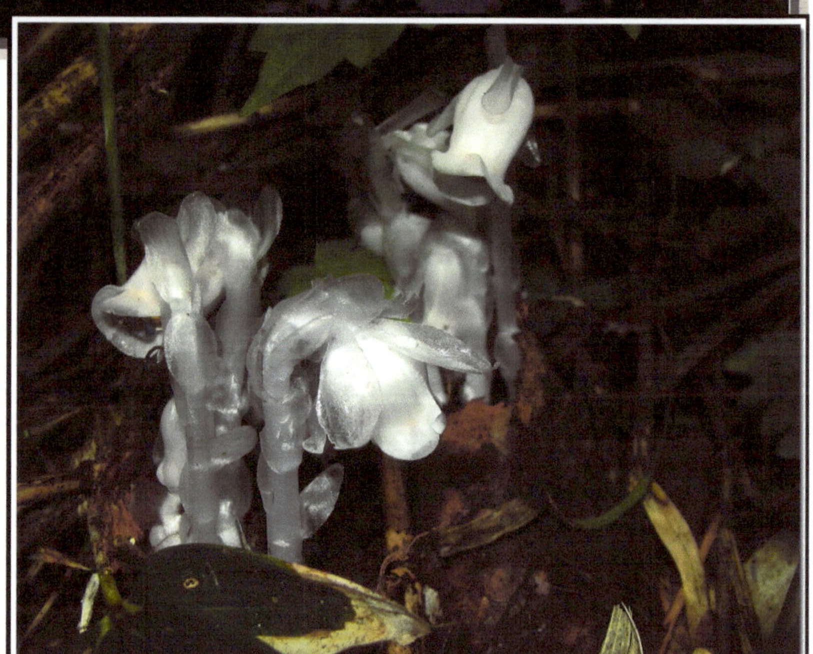

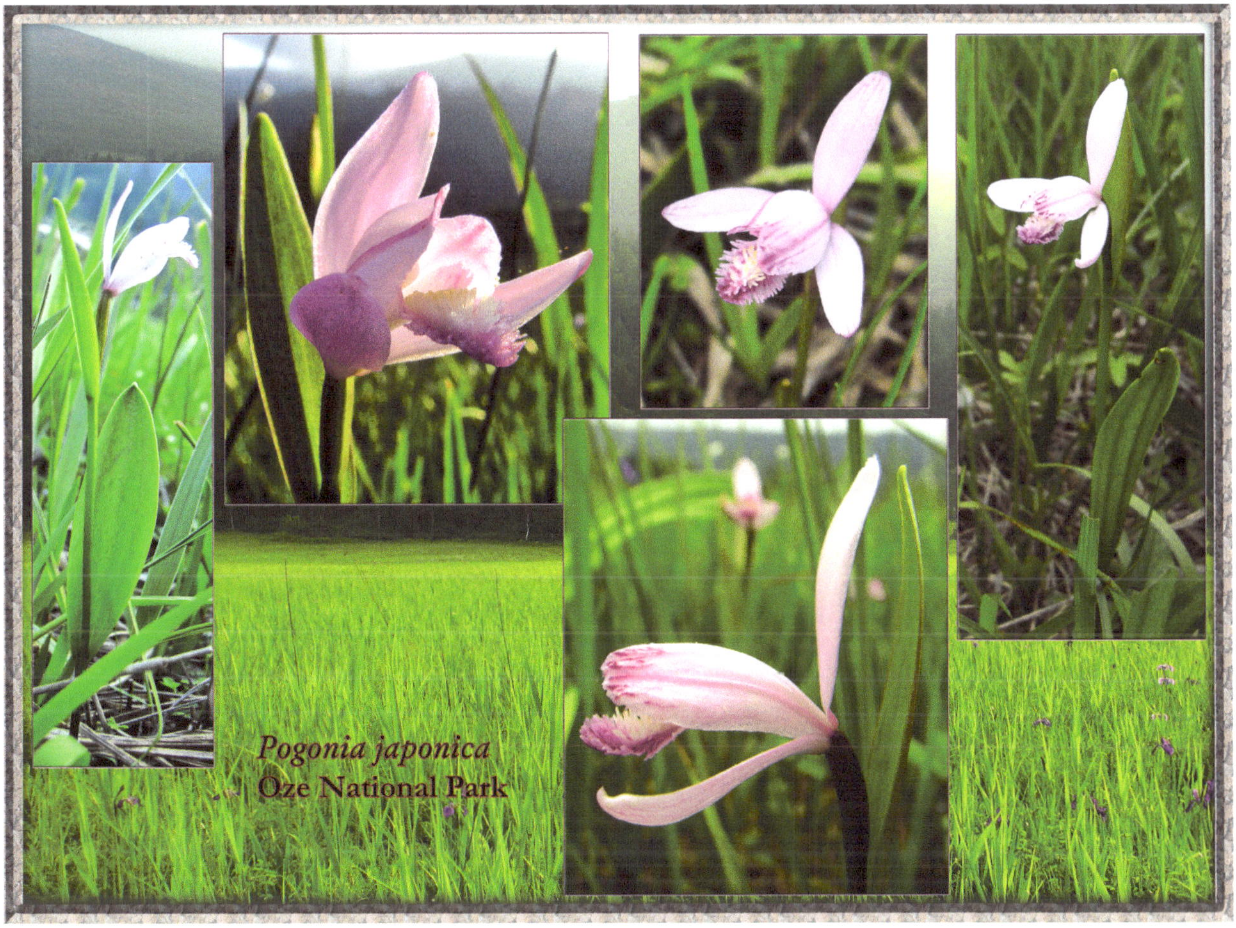

Here is a collage of ***Pogonia japonica* – an Orchid**. These photos were all taken in Oze National Park. The individual photos are set against a background where you could expect to find this flower. These five photos were taken at different hours during the day and therefore the lighting is significantly different. This is a rather spectacular orchid – a sight to rejoice at upon seeing.

We considered ourselves so very fortunate to have been able to come here at this particular time of the year. So very many flowers were at their peak that it was just amazing to walk around and enjoy what nature had to offer us in the way of colors, shapes and diversity. The weather, although rainy at night, was okay during the day. We could not complain about anything at all.

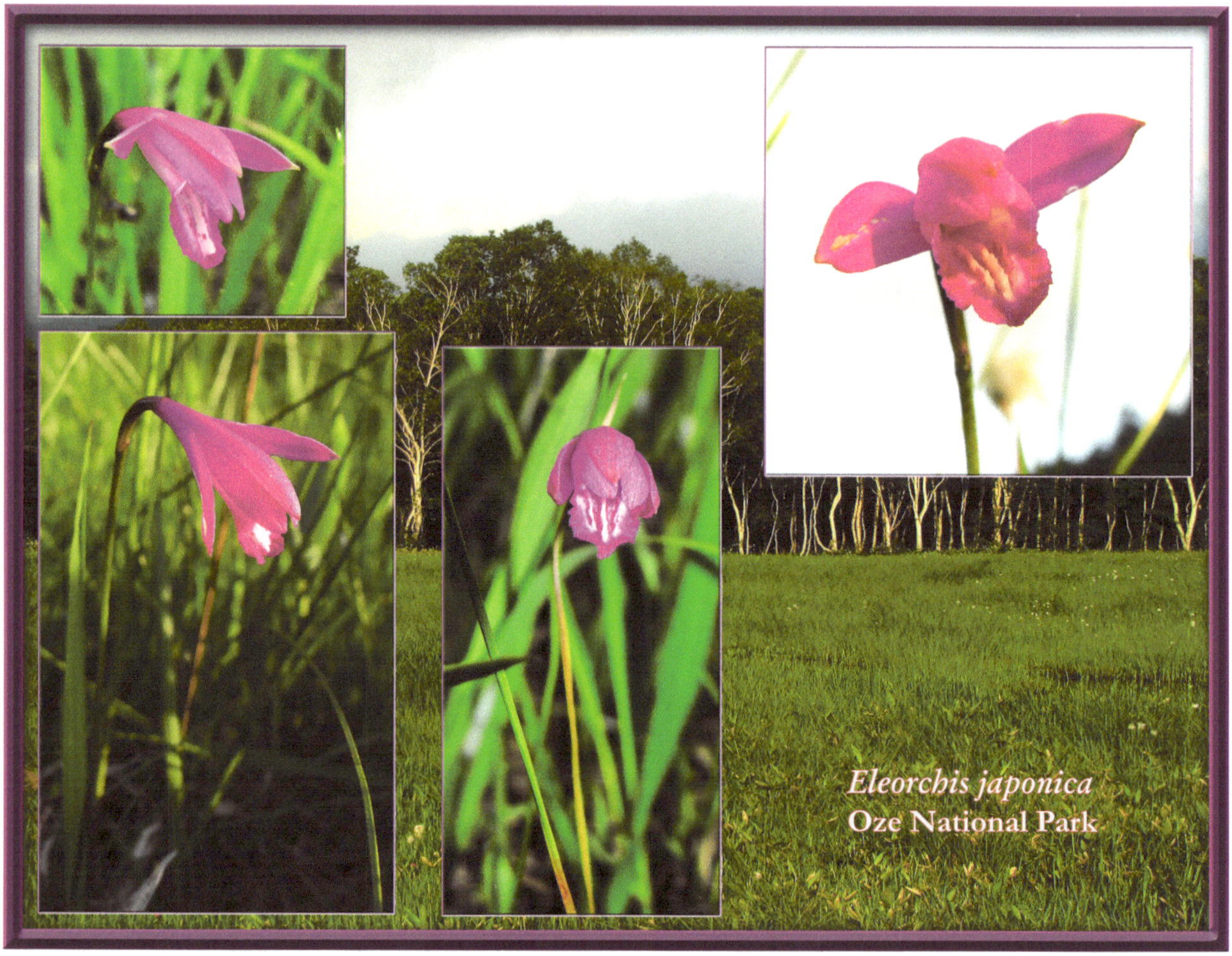

Here, immediately above, is another **Orchid** collage – this is ***Eleorchis japonica***. This one, as you can see, was quite red and it was amazing to see. The individual photos are inserted in front of a background photo which shows where one could expect to be able to find several of this flower during the proper season.

On the facing page is a collage which was created from several photos taken during our stay in Oze National Park. You see some photos and some flowers which you have already seen as well as some new ones. Of special note is the ***Vaccinium oxycoccos*** – **Cranberry** – shown in the upper right corner of the collage.

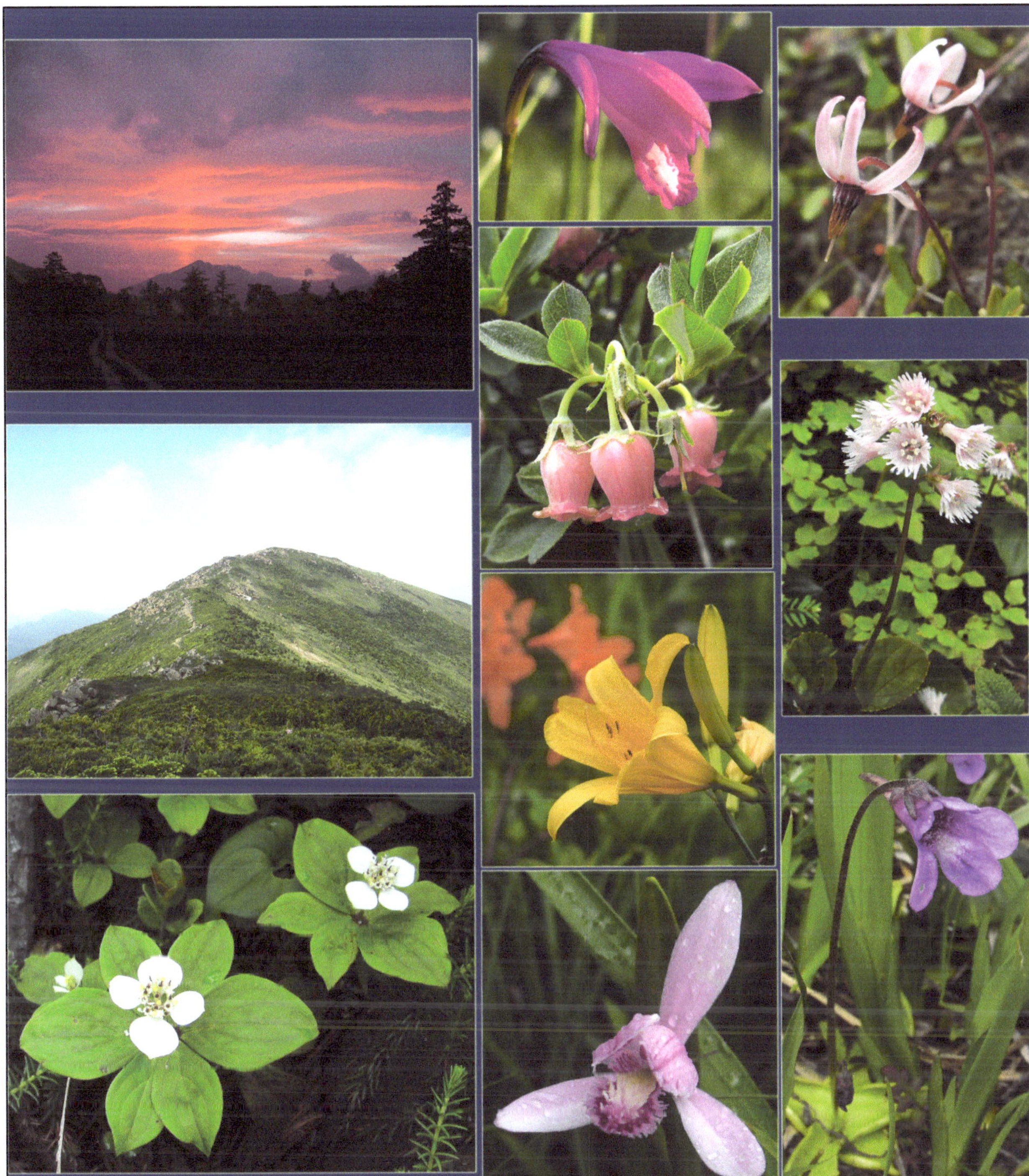

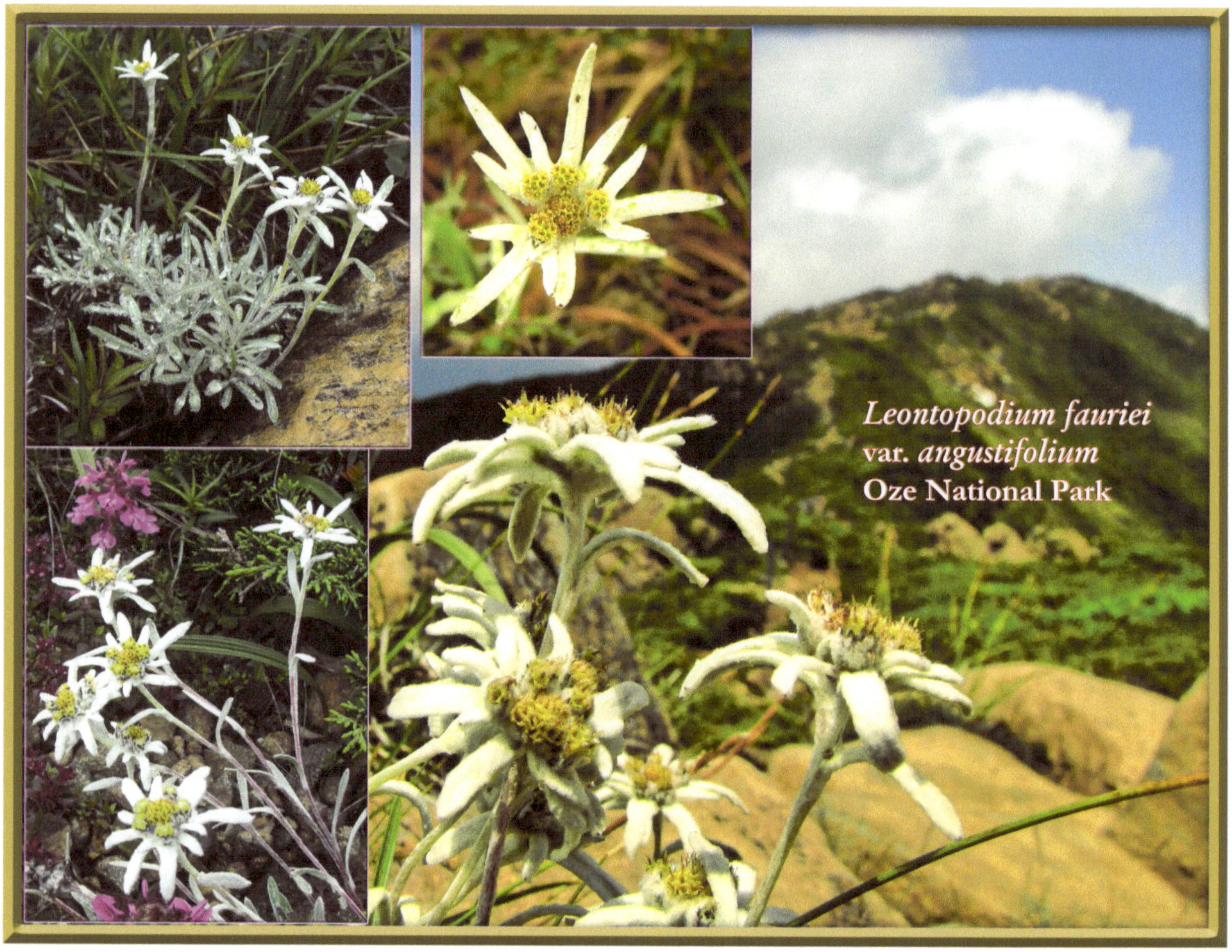

In the shot above you can see several photos of ***Leontopodium fauriei* var. *angustifolium*** – a species of **Edelweiss**. We found this, as well as another species of **Edelweiss**, ***Leontopodium japonicum* var. *shiroumense***, on this adventure (on Mt. Shibutsu – not in the marsh). The ***Leontopodium japonicum* var. *shiroumense*** was not as photogenic as the Edelweiss shown in this collage. The background of this collage is Mt. Shibutsu.

On the facing page is a final scenery and flowers collage created from the photos taken in Oze National Park on this adventure. This will be the final photo of this trip to Oze National Park, and in fact it will be the final shot of Oze National Park that you'll see in this book.

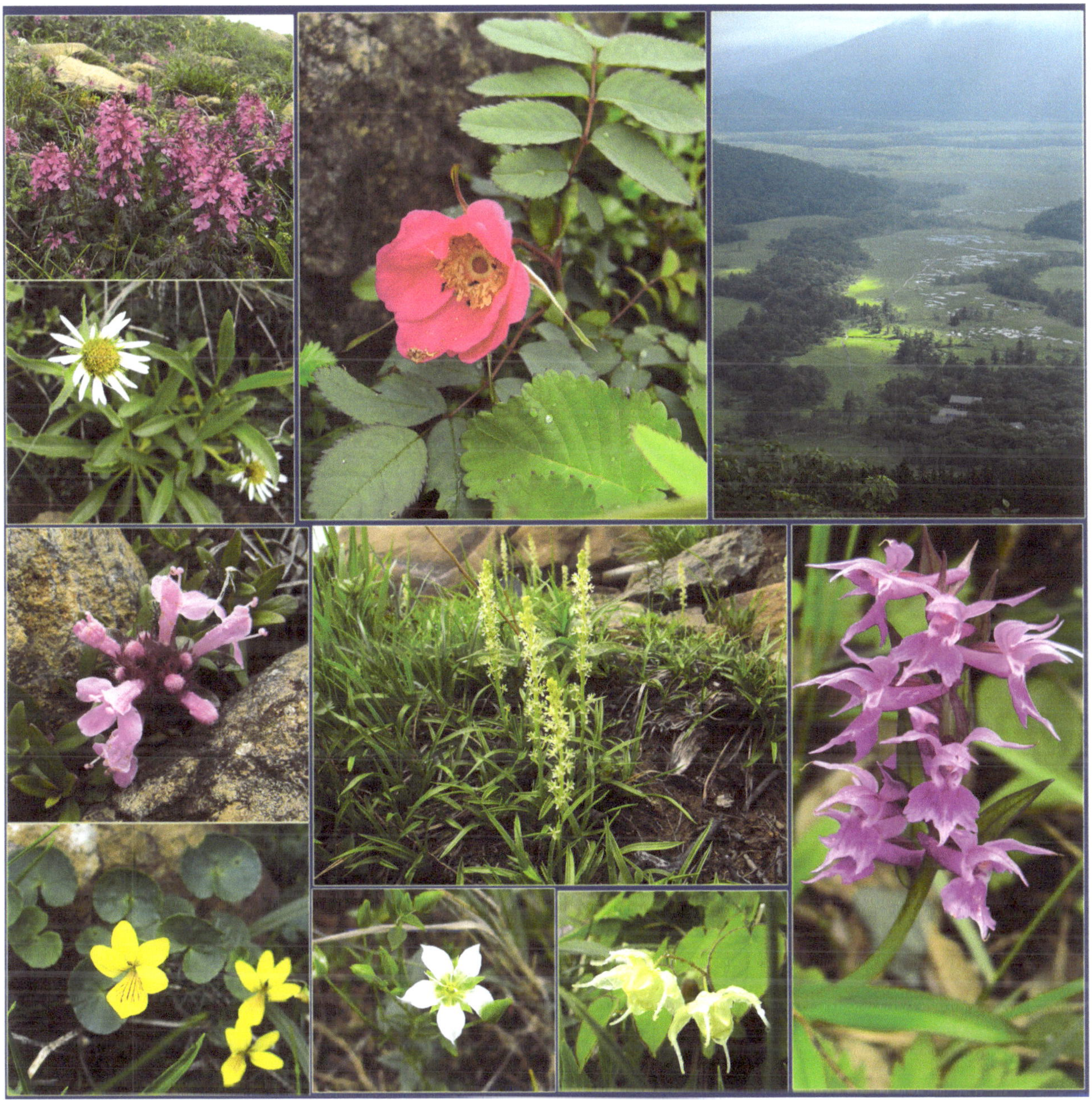

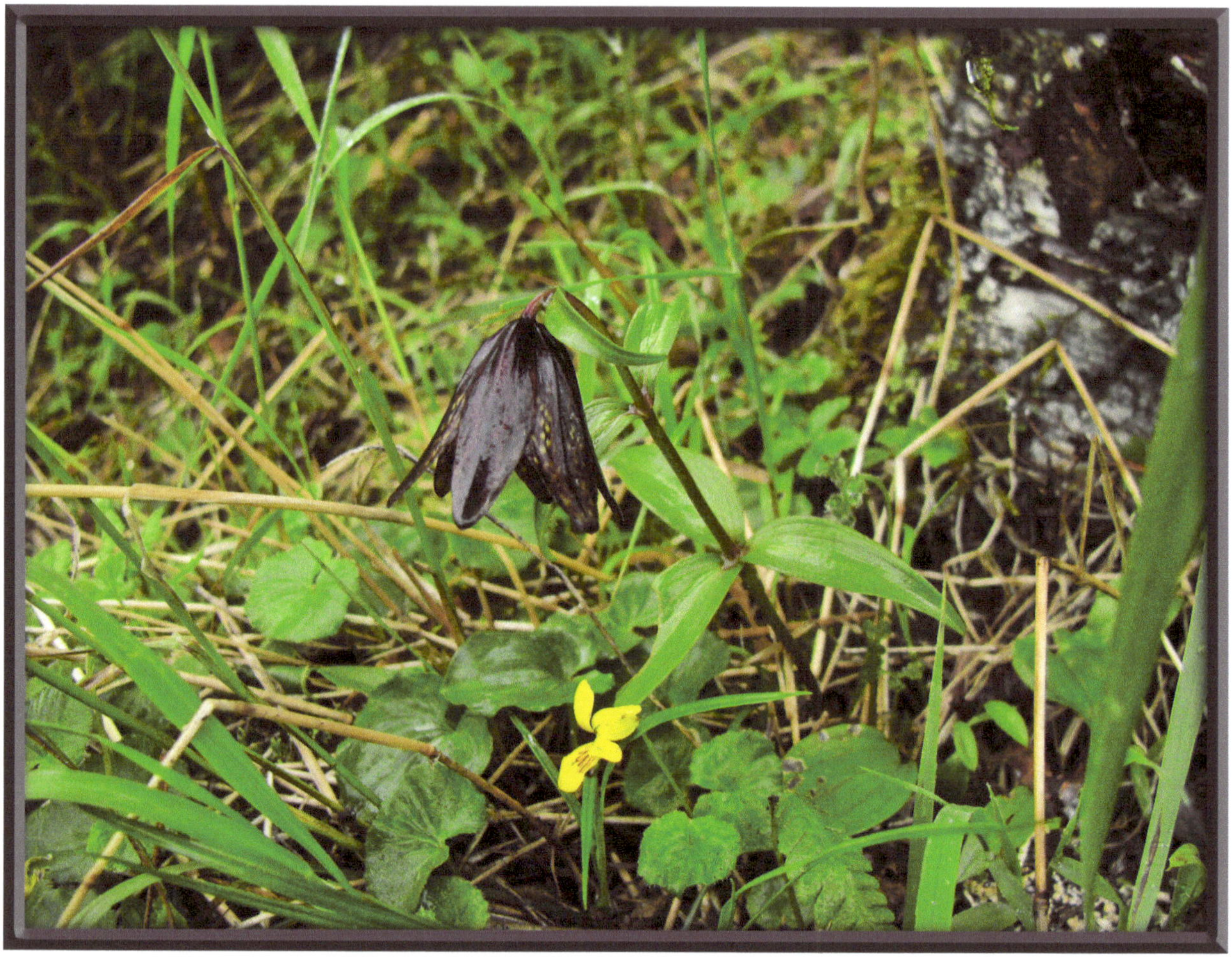

Now we're going to return to **Mt. Yatsugatake**. We last saw this mountain range back on pages 80 – 87. You may recall that the **Yatsugatake Mountains** are a volcanic mountain range on the border between **Nagano Prefecture** and **Yamanashi Prefecture**. The photo on this page shows a **Chocolate Lily** (***Fritillaria camschatcensis***). This is quite a rare flower to find. We were specifically searching for it in the rain and near whiteout conditions on this first day of climbing – and we found it.

The two photos on the facing page show, first of all, the near whiteout conditions which we experienced on the first day of our climb – it was so extreme with the clouds and the wind that we were actually quite concerned. The second photo on the facing page shows somewhat clearing weather in the morning of the following day. If you study the second photo very closely you can see a vague **Brocken Spectre**. We'll show you a better photo of a **Brocken Spectre** later on during this month and explain it to you at that time.

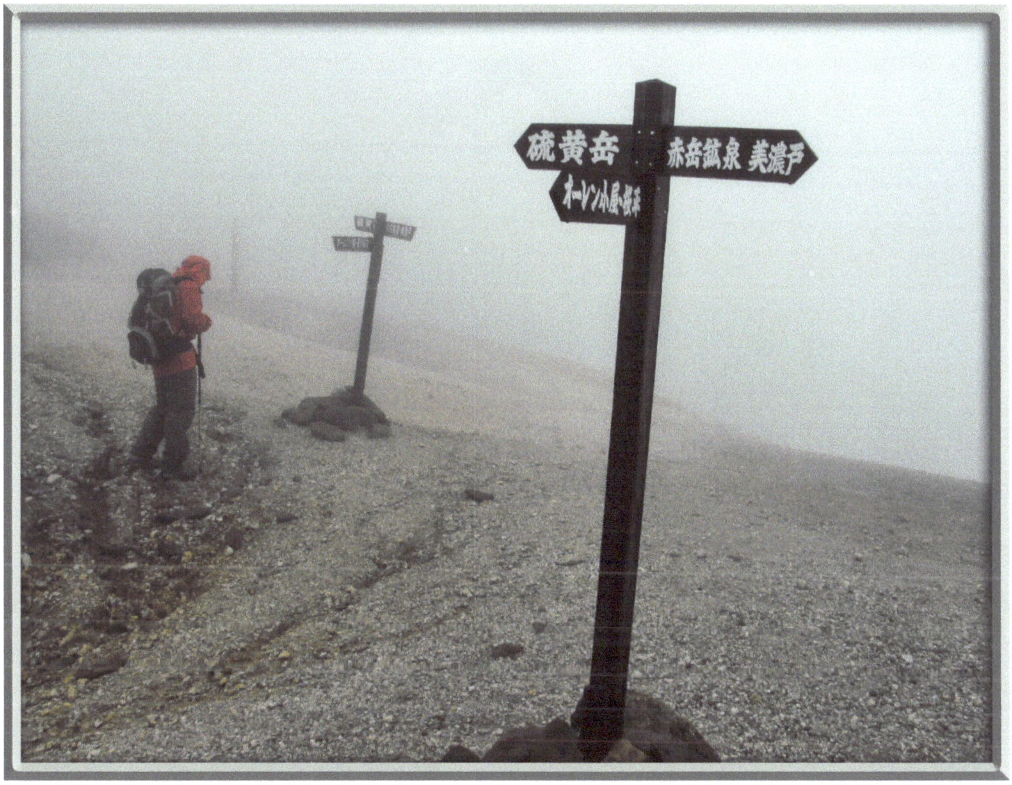
硫黄岳
赤岳鉱泉 美濃戸
オーレン小屋・桜平

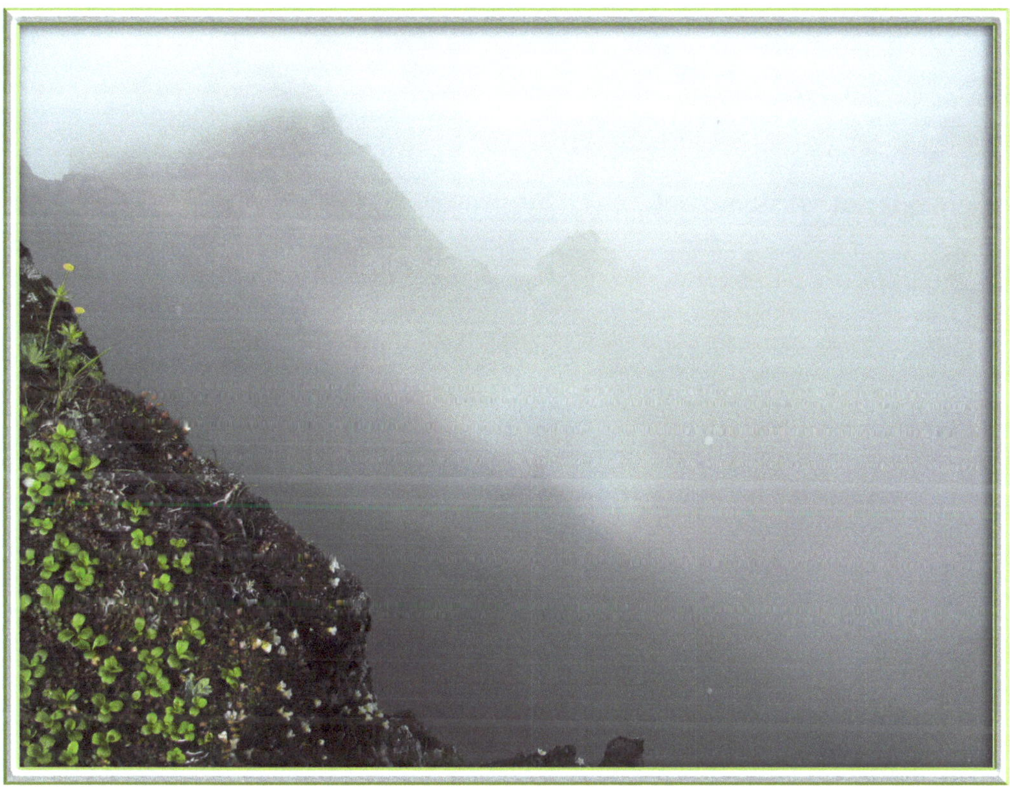

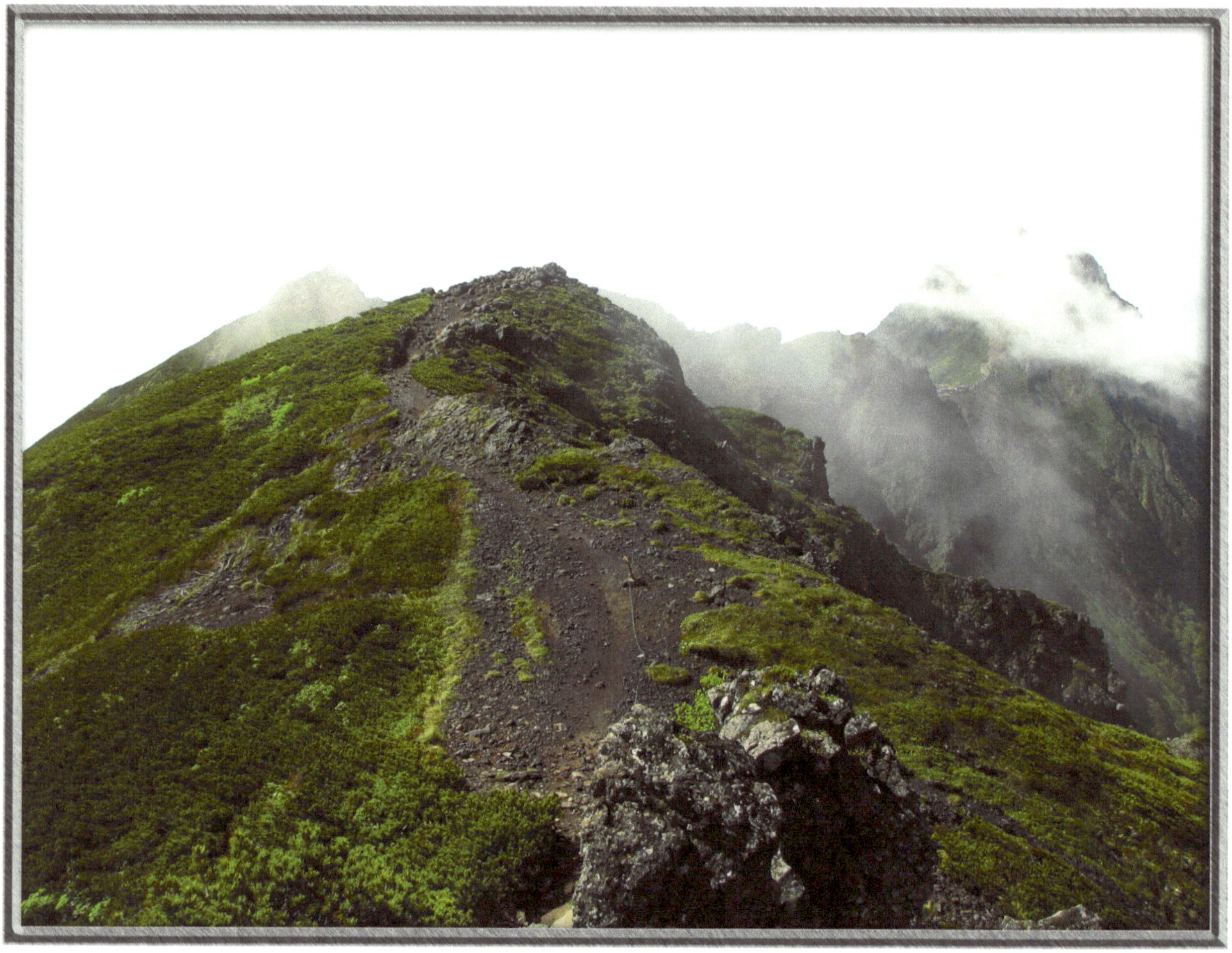

Above is a photo taken as we hiked along the **Bunzaburou Ridge** towards **Mt. Akadake**. Mt. Akadake is the mountain barely visible on the right side of the photo. Akadake is the mountain we attained the summit of back on page 84. As you'll note, the weather is clearing nicely at this point. We are hoping that it will get 100% clear later in the day.

The photo on the facing page gives just an idea of some of the terrain we crossed as we hiked out towards Mt. Akadake. This ladder was near **Mt. Sansha**, also along the **Bunzaburou Ridge**. That is Kazuya coming down. Also note the green rope – supposedly to keep people from wandering off the edge of the cliff in a storm or whiteout.

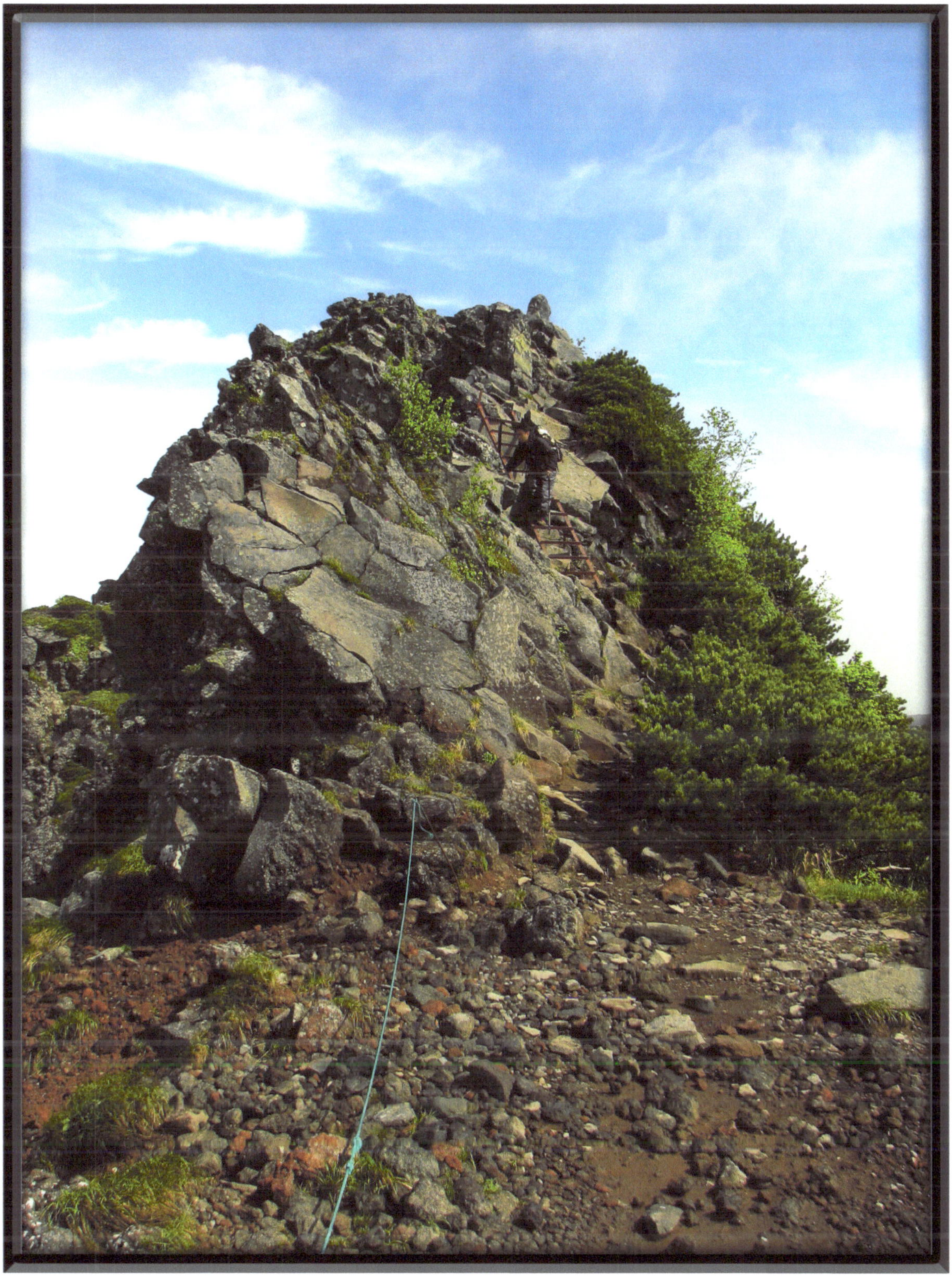

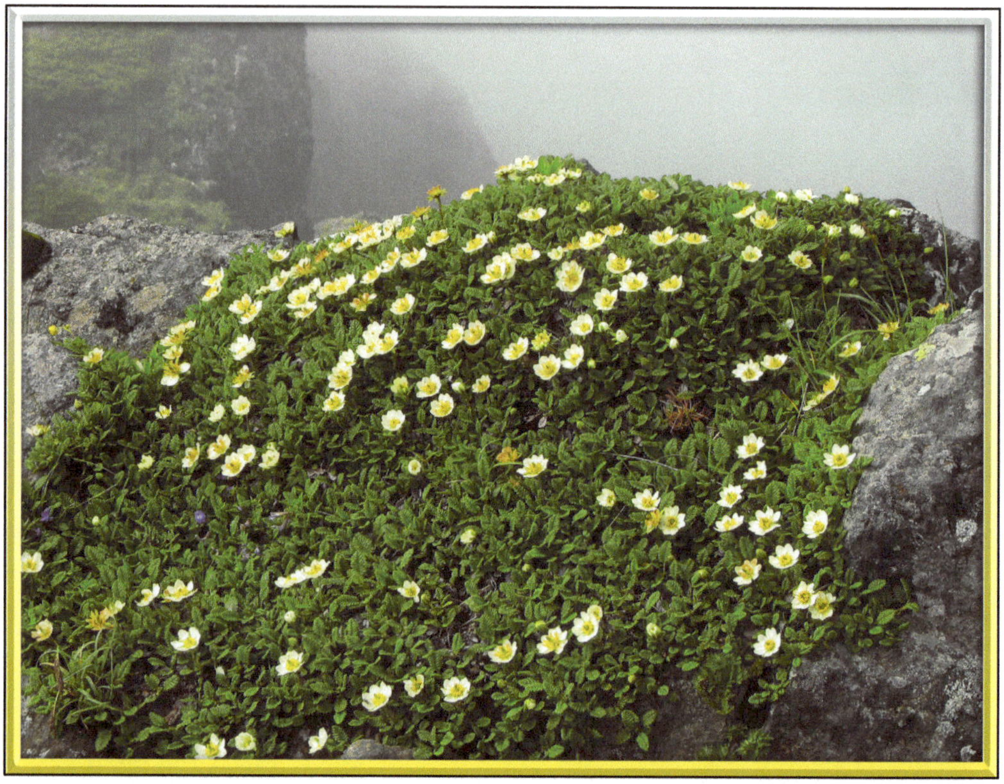

This photo is a flower and scenery shot. The flower is ***Dryas octopetala* var. *asiatica***. Scenes like this were not rare to see when we climbed **Mt. Yatsugatake**. We were very impressed by both the scenery and also by the abundance of flowers and the abundance of species of flowers.

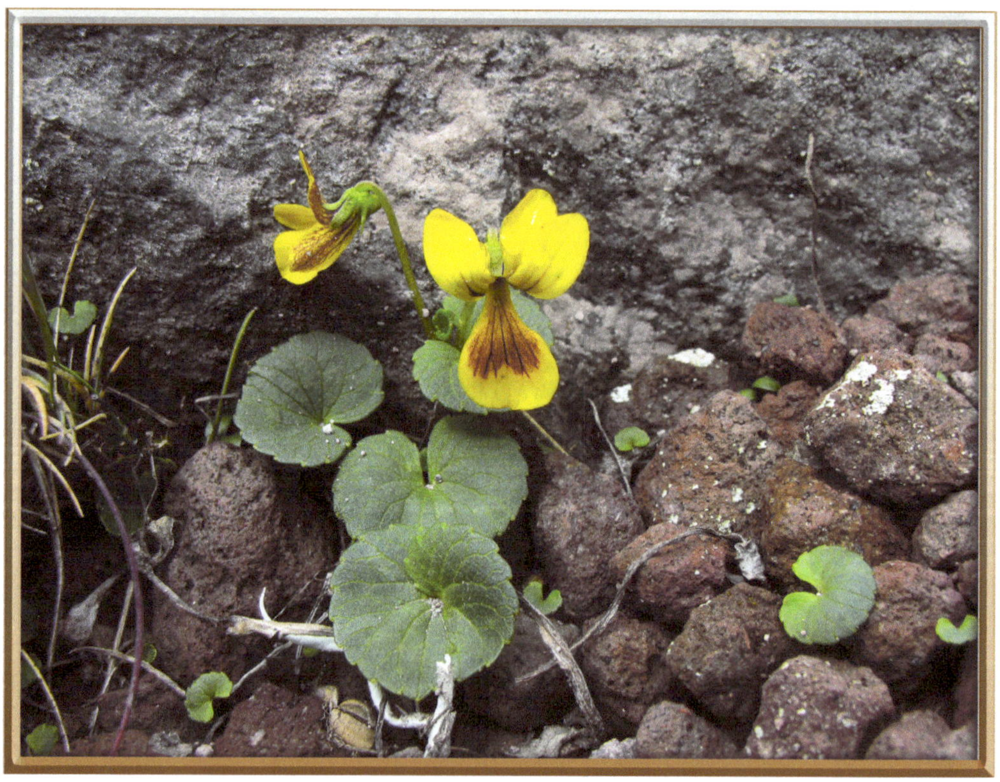

The shot to the right is a **Yatsugatake Violet** – a ***Viola crassa* ssp. *yatsugatakeana***. This species is pretty much only found around this mountain.

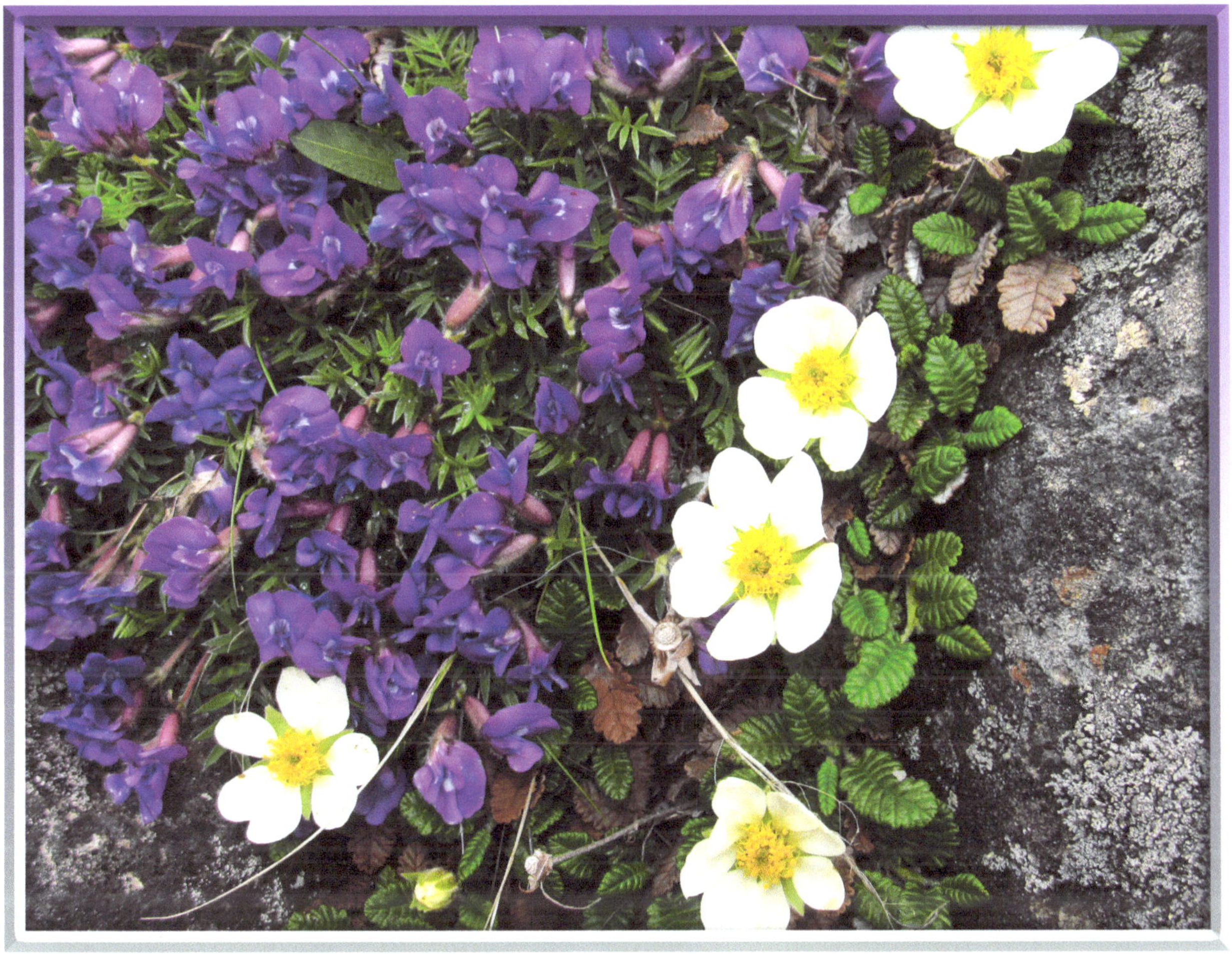

Here is a photo of ***Oxytropis japonica*** (the purple flower) and ***Dryas octopetala* var. *asiatica*** (the white flower). These two flowers growing together offer a rather astonishing color contrast.

The photo on the following page shows a blue ***Lagotis glauca***, a white ***Dryas octopetala* var. *asiatica*** and a dark pink or light red flower which is most likely one of the species of ***Pedicularis***. This also shows the relative steepness of the terrain we were hiking through. Down below is nothing except the bottom of the mountain.

There were so many flowers and so many colors that one barely had to try, and still ended up with several different flowers and many different colors in the same photo.

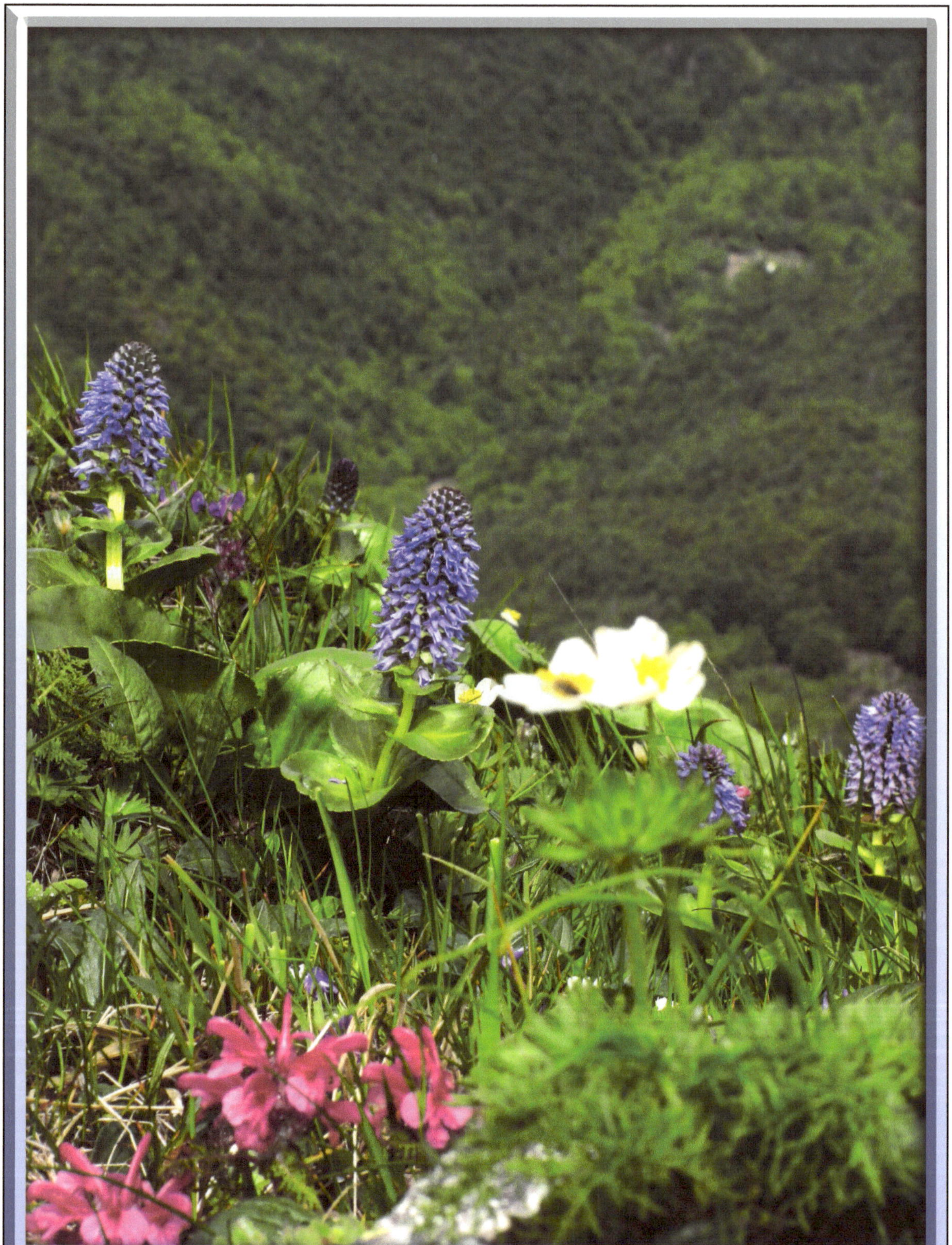

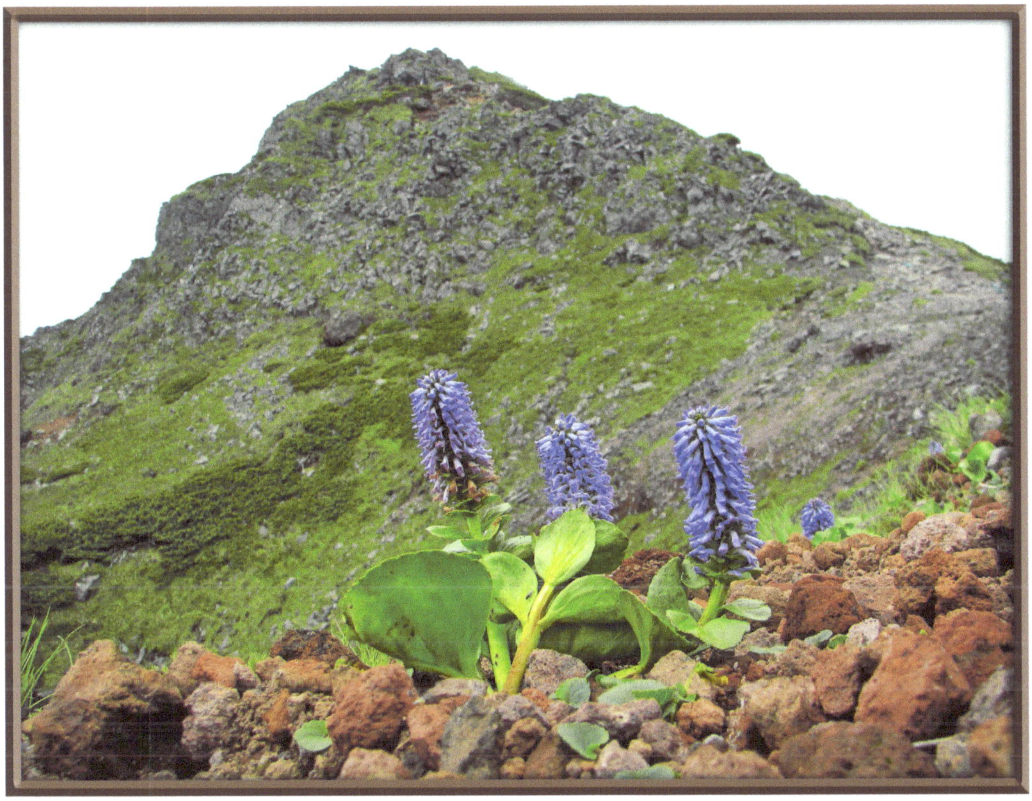

Here (above) is one additional photo of ***Lagotis glauca***.

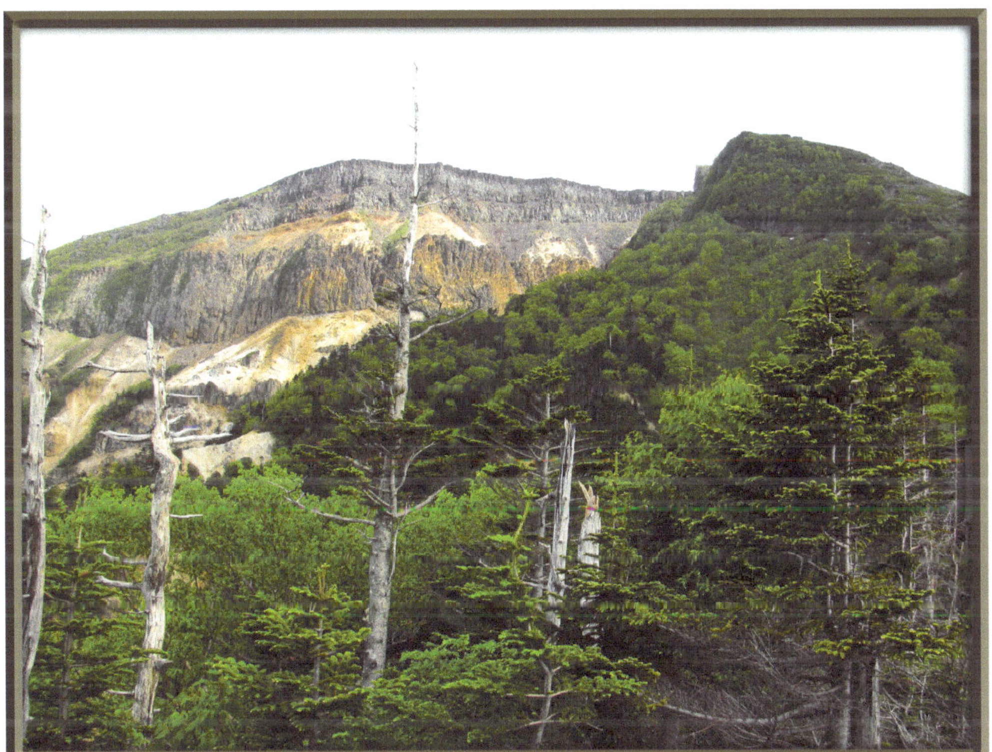

To the right is a scenery photo which was taken north of **Mt. Io-dake** and looking back towards **Mt. Iodake**.

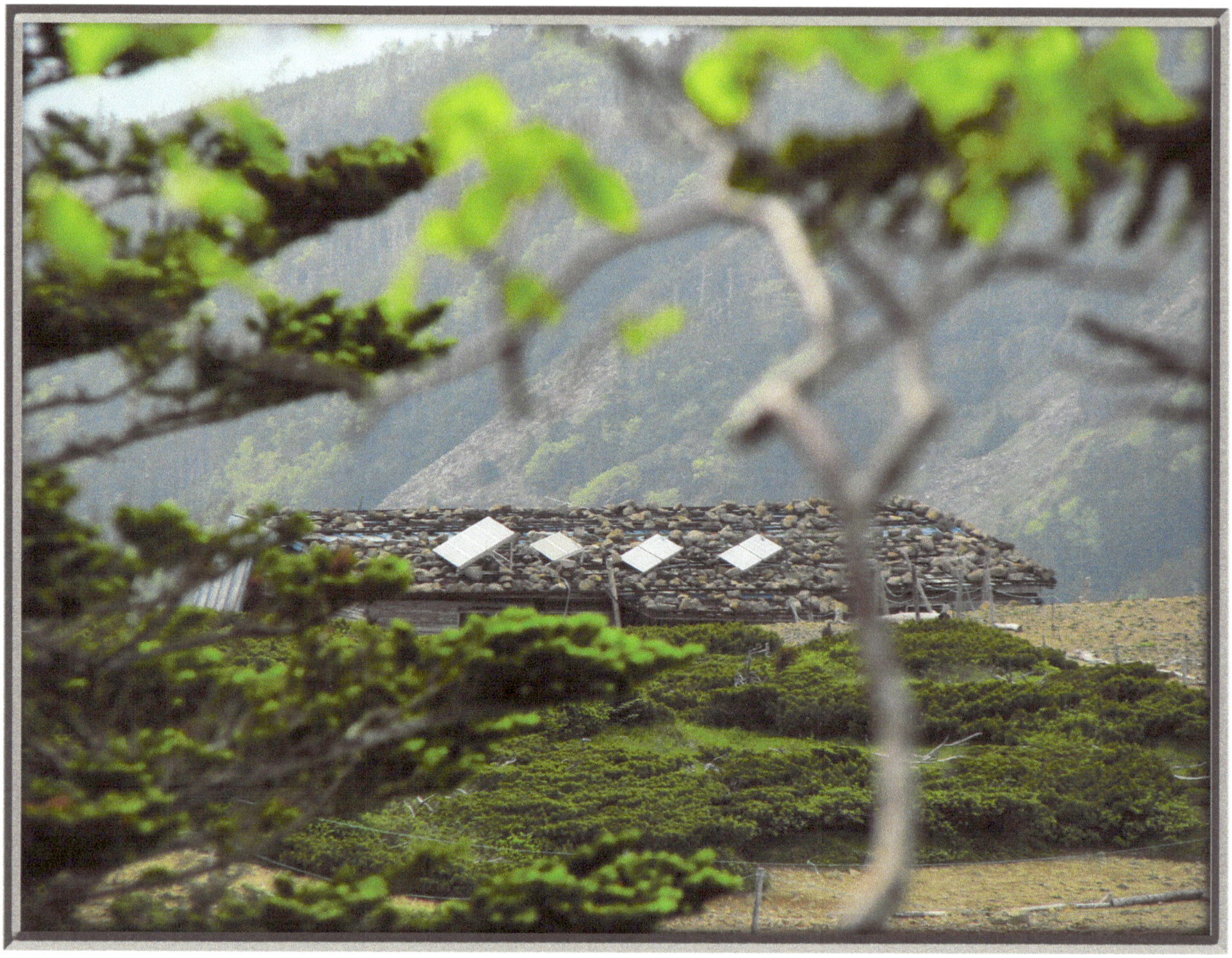

The photo above shows the **Mt. Neishi Hut** taken from quite a distance away. It's an interesting shot of an interesting hut. You can see solar panels on the roof, which supply the electric power, but more amazing to observe are the great number of rocks which seem to be holding down the roof. We assumed that there are often some very strong winds in this area. That would not be surprising, as this was right at a mountain pass. This hut offered a hot bath! We heard that this hut closed down the year after we stayed here, although we were not sure if that was true or not.

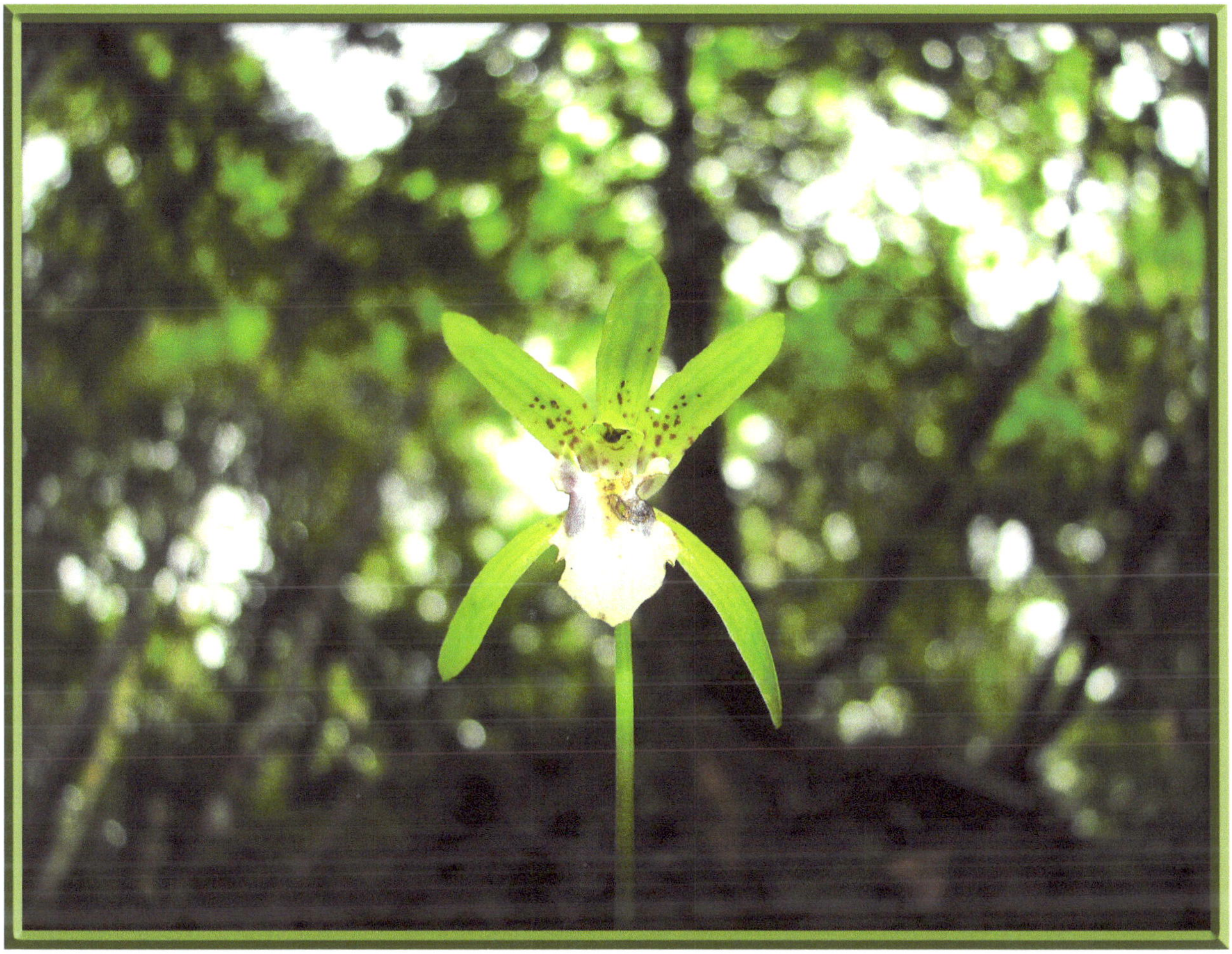

Here is a shot of a ***Dactylostalix ringens***, the "One-Leaf Orchid". This species is surely found in far-eastern Russia and in Japan. We assume that it must be found in other countries, but it is at least found in those two countries. This species can be found in cold areas and the flower appears in the spring on a 10 – 20 cm (4 – 8 inch) stem. Each plant has only one flower.

On the following two pages you will find two collages of mountain flowers and mountain scenery from our **Mt. Yatsugatake** adventure. As is usual, you have already seen some of these photos and you have not seen some of them. These following two collages will end the **Yatsugatake adventures** which you'll find in this book. Which photo in these collages is the most impressive for you?

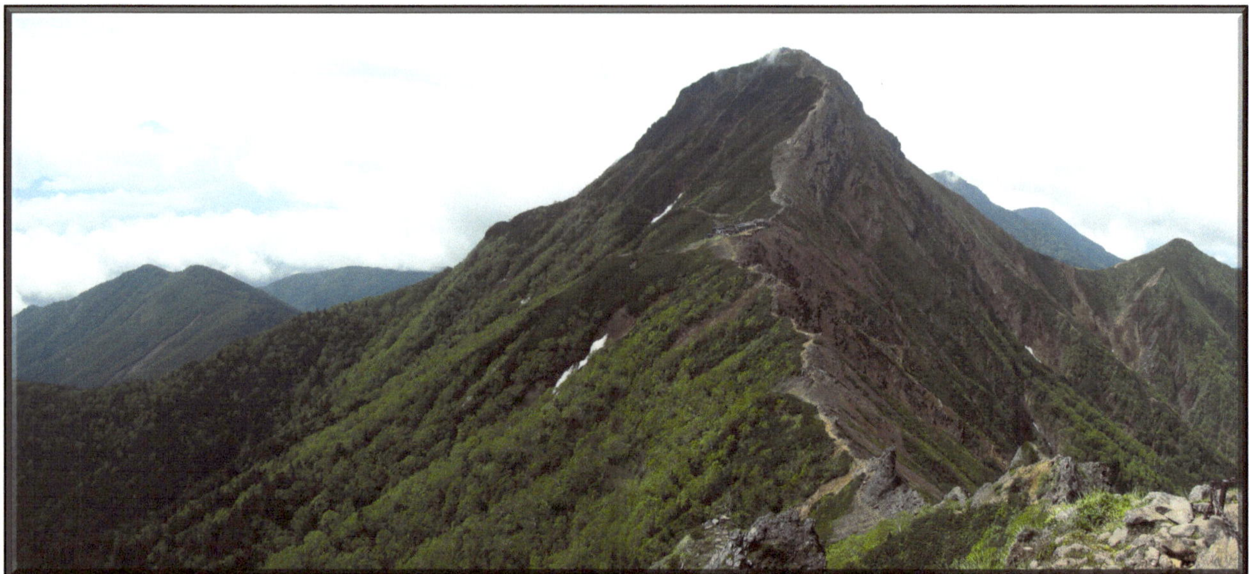

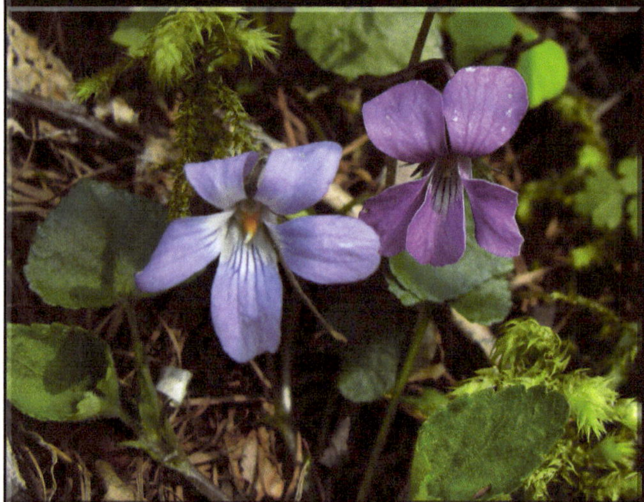

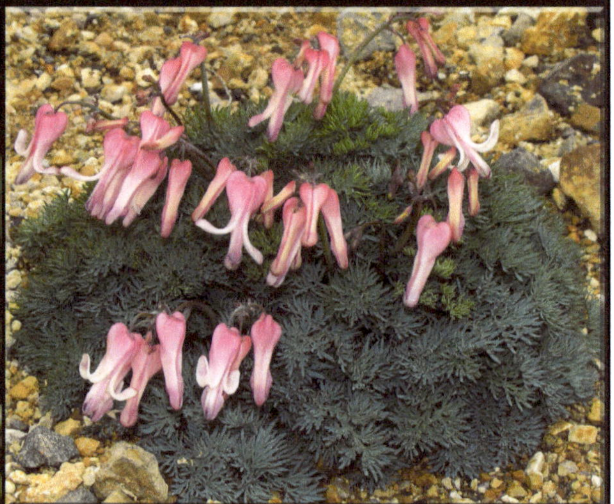

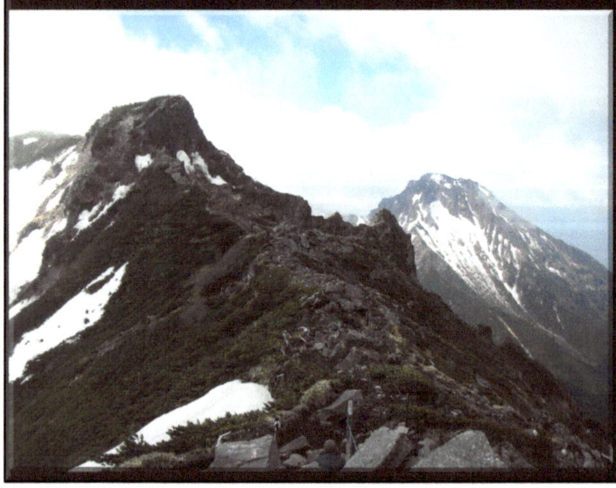

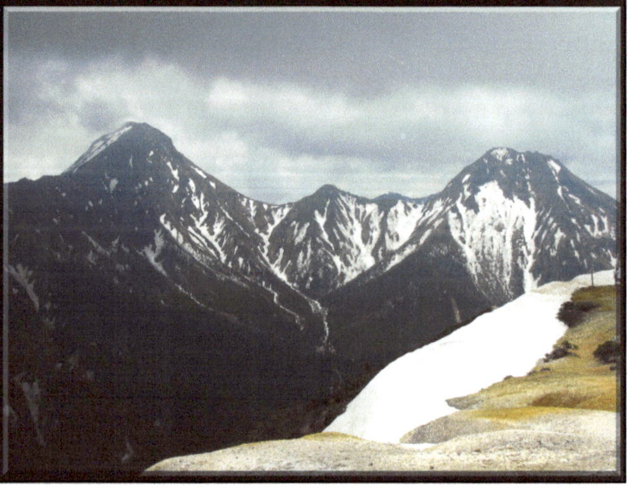

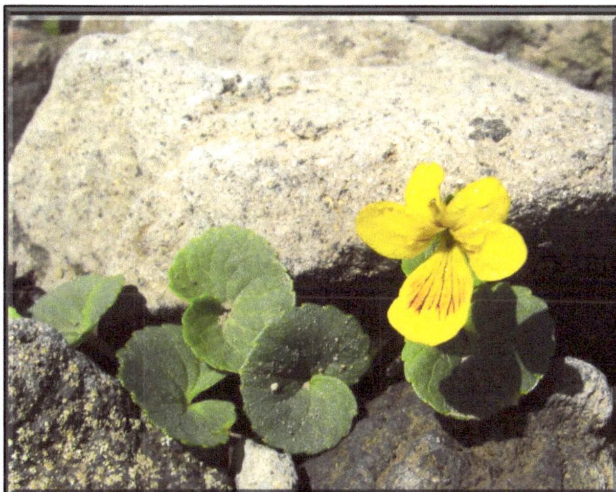

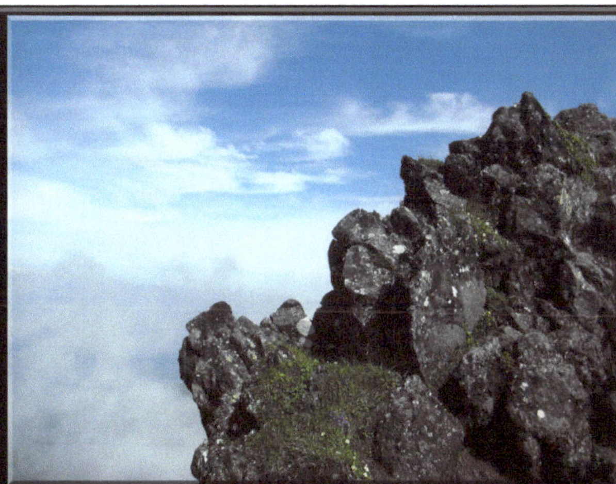

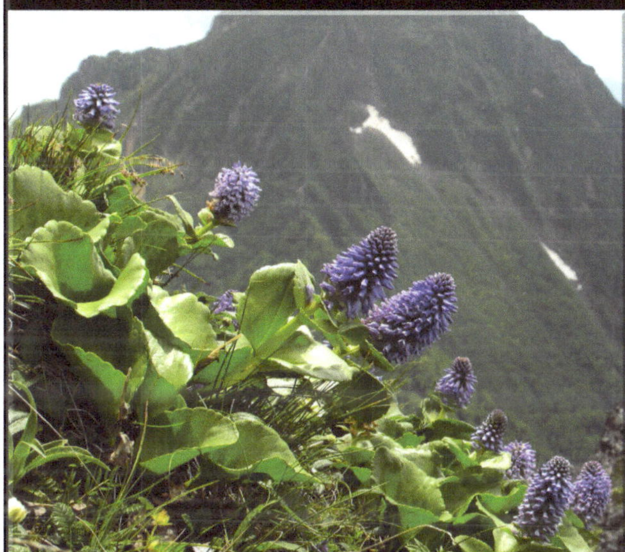

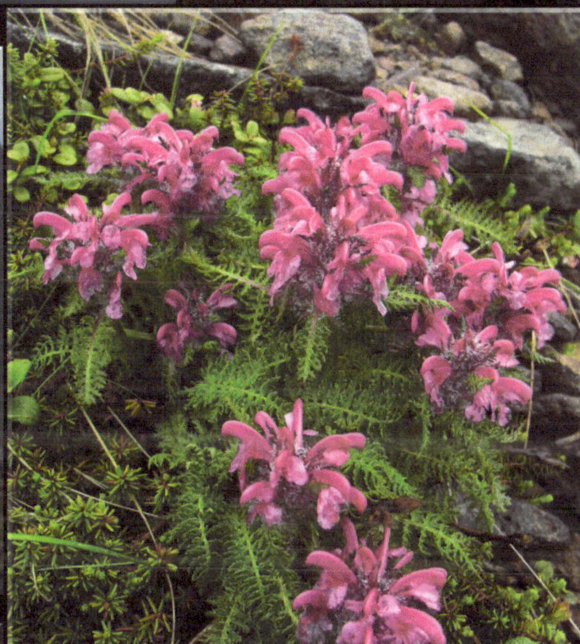

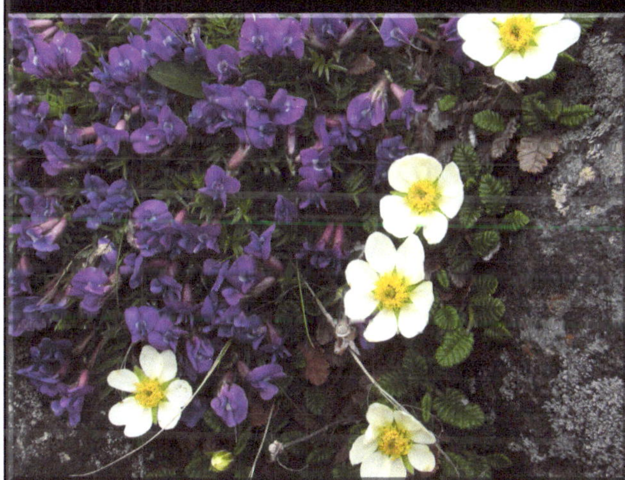

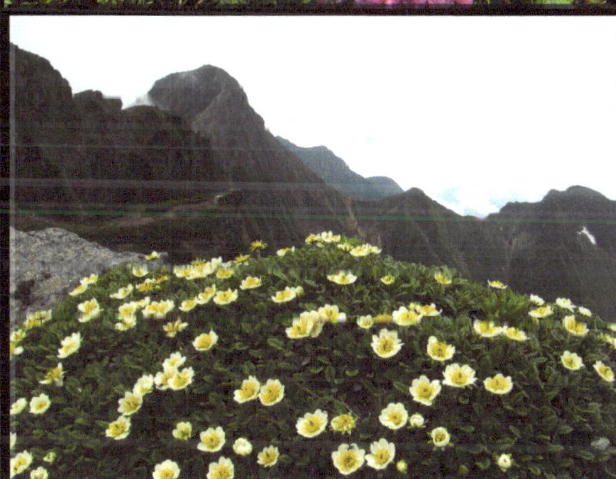

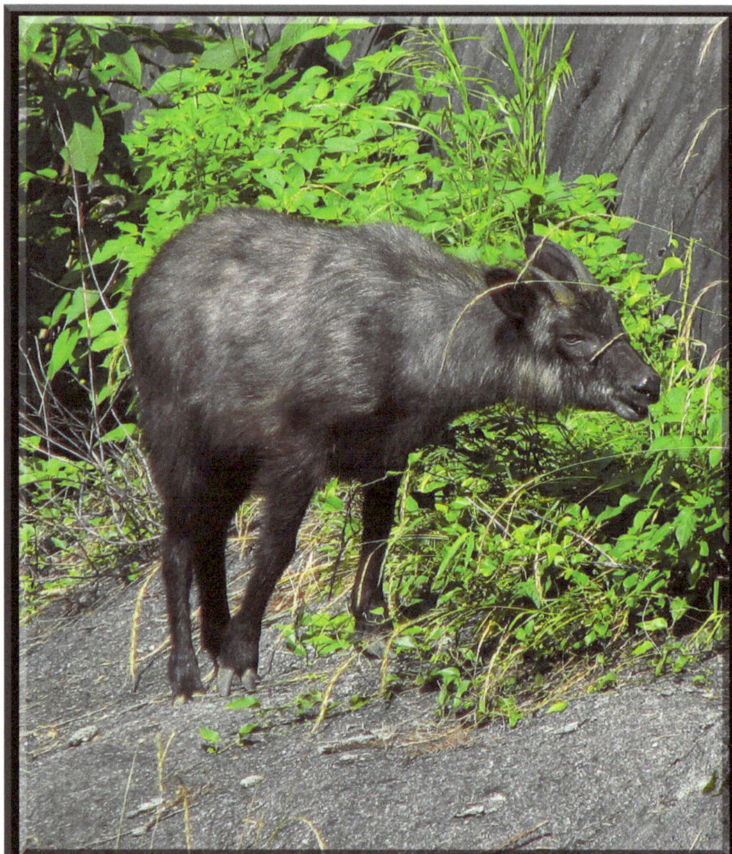

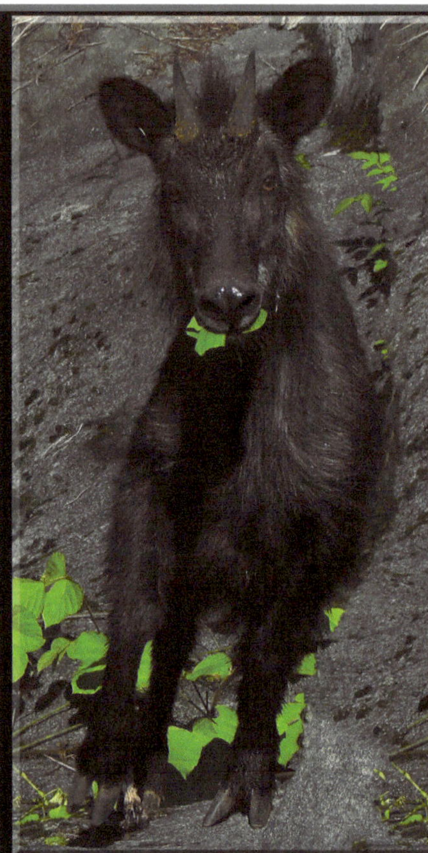

Way back on page 48 we showed you a photo of a ***Capricornis crispus***, a **Japanese Serow** (***Kamoshika*** in Japanese). In that photo the animal was dressed in its winter coat and the hair was so long that it was actually shaggy. Here (above) is a summer photo of this animal. The hair is now much shorter.

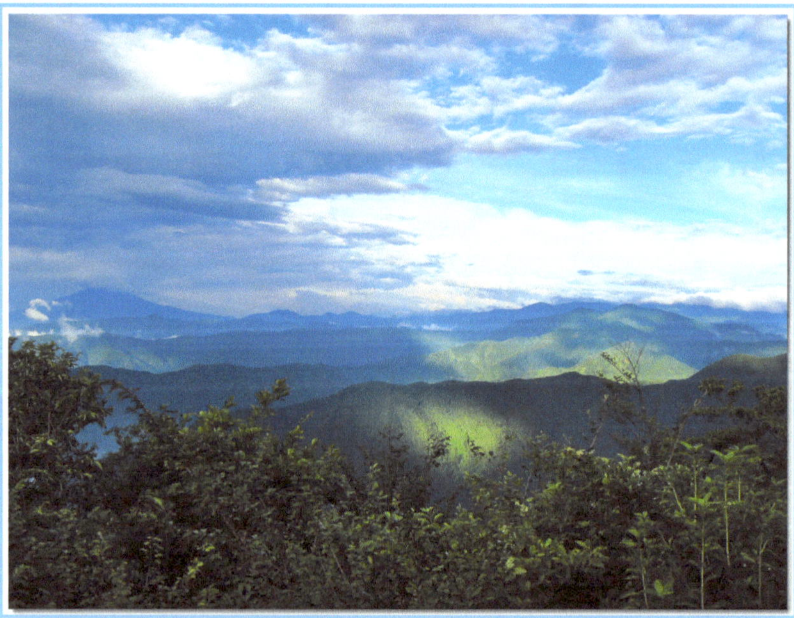

To the right is a very interesting photo taken in **Western Tokyo** – from the summit of **Mt. Ohtake** (1,267 meters = 4,155 feet). This was just a short time after the sun came up (about 6:00 AM). The clouds are interesting and the light is a strange color.

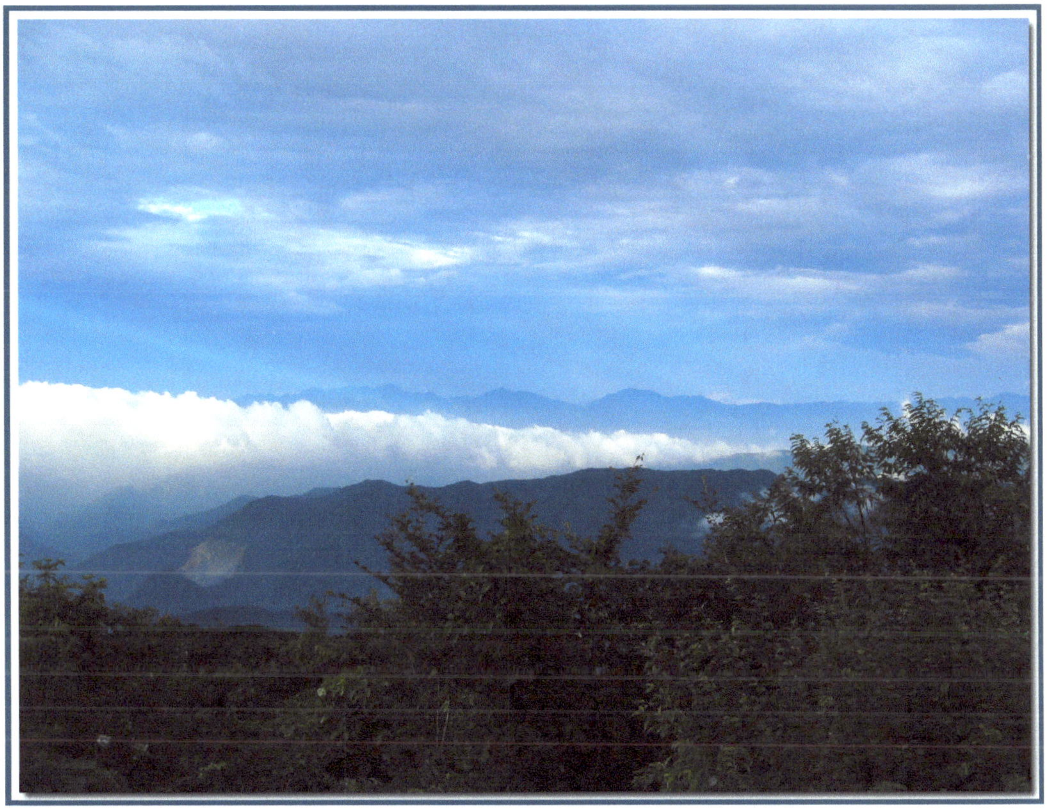

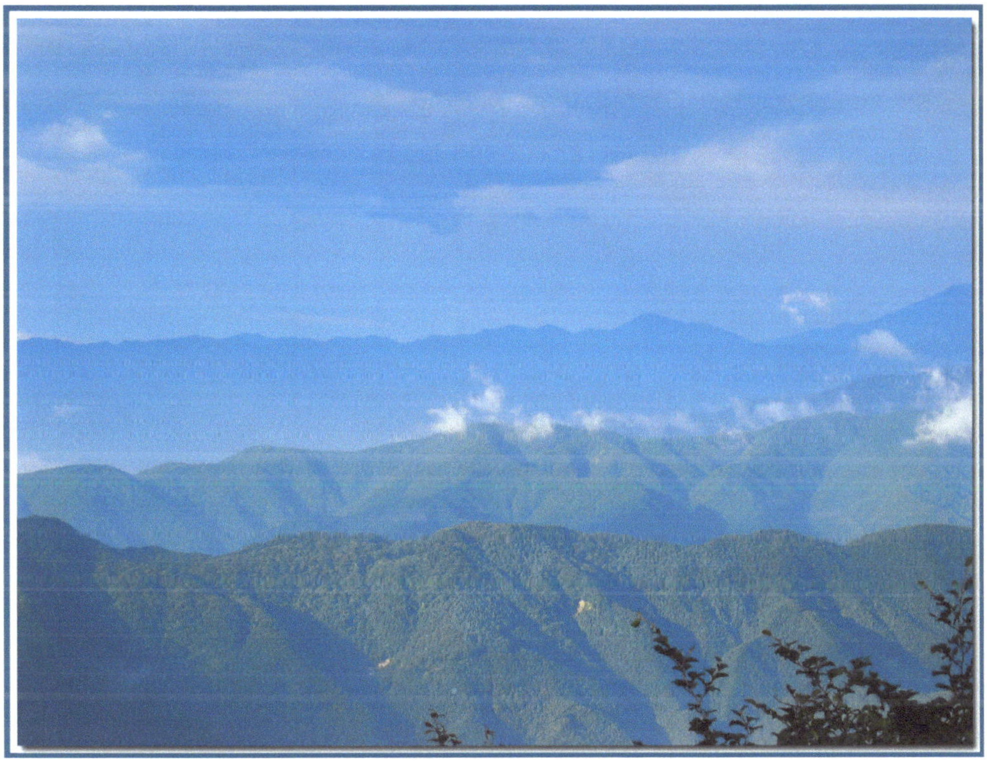

Here are two additional photos which were taken on the same morning as the one on the facing page. These show some interesting colors and clouds from the summit of **Mt. Ohtake**, in **Western Tokyo** at shortly after 6:00 AM in the month of July.

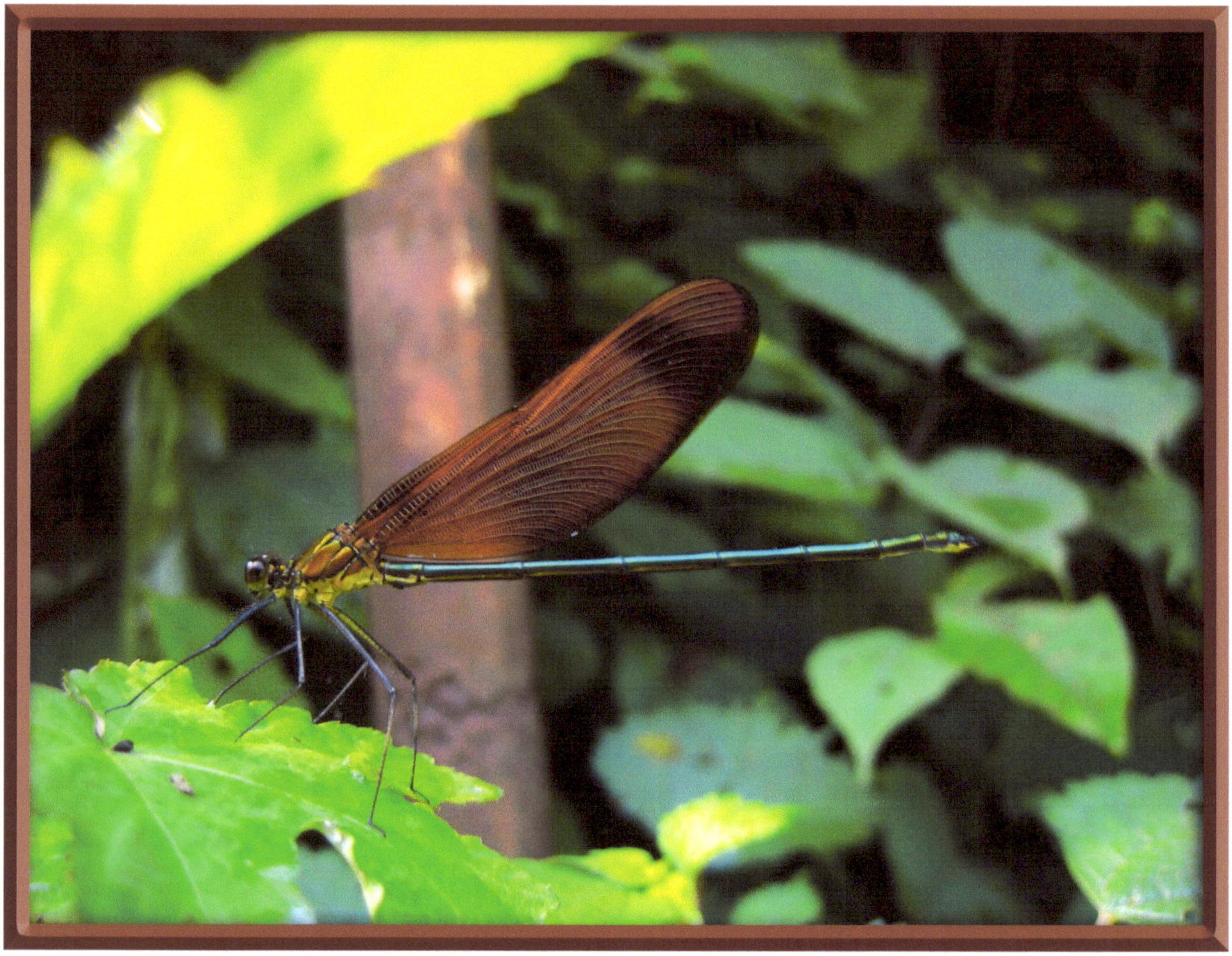

Here is an amazing photo of a blue and brown dragonfly. This was taken on **Mt. Hinode**. Every now and then we get to see some amazing insect just sitting and waiting for us to take its photo, this was one of those cases. Occasionally we get to capture the image of a nice butterfly too, but they are pretty difficult, though you will see photos of two different species of butterflies later this month.

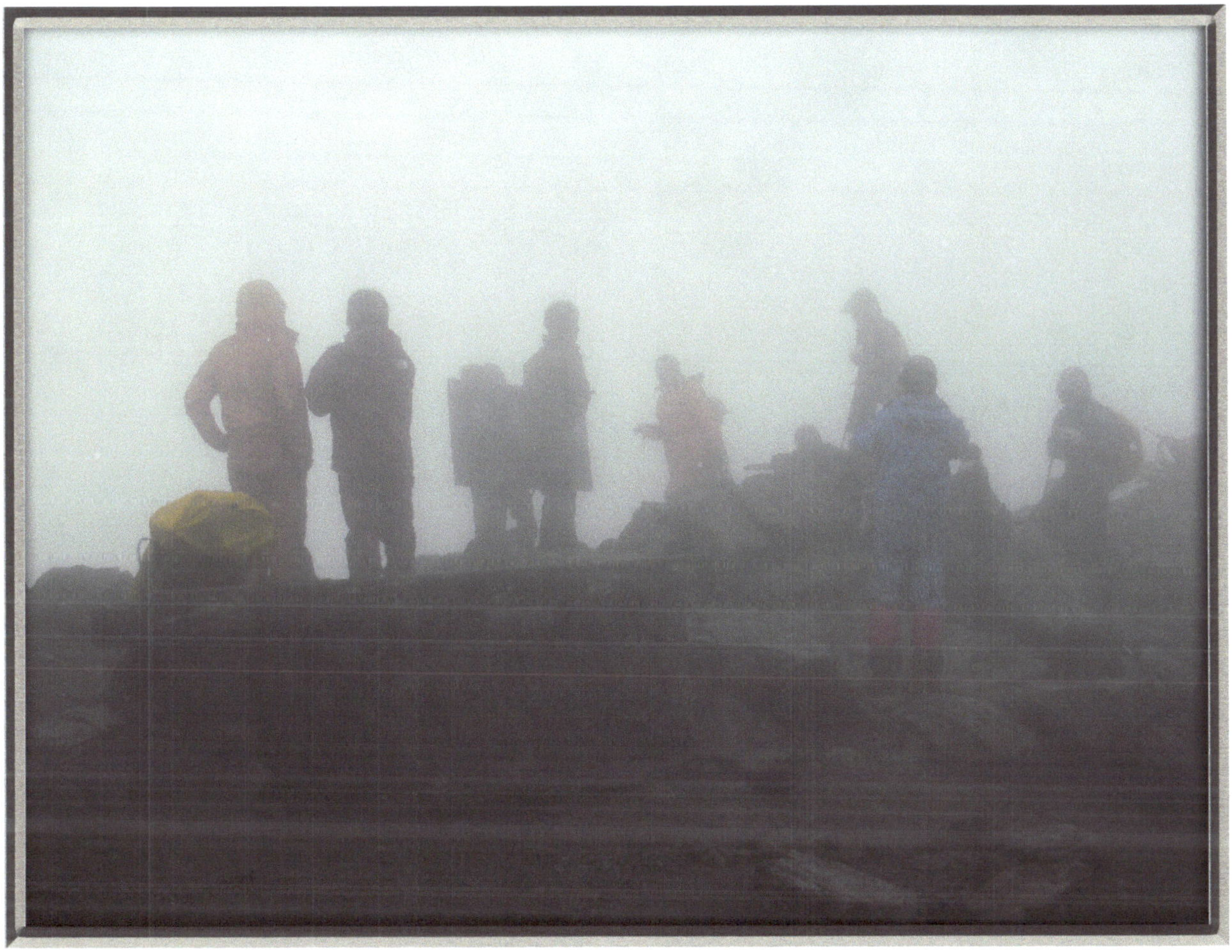

This photo was taken at the summit of **Mt. Kita-dake** (3,193 meters = 10,476 feet) on July 19th one year. We climbed up here in search of some specific flowers, which we were unable to find because the weather was pretty much like this – near whiteout conditions – for the entire two days we were here. You can see the summit sign in this photo – it is very close to the center of the photo. **Mt. Kita-dake** is the second tallest mountain in Japan, after Mt. Fuji. It is in the **Southern Alps Mountain Range**. It is in **Yamanashi Prefecture** and it is included in the **"List of 100 Famous Japanese Mountains"**. We hope to climb this mountain again at some point in the future.

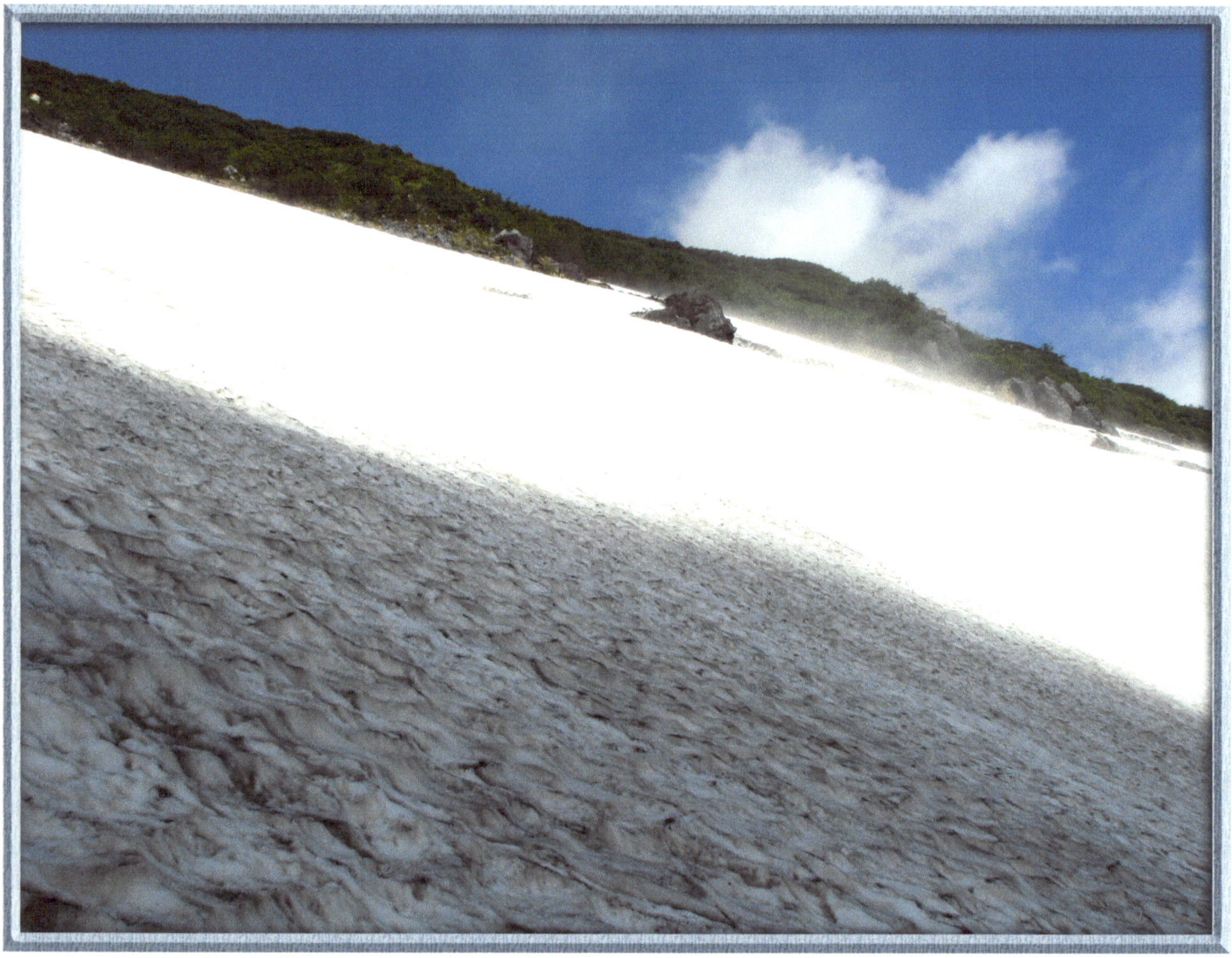

Let's take a return trip to the **Hakuba Mountains (Hida Mountains, Northern Alps Mountain Range) of Nagano Prefecture**. You visited these mountains with us back on pages 27, 28 and 29 – winter! Now it's July 23rd through July 25th. We'll spend three days here and see some spectacular mountain scenery and a few remarkable mountain flowers. We hope you'll enjoy this trip with us.

In the above shot we are already above the elevation we were at back on pages 27, 28 and 29. We crossed this snowfield on our ascent to the summit of **Mt. Shiroumadake**. The snow was soft enough so that we did not need crampons or any other technical equipment. We generally climb with one trekking pole each. Before this trip ended we would wish that we had crampons, but we made it home alive.

On the facing page are two photos of **Hakuba Pond**. The first image is an amazingly beautiful panorama shot and the second is not a panorama. This pond is above **Mt. Norikuradake** (2,436.7 meters = 7,994 feet) and below **Mt. Korenge** (2,766 meters = 9,075 feet).

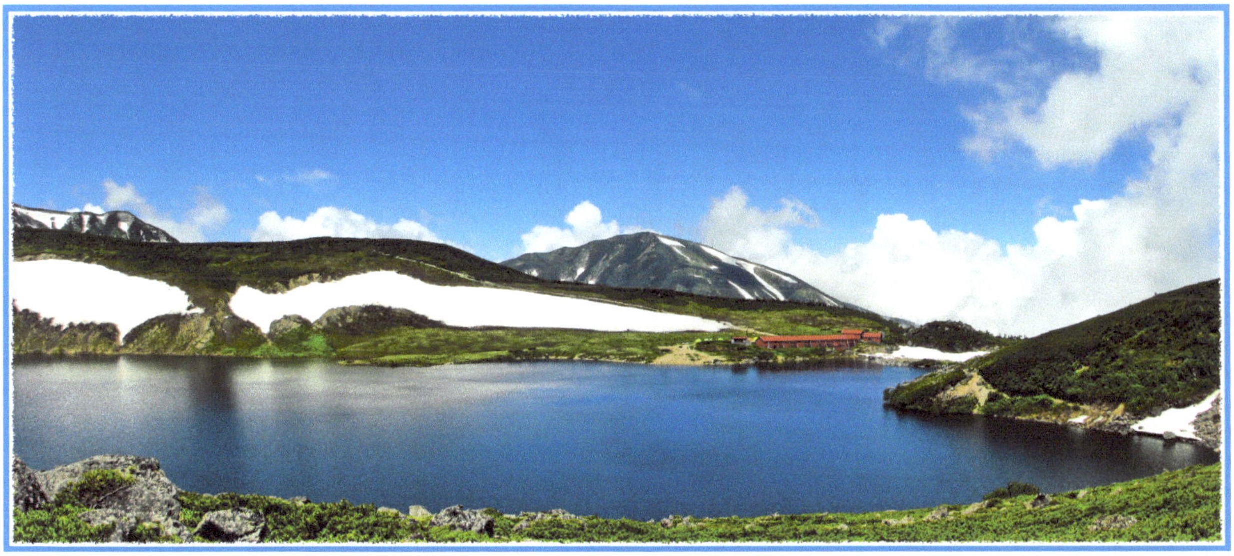

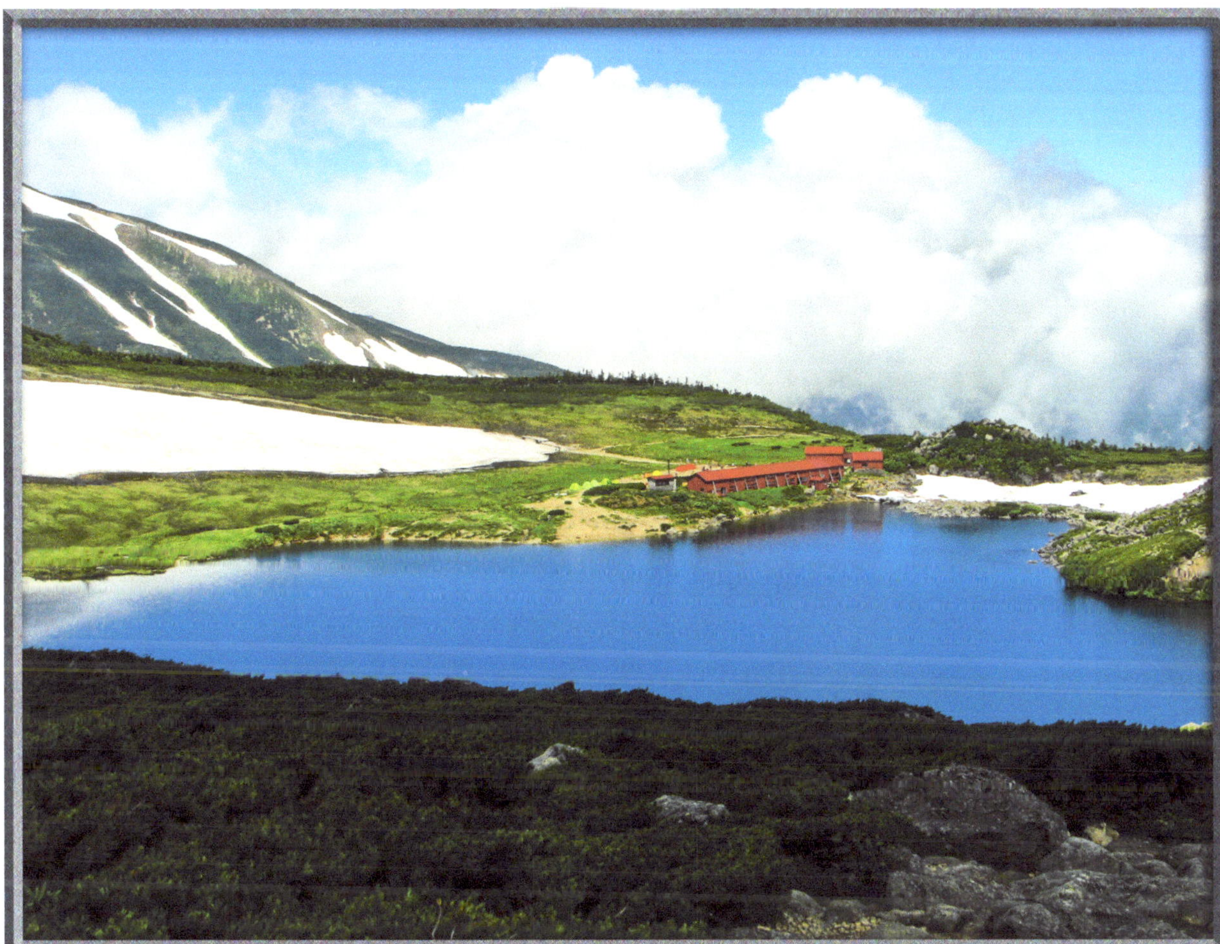

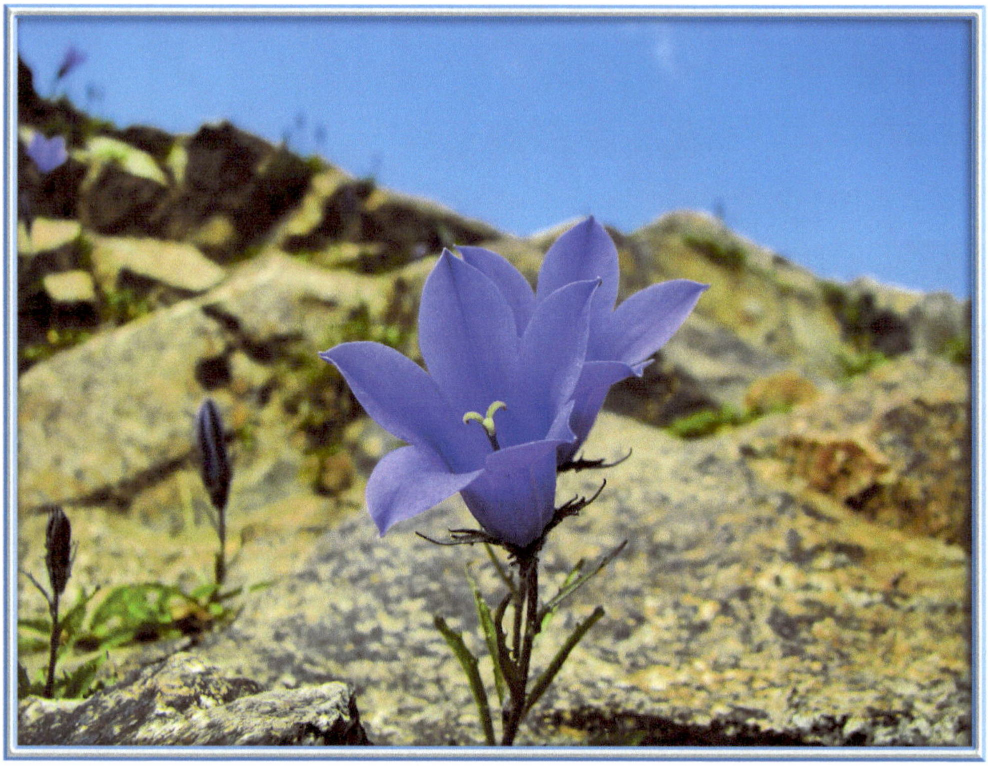

Here are 2 flower photos – both quite amazing in our opinion. The one to the left – the blue flower – is a ***Campanula lasiocarpa***. This color goes very well with the blue sky which we were able to see on this day.

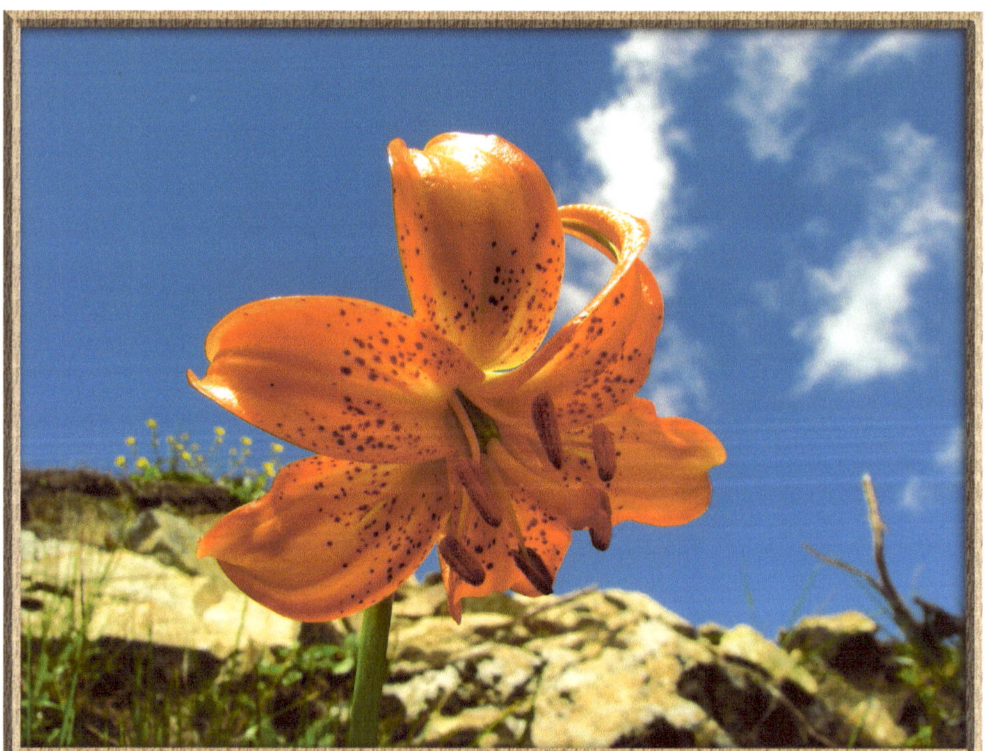

The orange flower to the right is an exceedingly beautiful lily – ***Lilium medeoloides***. We could barely believe how photogenic the flowers and the scenery were on this trip.

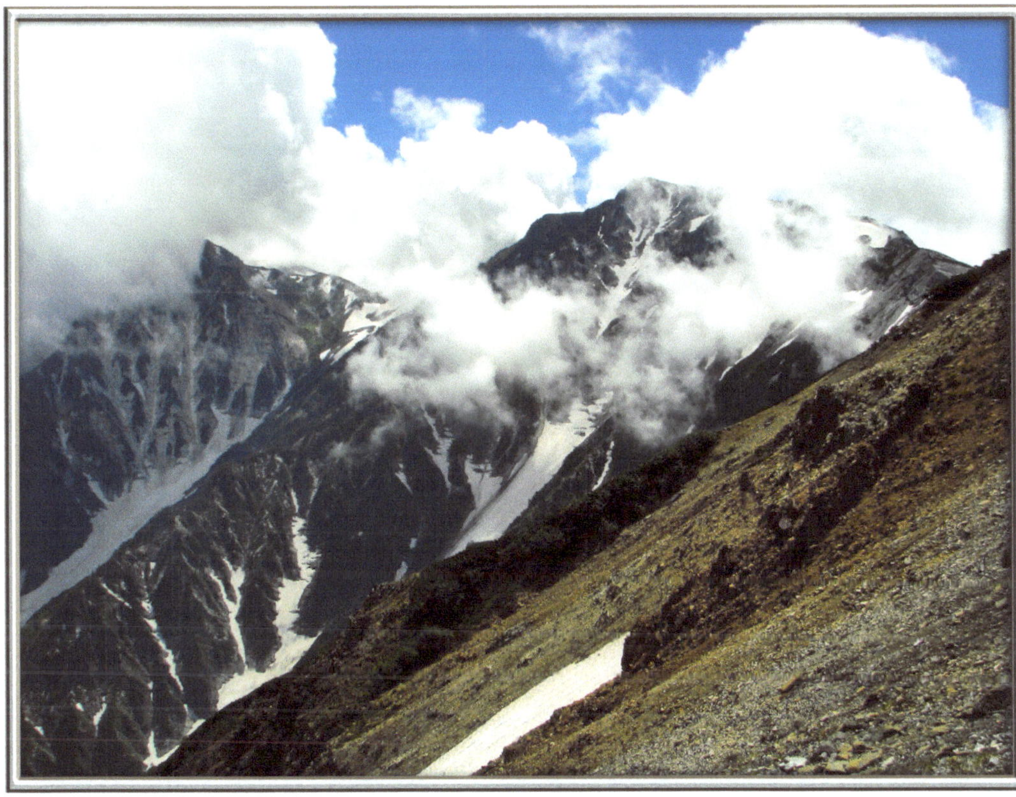

The upper photo on this page was taken from near the summit of **Mt. Korenge** (2,766 meters = 9,075 feet). What amazing colors and clouds.

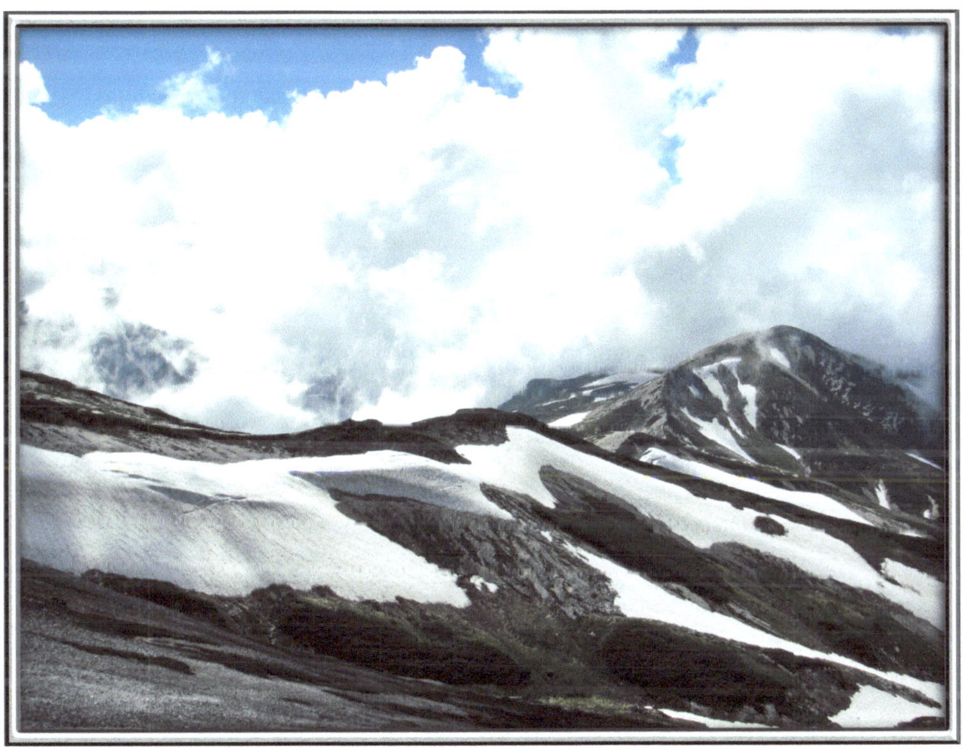

This lower photo was taken after we passed the Mt. Korenge summit and we were on our way to **Mt. Shiroumadake** (2,932 meters = 9,620 feet). Both of these photos show you some exquisite high alpine scenery.

You should also notice how much snow is still here.

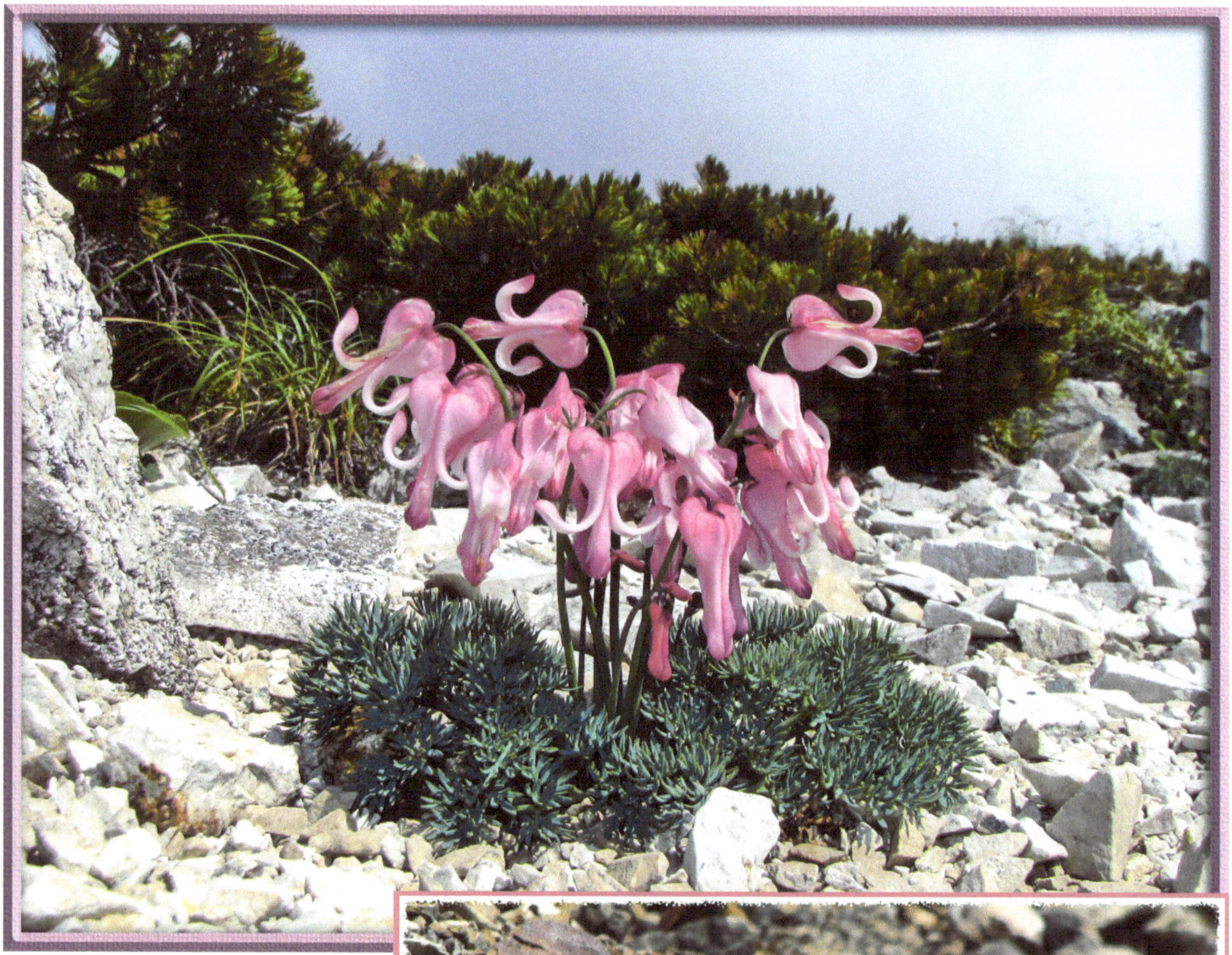

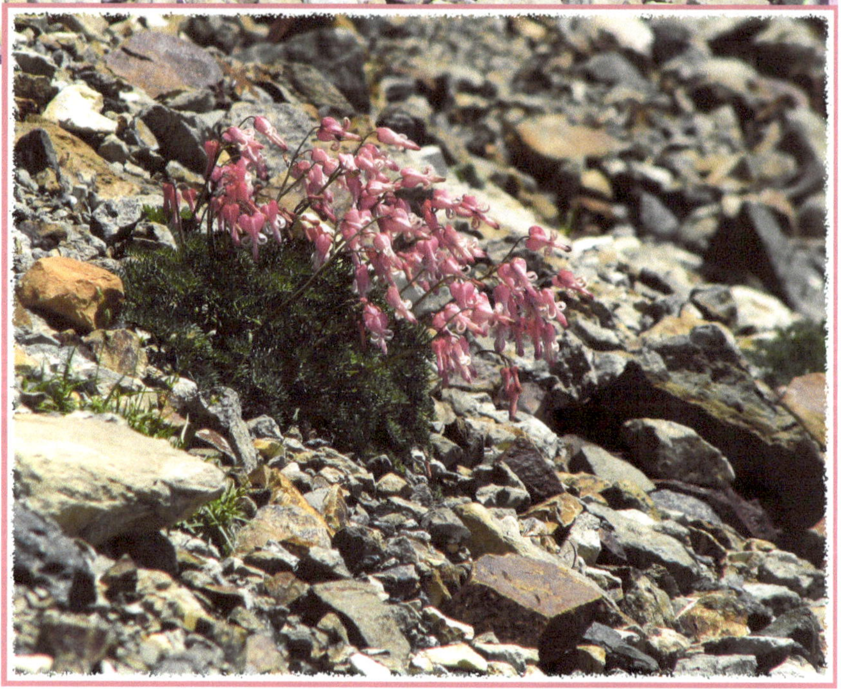

Here are two photos of ***Dicentra peregrina***, or **Bleeding Heart**. It is quite a treat to find this flower. It only occurs in high alpine country and only on scree slopes. It is in the family ***Fumariaceae*** – the Bleeding Heart family. There are only eight recognized species of ***Dicentra*** in the world. The above photo shows a near perfect plant.

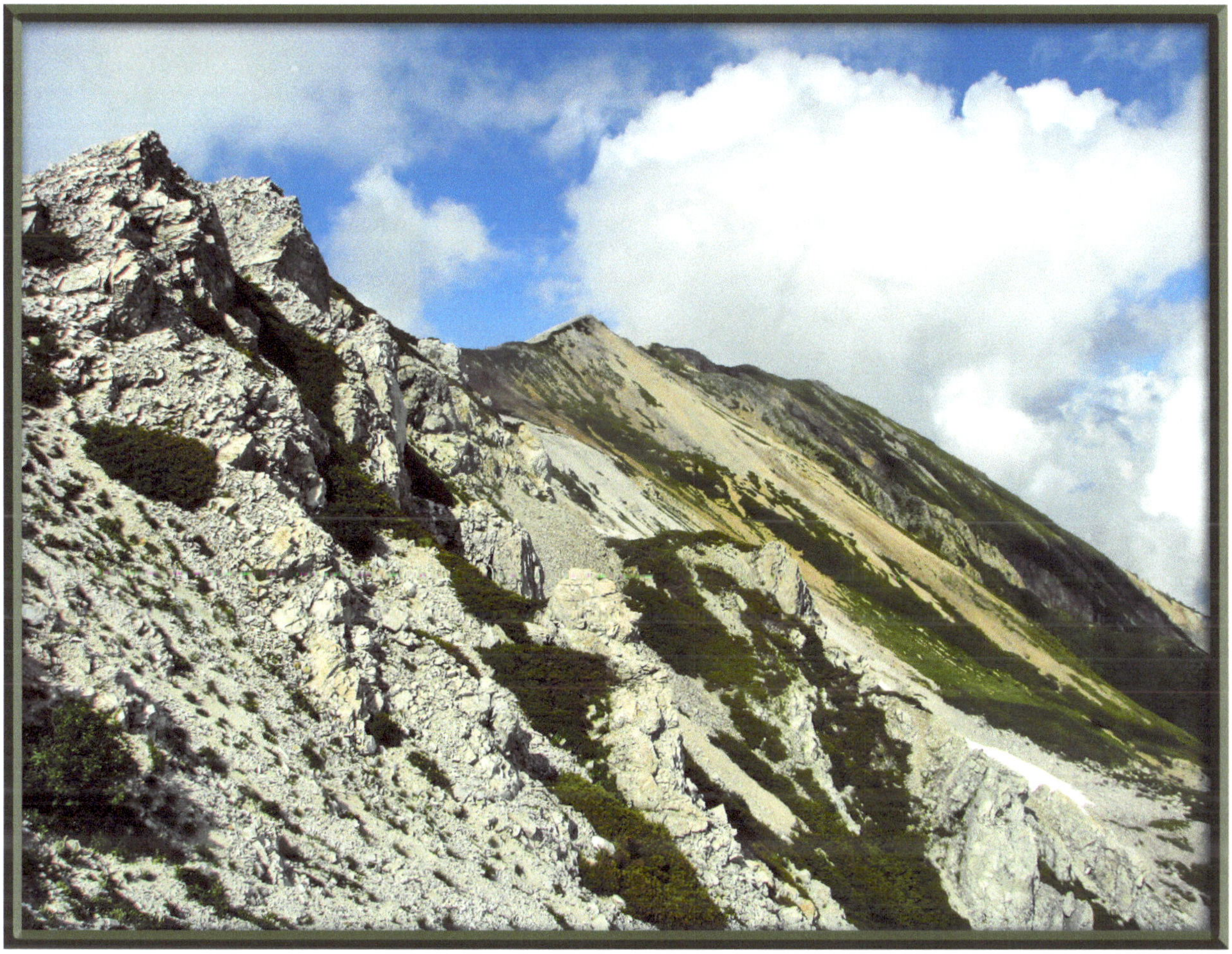

The photo just above was taken as we approached the summit of **Mt. Shiro-umadake**. It was getting later (3:15 PM) in the afternoon and the light was getting very interesting at this point. There was a threat of clouds coming in, we wondered what would happen with the weather and hoped that it would not cloud up and become whiteout or near whiteout conditions – or even begin to rain. It had been such a perfect weather day so far that we sincerely hoped that it would stay that way.

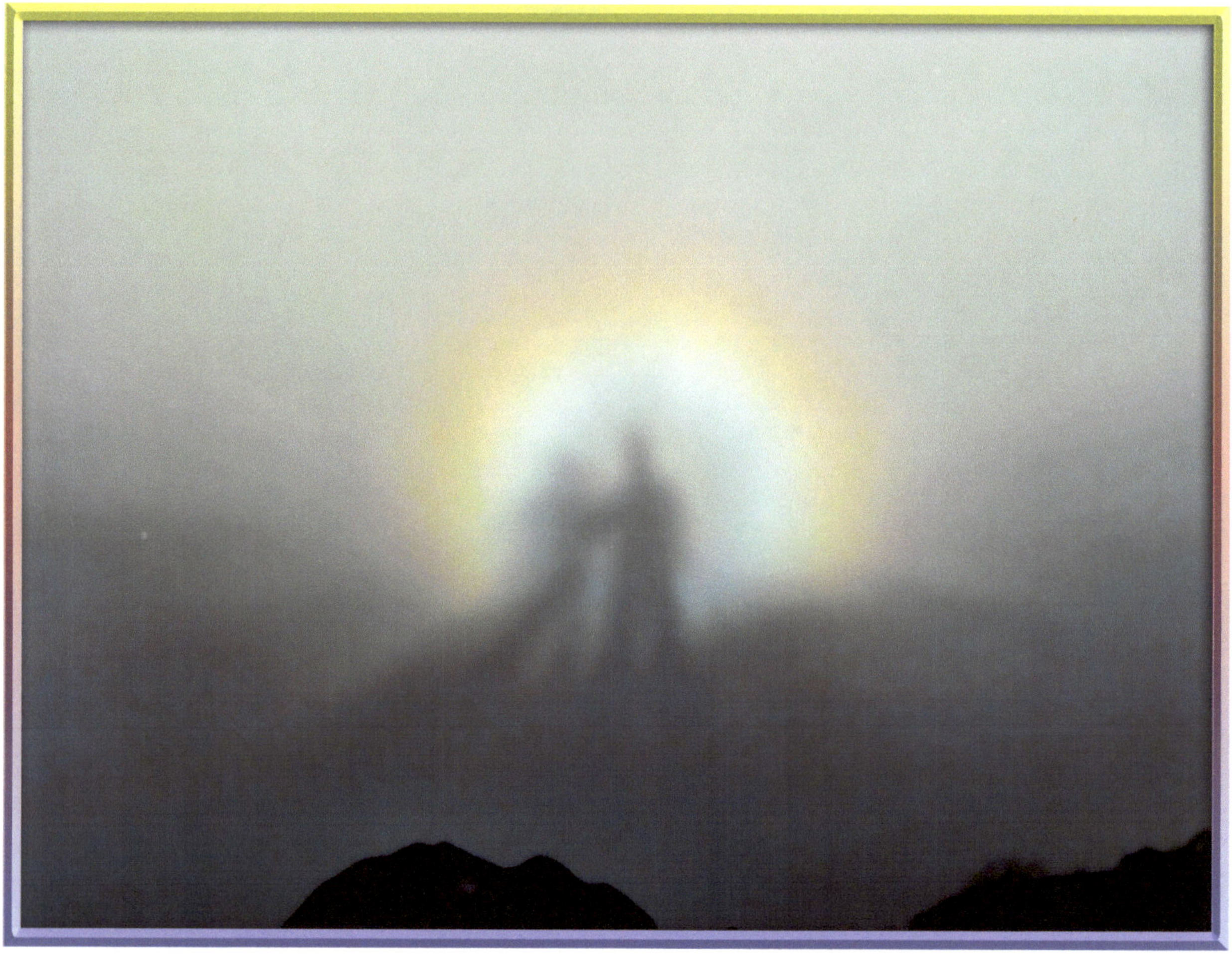

We promised you a better photo of a **Brocken Spectre** back on page 120. Here it is. Oh, as you'll note, it did cloud up as we continued our hike towards **Mt. Shiroumadake**. That is how we happened to see this phenomenon.

The **Brocken Spectre** is the apparently enormous and magnified shadow of an observer, cast upon the upper surfaces of clouds opposite the sun. The phenomenon can appear on any misty mountainside or cloud bank, or even from an airplane, but the frequent fogs and low-altitude accessibility of the Brocken, a peak in the Harz Mountains in Germany, have created a local legend from which the phenomenon draws its name.

The Brocken Spectre appears only when the sun shines from behind a climber who is looking down from a ridge or peak into mist or fog. The light projects the climber's shadow forward through the mist. By the way, we stood side-by-side to get this image, a person's shadow is not doubled as a part of the phenomenon.

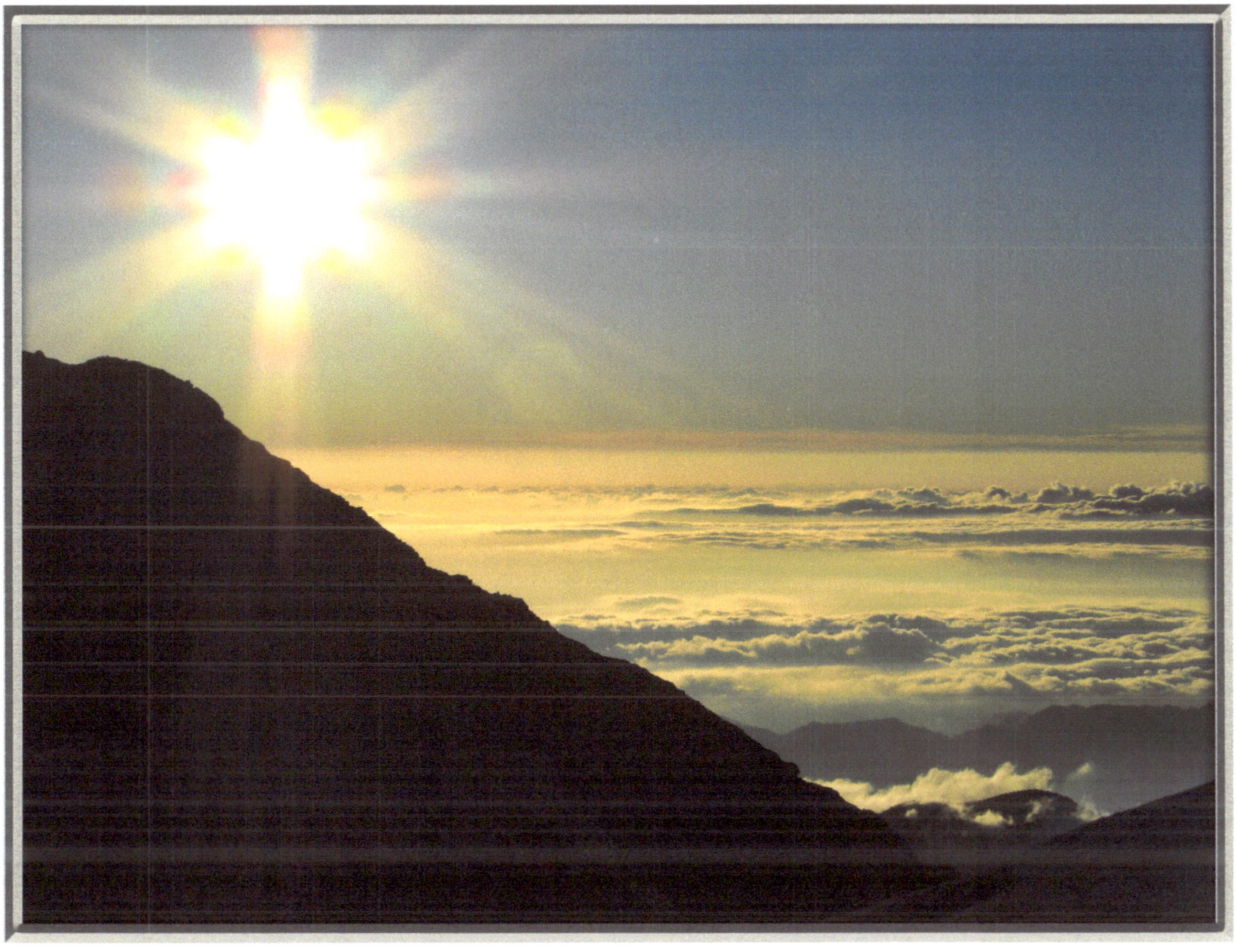

Immediately above is a photo which was taken while standing in front of the **Mt. Shiroumadake** hut. Obviously it was approaching sunset – the time was 6:32 PM. A sea of clouds was forming down below us and the star effect of the sun was perfectly natural – no filters were used. We were very fortunate all day today as far as weather conditions. We could only hope that the weather gods would continue to smile upon us tomorrow, as we continued on this adventure. We would be on this mountain range for an additional night after this – if the weather had deteriorated it could have been really miserable.

The photos from page 136 through this page were all taken on the same date. This is the most photos from any single day which can be found anywhere in this book.

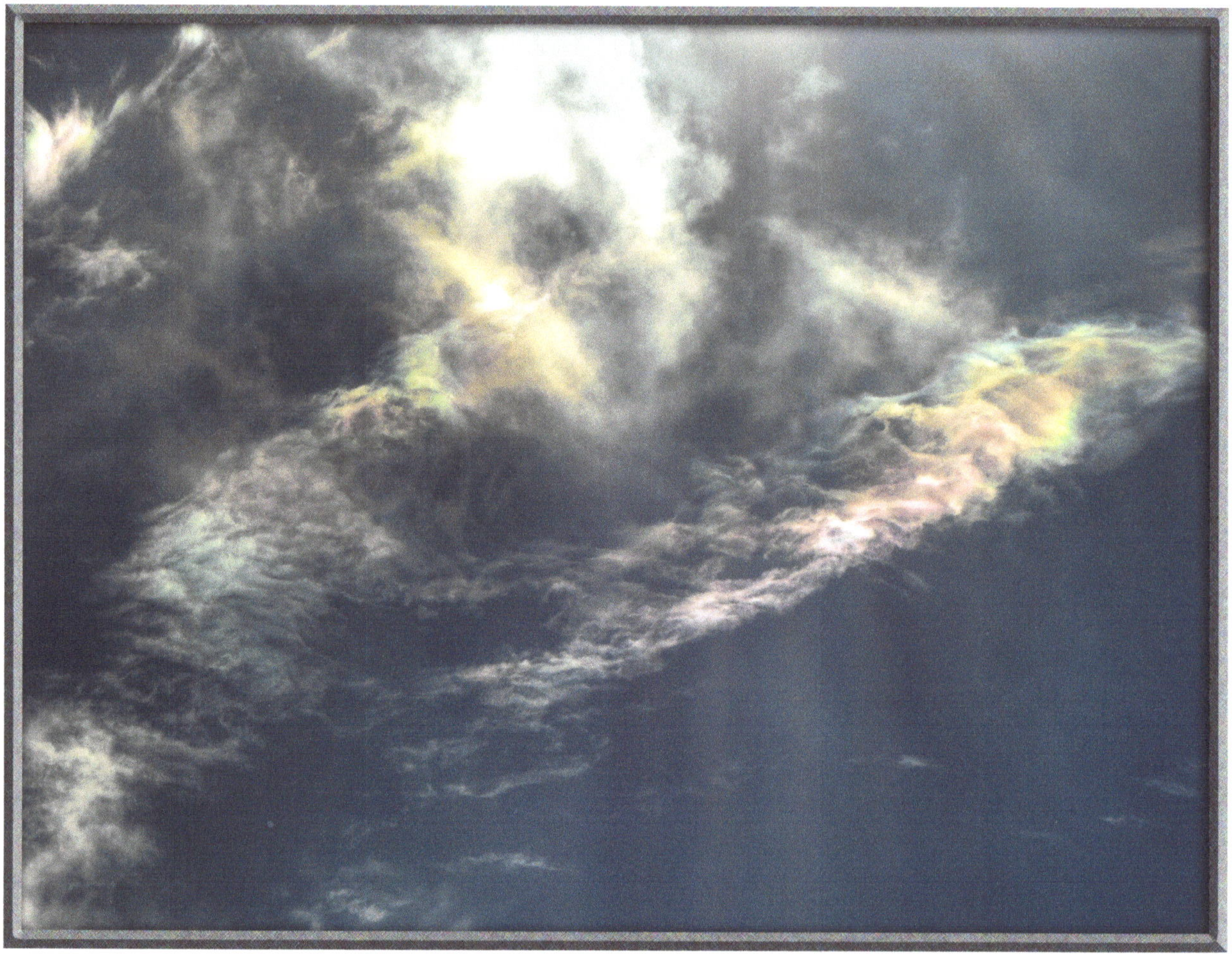

This above photo continues the next morning as we were hiking from **Mt. Shiroumadake** (2,932 meters = 9,620 feet) towards **Mt. Shakushidake** (2,812 meters = 9,226 feet) and then **Mt. Yarigatake** (2,903 meters = 9,525 feet). When we began we were in the clouds and could not see very far at all. When it began to clear up, at around 8:00 AM, it was impressive as we could see some exquisite mountain scenery. Then, at about 8:45 AM we were shown this cloud phenomenon – **iridescent clouds** (**cloud iridescence**).

This phenomenon occurs when parts of clouds are thin and have similar size droplets, diffraction can make them shine with colors like a corona. The usually delicate colors can be in almost random patches or bands at cloud edges. The bands and colors change – or come and go – as the cloud evolves. Iridescence is generally seen when part of a cloud is forming because then all the droplets have a similar history and consequently have a similar size. This is the only time we have ever seen this.

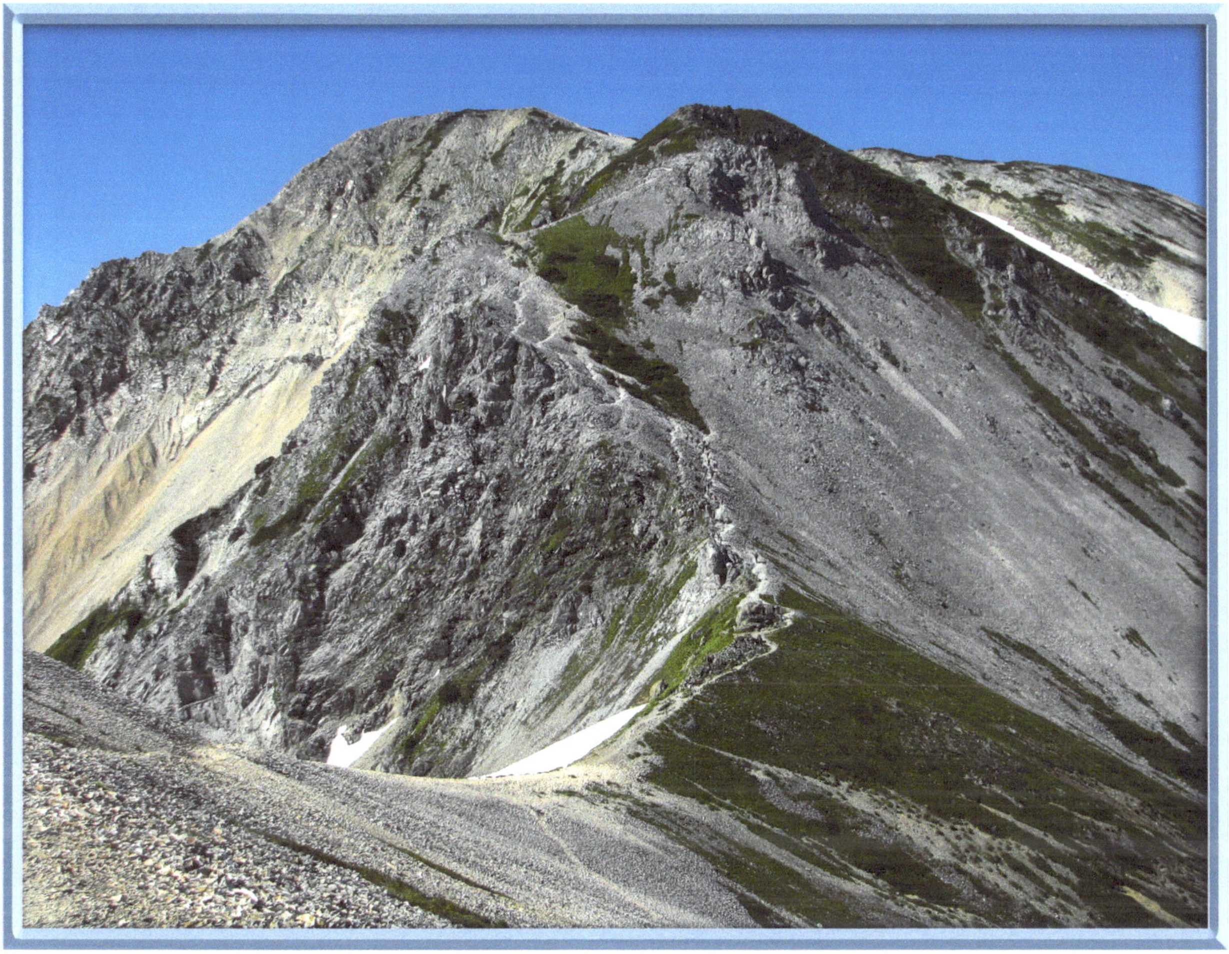

This shot shows **Mt. Yarigatake** (2,903 meters = 9,525 feet) ahead of us – to the left of the green-topped peak near the center of the photo. We are now coming off **Mt. Shakushidake** (2,812 meters = 9,226 feet). It is very difficult to see it in this photo, but there was a large group of climbers in front of us and going the same direction as we were. It is always very disappointing when one encounters these large and often noisy "organized" groups which show little respect for the wilderness experience of other people on the mountains. We ended up catching up with them at the green summit while they took a noisy break. We were fortunate in that we could pass them. We were unfortunate in that we had to see and meet them at all.

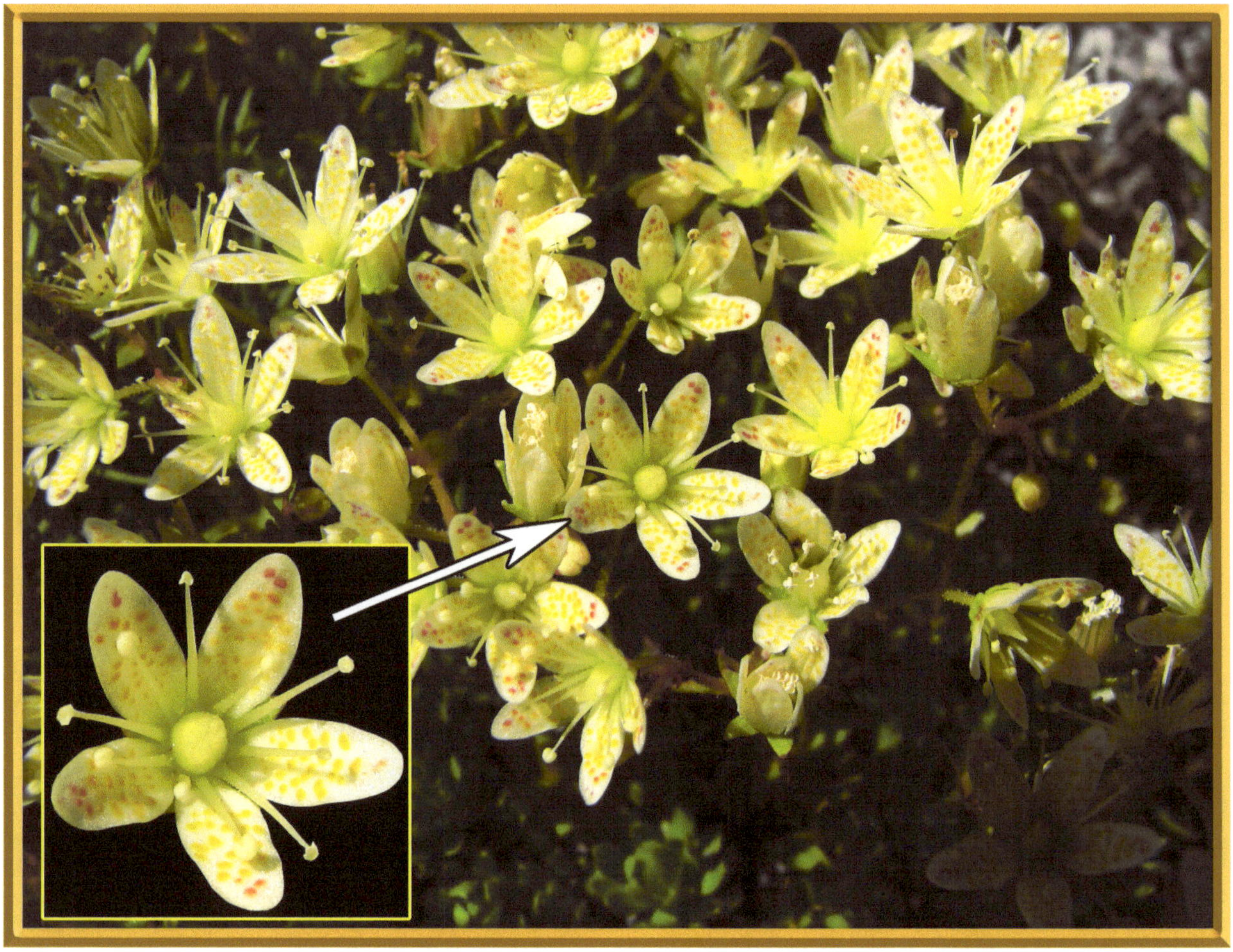

This flower is ***Saxifraga bronchialis* ssp. *funstonii* var. *rebunshirensis***. We really wondered what insect this plant depends upon for pollination so that it needs bright red or orange colors at the outer edge of the flower and then needs lighter and lighter colors near the center of the flower. The evolutionary history of this plant must be very interesting to end up like this.

On the facing page in top position is a magnificent photo looking back at **Mt. Shakushidake** and **Mt. Shiroumadake** as we climbed up towards the summit of **Mt. Yarigatake**. If you study this photo closely enough you can find the **Mt. Shiroumadake** hut – where we stayed last night.

In lower position on the facing page is a photo taken while looking back at **Mt. Yarigatake** as we were descending it. It exhibits a beautiful blue sky and if you study it closely you can see a few people coming towards us on the trail.

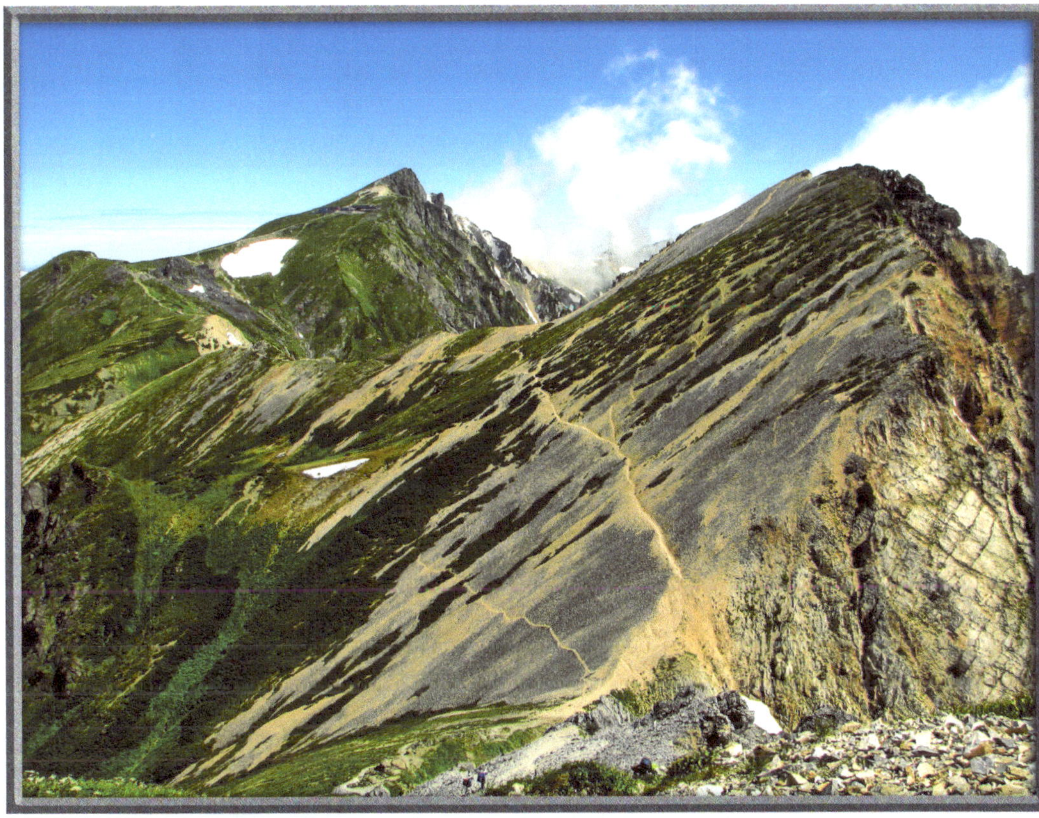

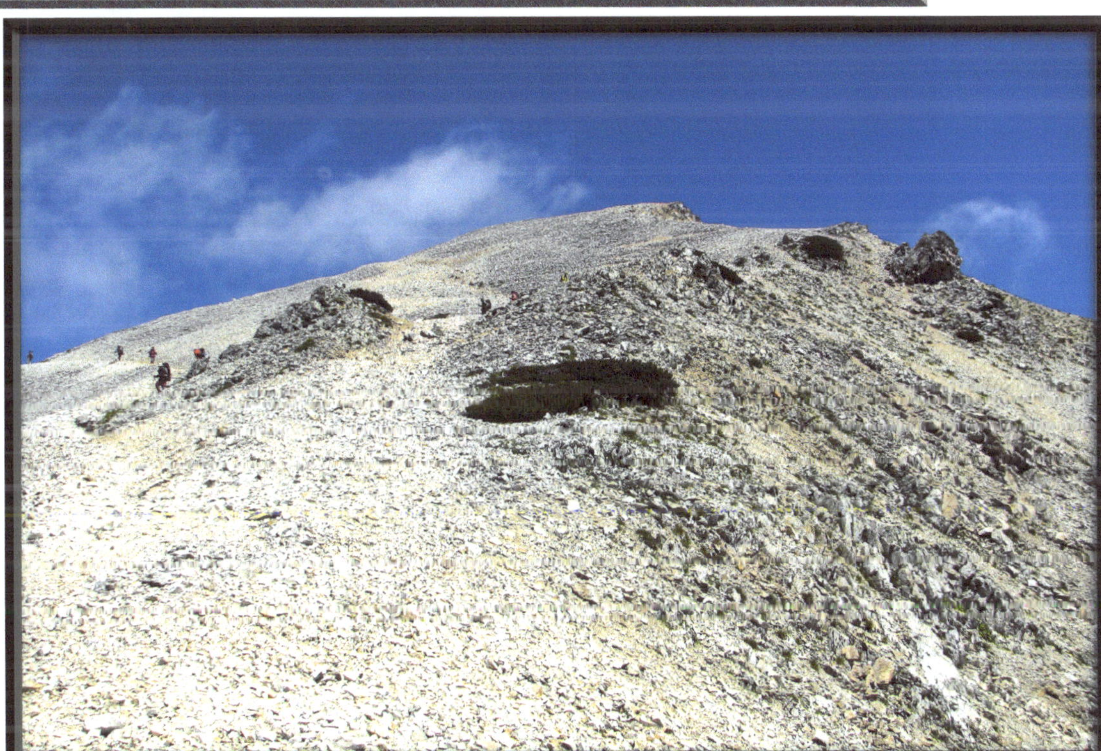

Shortly after we descended **Mt. Yarigatake** we arrived at our destination for the day. We arrived at **Yari Onsen** (Hot Spring) **Hut** at around 12:45 PM. We checked in (we had reservations) and then after a while we soaked in the hot spring. The waters of this hot spring are very hot – some folks say that they are 45° C. This is an amazingly high elevation hot spring too – it sits at about 2,500 meters. Some reports indicate that it is the highest elevation hot spring in Japan. We do not know if this is factual information or not.

What is factual is that after hiking for two days on the high mountain trails it was wonderful to get into a hot spring with no clothes on and soak our tired muscles and relax for several hours.

The following morning we had to head for home, unfortunately, as we were having such a wonderful time. The sunrise photo below was taken at 4:43 AM as we descended towards the bottom of the mountain.

The two photos on the facing page show incredible mountain scenery as we descended the mountain. You can actually see the **Yari Onsen** in the lower photo if you have very good eyes.

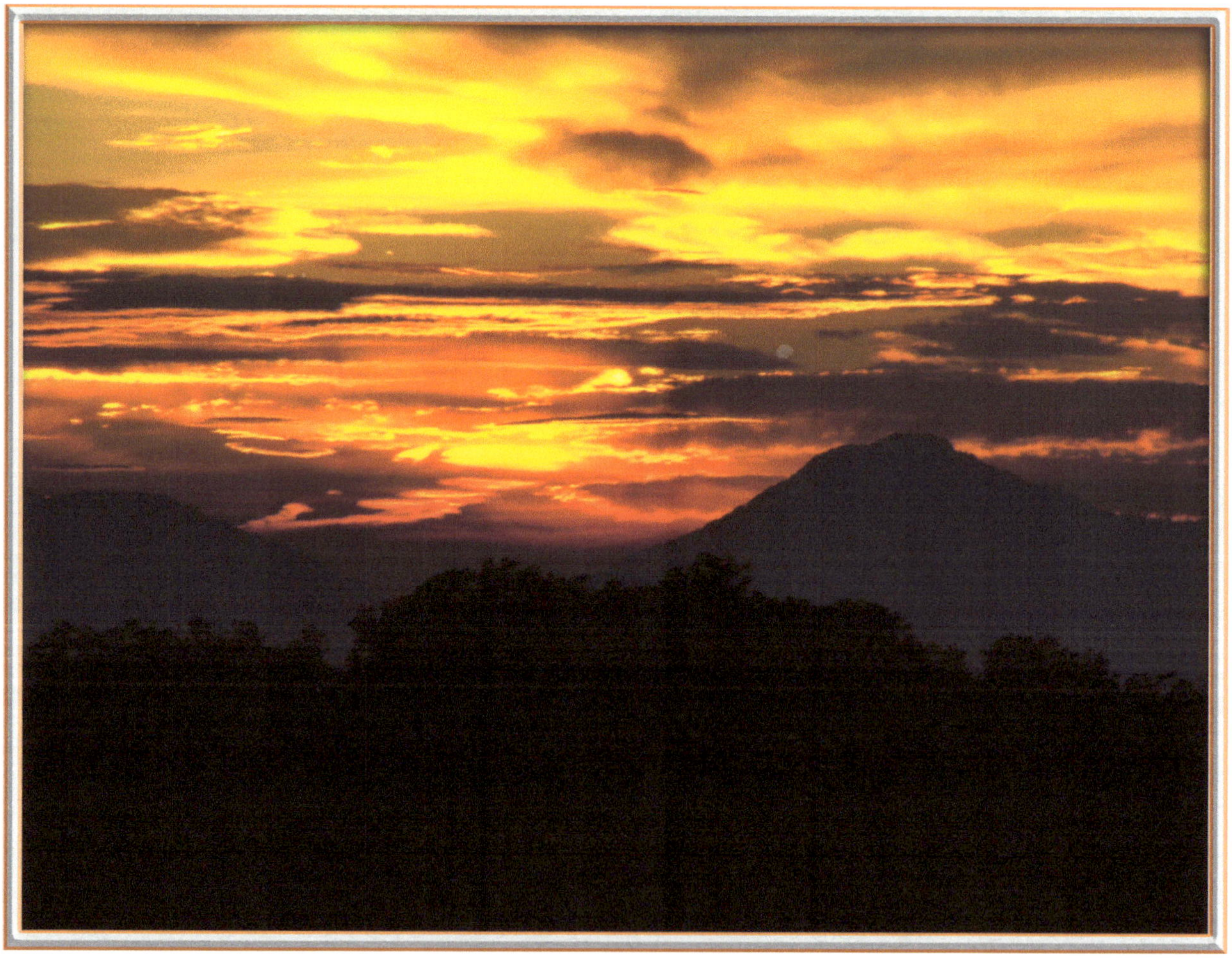

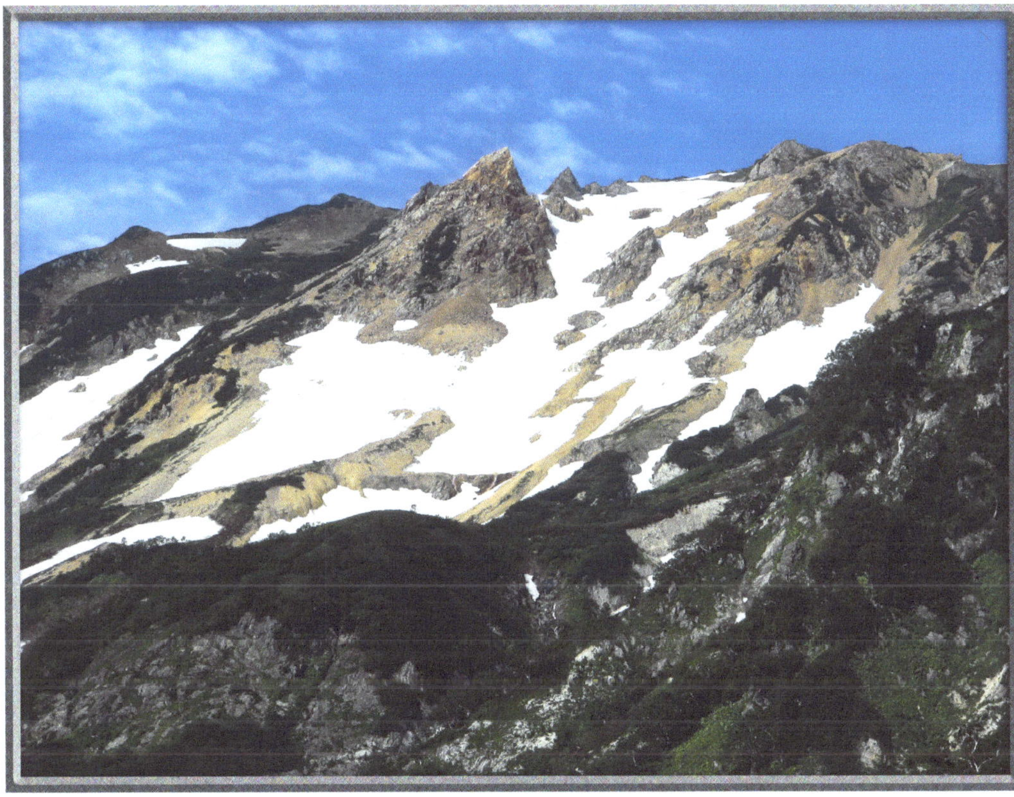

Yari Onsen

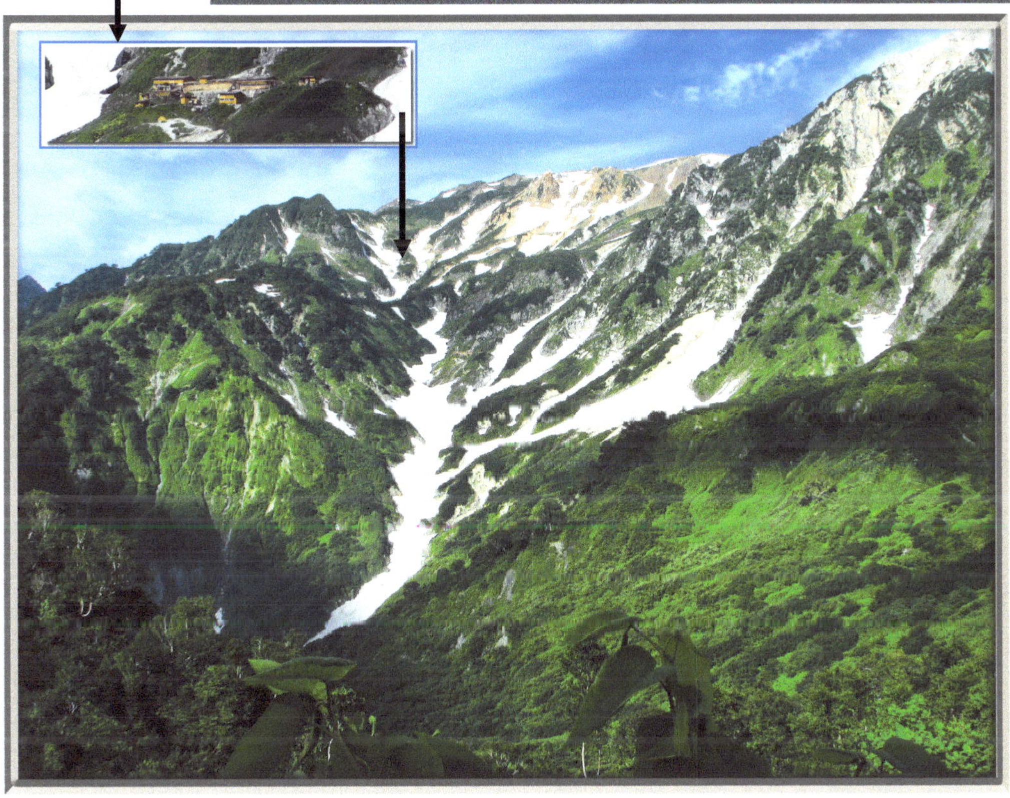

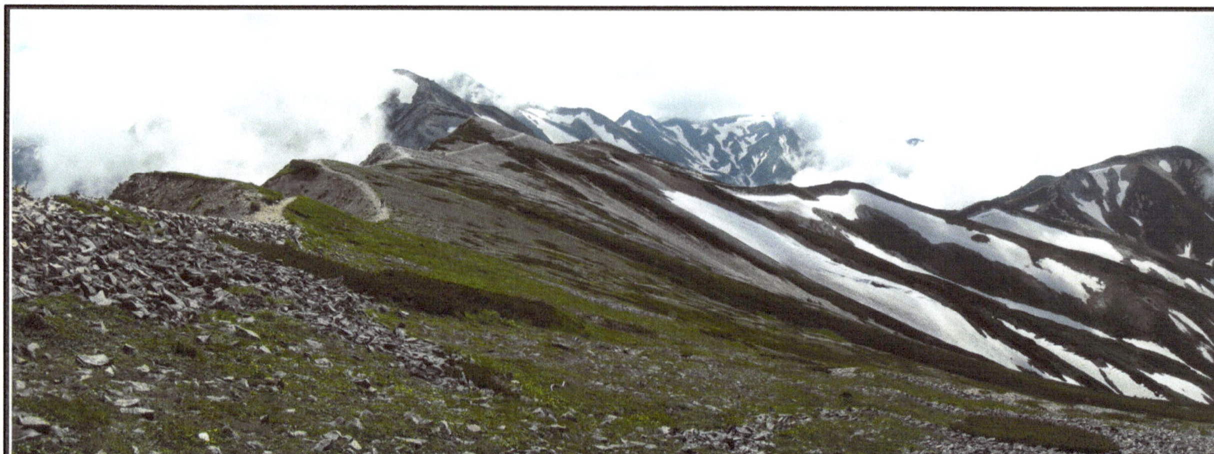

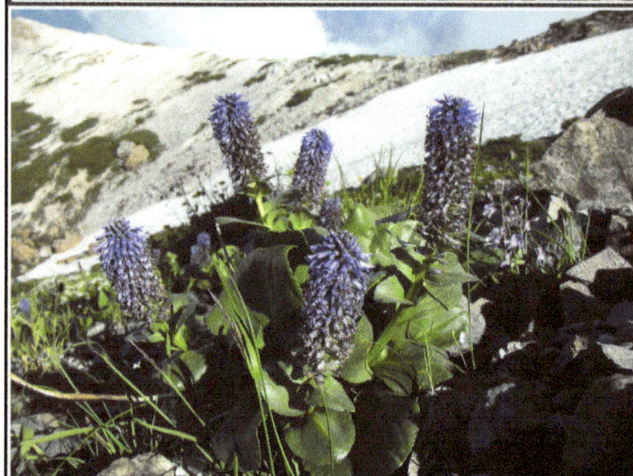

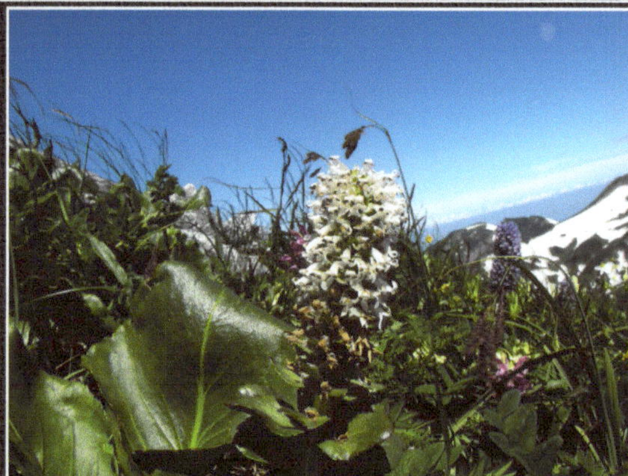

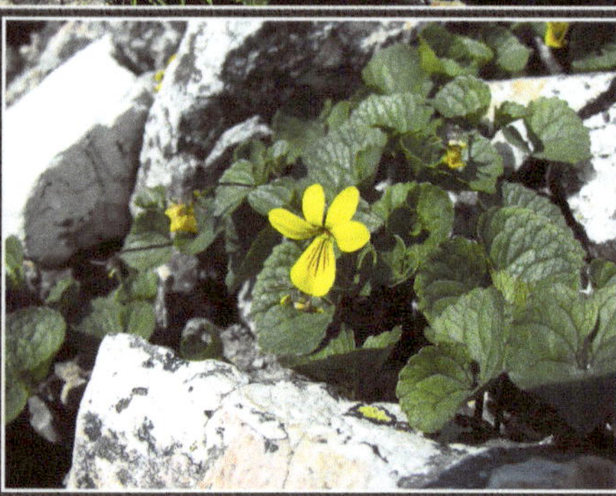

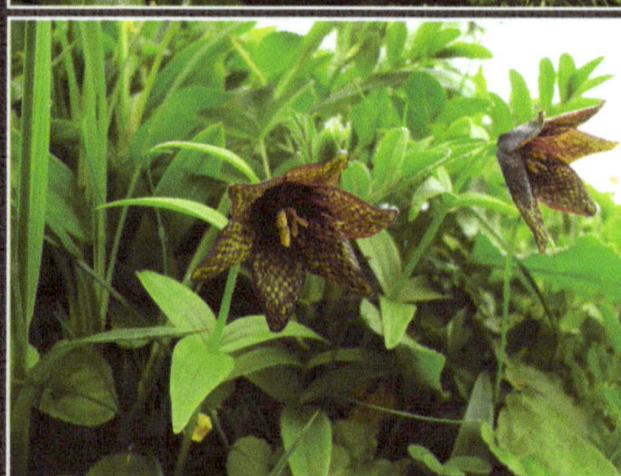

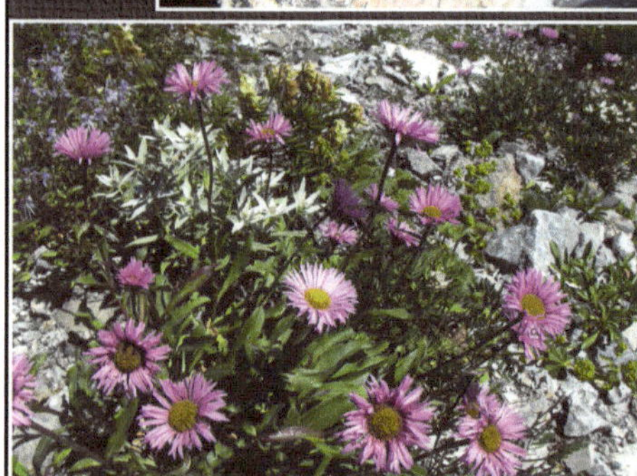

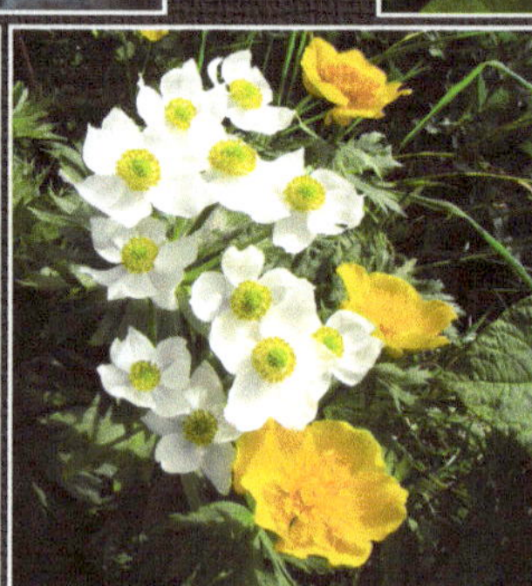

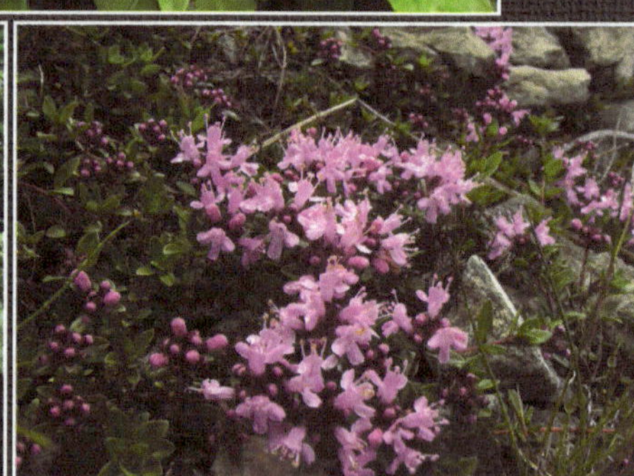

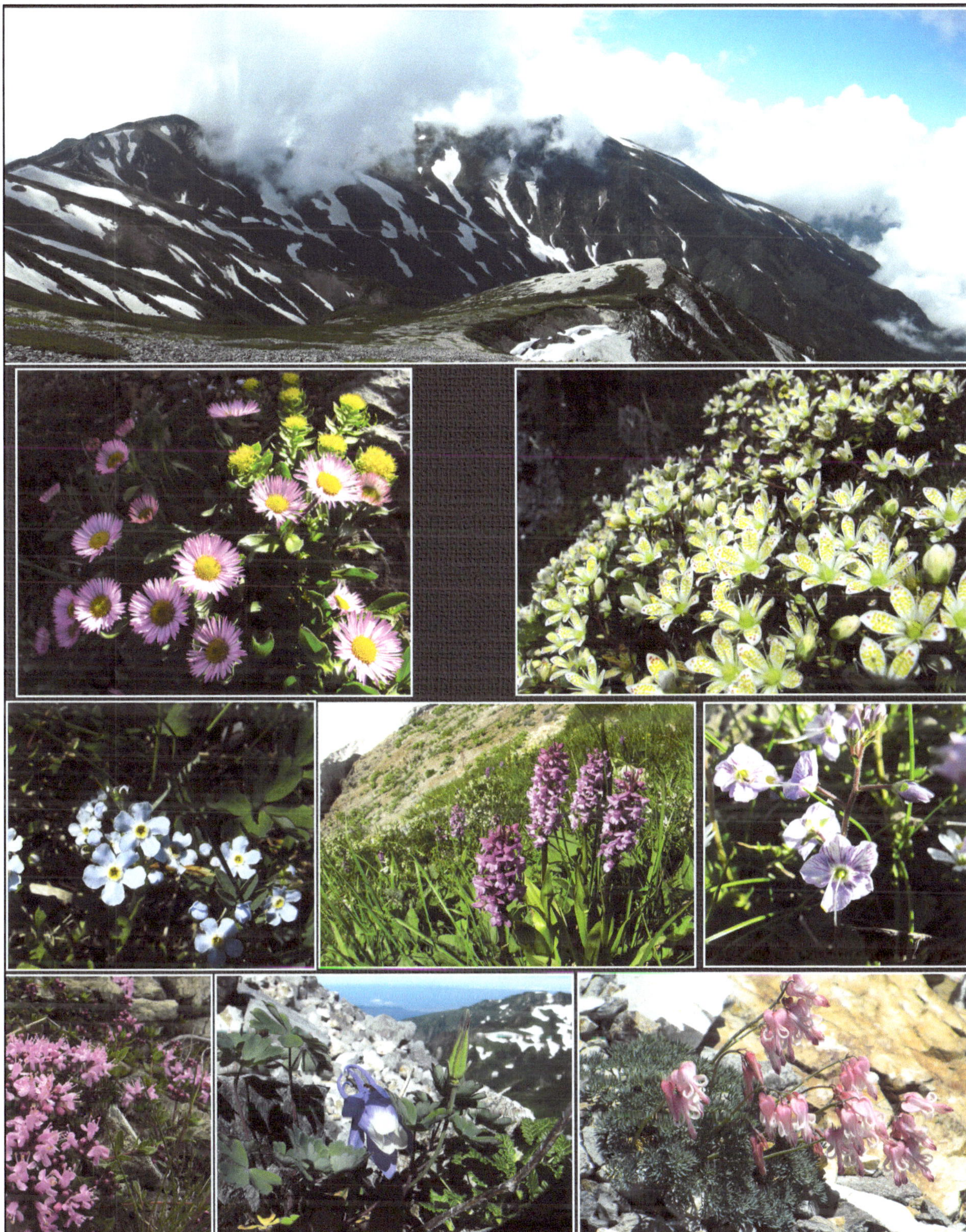

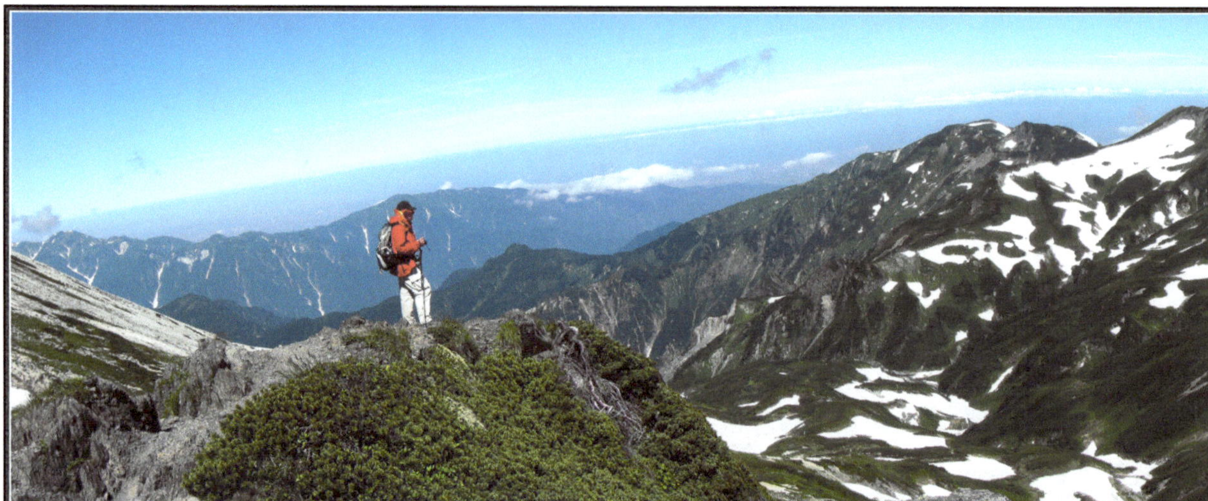

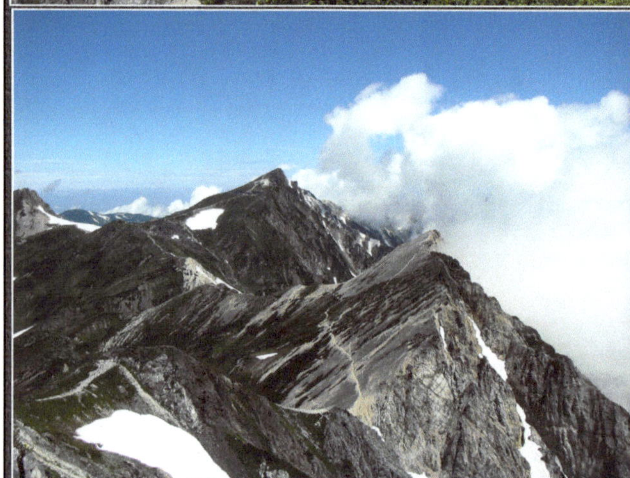

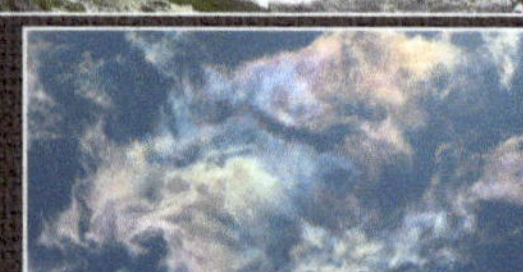

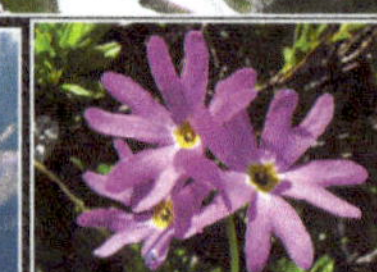

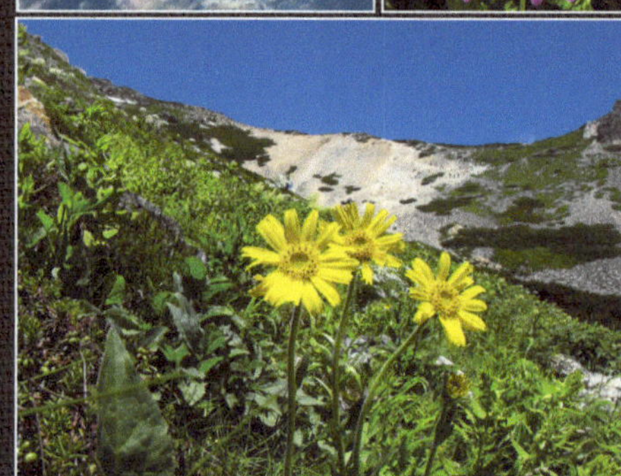

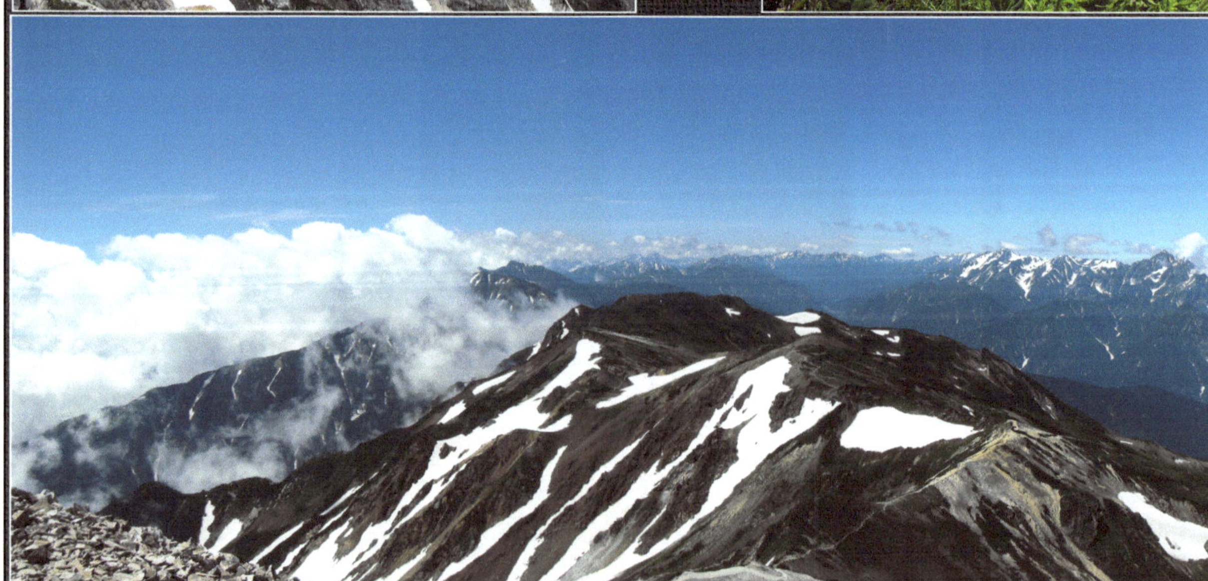

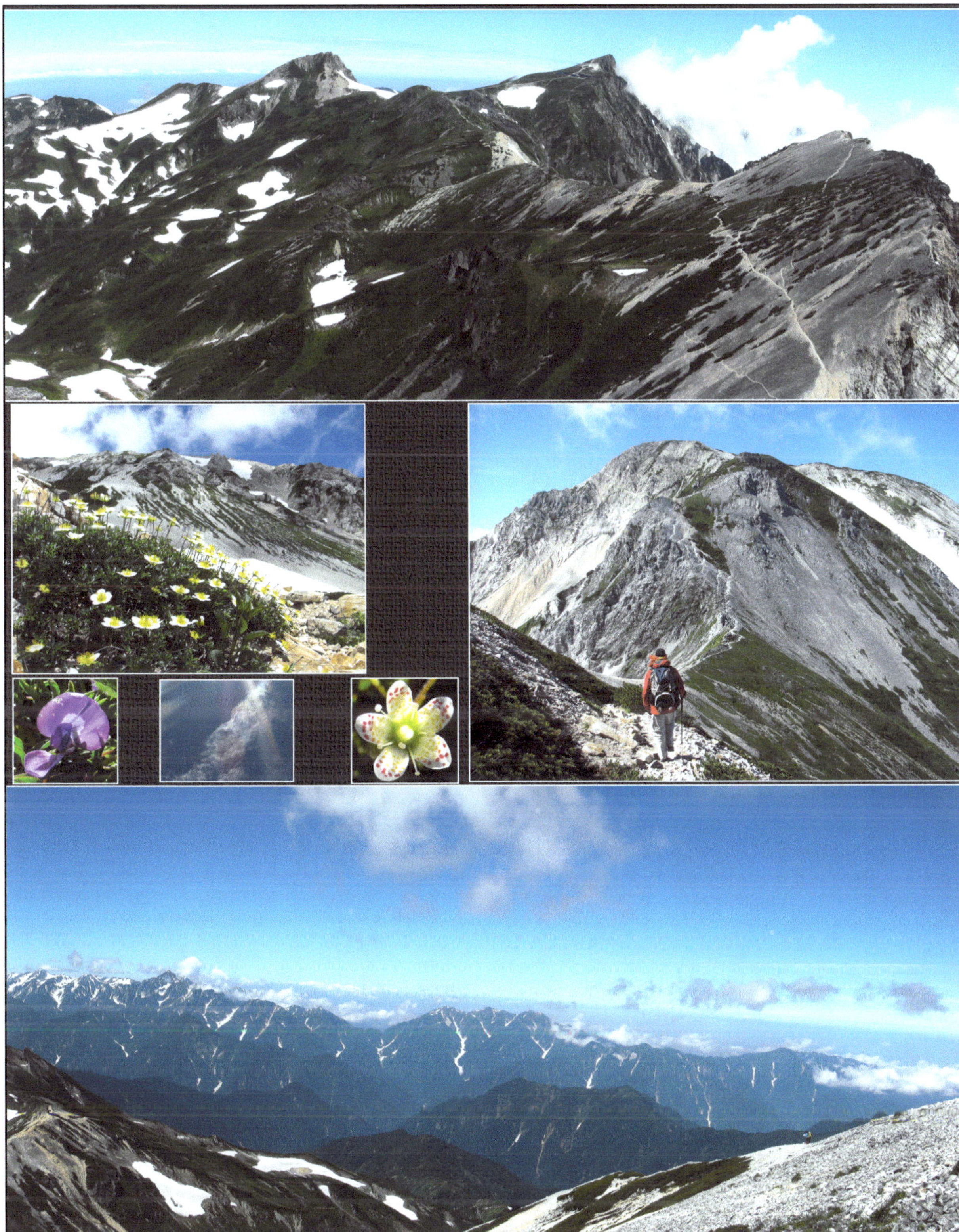

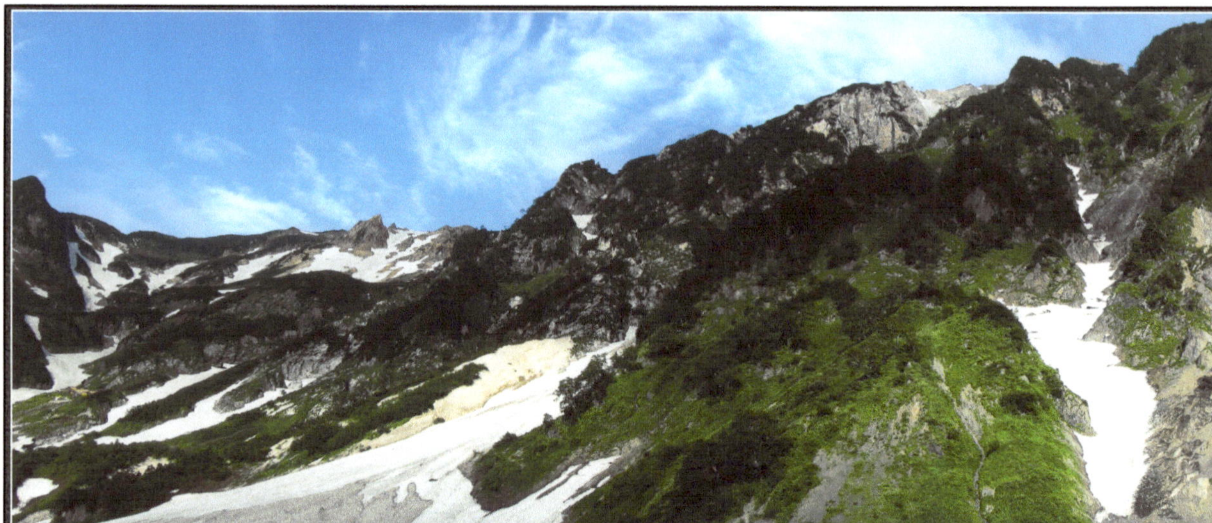

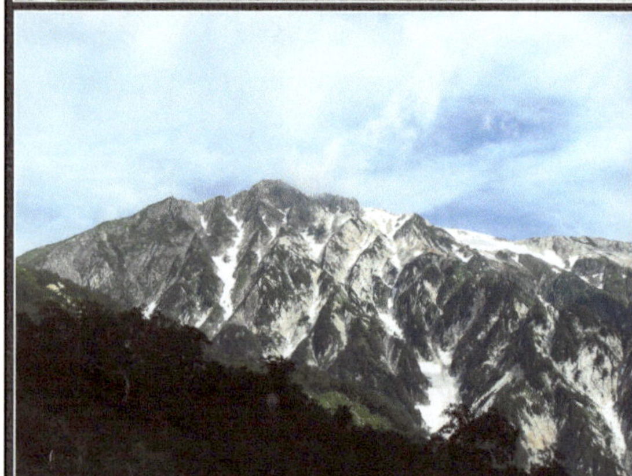

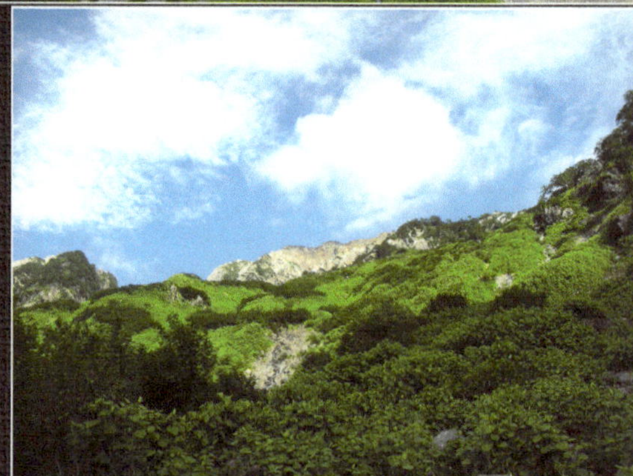

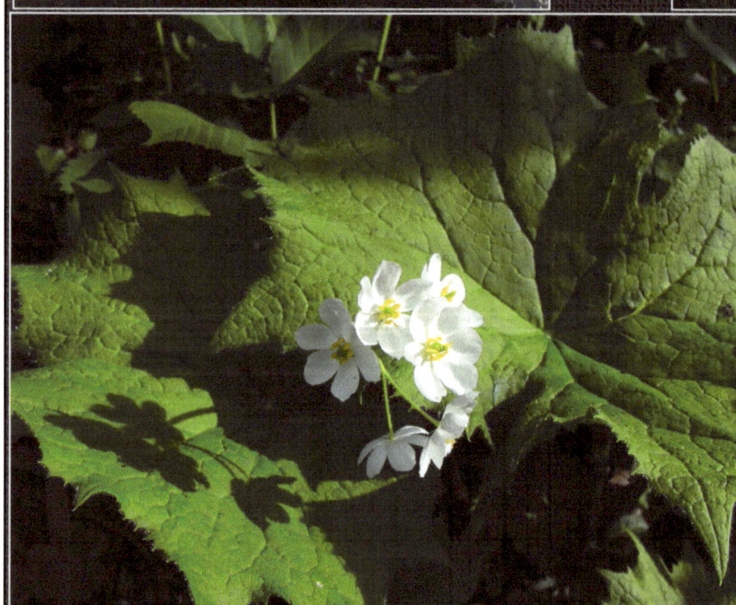

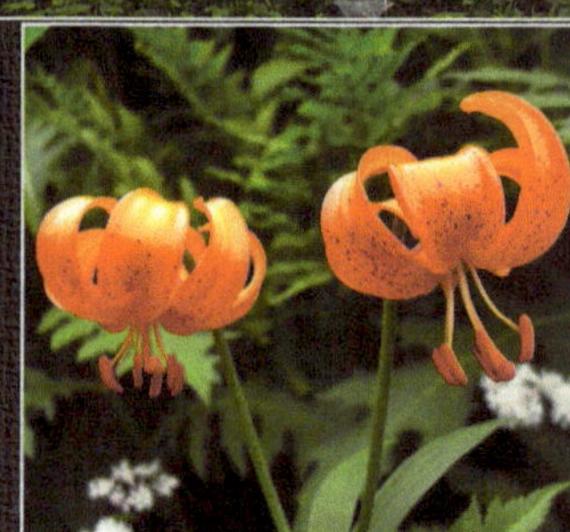

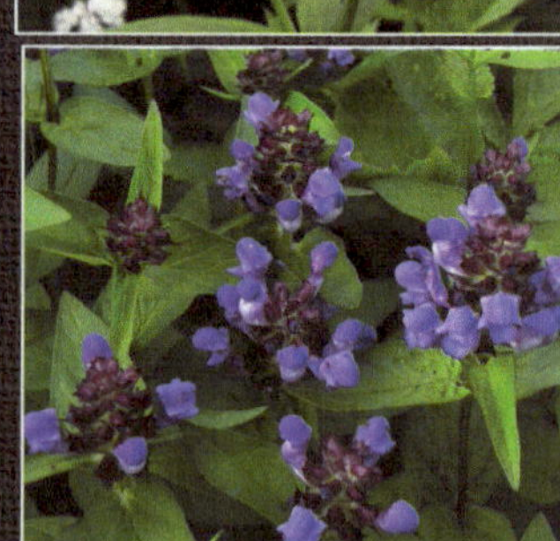

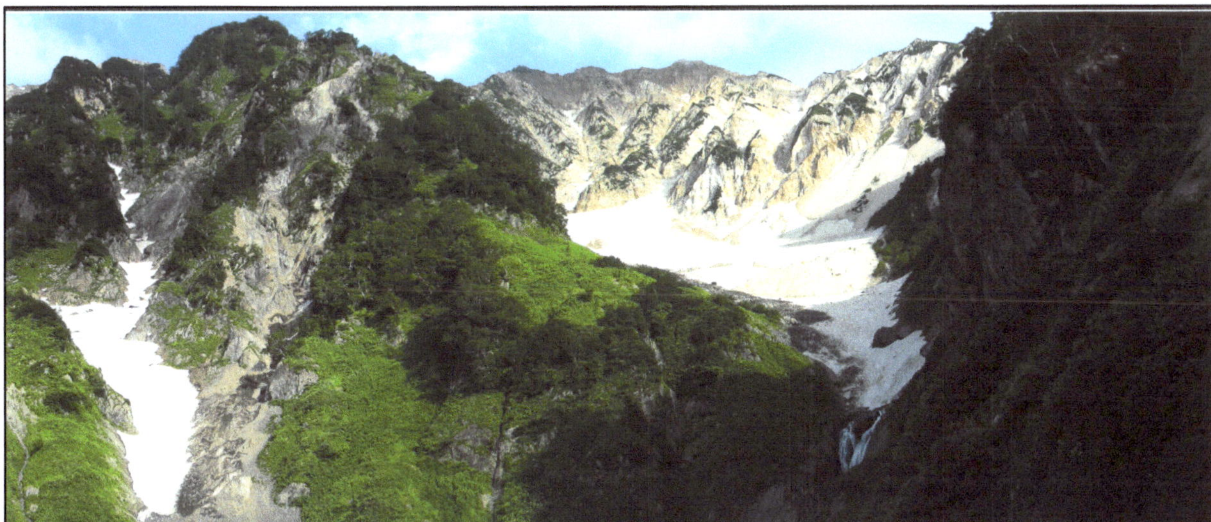

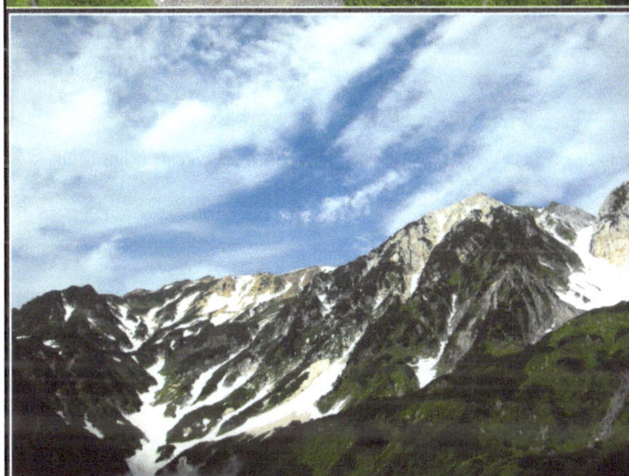

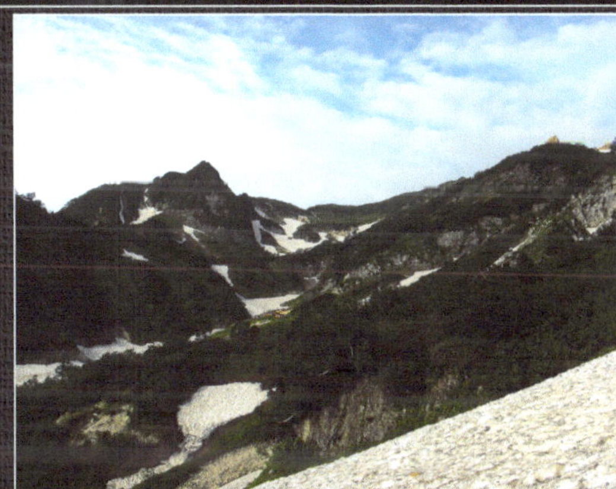

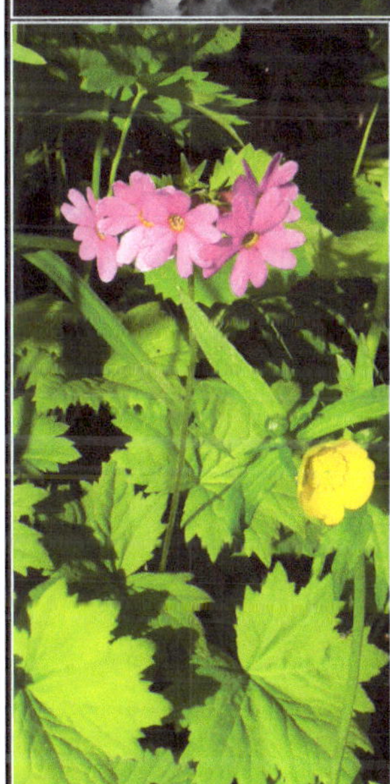

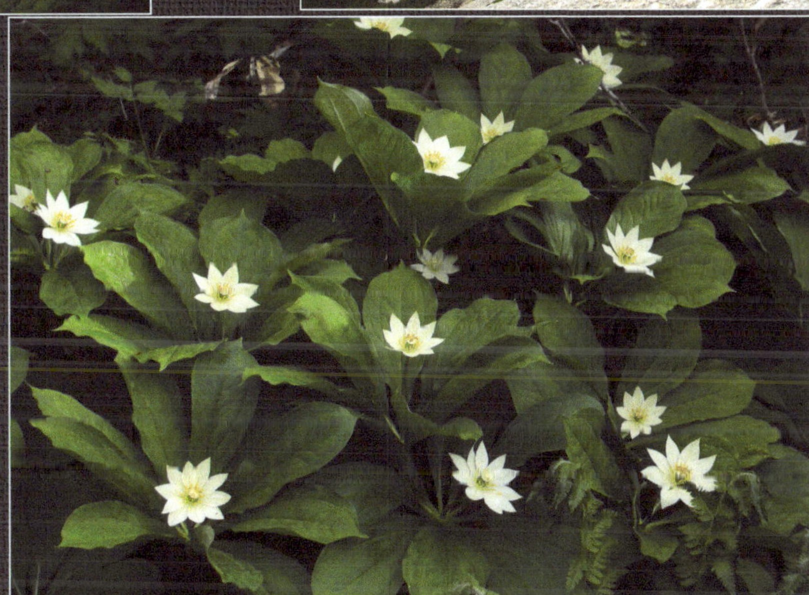

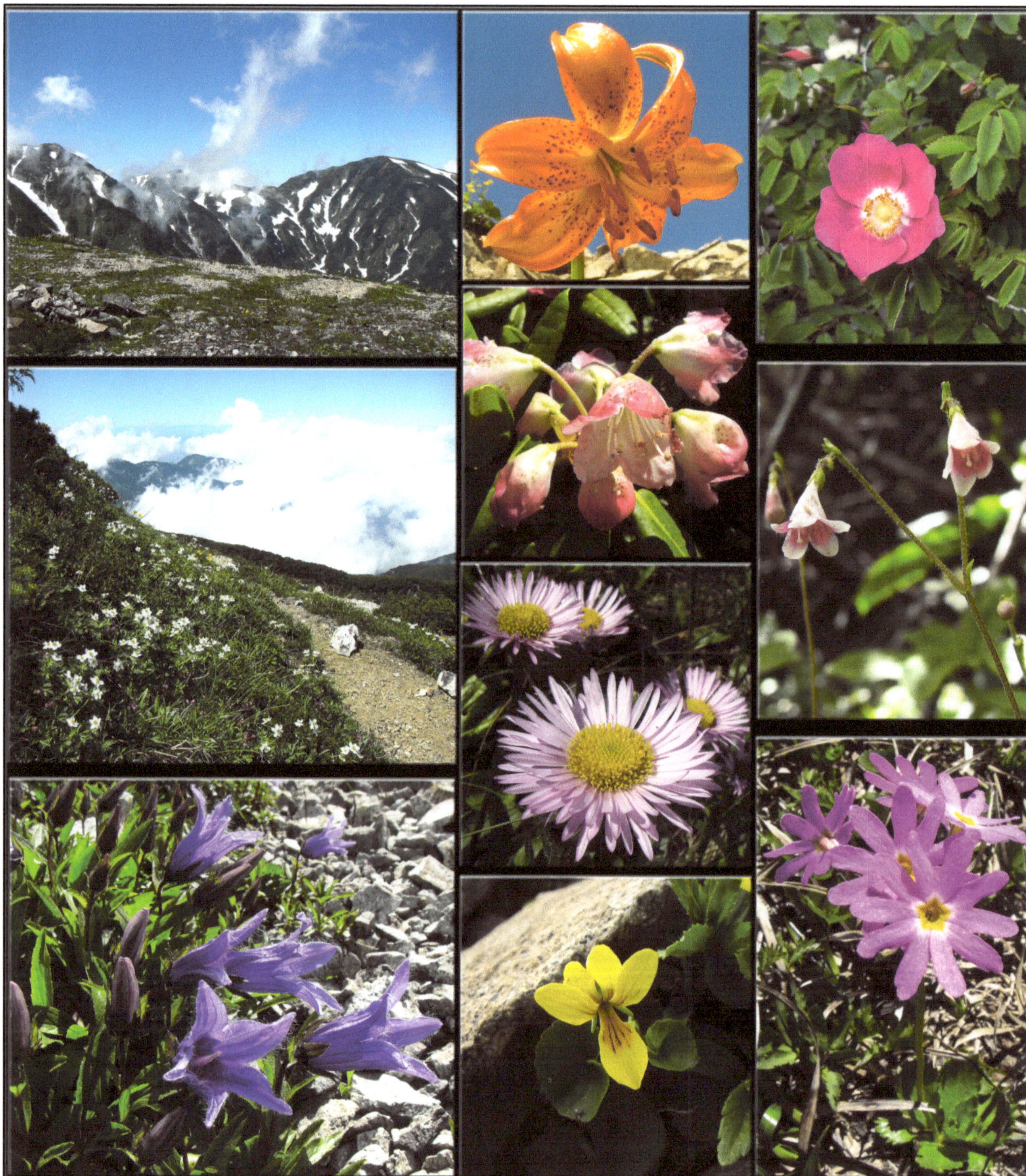

On the previous several pages we have shown you a number of collages of our **Hakuba Mountains** trip. Some of these photos are ones which you have already seen as we progressed through this astounding adventure and some of them are photos which you have not yet seen.

On pages 150 and 151 the photo at the top is a panorama and continues (with some overlap) from page 150 to page 151. Below that panorama you can see several flowers which we saw on this trip. You have also seen some of these species in association with other adventures.

On pages 152 and 153 the photos at the top and also at the bottom are panoramic images (with some overlap). The red-jacketed person in two of the photos is me.

On pages 154 and 155 the top photo is once again a panorama (with some overlap). Most (but not all) of these photos were taken on the final day of this adventure as we descended from Yari Hot Spring to the bus stop.

By the way, we failed to mention the fact that we had to cross some huge snowfields on the descent from **Yari Hot Spring** – something which we were not aware that we would have to do. When we started hiking it was only around 4:45 AM, so the snow was still frozen hard. We did not have crampons. It was very dangerous – so much so that we were scared that we were going to die. We did not show you any specific photos of the snow fields which we had to cross, but they were steep enough so that if we would have slipped there would have been nothing to stop us. We had no means of self-arrest. We would have slid until we hit the rocks at the bottom of the snowfields. As we descended over the snowfields we kicked in with our boots as much as we could and went very slowly! We weren't doing much talking or taking many photos while we were crossing the three snowfields which we had to cross. You can get an idea of what we crossed in the top panoramic image on pages 154 and 155.

The final photo collage of this adventure, on page 156 shows you some mountain scenery and also some flowers.

Now we will stay much closer to home for a while. The photo on the following page is a ***Cymbidium nipponicum*** a.k.a ***C. macrorhizon*** a saprophytic species of Cymbidium Orchid. It is a saprophyte on various species of tree roots. We find this species at **Jindai Botanical Garden** in the summer.

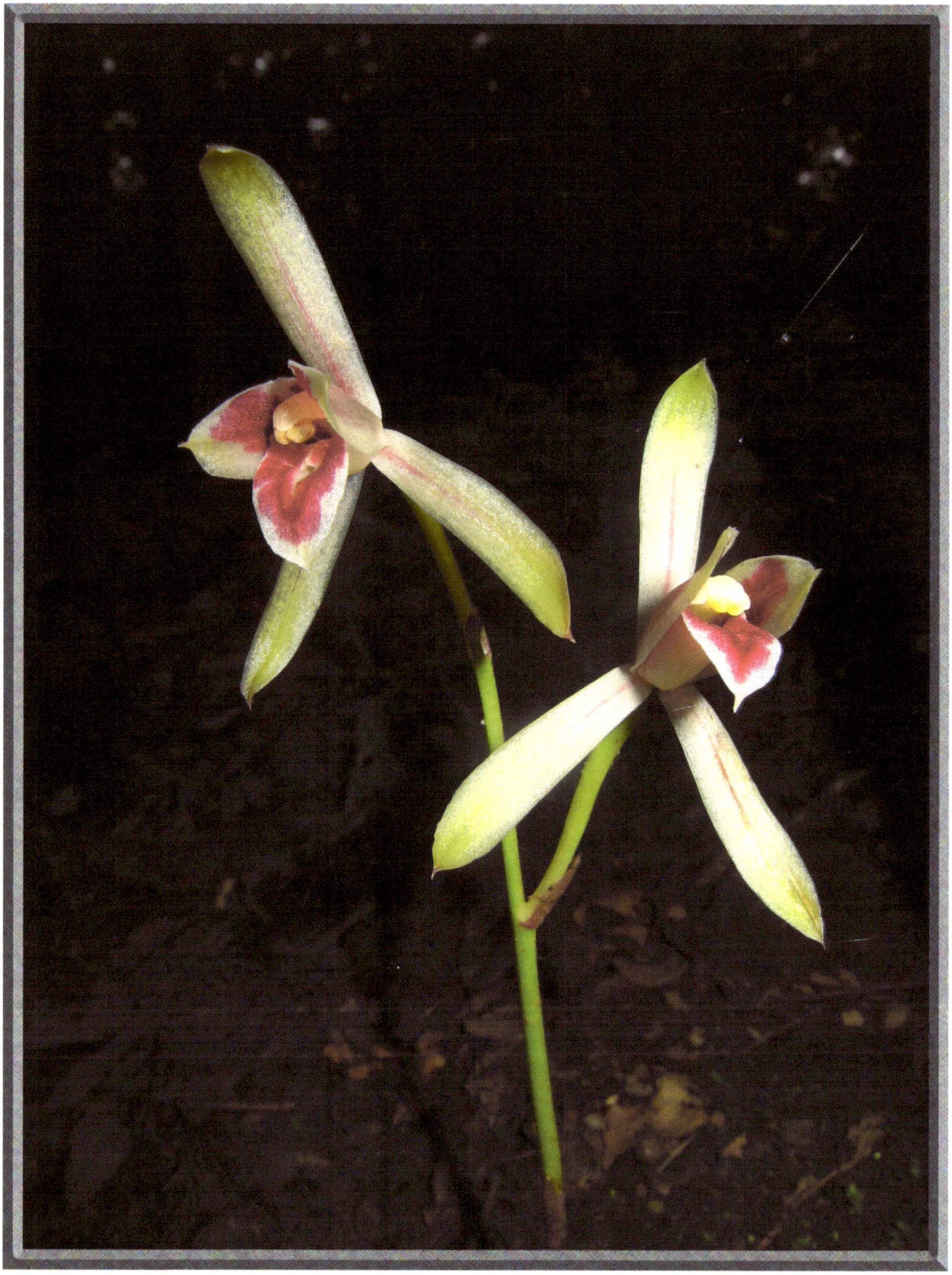

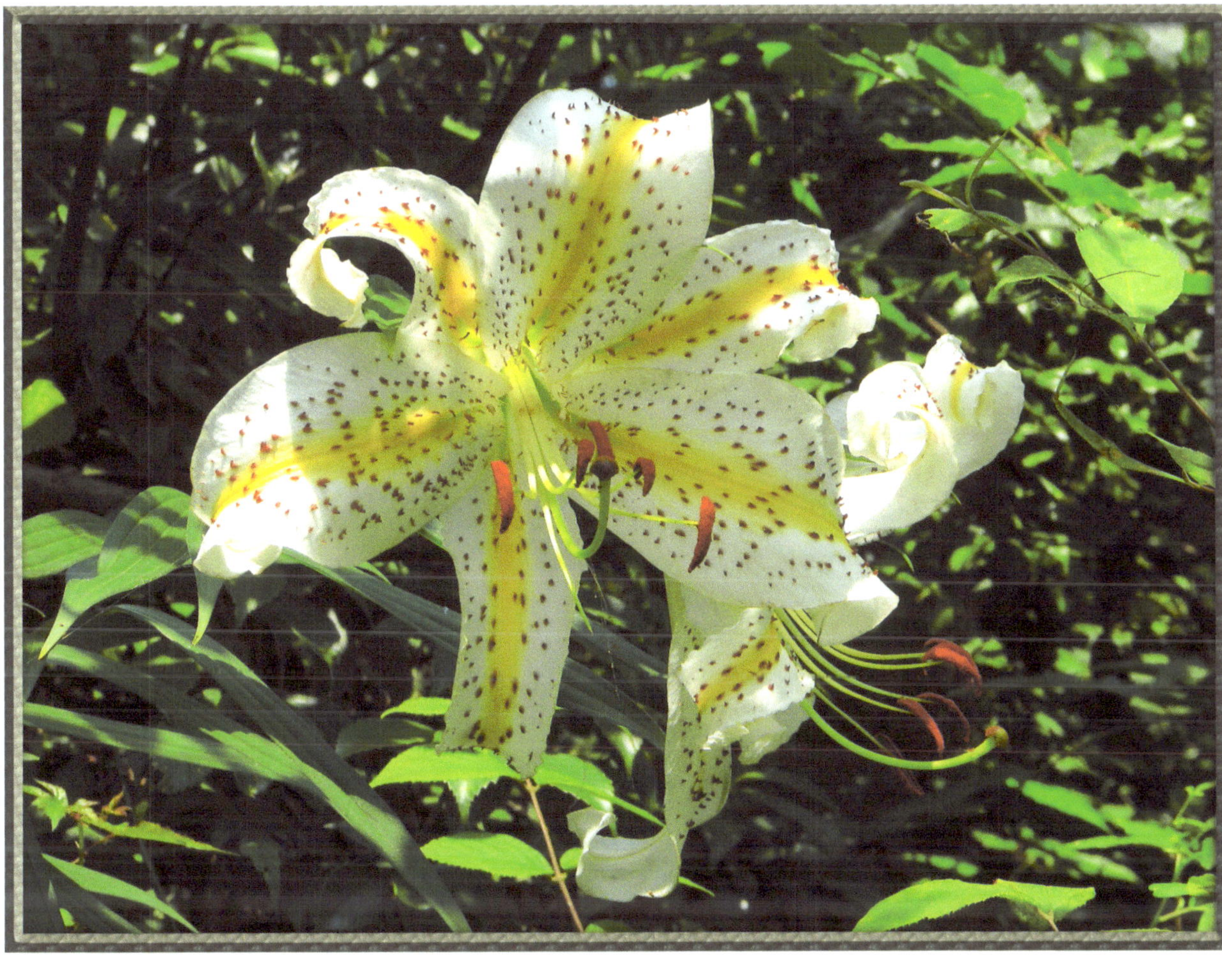

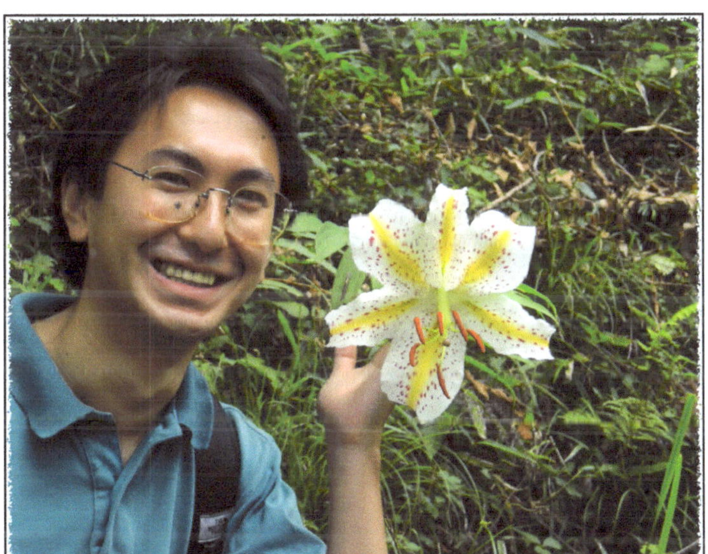

This flower is a **Mountain Lily** (***Lilium auratum***) or ***Yama-Yuri*** in Japanese. These huge lily flowers can be found in the mountains from late July into the first two weeks of August. This particular photo was taken at **Mt. Takao**. You would not believe how large these flowers are. In the above photo there is really nothing which you can use to judge the size of it. The photo to the left, therefore, gives you something to judge how large this flower actually is.

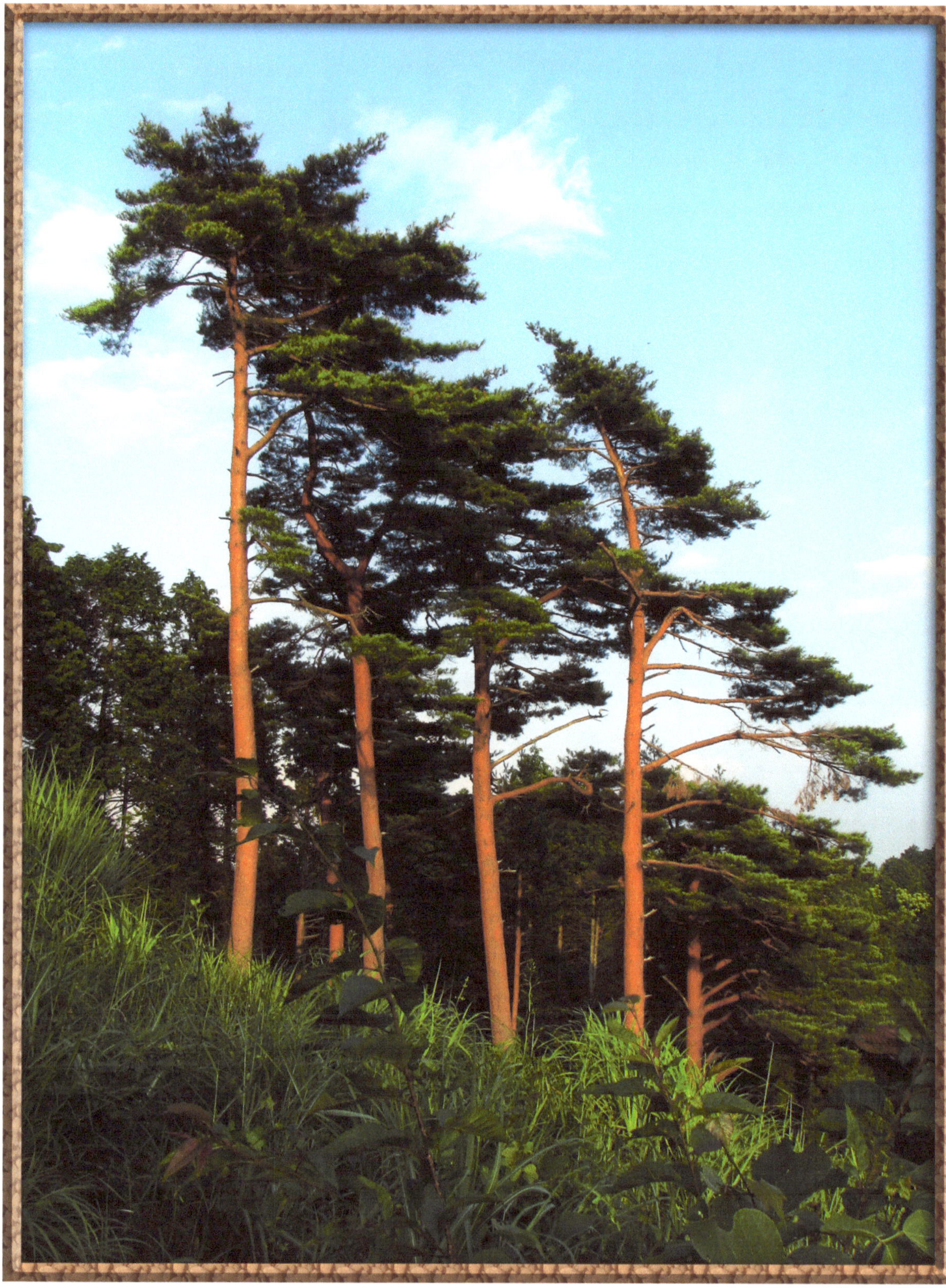

On this and the facing page are the final three photos for July. The photo on the facing page displays some setting sun colors on some Japanese Red Pine trees (***Pinus densiflora***) near **Mt. Takao**.

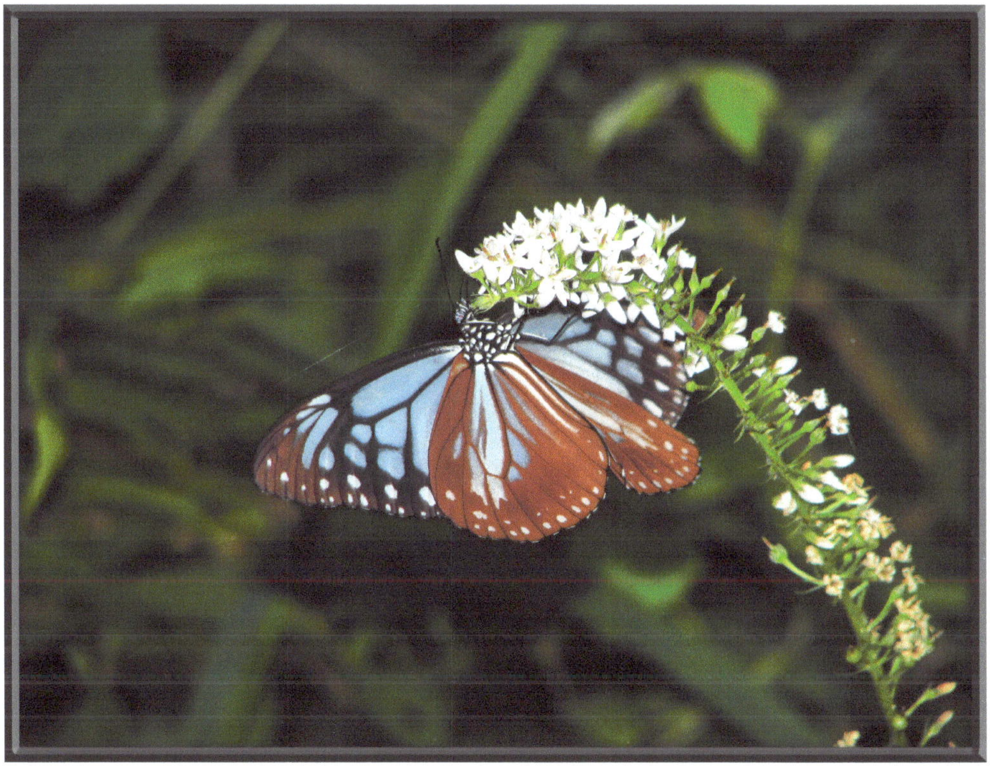

The two photos on this page show you two species of beautiful butterflies. On page 134 we promised that we'd show you two species of butterflies later in the month. Here are those two photos. Sorry, we don't know the scientific names of these butterflies.

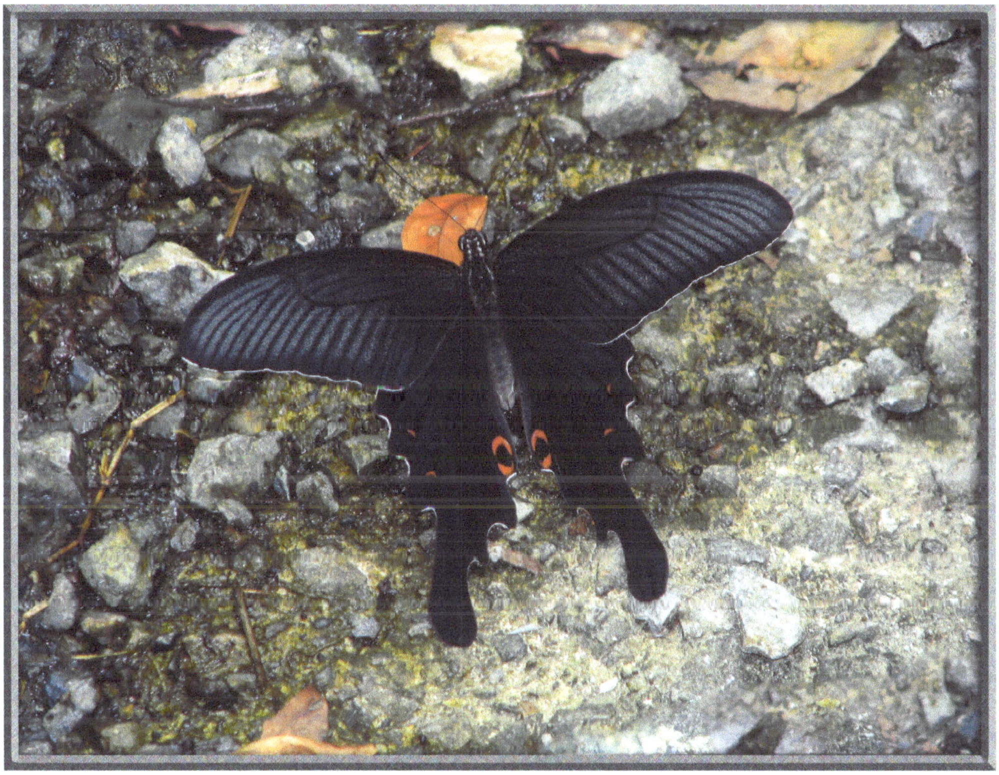

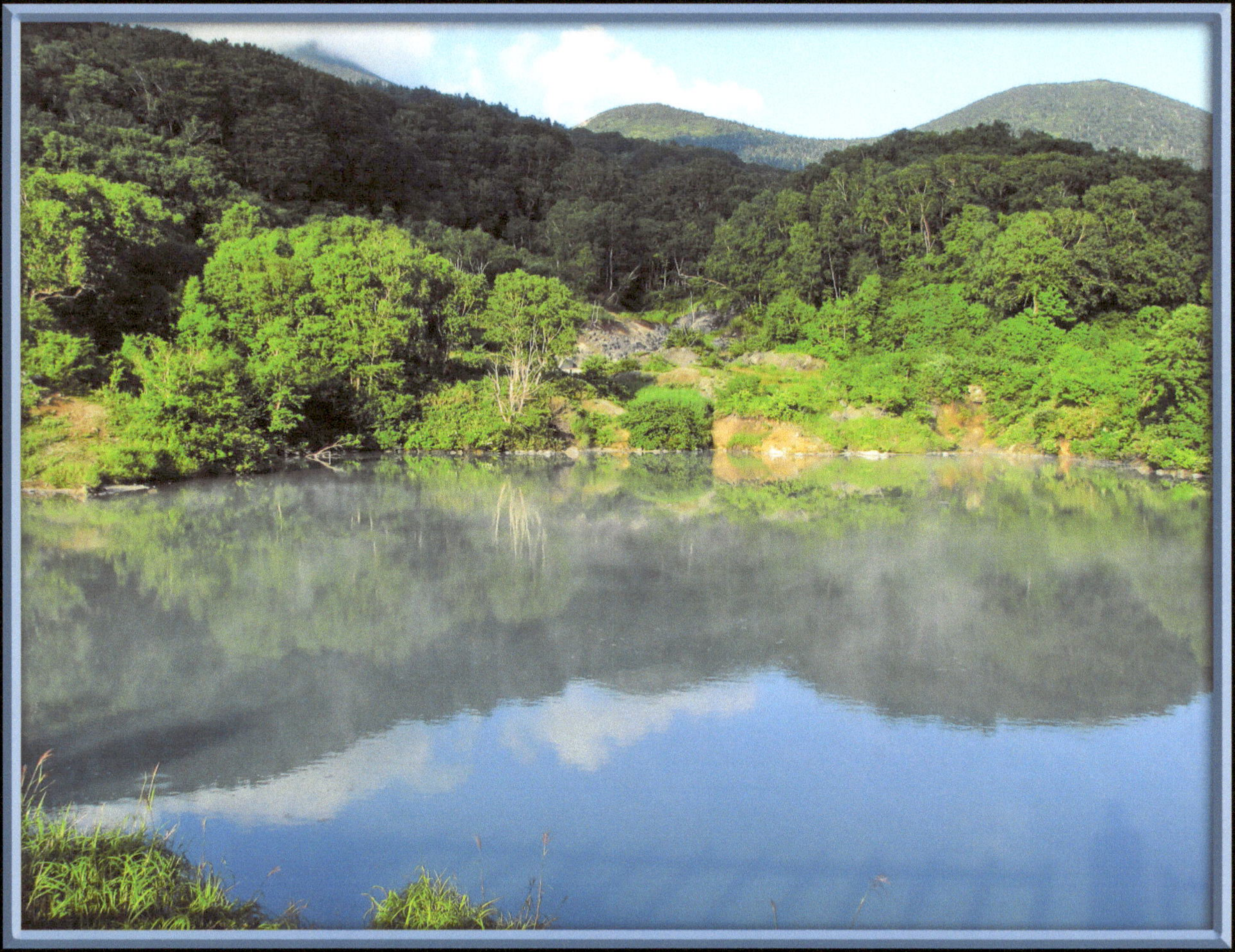

August Photos and Story

Here we begin August photos. The photo just above is **Jigokunuma**. Literally that translates as **Hell's Pond**. Why? That is steam rising off the surface of the water. Every minute 2,700 liters of highly acidic, 90° C water is coming up out of the bottom of this swamp. This is at the base of **Mt. Hakkoda** (1,584.4 meters = 5,198 feet) and very close to **Sukayu Hot Spring** – in **Aomori Prefecture**. You can see a portion of Mt. Hakkoda in the background of this photo. We climbed it the following day.

On the facing page is a stunningly impressive photo of an ***Abies mariesii* f. *hayachinensis*** – a **Maries' Fir**. It is named after the English plant collector Charles Maries (1851-1902), who introduced the species to Britain in 1879. This true fir was quite common on **Mt. Hakkoda**.

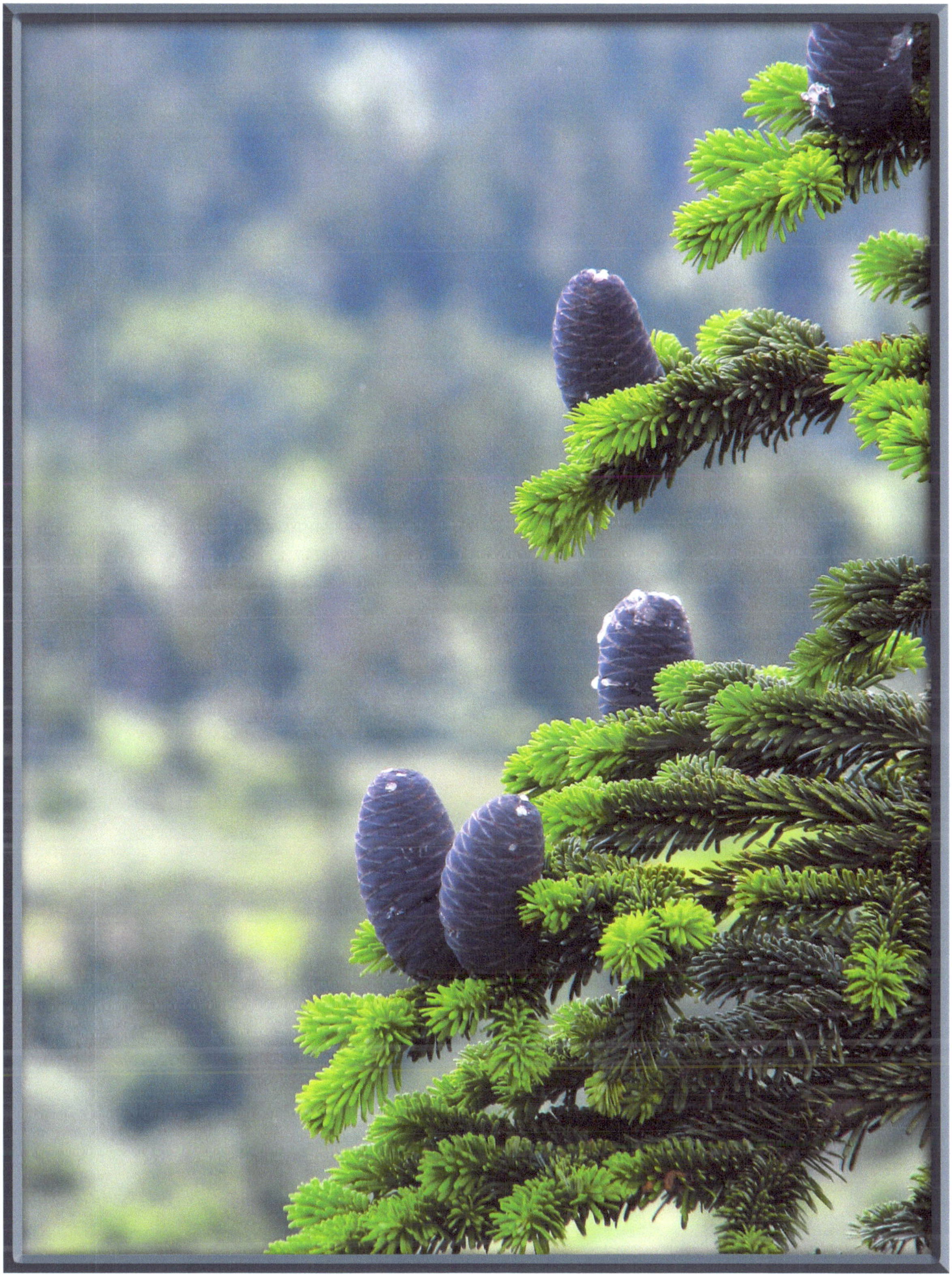

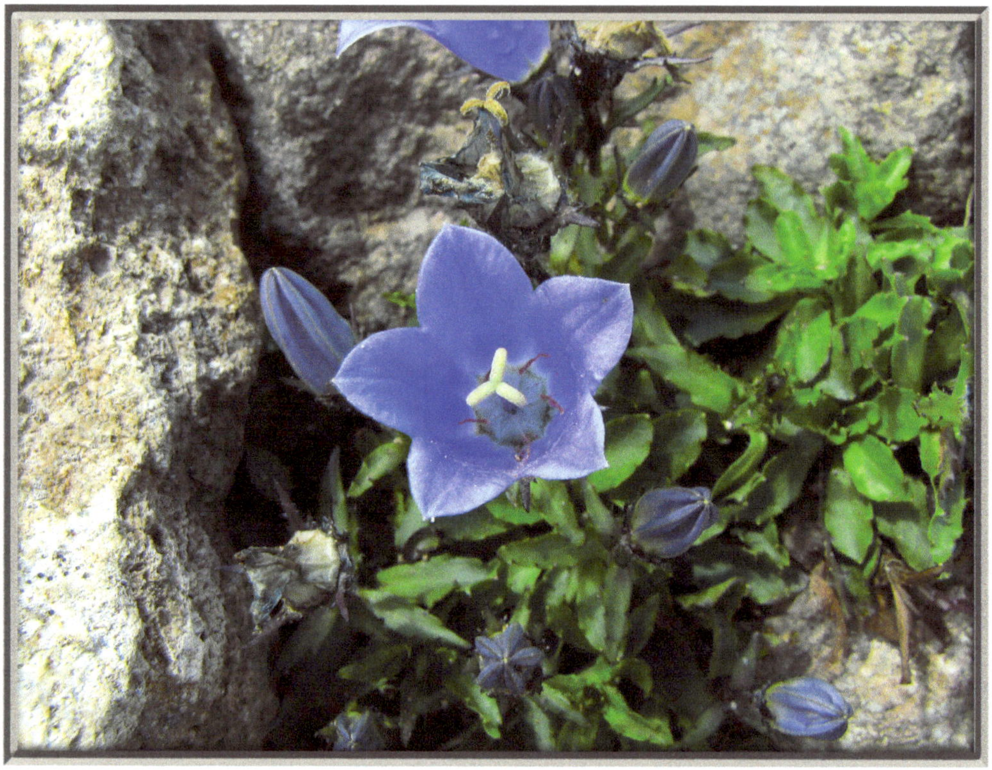

To the left is a photo of a ***Campanula lasiocarpa*** flower. This is a stunningly beautiful photo with its bright blue color. This was seen on our Mt. Hakkoda climb.

The photo to the right was taken at the summit of **Mt. Hakkoda** (1,584 meters = 5,198 feet). We called this **"Dragonfly Horror Movie"**. Of course the dragonflies did not attack us, but the sky was filled with them. It was the most dragonflies we had ever seen at one time or place.

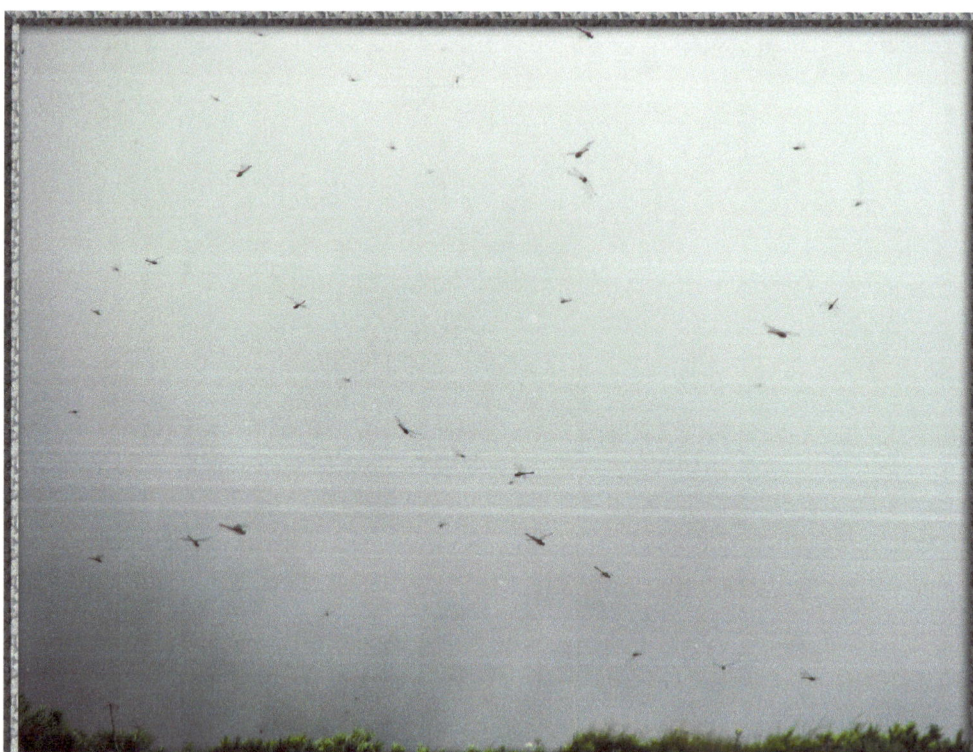

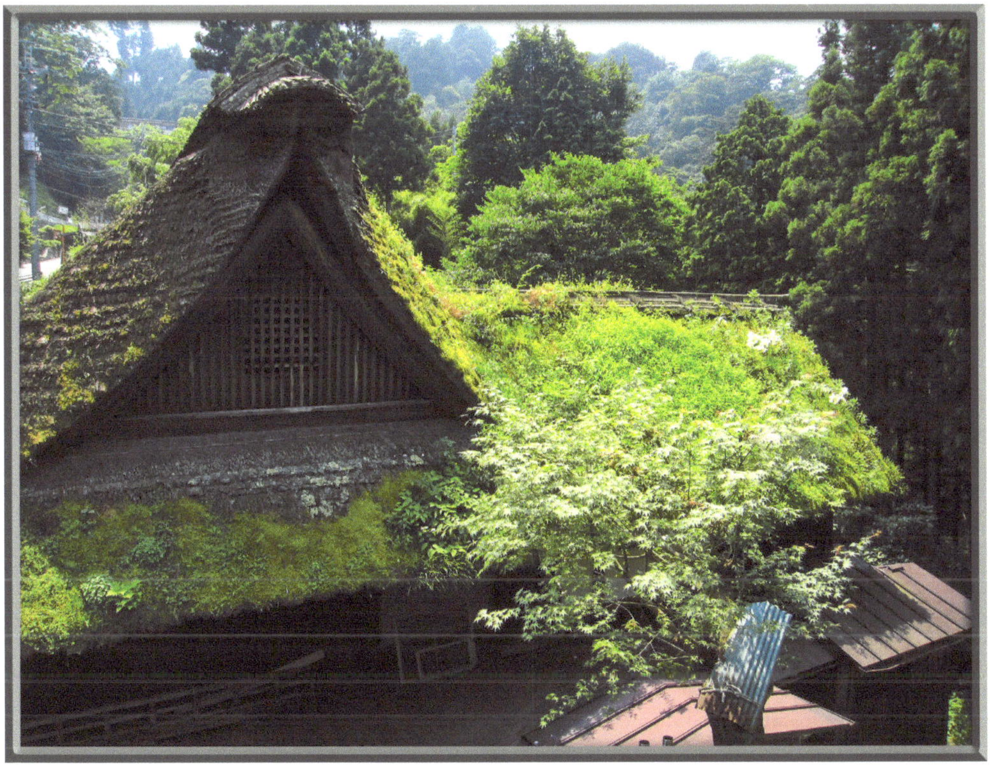

The photo to the left shows an amazing grass roof on an old building at **Mt. Mitake**. You may recall that **Mt. Mitake** is in **Western Tokyo** and it is 929 meters (= 3,048 feet).

To the right is a **"Plant-in-a-Bottle"**. This was totally natural. I was walking on a mountain trail and felt something hard and unnaturally even under my feet. I bent down and brushed aside the soil and found this bottle. We cleaned off some of the dirt, photographed it and stuck it back under the ground where we found it. Amazing!

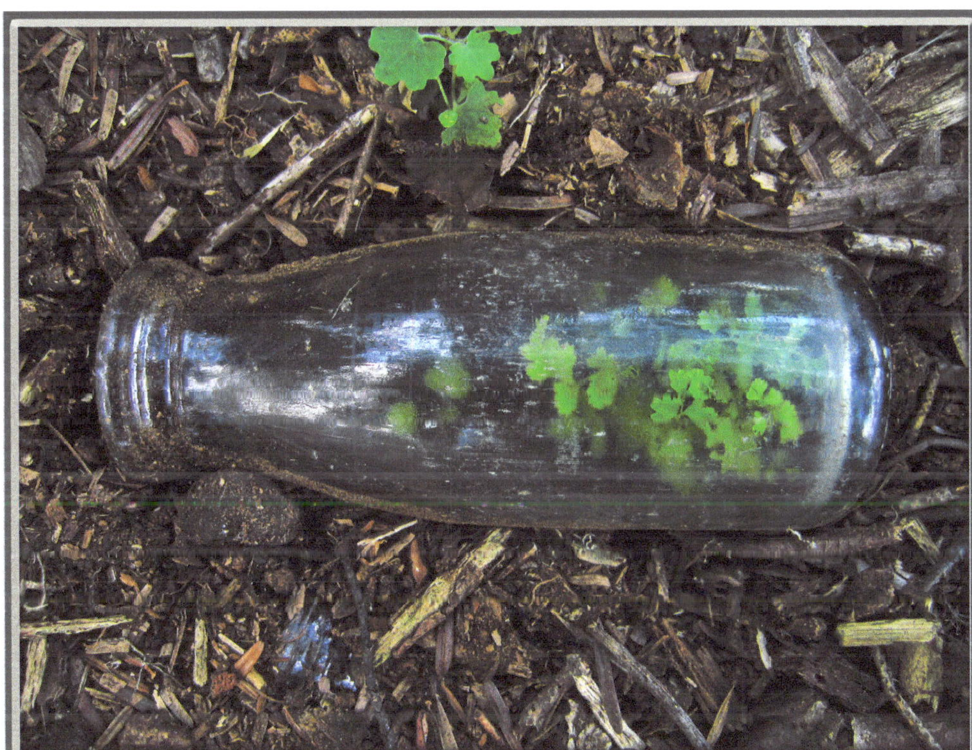

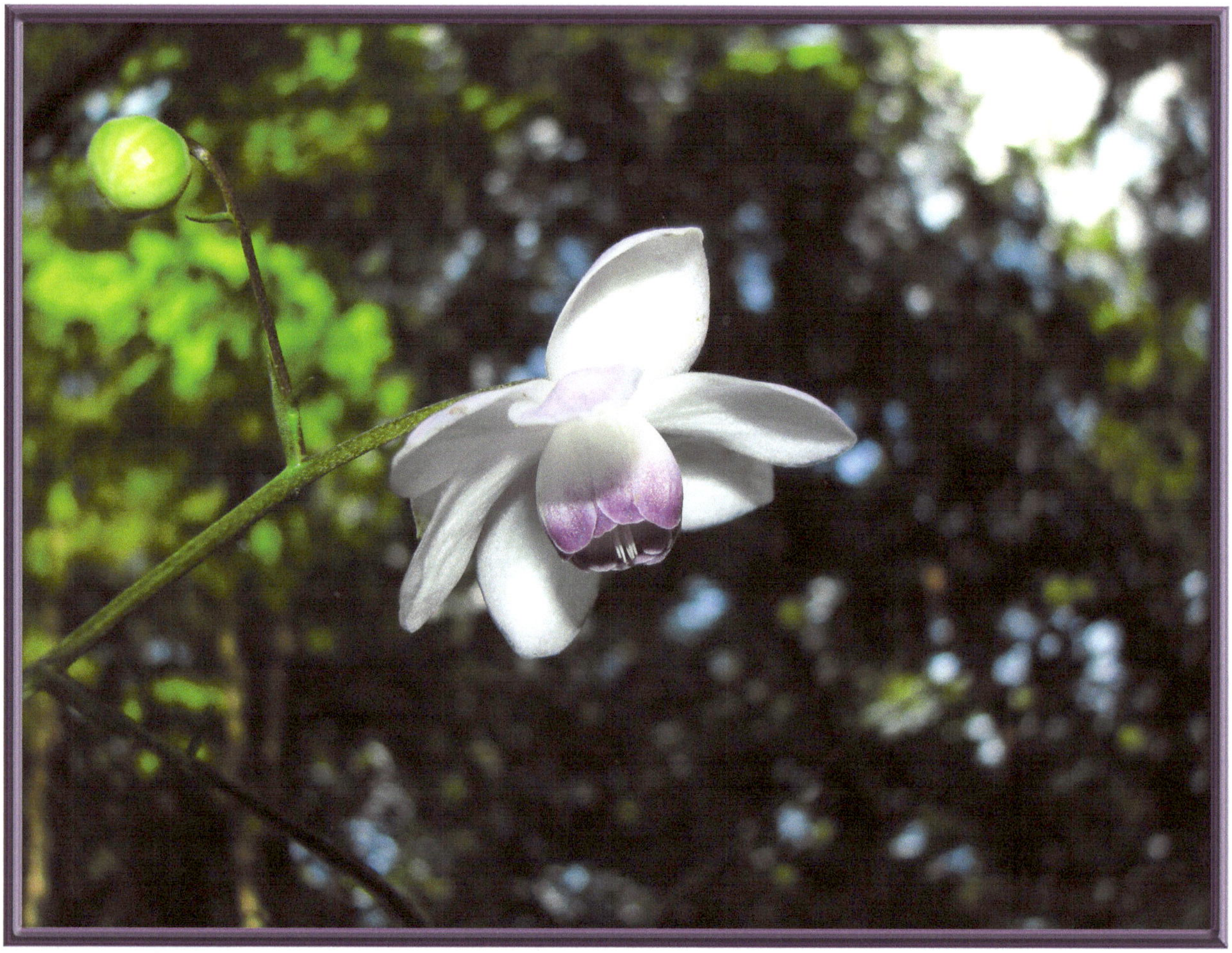

Every year near the beginning of August – maybe up to the end of the second week of the month – we try and go to **Mt. Mitake** for the ***Anemonopsis macrophylla*** a.k.a. ***Anemonopsis heterophylla***. This plant is commonly called the **False Anemone** (***Rengeshouma*** in Japanese). There is a single area on the side of Mt. Mitake where this plant grows in great abundance. There is an annual festival and many people visit here specifically to see this flower.

The photo on the facing page is also an ***Anemonopsis macrophylla*** – a two photo collage. In both of the photos in this collage you can see some buds in addition to the flowers. If you are in the Tokyo Area during the first half of August it is worth the time and effort to visit Mt. Mitake to see this flower.

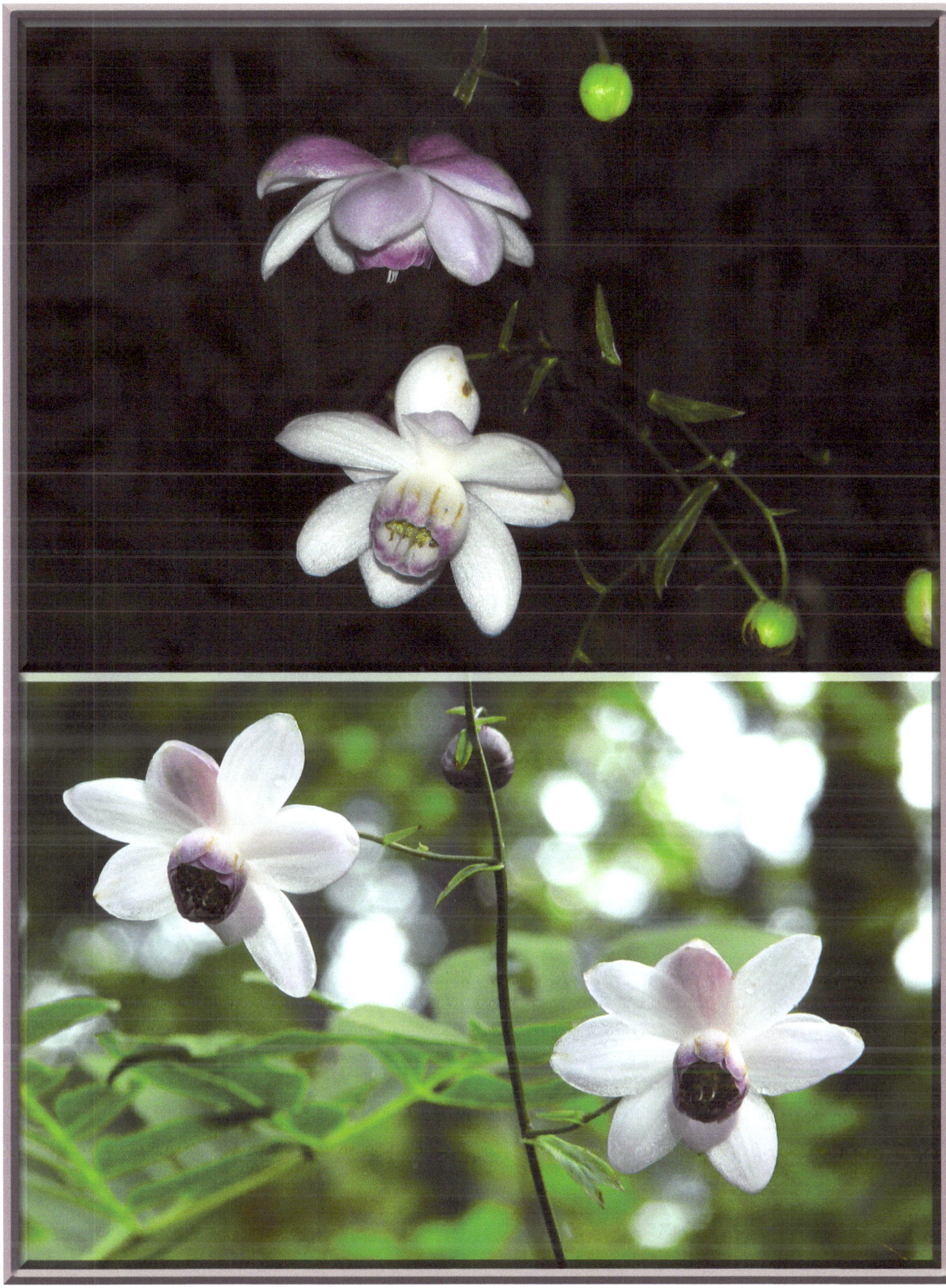

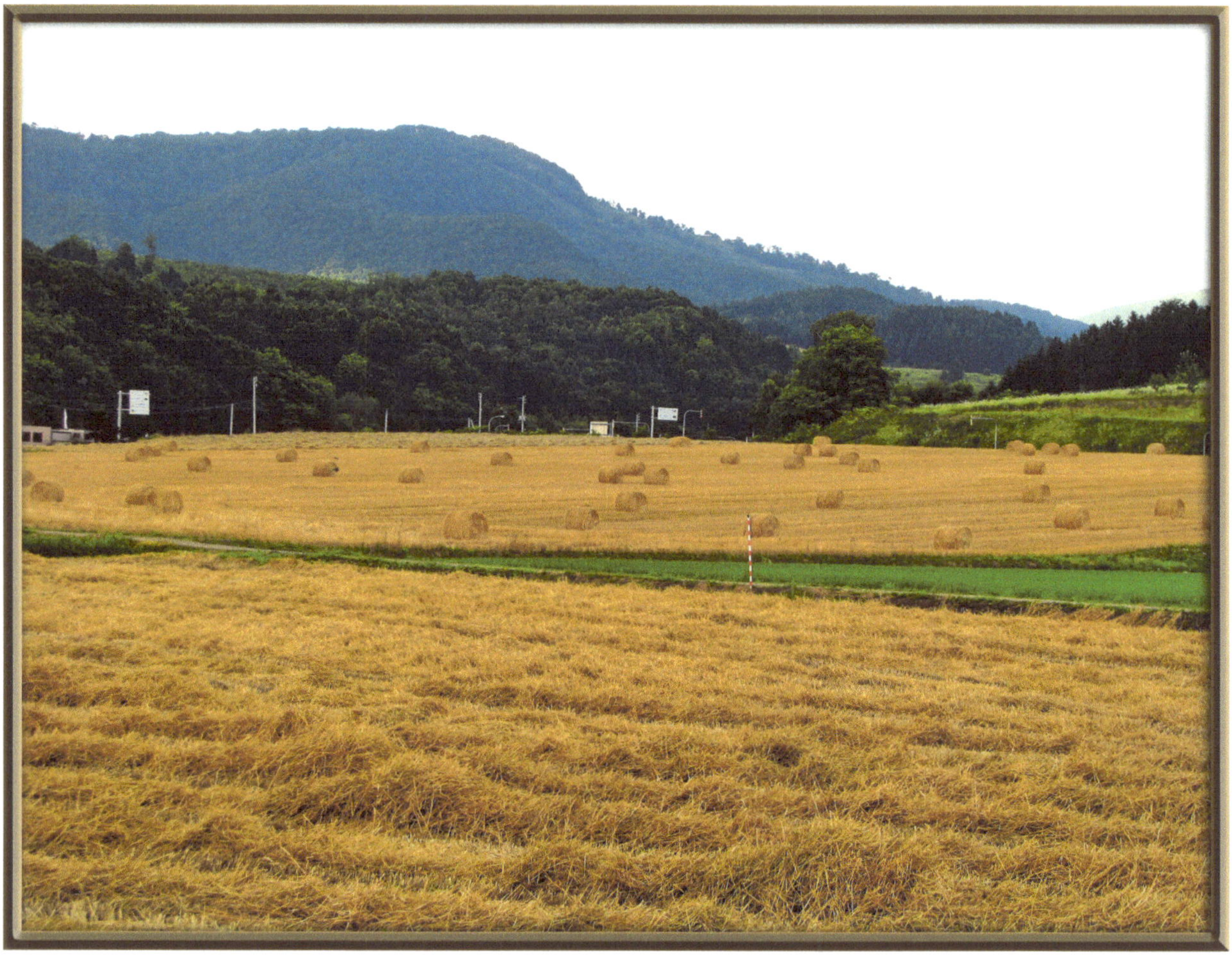

We have gone to **Hokkaido** for our August vacations two times. This photo of a hay field was taken near **Nisshin, Hokkaido.** We found a Youth Hostel north of **Asahikawa** and Nisshin was where it was located. This picturesque hay field was near the Youth Hostel.

On the facing page (upper photo) you can see the **Nisshin Train Station** in top position. Not very big is it?

On the facing page in lower position is another train station which we passed on Hokkaido as we traveled north to **Wakkanai.** This one is impressive for its "handicapped ramp". We were told that the temperature can drop to minus 30° C here in the winter. Nice that there is a heated "station" (note the small chimney) isn't it. We had to wonder if there are an abundance of train delays when the temperature is minus 30° C.

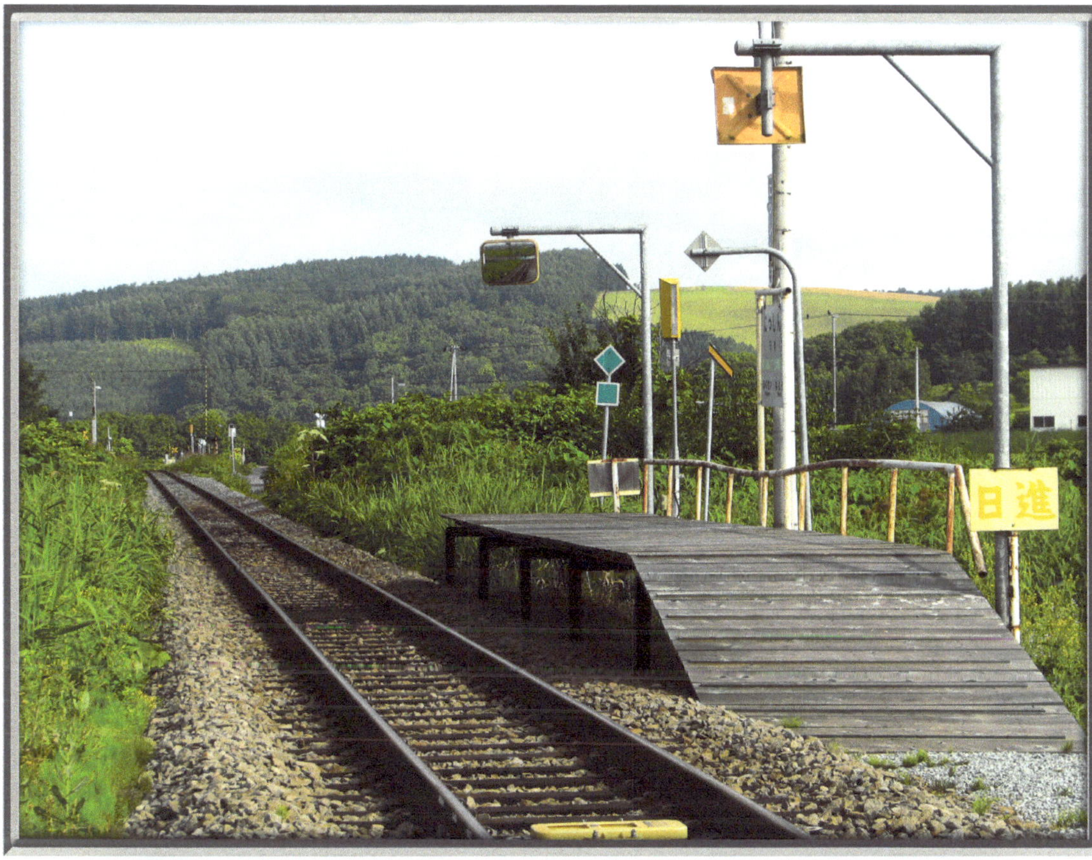
日進

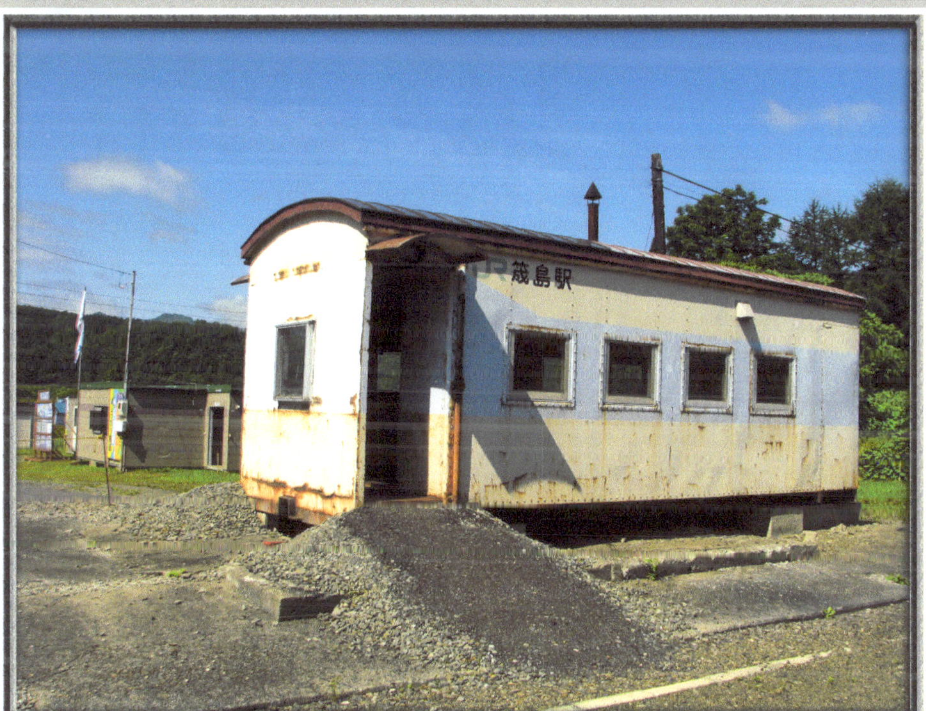
筬島駅

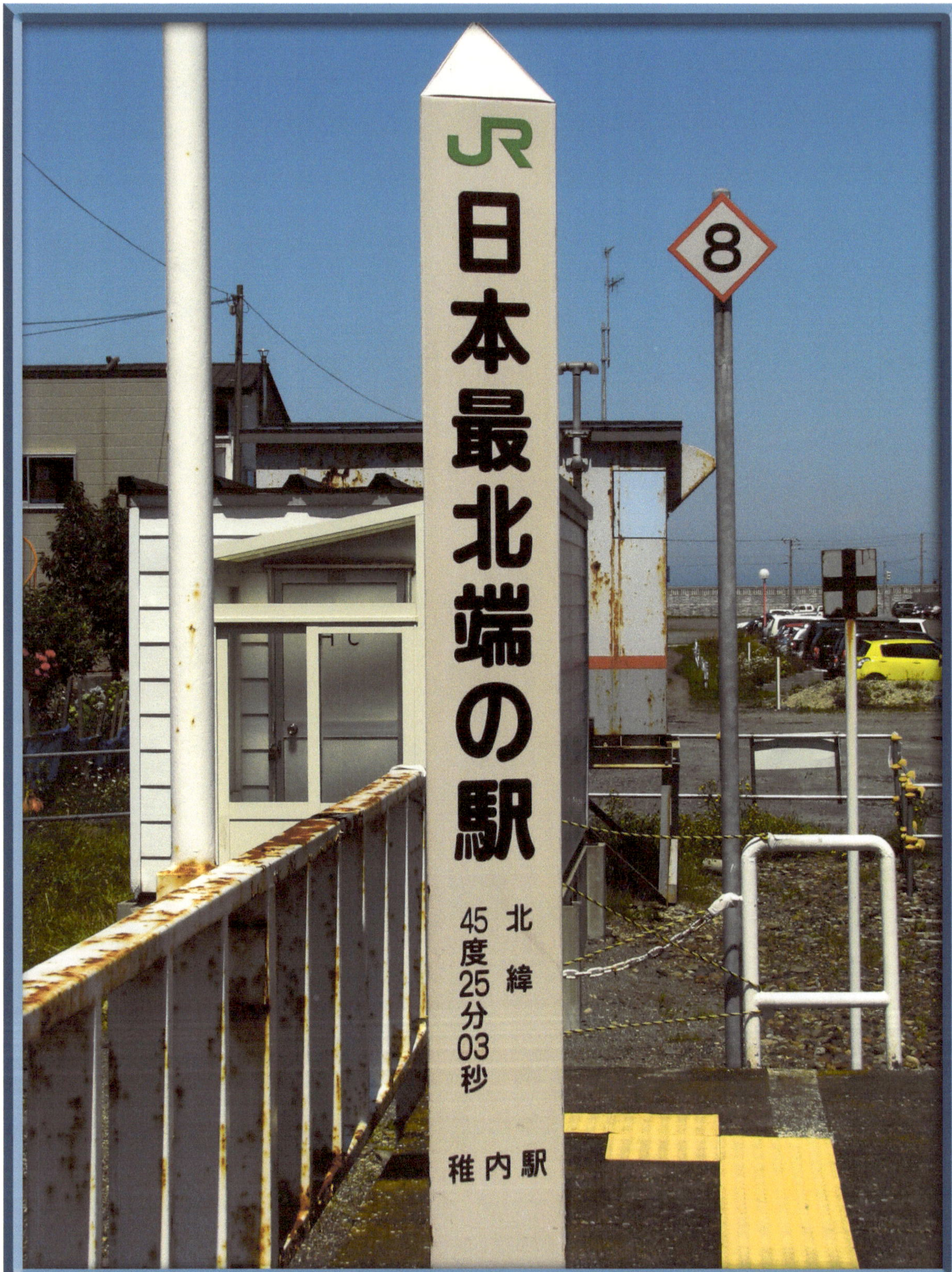
JR
日本最北端の駅
北緯
45度25分03秒
稚内駅
8

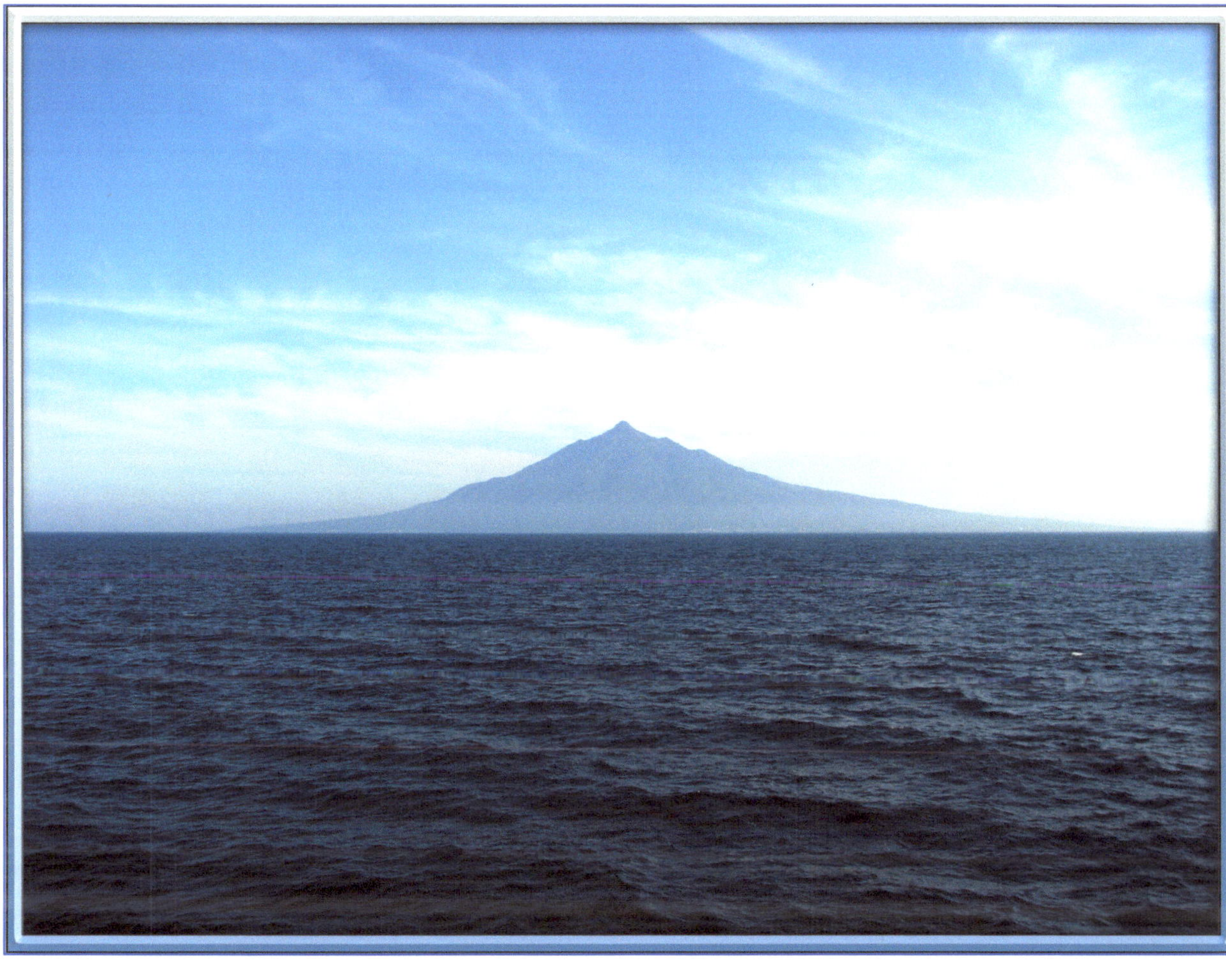

The photo on the facing page is of a sign at **Wakkanai Train Station** on **Hokkaido**. It notifies people that this is the furthest north train station in Japan. It says that we are at 45° 25' 03" North Latitude. Wakkanai is an interesting small city. This is very close to **Sakhalin Island, Russia**. There are many Russian speakers here and most of the signs in town are in Japanese, Russian and English.

The above photo is of **Rishiri Island**. From **Wakkanai** we took a ferry to **Rebun Island**. While on the ferry we passed by **Rishiri Island**. **Mt. Rishiri** is 1,721 meters (= 5,646 feet). We did not visit Rishiri Island. We went directly to **Rebun Island** and hiked around there for two days. We thoroughly enjoyed every moment of this vacation. By the way, it may interest you to know that Hokkaido is often called **"The Alaska of Japan"**. This means that it is the furthest north part of Japan and also the most "wild" place in Japan. It is true too – we have seen a bear on each visit we have made to Hokkaido.

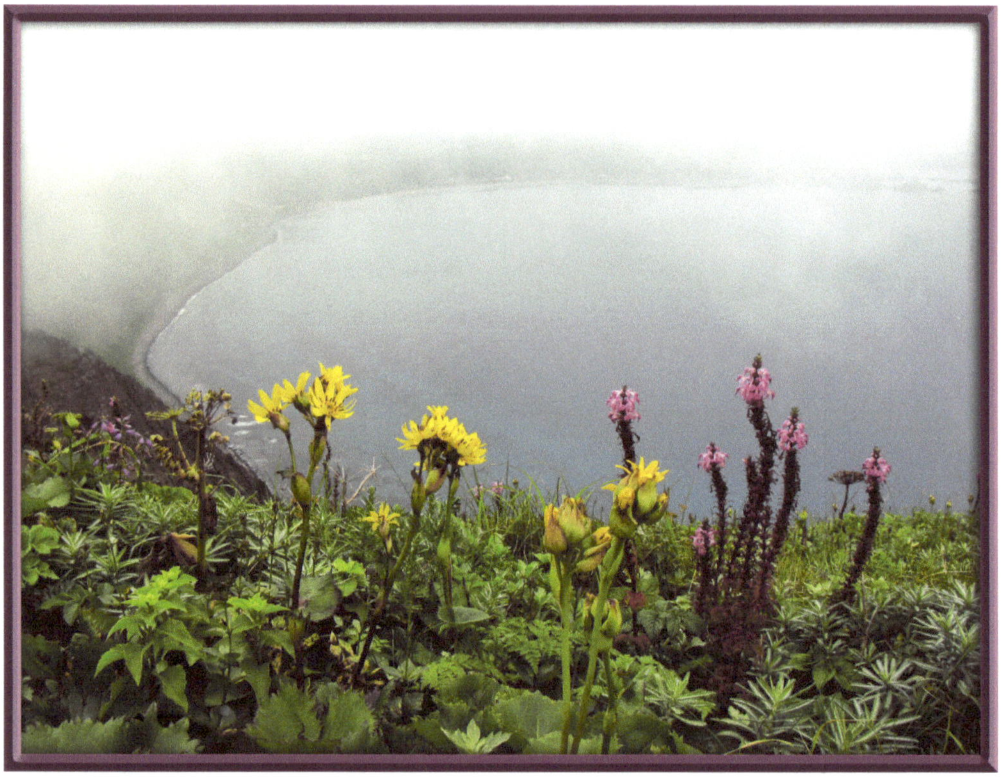

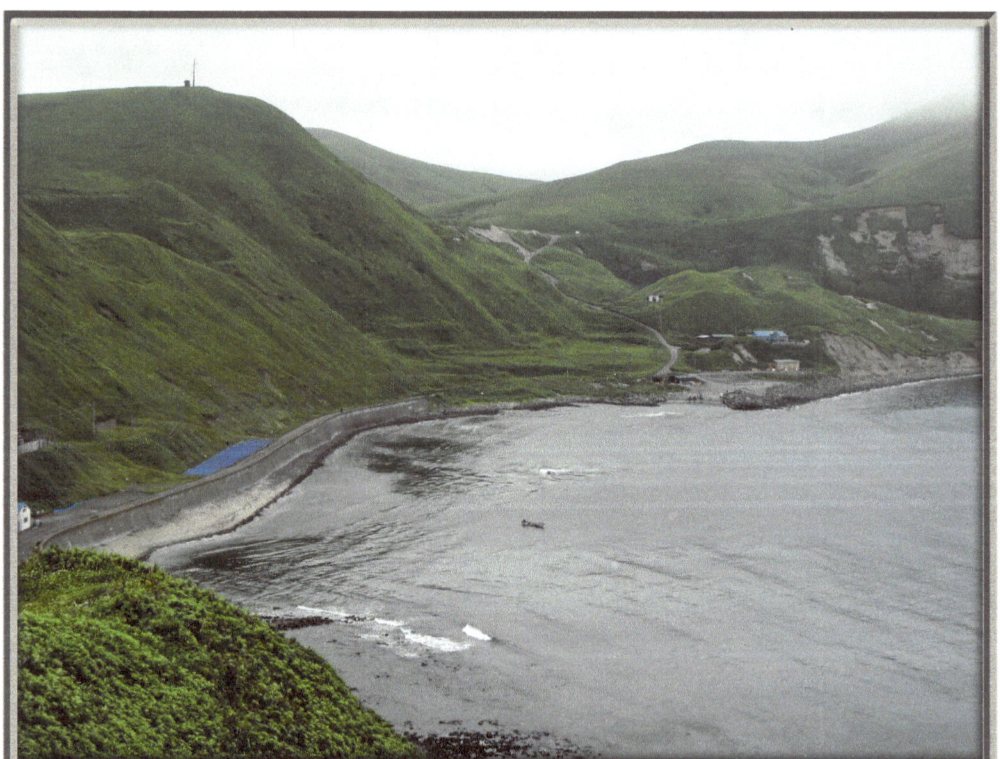

The first night we were on **Rebun Island** we stayed at a place called the **"Field Inn"**. It is located pretty much on the northern tip of **Rebun Island**. The next day we hiked southward and these two photos – show two different locations we hiked past. The upper photo was taken between **Cape Sukoton** and **Cape Gorota** and is pretty for its clouds, ocean and flowers. The lower photo was also taken as we hiked from **Cape Sukoton** to **Cape Gorota**. It was still somewhat cloudy, but less so than in the upper photo. Note the lack of much civilization.

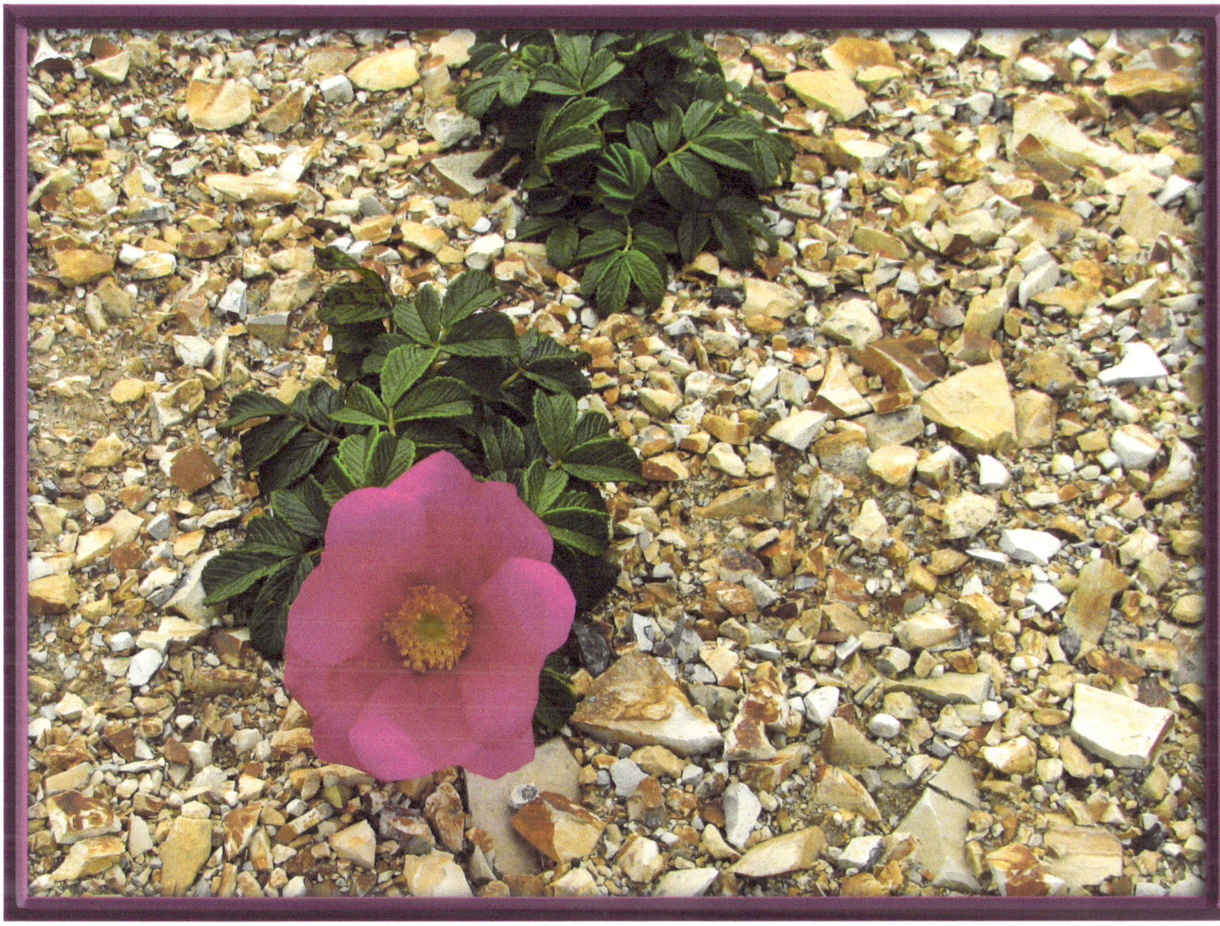

Here (above) is an amazing rose which we found. This is ***Rosa rugosa***. It is such a small and beautiful little member of the rose family. There were not very many of this plant. And, look at the conditions which it grows under! The soil here is a solid rock scree slope. We found so many amazing flowers as we hiked south.

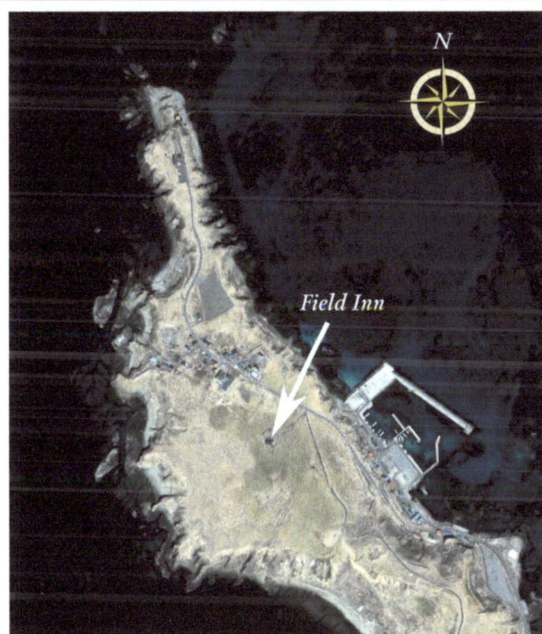

By the way, the **Field Inn** – the Inn where we stayed last night – can be found on **Rebun Island** using **Google Earth**. The location is 45° 27' 21.07" North Latitude and 140° 58' 17.48" East Longitude. We have borrowed the image to the right from Google Earth. This shows only the very northern tip of Rebun Island.

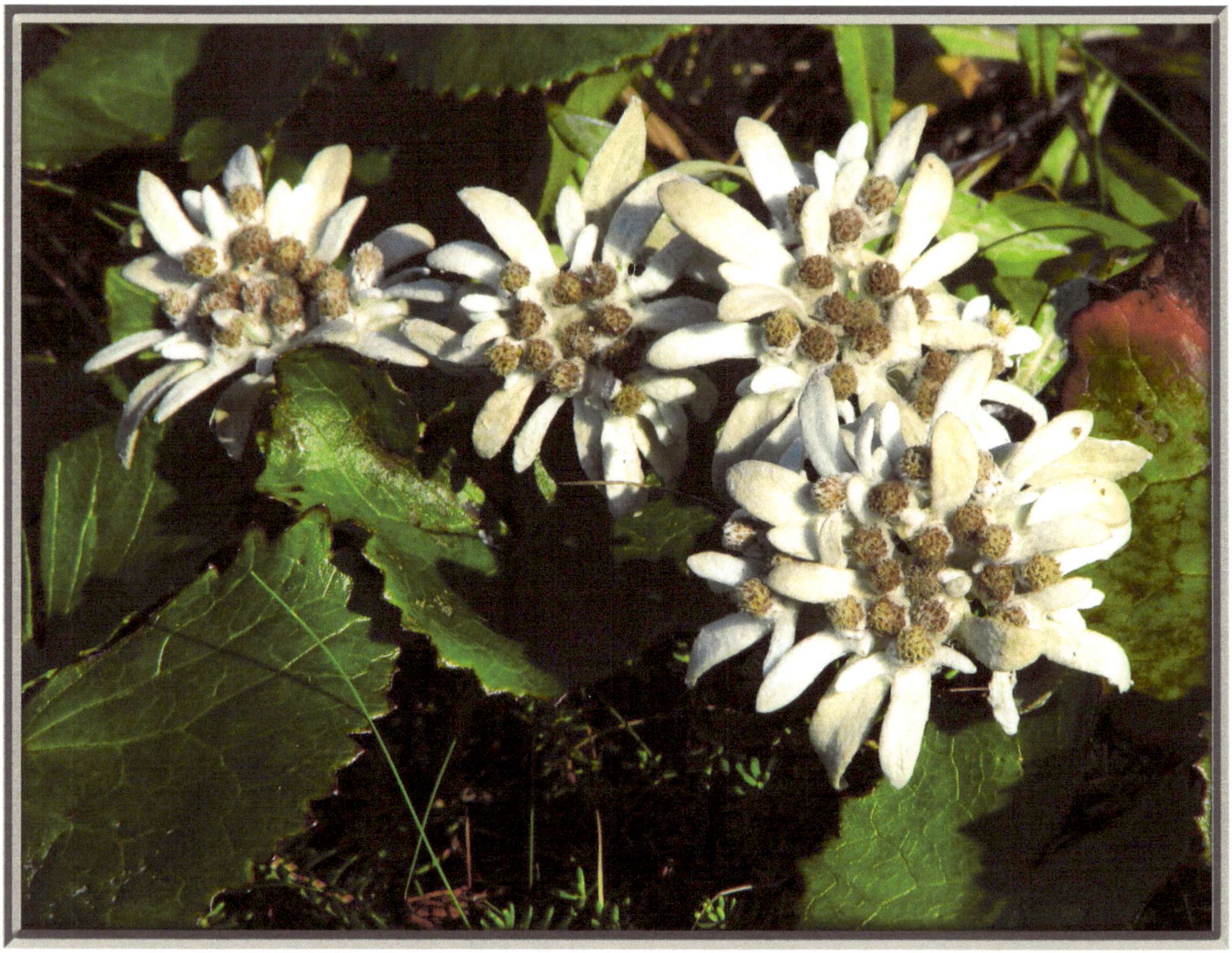

The above shot is the type of **Edelweiss** we found on **Rebun Island**. It is ***Leontopodium discolor***. Most of the leaves you can see in this photo do NOT belong to the Edelweiss. The Edelweiss leaves are the long and skinny ones near the upper right hand corner of the photo. We were amazed to find this species in the numbers which were present. We had read about this plant on the internet and we had hoped to find it, but we did not expect it to be as common as it was in the area where it is found.

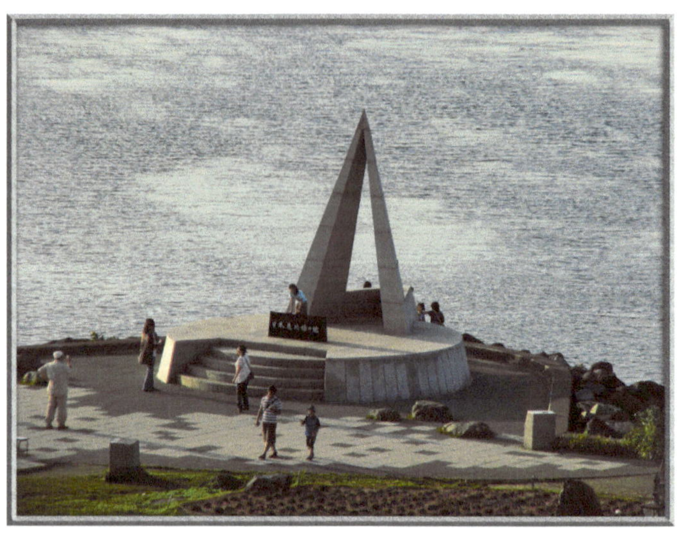

The photo to the right shows the northernmost point in Japan. It is **Soya Misaki**, or **Cape Soya**; it is located at 45° 31' 22" North Latitude.

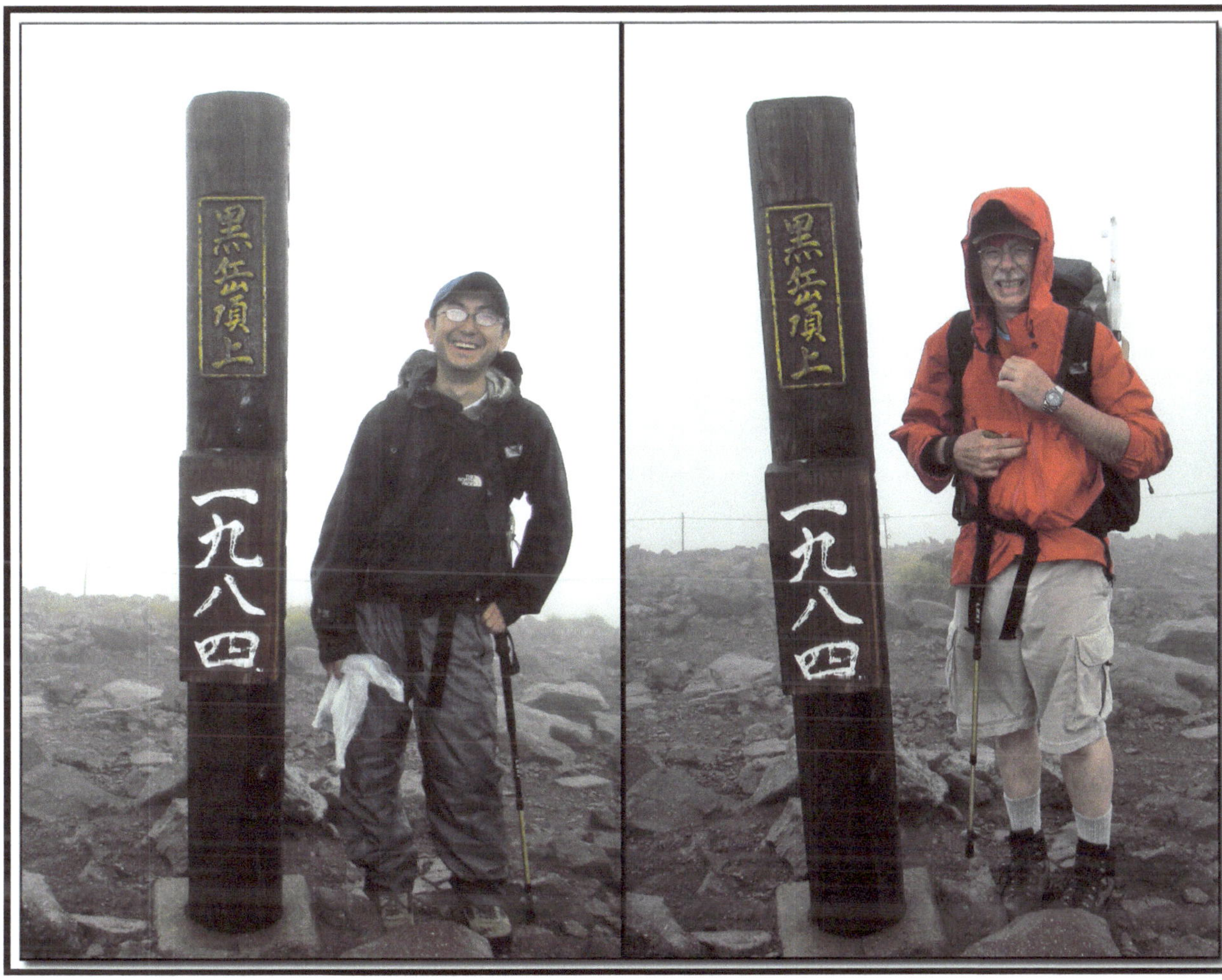

The next several photos were taken in **Daisetsuzan National Park** on **Hokkaido**. We have visited there in two different years. One year it was sunny and nice and one year it was rainy and cloudy; that is why some of these next several photos show it to be sunny and nice weather and others show clouds and rain. Daisetsuzan National Park is where **Mt. Asahidake** is. There are also several other mountains in this park. We went there for mountain climbing adventures.

The above photo shows Kazuya and myself at the summit of **Mt. Kurodake** (1,984 meters = 6,509 feet). As you can see, the weather was not very nice. You may be able to tell, though, that we are happy with what we are doing. Our faces show smiles combined with grimaces. It did not clear up at all on this day. We stayed in the hut at Mt. Kurodake this night. This hut did not serve meals. We had to carry our own food and cook it on our cook stove. Water, however, was available.

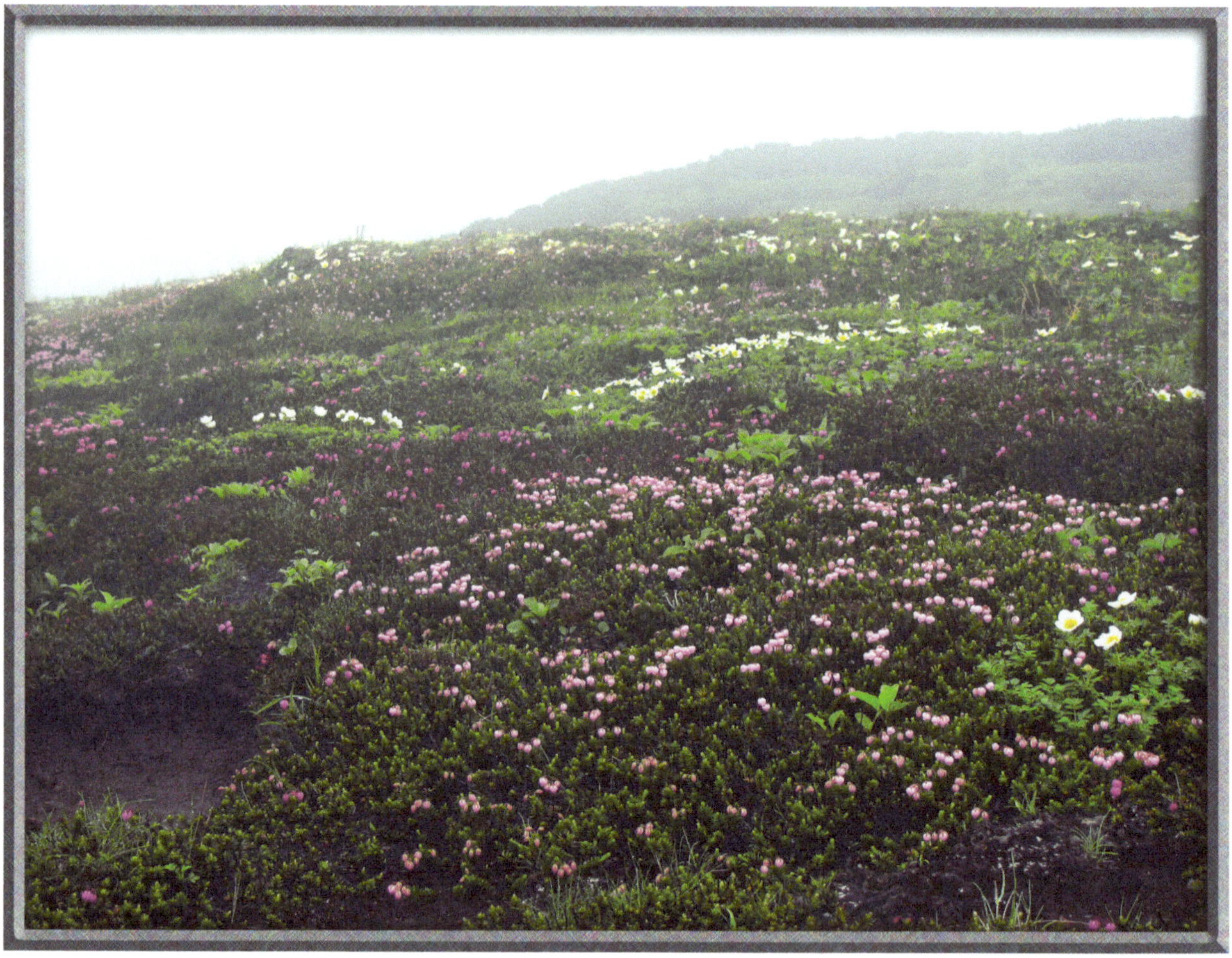

In this photo, taken as we descended Mt. Kurodake towards the hut, you can see that it is still raining and you will also note that this small valley is literally filled with ***Phyllodoce caerulea* var. *yezoensis*** flowers – the pink colored ones – and ***Geum pentapetalum*** flowers – the white colored ones. We could not even believe our eyes. We stopped and shot so many photographs of this area that it could probably be considered ridiculous.

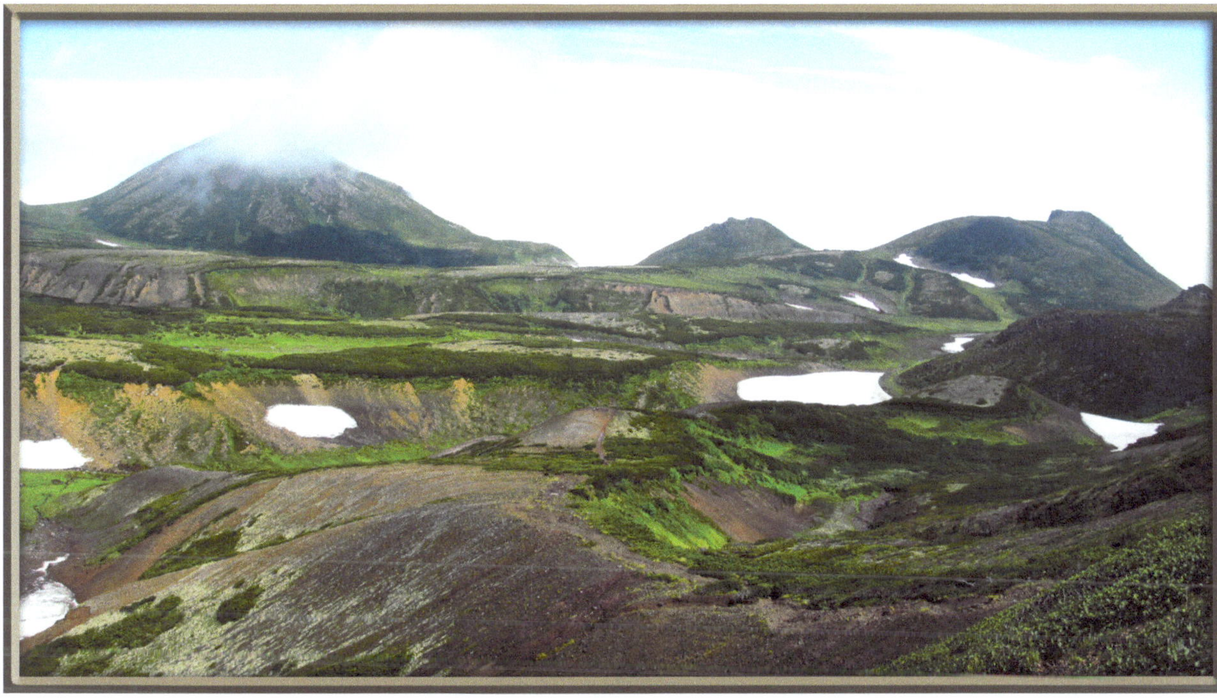

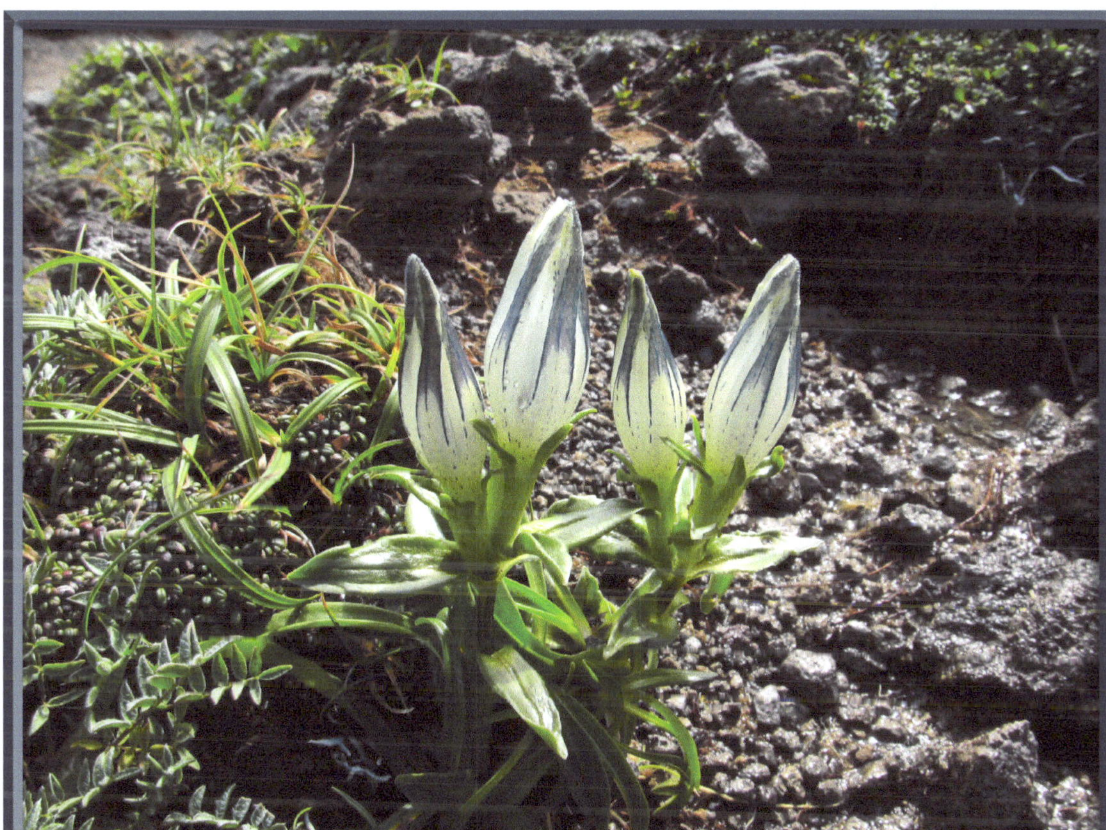

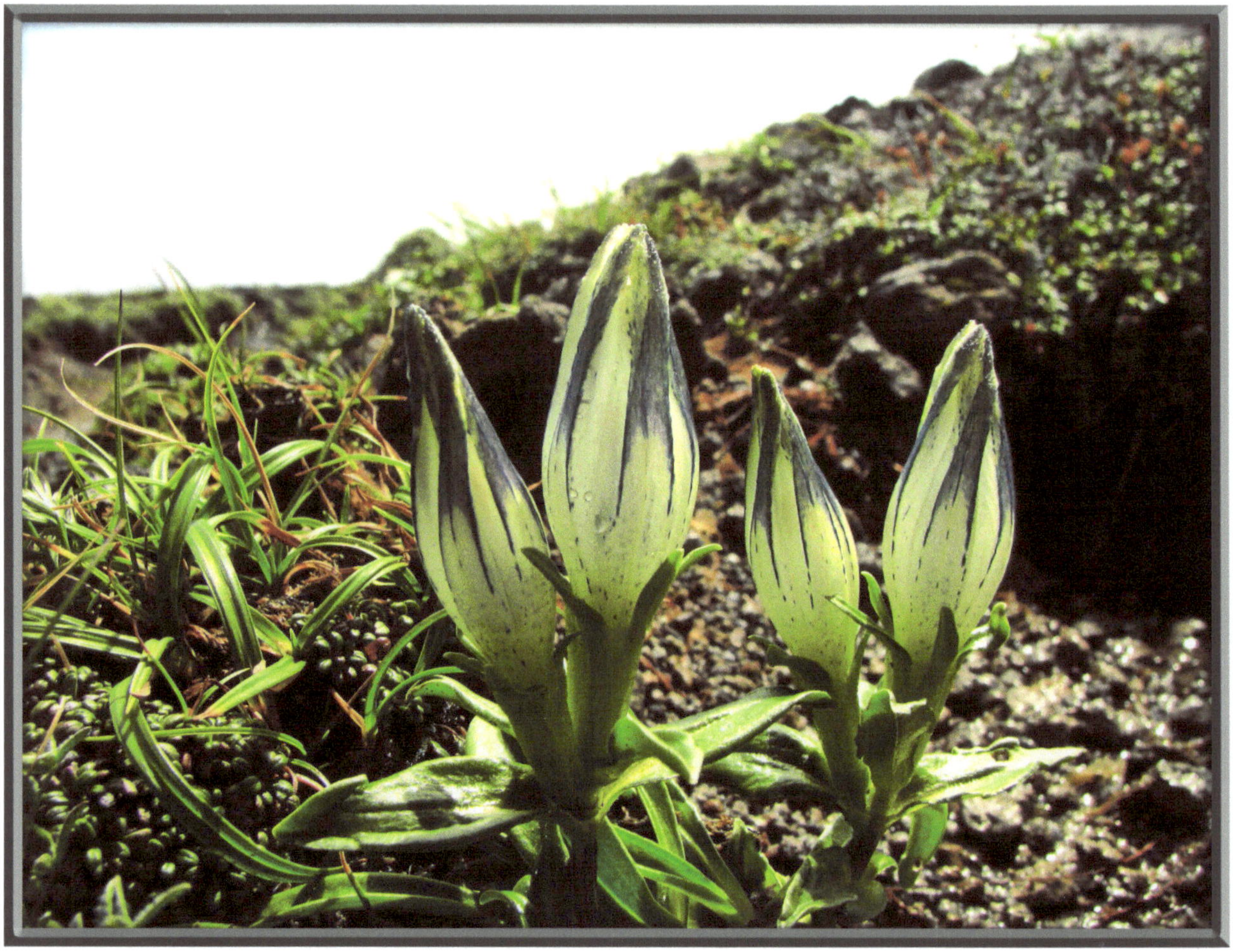

The two photos on the previous page were taken the following day. The weather cleared up somewhat and we had some pretty good views. The top photo shows the scenery as we hiked from the **Mt. Kurodake Hut** towards the summit of **Mt. Hokkaidake** (2,149 meters = 7,051 feet). In this photo **Mt. Kurodake** is the mountain just to the right of the center of the photo – not the one with the cloud over it. The one with the cloud on top of it looks higher, but it is not, it's just closer.

The lower photo on the previous page, and the photo on this page show ***Gentiana algida* f. *igarasii***. This plant is quite rare and we only saw one small patch of it here. We found this plant as we hiked the trail from **Mt. Hokkaidake** to **Mt. Hakuundake** (2,229.5 meters = 7,315 feet). We were very excited to find this plant.

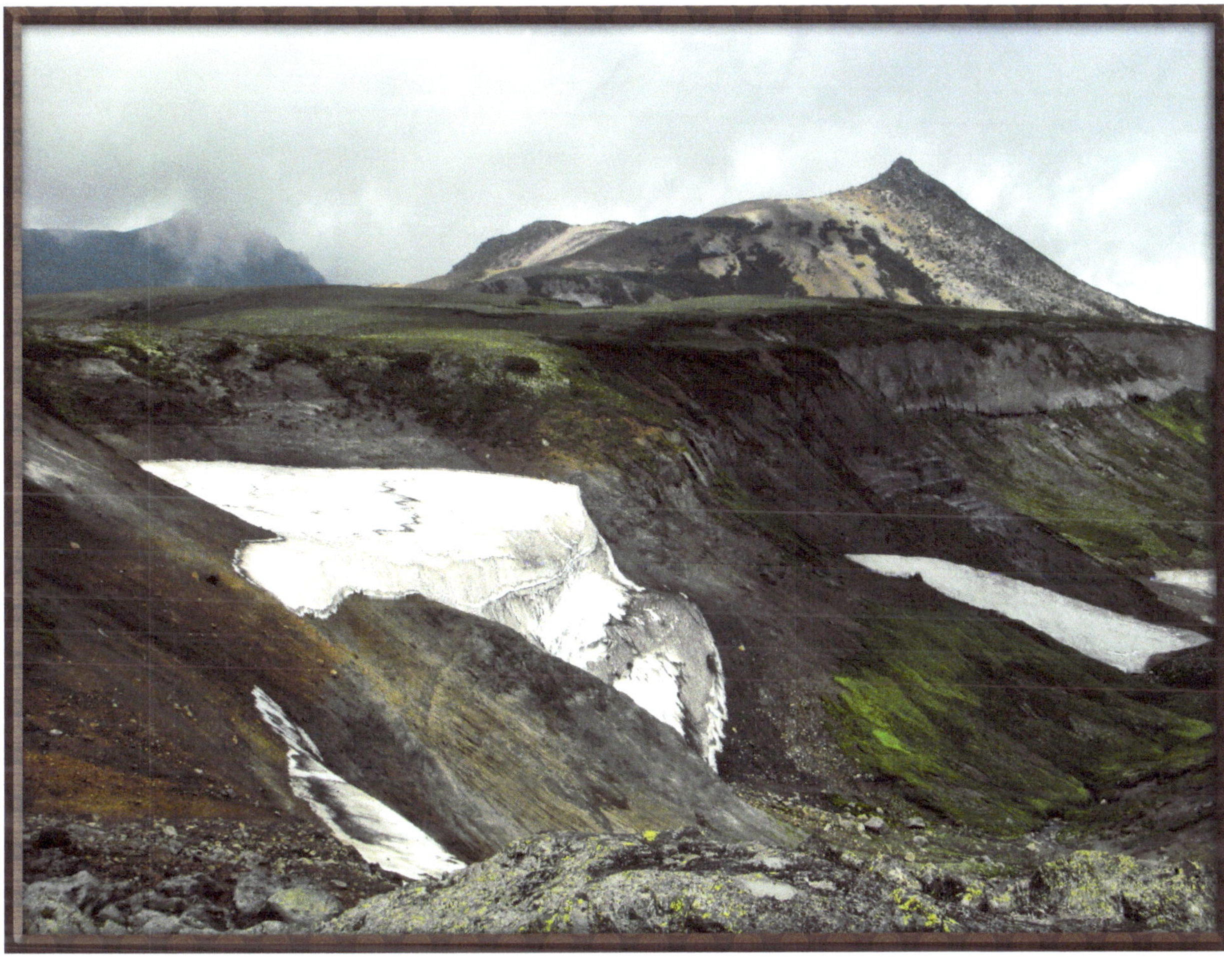

The photo on this page is a scenery shot taken as we continued to hike from **Mt. Hokkaidake** towards **Mt. Hakuundake.** The primary reason this photo was taken was to show the incredible snow depth in that small valley on the left side of the photo. Keep in mind that this was August. Maybe you can deduce that the snow never totally leaves this mountain. You can see that there are many shadows passing over the ground in this photo. The clouds kept blowing around and the conditions were quite cold and very windy. The rain had mostly stopped by this point though.

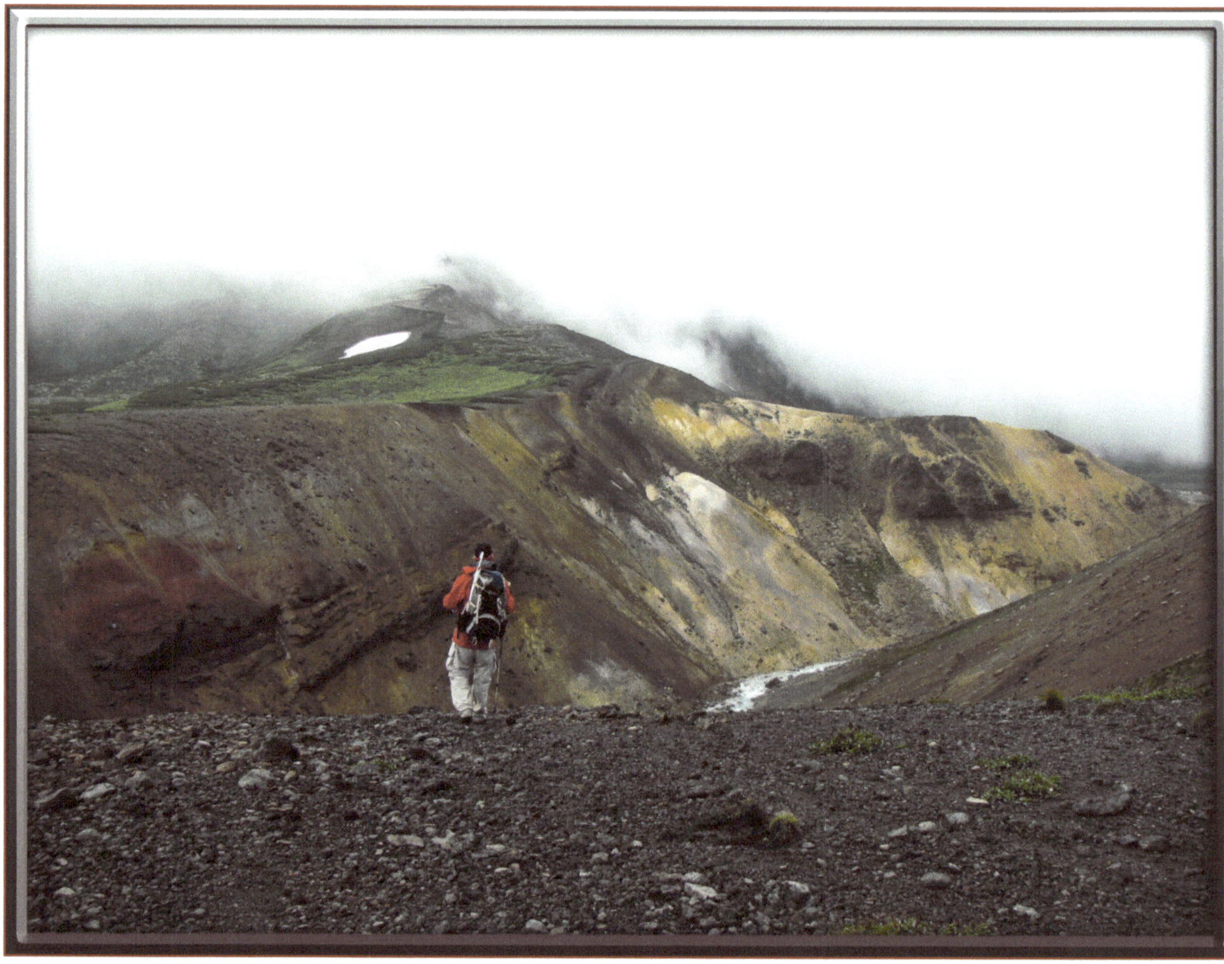

The above photo was taken the following day. The person is me. This was taken as we hiked from the **Mt. Kurodake Hut** towards **Mt. Hokuchindake** (2,244 meters = 7,362 feet).

The top photo on the facing page – in near whiteout conditions – was also taken on the trail to **Mt. Hokuchindake**. We had to cross another dangerous snowfield, but after the **Hakuba Snowfields** of last month this one was a piece of cake. We had a third person following us across the snowfield and he was really scared and asked us to make sure that he got across it alive, so we waited for him as we went. This photo shows Kazuya and the third person. We were in the clouds, so there was no visible trail and it was questionable which direction to go. I led and assumed we had to go uphill (according to the map) and I finally saw yellow paint marks on the rocks ahead – that is how they mark the trails here — WHEW!!

The lower photo on the facing page shows **Reindeer Moss** (***Cladonia rangiferina***), also known as **Reindeer Lichen**. It is a light-colored lichen belonging to the family ***Cladoniaceae***. It is found primarily in areas of alpine tundra and is extremely cold-hardy. This was after we crossed the summit of **Mt. Hokuchindake**.

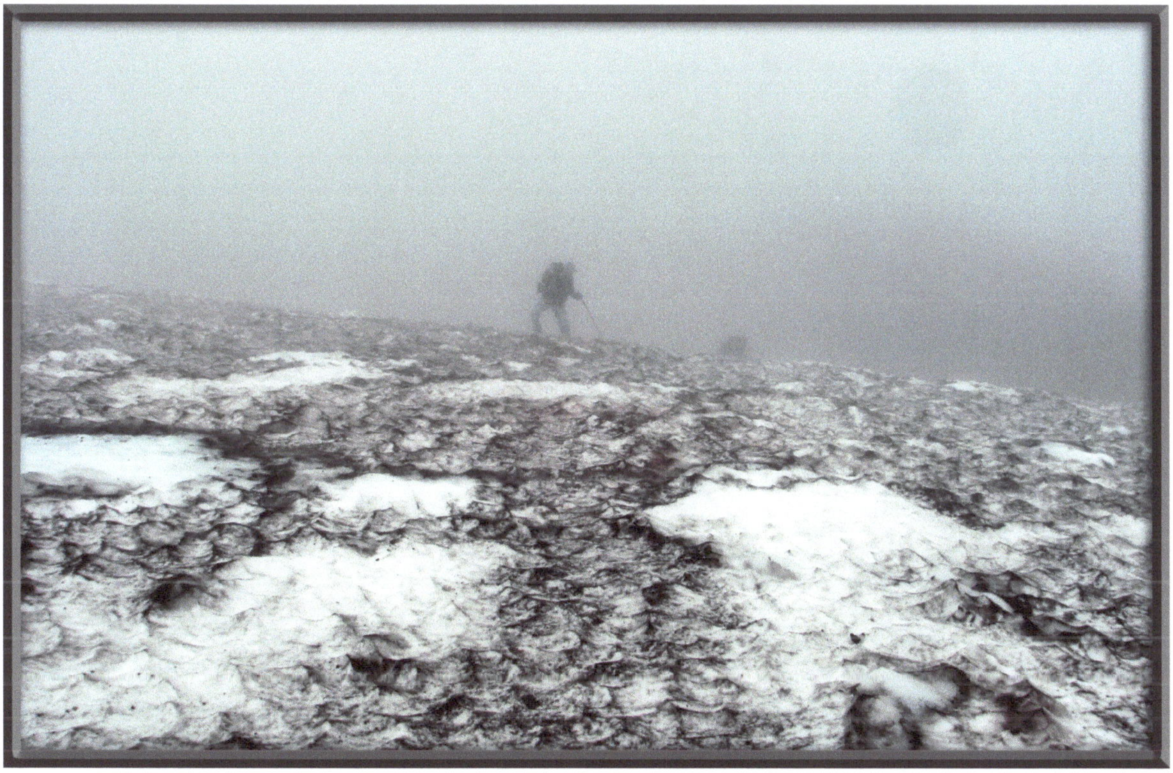

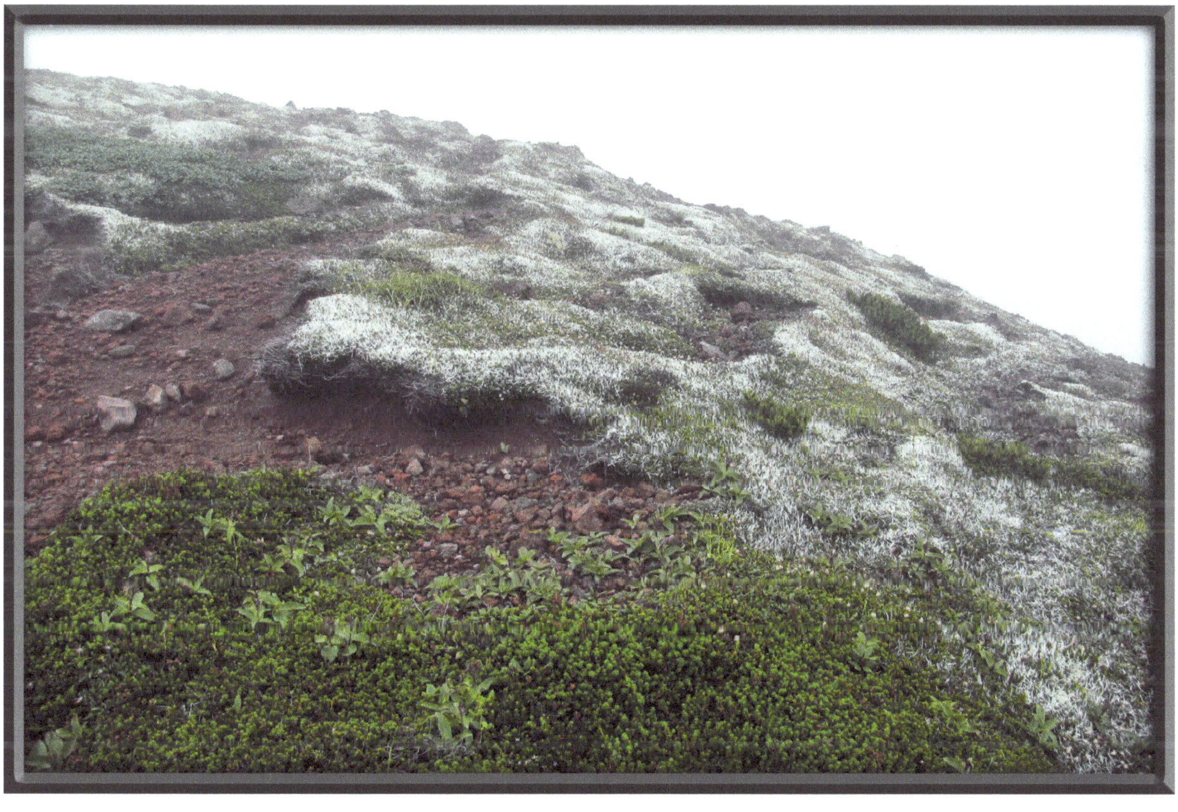

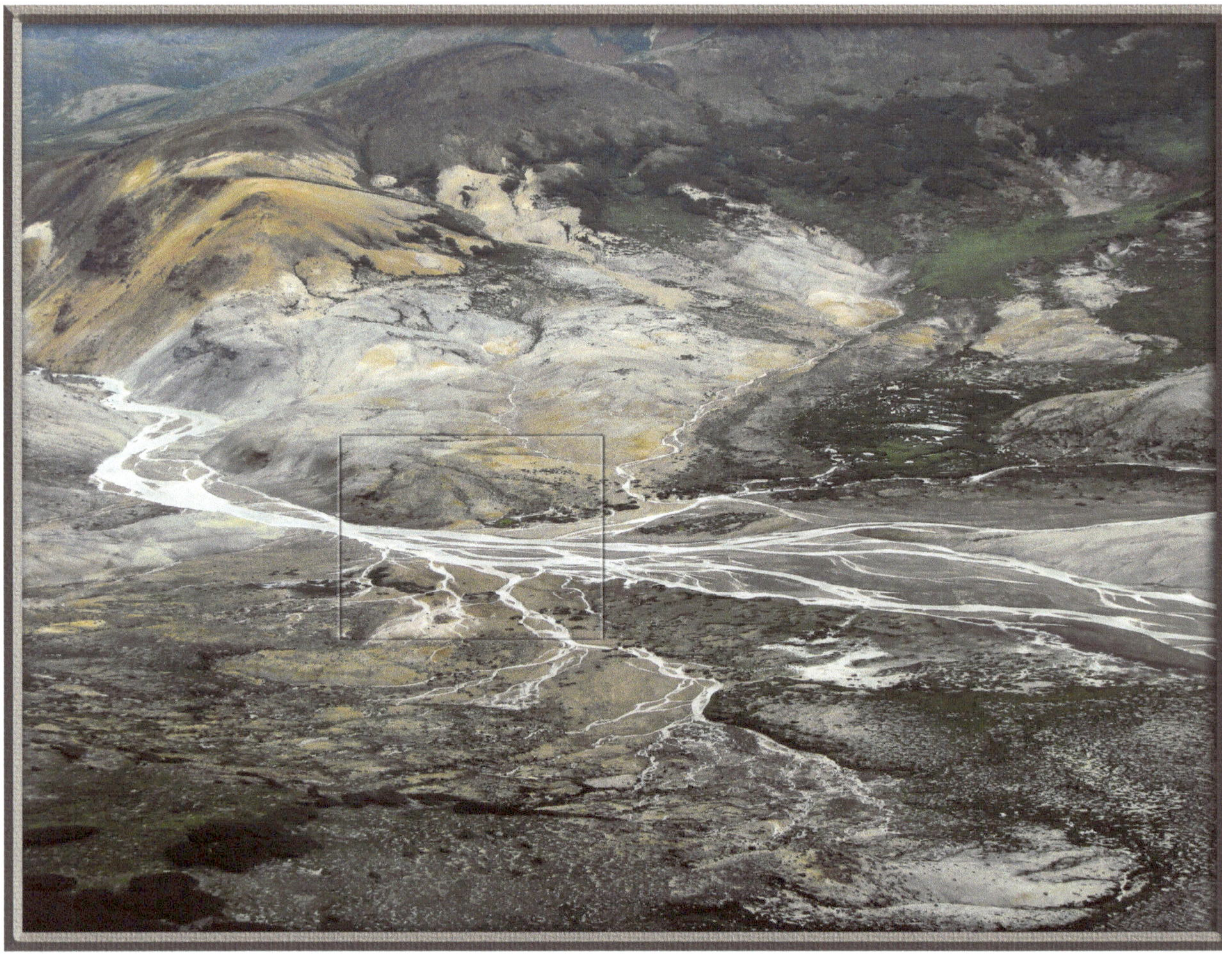

In **Daisetsuzan National Park** there is a valley (shown above) with no trails crossing it. There is supposedly a poison hot spring here and therefore we refer to it as **"Poison Hot Spring Valley"**. There are trails on all of the ridges which surround this valley. When the wind blows up out of the valley you can smell a very strong odor of sulfur. **Mt. Hokkaidake** is on the southeast side of this valley, **Mt. Hokuchindake** is on the northwest side of the valley, while **Mt. Araidake** and **Mt. Mamiyadake** are at the head of the valley. As you can see in this photo, there is very little vegetation growing in this valley. The second time we were here we could even see an area which appeared to have been burned. We assumed that was due to an eruption of extremely hot or poisonous water from the hot spring.

The embossed area in the above photo outlines the approximate area which is shown in the photo on the facing page. There is a lot of water for such a small valley.

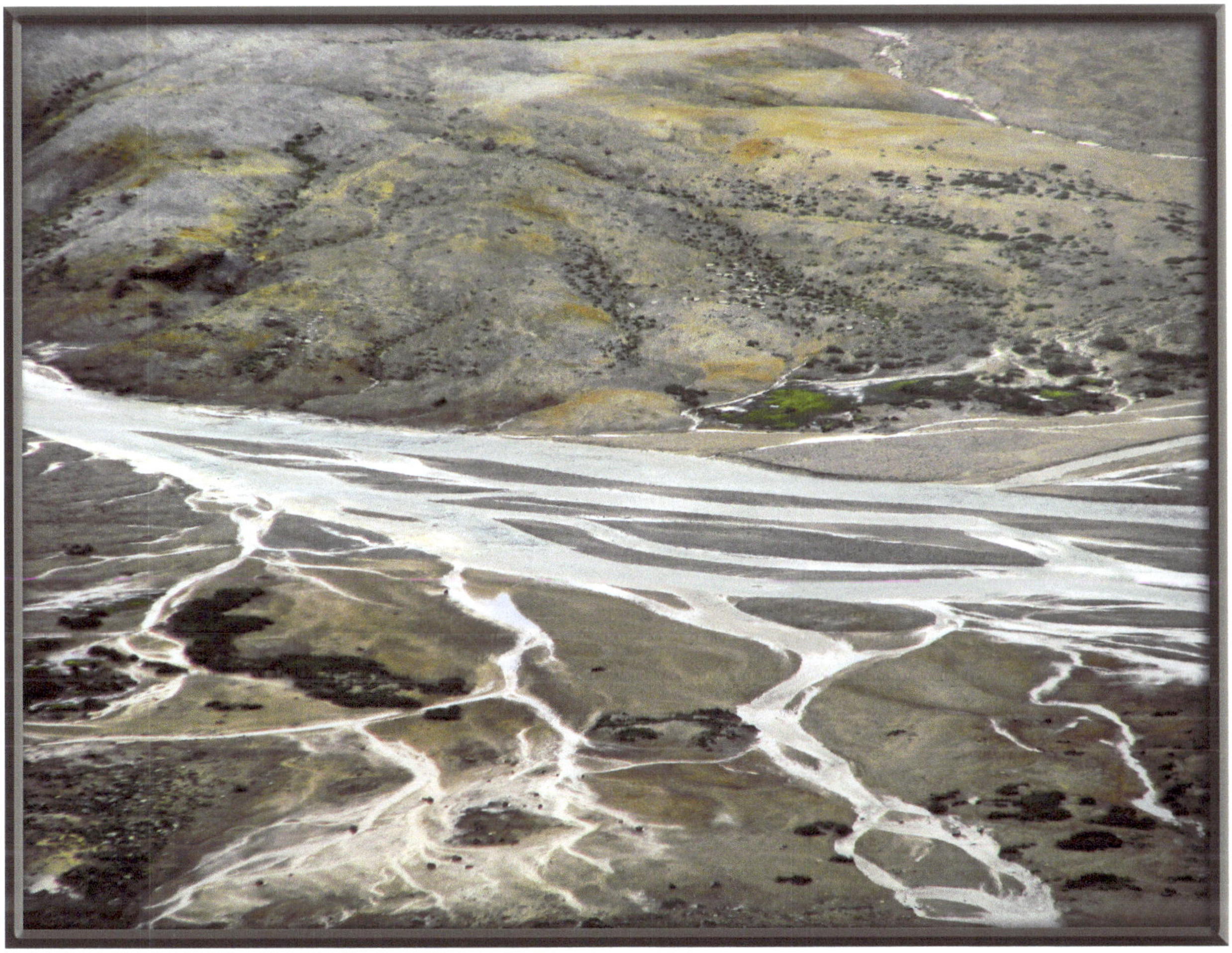

Here is a zoomed-in photo showing the approximate area outlined in the photo of **"Poison Hot Spring Valley"** on the previous page. As you can see, there is a substantial amount of water coming out of this valley. It amazes us that this kind of place can exist here. This entire area is an active volcano – later on we'll show you photos of steam fumaroles with large quantities of steam rolling up out of them. There is, in addition, one **Hot Spring** (**Nakadake Onsen**) on this mountain which is right beside a trail, is not poison and, depending on the time and the day, is remote enough to be able to undress and soak in without being disturbed by other hikers.

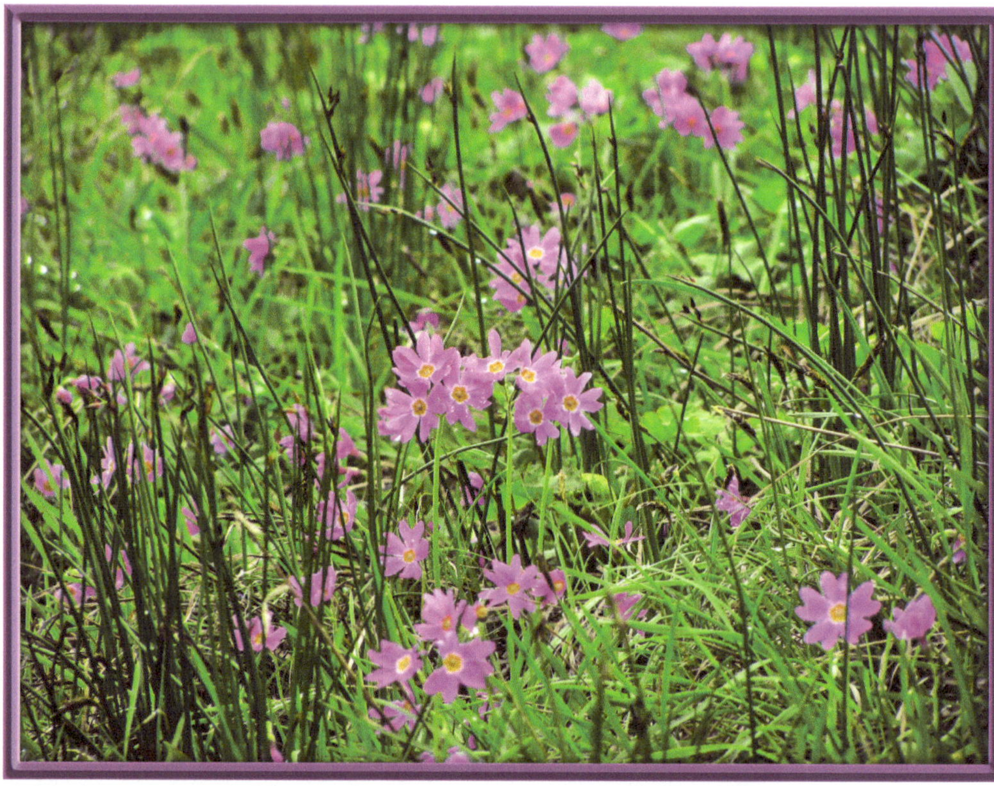

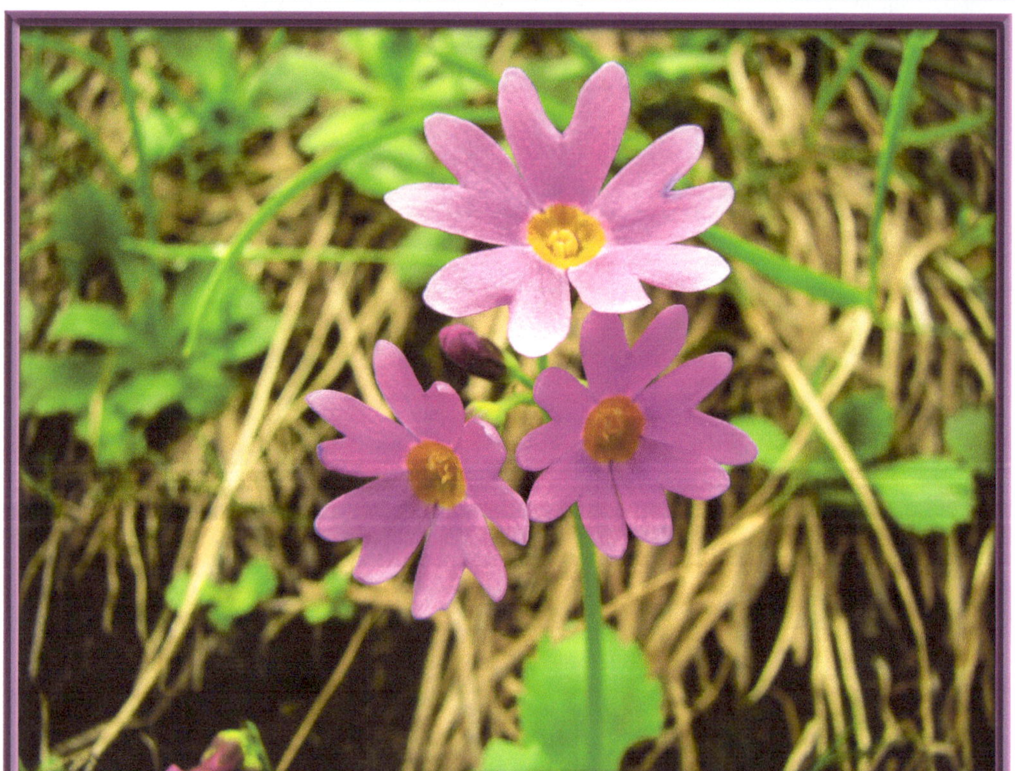

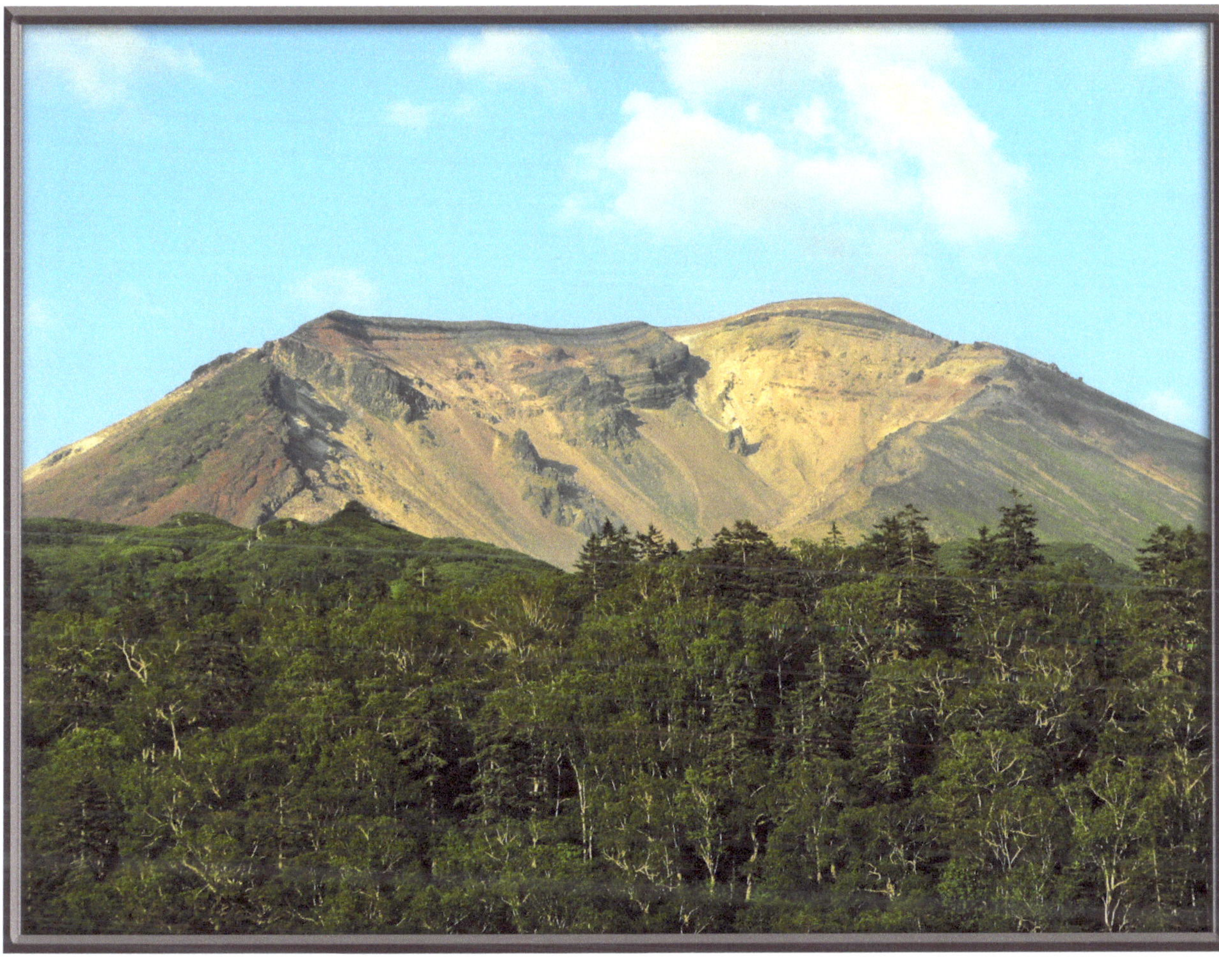

The two photos on the facing page show ***Primula cuneifolia***, a Primrose. It was unbelievable how abundant this species was in some small areas. We took quite a few photos of this flower. The upper photo shows a group of the flowers and the lower photo shows a single stalk with three flowers on it. We hope that it is obvious that these two photos were taken at different places on **Mt. Asahidake**.

The image immediately above shows **Mt. Asahidake** as sunset approaches. This photo was taken from the bottom of the ropeway in the year the weather was good most of the time we were there. Isn't it a beautiful color!

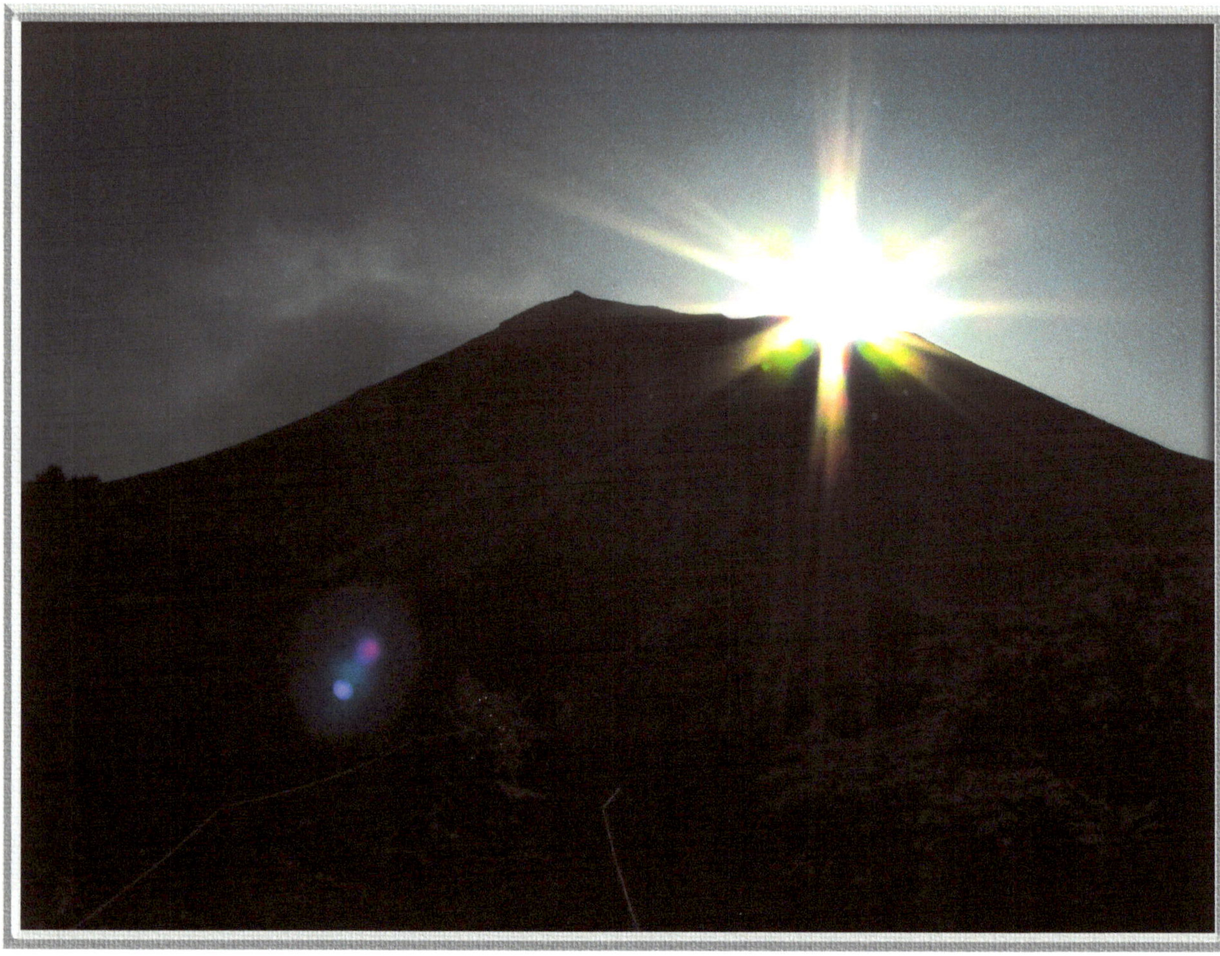

This photo shows **Mt. Asahidake** (2,291 meters = 7,516 feet) as the sun rises over the top of it. This photo was also taken in the year we were here and the weather was nice. The time of this photo was 6:11 AM. The place was along the trail as we hiked from the top of the Ropeway up towards **Sugatami Pond**. In a little less than three hours we will be at the summit. Mt. Asahidake is the highest mountain on **Hokkaido**. We also climbed the second highest mountain – **Mt. Hokuchindake** – we mentioned that a few pages back, but we did not show you a photo of us at the summit in the clouds – there was not much to see.

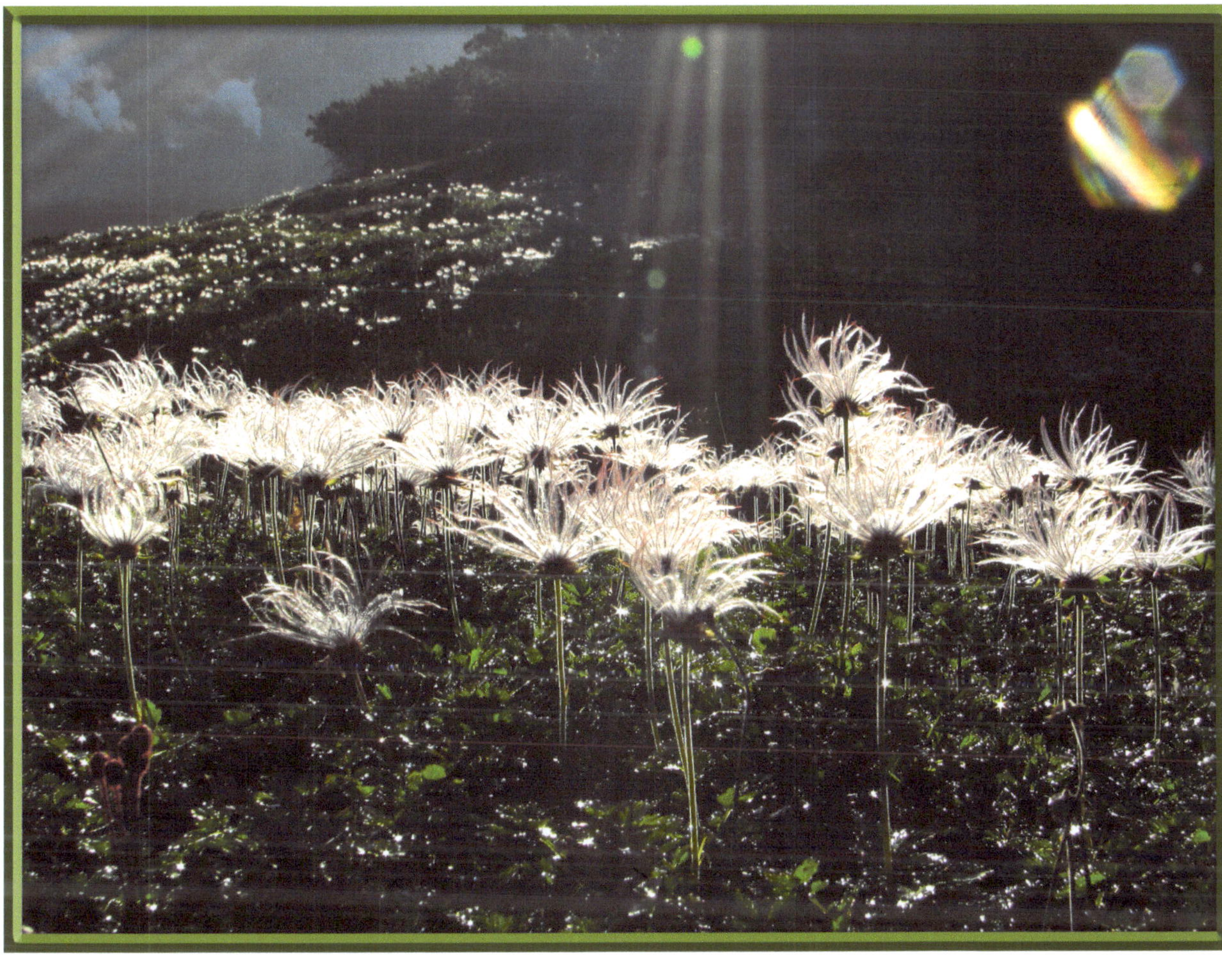

The shot above is a rather amazing backlit example of ***Geum pentapetalum***. This photo was taken just three minutes after the previous photo and also looking the same direction as the previous photo. You may be wondering why we did not do something with imaging software to eliminate the lens flare in the upper right corner of this photo. The reason is simple to explain – we did experiment with eliminating the lens flare and the photo was not nearly as impressive as it is with the lens flare, so we discarded the experiment and went with the original photo in its unaltered state.

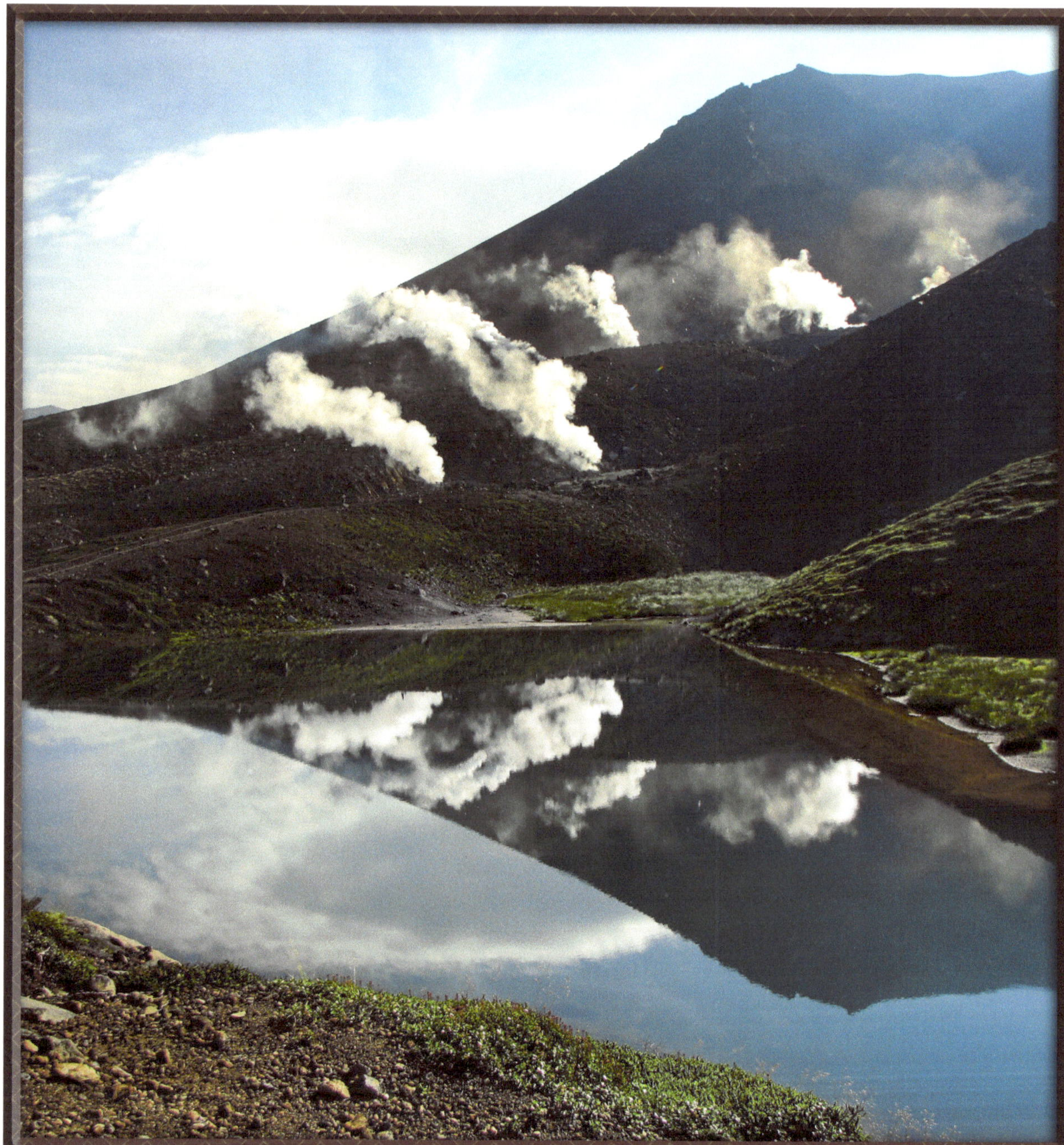

This vertical panoramic image was taken from the scenic overlook at **Sugatami Pond** as one begins the ascent of **Mt. Asahidake**. This is the first photo which really shows you that this is an active volcano. The steam fumaroles are very evident here. You can also see the shoulder of Mt. Asahidake in this image.

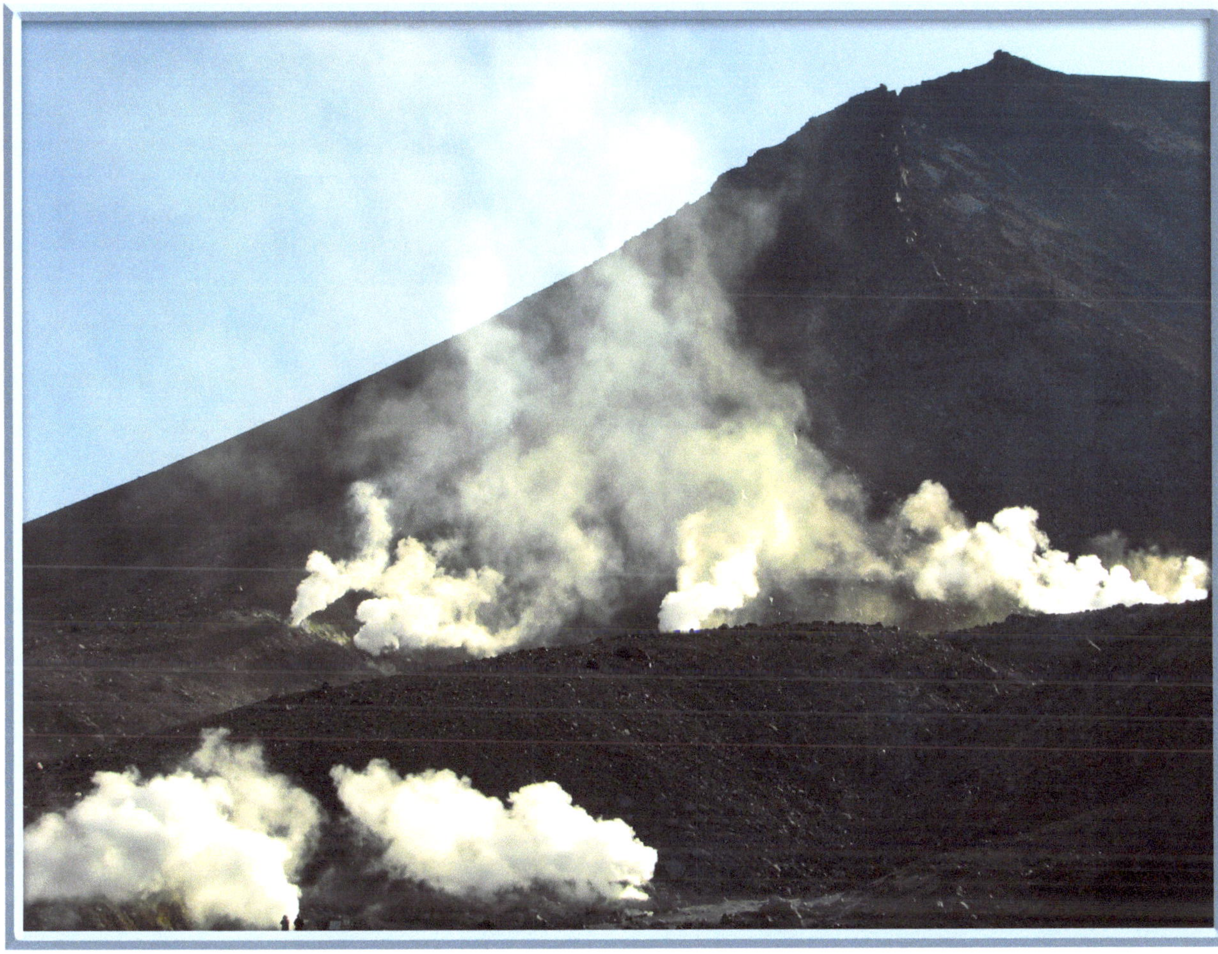

This photo was actually taken in a different year than the one on the facing page. This one was also taken from a different trail than that photo. It was taken from a trail near **Sugatami Pond** and it shows the shoulder of **Mt. Asahidake** as well as several steam fumaroles. The color of this photo is very interesting due to some strange lighting conditions at this time of day. If you study this photo closely you can see some people right at the bottom edge of it – one of them is in front of the steam.

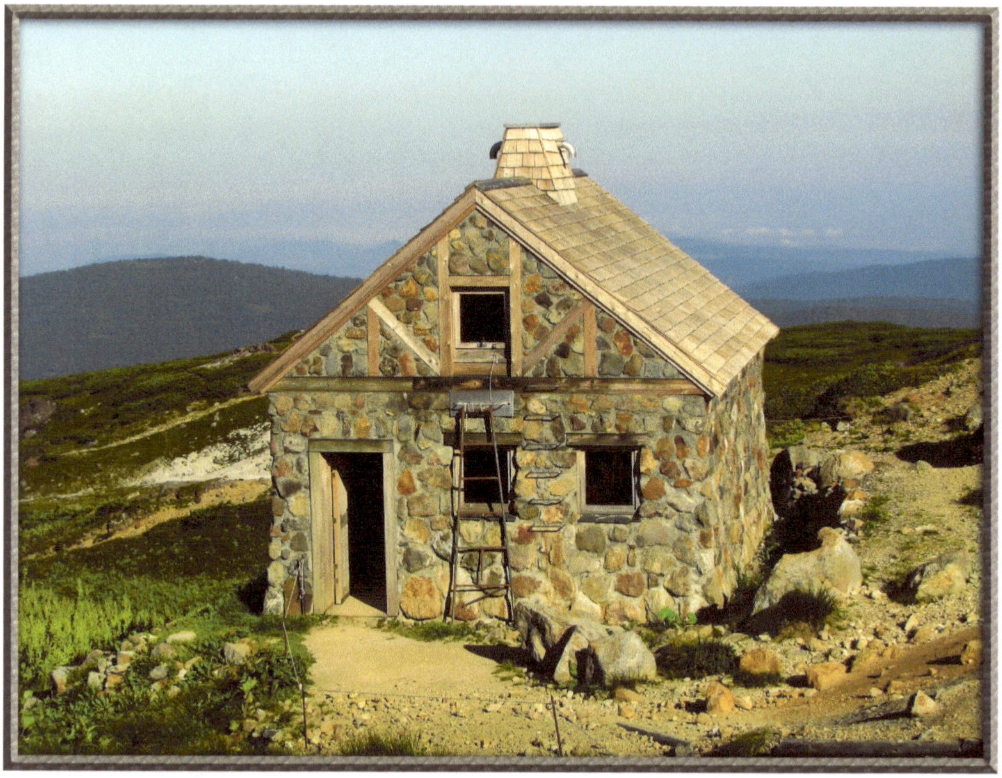

This photo features the emergency shelter at **Sugatami Pond**. It looks very sturdy does it not? There is a warning sign here stating that this shelter does not have a toilet. This shelter is very photogenic.

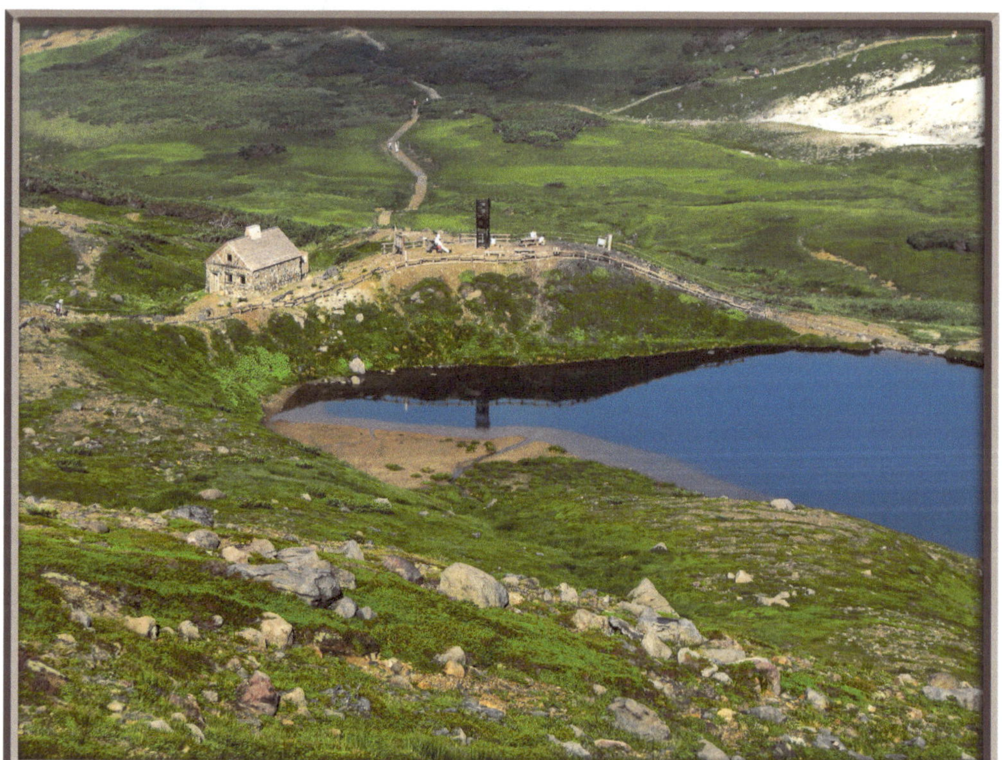

This photo was taken as we were on the trail to the **Mt. Asahidake** summit. That is **Sugatami Pond** and the emergency shelter down there.

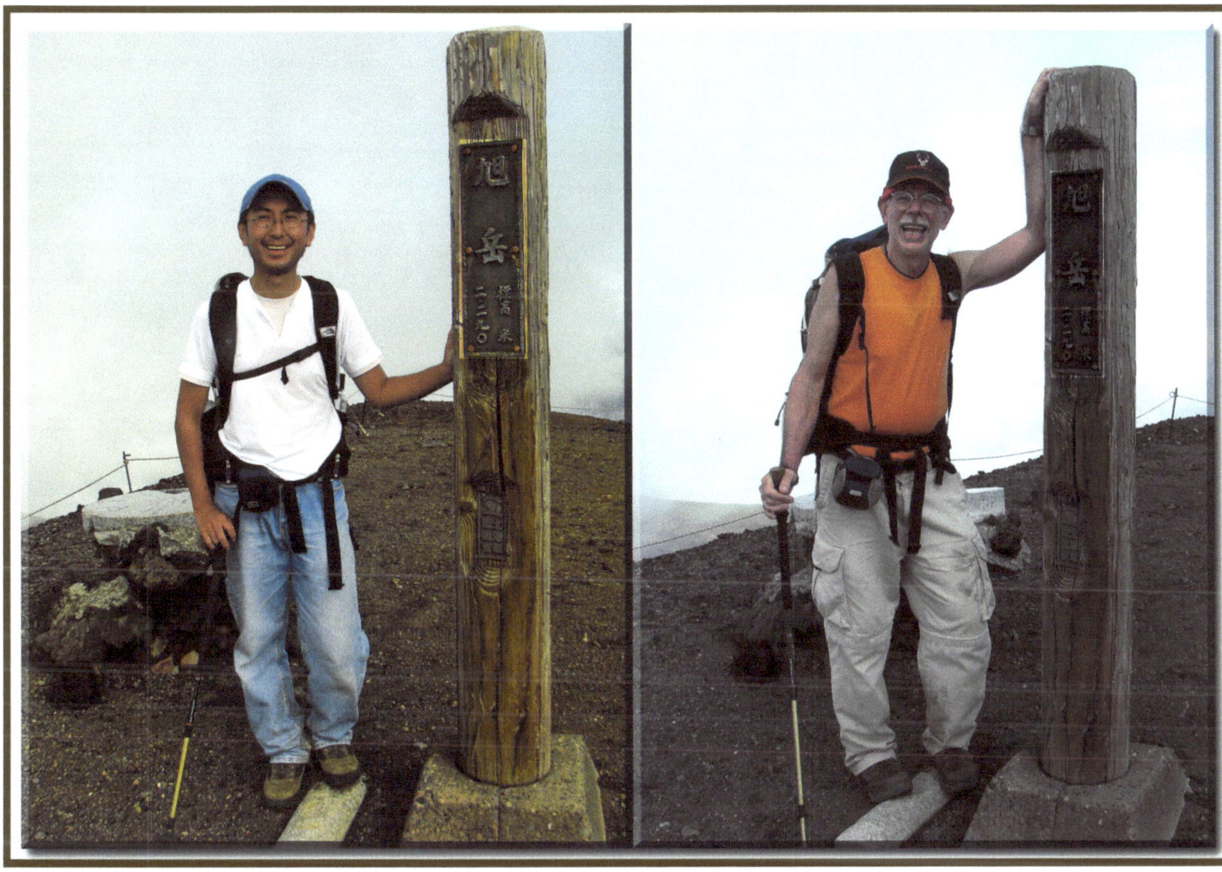

Here are two separate photos of us at the summit of **Mt. Asahidake**. You may be able to read the sign – it states the elevation (2,290 meters = 7,510 feet) and the name of the mountain. Note that once again, we both look very happy.

I once read somewhere that the fifth day of hiking/climbing is kind of a magical day in that your heart stops beating so fast, you don't get winded as easily and in general, your body is suddenly in condition for it. Well, we can both say that the fourth day is equally as magical – and for the same reasons. We attained the summit of Mt. Asahidake in about one hour less time than it should have taken us – certainly due to this phenomenon. My 62 (nearly 63) year old body felt pretty fine. We wished we could climb for ten days straight – what would we feel like then?!

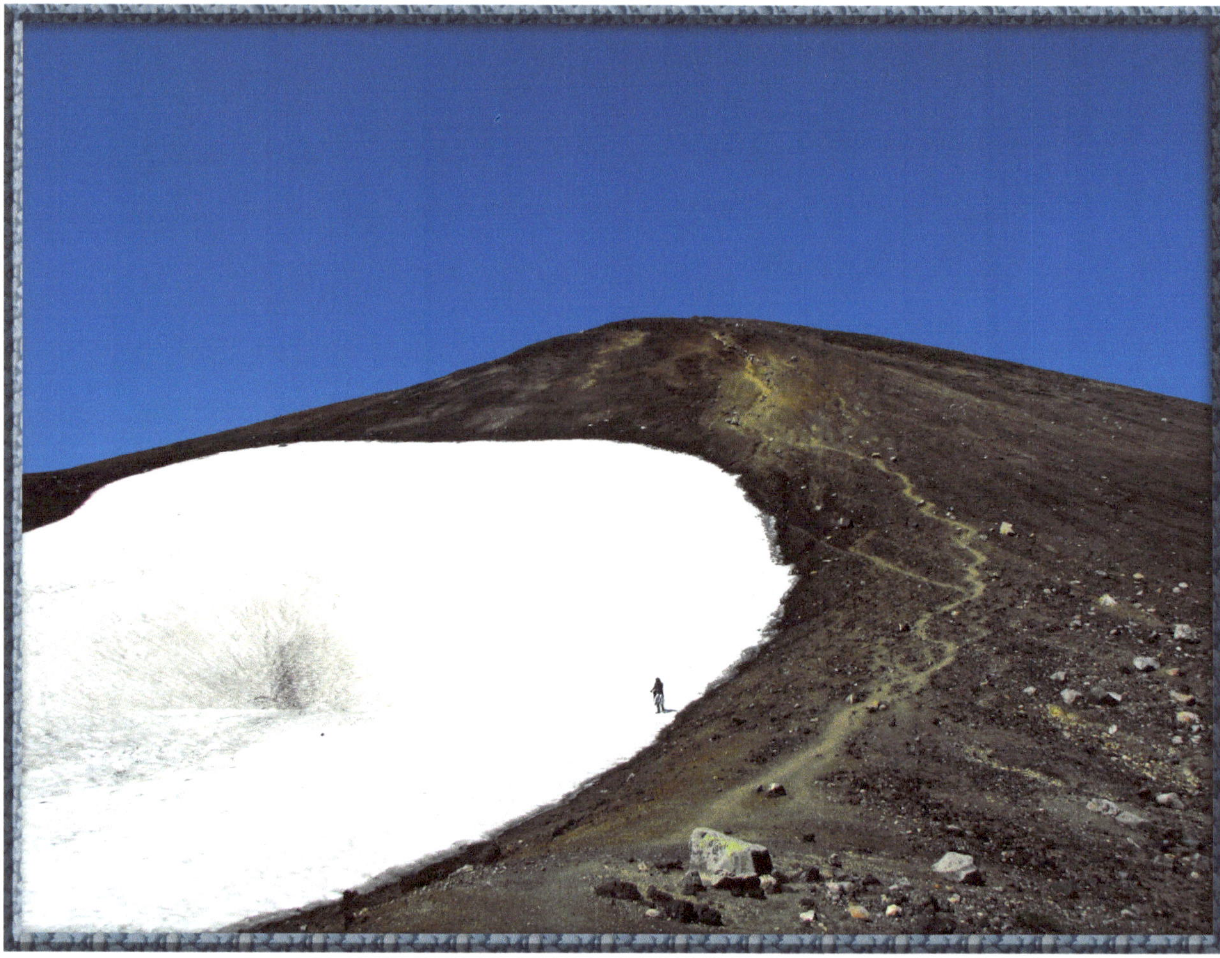

This photograph was taken as we continued our day of climbing – this was shot while going down the backside of **Mt. Asahidake** and towards **Mt. Mamiyadake** (2,185 meters = 7,169 feet). Look at that large snowfield. It's rather nice that a person happened to be coming by – it really makes for a much better presentation of the scale of everything than you would get if there was nothing there for size comparison.

The blueness of the sky is also amazing in this shot. It should be noted that no filters were used and there was no additional processing done with imaging software. This shot is just as it came from the camera – except for being framed, of course.

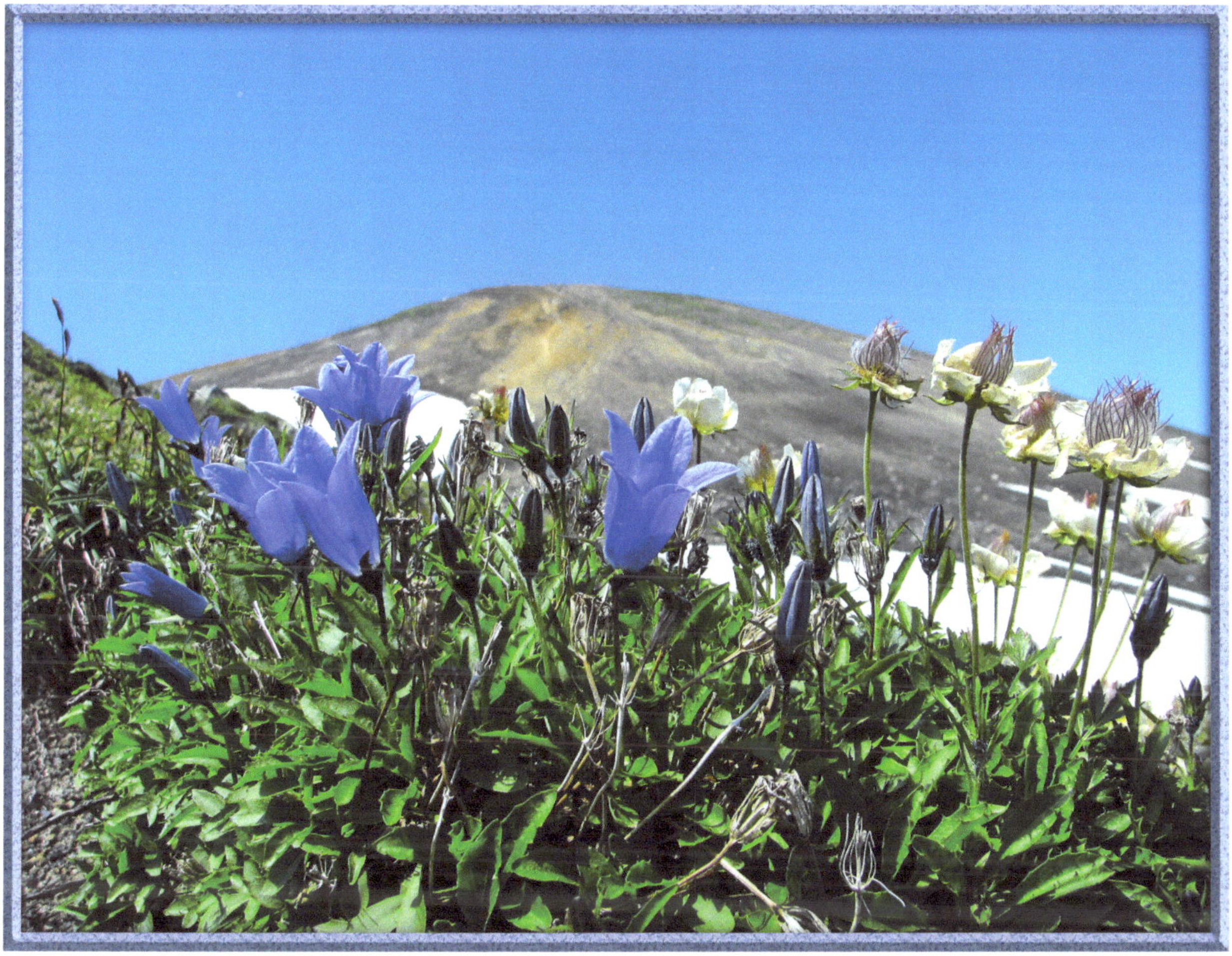

The photo immediately above shows an exquisitely beautiful example of ***Campanula lasiocarpa*** as we descend the backside of **Mt. Asahidake** and hike the trail towards **Mt. Mamiyadake**. The snowfield which you can see on the far left is the same snowfield which is shown in the previous photo (page 192). The white flowered plant is ***Geum pentapetalum***, which you have seen other photos of. The blue of the ***Campanula lasiocarpa*** really closely matches the blue of the sky, wouldn't you agree? The round top mountain back there is **Mt. Asahidake**.

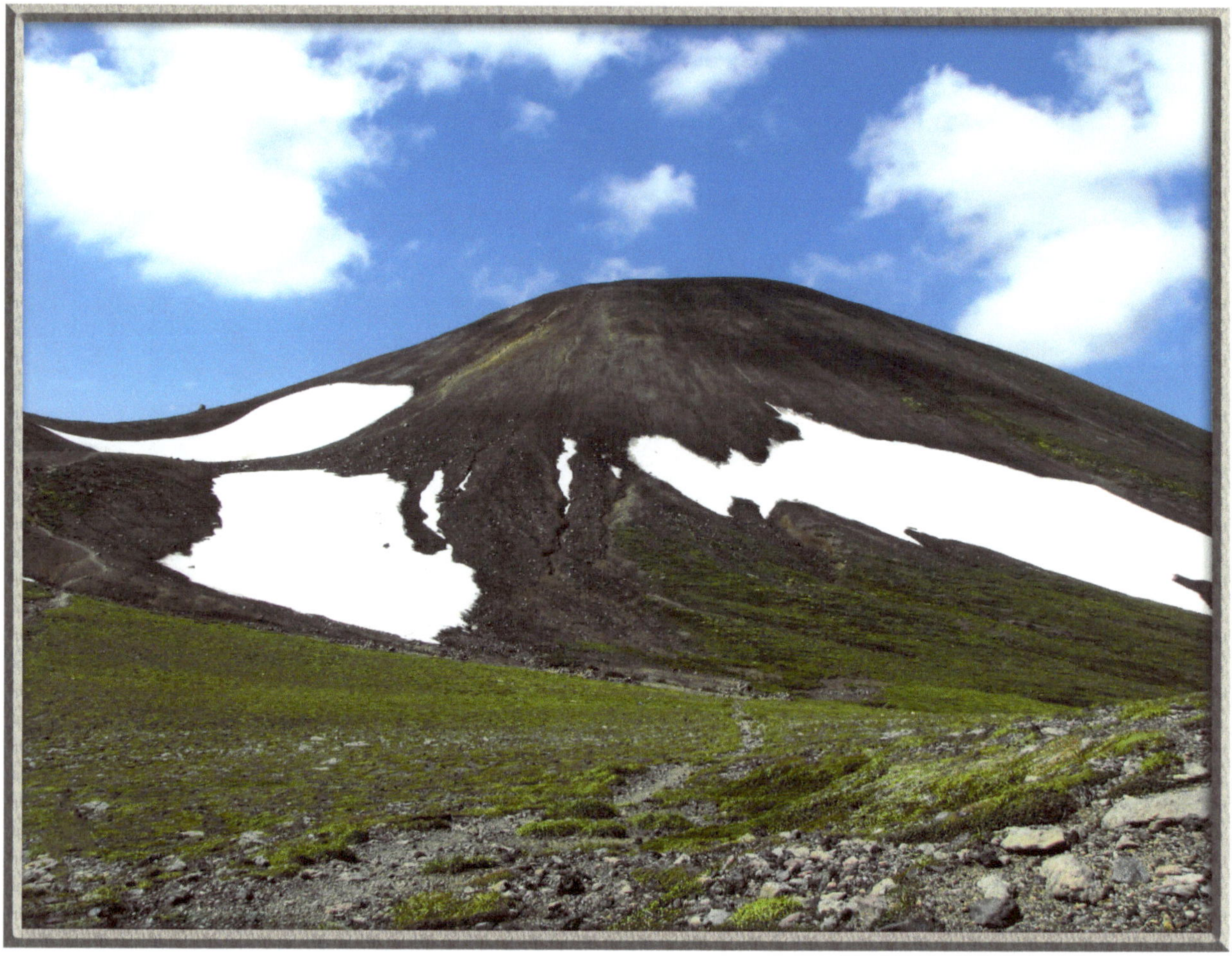

Here is a final photo of **Mt. Asahidake** from the backside. This was taken as we crossed the valley between **Mt. Asahidake** and **Mt. Kumagadake** and started up the slope of Mt. Kumagadake. You should note the presence of clouds in this photo. The photo on the previous page (page 193) was taken only nineteen minutes previous to this one and there were no clouds at all. Even the photo back on page 192 was taken only thirty-five minutes previous to this one and it showed not even a hint of a cloud. That is how quickly the weather can change here in the mountains. The snowfield you can see on the far left – in the bowl of the mountain – is the same one as seen on page 192.

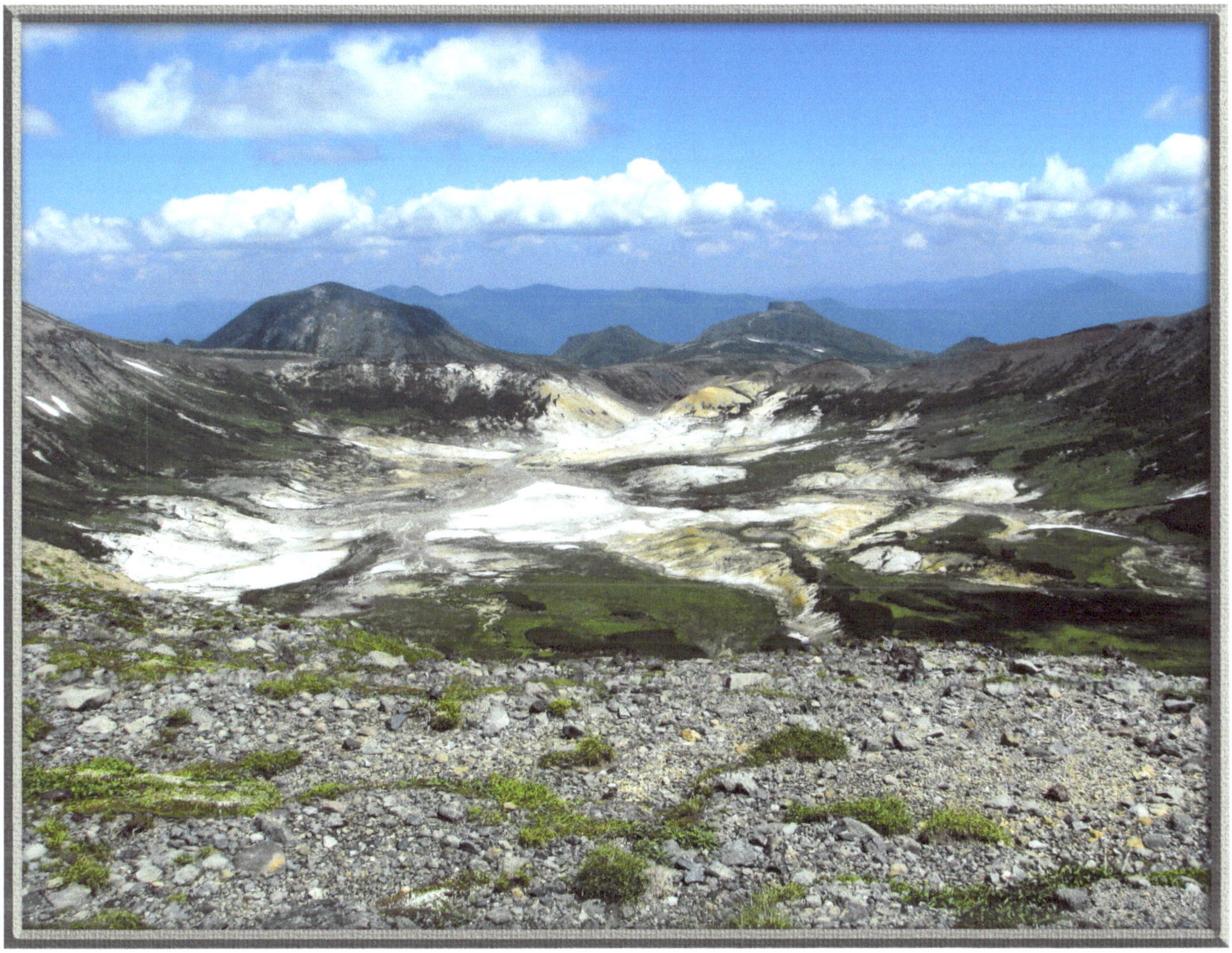

Here is a final photo of **"Poison Hot Spring Valley"** as seen from close to **Mt. Mamiyadake** (2,185 meters = 7,169 feet). On pages 182 and 183 you saw photos taken from the northwest side of **"Poison Hot Spring Valley"** – this photo was taken from the southwest side of the valley. In this photo we are looking pretty much right down the center of the valley.

From here we will proceed to **Mt. Nakadake** (2,113 meters = 6,932 feet) and then continue down to **Nakadake Onsen** (Hot Spring). We mentioned **Nakadake Hot Spring**, or **Nakadake Onsen** on page 183. This day there were few enough people so that we were able to bathe naked in **Nakadake Onsen**. Eventually we will end back at our starting point.

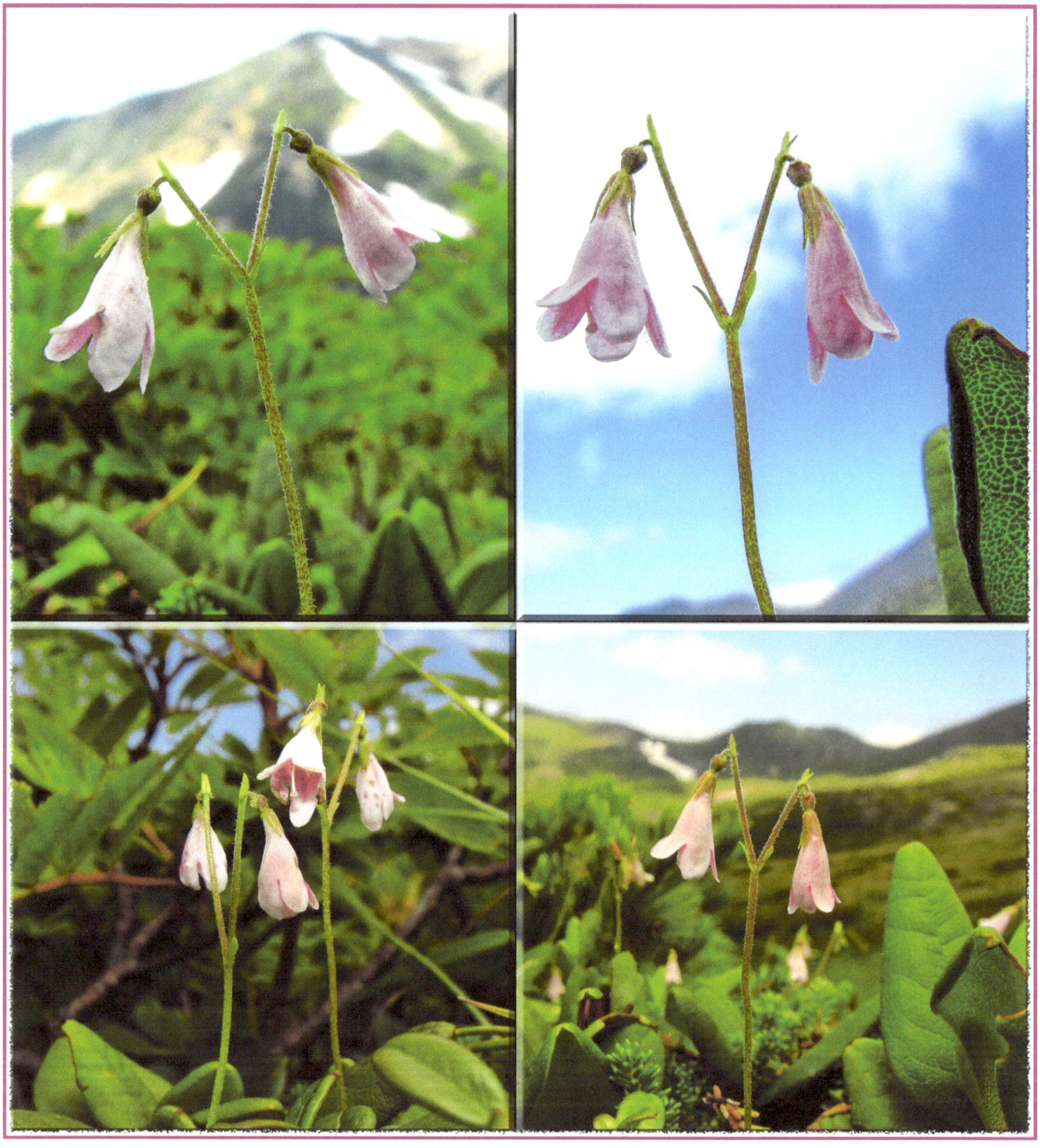

Here is a four-photo collage of ***Linnaea borealis*** – commonly known as **Twin-flower**. This is a very uncommon flower which is always a treat to see – we have seen it in only about three different locations in our ten years of hiking in Japan.

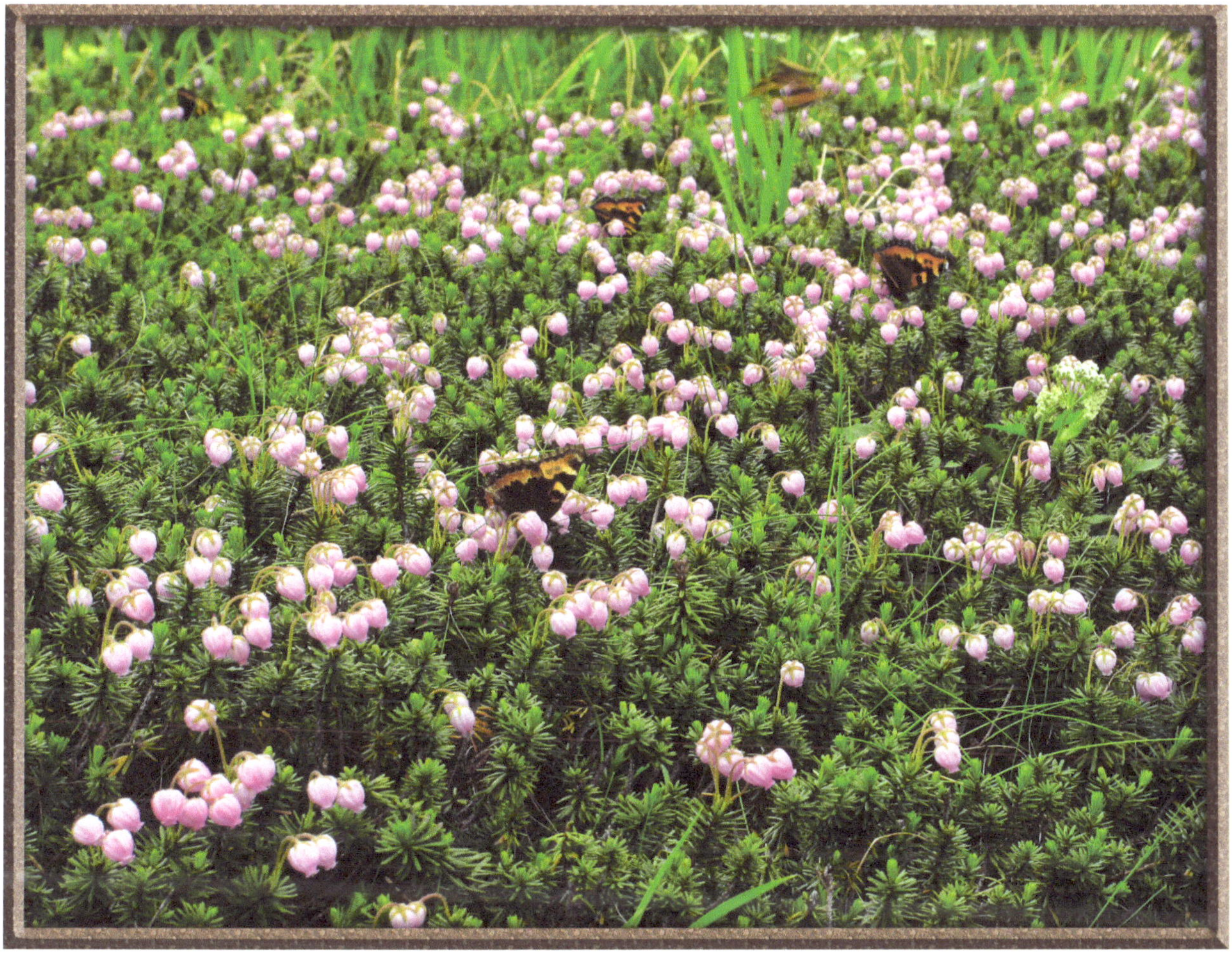

All of the photos on the facing page and on this page were taken on the lower northwest slopes of Mt. Asahidake as we hiked from Nakadake Onsen back towards the top of the ropeway.

Above, is an astounding photo of ***Phyllodoce caerulea* var. *yezoensis*** – there was such an accumulation of it here in a small valley that we could not believe our eyes. But, what was even more incredible on this day with the sun shining, was the number of butterflies which were feeding on the nectar of this flower. When we saw this flower on previous days it was cloudy, cold and windy and there were no butterflies around at all (page 176). So, when we saw the number of butterflies we were amazed.

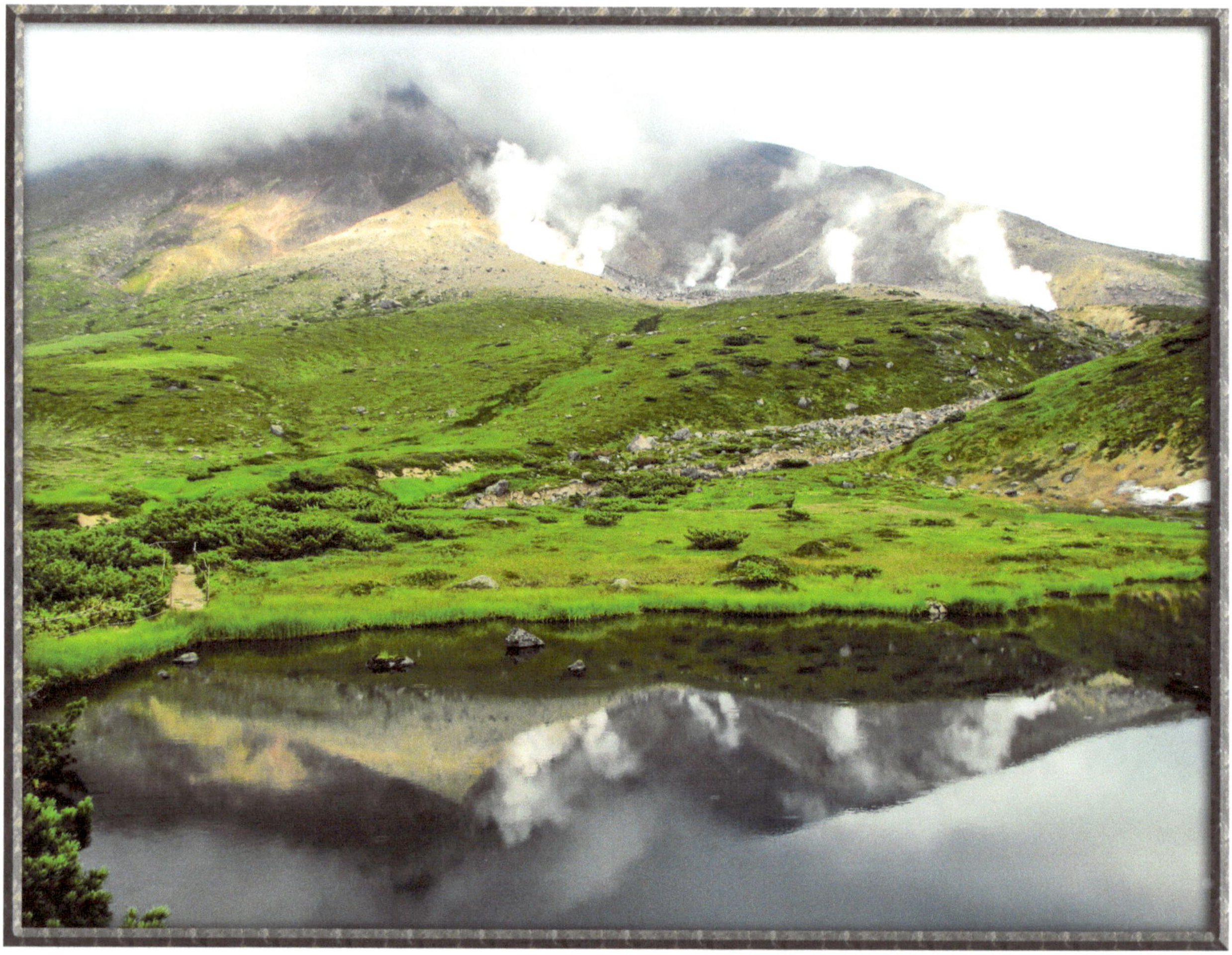

This is the final shot of **Mt. Asahidake**. This was taken as we neared the top of the ropeway which would take us to the bottom of the mountain. As you can see, the clouds have rolled in since the photos back on pages 192 – 195, and we can no longer see very high up on **Mt. Asahidake**. The reflection in the pond is quite nice. You should note that this is NOT the same pond as was shown back on pages 188 and 190 – this pond is actually quite far from that pond.

The photo on the facing page was taken as we rode the ropeway down to the bottom of the mountain. It shows a beautifully **"silvered out"** dead tree with the dark green living forest behind it as contrast. The photos shown on this and the facing page are the final ones we want to show you which were taken during our two different **Daisetsuzan National Park** adventures. We hope that you enjoyed these adventures nearly as much as we did.

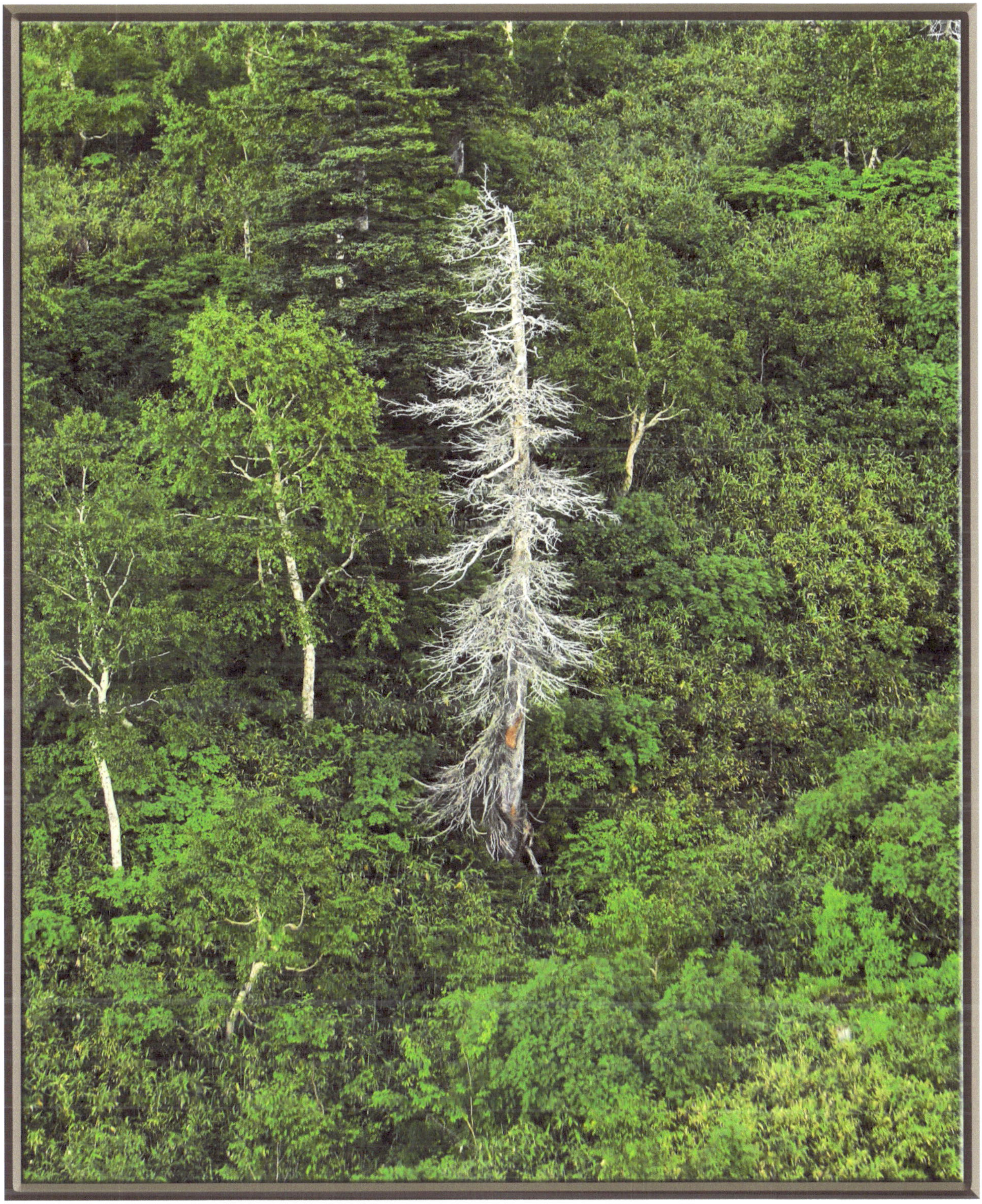

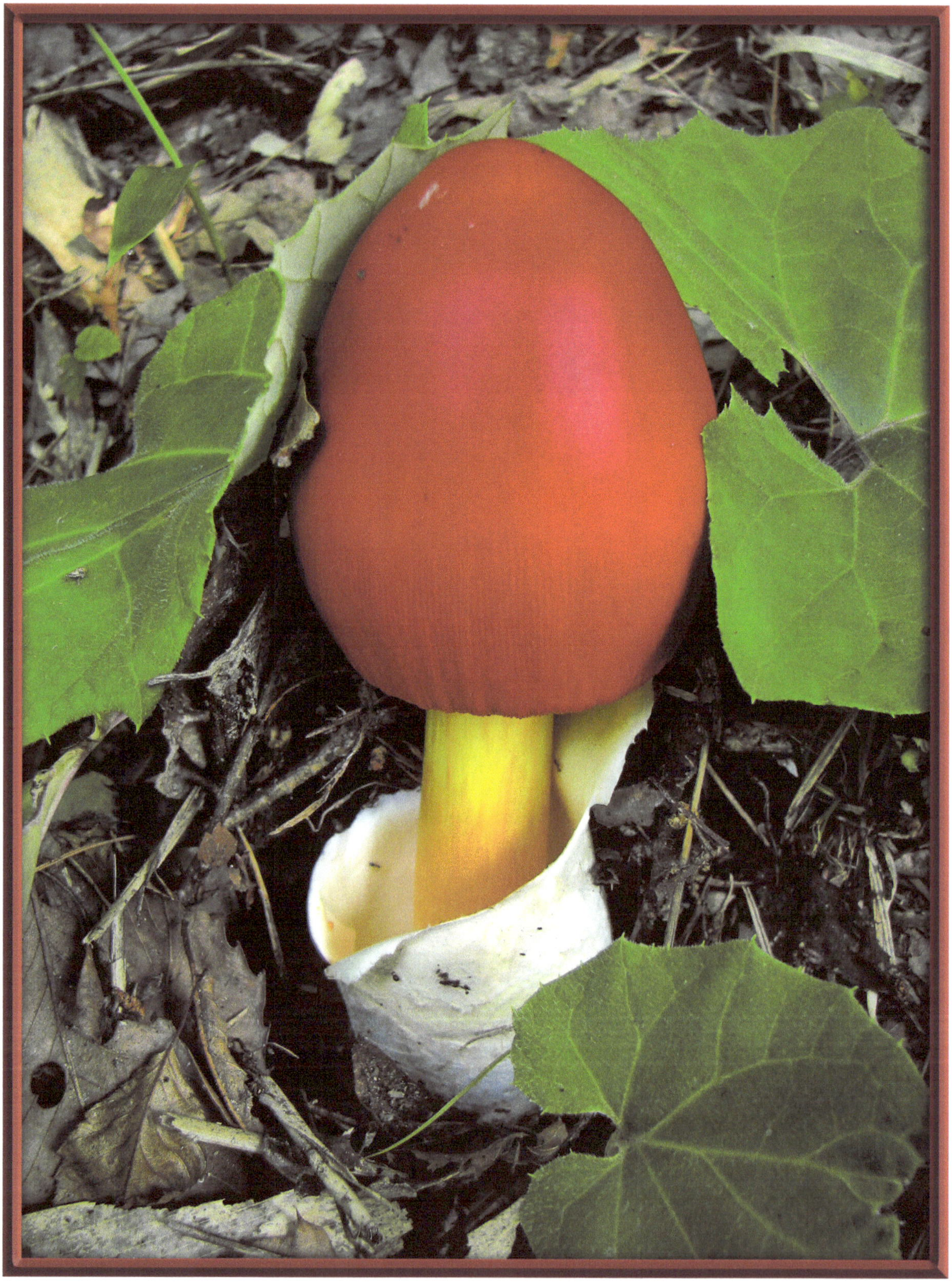

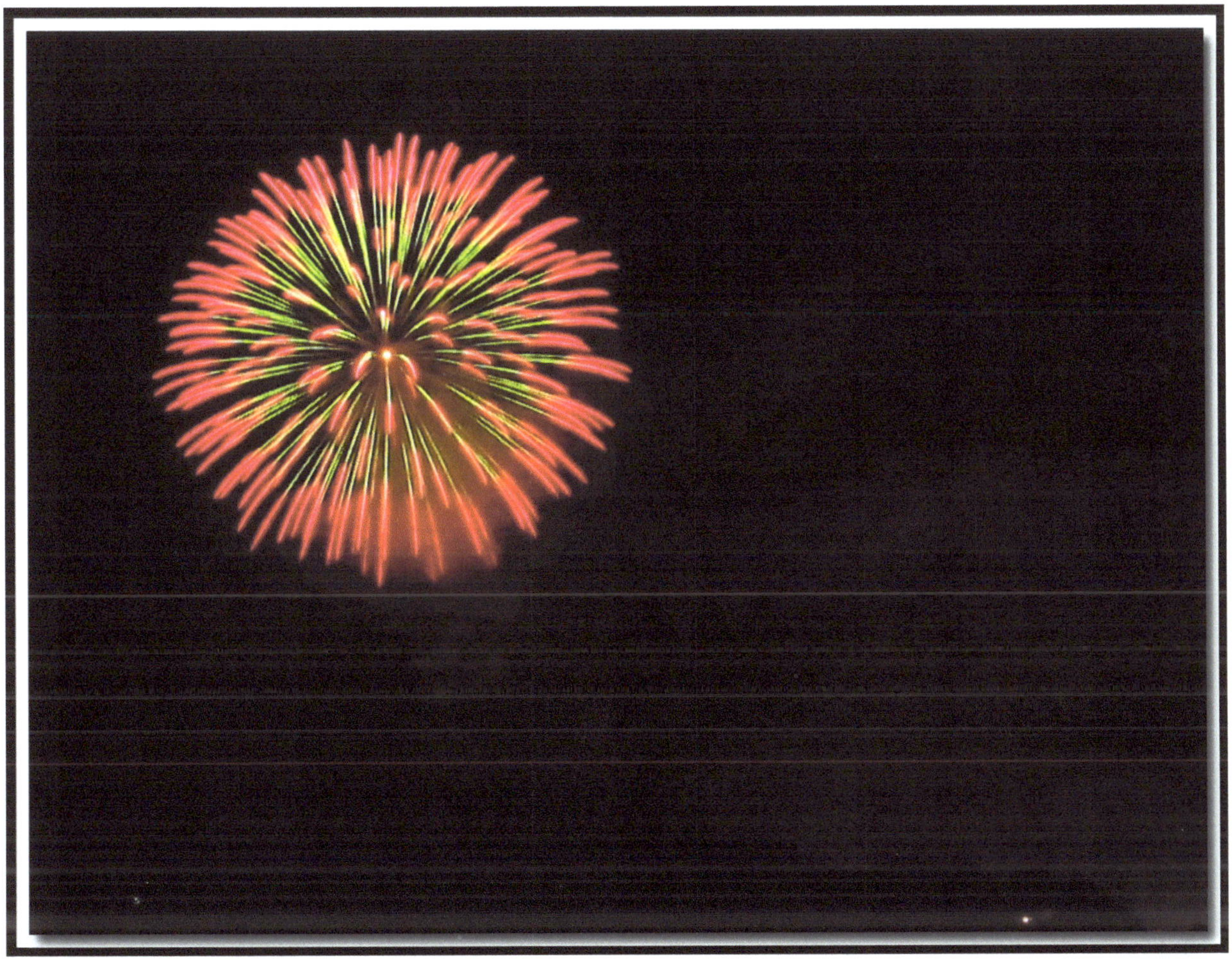

Now we're going to take a trip to **Yamagata Prefecture**. We'll spend a day in Funagata Town – Kazuya's hometown – and then travel to **Sakata City** and climb **Mt. Chokai** (2,236 meters = 7,336 feet). **Mt. Chokai** is on the boundary between **Yamagata** and **Akita Prefectures**.

On the facing page is a beautiful photo of a **Fly Agaric** or ***Amanita muscaria*** mushroom. This is a very poisonous mushroom, but its red color, often with white spots makes it very attractive to photograph and to look at.

On this page is a photo taken at a fireworks festival. Fireworks are difficult subjects to photograph because everything happens so fast. We were on a bridge over a river when we took these photos in **Yamagata Prefecture** and we were able to set our cameras directly on the concrete bridge rail, so that they were very stable.

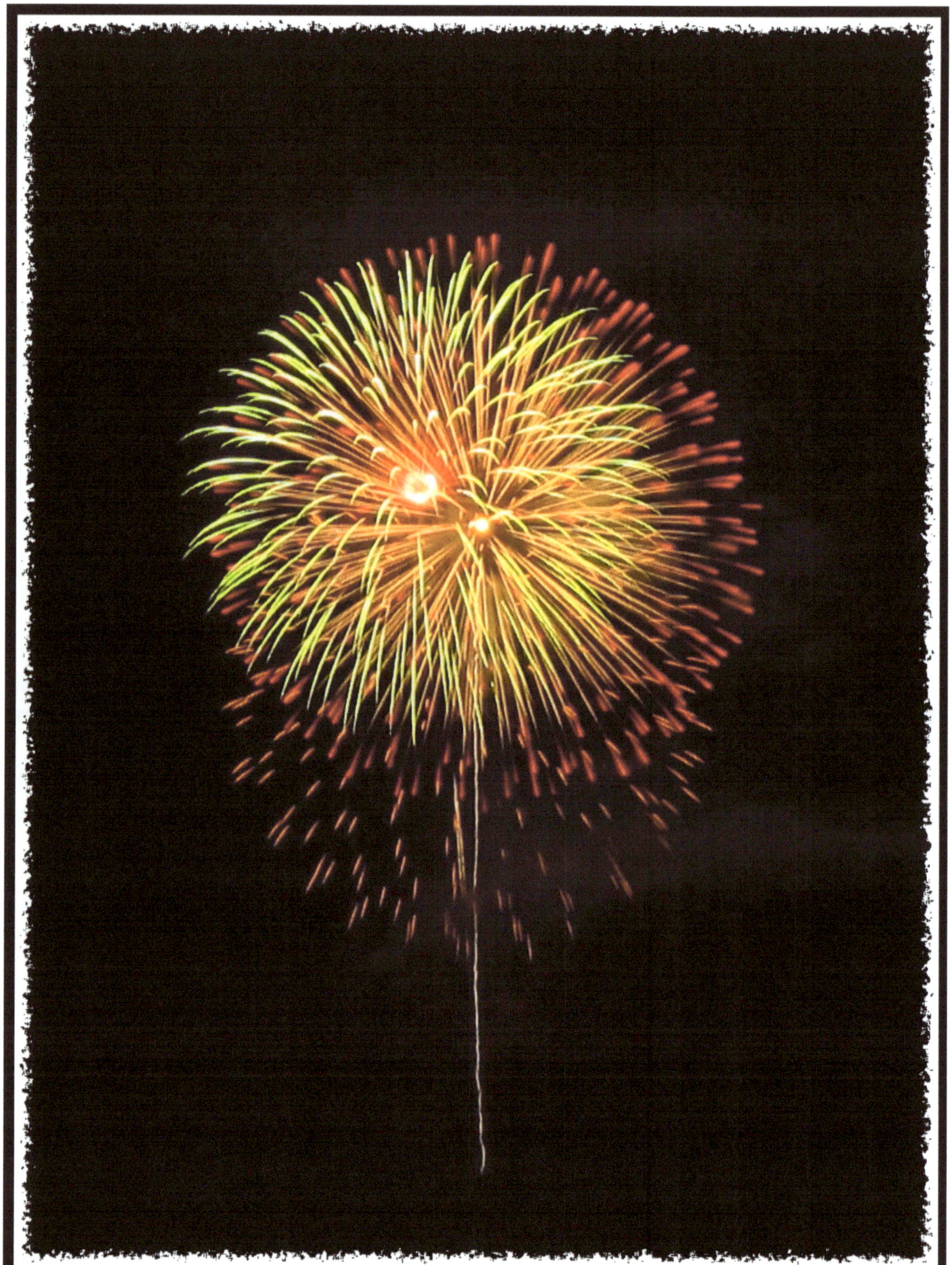

The facing page photo is another, and the final one, which was taken at the fireworks festival in **Yamagata Prefecture**.

The shot below is the first photo you see as we climbed **Mt. Chokai**. At 2,236 meters (= 7,336 feet), Mt. Chokai is the second highest mountain in the **Tohoku Region** of Japan. **Mt. Hiuchigatake**, at 2,356 meters (= 7,730 feet) is the highest mountain in the **Tohoku Region**. As we said previously, **Mt. Chokai** is on the boundary between **Yamagata** and **Akita Prefectures**. In this photo you can see the summit of **Mt. Chokai**. In the area of the right background you see a higher elevation place and on the left side of that higher elevation place you can see a series of four peaks. The summit of **Mt. Chokai** is one of those four peaks.

Note what beautiful weather we are having for this climb – at least so far!

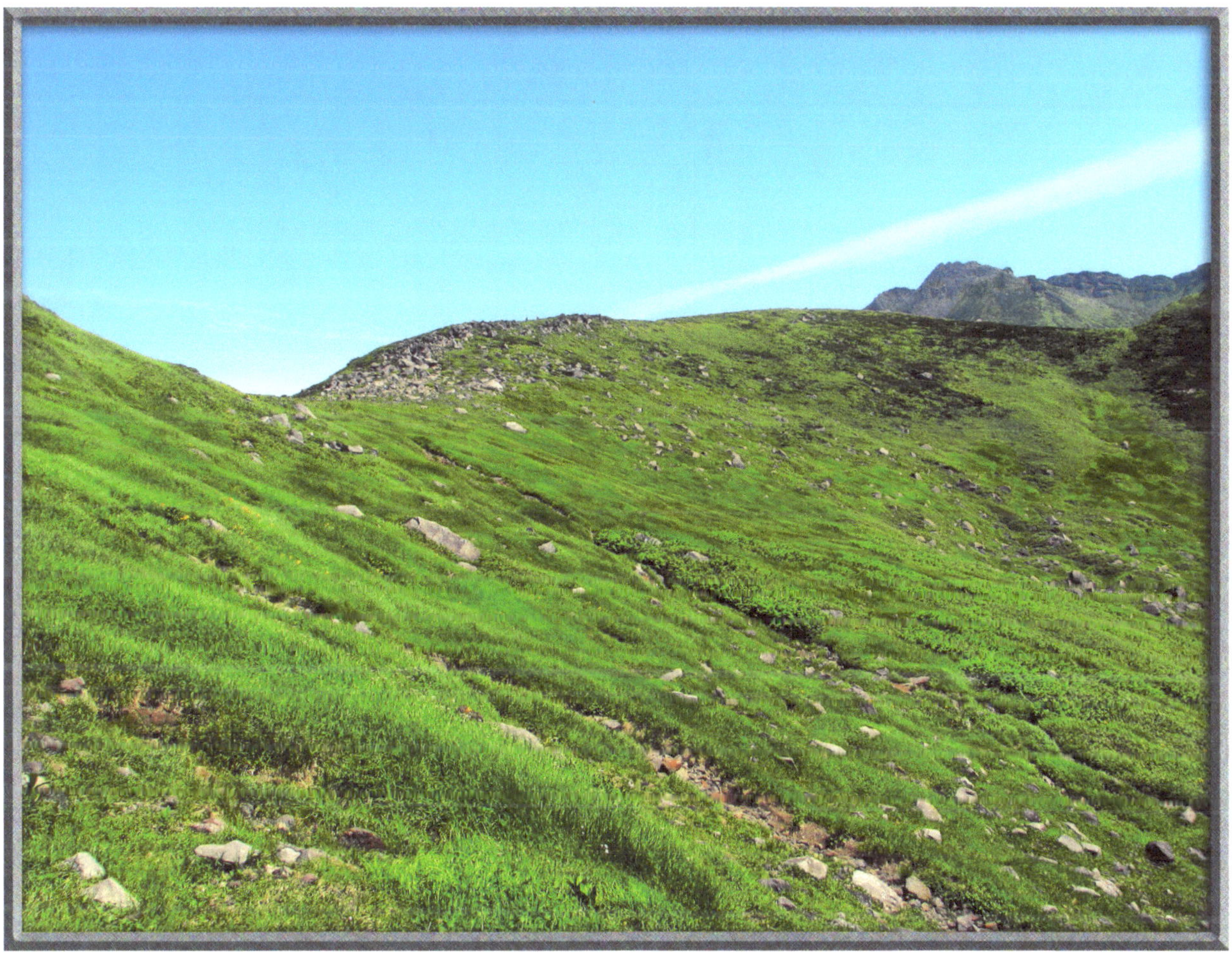

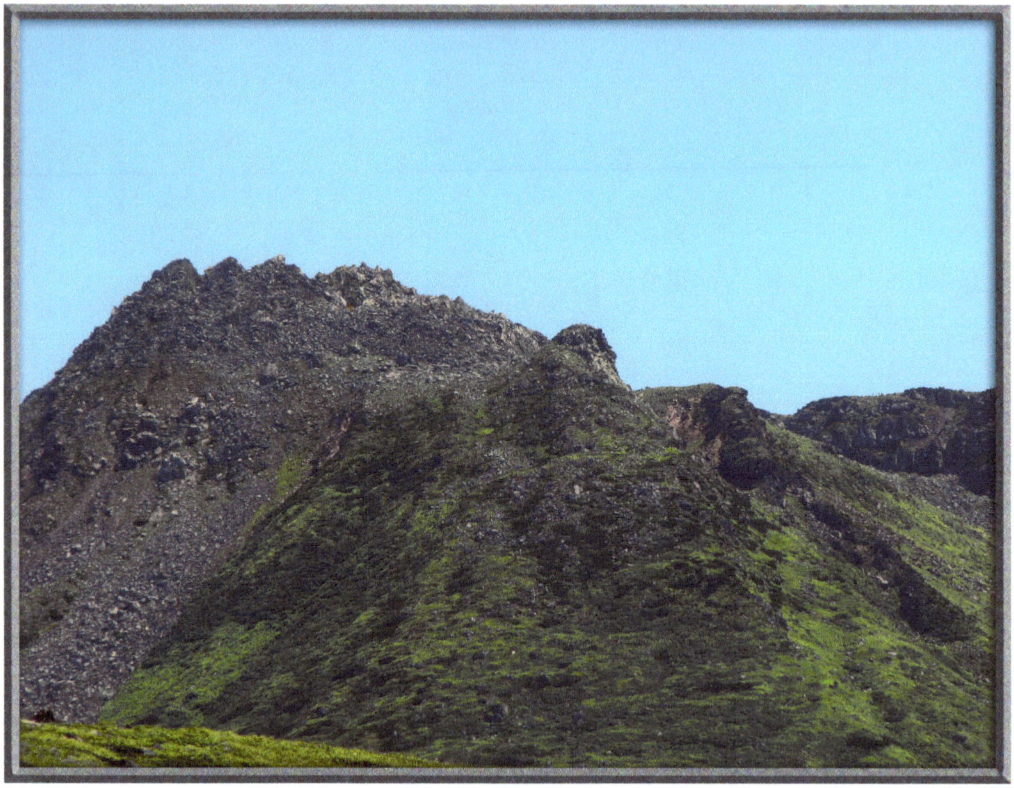

These two photos of the summit area of **Mt. Chokai** are rather similar, but we wanted to show you both of them due to the fact that the colors are impressive and also to show you how rugged the peak area is.

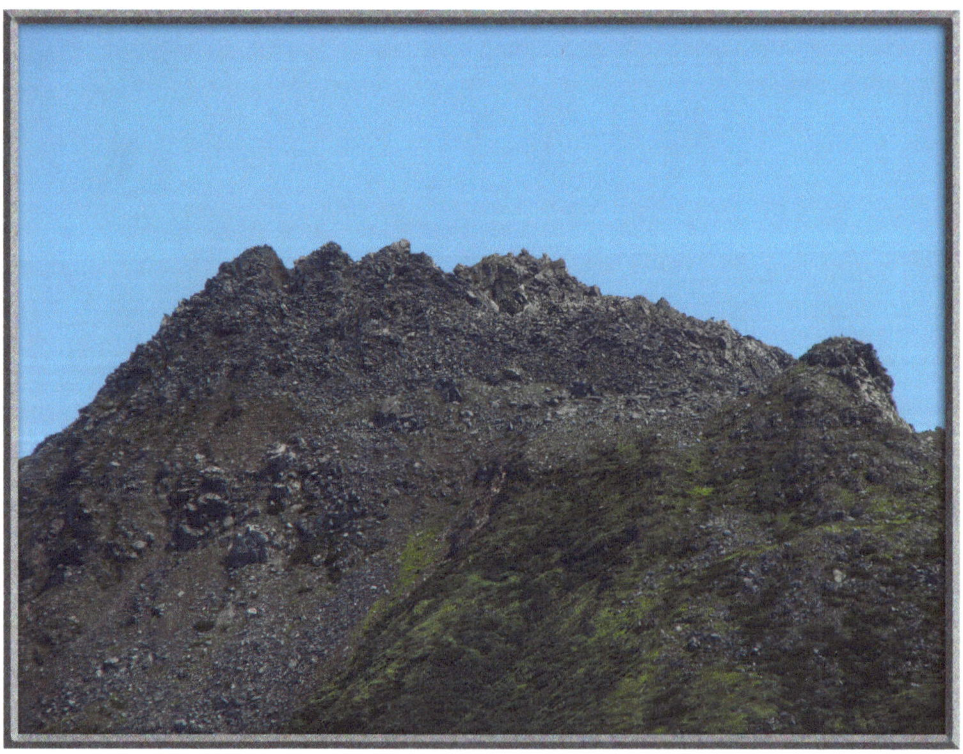

In this lower photo one of those bumps on the left is the summit.

The facing page shows a beautiful photo of ***Hemerocallis middendorffii* var. *esculenta***.

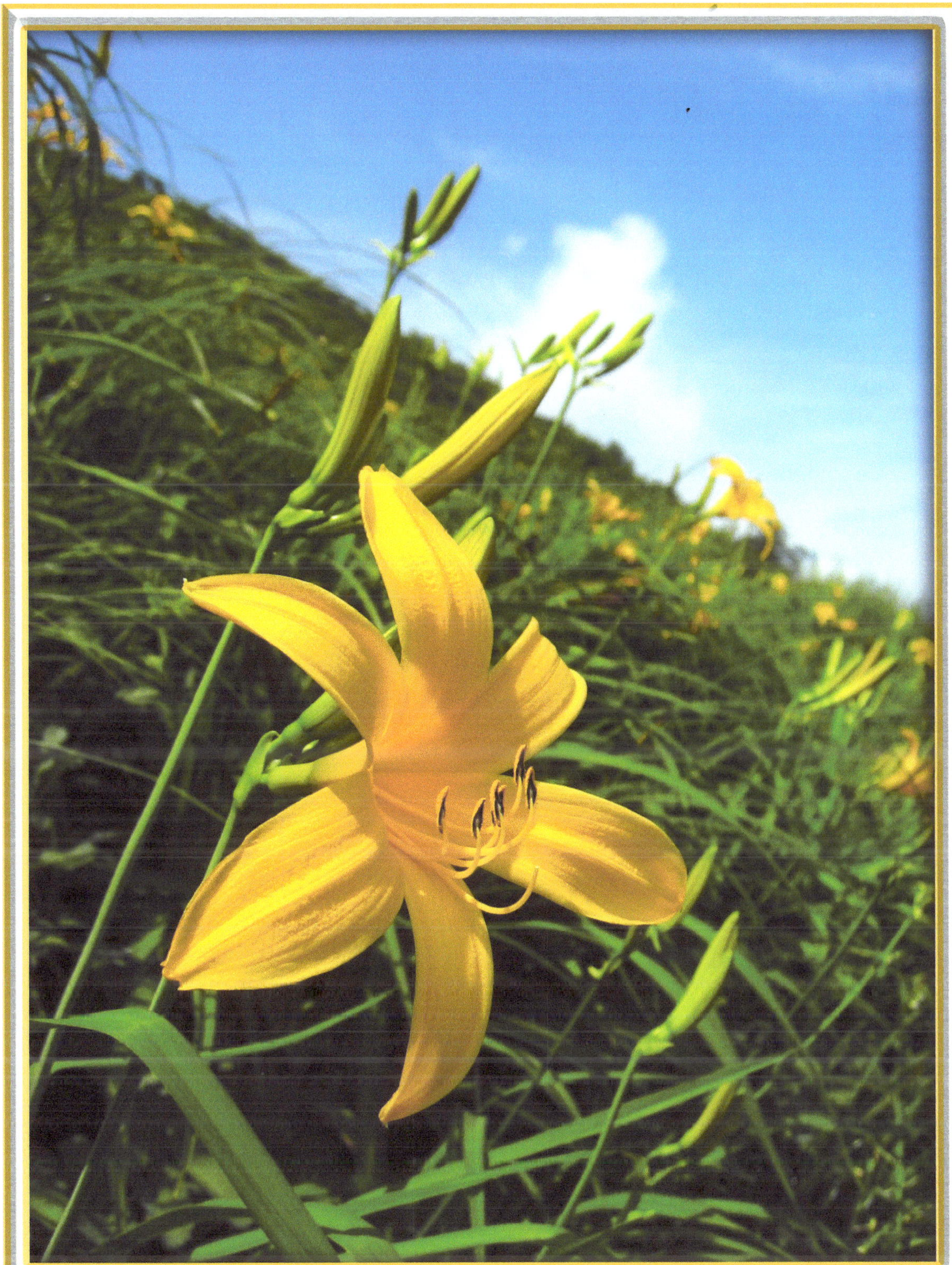

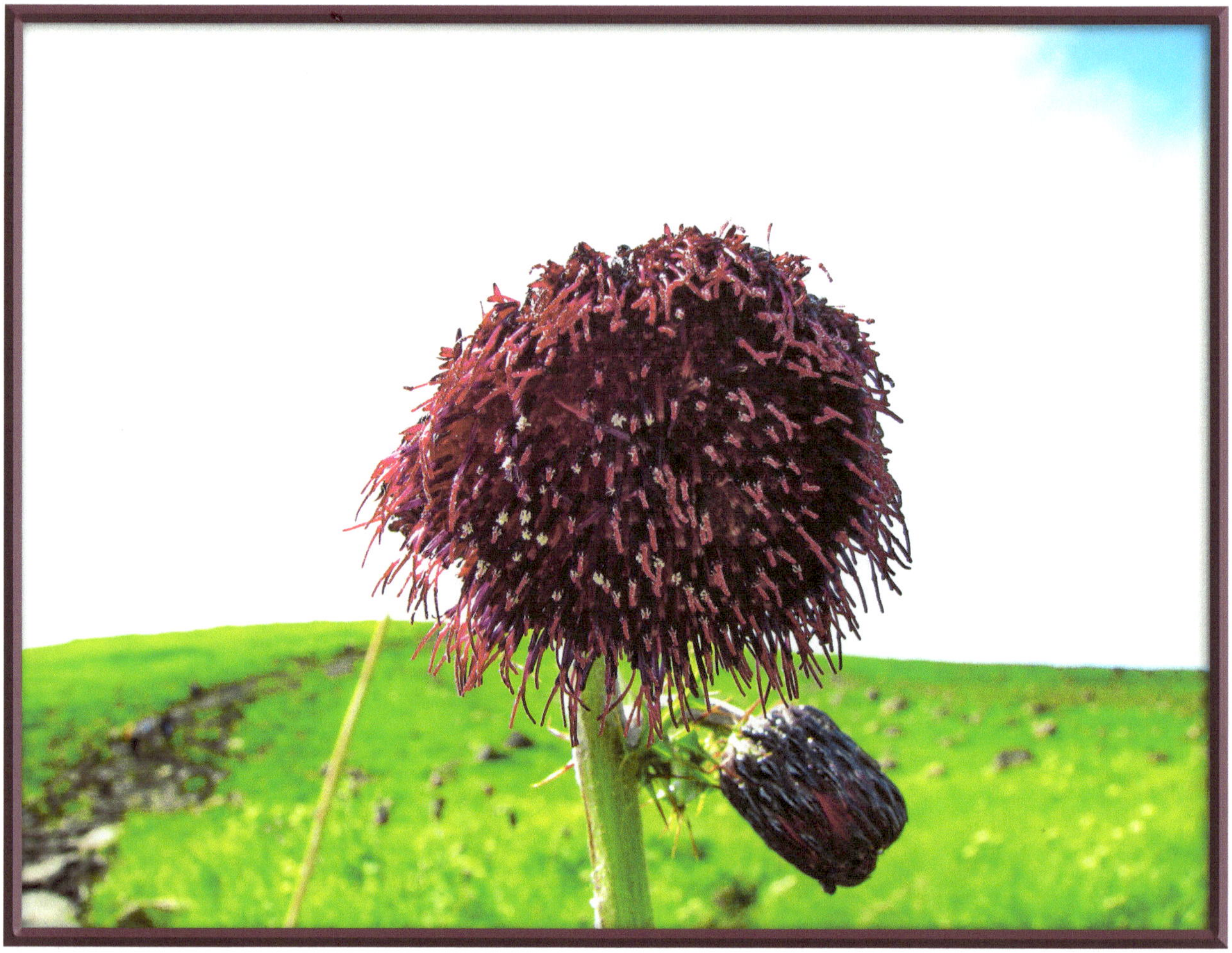

The above photo is of a **Chokai Thistle** (***Cirsium chokaiense***). This plant is found only on **Mt. Chokai** and in the immediate vicinity of Mt. Chokai.

The top photo on the facing page was taken as we neared the summit hut. Of course the summit hut is not actually at the summit, but it is within a thirty minute hike of the summit. The actual peak of this mountain is only large enough so that about ten people can stand on it at a single time. By the way, you might want to notice the people on the snowfield.

The lower photo on the facing page was taken from the summit of **Mt. Chokai** (2,236 meters = 7,336 feet). The time was 5:58 PM – nearing sunset. The elongated island you can see out there in the **Sea of Japan** is **Tobishima** (Tobi Island).

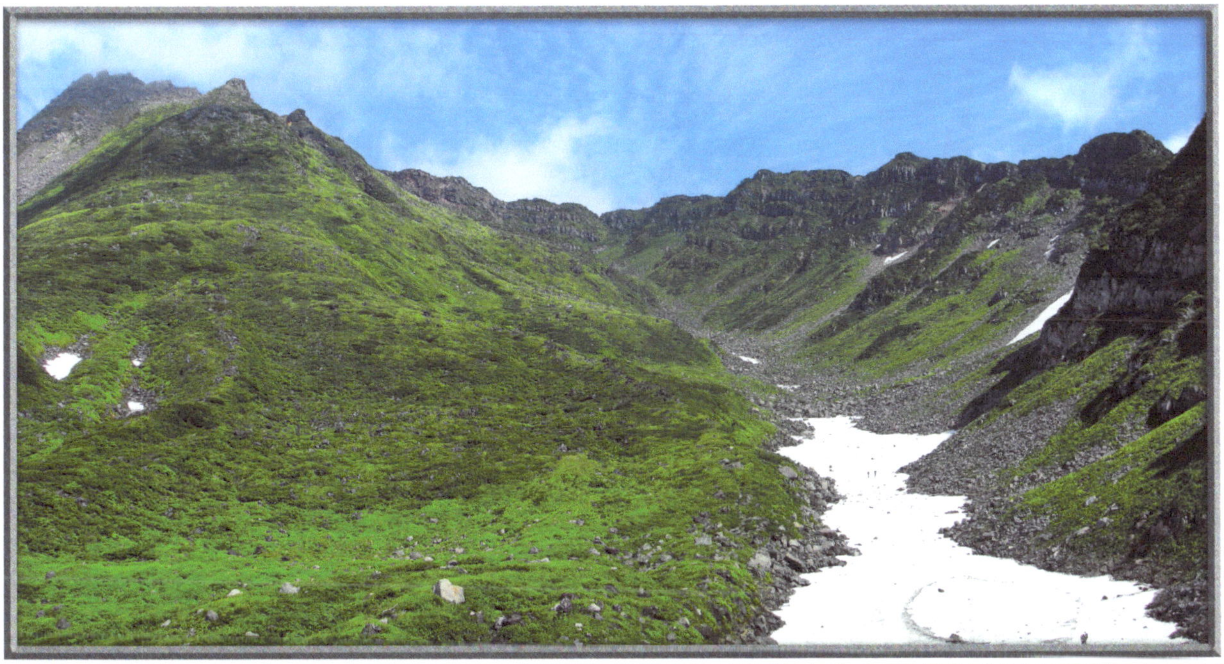

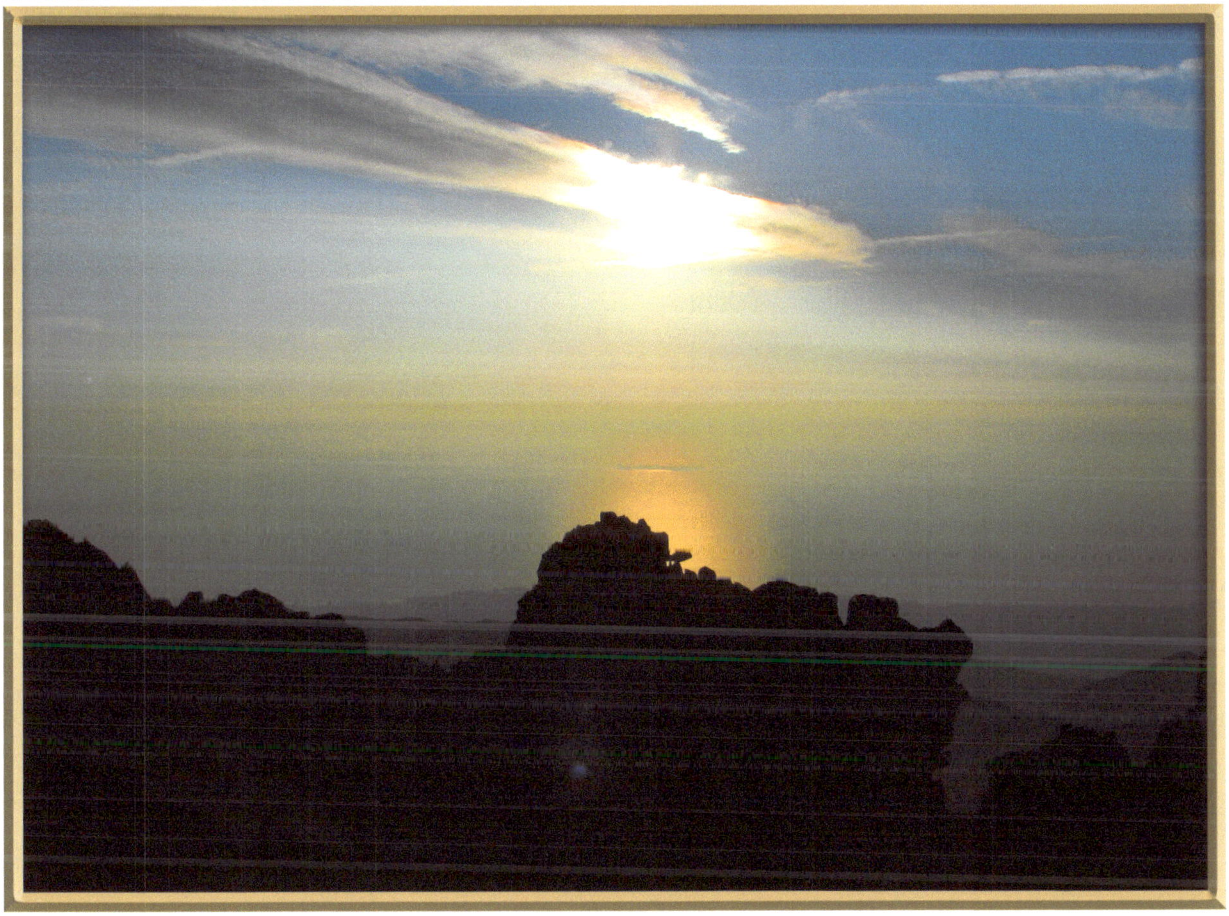

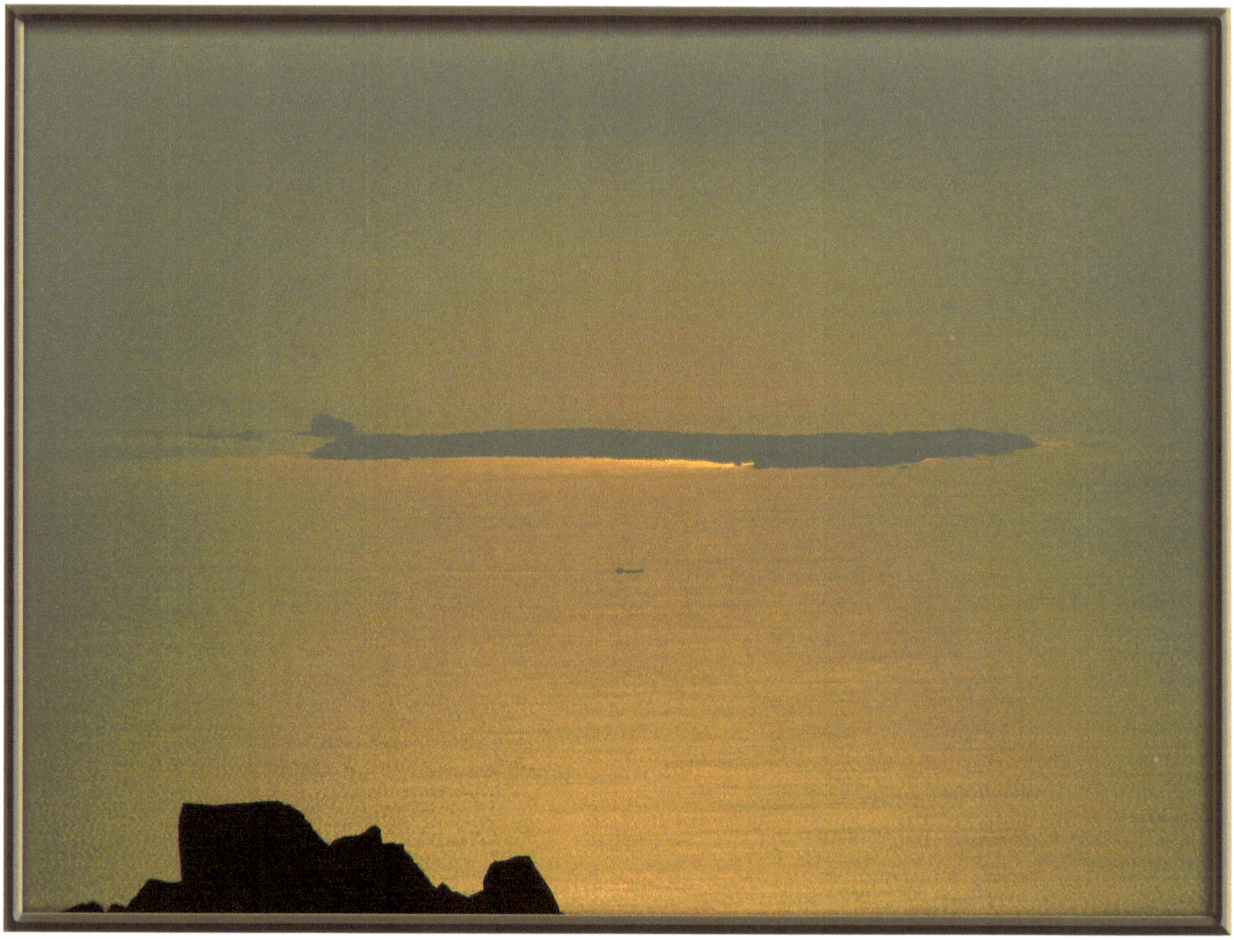

Just above is an additional photo of **Tobishima** (**Tobi Island**) which was taken from the summit of Mt. Chokai. The time of this photo was also 5:58 PM, but this photo is zoomed in to show a larger view of **Tobishima**. In this photo you can also see a boat or ship crossing between the mainland and **Tobishima** in the **Sea of Japan**.

On the facing page is a final image which shows **Tobishima**. This photo was taken at 6:00 PM and the light has changed just enough in the two minutes since the shot you saw on page 207 to make this interesting to look at. Of course you will also note that this photo is zoomed in much more than the one on page 207.

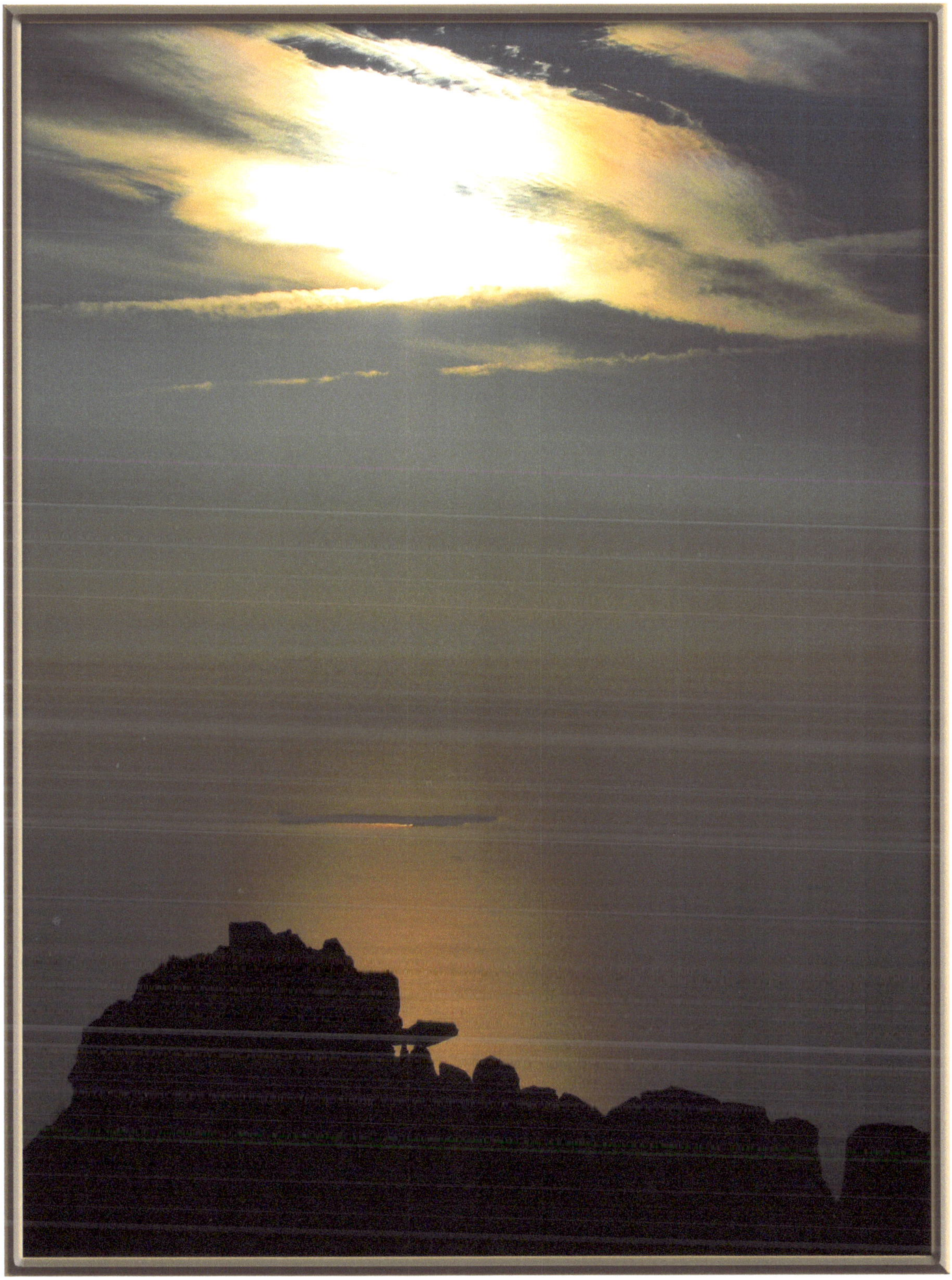

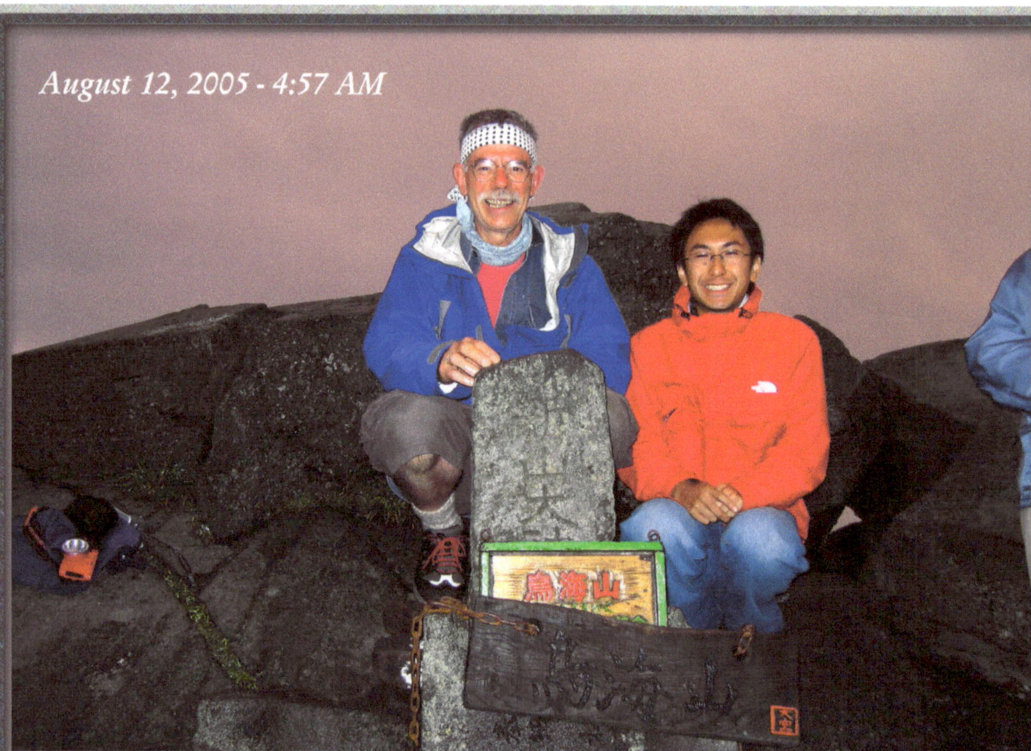
August 12, 2005 - 4:57 AM
鳥海山

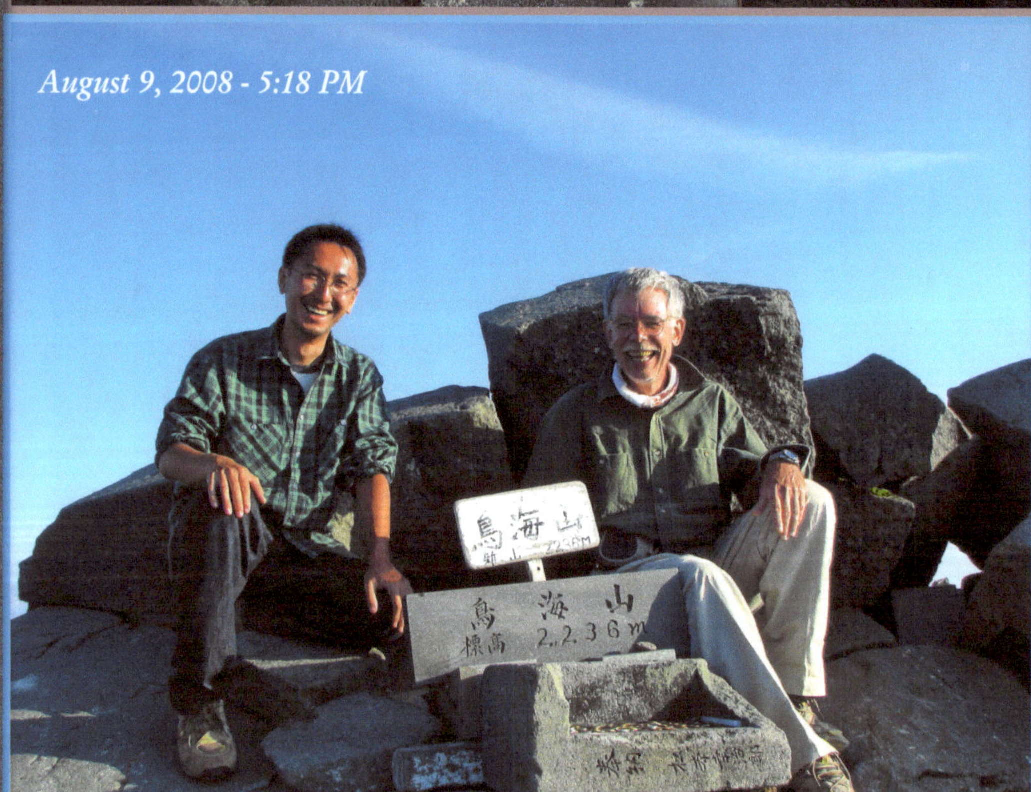
August 9, 2008 - 5:18 PM
鳥海山
鳥 海 山
標高 2.2.3 6 m

The facing page photo shows us at the summit of **Mt. Chokai** (2,236 meters = 7,336 feet) on August 12, 2005 at 4:57 AM and again on August 9, 2008 at 5:18 PM. In 2005 we attempted to go to the summit in the evening, but the trail through the boulders was not clearly marked and we ended up on a false summit. The following morning we were more careful to search for the trail markers (the white paint marks on rocks) and we successfully attained the summit and witnessed the sunrise.

In 2008 when we again climbed Mt. Chokai we knew where to search for the summit and we successfully found it in the evening to see the sunset. It was fortunate for us that we went to the trouble to summit the mountain in the evening, because on the following morning we were totally in the clouds and could not see anything even resembling a sunrise.

That photo is the final one from our climbs of Mt. Chokai. Below is a photo from **Mt. Gassan**, in **Yamagata Prefecture**. **Mt. Gassan** is 1,984 meters (= 6,509 feet) in elevation and has many flowers. This was our first time to find **Edelweiss** flowers, but they were rather dried up and not so attractive so we will not show you any photos of Edelweiss from this adventure. In the below photo – taken as the sun lowers (4:41 PM) – you can see such an amazing variety of alpine flowers that we think you'll be impressed by the beauty.

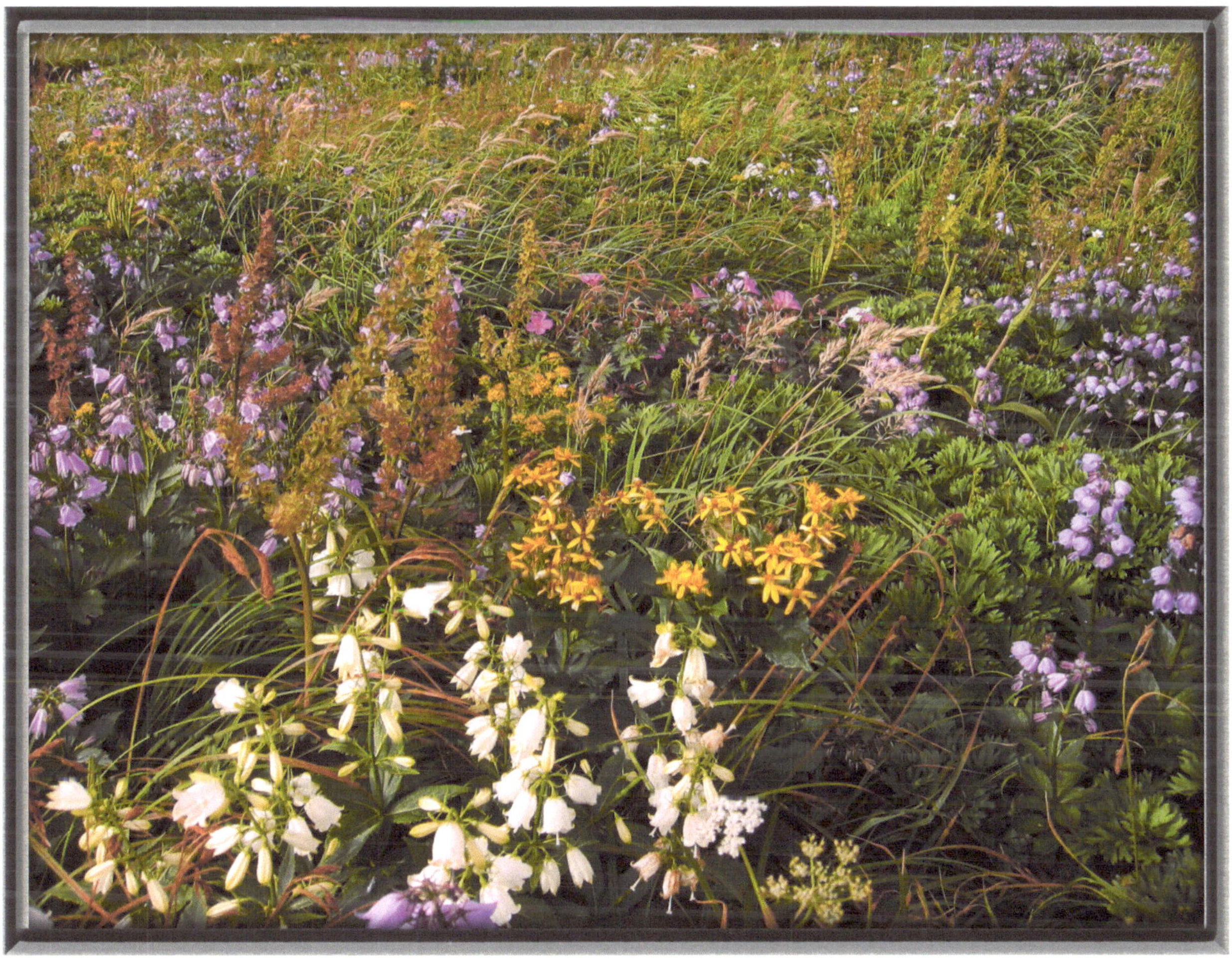

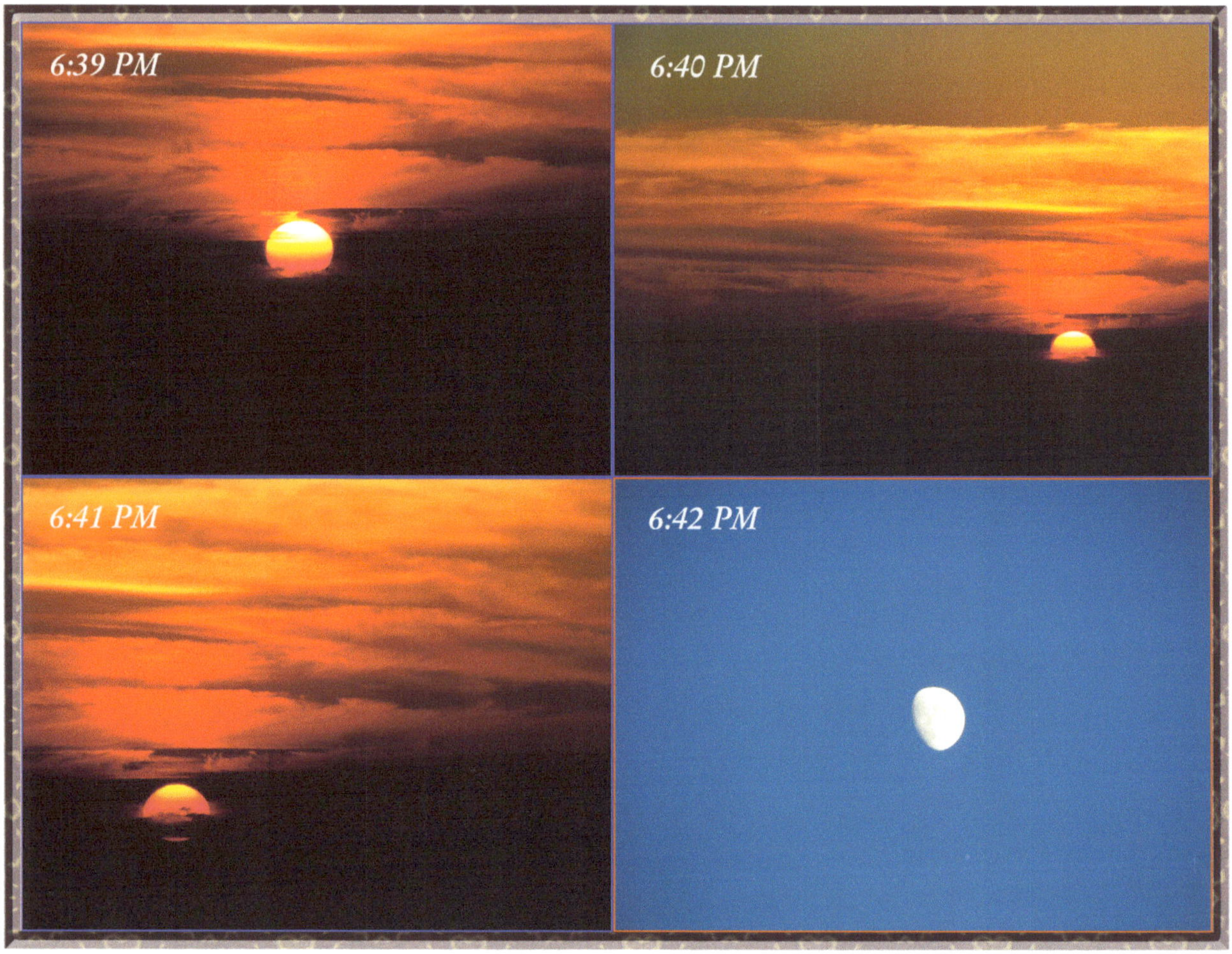

This photo collage shows three shots of the setting sun which we witnessed from the summit of Mt. Gassan. This sunset was rather amazing in that it looked like a bright orange light sinking through layers of oil. We took about seventy-five photos of the sunset in just a few moments. The fourth image in this collage was taken while looking in the opposite direction – at a ¾ moon as it makes its way across the sky.

The photo on the facing page was taken the following morning as we descended Mt. Gassan. There is a tiny lake or pond down there which caught the sun's rays and reflected them back to us in this incredible star shape. No filters or special lenses were used to capture this phenomenon – this photo is just as taken with our stock lens and also just as it appeared to our naked eyes.

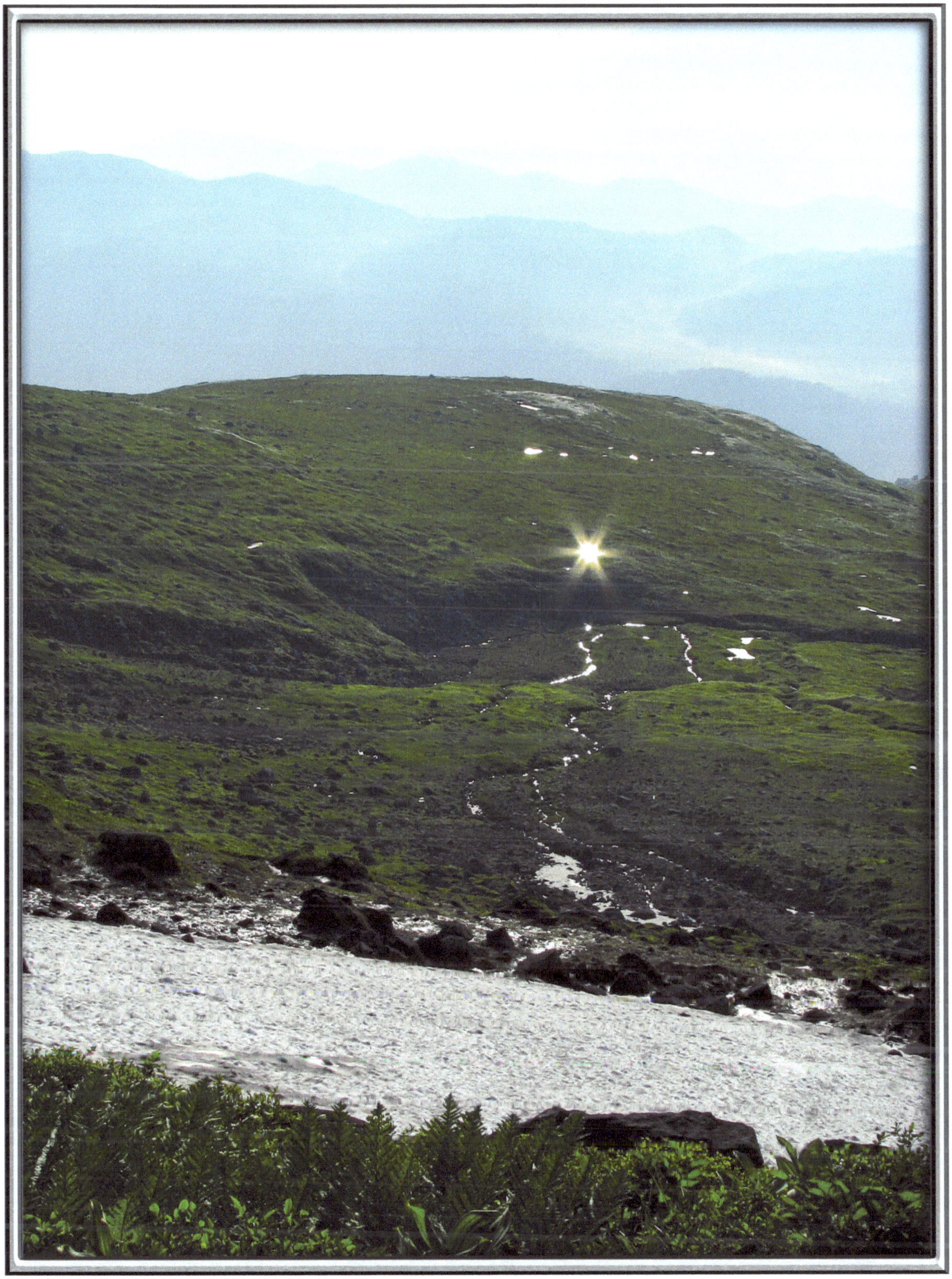

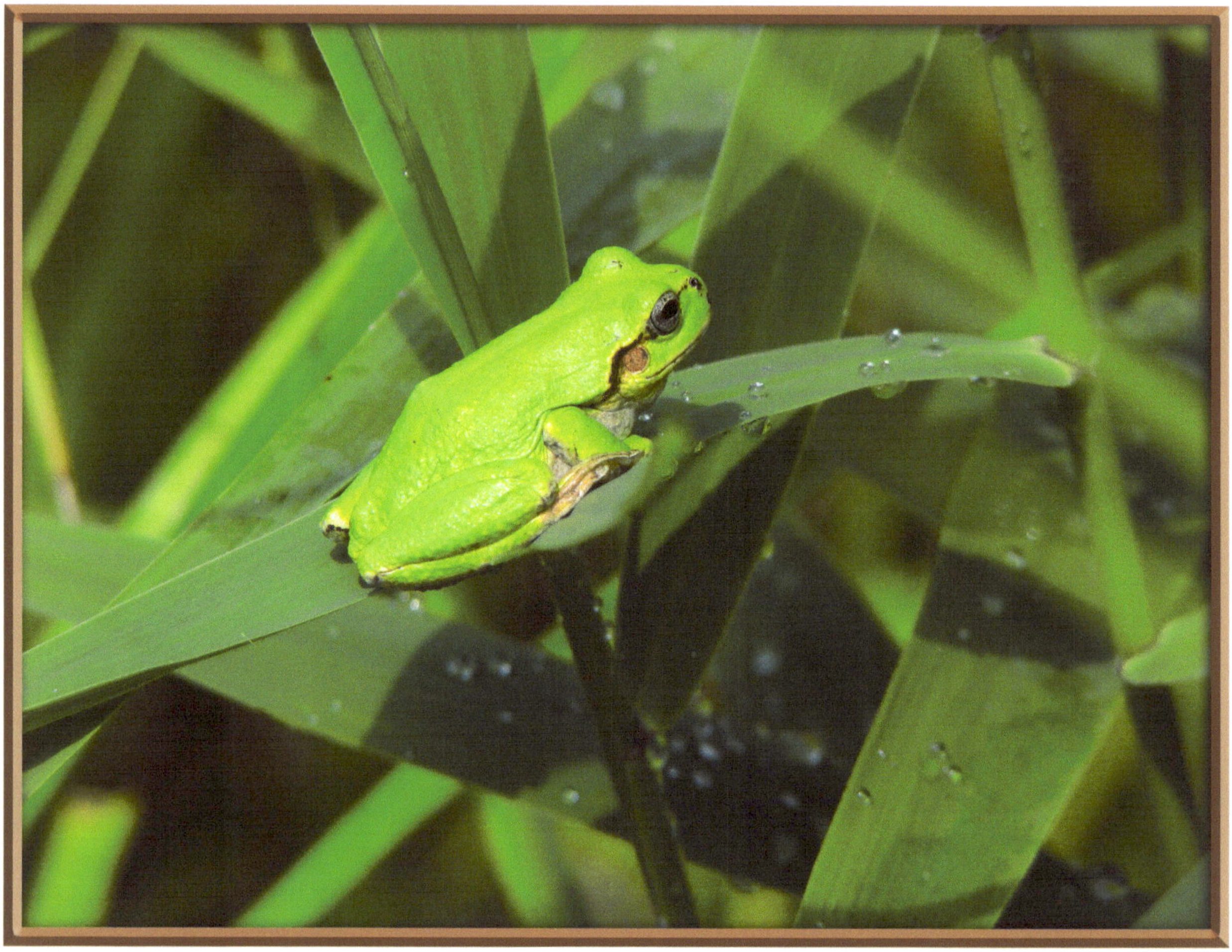

Isn't that a cute little frog sitting on the leaves of the bamboo grass? It was so very cooperative in our efforts to photograph it too. It just sat there and didn't hop away as we shot about ten photos of it. It never turned around and looked right at us and the location made it very difficult for us to move around and get in front of it, so we were quite satisfied with a series of profile shots. This shot was taken in **Funagata Town** in **Yamagata Prefecture**.

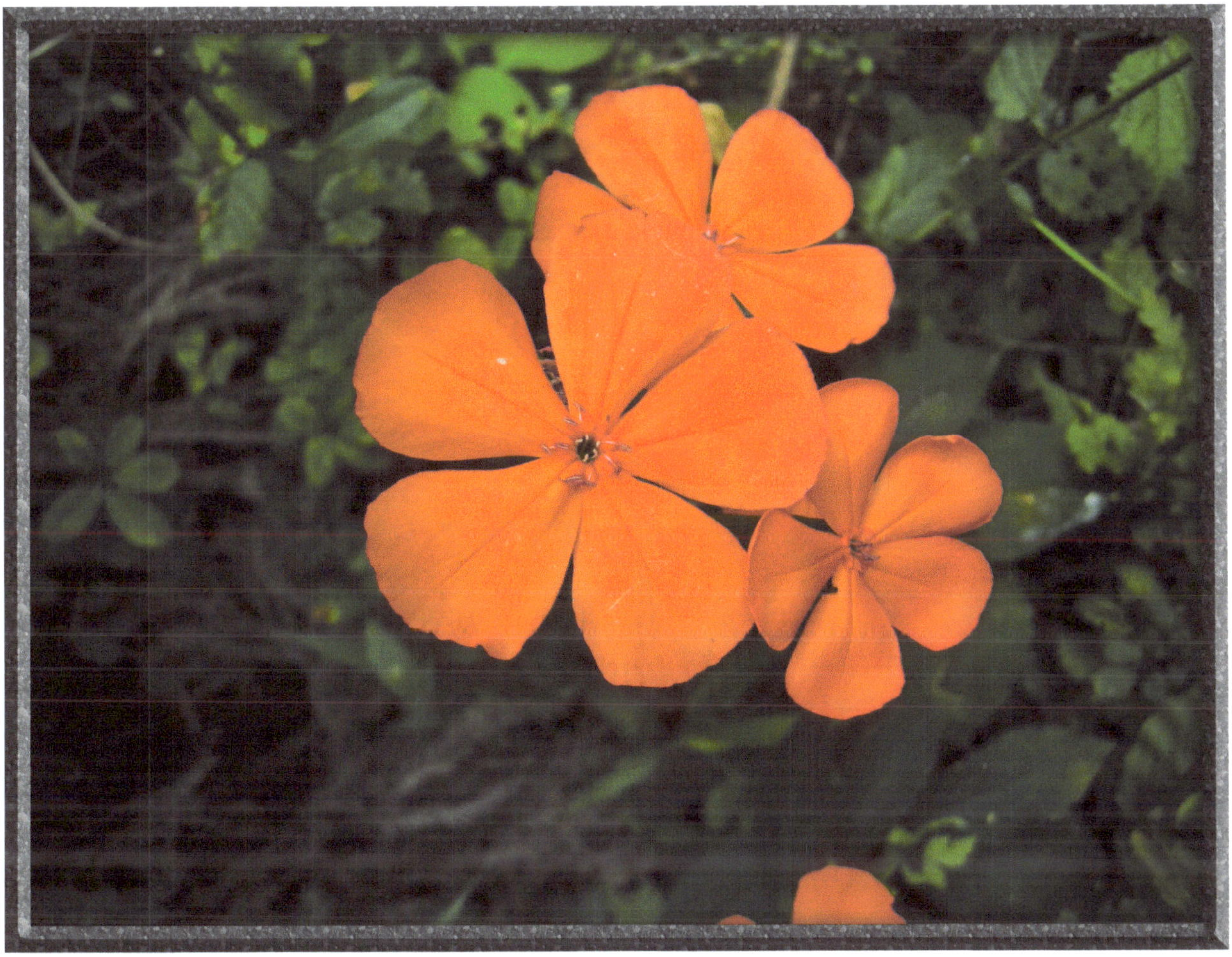

Now we're going to return to our home territory to finish off the month of August. This photo of ***Lychnis miqueliana*** is the first of the final three shots from August. We are once again climbing **Mt. Kumotori**, in **Tokyo**. You may recall from pages 64, 66 and 79 that Mt. Kumotori, at 2,017.6 meters (= 6,619 feet), is the highest point in Tokyo. In actuality, late August is quite late to be able to find flowers on Mt. Kumotori, but these were found down near the start of the trail which takes us to the summit. By the time we get to the summit in late August it is already approaching autumn weather.

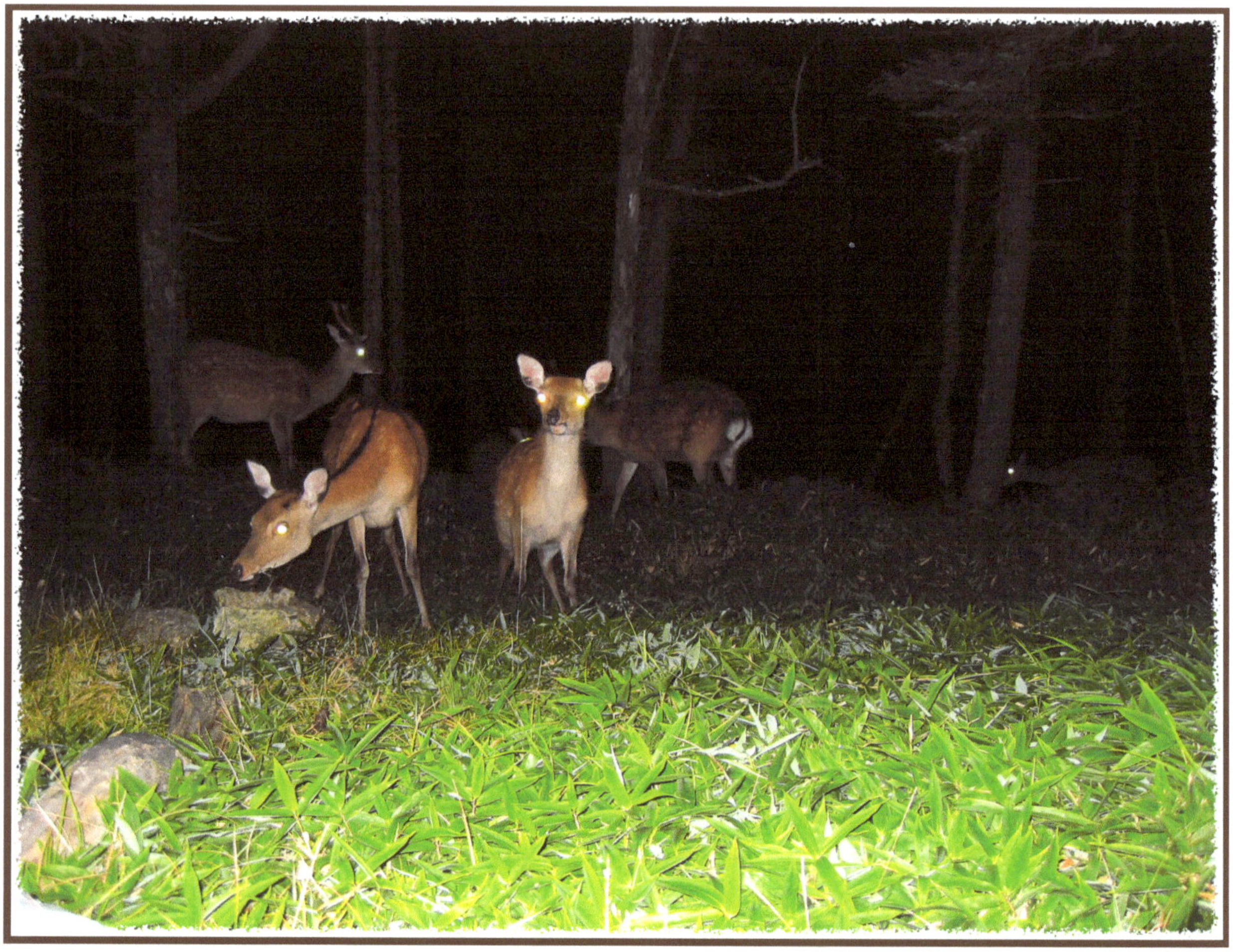

This photo was taken from directly outside of our tent on **Mt. Kumotori**. If you study this photo carefully you can find six deer here. What are they doing? Well, the deer population on Mt. Kumotori is so high that it crashes every few years due to lack of enough winter food resources. There is also a severe lack of anything with salt in it. These deer are going after the salt in our urine. Yes, we urinated here on the mountain, rather inevitable isn't it, when one is camping out on a mountain and the nearest toilet is some kilometers away.

The facing page photo is the final photo from August. It is the sunrise on **Mt. Kumotori** in late August of this particular year. In this photo you can see another sun pillar (page 10). Mt. Kumotori is situated with the peak facing in such a direction that one can get both incredible sunrises and incredible sunsets from here.

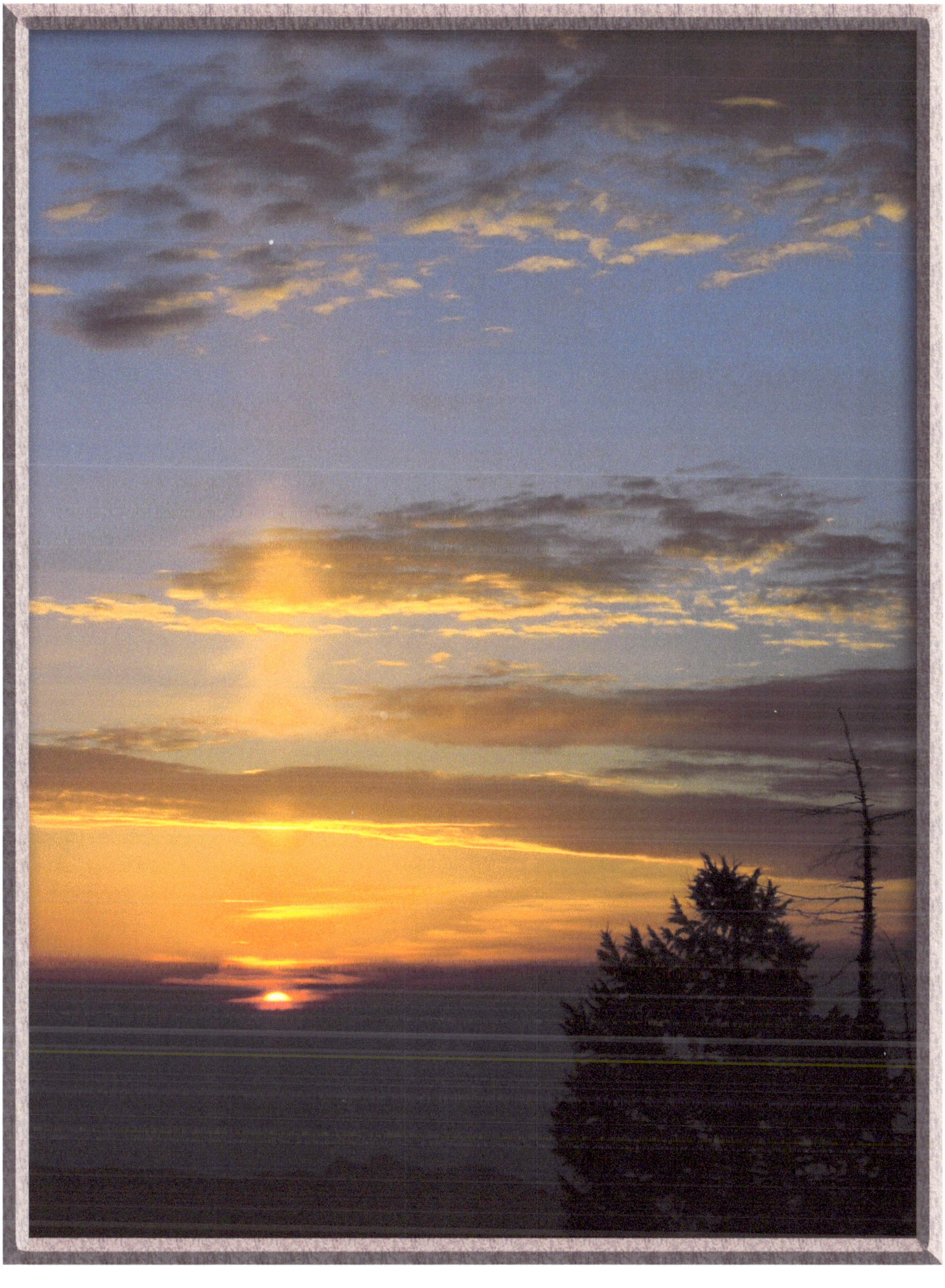

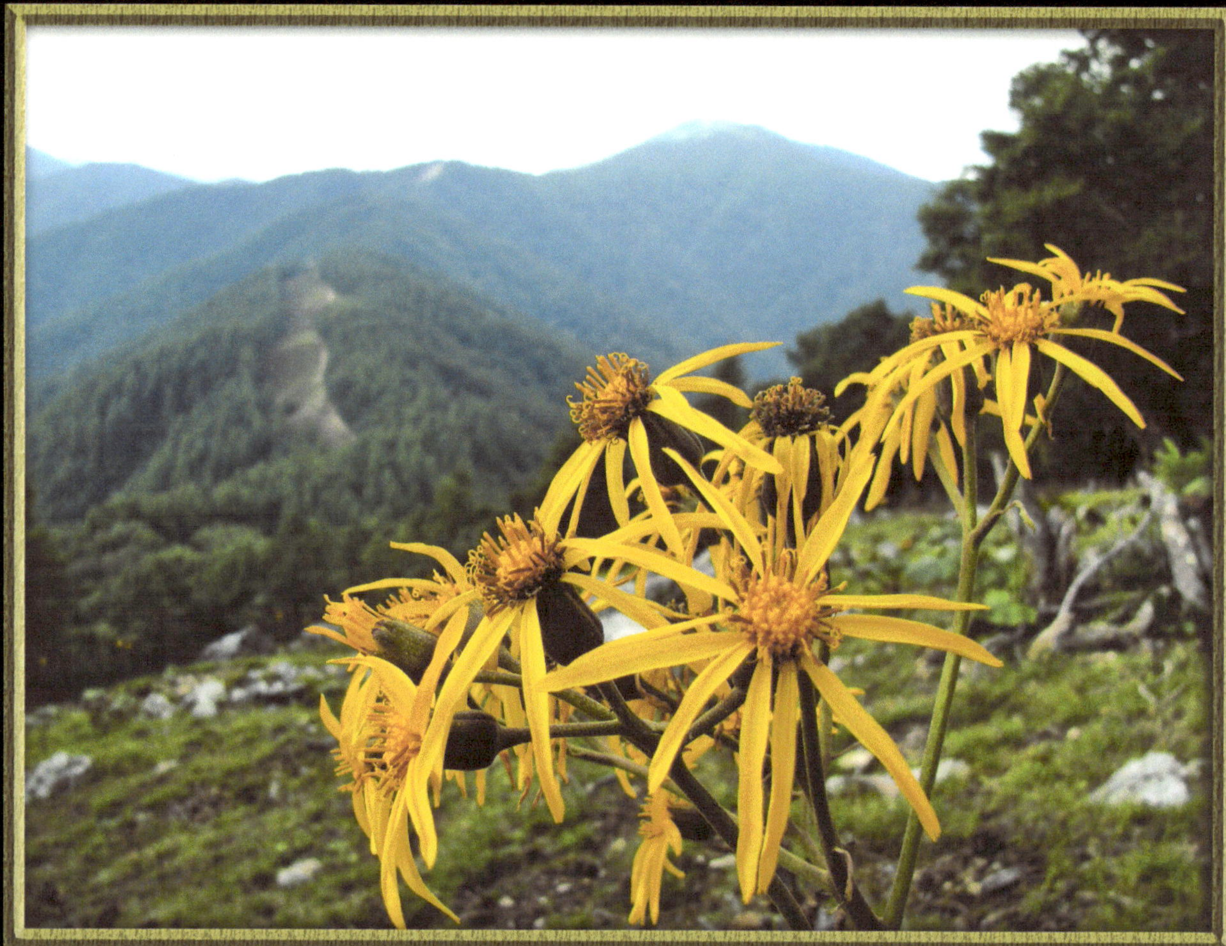

September Photos and Story

Amazingly enough, we ended August on **Mt. Kumotori**. Now, it's September and we begin with another trip to **Mt. Kumotori**. Of course this is a different year than the previous photos.

The photo above is a shot of ***Ligularia dentata*** (***Marubadakebuki*** in Japanese). This was taken at the summit of **Mt. Nanatsu-ishi** (1,757 meters = 5,765 feet). ***Ligularia dentata*** is a very late summer flower (of course it's already autumn up here at this elevation).

In the background you can see the ridgeline firebreak cut through the forest and on the right side of the photo, way in the background, with a cloud around its summit, you can see **Mt. Kumotori**.

On the facing page we are at the summit of **Mt. Kumotori**. The top photo was taken at 5:13 AM, it's sunrise time. The lower photo, a panorama showing Mt. Fuji and the summit sign, was taken at 6:10 AM.

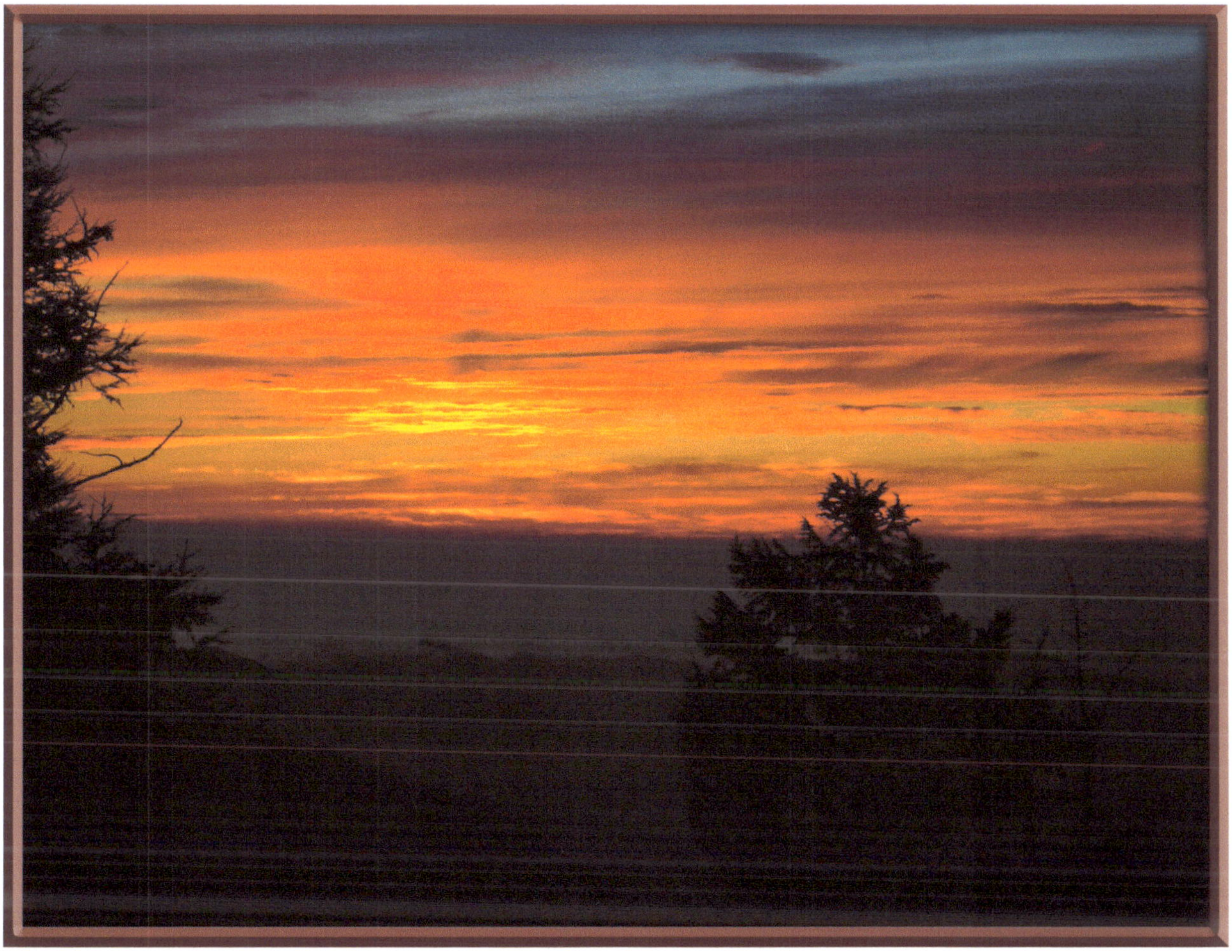

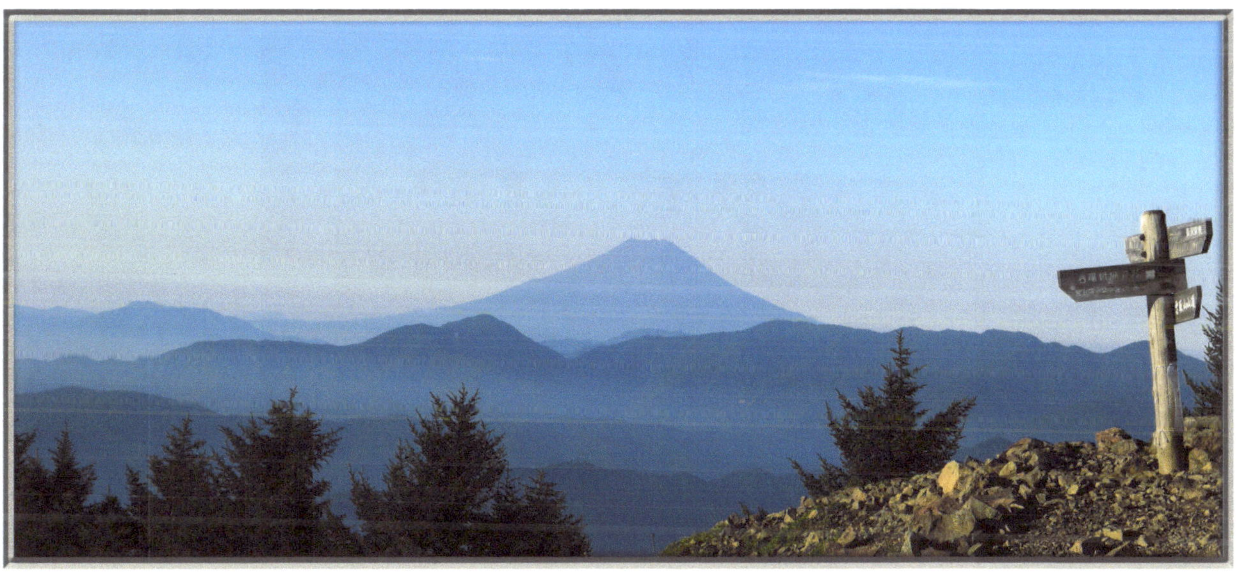

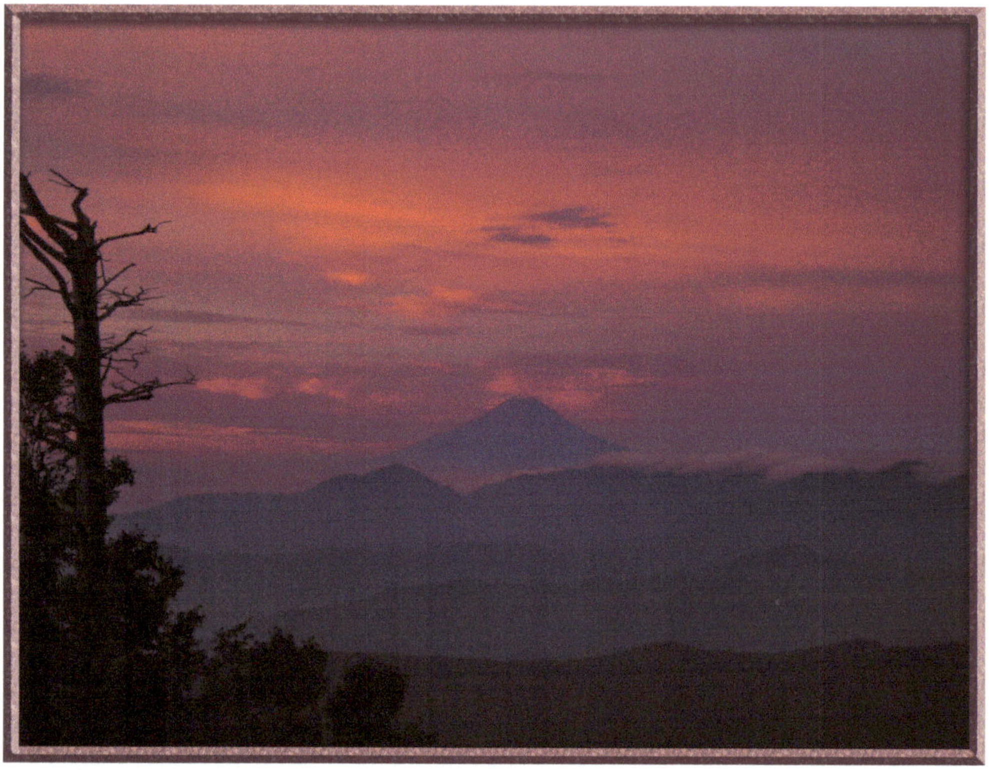

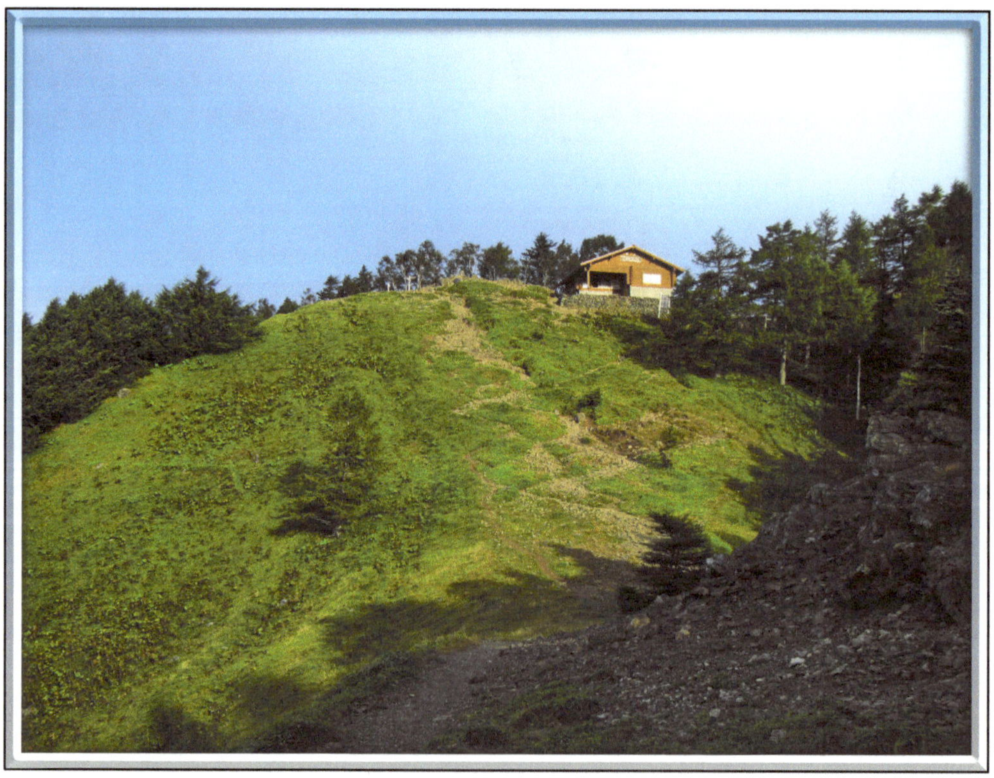

The upper photo on this page is another sunrise photo taken from the summit of **Mt. Kumotori**. The time here was 5:19 AM and it is a different year once again. That is **Mt. Fuji** back there.

The lower photo shows the summit hut on **Mt. Kumotori** from just below the summit. This photo was taken in the same year as the photo just above.

The facing page photo was taken as we descended **Mt. Kumotori**. It is another ***Ligularia dentata*** with some of the native forest as a background. Note the huge leaves which this plant has.

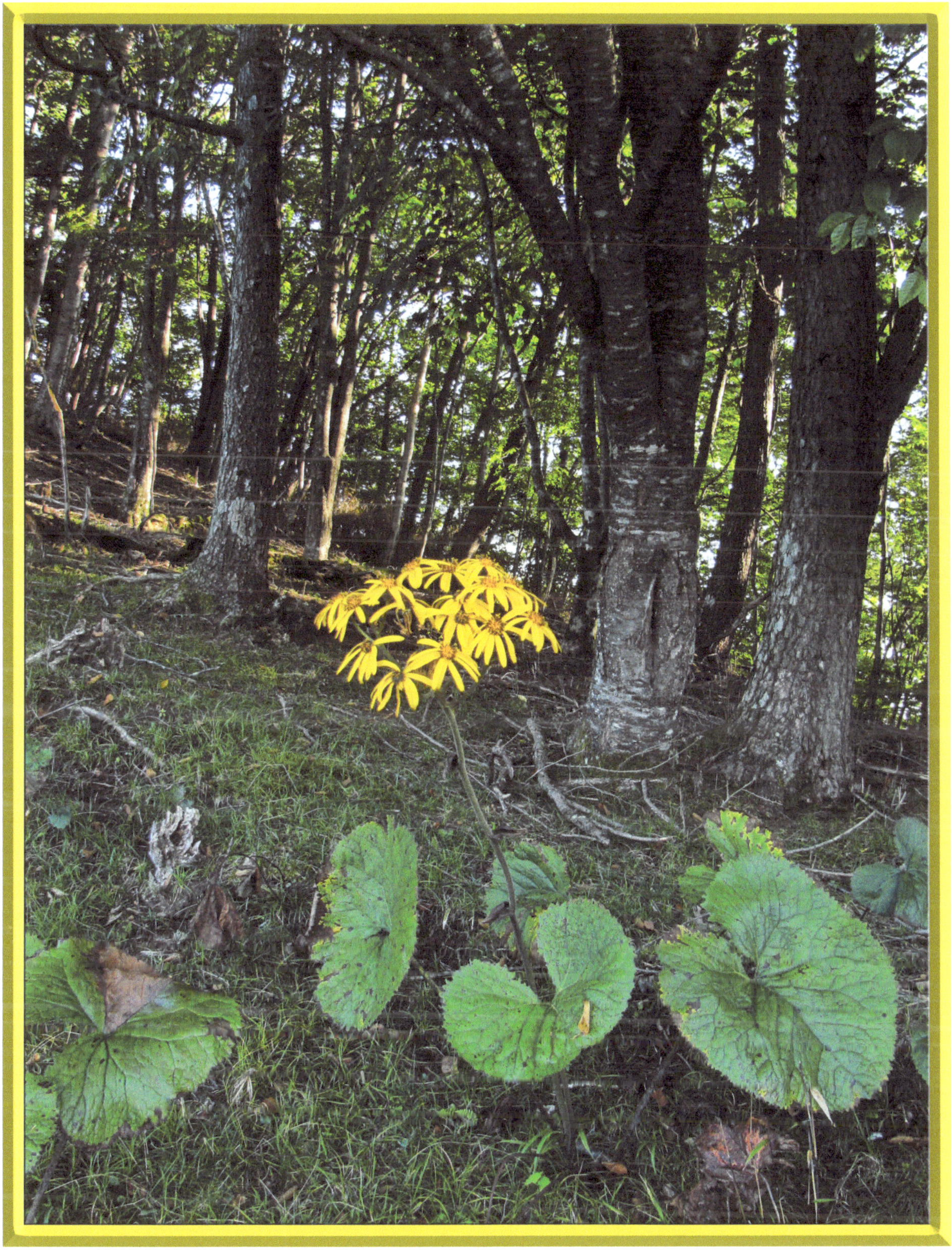

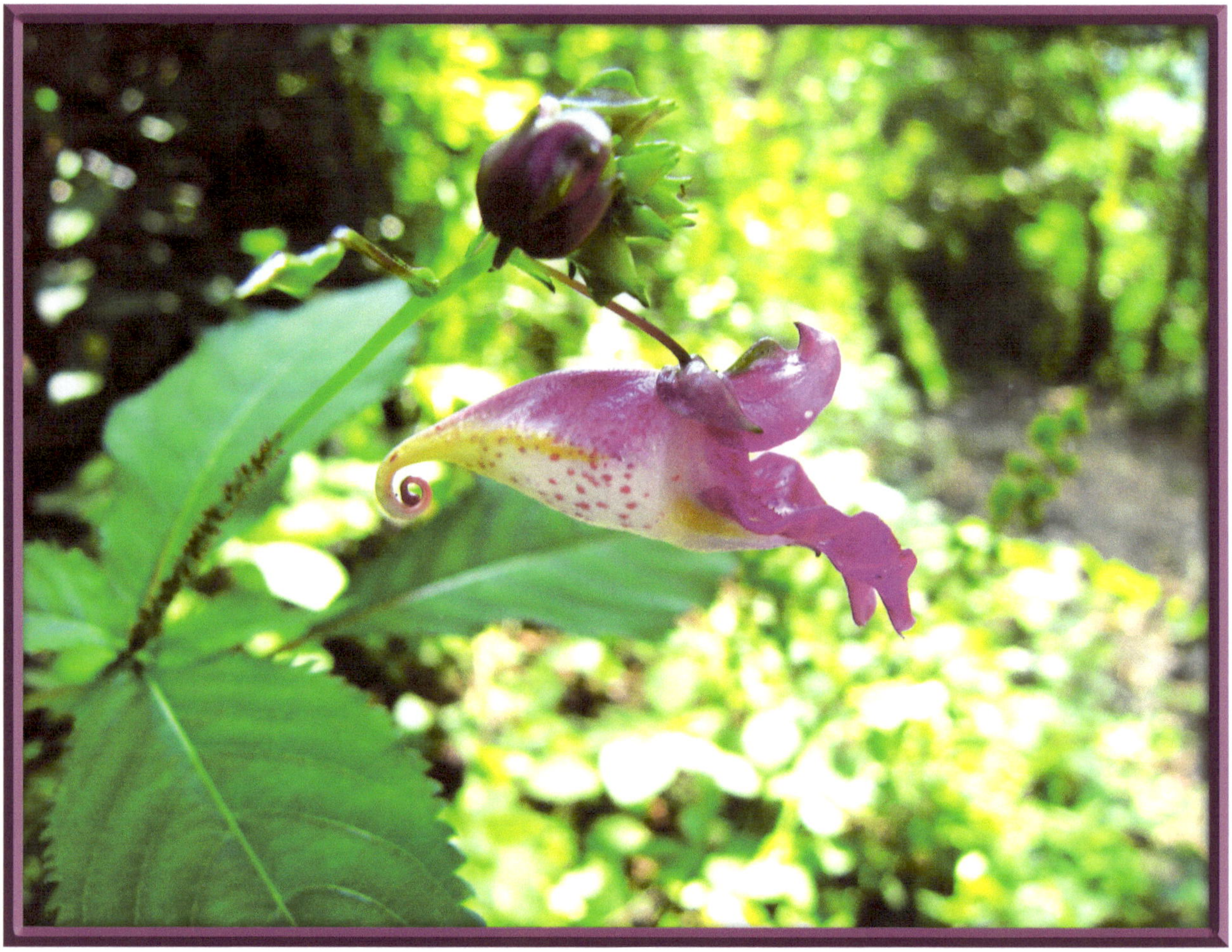

Above is a shot of ***Impatiens textorii*** which was taken as we descended **Mt. Kumotori**. We descended via a somewhat different trail on this trip and we found some different flowers than we usually find.

In addition, we also got the shot on the facing page of an interesting ***Geranium* sp**. plant with its seedpods. We have, at this writing, climbed **Mt. Kumotori** a total of seven times between the months of May and November from 2002 to 2010. So, what that means, is that you should probably expect to see photos taken on Mt. Kumotori one more time – with the November photos.

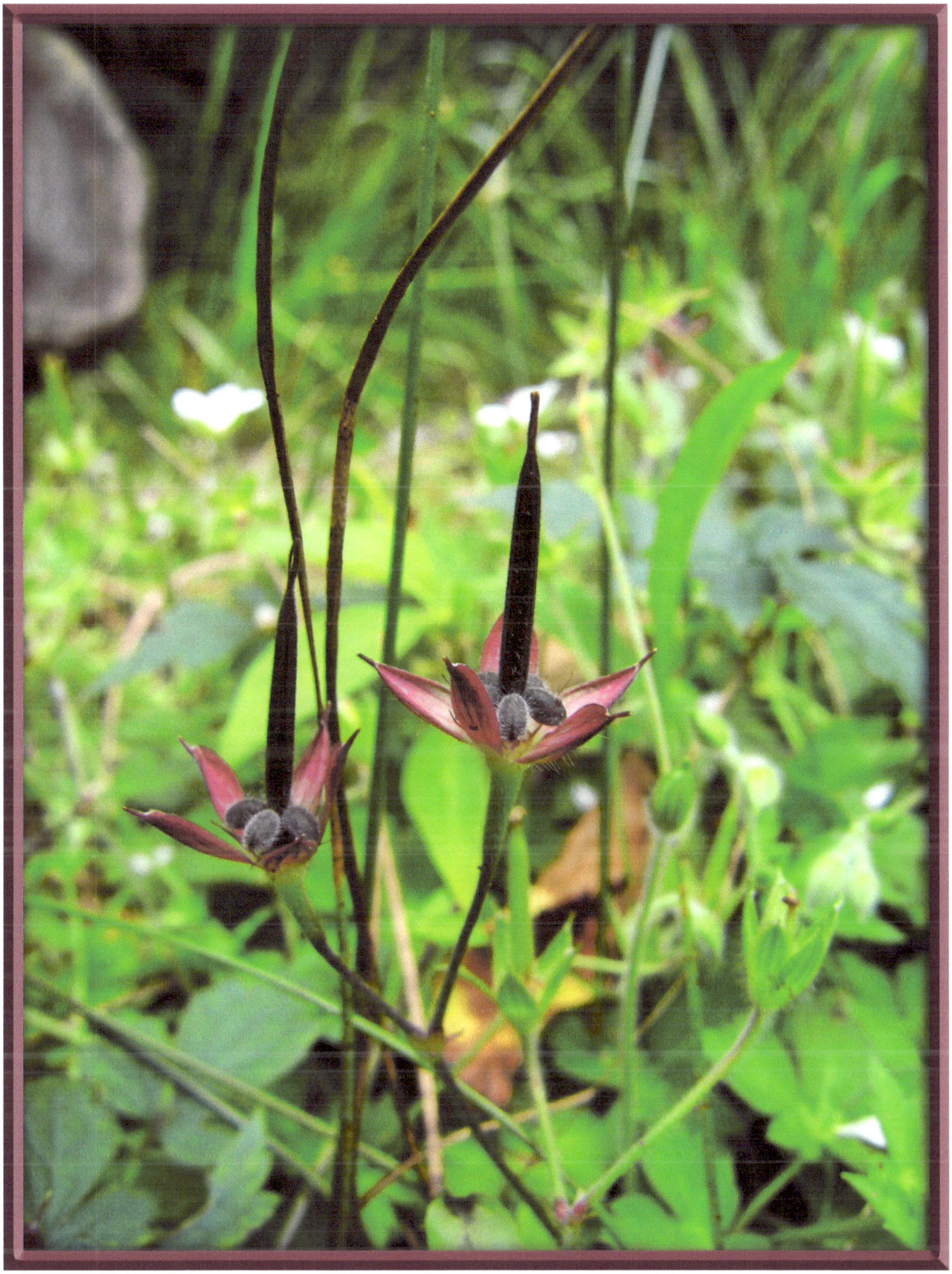

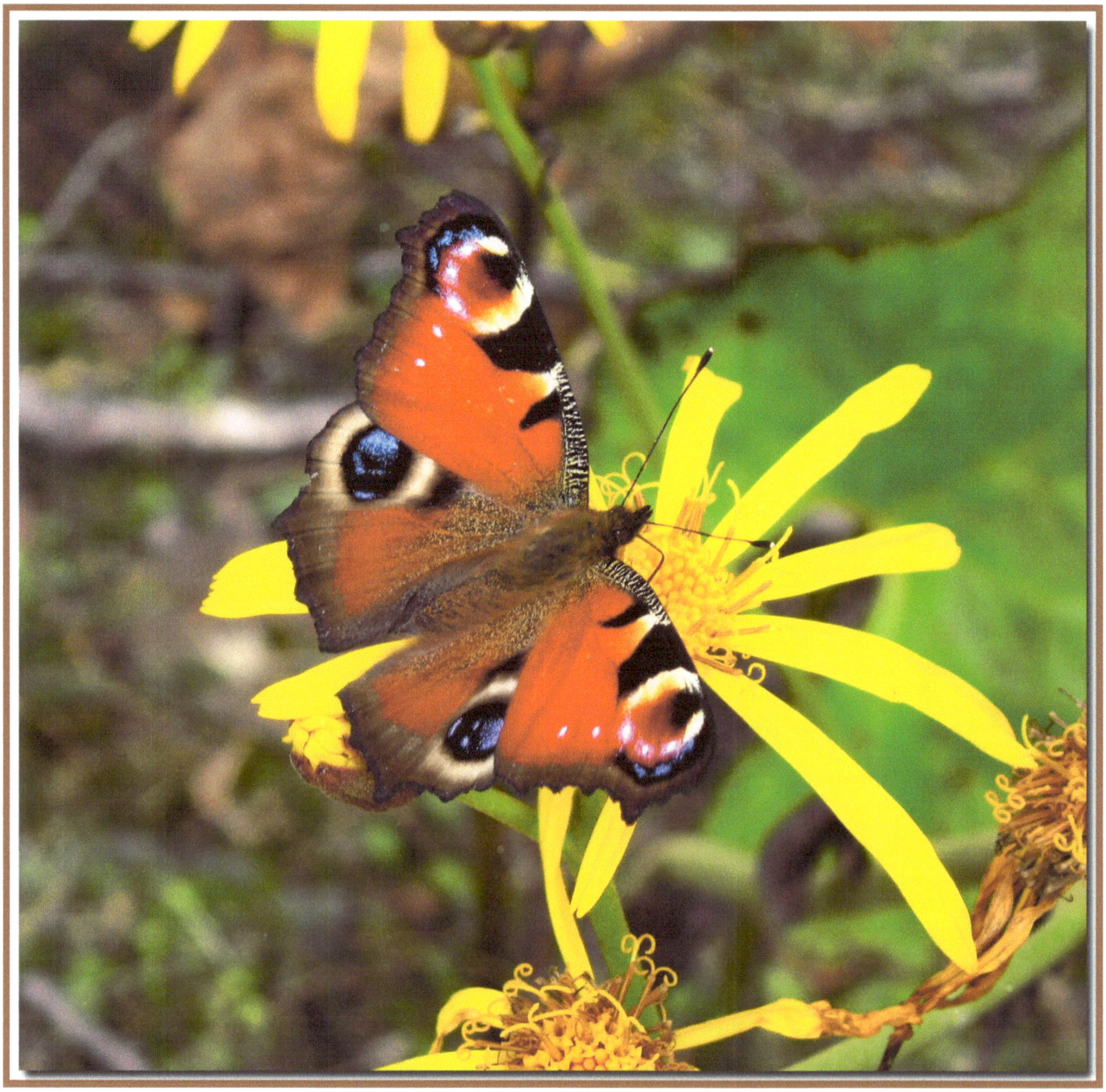

Here is a final shot which was taken during the descent of **Mt. Kumotori**. It shows a very beautiful butterfly working to gather the nectar of the ***Ligularia dentata*** flowers. There are certainly a lot of brilliant colors in this photo.

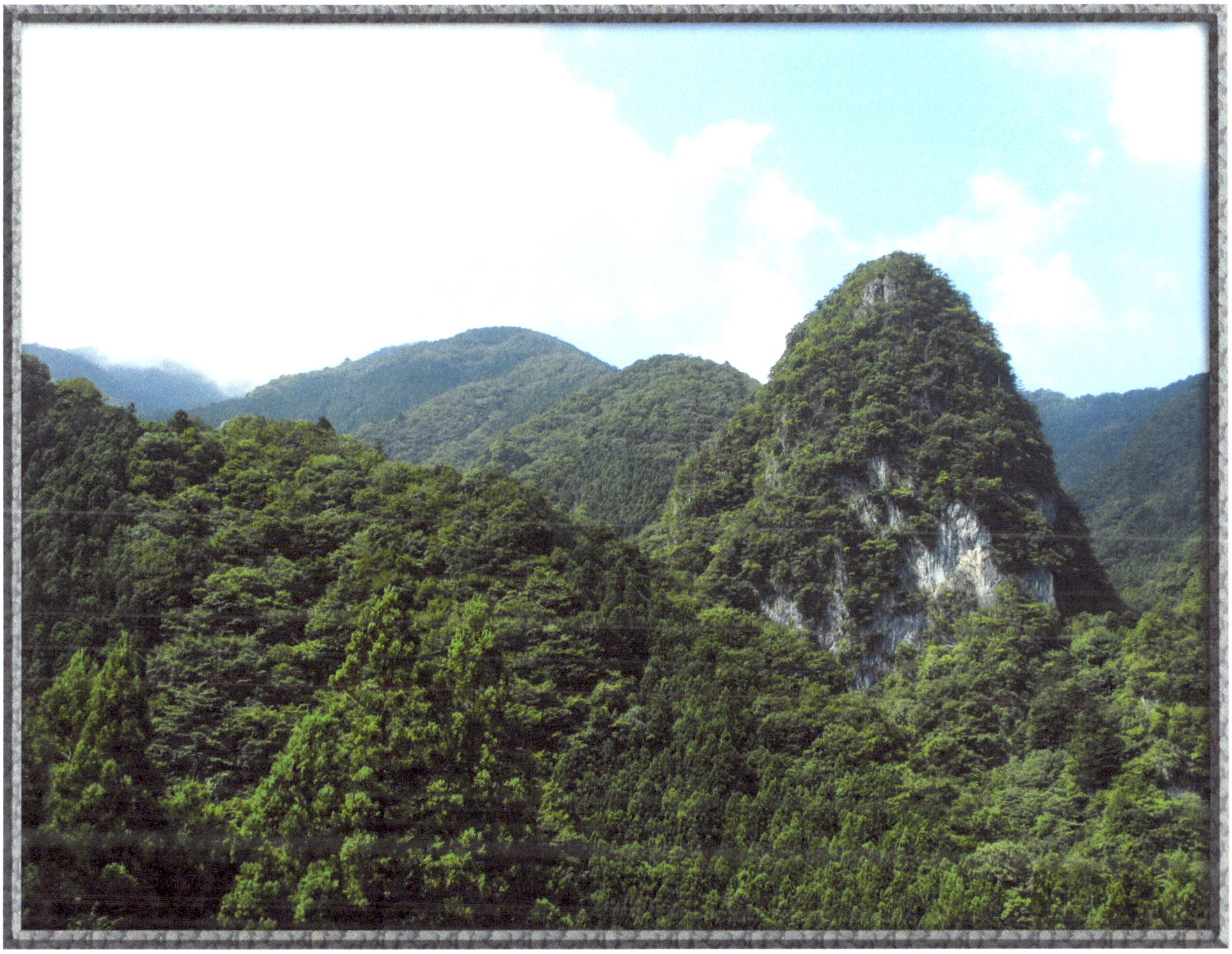

Here is a pretty amazing rock. This is in **Western Tokyo**, rather near **Okutama Train Station**. The name of this rock is **Inamura-iwa**. It is near the village of **Nippara**. You can take a bus from **Okutama Station** to **Nippara** and then walk to a limestone cave from the bus stop. You will pass this rock.

There is also one trail which you can climb to or else descend from the summit of Mt. Kumotori, which will take you past this rock. It is difficult to explain, but you will come down on the right side of the rock as seen from this photo. There is even a trail from the back side which will take you to its summit.

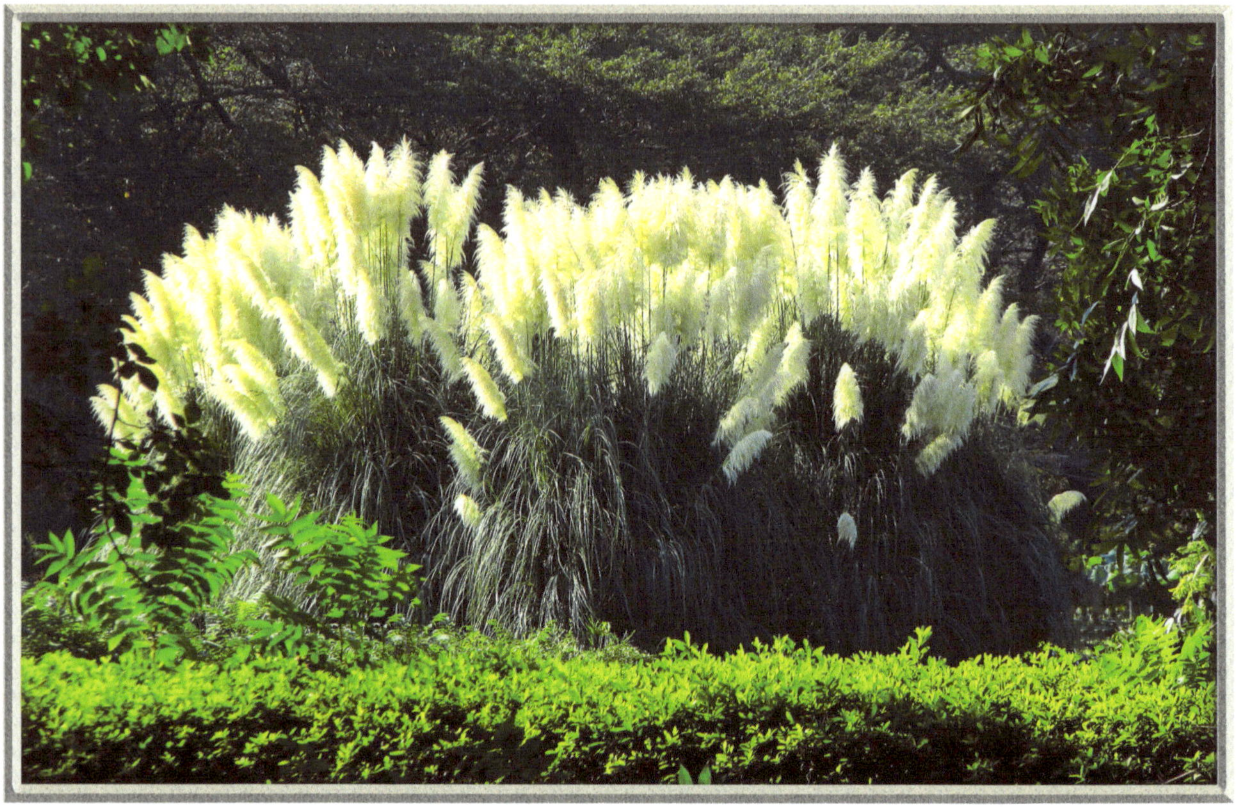

The above photo was taken at **Jindai Botanical Garden**, on the western side of Tokyo. This is ***Cortaderia selloana*** commonly known as **Pampas Grass**. Jindai Botanical Garden has been mentioned enough times (see pages 14, 22, 75 and more) so that we don't think that we need to make any more comments about its location.

When we first started visiting Jindai Botanical Garden, several years ago, this patch of **Pampas Grass** was not very large at all. It has increased in size and in beauty every year. There is nothing in this photo which can be used for scale, but the seed stalks are at least 4 meters (12+ feet) in height. If you should visit the west side of Tokyo any time in the late summer or autumn you should certainly visit here to see this.

On the facing page is an additional photo of this Pampas Grass – the seed stalks against a beautiful blue sky.

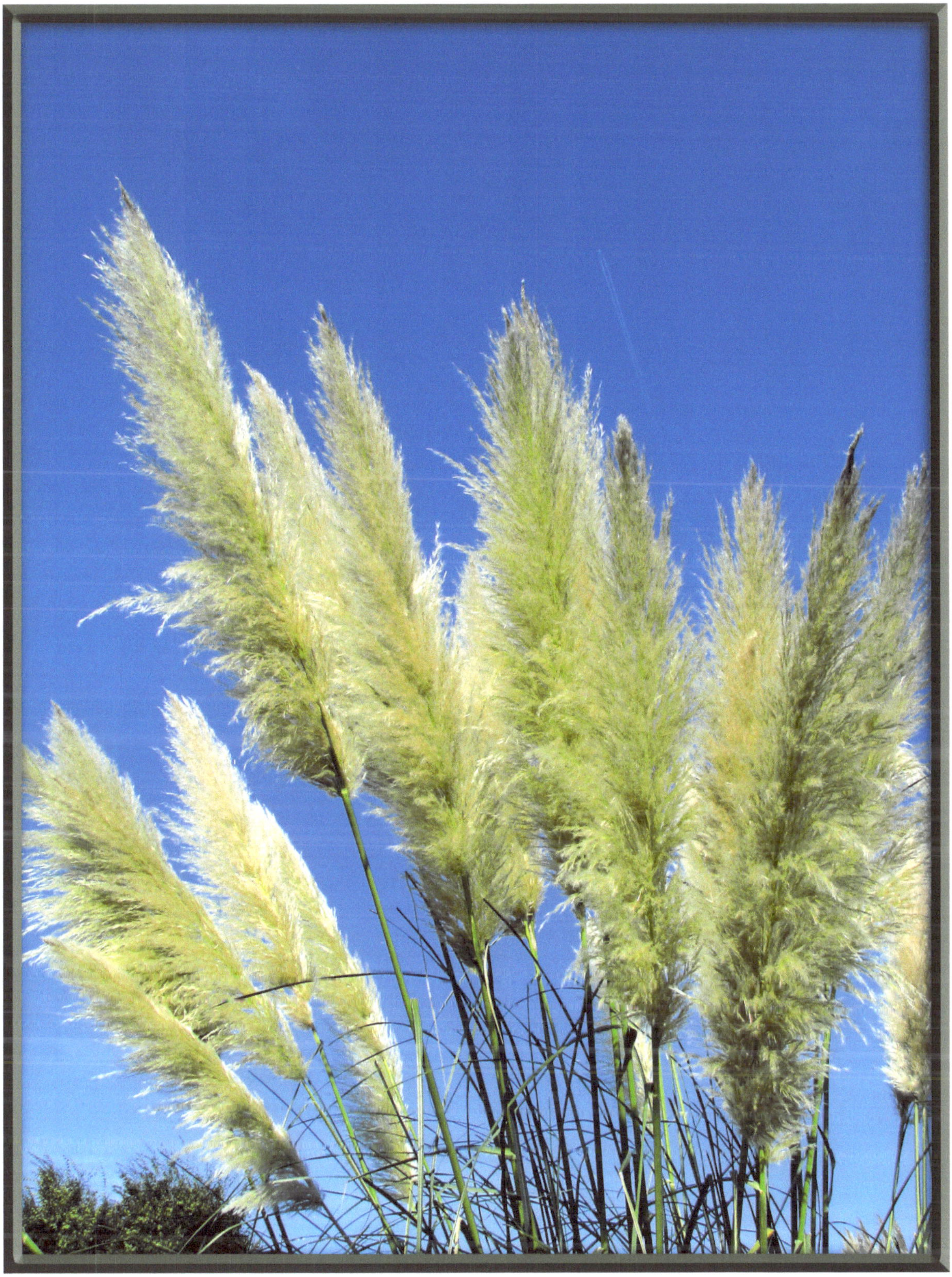

PART 4: AUTUMN

Okay, it's now September 21st, so we need to begin Autumn here.

Way back on page 106 we showed you a photo of a **Lotus Flower** (***Nelumbo nucifera***). At that time we also promised that we'd show you a photo or two of the seed-heads of this plant. Well, here is the first of these photos. This very nice shot was taken at **Showa-Kinen Park** in Western-Tokyo. We'll show you one more shot of some seedheads later in September.

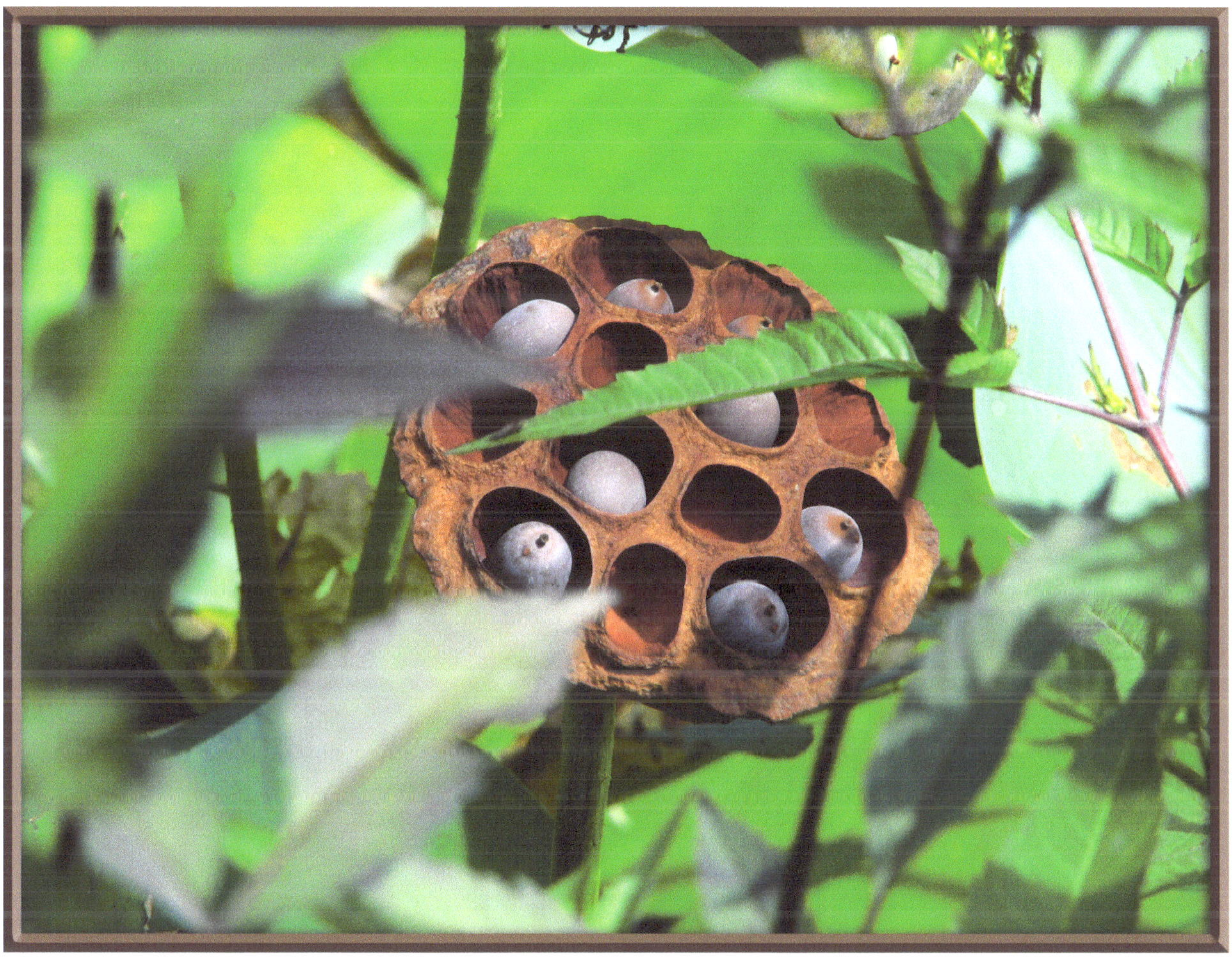

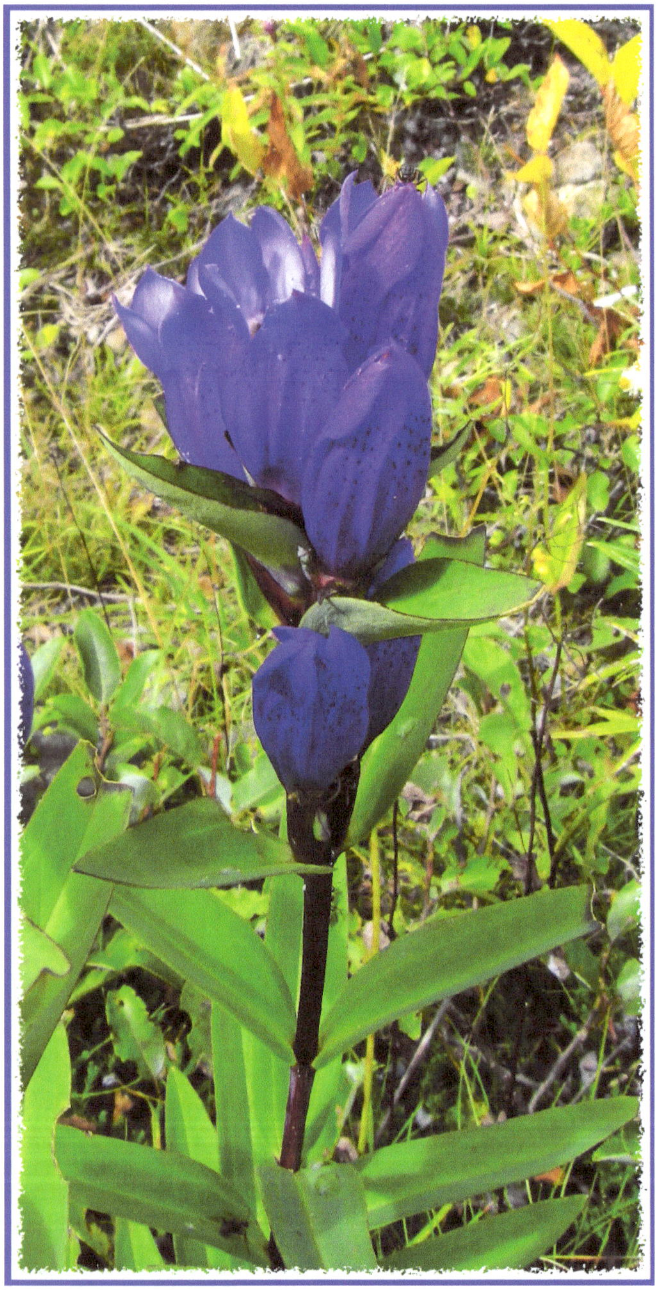

Now let's take a return trip to **Kusatsu,** in Gunma Prefecture. We last visited **Kusatsu** back on page 43. We seldom go to **Kusatsu** in the summer as the best thing to do there is to soak in the many hot springs in the area. Therefore we like to go there when the weather is cool or cold. The photo to the left is a ***Gentiana scabra* var. *buergeri***. This beautiful blue autumn mountain flower is right at its peak in this photo. This photo was taken near **Mt. Shirane**. Mt. Shirane (2,160 meters = 7,087 feet) is a mountain which overlooks a very odd colored caldera lake. The name is **Yugama Crater Lake** (see facing page).

On the facing page you see two photos of the odd colored **Yugama Crater Lake**, which is visible from **Mt. Shirane**. The upper photo on the facing page is a two shot panorama which shows the entire lake, while the lower photo is a single photo which shows most of the lake.

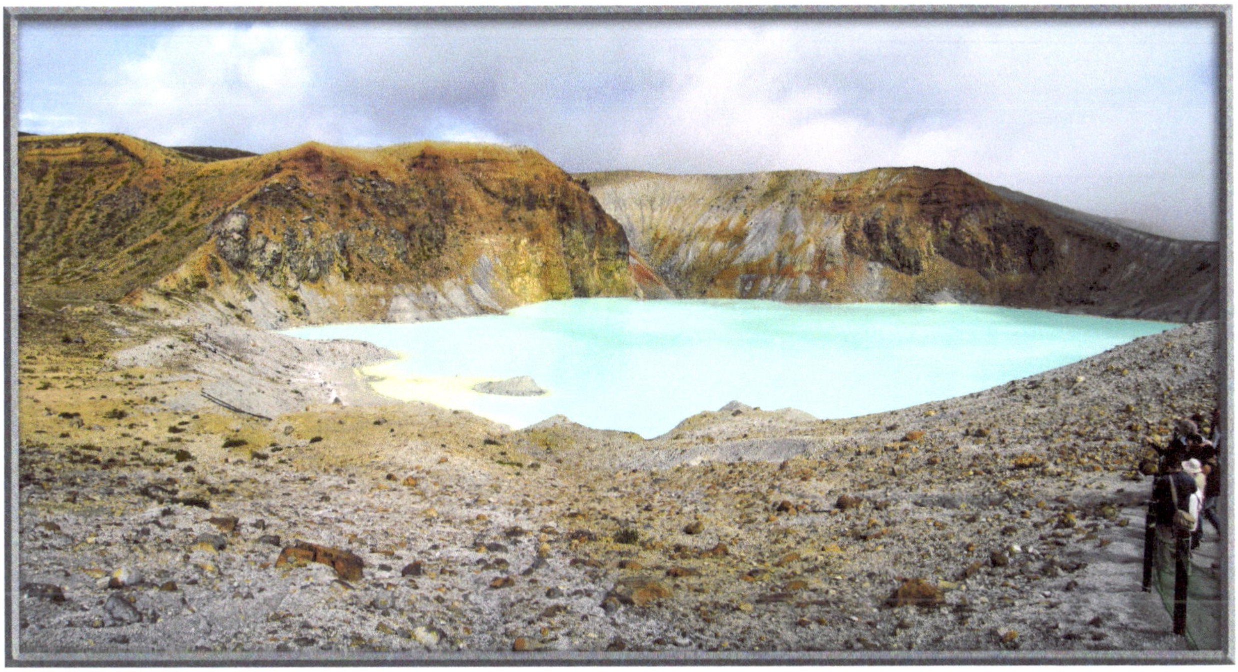

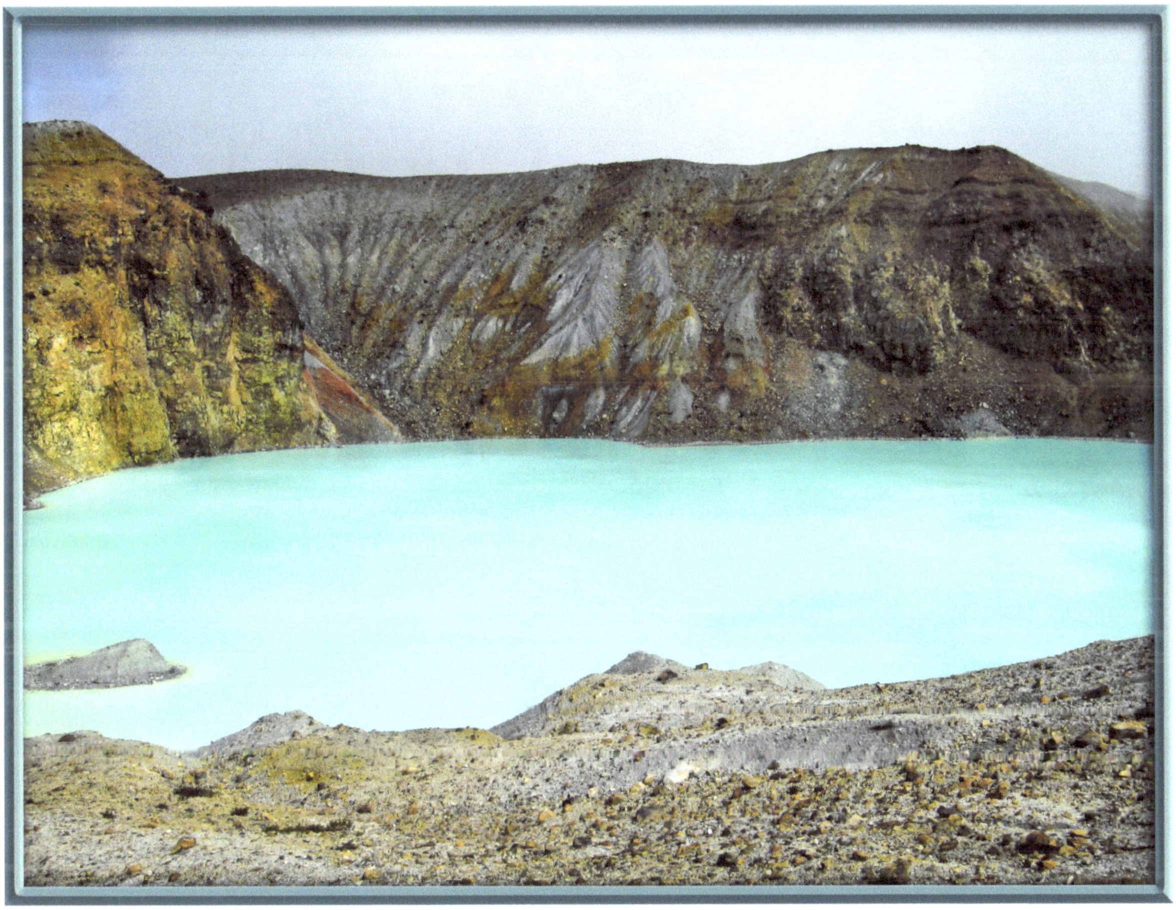

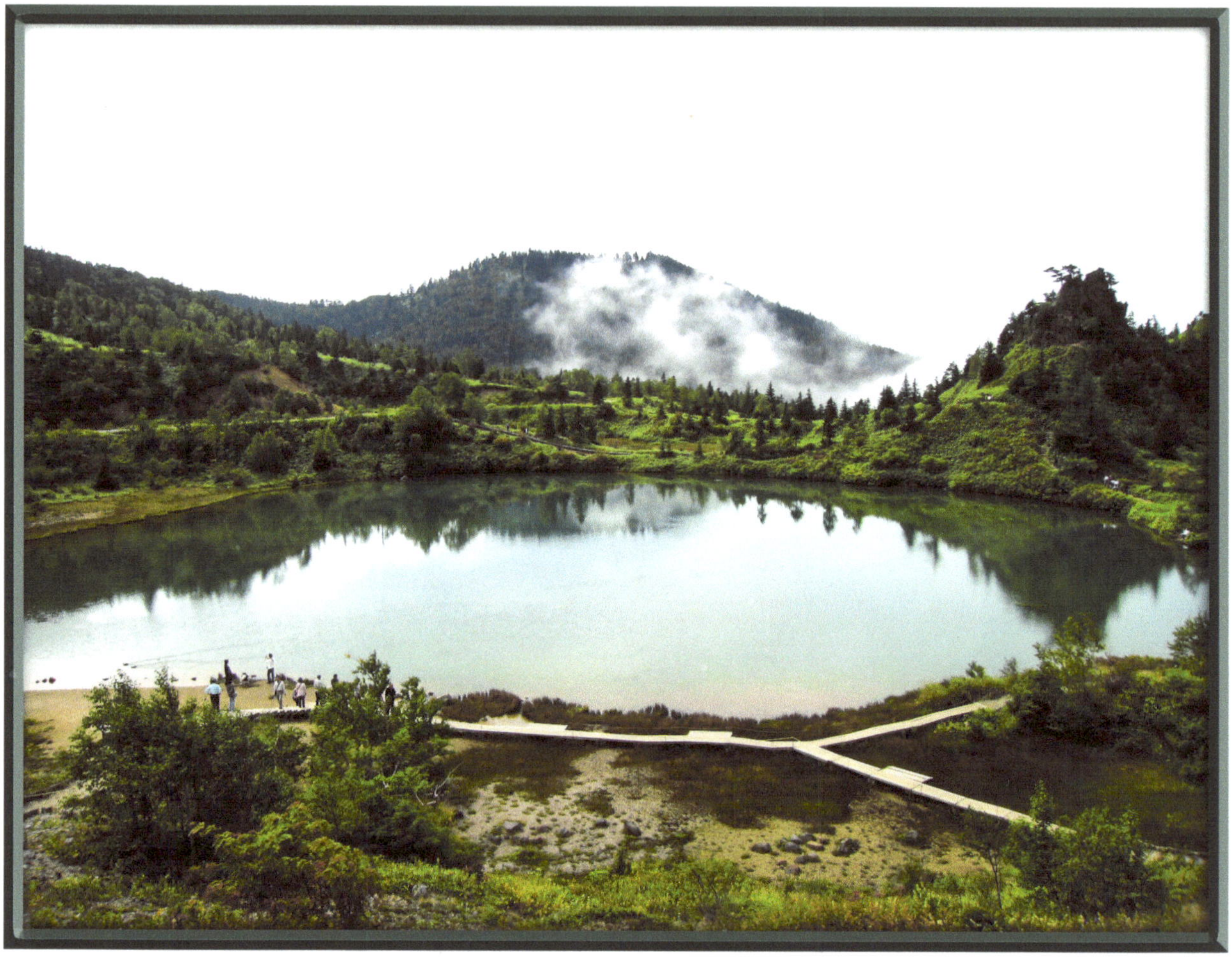

The above photo is not Yugama Crater Lake, this is on the opposite side of the highway from Mt. Shirane and also opposite the Shirane Rest House. The name of this body of water is **Yumiike (Yumi Pond)**. As you can see in this photo, it is totally surrounded by a trail and several branching trails. From here it is possible to hike to several different points in the **Mt. Shirane** and **Mt. Moto-Shirane** (2,171 meters = 7,123 feet) area.

In the above photo you notice a rock sticking up on the right side of the photo. The photo on the facing page is a closer shot of that rock and shows the beginnings of some autumn colors.

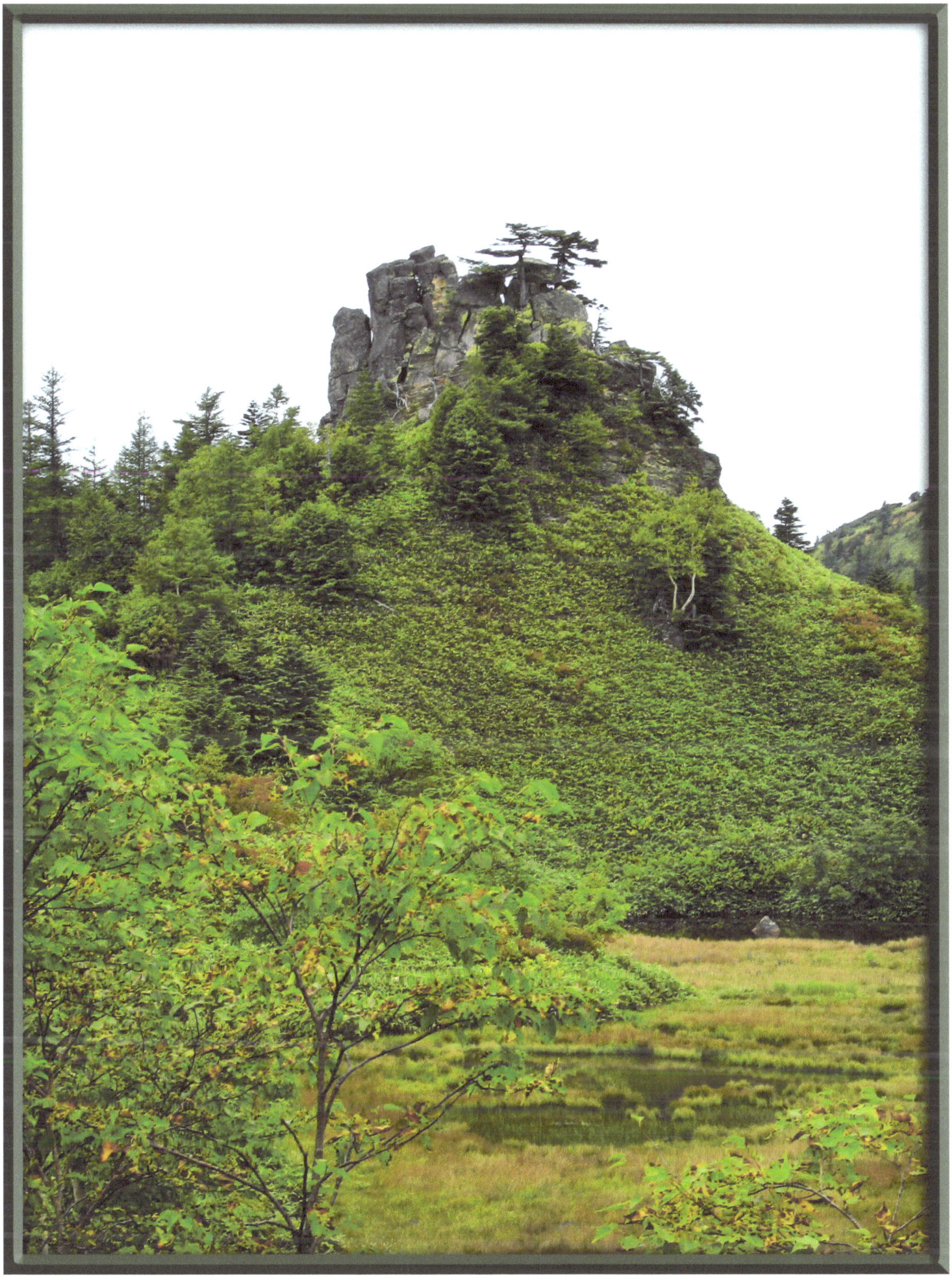

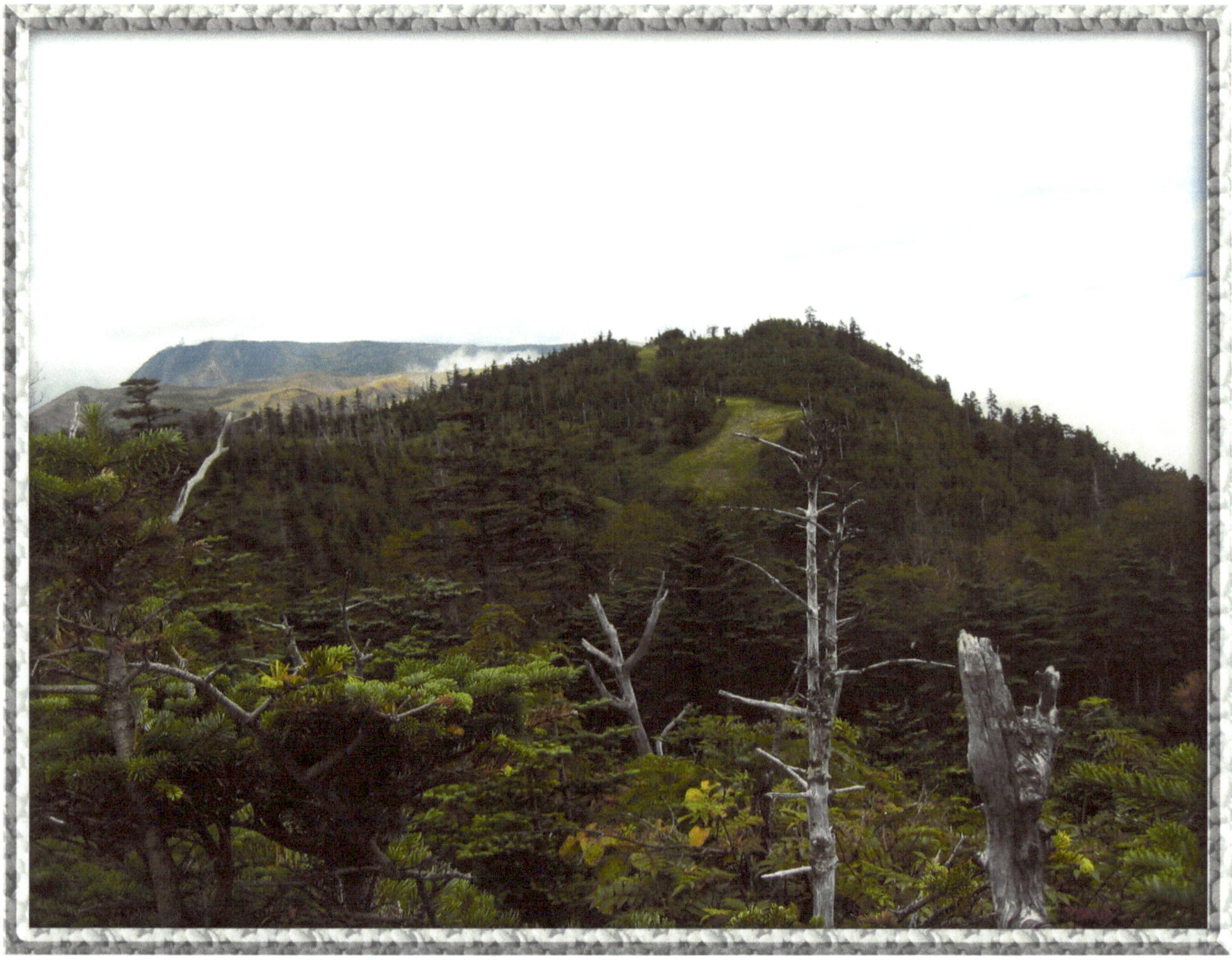

The above photo was taken as we hiked around the trail from **Yumiike (Yumi Pond)** towards **Mt. Moto-Shirane**. In this shot, you can also see the beginnings of some autumn colors. You might notice the number of snags (dead trees) in this photo. There will be a photo in October which will show a weird lighting phenomenon with these snags. This is also a ski area and the cleared slope on the opposite hill is a ski slope.

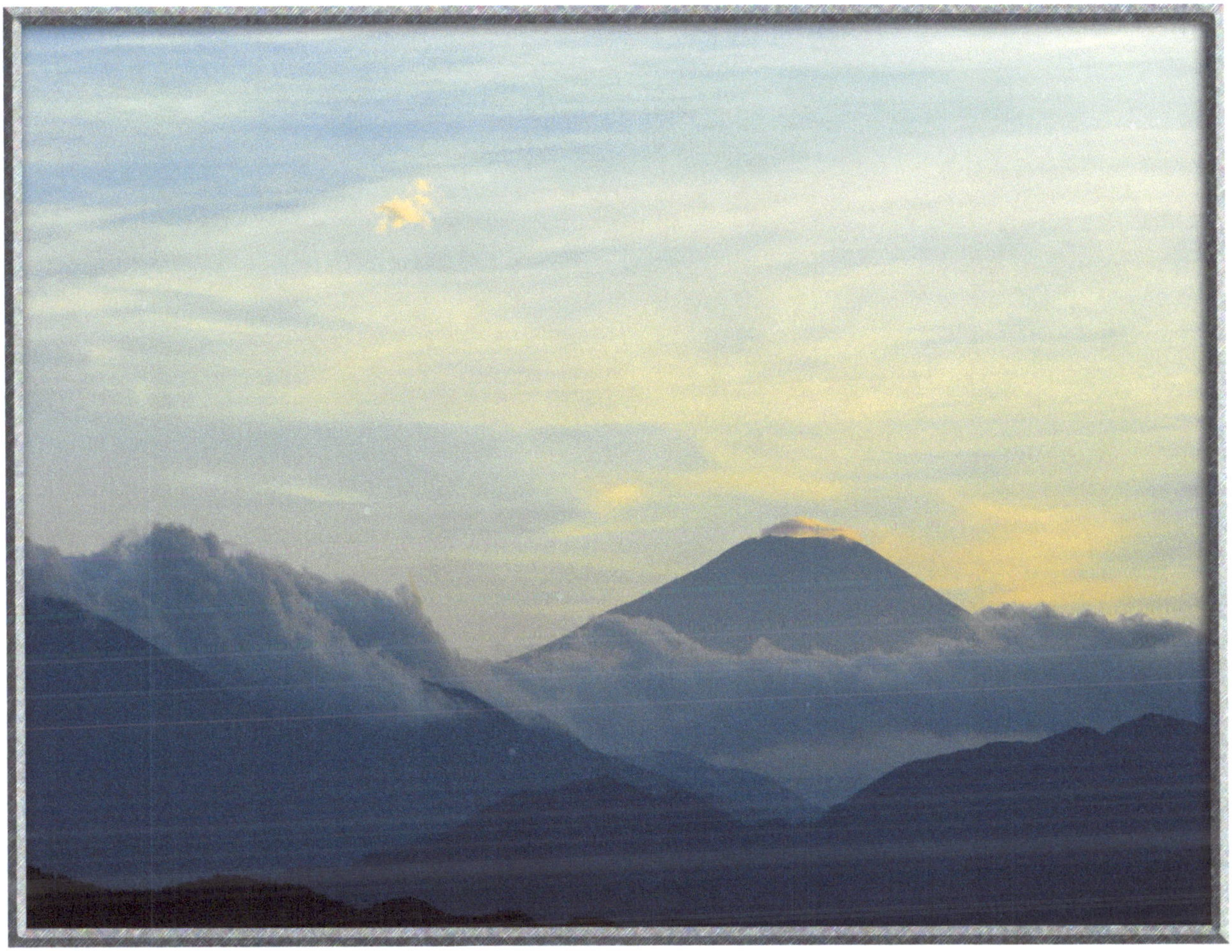

In this photo we have returned once again to **Mt. Takao** (599 meters = 1,965 feet). We are standing at the summit of Mt. Takao (Takao-san) and looking at **Mt. Fuji**. The phenomenon we are witnessing here is referred to as **"Mt. Fuji with an Umbrella"** (***Fuji no Casa*** in Japanese). In this particular shot the umbrella is not so large, but occasionally one can see Mt. Fuji with a very large umbrella over it. This photo is also interesting because of all of the other clouds in the scene. As you may surmise – we felt fortunate to even be able to see Mt. Fuji at all on this day.

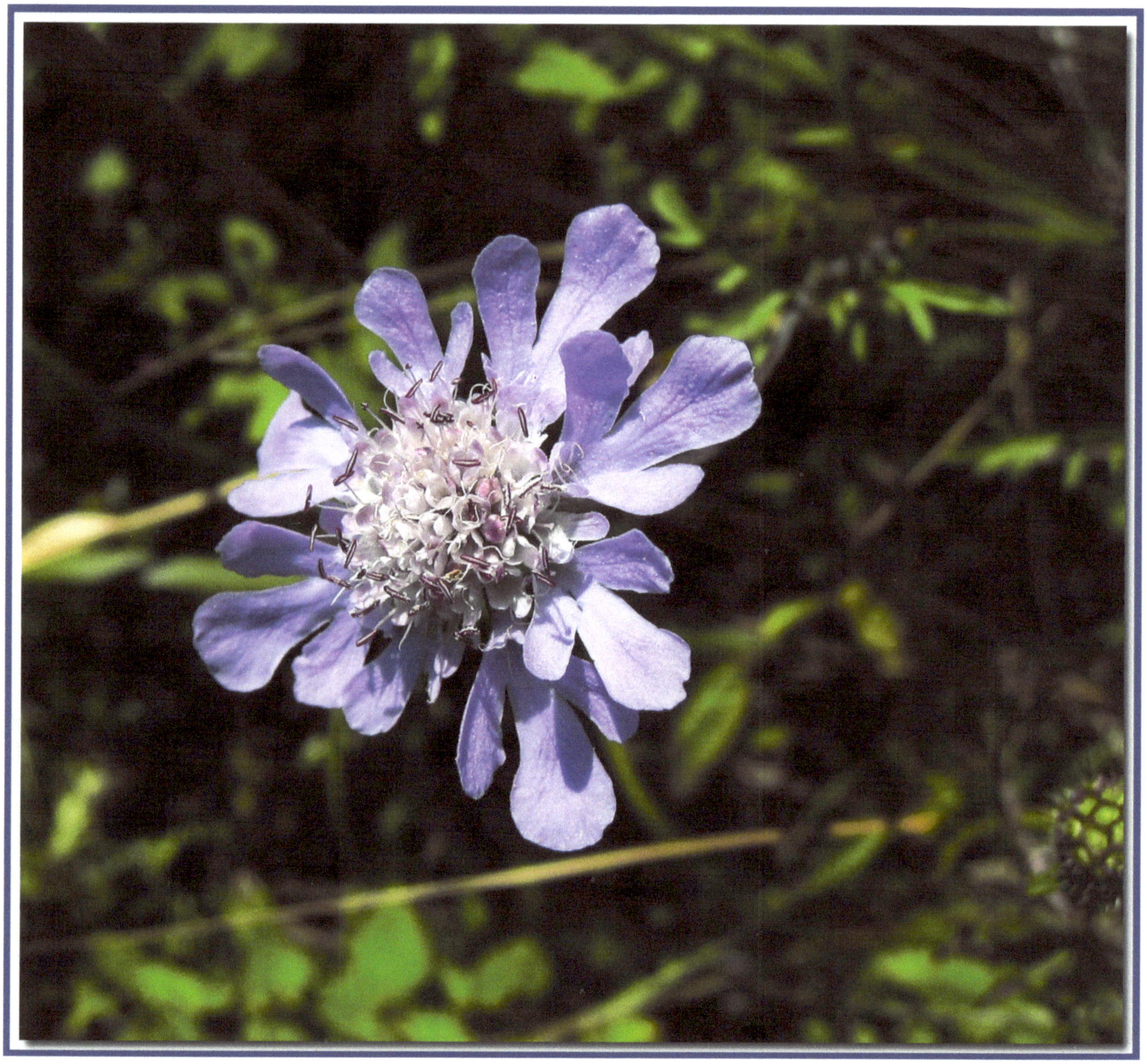

Now we are going to go, once again, to **Yamanaka Lake** (pages 9 & 74), in **Yamanashi Prefecture**. One year we went there for a September Full Moon and camped out on **Mt. Myoujin** (1,291 meters = 4,236 feet) with the intention of taking photos of **Mt. Fuji** by the light of the full moon. The above shot shows a flower, ***Scabiosa japonica***, which we had never seen before this. It was in great abundance here and we shot many photos of it. This is one really great example.

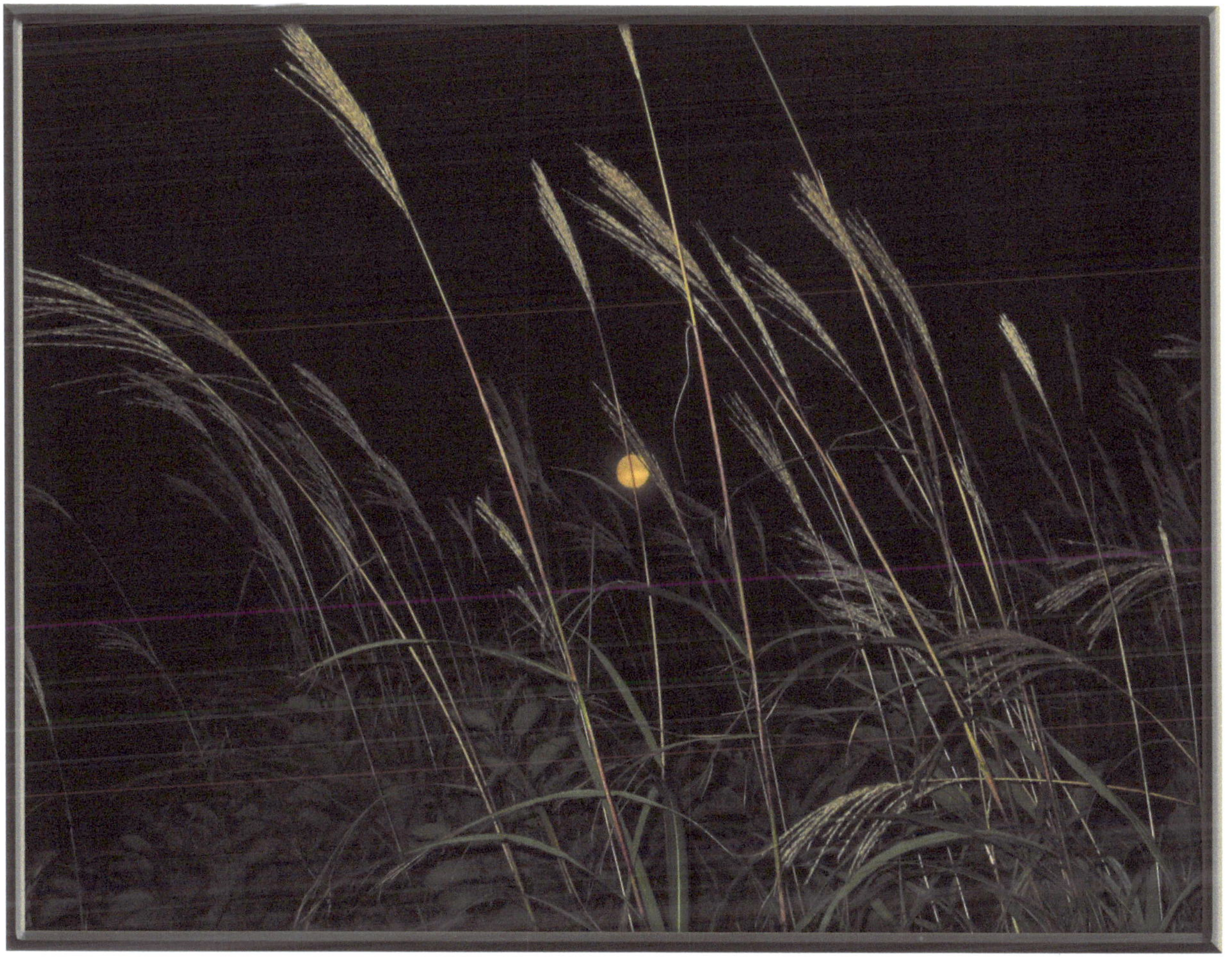

This photo above was taken on **Mt. Myoujin** as the full moon was rising. It shows the full moon and the tall grass. We think it came out nicely. It was taken at 6:44 PM, the sun had not been gone very long and this full moon had not been up very long. As you may know – the full moon rises just about the same time as the sun sets. Due to the lack of natural light and other conditions this photo lacks much saturation, but it is nice.

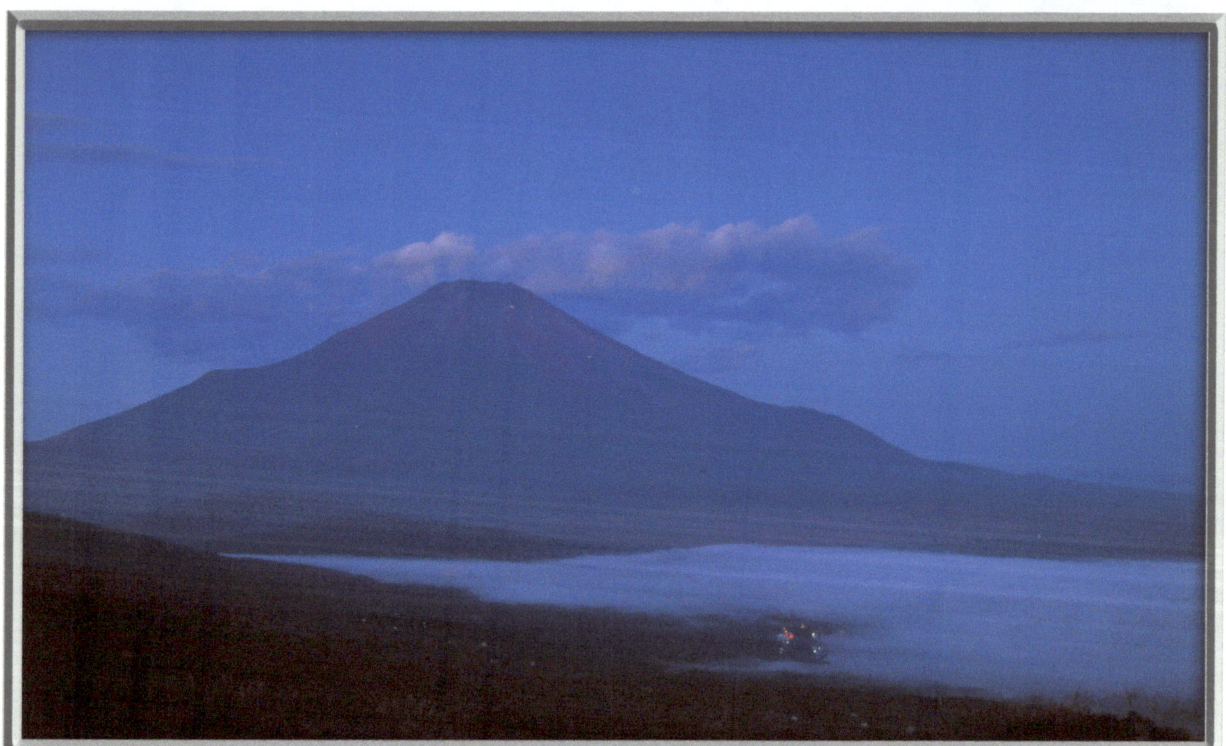

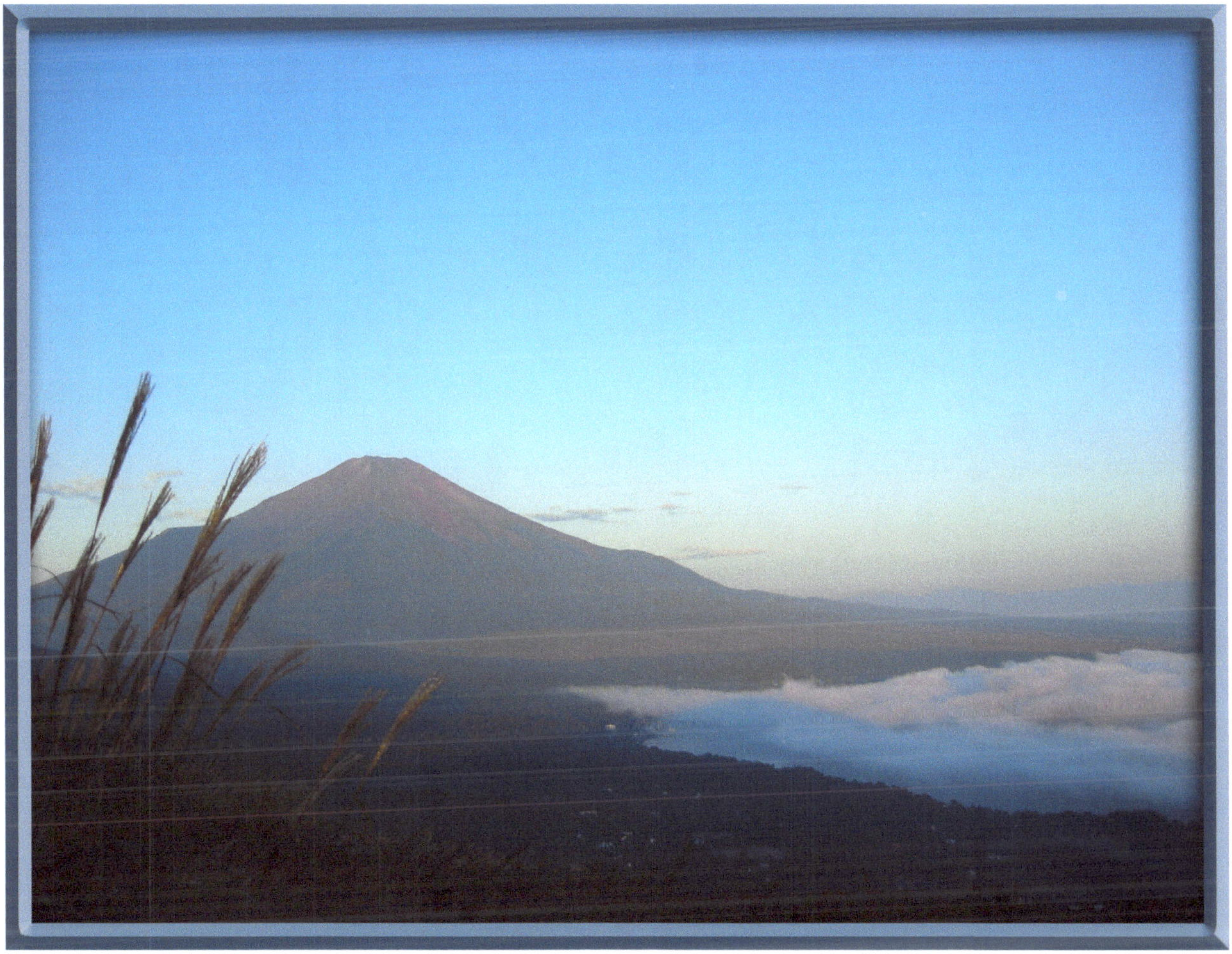

The upper photo on the facing page was taken by moonlight. That is, of course, **Mt. Fuji** out there. You can also see a blanket of fog sitting on top of **Yamanaka Lake**. If you look very closely you can see flashlights on the side of Mt. Fuji as zealous climbers attempt to attain the summit to witness the sunrise. This photo was taken at 2:59 AM.

The lower photo on the facing page shows approximately the same area as the upper one, but daylight is now approaching. The time is now 5:05 AM. You can still see some flashlights on the side of the mountain. They are not going to make it to the summit for the sunrise – it is only a few moments away.

In the above photo, taken at 5:49 AM, you can see that the sun has come up and is shining on Mt. Fuji and you can see the shadow of **Mt. Myoujin**, the mountain we are standing on, down below us. The blanket of fog still covers **Yamanaka Lake**. The climbers who succeeded in getting to the summit of Mt. Fuji in time for the sunrise were probably disappointed as the actual moment of sunrise was obscured by a bank of clouds on the eastern horizon.

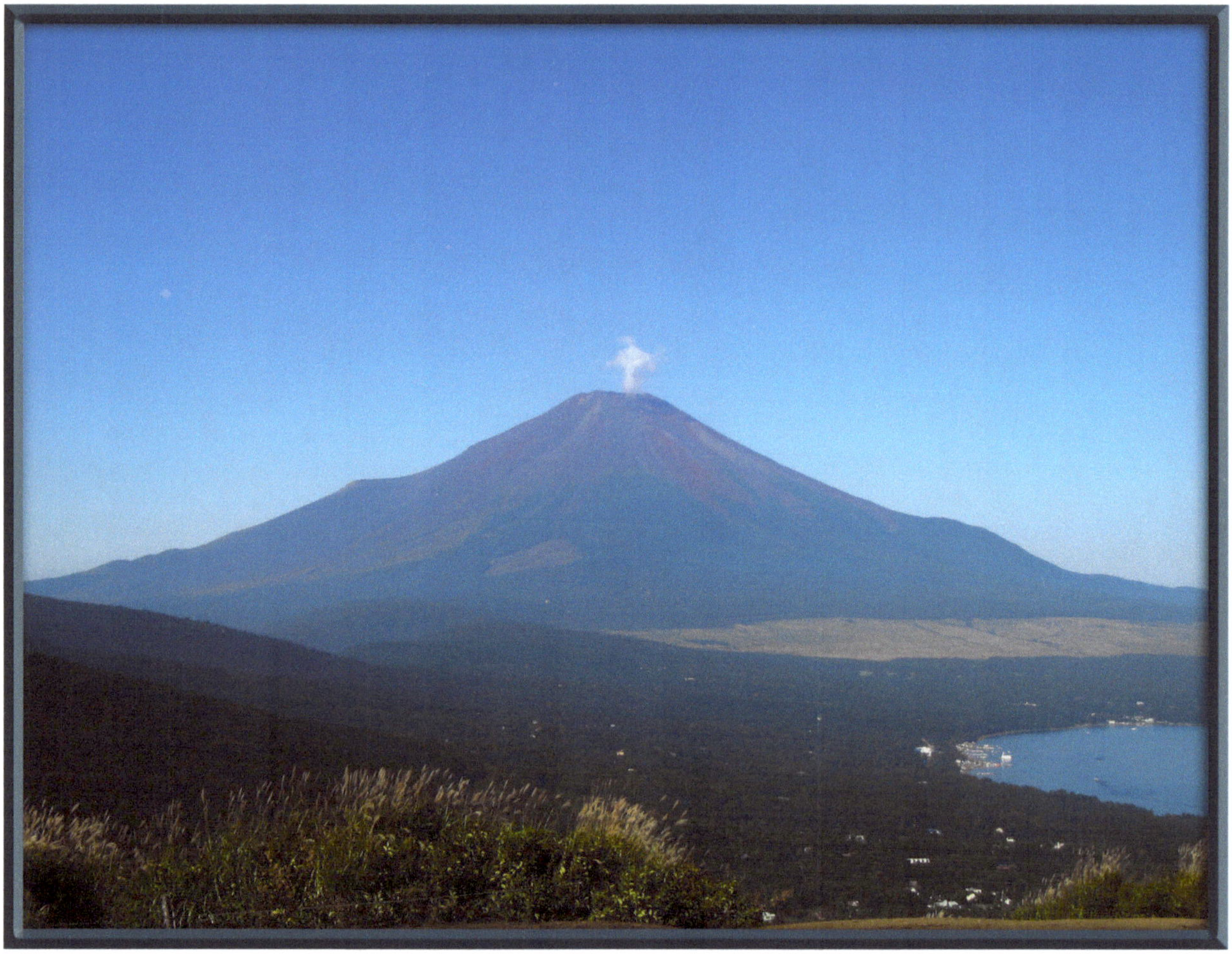

This attractive scene, taken just as we had finished breaking camp and were doing our final preparations to leave at 7:59 AM, shows a cute little cloud which seems to be rising directly off the summit of Mt. Fuji – it looks like there is steam or smoke rising from the mountain itself. Of course it is not, it's just an interesting cloud phenomenon is all. The clouds around Mt. Fuji come and go constantly – in this case the cloud had totally dissipated less than a minute later. So, that means that we were fortunate that we even noticed it and managed to capture it in a photo.

You may find it surprising to learn that we have never climbed Mt. Fuji. Why? Because we have no desire to battle the crowds of people scrambling to the summit. We have seen TV specials of the lines of people climbing to the summit, have heard stories of having to wait behind a line that is not moving and nobody has any idea why the line is not moving. Apparently once on the trail you are not permitted to pass the slower people, so if a great-grandfather a kilometer ahead of you stops for a thirty minute break then everybody behind him has to stop too. To us that does not sound appealing.

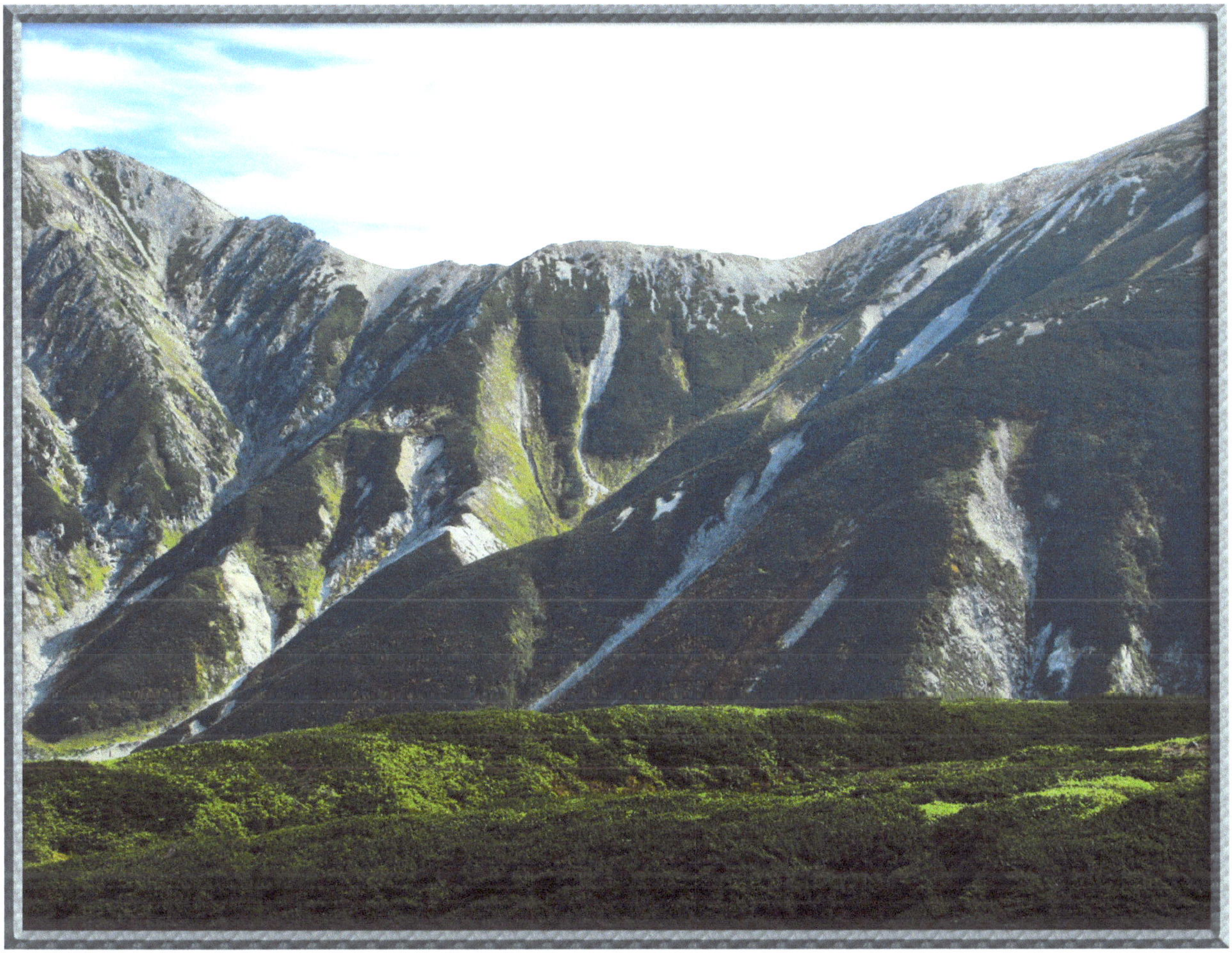

Now we're going to take a trip to **Toyama Prefecture**, in the **Chubu Region** and return to the **Hida Mountains** – also known as the **Japanese Northern Alps Mountain Range**. We visited a different part of the Japanese Northern Alps back on pages 27 – 29 and 136 – 157. We'll be climbing five peaks in this section of mountains. The mountains we'll be summiting are **Mt. Oh** (**O-Yama**) (2,992 meters = 9,815 feet), **Mt. Oonanji** (**Tateyama**) (3,015 meters = 9,892 feet), **Mt. Masago** (**Masago-dake**) (2,861 meters = 9,386 feet), **Mt. Bessan** (**Bessan**) (2,874 meters = 9,429 feet) and **North Mt. Bessan** (**Kita-Bessan**) (2,880 meters = 9,449 feet).

The photo above shows the central part of the ridgeline which runs from south to north. Note that this entire area is above tree line. The tallest vegetation which grows here are the bushes which you can see. The maximum height of the vegetation is about 2 meters (about 6 feet). You'll see some autumn colors on this trip too.

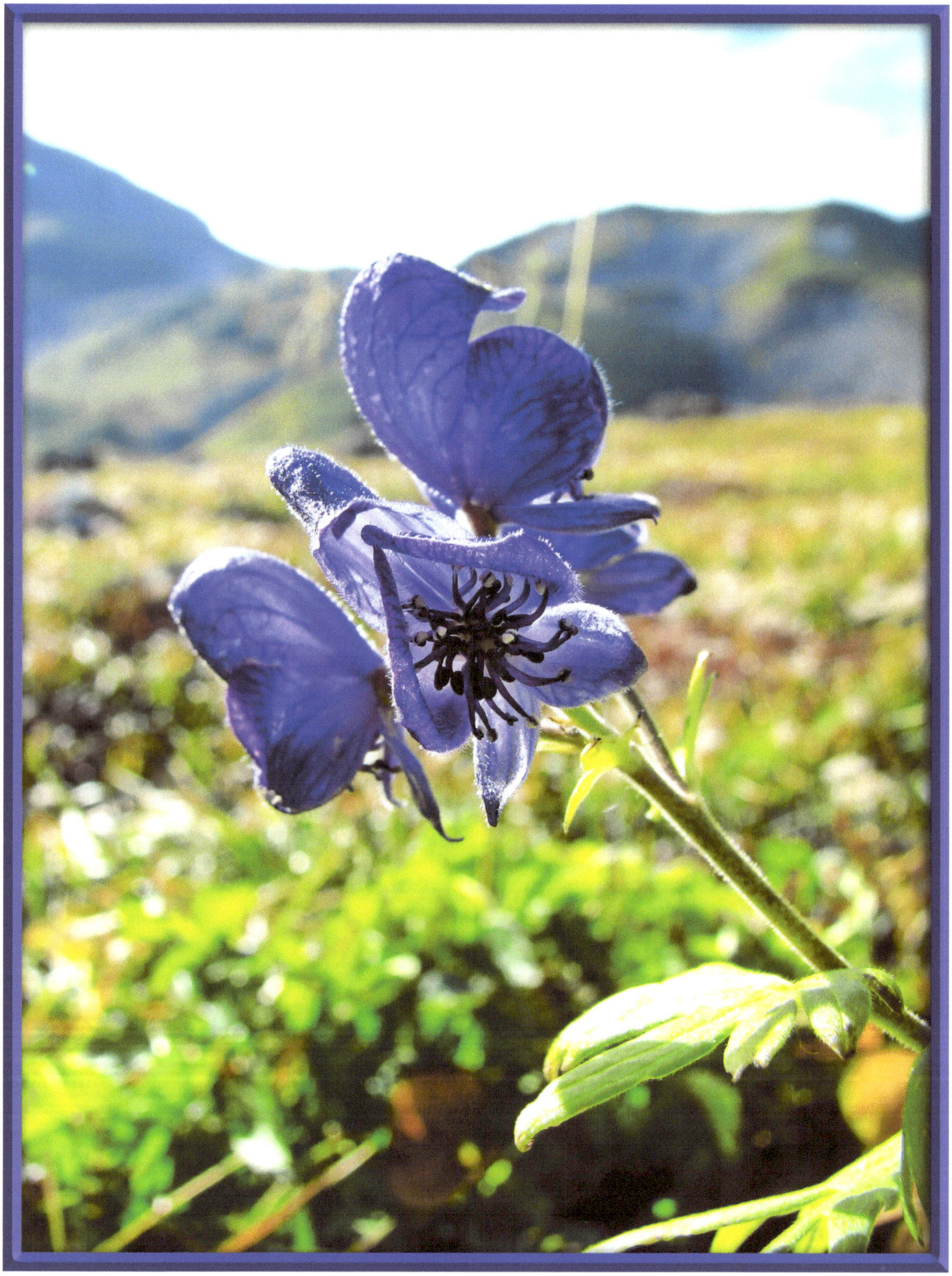

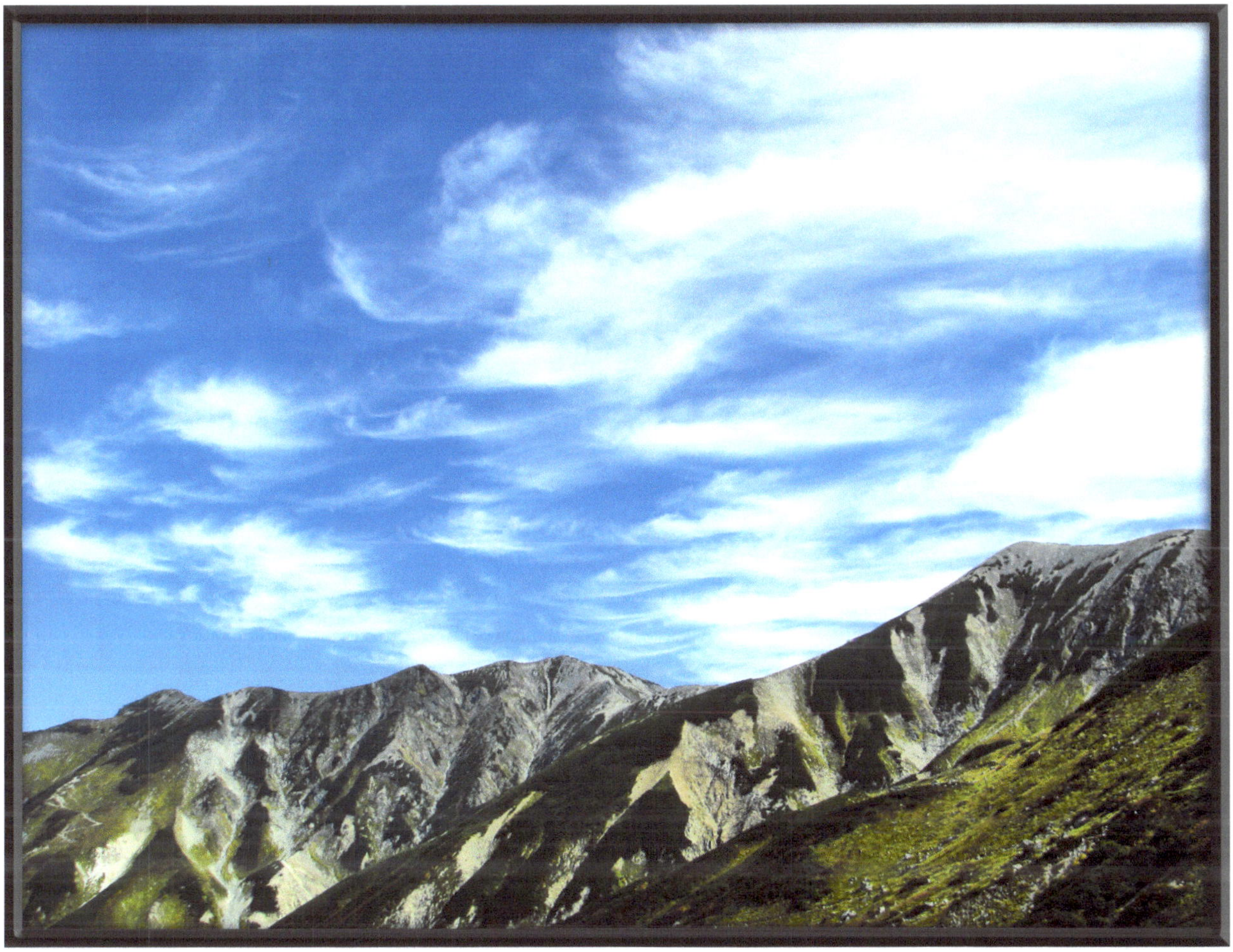

The photo on the facing page is a beautiful ***Aconitum* sp.** flower. There are over 250 species in this genera, so it's not possible for us to definitely identify it. You are probably aware that this plant is also known as wolfsbane, monkshood, aconite, Devil's helmet and blue rocket in addition to others. It is in the buttercup family (***Ranunculaceae***). Several species of ***Aconitum*** have been used to poison arrows in times gone by. It is extremely poisonous.

The photo just above was taken as we climbed along the trail from **Murudo** to the **Ichinokoshi Hut**. The multiple purposes of this photo were to capture the astounding clouds and the blue sky in addition to the mountain scenery.

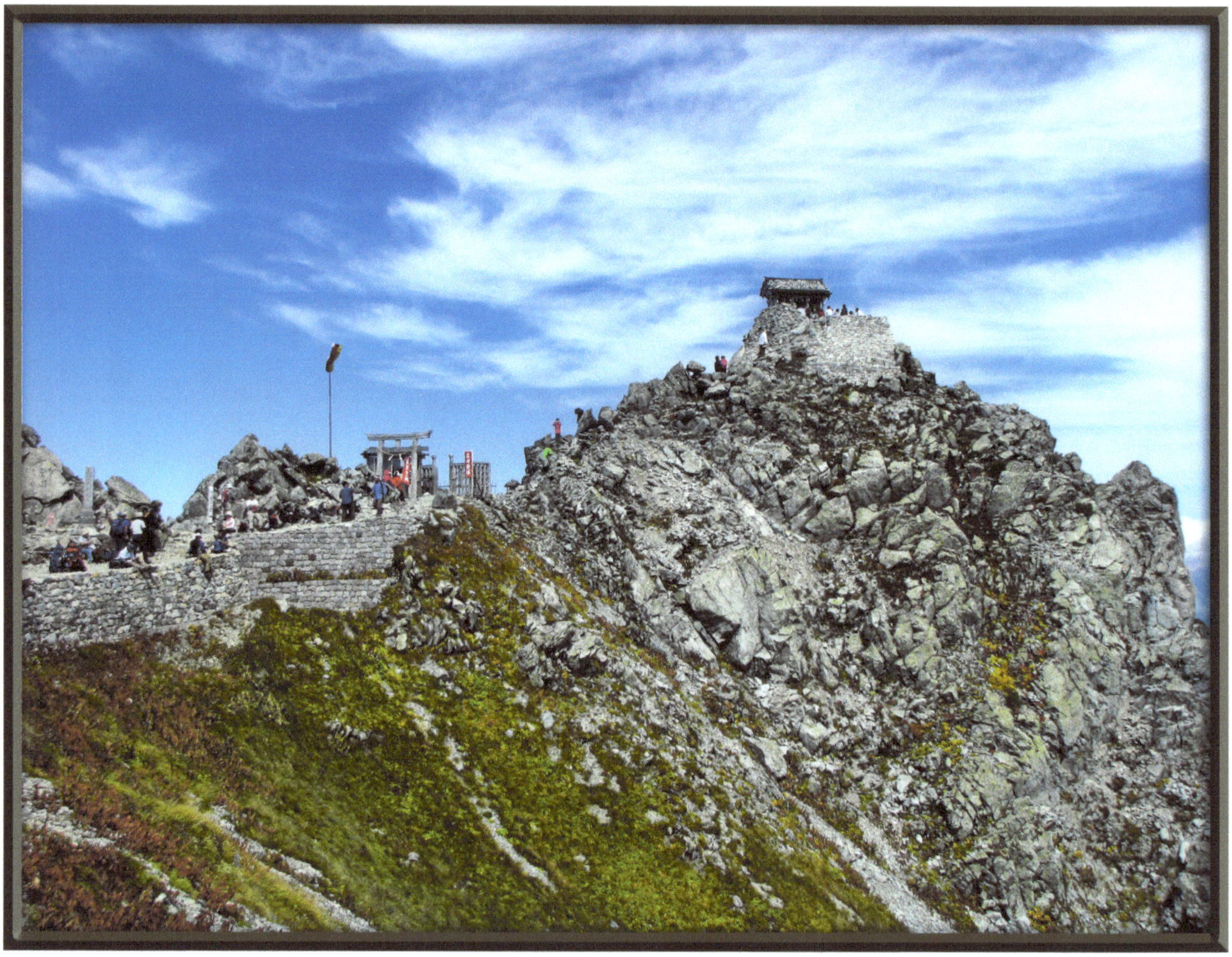

This is the **Oyama Shrine**. This small shrine is located at one of the peaks of **Tateyama**. It is actually the summit of **Oyama** (**Mt. Oh**) (2,992 meters = 9,815 feet). You cannot see it in this photo, but there is a monk standing there welcoming people. In addition, it is not free to go up there, so that monk also collects the money. We did not go up, so we don't know how much it costs – it may be a donation or it may require a flat fee. Many of the shrines at mountain peaks in Japan require a flat fee, so that's probably what is required here too. With the mountain colors and the autumn clouds it is a very attractive place to sit and take a break.

On the facing page is a scene with a large rock and some incredible clouds in top position. In lower position is a photo taken looking back towards **Oyama Shrine** as we approached **Mt. Oonanji** (**Tateyama**) (3,015 meters = 9,892 feet) – can you find the shrine and the monk? Once again, you should also notice the clouds.

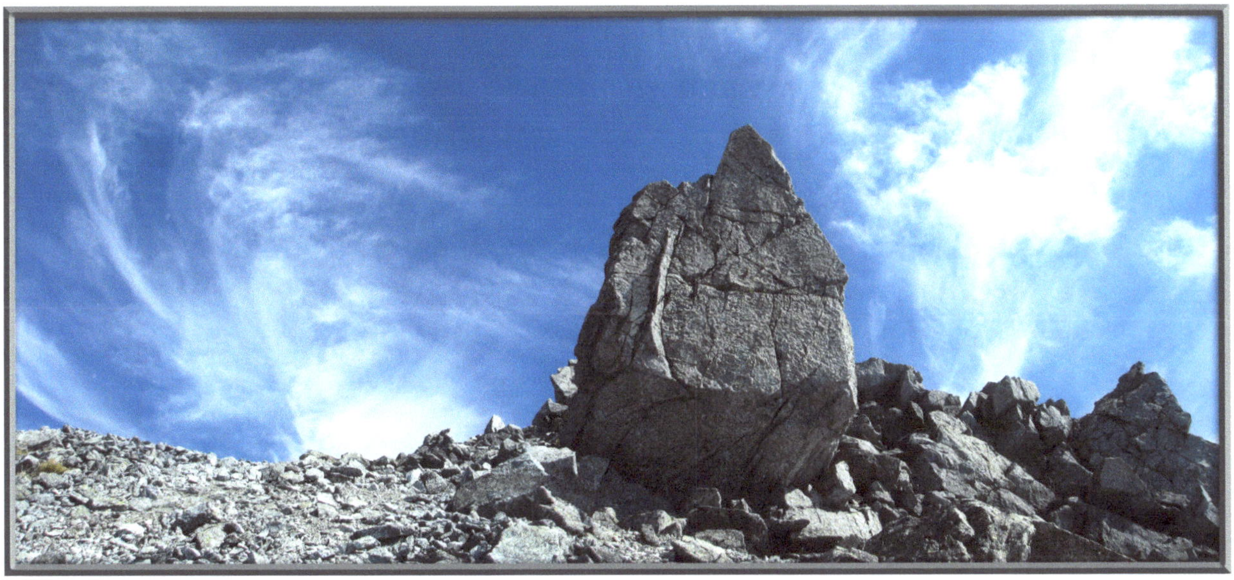

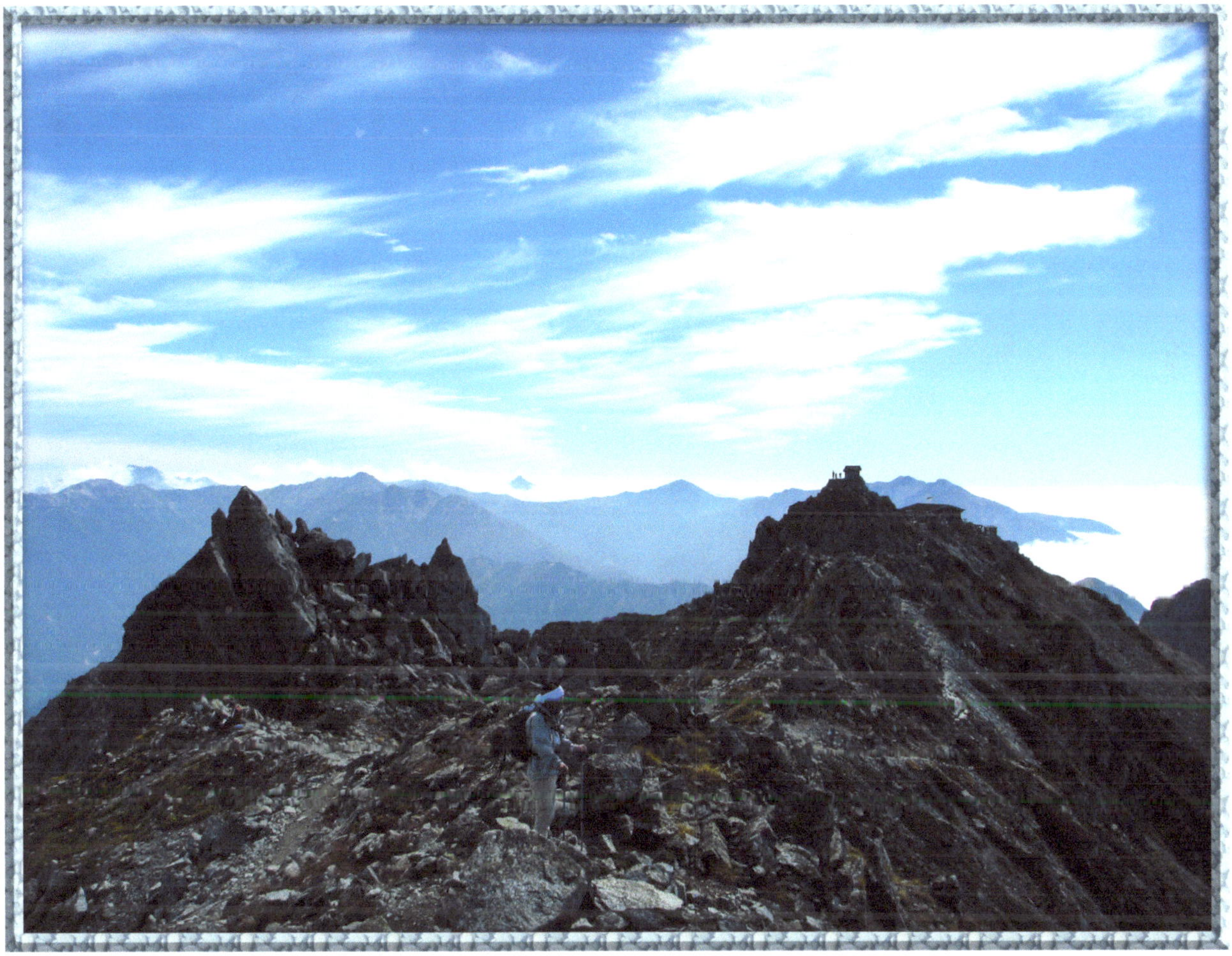

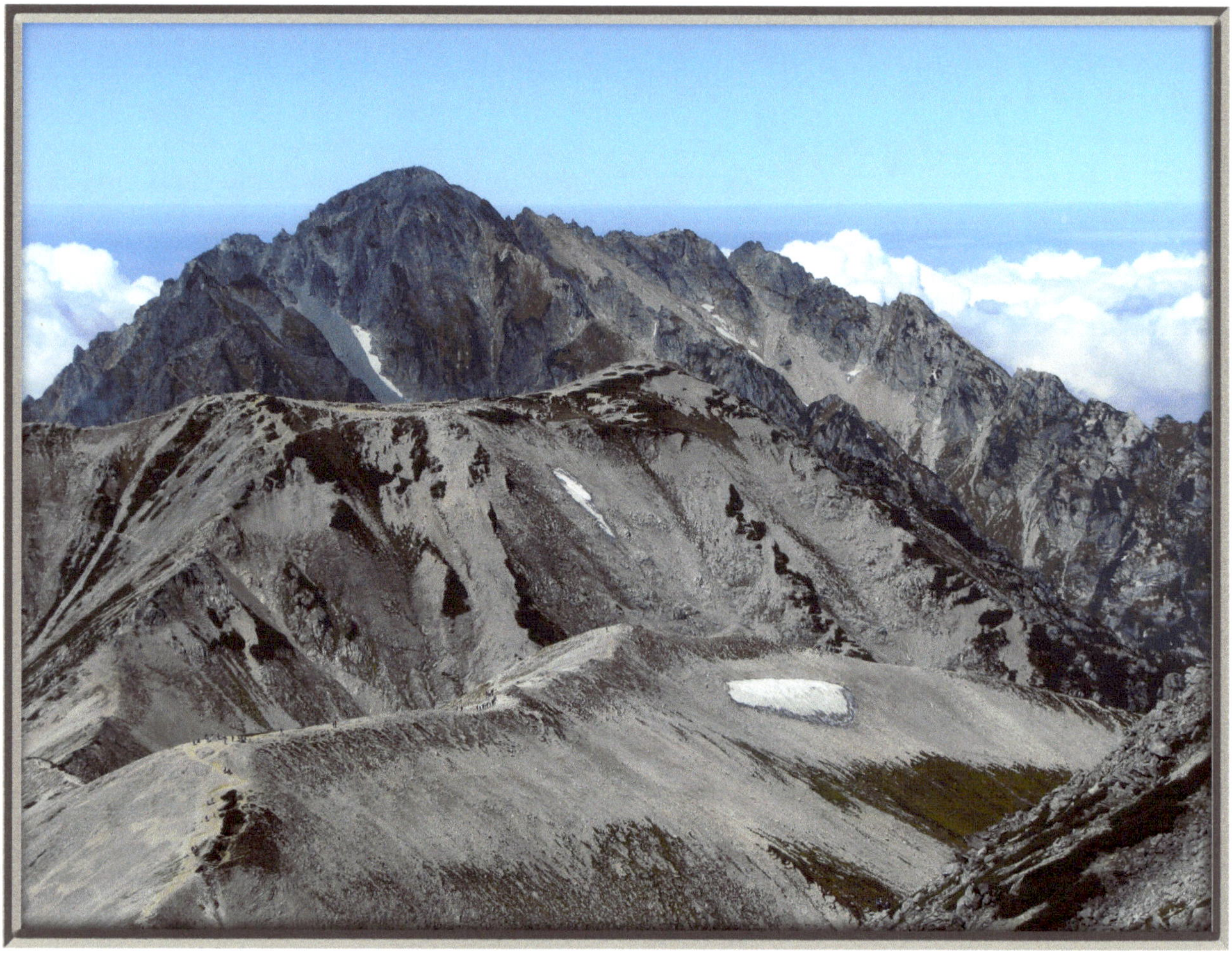

Not much grows here, as we mentioned back when we showed you the very first photo of this area. Now we are still approaching **Mt. Oonanji (Tateyama)** (3,015 meters = 9,892 feet), the highest peak. Kind of off in the distance – is **Mt. Tsurugidake** (2,999 meters = 9,839 feet). While not the highest peak in these mountains, **Mt. Tsurugidake** is called Japan's **"most dangerous climbable mountain"**. Tsurugidake has a number of routes which approach world class long routes.

In this photo you can probably identify tiny specks on the ridge in front of us – those are people on the trail. **Tsurugidake** is so far away so, although you cannot see them, there are probably one hundred people on its peak right now. We'll show you a photo showing people at the summit of Tsurugidake just a short while later on. We did not climb Tsurugidake. We didn't feel like we wanted to chance dying on this trip.

There was even a Japanese movie produced in 2009 which chronicled the first military climb and mapping of Tsurugidake. It is a very impressive movie. Of course the title is merely **"Tsurugidake"**.

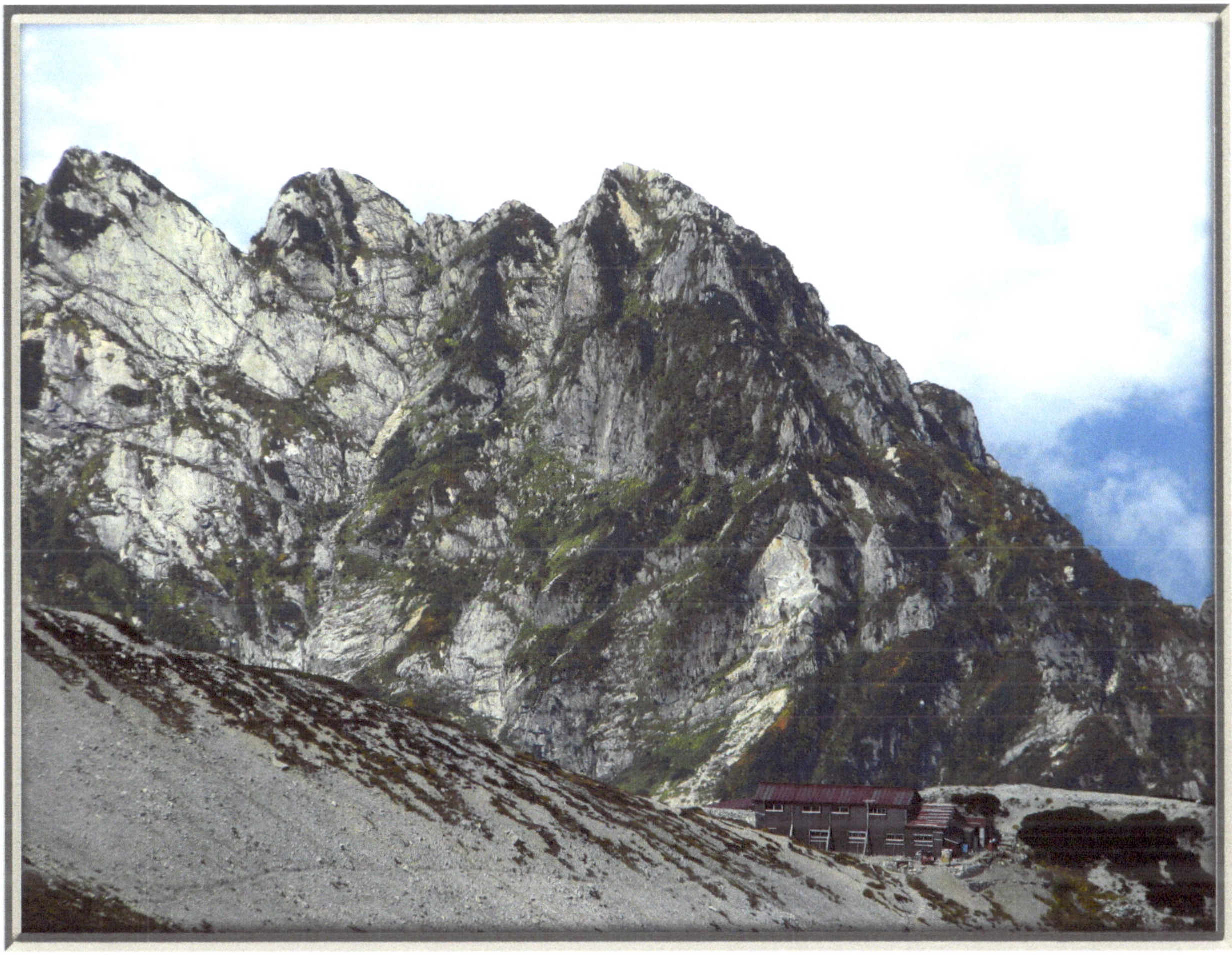

This photo shows a small part of **Mt. Tsurugidake** and, more importantly, at least to us, it shows the **Kuranosuke Hut**. The **Kuranosuke Hut** is where we are will be staying tonight. At this time we have just crossed the summit of **Mt. Oonanji (Tateyama)** (3,015 meters = 9,892 feet) and this is our first sighting of the end of the line for us for today. It has not been an extremely difficult climb, but it has been long and – despite the fact that the hut now looks close, it is not. This shot was taken with a telephoto lens! It's only 2:04 PM and we will not arrive at the hut until about 3:04 PM – another hour to go.

If you study the photo on the facing page, although the peaks in this photo are not visible, you may be able to guess that they would be to the right of the area shown in that photo.

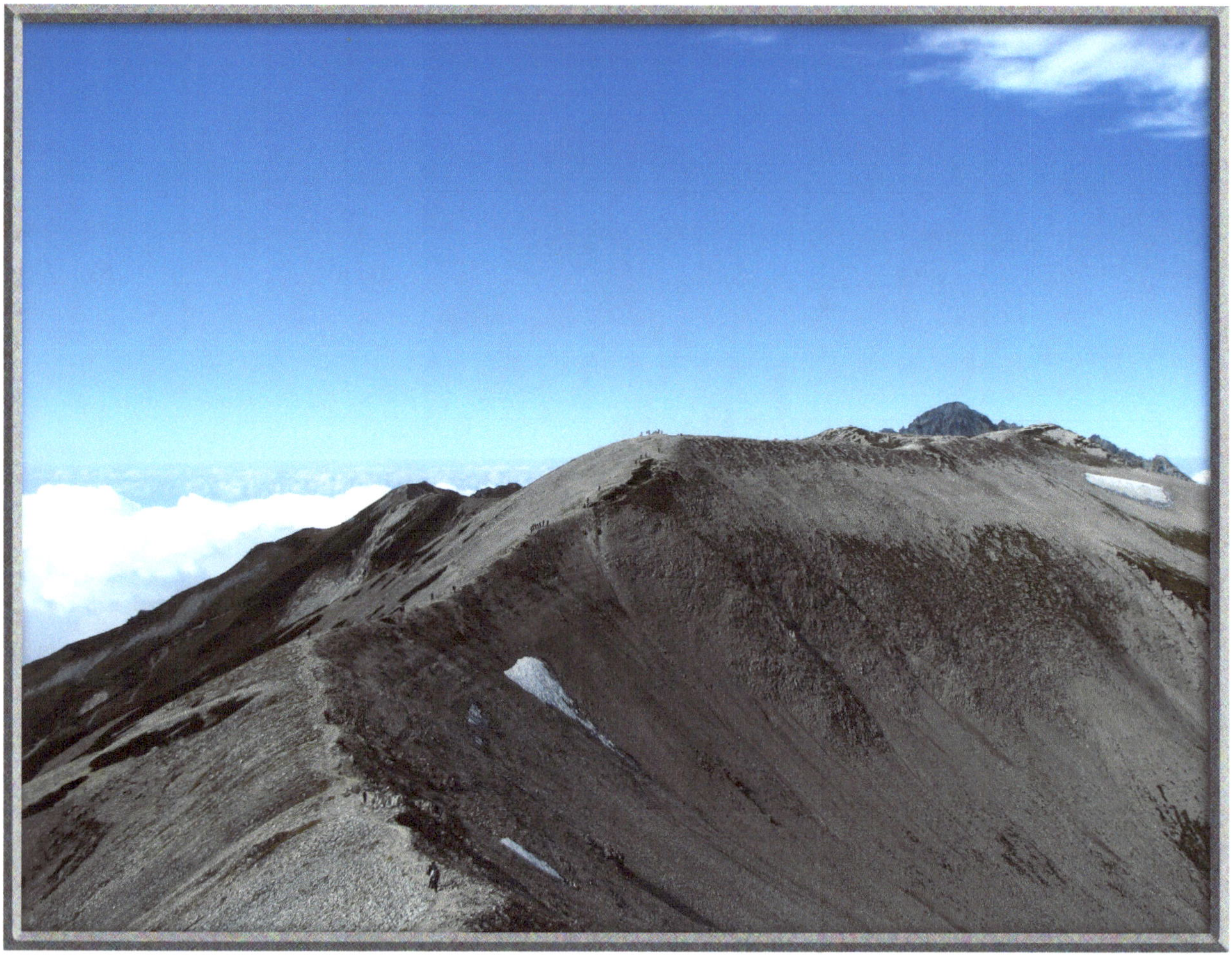

This scenery and color shot was taken as we continued to hike out the ridge shown in the photo on page 246. You can probably match the snowfield near the right hand edge of this photo with the snowfield which is just to the right and just below the center of the photo on that page. If you study carefully you can identify several people in this photo. This is a very popular mountain area for climbers in Japan. This is probably especially true now as the autumn colors begin to appear.

Notice off to the left side of this photo that it appears that the valley down there is under the clouds. When we arrived at the summit of the next peak – **Mt. Masago** (**Masago-dake**) (2,861 meters = 9,386 feet) – we saw that this was in fact the case.

On the facing page, the upper photo was taken from just above our destination for the day – the Kuranosuke Hut. It shows **Mt. Bessan** (**Bessan**) (left) and **North Mt. Bessan** (**Kita-Bessan**) (right). The lower photo shows **Mt. Tsurugidake** from **North Mt. Bessan** on the following morning. The small insert shows the large number of people who have risked their lives to attain the summit of Mt. **Tsurugidake**. The time of this photo was 8:29 AM.

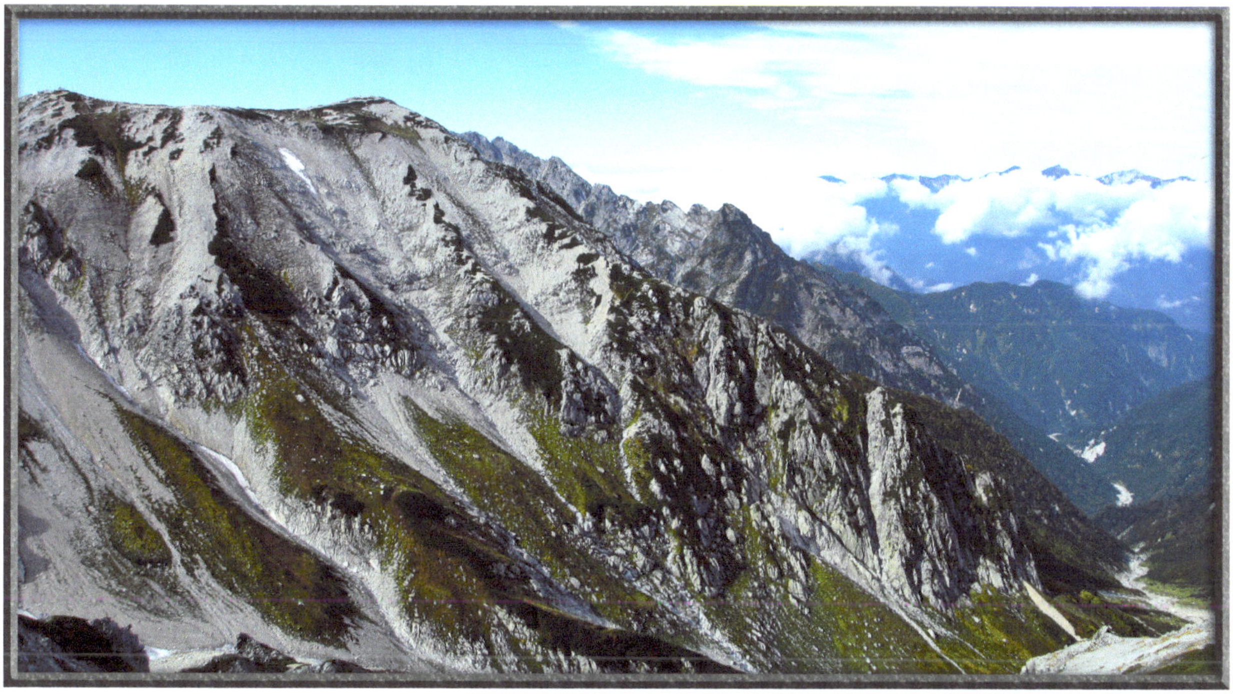

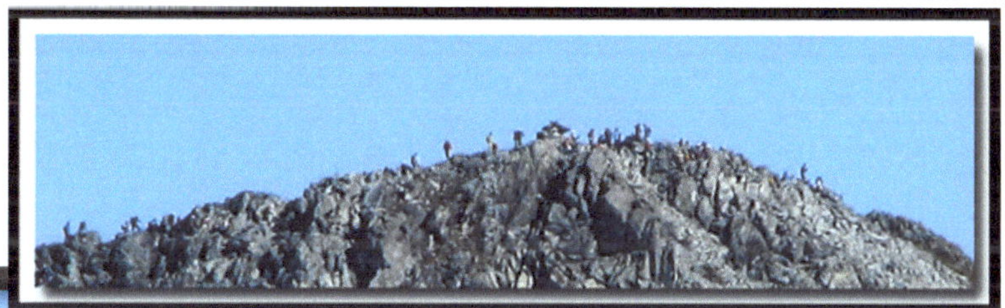

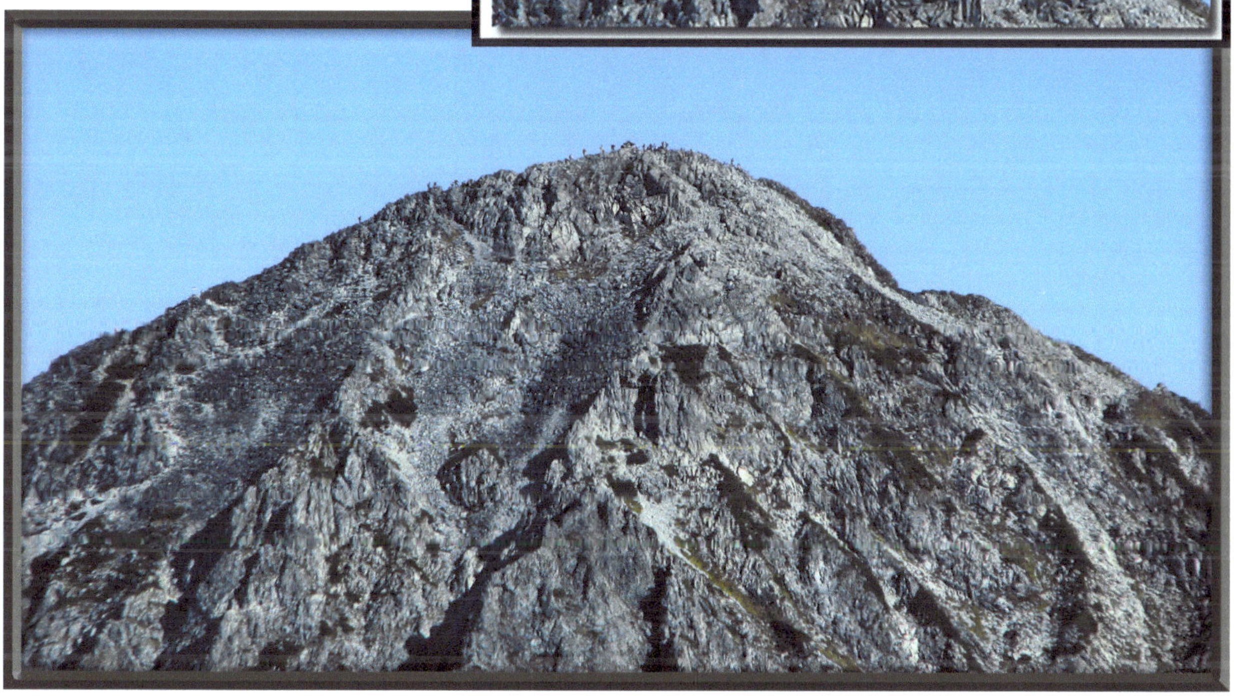

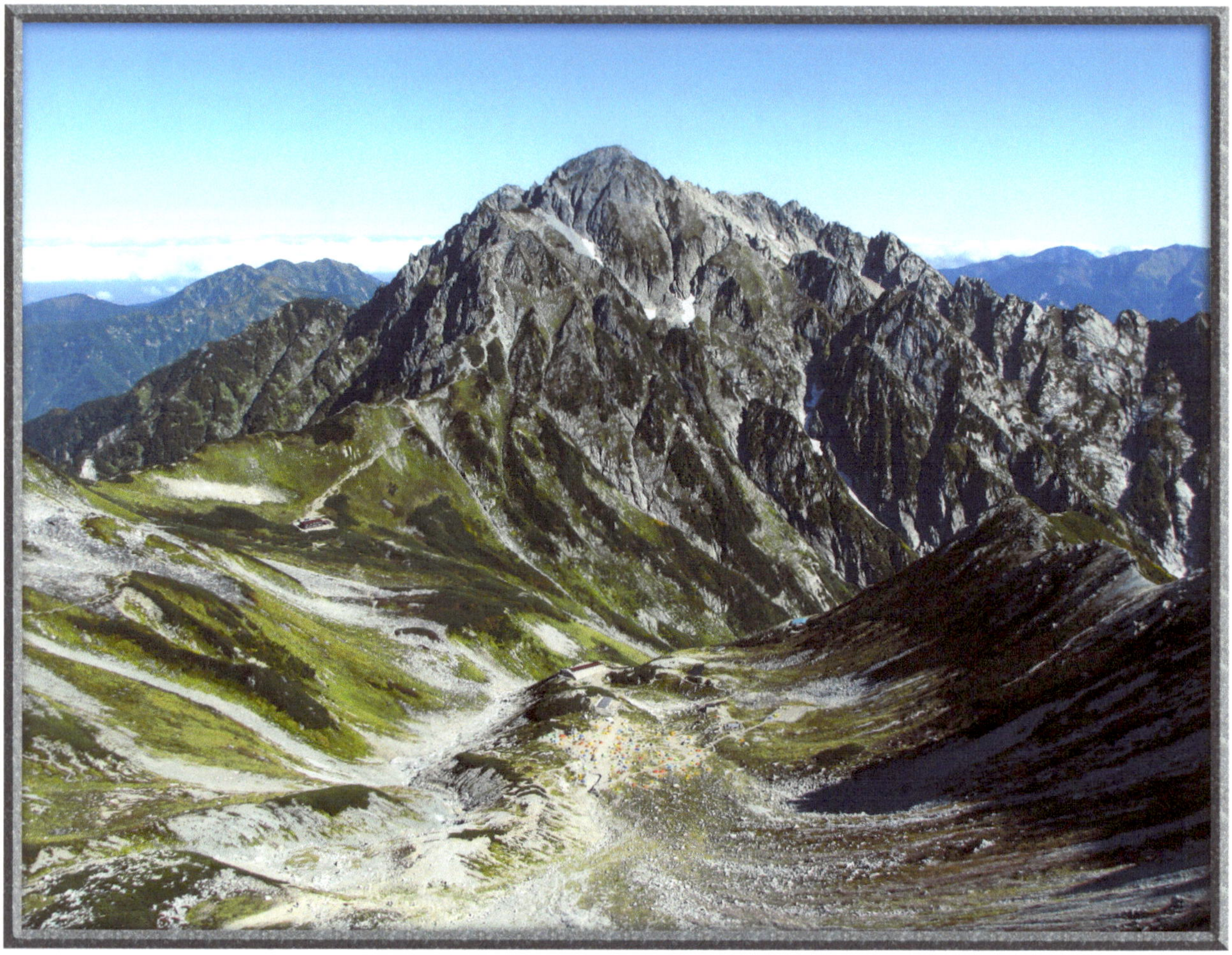

Here is an amazing shot of **Mt. Tsurugidake** (2,999 meters = 9,839 feet). This shot was taken from the ridge as we hiked from **North Mt. Bessan** (**Kita-Bessan**) down towards where we started. This was our final day on this climbing adventure.

In the photo above, you probably cannot distinguish enough to be able to notice that there is a very large mountain hut down in that valley and that there are probably at least one hundred tents set up, in addition to the accommodations which are available at the hut. We had no idea that anywhere near this number of people would be attempting to climb Japan's **"most dangerous climbable mountain"**. Do they have a death wish or what?

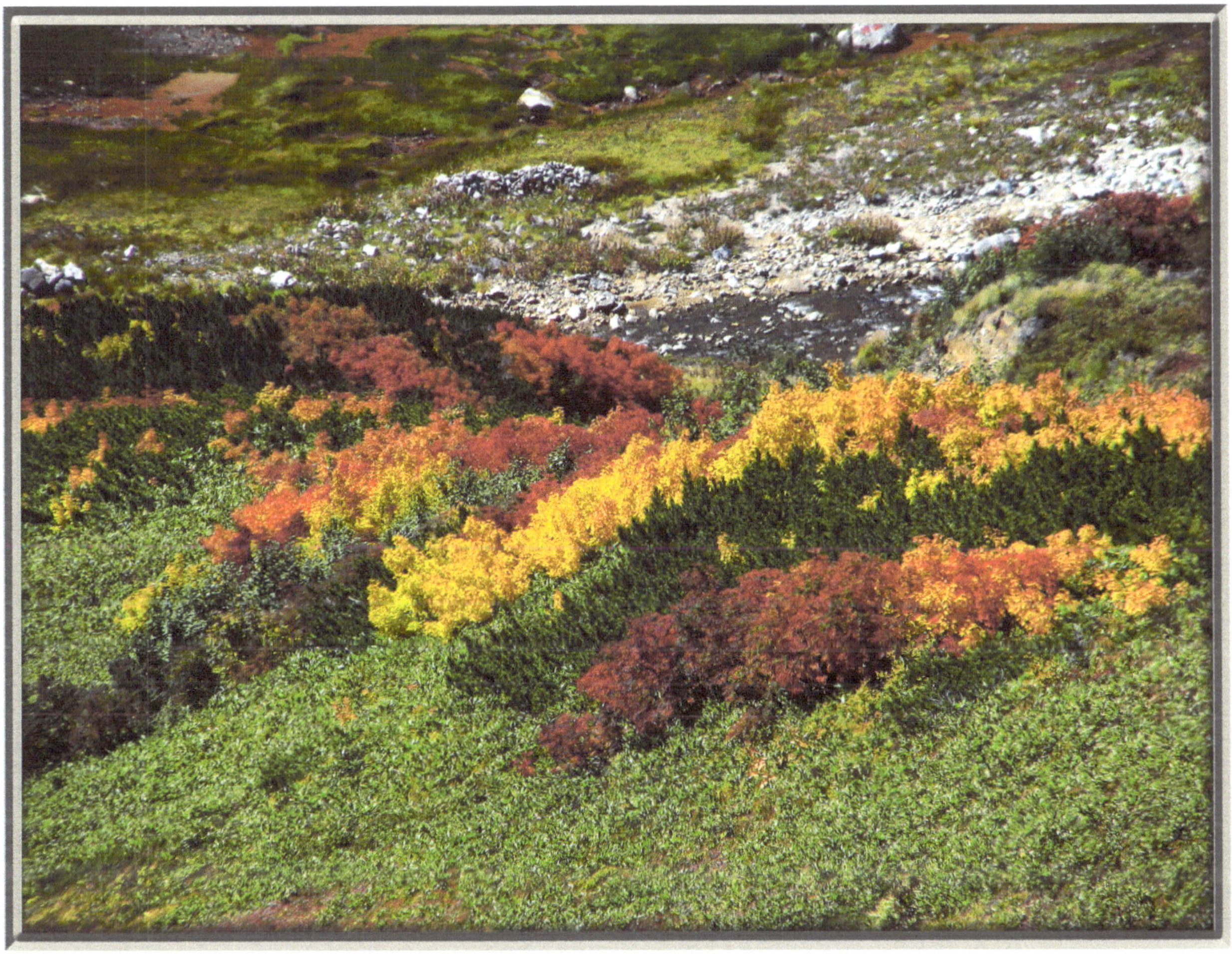

We have now descended low enough so that there is some vegetation which is affected by cold weather and we've found some of the most incredible fall colors. This is just barely into the actual season of autumn, but it is certainly autumn at this elevation on the mountain. We were amazed to see this kind of coloration already and we ended up taking many photos of it.

We wonder what the best season to climb in this area probably is. It is obvious that we had some fantastic autumn sky and clouds and now that we are getting down to an elevation where there is vegetation, we can even enjoy autumn colors, but we have certainly not seen many flowers during this adventure – it is too late in the season for most all flowers.

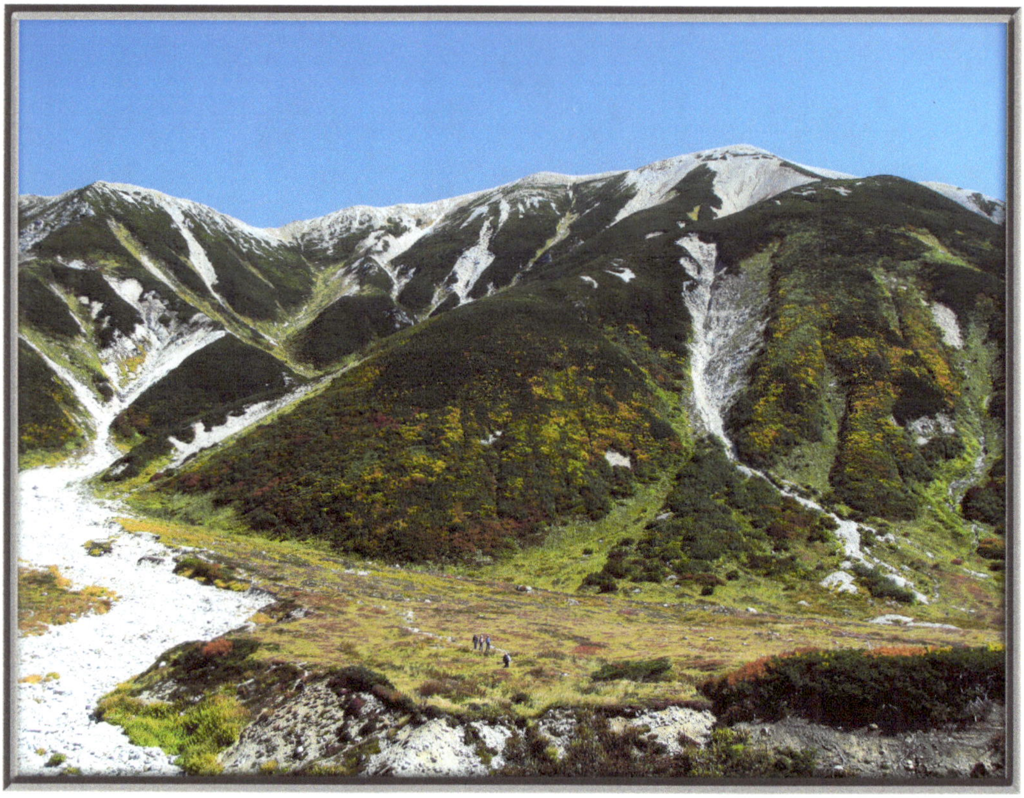

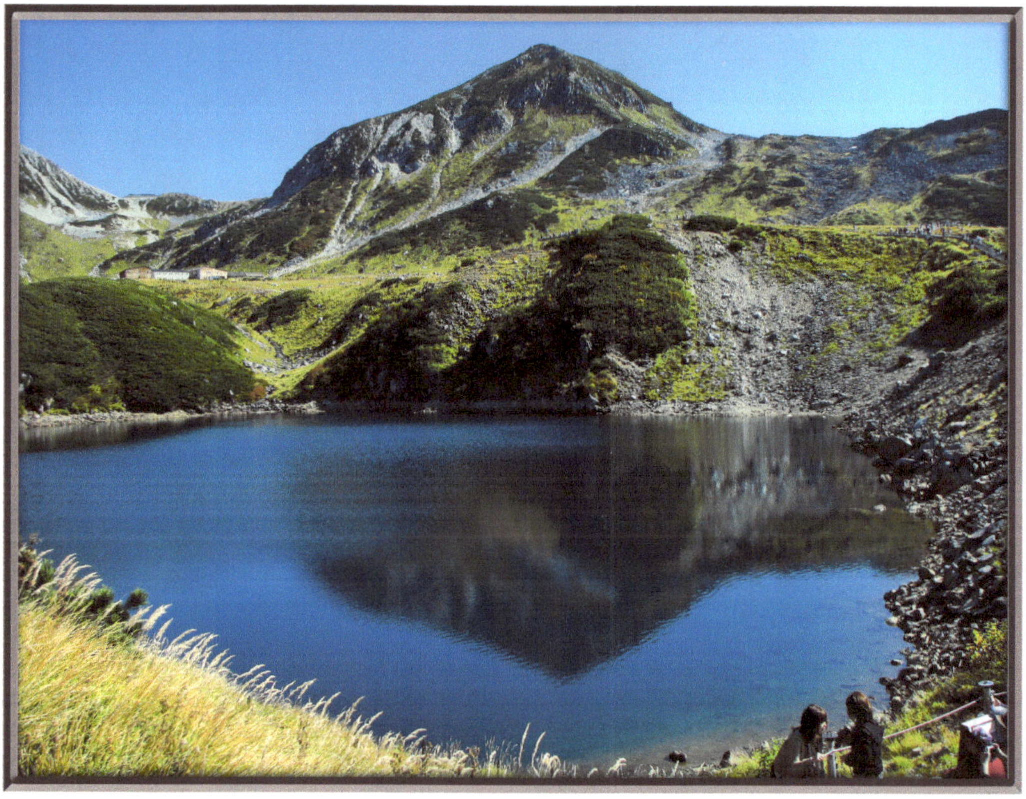

The two photos on the facing page are the final two from our **Mt. Tateyama** adventure. The upper photo shows the final ridgeline we hiked and now we are on a very minor ridge on our way to **Jigokudani – Hell's Valley**. We have not included any photos of it, but there is still an area of very active volcanism here. It has steam vents shooting steam up into the air and large bright yellow sulfur cones sticking up around the steam fumaroles.

The lower photo on the facing page is a pond with a nice reflection.

The photo on this page is a grass-roofed house at **Shirakawa-go**, a **World Heritage Site** which we visited before returning home to Tokyo. There are many homes and businesses in Shirakawa-go which are grass-roofed. It is a most stunning area to visit if you ever have the chance.

We'll show you three photos from this area before we leave and then we'll continue on to the next adventure.

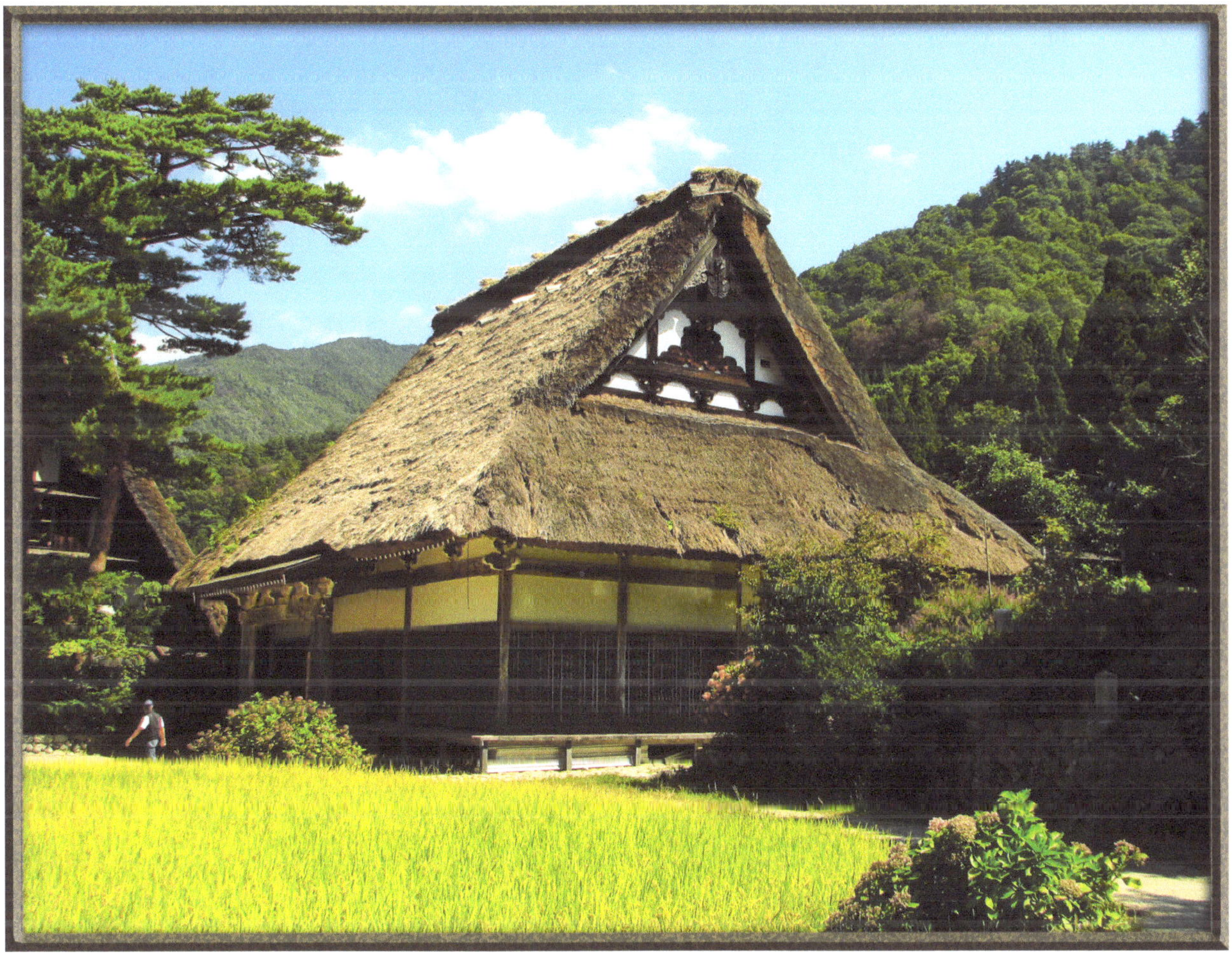

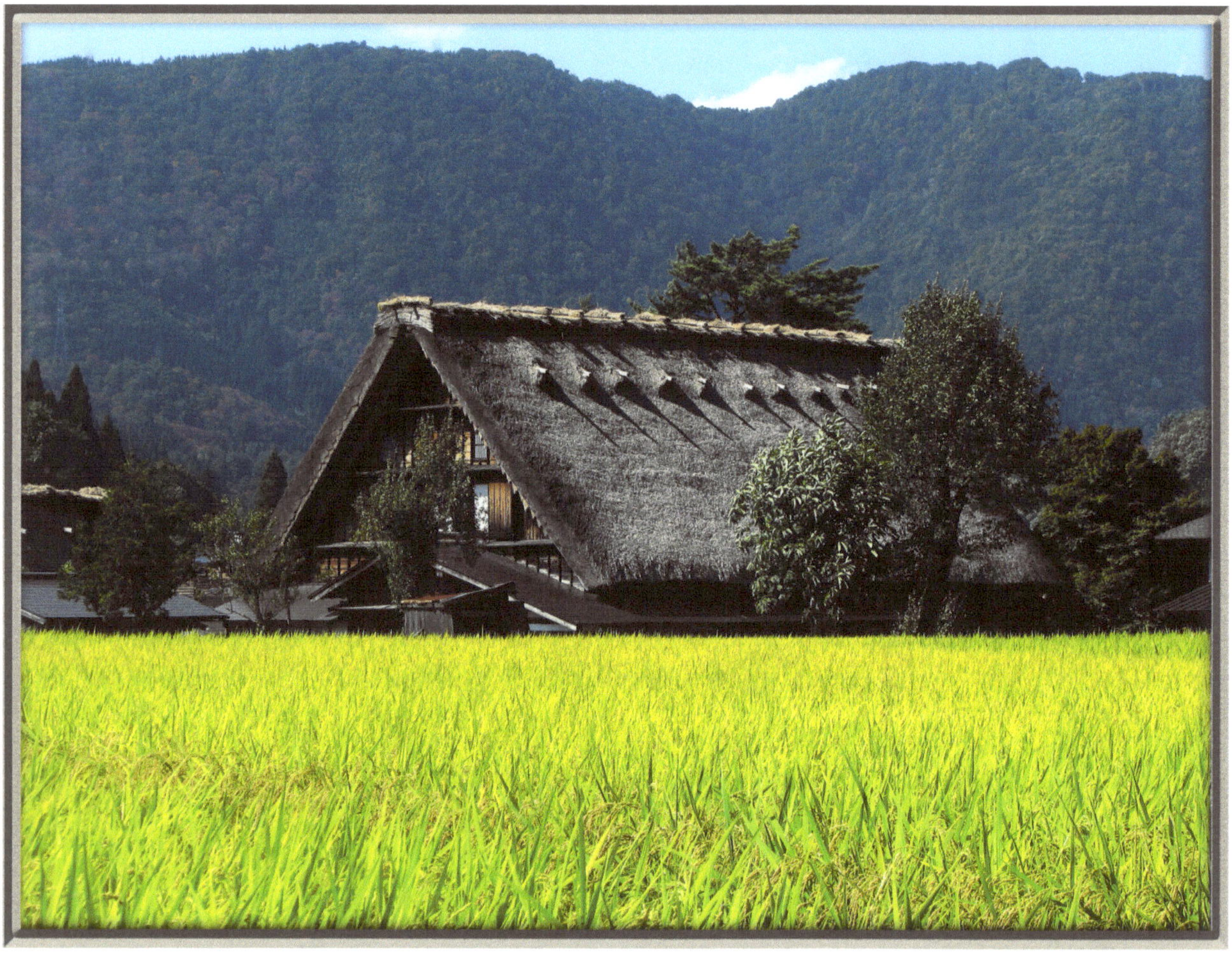

Here is another shot of a grass-roofed home at **Shirakawa-go**. It is located in **Gifu** and **Toyama Prefectures** – in the **Chubu Region**. We were very fortunate to have visited here in late September when the rice was ripening and so very nice and yellow in color. We were treated to some fascinating sights. Of course many other people had the same thought and the highways to get here were packed. We were on a bus, so we could sit back and relax and let the bus driver worry about traffic. However, personally I do not like sitting on a highway with traffic not moving, so it was not enjoyable for me to travel here. Kazuya has more patience than me about traffic, so it did not bother him as much.

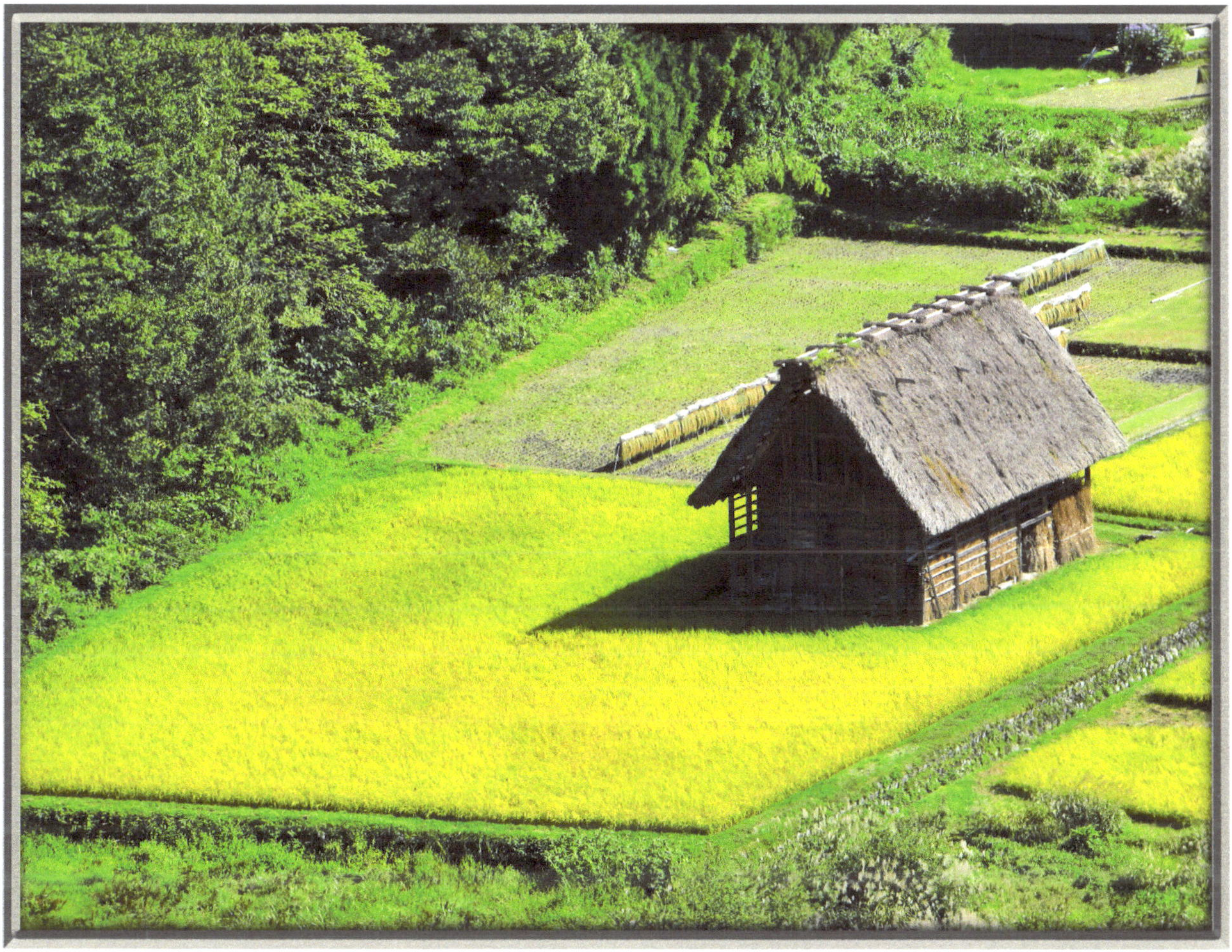

Here just above is one final shot taken at Shirakawa-go. On one side of the town there is a hill and an overlook which you can walk up to and look down on the entire town. We walked up there and on the way we passed this scenic older building. It is not a home, more likely it's a barn or tool building of some sort. The ripening rice around it offers a very nice gold color and all in all it is very attractive.

Now it's time for us to leave and head back towards Tokyo and start on a one day adventure. It's also getting to be very close to the end of September – there are only three photos left for this month.

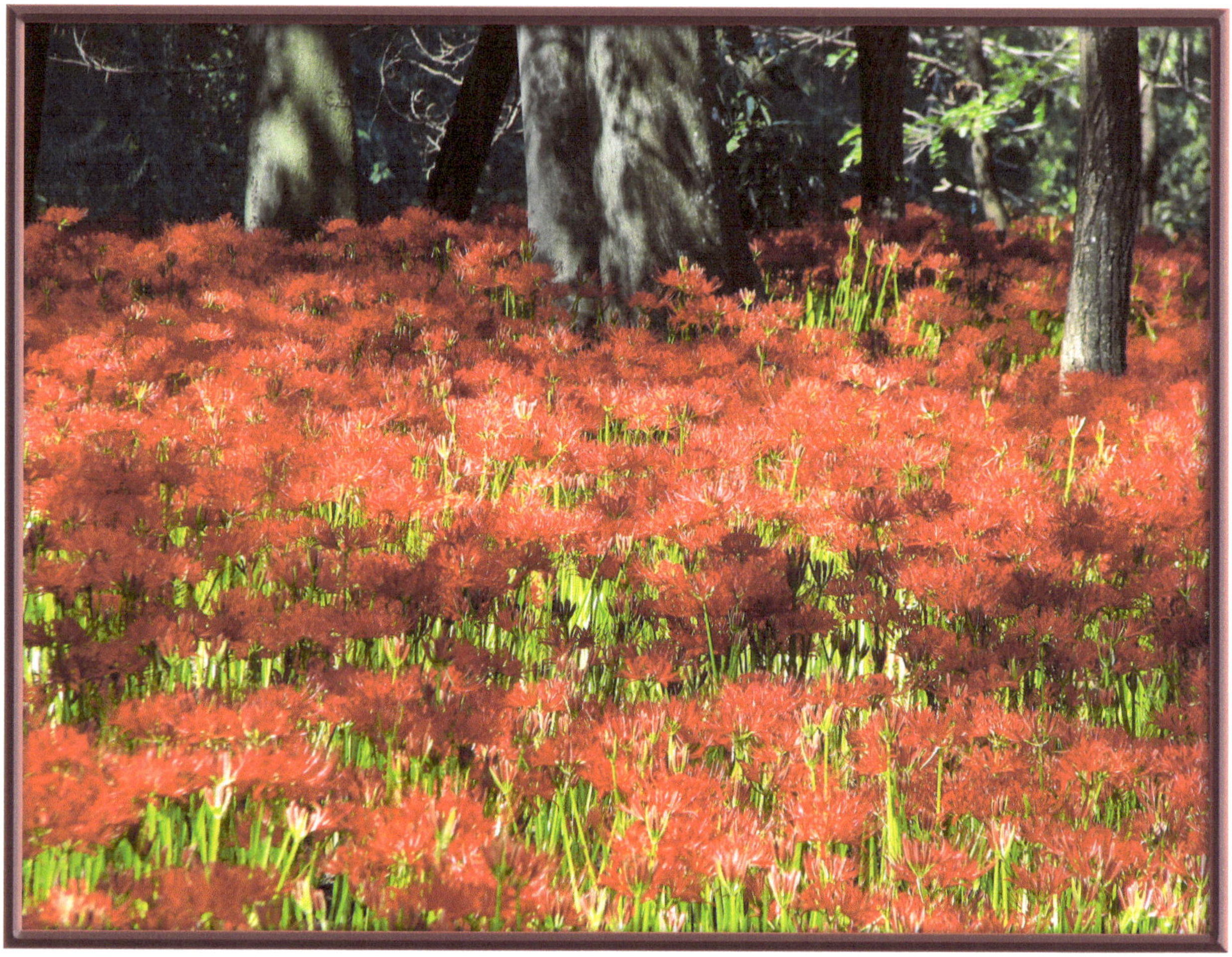

This shot was taken in **Saitama Prefecture** at a place called **Kinchakuda**. The amazing red flowers are **Cluster Amaryllis** (***Lycoris radiata***) (***Higan-bana*** in Japanese). This is a very late September flower and at this particular place it grows in the bend of a river. This smallish river park is filled with this plant and in this season so many people come here to see this amazing phenomenon that it's barely fun to have to fight the crowds in the park. It is very difficult to get photos with no people in them. This is a relatively small area pictured above, and it's right on the bank of the river, so there are probably people down there behind this photo walking on the riverbank.

On the facing page is an additional shot of Cluster Amaryllis. In this shot you can see some people without searching too hard.

On pages 106 and 229 we showed you **Lotus** plants (***Nelumbo nucifera***). Here is a shot of a Lotus garden at **Kinchakuda** in which you can see several seedheads. This (facing page) is the final photo of Lotus. This is also the final photo of September.

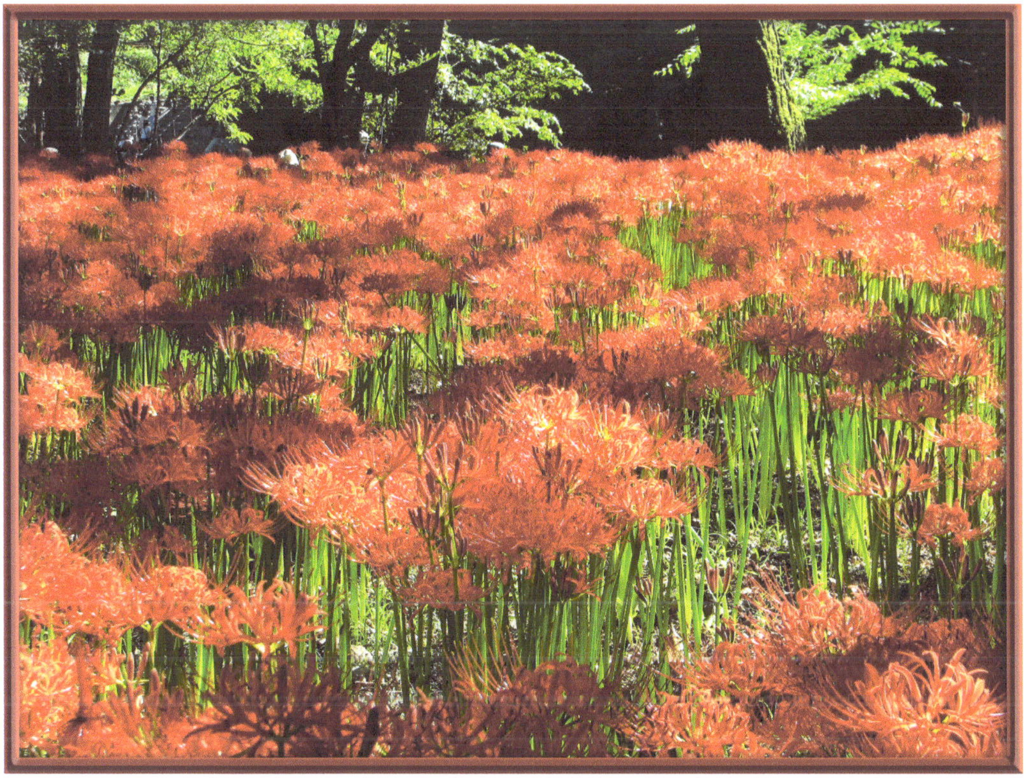

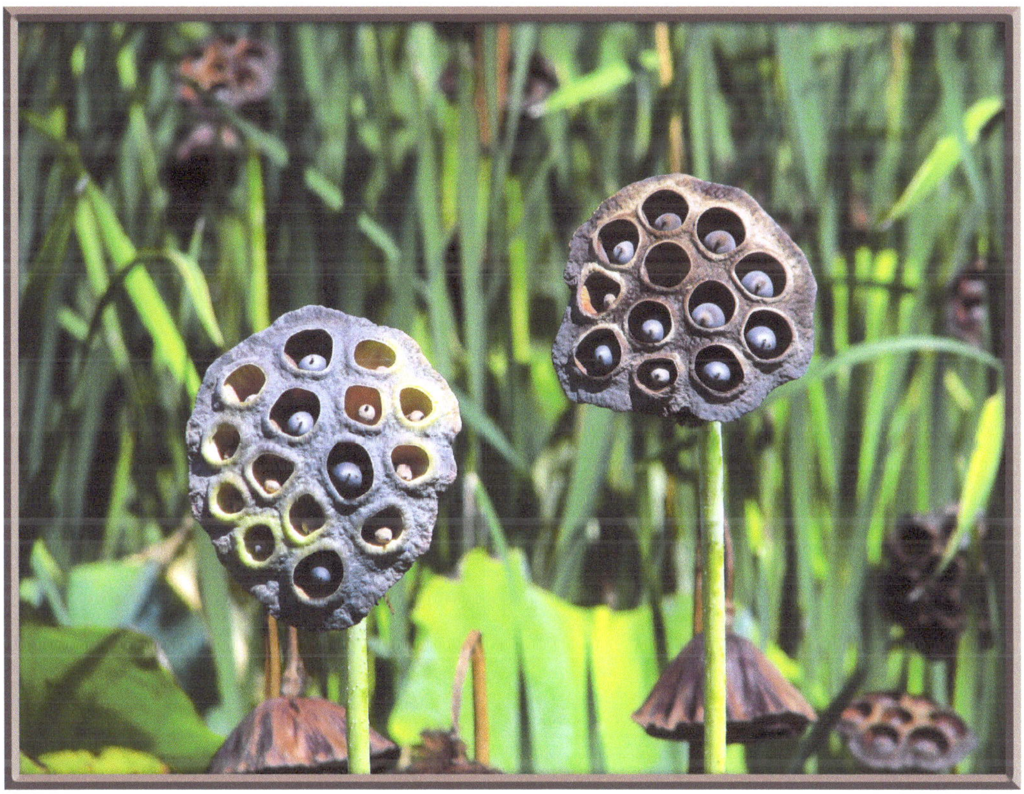

October Photos and Story

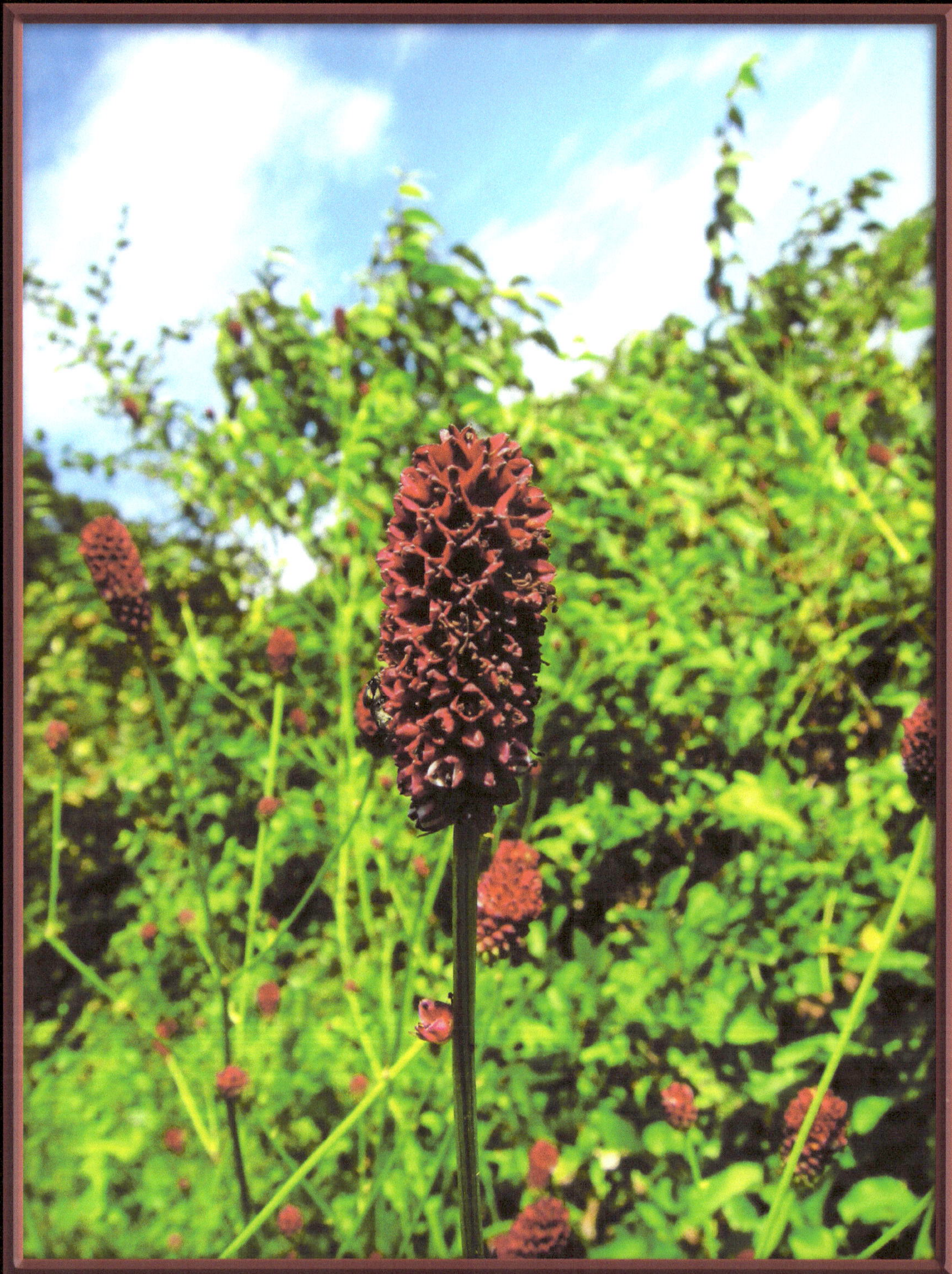

The image on the facing page, that weird red flower, is a ***Sanguisorba officinalis*** – ***Waremokou*** in Japanese. We have once again returned to **Mt. Mitake** and **Mt. Hinode,** (pages 79, 165 and 166) in Western Tokyo, and are checking out the autumn flowers. On this particular date the Waremokou was just about the only interesting thing we found. As you can see, this flower is plentiful here.

The photo below was taken after we finished up on Mt. Hinode and Mt. Mitake, took the cable car down to the bottom and then hiked down to the **Upper-Tama River**. As you will note, this river – here in the mountains – is very clear and beautiful. It rushes through and around the rocks and is a favorite multiple-use area for kayakers, rafters, rock climbers, picnickers, photographers and young lovers. It is a multiple-use area in the strictest sense of the word.

In the hot summer months this is a favorite place to cool off too. Sitting beside the river with ones feet in the water, sipping on a cool beer and watching people is a nice thing to do to relax after hiking in the local mountains.

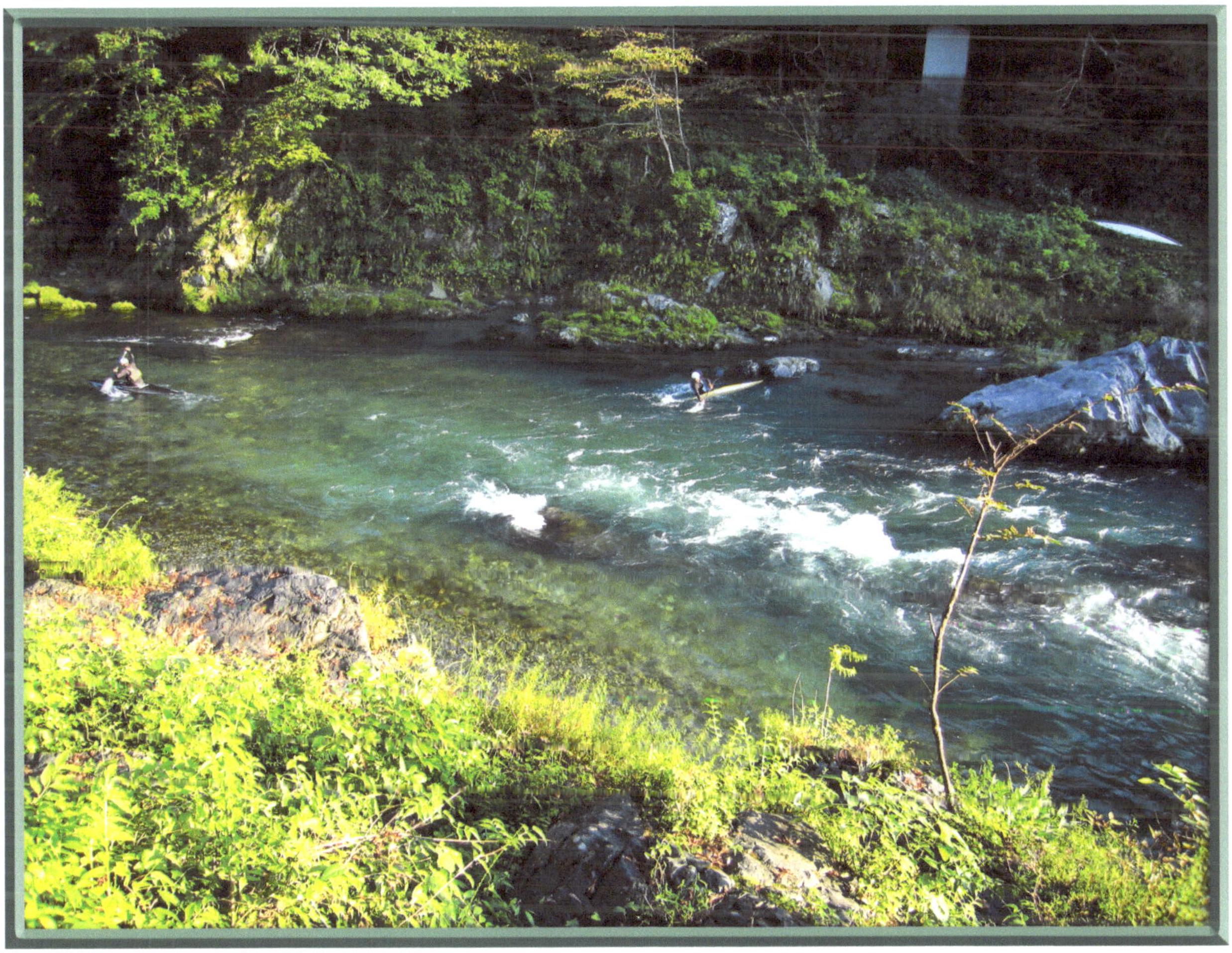

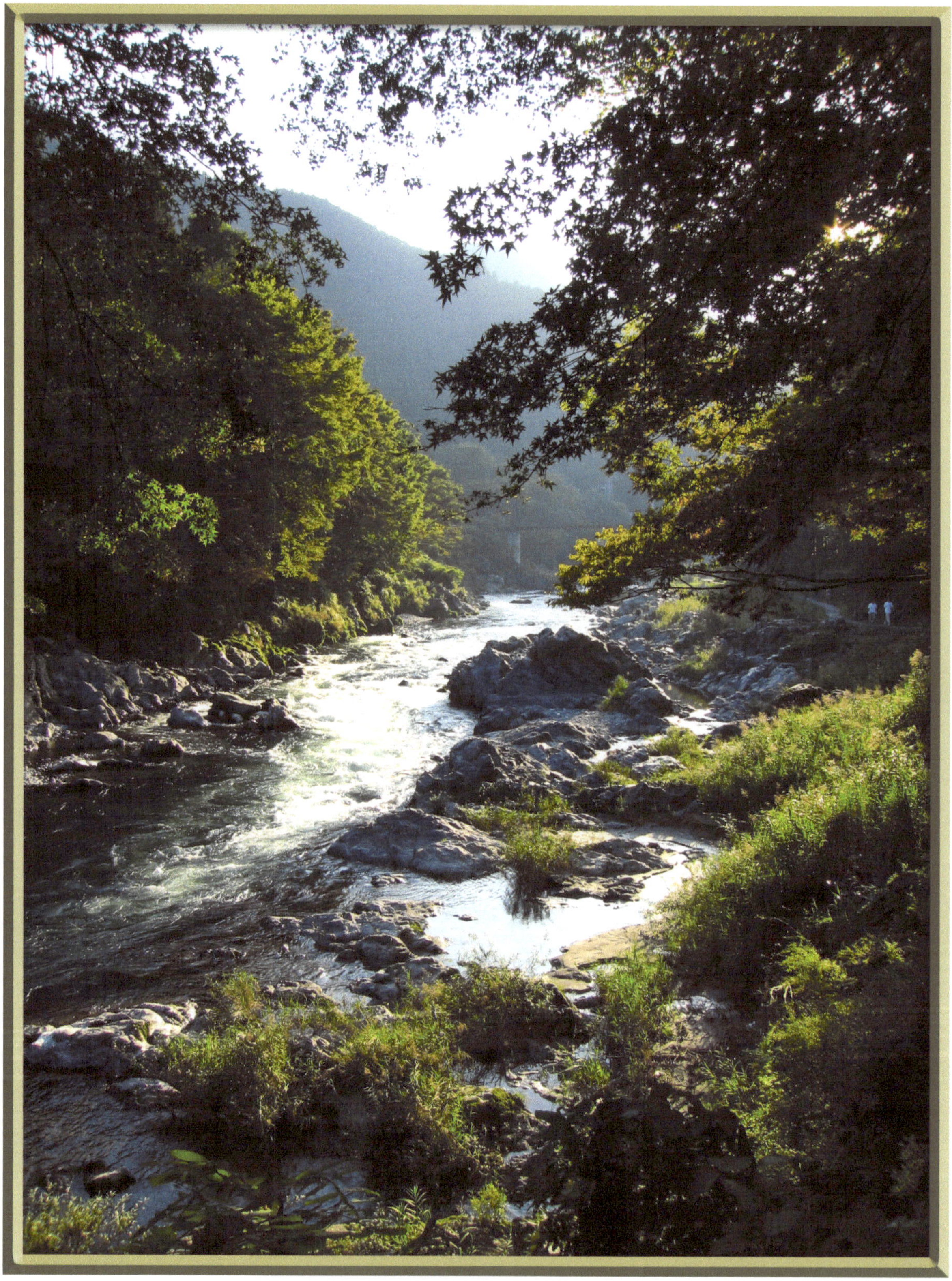

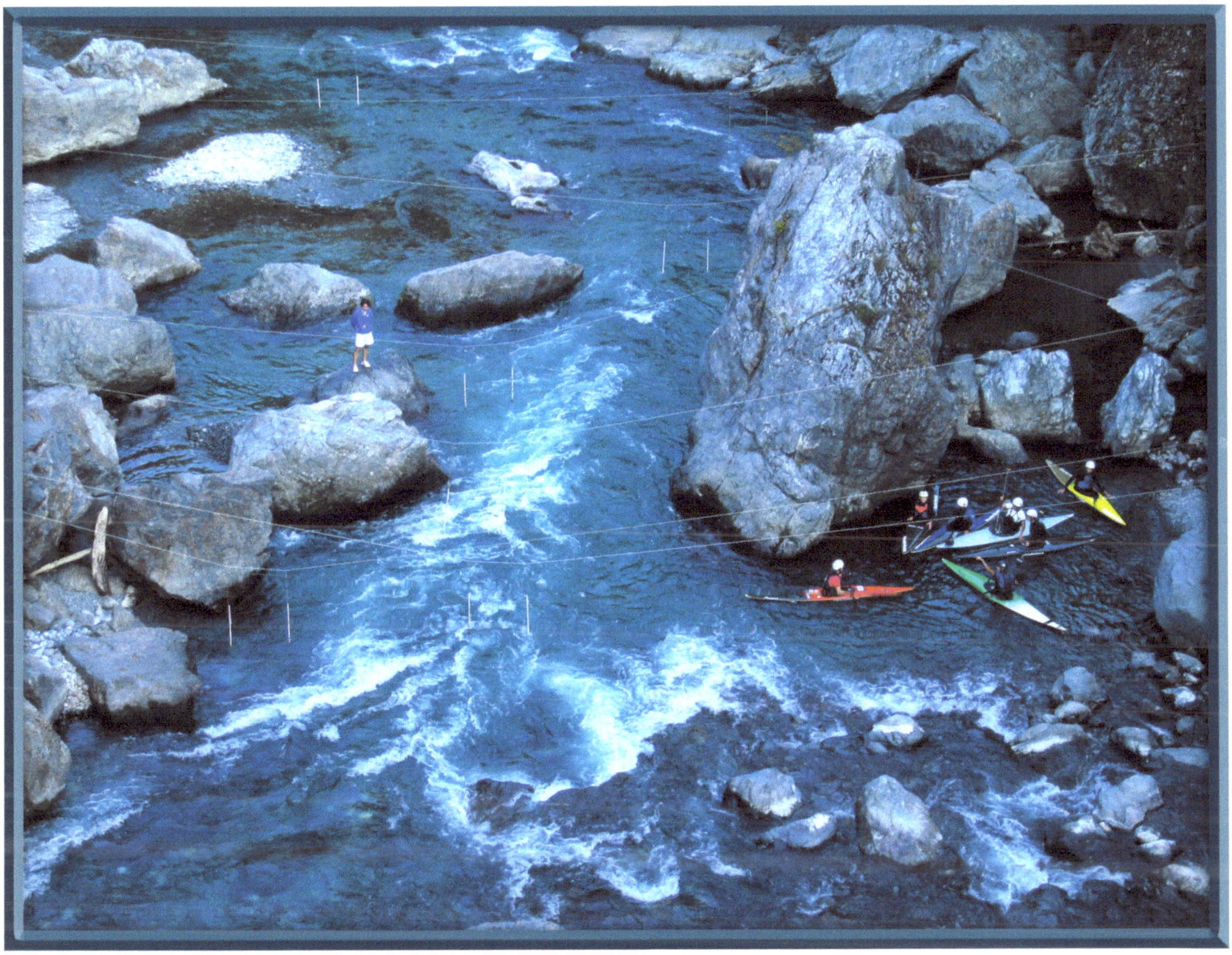

The facing page photo shows the Upper-Tama River looking upstream from a spot near Mitake. The sun is going down and reflecting on the river in this very attractive scene. On the right side of the photo you can see some people walking along the developed trail and quite a distance upstream you can see a footbridge.

The shot on this page shows an amazing blue cast to the entire photo due to the particular lighting conditions, shadows and so on. Nothing special has been done to this photo to make it more blue than it naturally is. You can also get a good idea of scale due to the kayakers, the person standing on the rock and the ropes with poles hanging on them – which the kayakers attempt to go through – either from upstream or from downstream. They have several kayak events here every year. Fortunately they remove the ropes and poles between events.

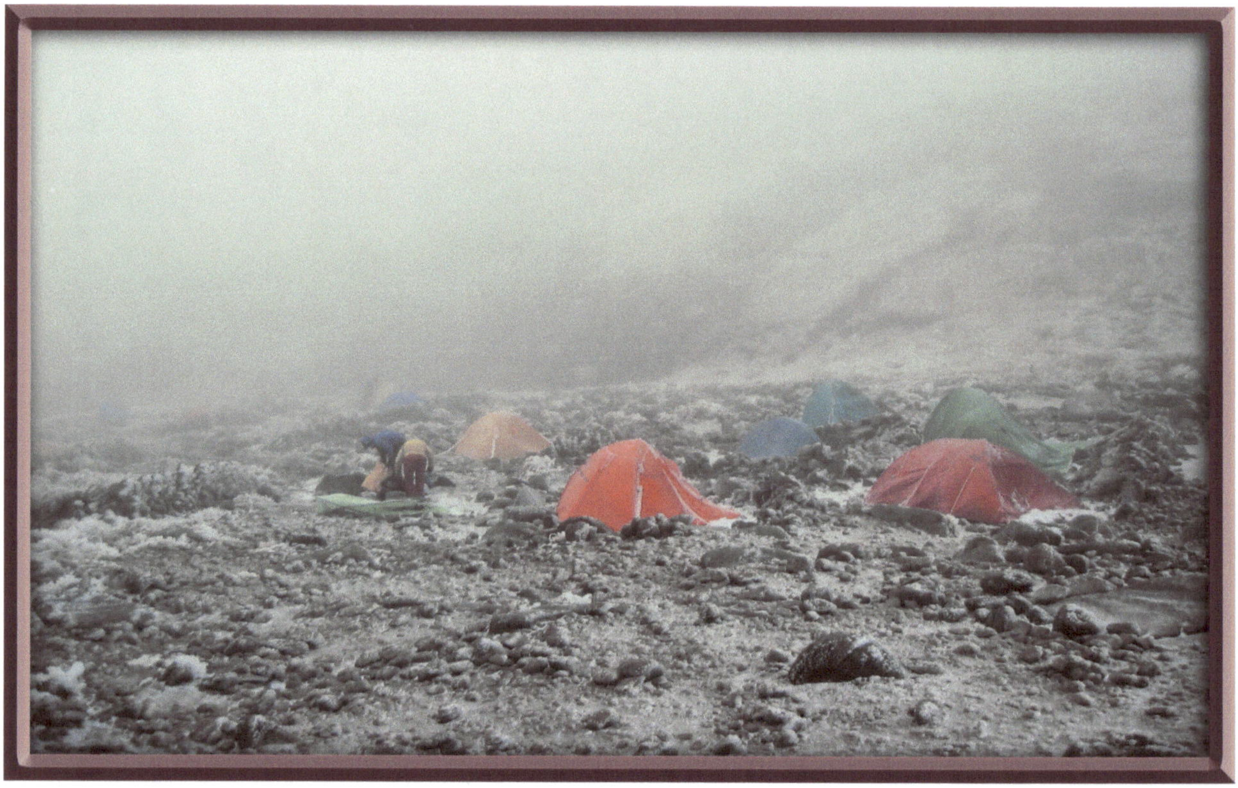

Now we're going to take a trip to **Nagano Prefecture** and climb **Mt. Kiso-Komagatake** (2,956 meters = 9,698 feet). It is the highest peak in the **Japanese Central Alps Mountain Range**. It was pretty cloudy as we climbed from the top of the Gondola to the hut where we had our reservations at. It was getting cold and blustery, but we didn't think too much of it – we were not worried for our safety or anything like that.

The photo above shows what it looked like outside of the hut on the following morning. The white is **ICE**. We realized that it was cold and of course we knew that it was raining and very windy during the night, but we were tucked warm and cozy under our blankets and did not realize that the rain was turning to ice on everything it struck. When we looked outside the next morning we hoped that the people who were in tents had plenty of warm gear with them. We knew that we were not prepared to descend the mountain in these conditions.

The facing page shows what we saw as we began our descent of the mountain back towards the top of the Gondola. That white stuff is ice. The trail was extremely slippery, we had no gloves, warm hats, long underwear or anything adequate for this kind of weather. It was scary.

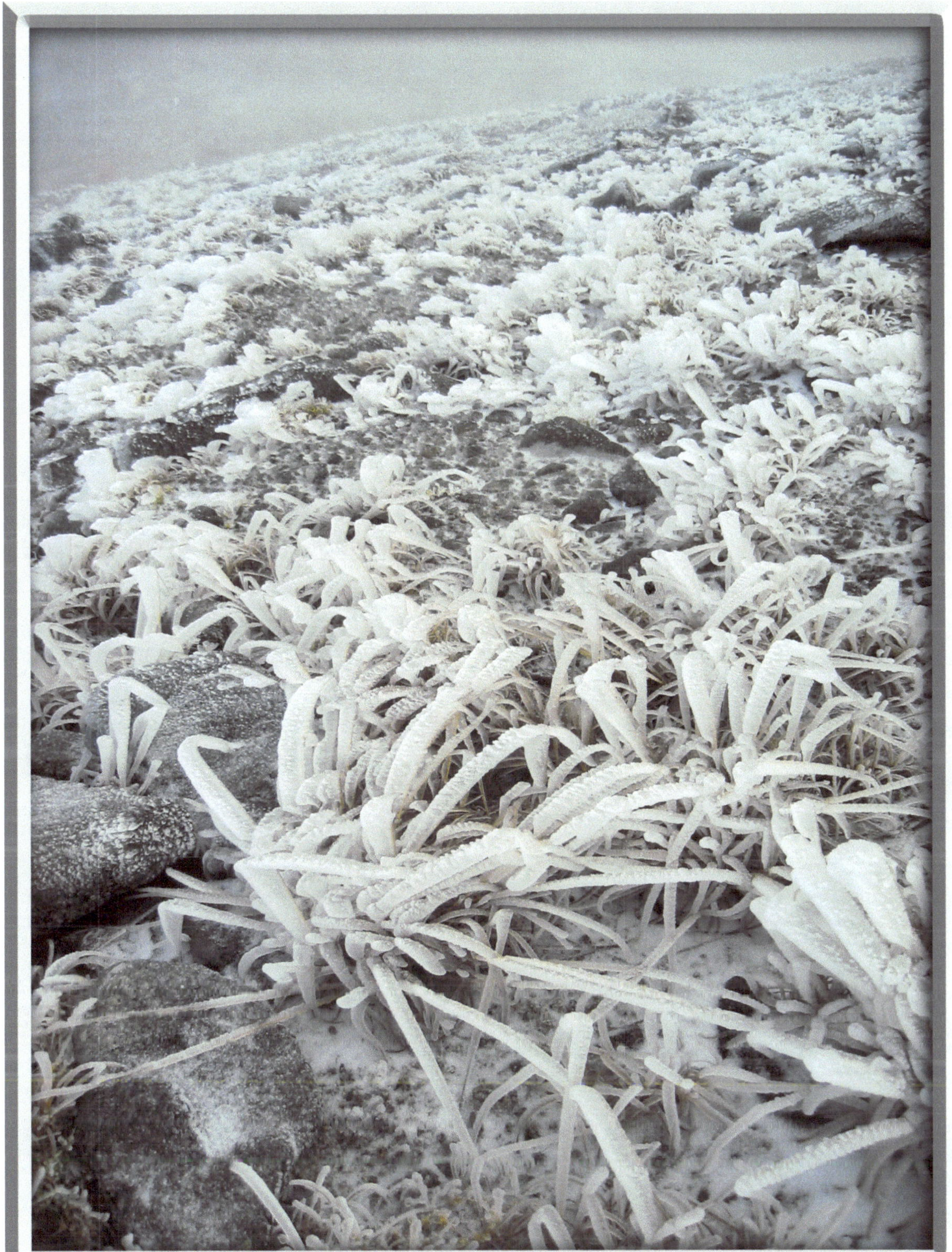

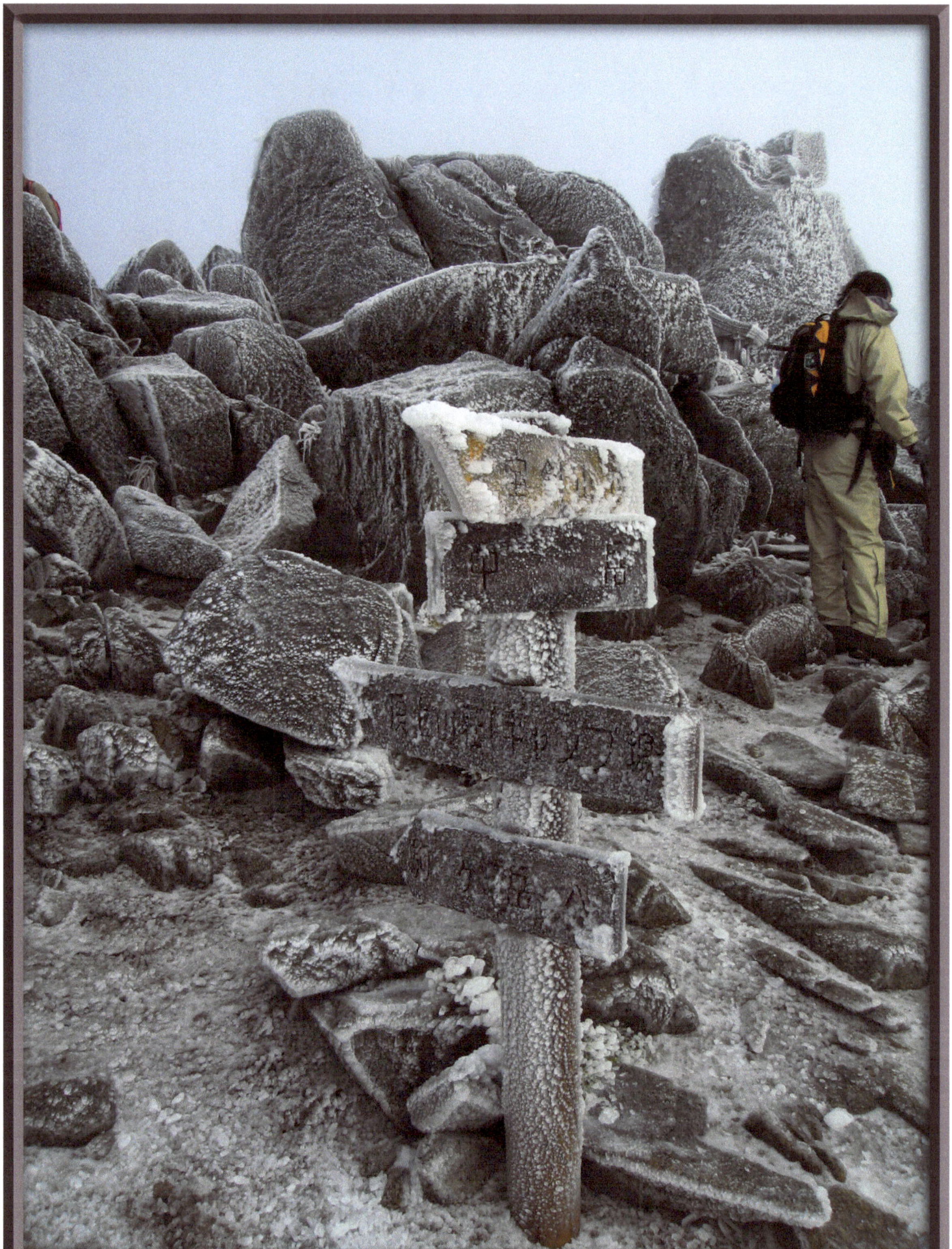

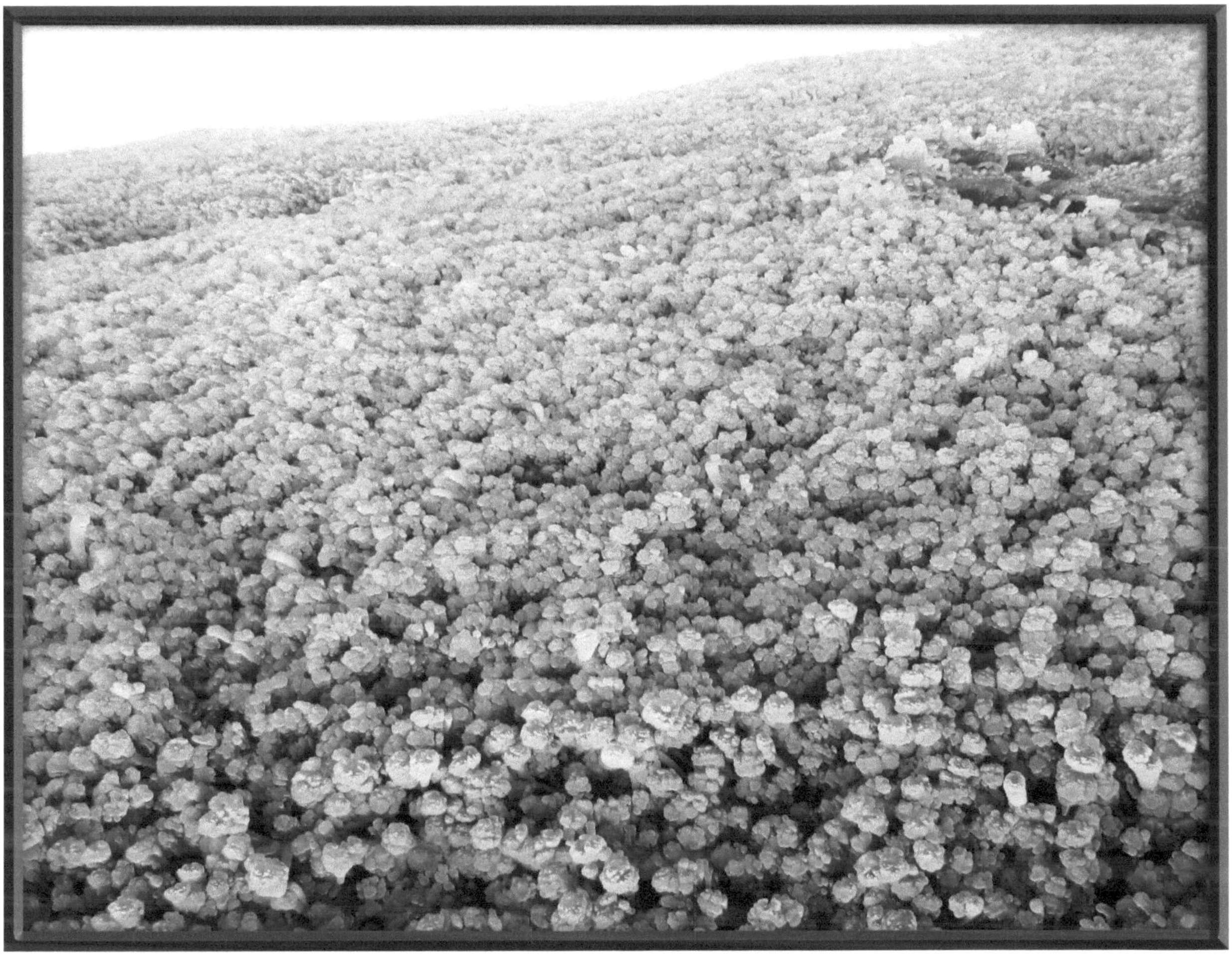

The facing page photo shows a sign along the trail as we descended to the Gondola. The person in the photo is a stranger. Look at the amount of ice which is on the horizontal surfaces – as we mentioned above – we were not at all prepared for this. The hoarfrost was developing on our caps and jackets, our fingers were numb, our toes were numb and the weather was not relenting as we went down. Silly people were also coming up as we were going down. We felt that the smartest people we encountered all day were the ones which turned around and went back down when they saw us on our way down. They probably noticed the hoarfrost on our clothing and decided that, like us, they were not prepared for these conditions.

The photo on this page is an additional shot which gives you more of an idea of how much ice was on everything as we descended along the trail.

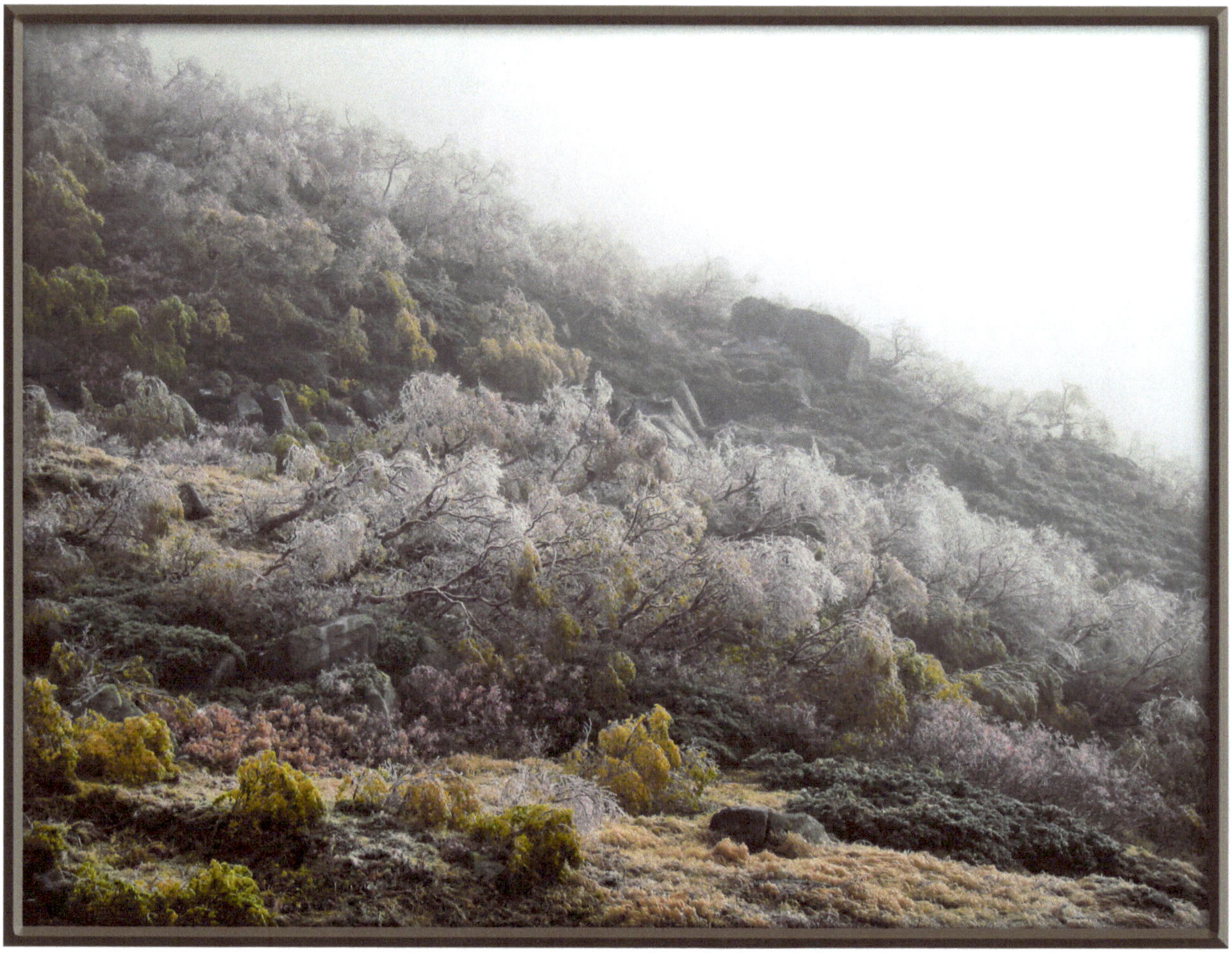

This photo just above shows some of the amazing beauty of the icy scenery. We are presently approaching the bottom of the trail and getting close to the Gondola. We are still alive, we have not slipped on the ice and ended up going head over heels off the mountain, so now we can begin to appreciate the beauty. Here you can note some autumn colors, the clouds still all around us and – of course – the ice on all of the bushes. One of the reasons we came here was for autumn colors. This is actually the first chance we have had to be able to see and appreciate them.

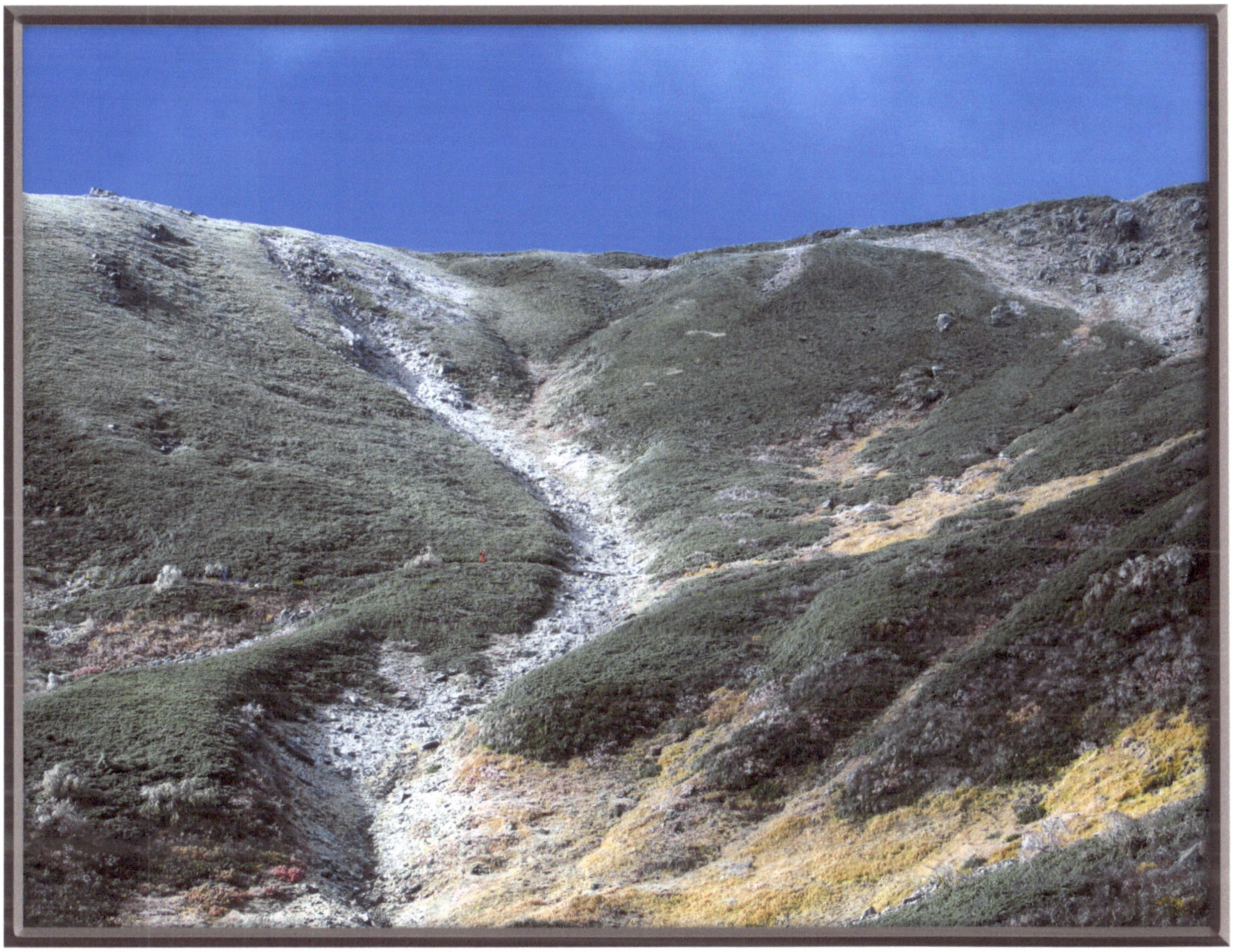

Is it going to clear up or not? The clouds are presently coming and going and this is the best scene we have had since we've been here. This was taken from very close to the top of the Gondola. This is also the first time we've seen this much blue sky since we've been here. We have decided to wait and see if it might possibly clear up even more before proceeding down! There is such an amazing difference between the weather now and when we first started com ing down the mountain. Apparently we should have spent more time loitering at the hut before beginning our descent.

The clouds – do they want to come or do they want to go? They seem to be unsure about what they want to do!

9:01 AM

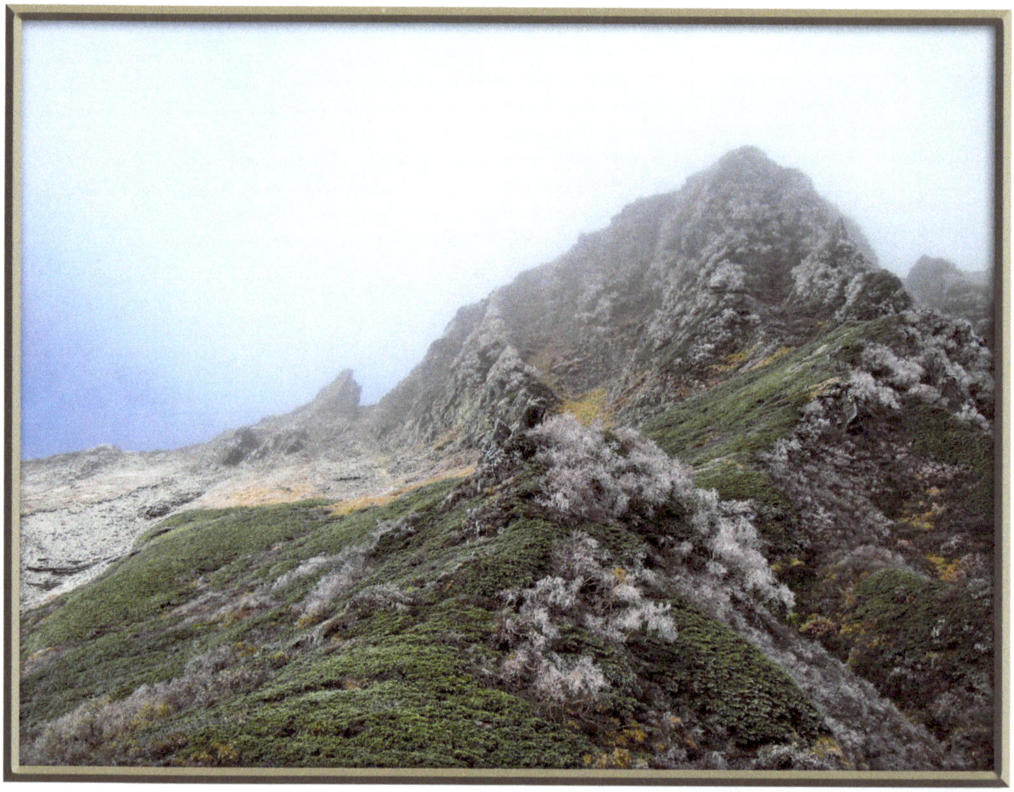

9:02 AM

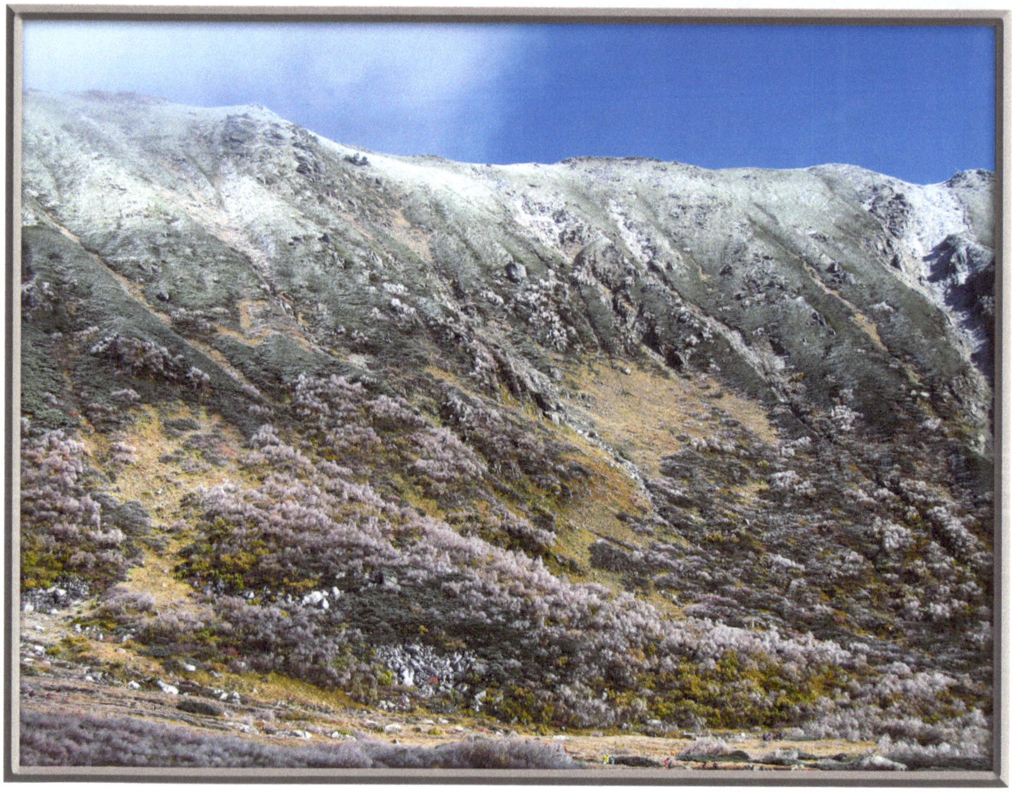

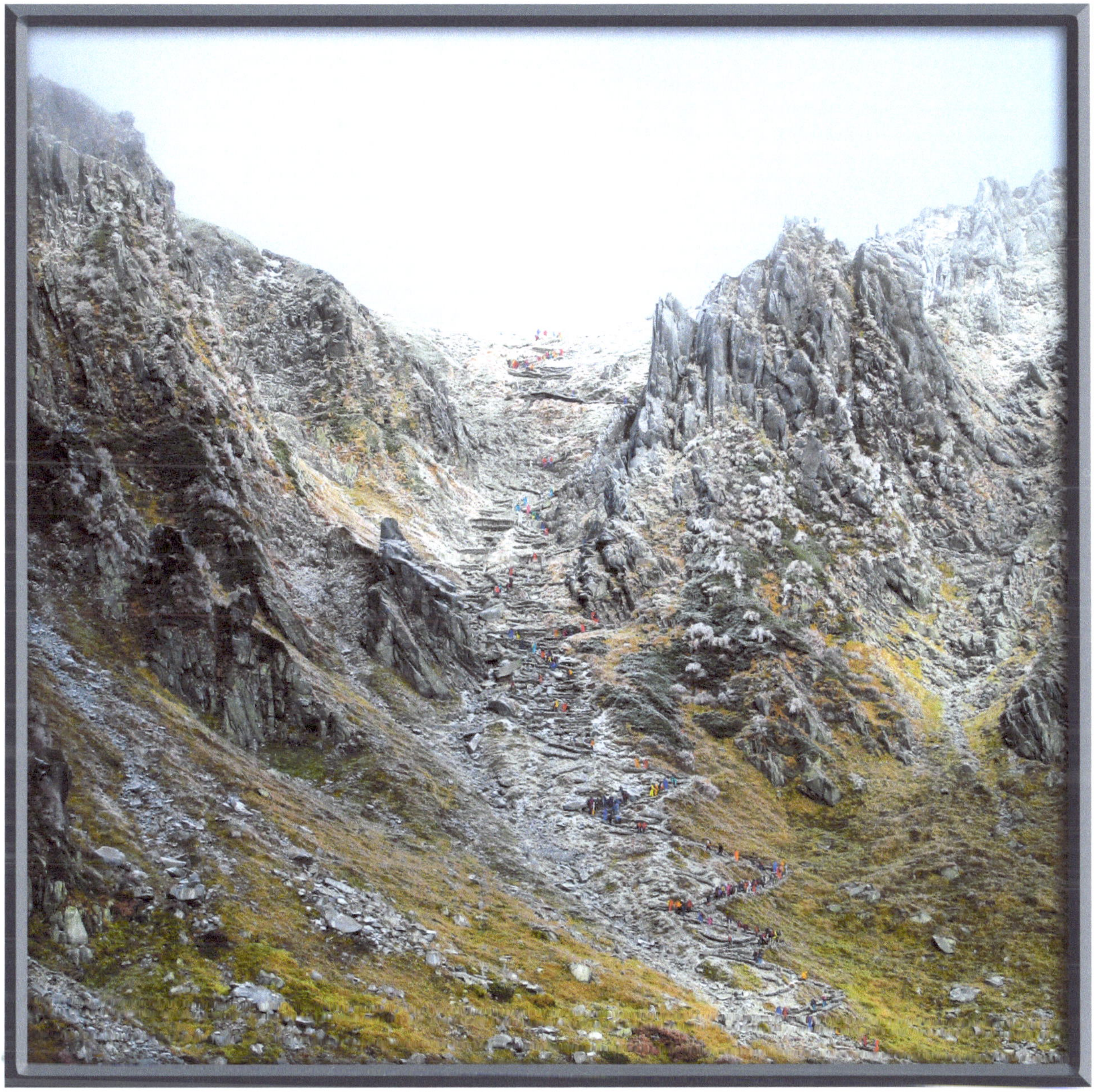

This photo shows the trail – the amazing series of switchbacks – which we traversed on both our climb and again on our descent. This was the first time we had been able to see what we had walked up and down – we were absolutely amazed to see this landscape. Each one of those small colored dots is a person. The clouds are still coming and going – will they finally all disappear or will they not?

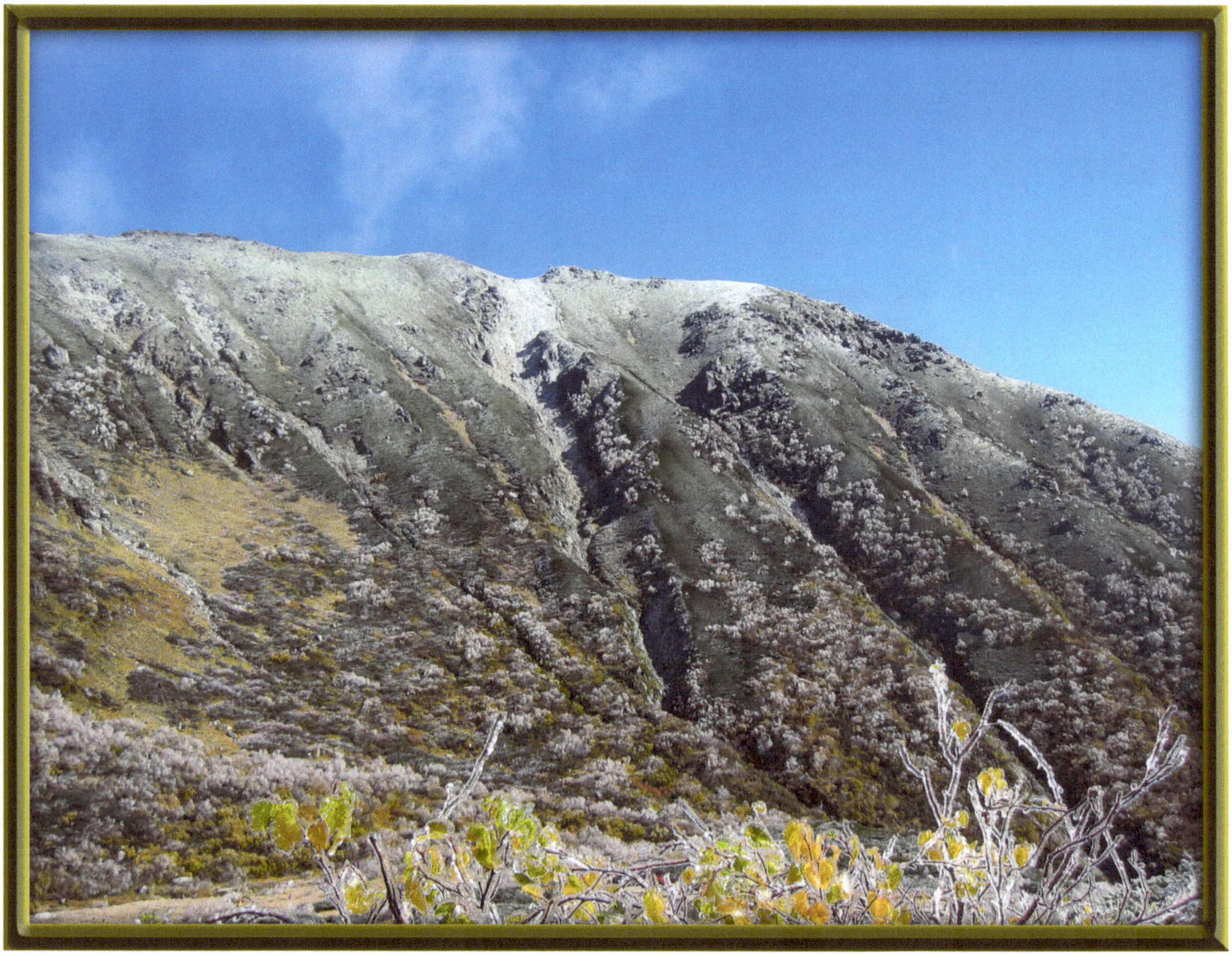

This photo shows the ridge-top still snowy and the nearby bushes still covered with ice. The clouds seem to be going away, but we still cannot be sure of what it going to happen. We are hesitating to take the Gondola down for fear that the weather will get beautiful if we leave now. At this time we still have not been able to see 360°.

The facing page photo shows one of the scenes we saw as we rode the Gondola Car down to the base of the mountain. Is this country steep? We think so! Now you can see some of the autumn colors which we had hoped to see. This is the first we've seen them too. Yesterday, when we rode the Gondola up, it was 100% cloudy.

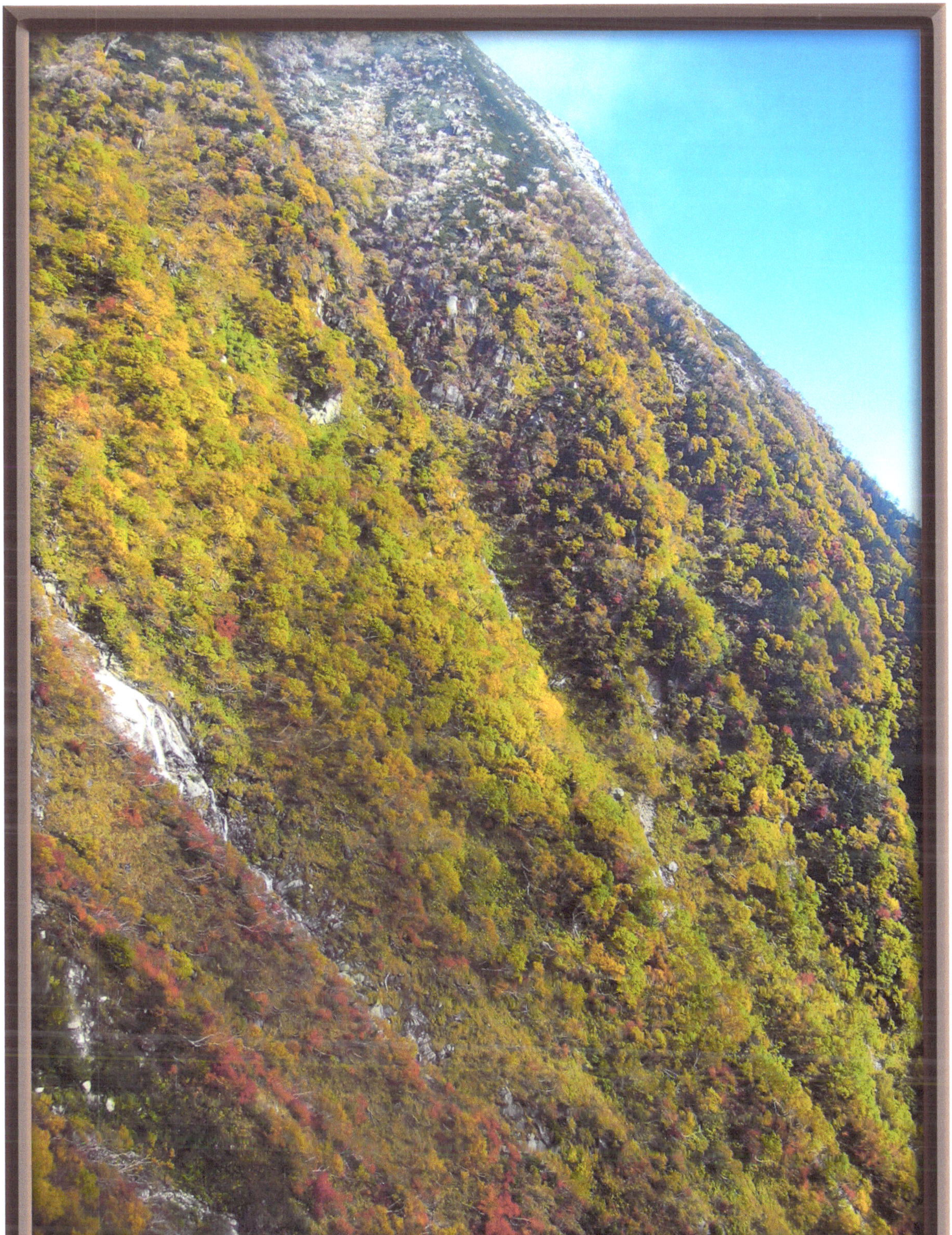

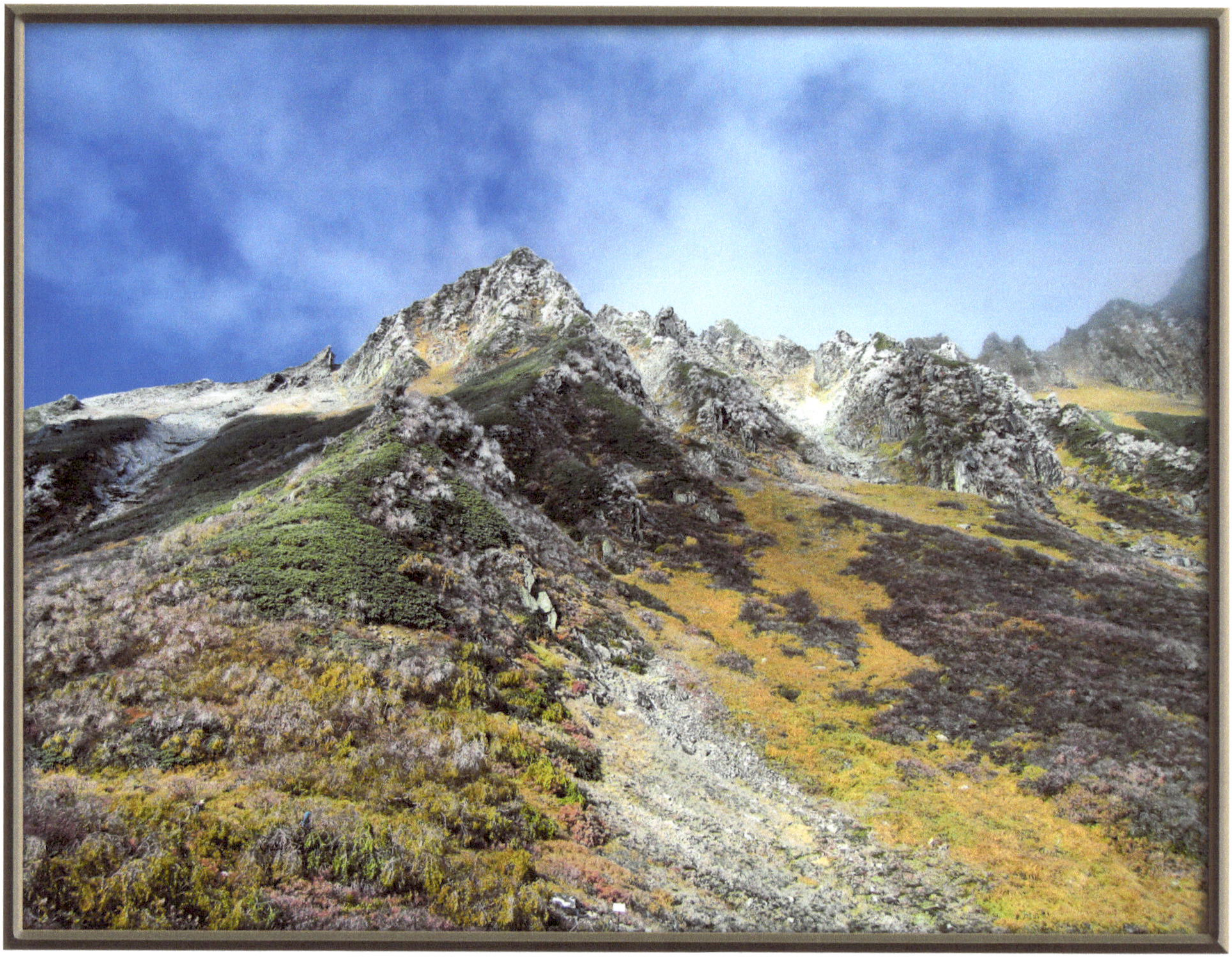

Here is an additional (and final) shot which was taken before we started the Gondola ride to the base of the mountain. We put it here (out of chronological order) so that we could have this space to be able to make comments on the facing page photo as well as this one. You'll note that the clouds never did disappear 100% before we began our descent. Such is life.

The facing page photo is another which was taken as we descended in the Gondola. Such amazing colors and contrasts. We hope to be able to return here again someday in the future.

The photos on pages 274 and 275 were also taken as we descended in the Gondola and show you more scenery and autumn colors.

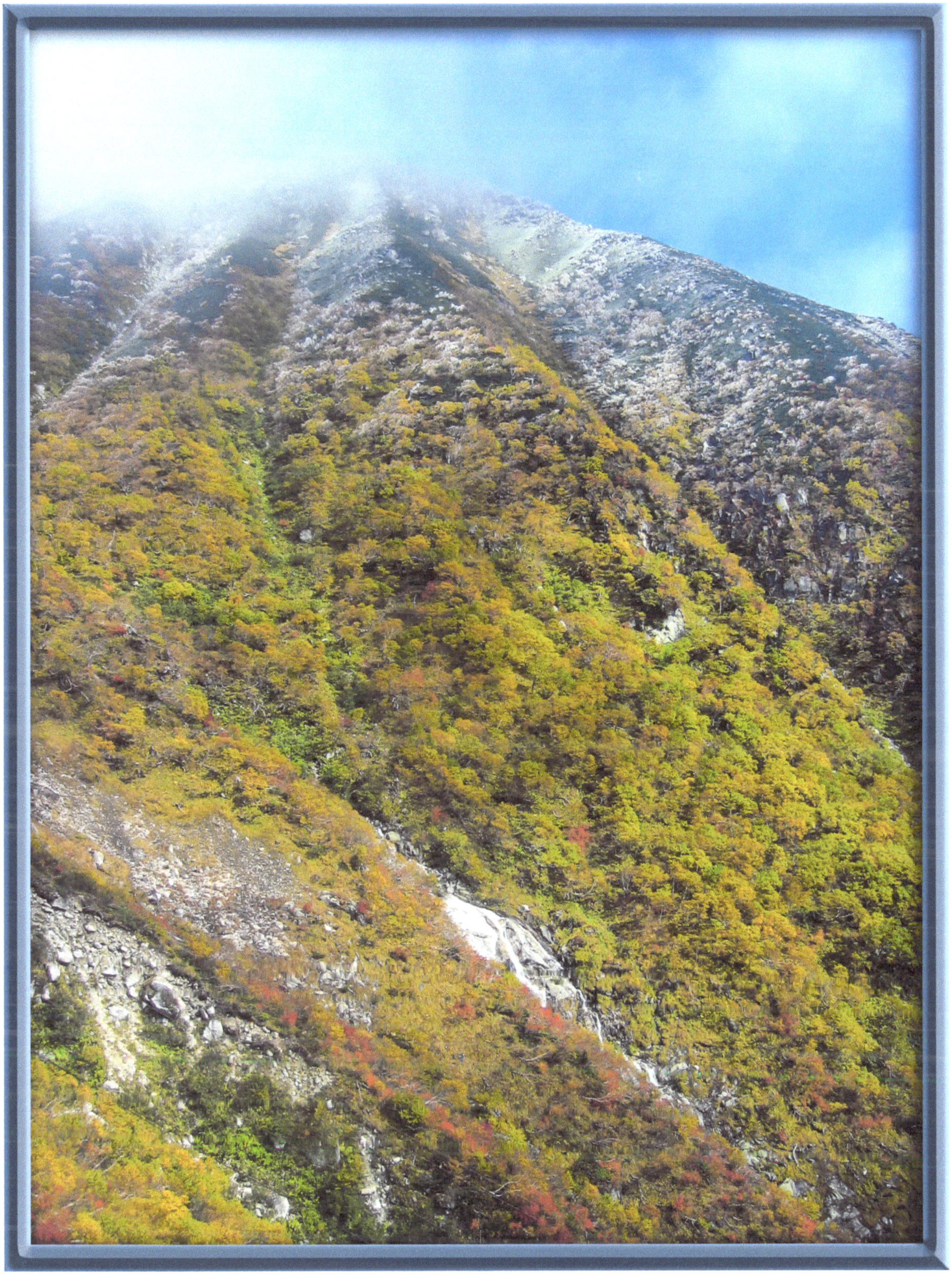

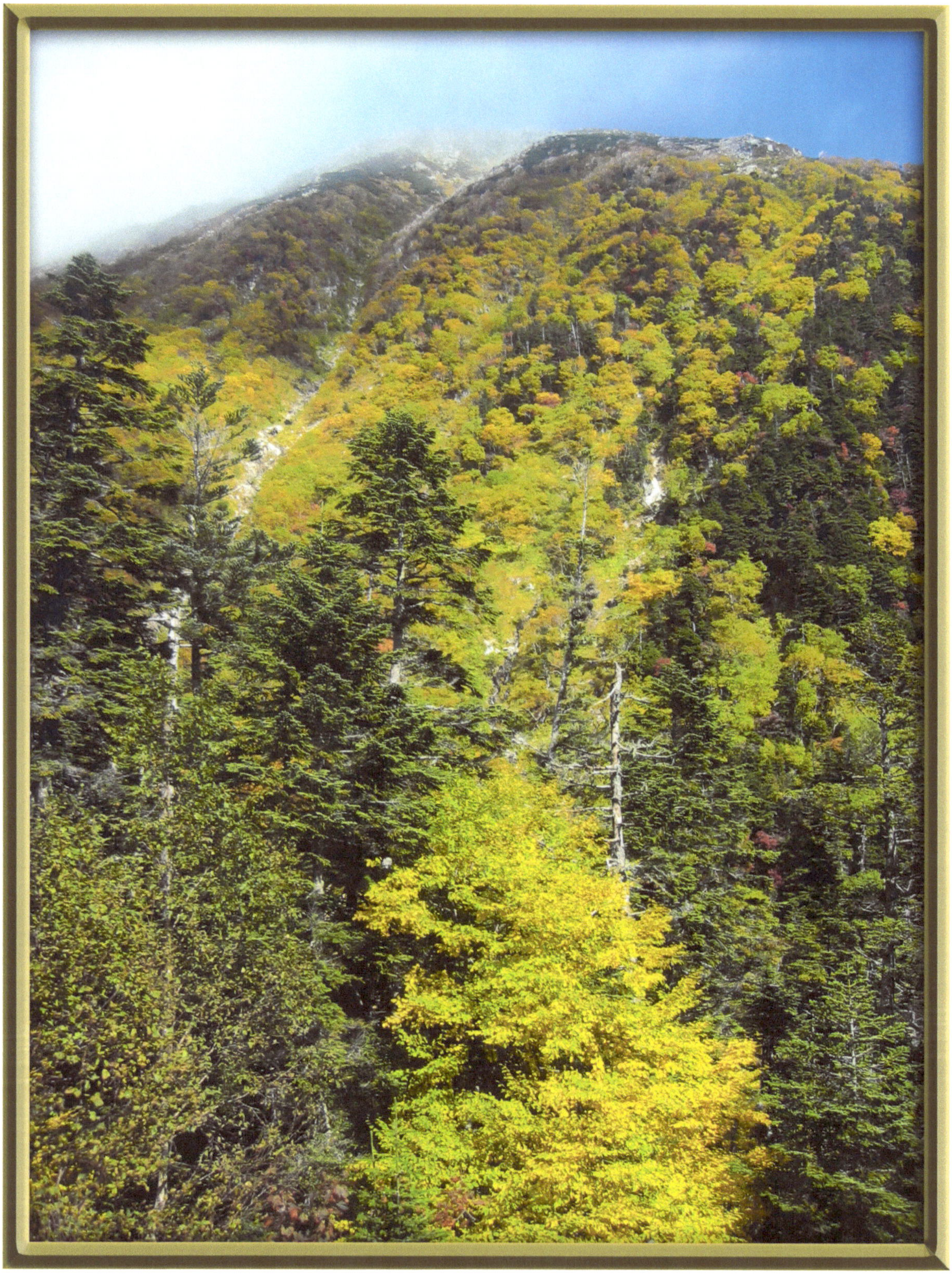

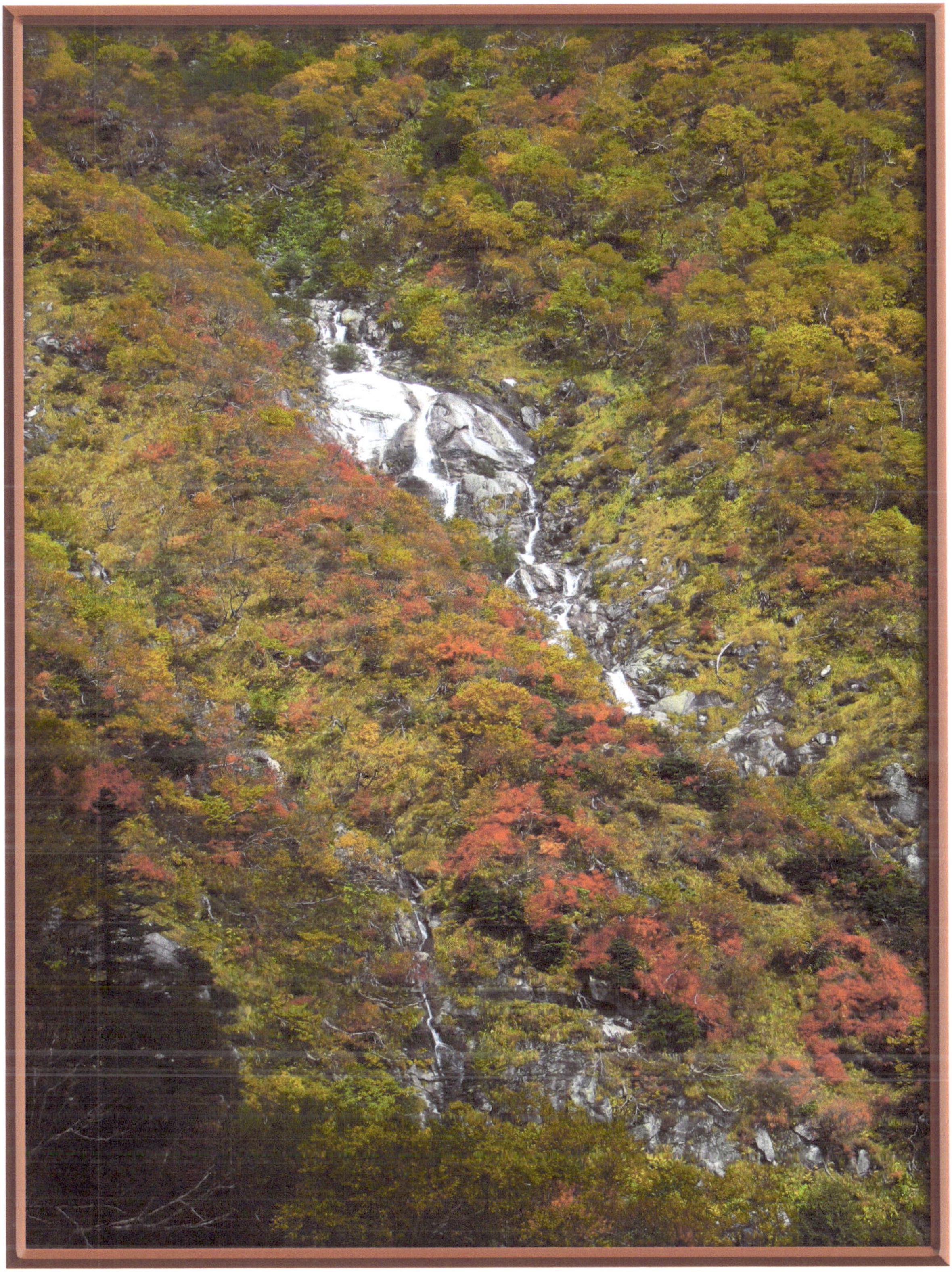

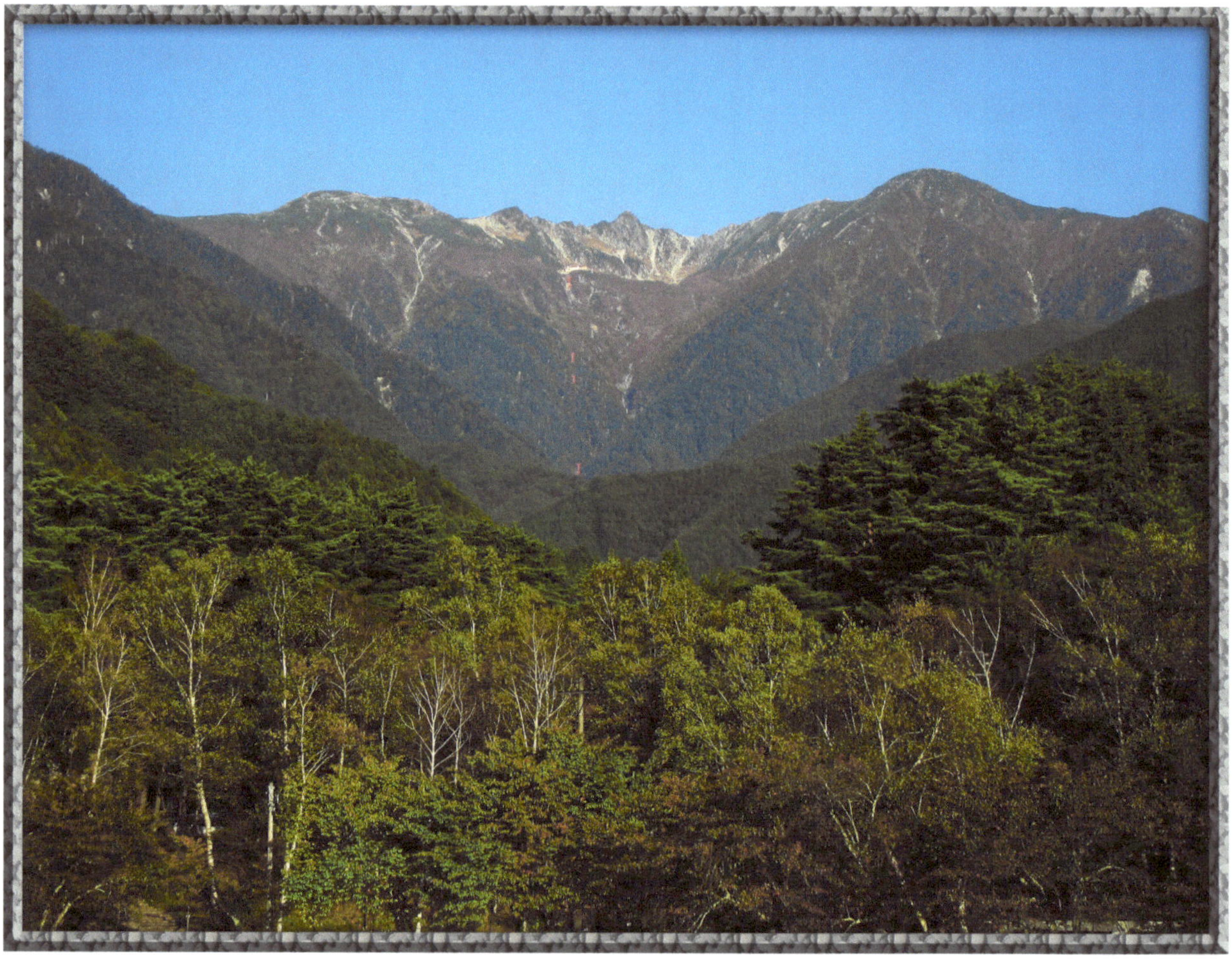

This is the final photo from our **Mt. Kiso-Komagatake** adventure. This was taken from near the Youth hostel we stayed at. Mt. Kiso-Komagatake is the rocky peak just about in the center of this photo. If you study carefully you can discern the route of the Gondola and you can see some orange towers – they are the cable towers for the Gondola. You'll note that – yes – it finally did clear up 100%, but we were not there for it. We were quite cold – in fact chilled to the bone – when we got down here. The first thing we did was go to a Hot Spring and soak until we got thoroughly warmed up. After that, we went out to lunch.

We did not realize it until later, but this freak storm on October 7th and 8th in the Central Alps Mountains resulted in the deaths of nine people. Personally, I learned of it when I returned to work on Tuesday, October 10th and people were thrilled to find me among the living. I was shocked until they explained why they were concerned.

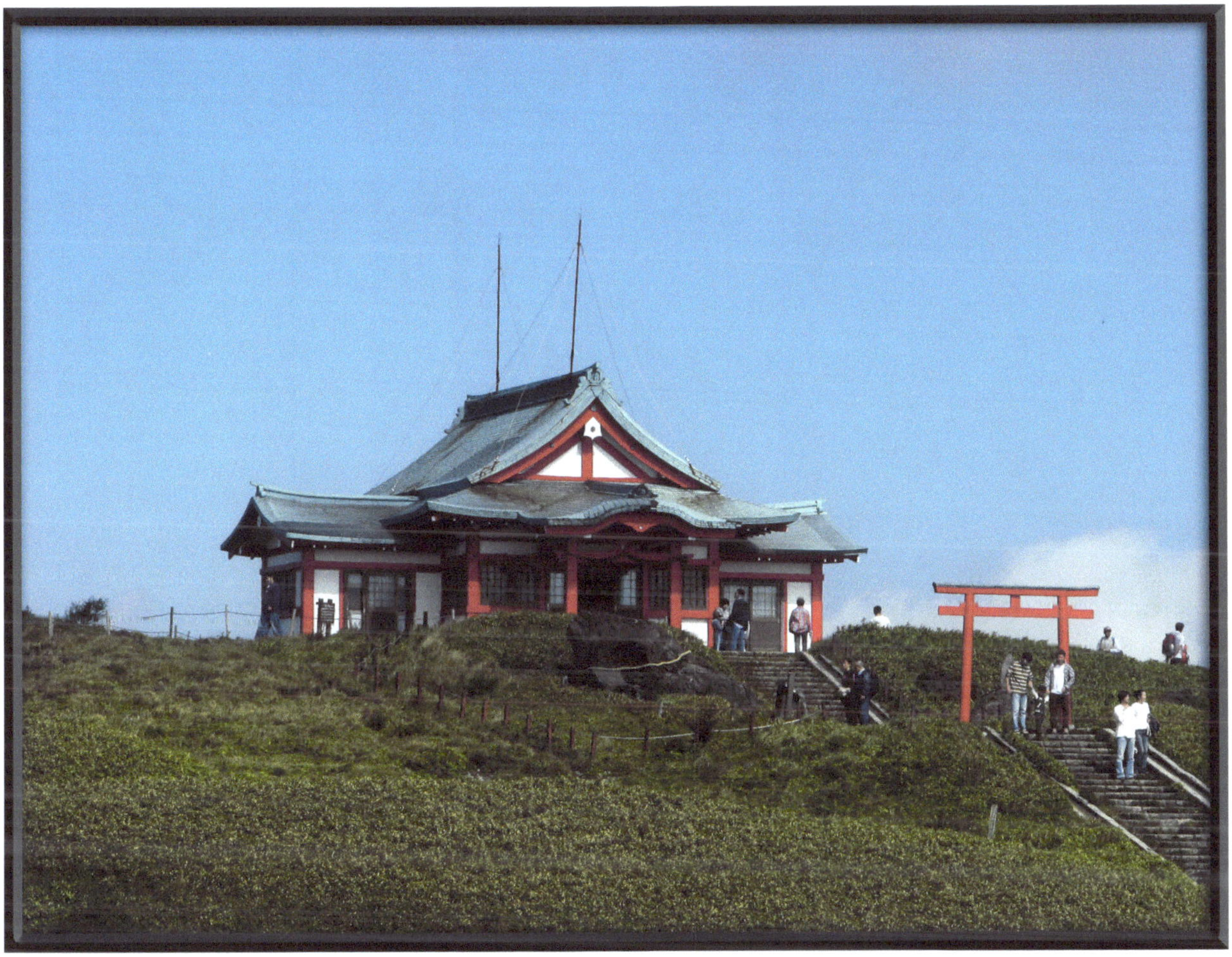

You may think this looks familiar. That's because you saw this shrine, at the summit of **Hakone's Mt. Komagatake** (1,357 meters = 4,451 feet) back on page 96. That shot was taken in the early part of June and the sky was somewhat overcast. In addition that photo was taken from a different angle. This photo was taken in October with a beautiful blue sky background and from the left front of the shrine. We hope that you don't mind seeing this photo. You may recall that this **Mt. Komagatake** is the high mountain on the east side of **Hakone's Lake Ashi** and there is a ropeway to the summit. You should not confuse this with the **Mt. Kiso-Komagatake** of the previous several pages.

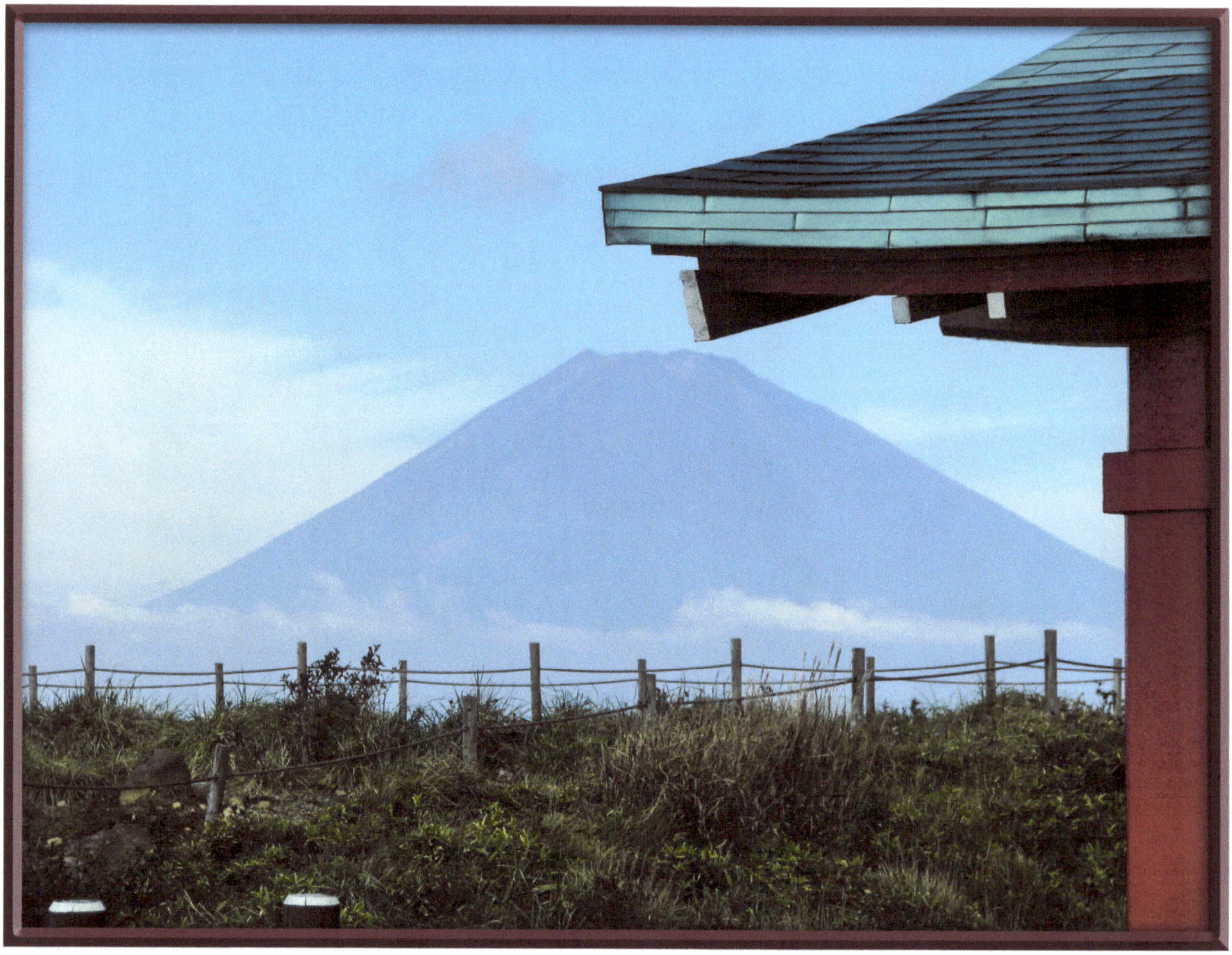

Here is a pretty shot of **Mt. Fuji** taken from beside the shrine shown on the previous page. We have been to this Mt. Komagatake several times now in different seasons and we have never again been able to even approximate a shot similar to this one. The roof of the shrine is copper plate and that is the reason it has such an intriguing blue color.

As mentioned earlier, there is a ropeway to the summit of this mountain. We did not mention earlier, however, that from here, you can hike across **Mt. Kamiyama** (1,438 meters = 4,718 feet) and end up at **Owakudani**. It is a little steep and it is a bit long, but it can be done in a couple of hours with no problem. From Owakudani, of course you can take the ropeway back down to **Lake Ashi**, or down the other direction towards **Gora**.

On the facing page we're at **Showa-Kinen Park** in **Western Tokyo** once again (page 229). This flower is ***Osmanthus fragrans* var. *aurantiacus*** (**Kin-moku-sei** in Japanese). This is an amazingly fragrant flower and the fragrance absolutely fills the air for a long ways around these trees. It's a very interesting flower isn't it.

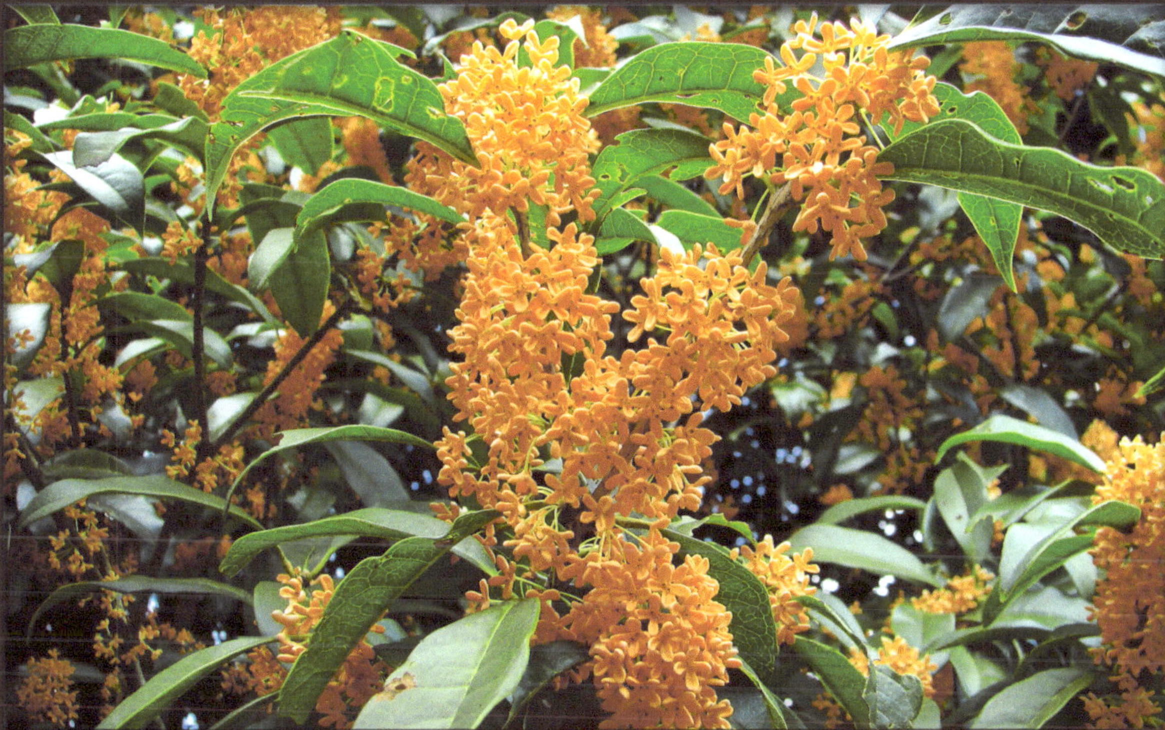

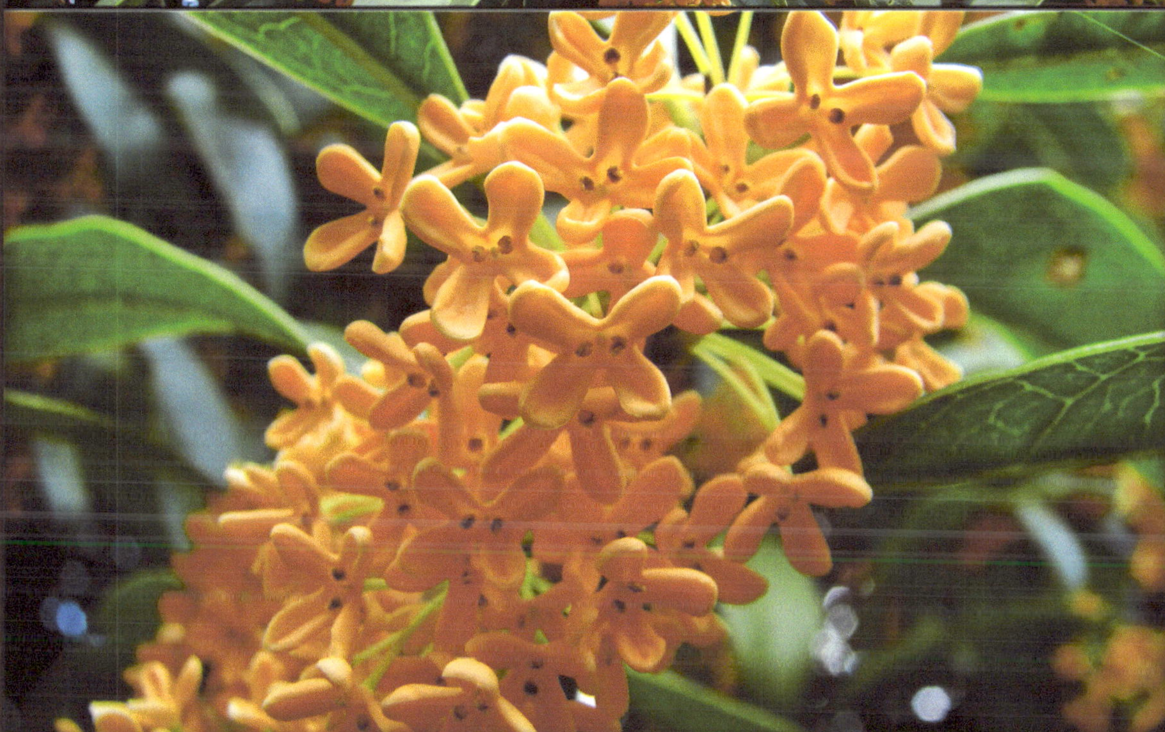

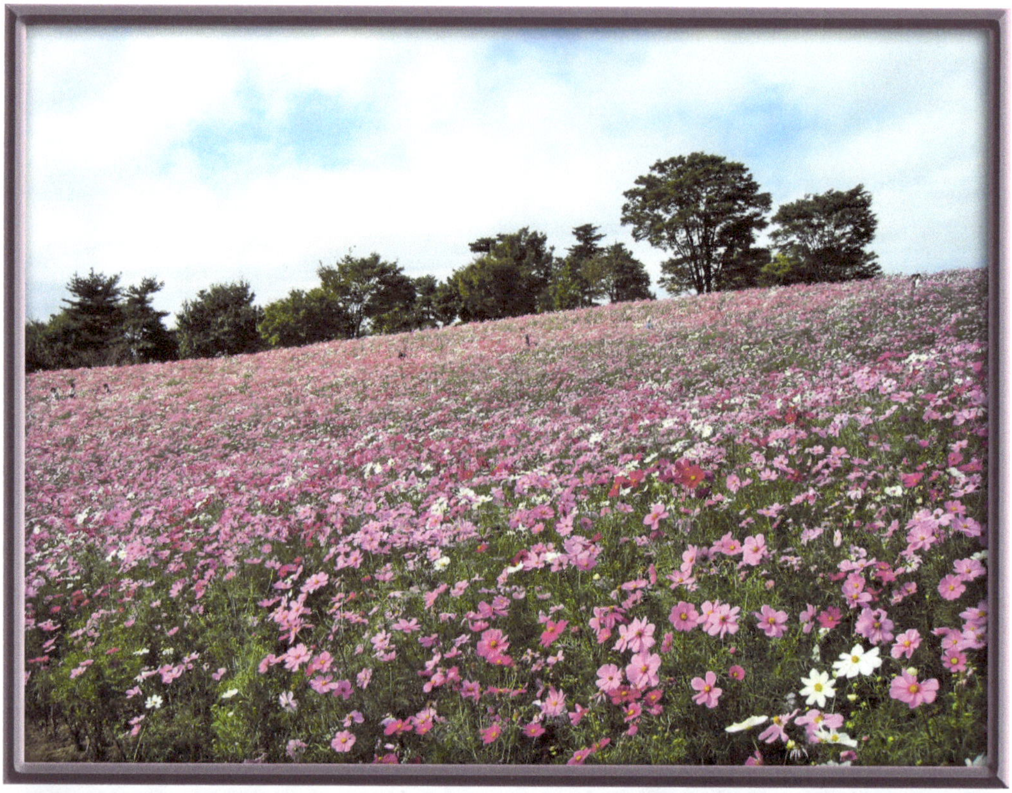

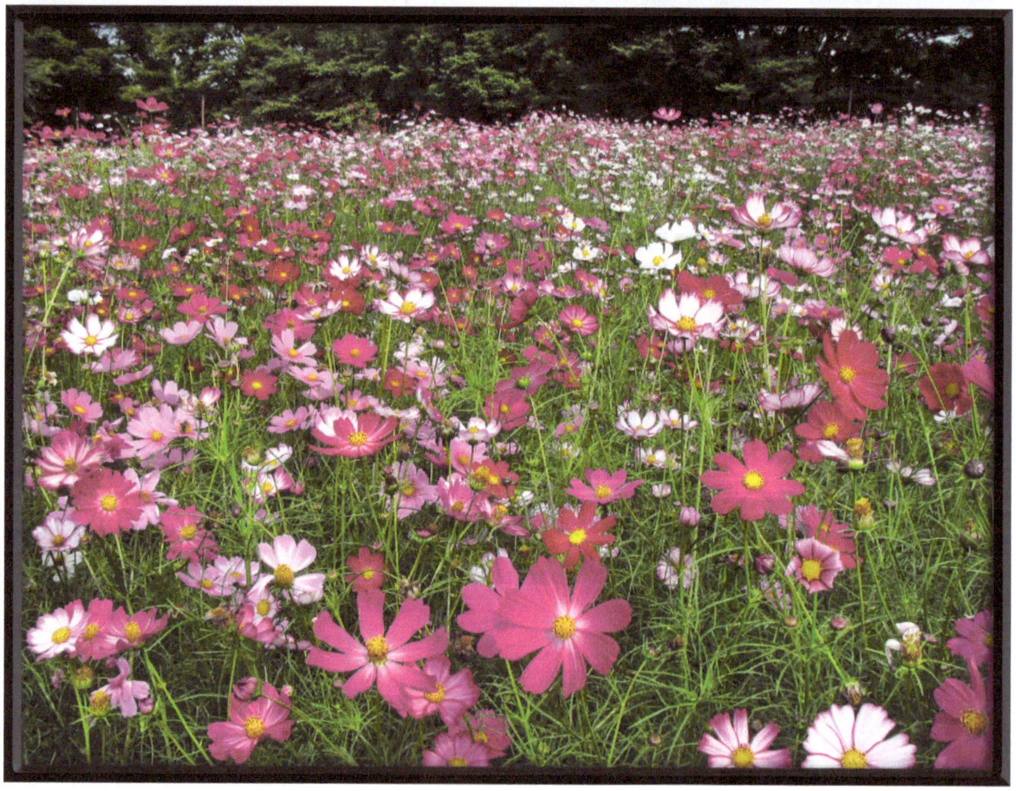

These two photos were also taken at **Showa-Kinen Park** in late October. They show you some ***Cosmos* sp.** flowers. This park plants an entire hill (to the left) with Cosmos seeds every year. In the fall, when it is at its peak of flowering, it is a sight to see. It's hard to imagine how large of an area this is. If you look closely you can see some people up on the hillside. As you'll probably note, the main color of Cosmos flowers is shades of red. There are some yellow ones, but not many.

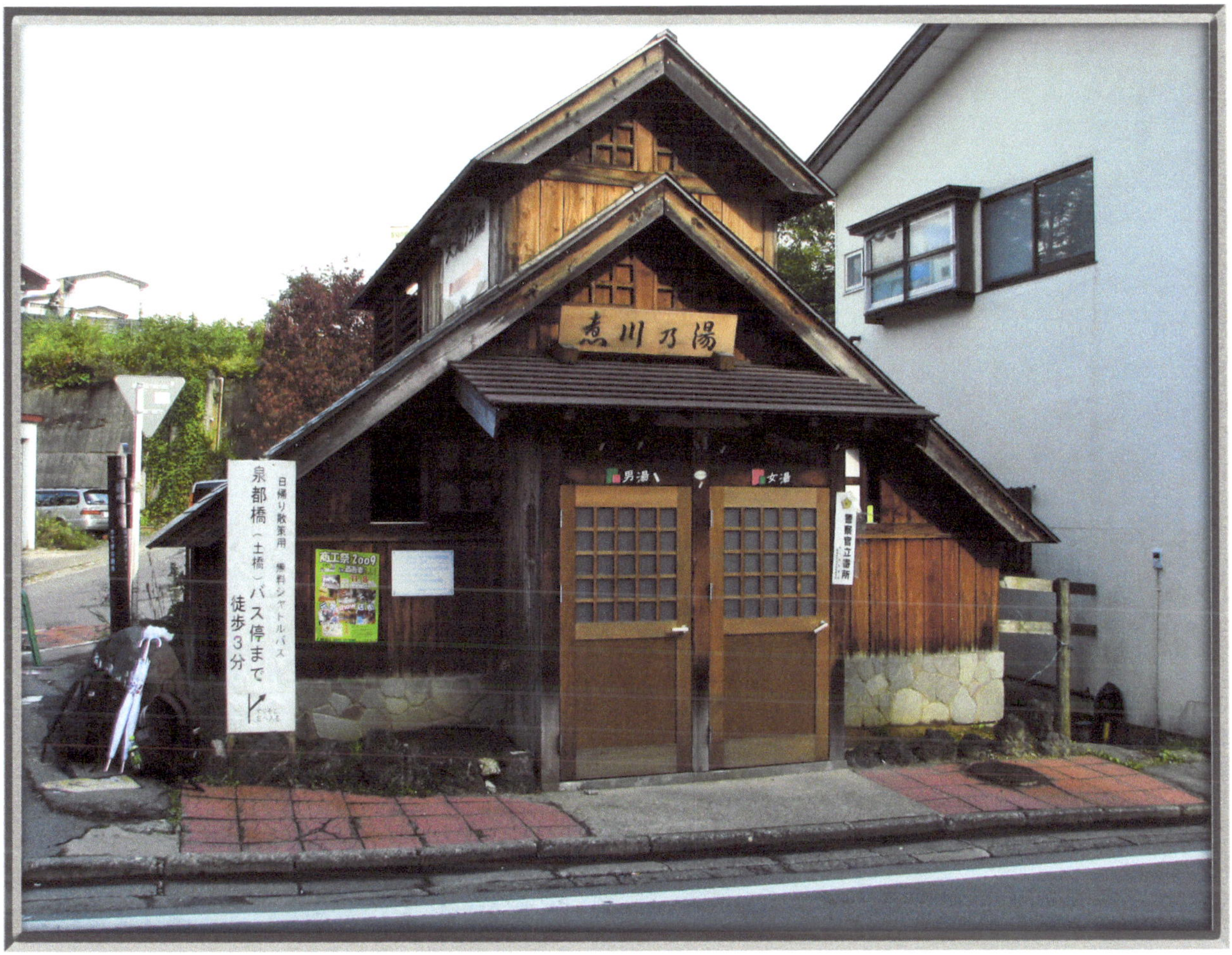

Now let's return to **Kusatsu** (previously seen on pages 43, 230 – 234) in **Gunma Prefecture**. We've mentioned that we like to visit this place in the cool and cold weather because the best thing to do here is to soak in the many hot springs. This little building is one of the free public hot baths which you can find in Kusatsu. The men's part is through the left door and the ladies part is through the right door. Notice the cupalo on the building to permit easy exit of the steam.

In Kusatsu there are about eighteen free public baths. They are scattered all over town and therefore some of them come from different hot water sources than others. They are all characterized as being very hot. You have to ease yourself into the water and then once in the water it's painful to move around. You can't stay in the water for very long – you have to get out and cool off. That's another good reason for coming here during the cool season of the year, so that you can cool off outdoors!

We called this the "burning bush" – what an amazing shade of red. It was the brightest red anywhere near this area. This was close to the Mt. Shirane trail (pages 230, 232 and 234).

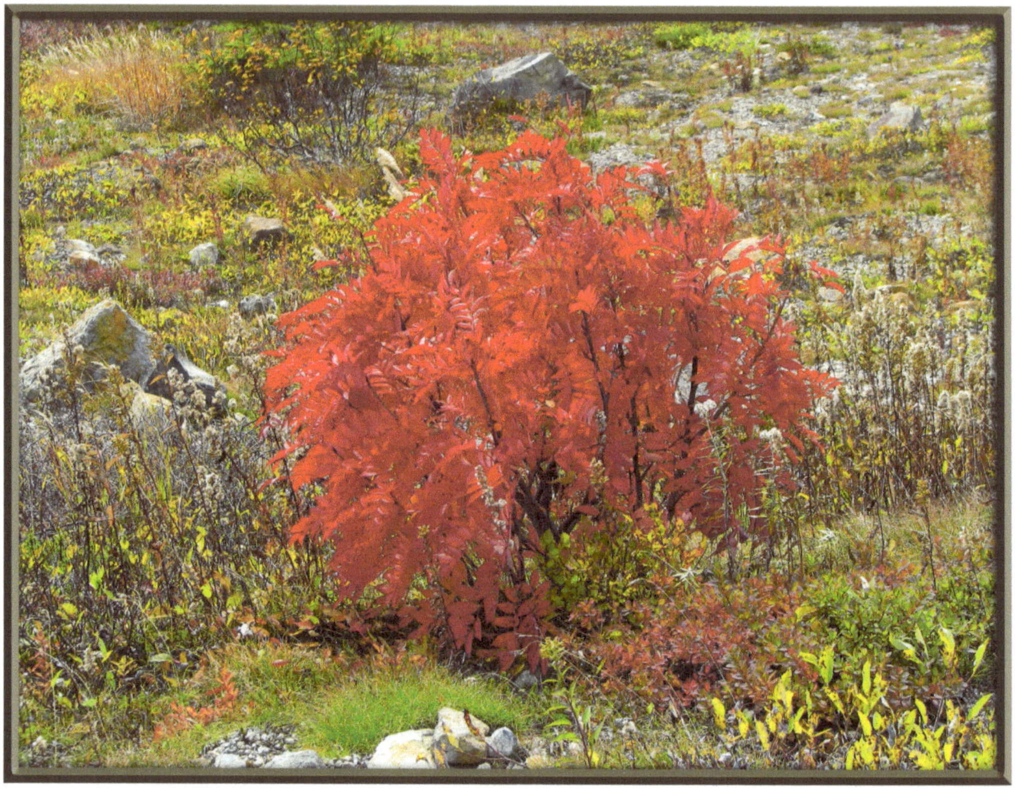

This is the same rock which was pictured on page 233 at **Yumiike** (Yumi Pond). The angle is different and the autumn colors are much more apparent here than they were back on page 233.

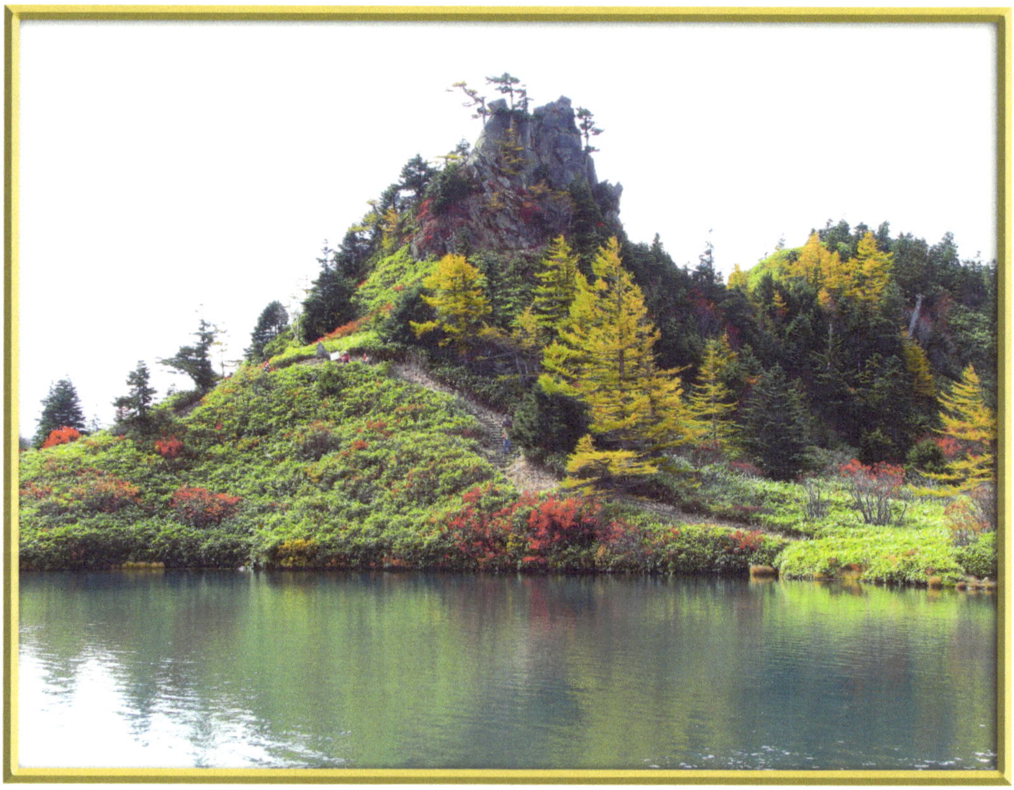

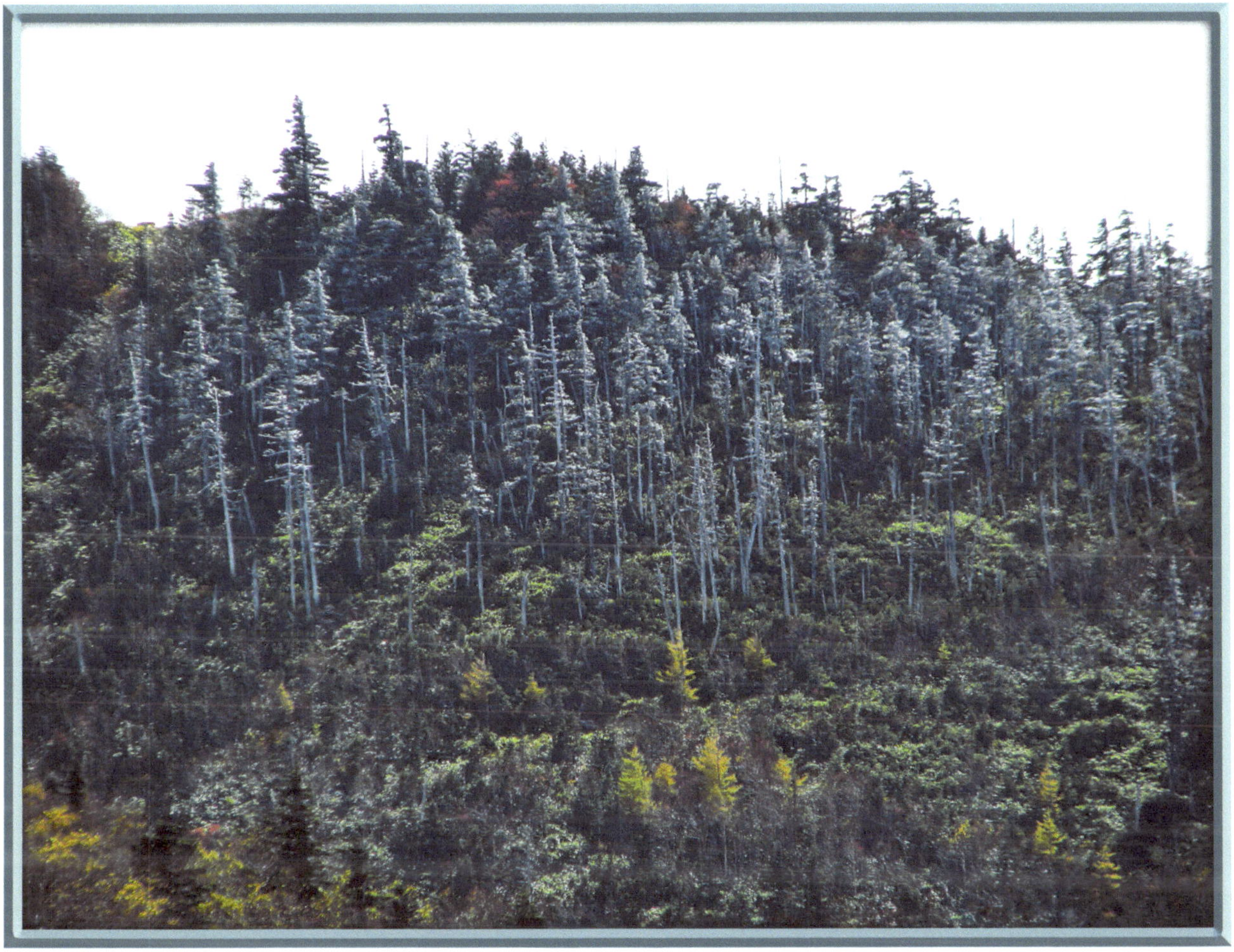

Back on page 234 we showed you a photo with a number of snags (dead trees) in it and we promised that we'd show you an October photo which shows a weird lighting phenomenon. Well, this is that photo. The weird lighting is the effect which makes it appear that the trees are ice-covered. We studied this very closely to be sure that it was not ice on the trees. There was some scattered snow and ice on the ground here – it had, apparently snowed during the previous night – so we really thought we were looking at a layer of ice on these trees. We finally decided that it was not possible, and then a few moments later the lighting conditions changed and we were sure that it was not ice, but merely the lighting.

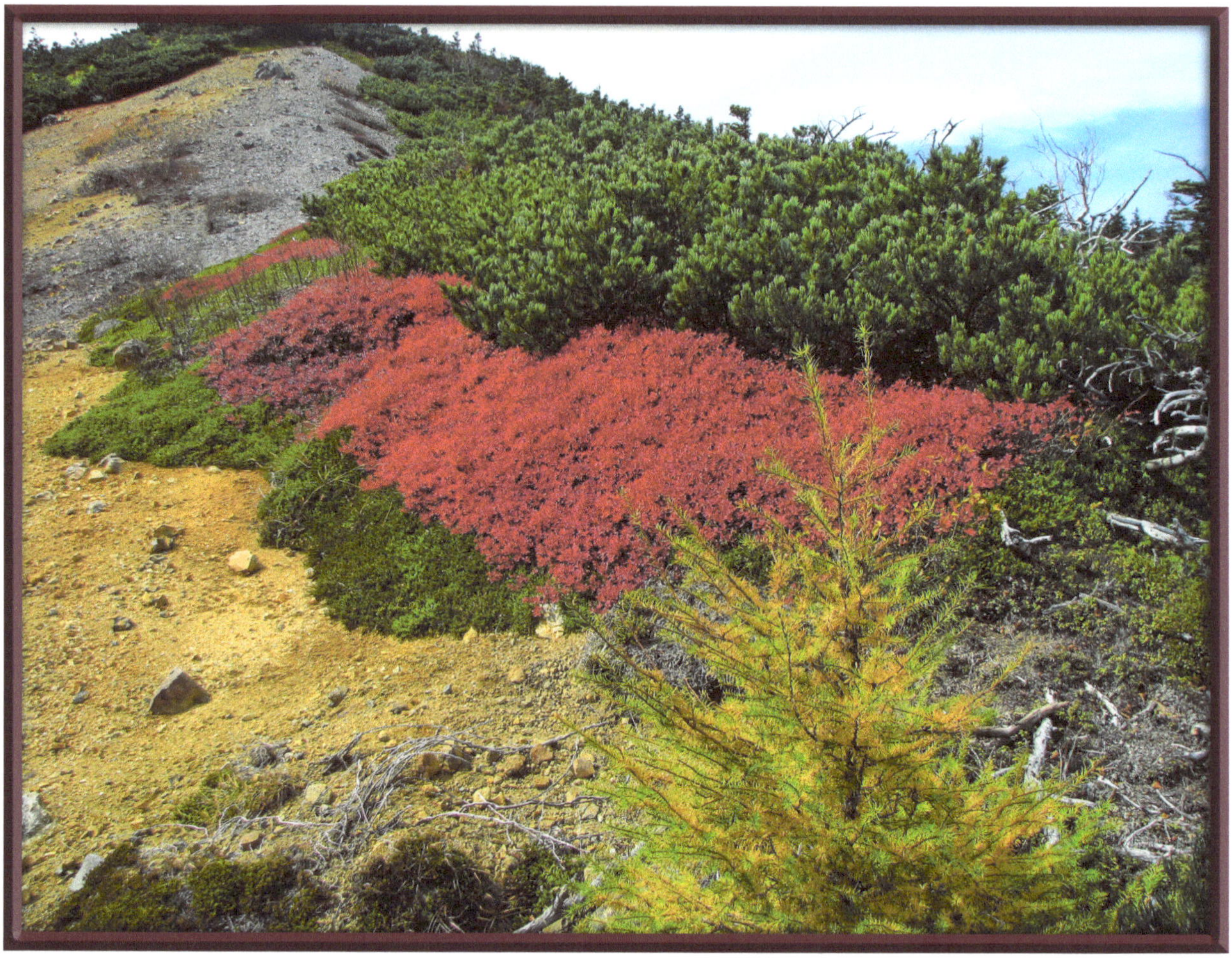

This shot, taken as we hiked from the **Mt. Shirane** area towards **Mt. Moto-Shirane**, shows some rather stunning autumn colors. The red-leafed plant is a kind of blueberry – wild of course. The stunted pine trees are a kind of mountain pine and the yellow needle tree right in front of the camera is a larch tree (***Larix* sp.**). Note that there are also many colors of soil as you descend the scree slope here. We did not come down this way, we came around from the right on the trail. We found blueberries, crowberries, snowberries and a few other berries on this hike. Not all of them were delicious – or even edible – but the ones which were edible, we enjoyed as we hiked along.

The upper photo on the facing page was taken looking back towards this area. The above spot would be on the extreme right edge of the upper photo and looking uphill.

The lower photo on the facing page shows **Mt. Moto-Shirane** (2,171 meters = 7,123 feet). You can easily see people hiking to its summit in this photo.

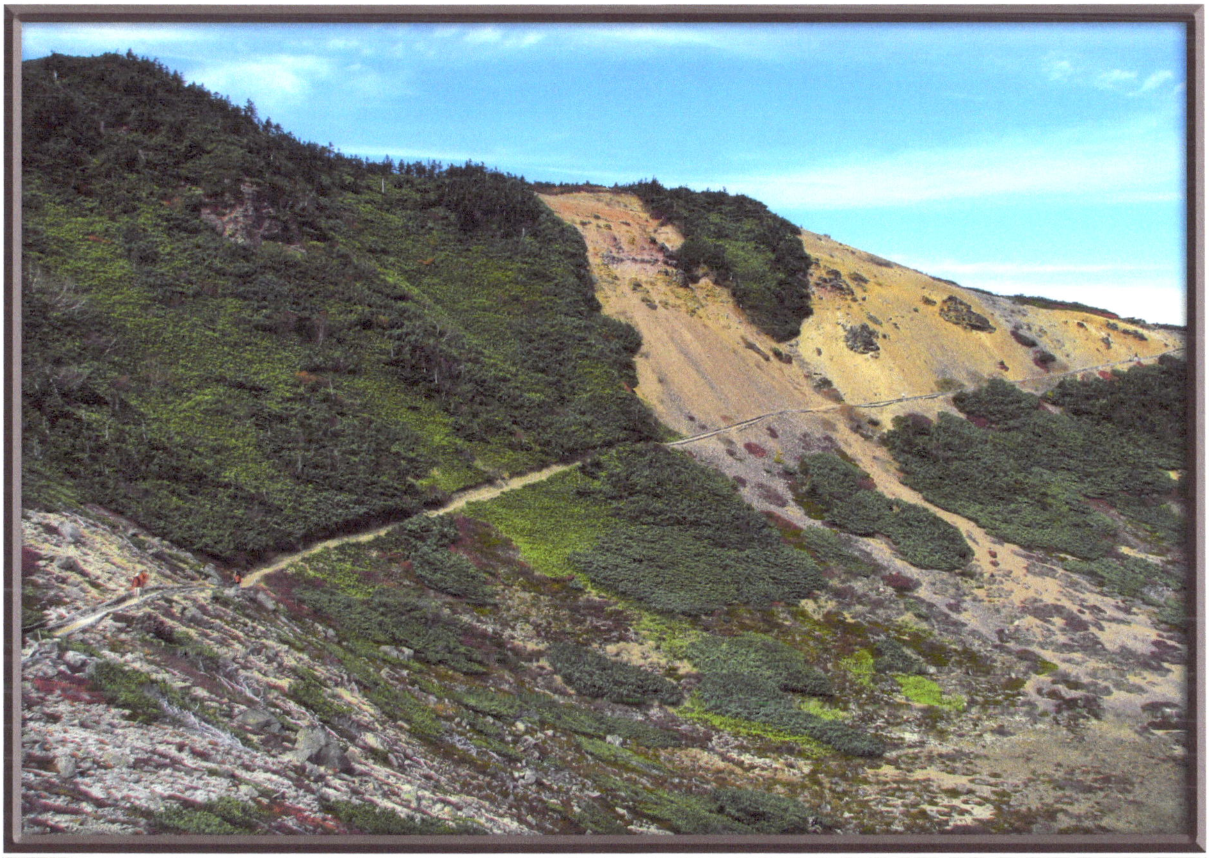

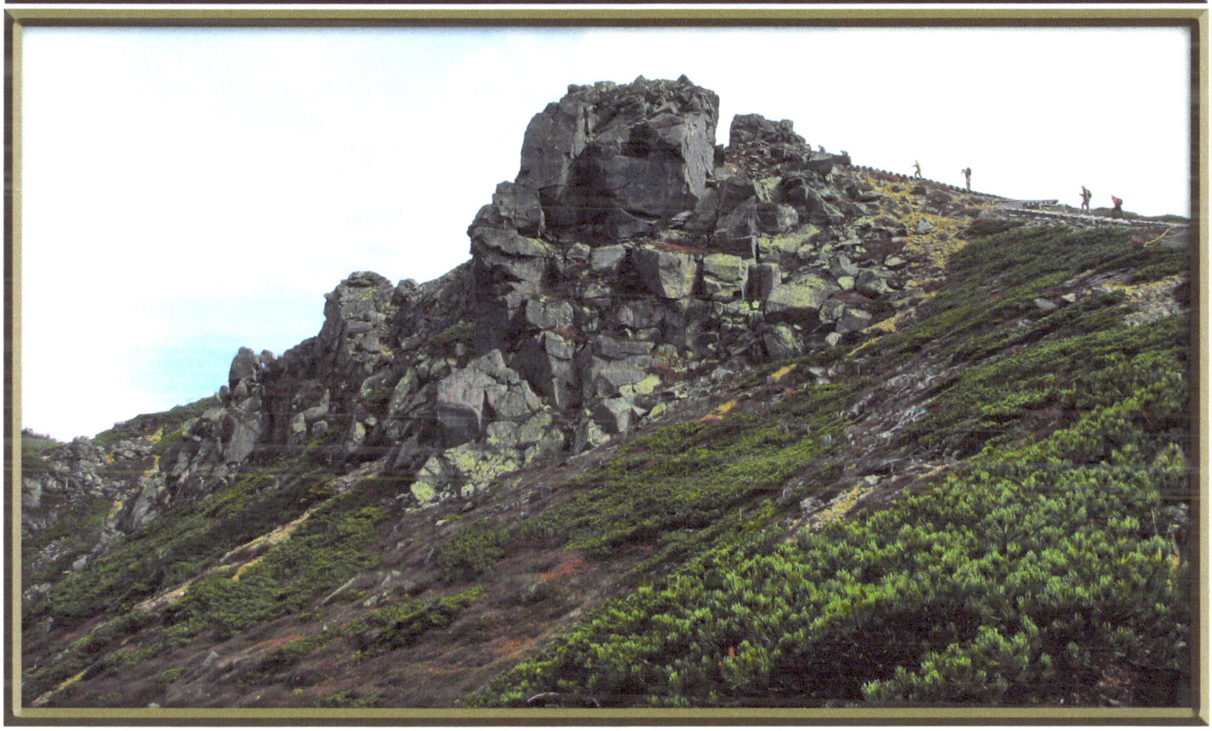

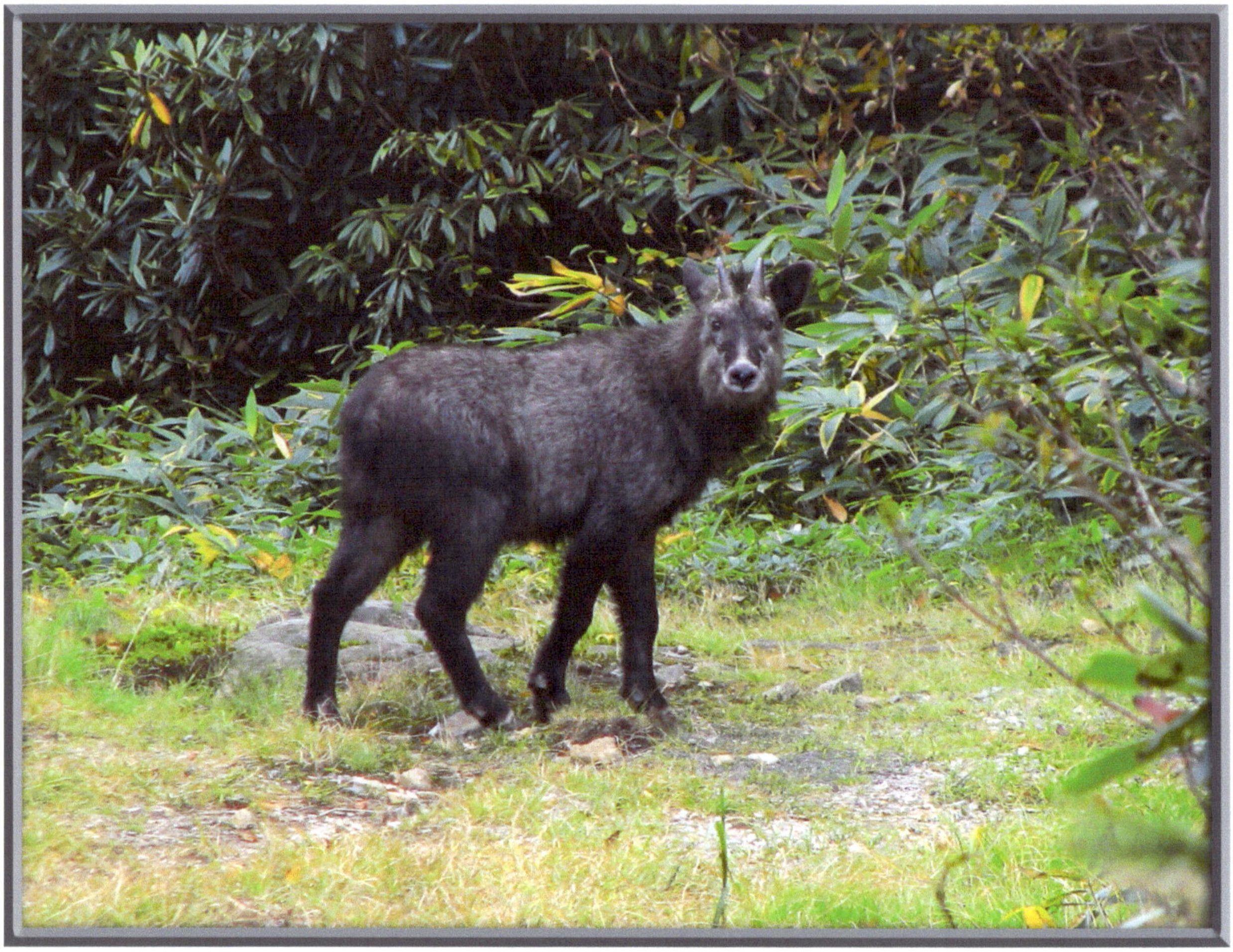

Here is the final photo we'll show you from this trip to Kusatsu. By now you should know what this animal is, right? You've seen this species on pages 48 and 132. Can you recall? It is a ***Capricornis crispus***, a **Japanese Serow** (***Kamoshika*** in Japanese). This one strolled down the trail ahead of us for quite some time and gave us several chances to get photos. Unfortunately it tended to stay quite a ways out in front of us – it did not want us to get very close at all. This shot was taken at the maximum zoom range of my camera. Finally it got tired of us and it went off the trail and into the thick brush where we absolutely did not want to follow. It was probably getting to the edge of its home range and didn't want to go any further.

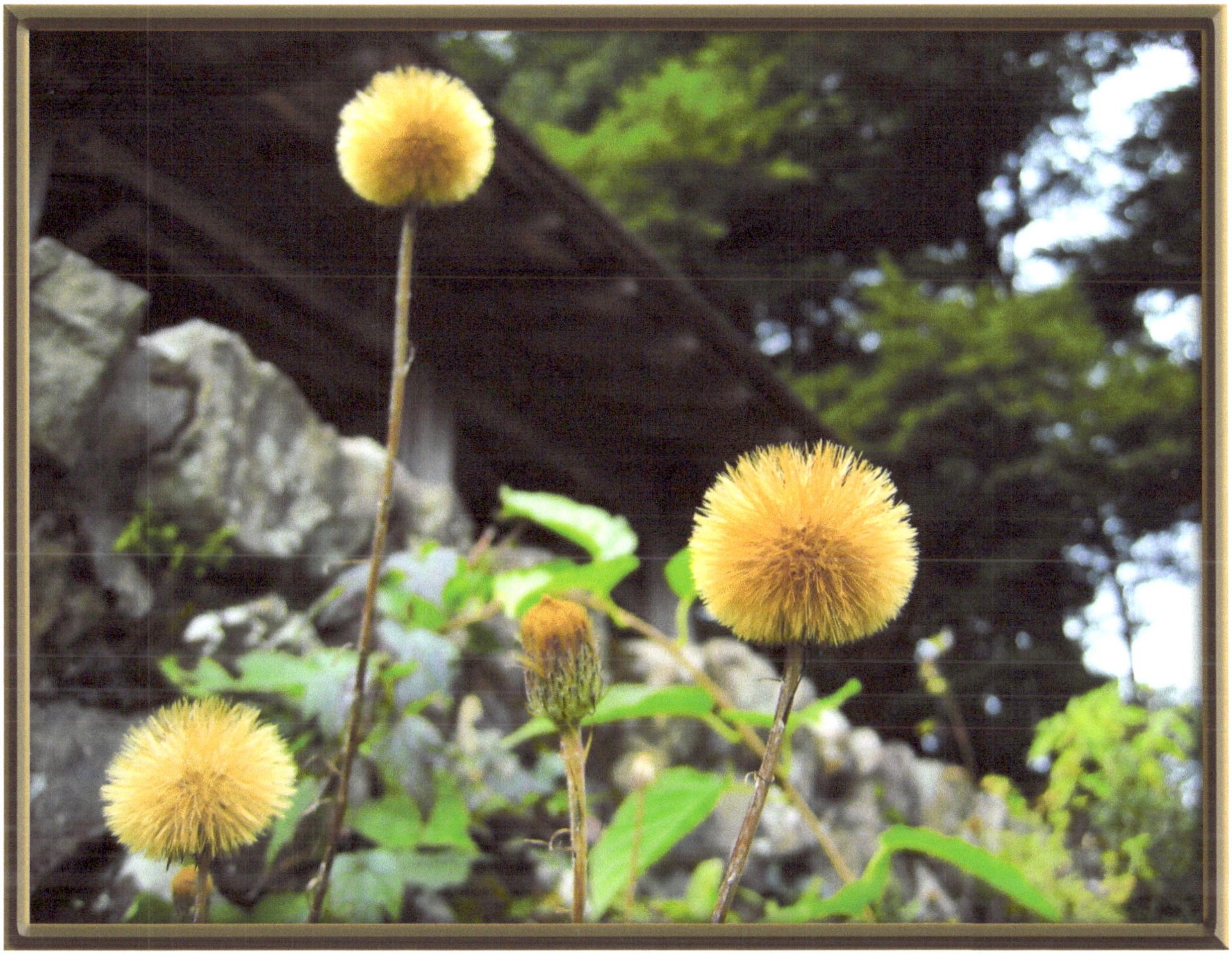

Now let's take a very brief trip out to **Mt. Mitake** (929 meters = 3,048 feet). The only photo which will be included from this trip is the one above. We don't know what kind of a seedhead this is, but it is very photogenic. We see these seedheads every now and then in the fall and we often take photos of them when we see them, but this is the best shot we've ever ended up with. They are an interesting color and appealing to the eye. This one was found in a spot at the end of a side trail near Mt. Mitake Shrine. The building above is a shelter where one can eat lunch if it's raining or snowing.

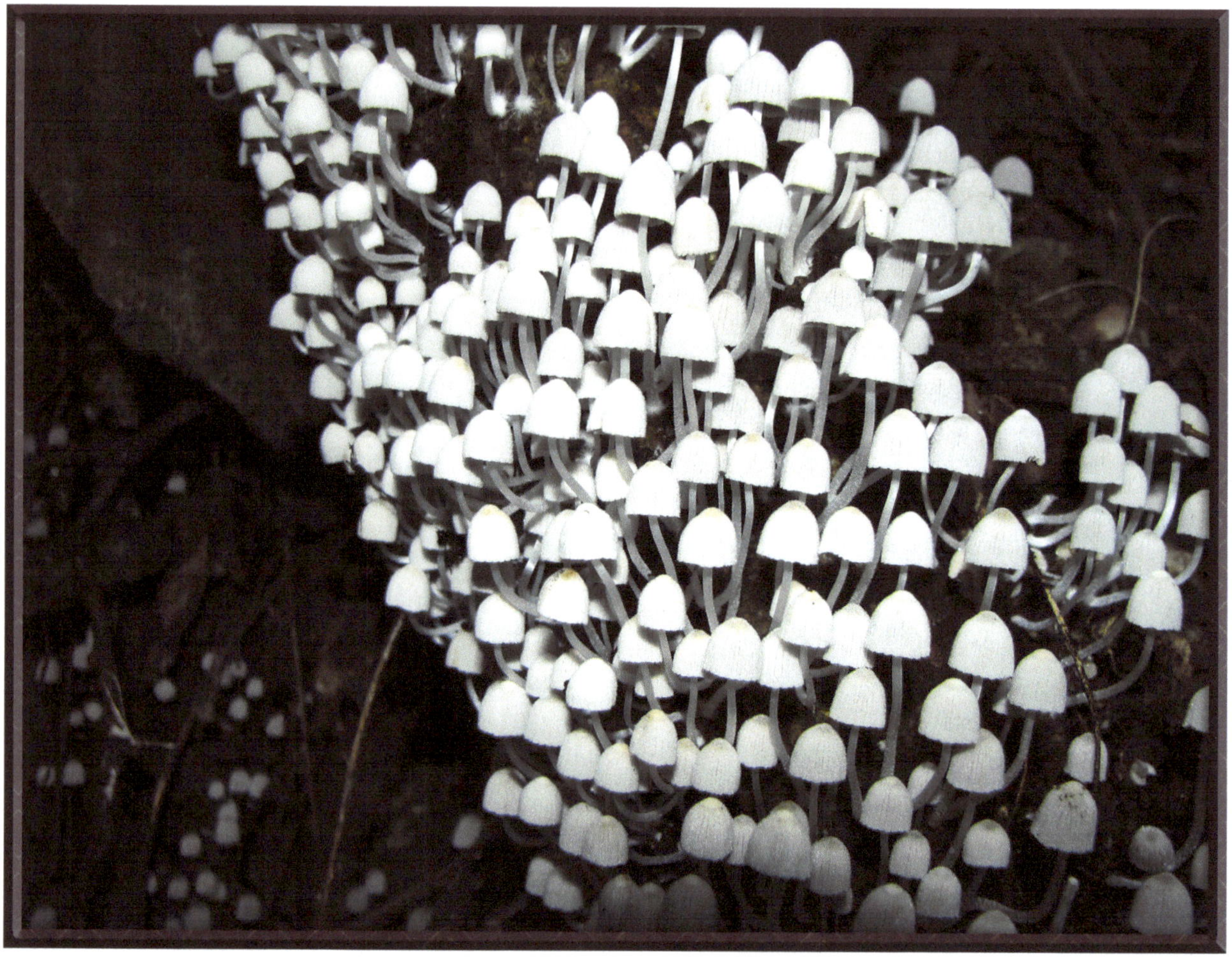

Here is another very brief trip. This was a colony of a very small mushroom on one of the slopes of **Mt. Takao (Takao-san)**. On this day we found several different species of mushrooms and fungi, but this one was by far the most intriguing. Each tiny cap is probably only about 0.25 inches (6 mm) in diameter. You'll note that they are also scattered on the ground below the log which this large colony is growing upon. We had never seen anything like this – and, to date – we have not seen anything like it since this sighting. We have not shown you many mushrooms or fungi in this compilation of photos. We believe that they should not be entirely overlooked though.

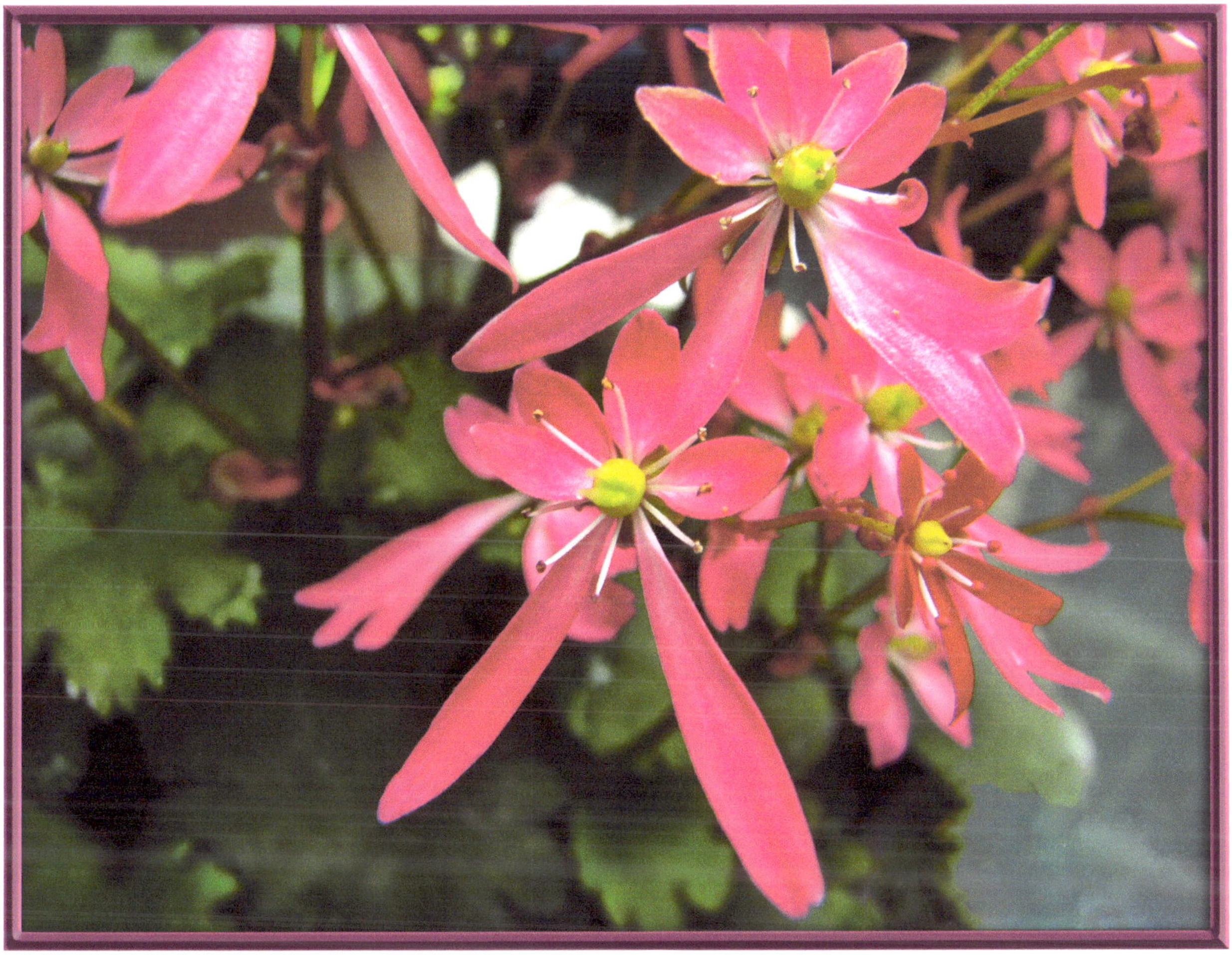

We showed you the "wild" version of this flower back on page 102 – do you remember what it is? The photo here shows a cultivar of ***Saxifraga* sp.**, but we have no idea which one. You may recall that in Japanese it is called the ***"Dai"*** flower as it assumes the shape of the kanji character Dai (大). We found these in a park greenhouse in **Gora**, which is a stop on the ropeway which takes you up to Owakudani. On this trip to **Owakudani** it was once again cloudy and it looked very similar to the scene on page 34 when we arrived at the summit. We didn't spend much time there, we hiked up to the black egg place and ate some eggs and then we continued on our way down to **Lake Ashi**. From there we took a bus to Sengokuhara and we'll show you some photos of that area on the next few pages.

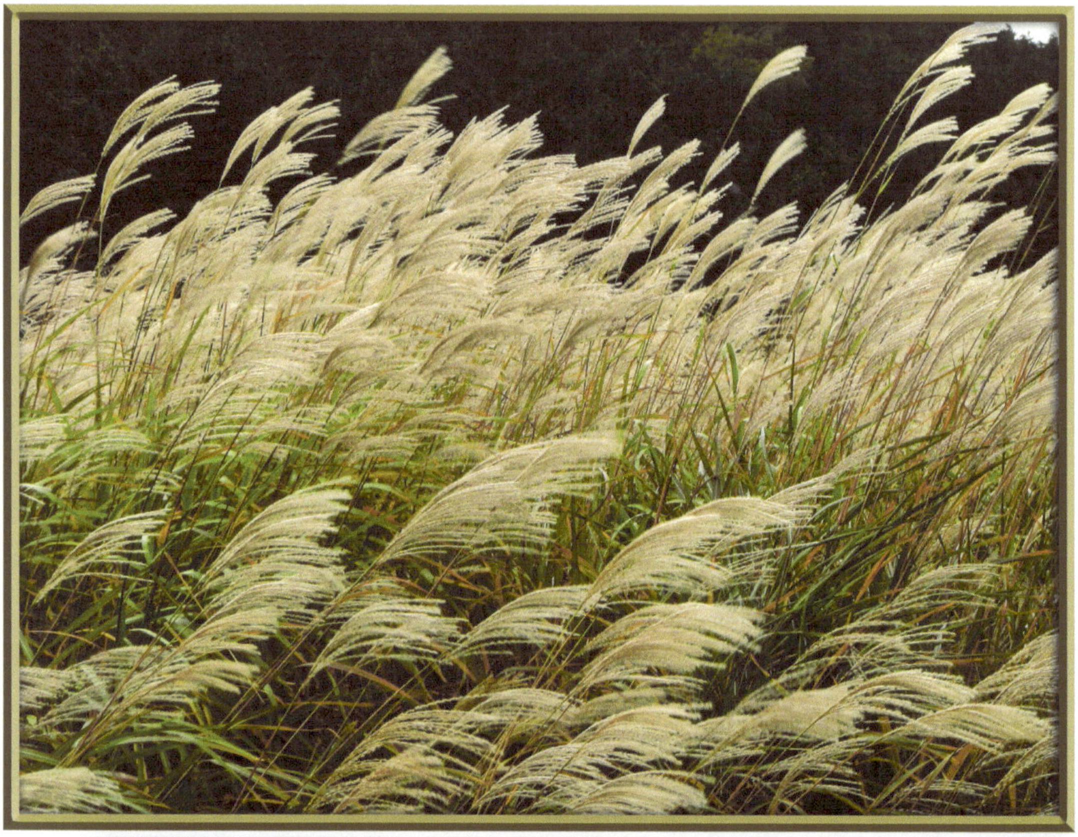

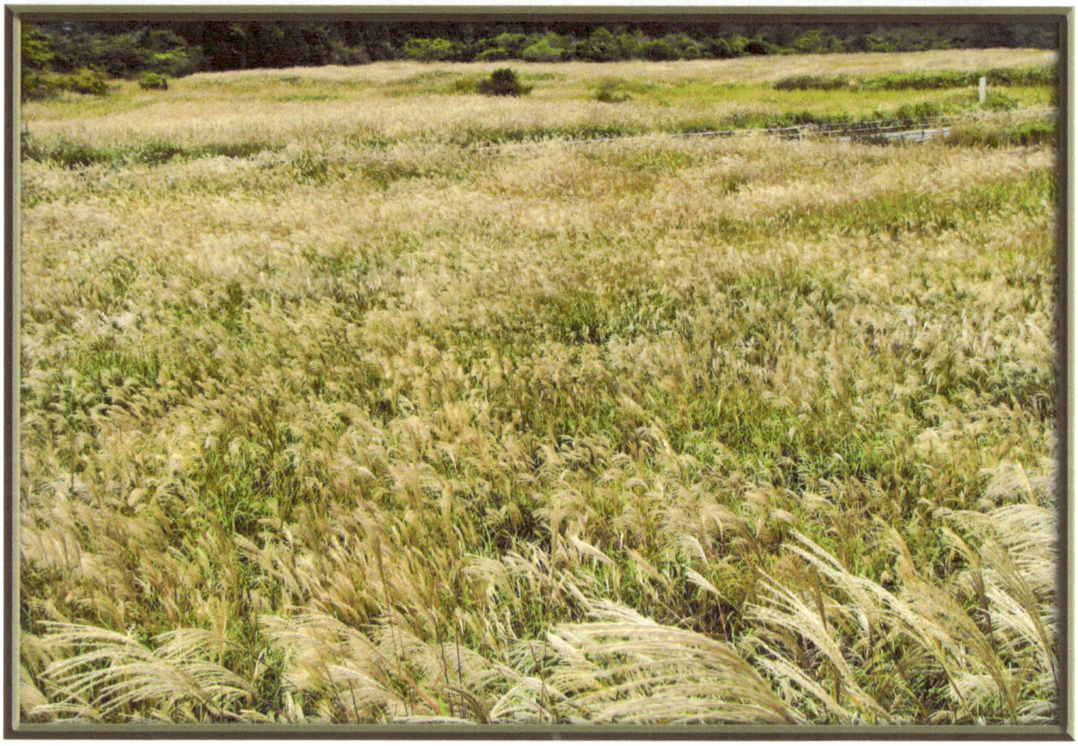

The two photos on the facing page show two excellent examples of **Susuki Grass** (***Miscanthus sinensis***). The **Sengoku-Kogen** area of **Sengokuhara** is famous for this huge field of **Susuki Grass**. We have no idea how large it is. In the lower photo you can get a slight feel for the size of it, but only a slight feel. In the autumn when this field is at its peak of beauty the single trail which goes through the center of this field is filled with people. It's probably around a mile (1.2 kilometers) in length, so it can take a good hour or more to hike up to the top of the hill by the time you stop every few yards (meters) and take a couple of photos. Depending on the exact lighting conditions, the grass can appear many different colors to the camera. The shots on the facing page certainly appear golden.

The below photo, of course another of Susuki Grass, and on the same day, appears to be a very different color than the ones on the facing page. We cannot explain precisely why this is, but this photo is definitely more of a silver shade than it is a gold shade. Did it suddenly get more cloudy, did the clouds get more gray in color, what happened? This was not a sunny day, not at all, but the sun was appearing now and then, so that could be the explanation.

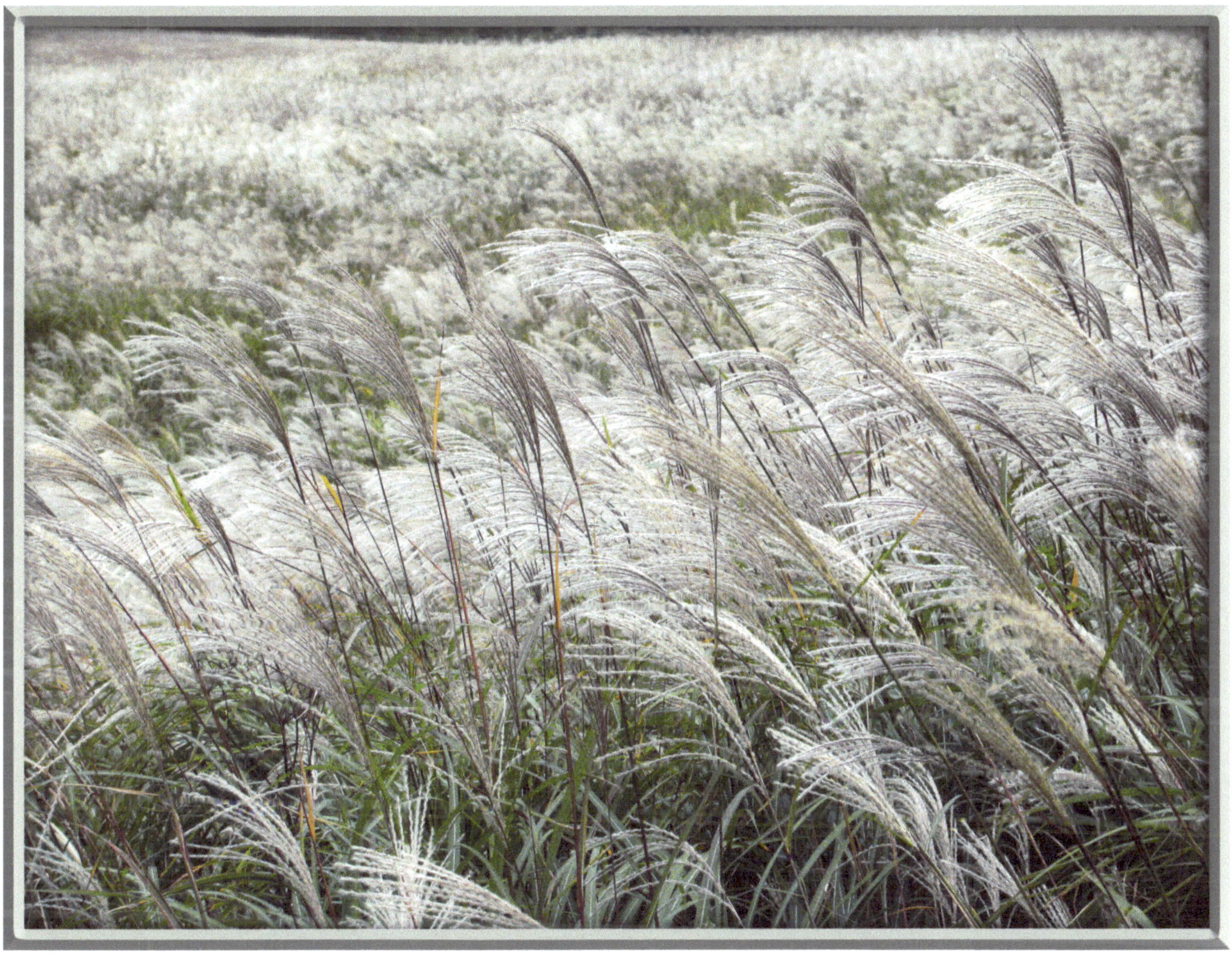

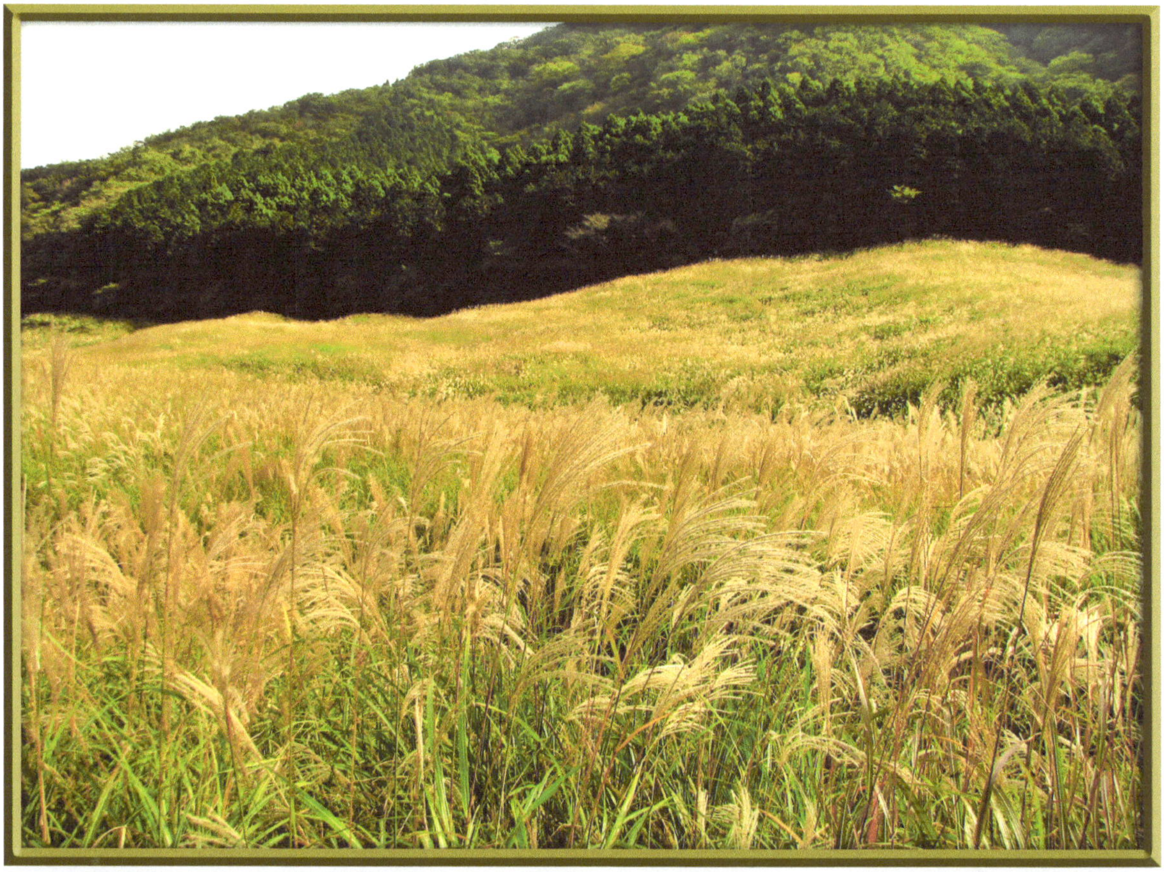

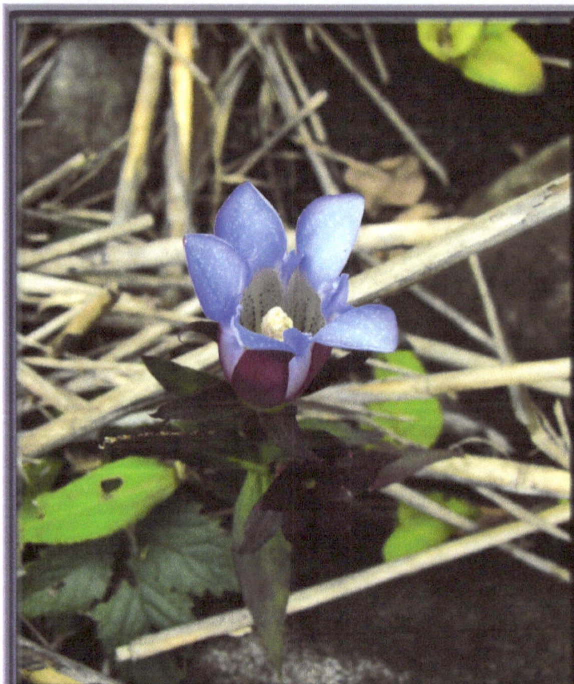

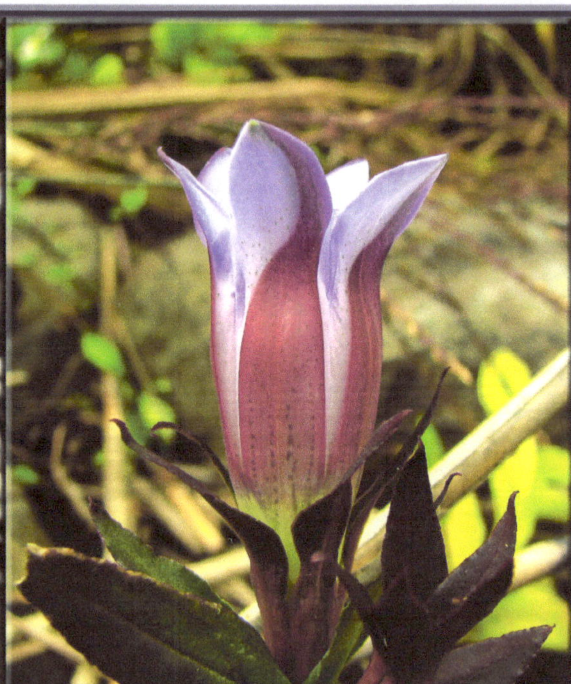

The upper photo on the facing page is the final one of **Susuki Grass** (***Miscanthus sinensis***) taken at Sengoku-Kogen. You may note that this one once again appears golden in color.

The lower collage is ***Gentiana scabra* var. *buergeri*** showing a shot from the side and a shot taken looking right down into the plant. This was also found at **Sengoku-Kogen**. It was along the trail as we hiked up towards the top of the Susuki Grass field. We were rather surprised to find it here.

The photo on this page was taken the following day as we rode the Cable Car from Lake Ashi up towards Owakudani. You may recall that it was cloudy yesterday when we passed through this area. This shot below was taken in the relatively early morning (first cable car) (9:02 AM) and shows the steam rising from the volcanic area. The black egg cooking place is the building which you can see just below, and to the left, of the steamy area on the right side of the photo.

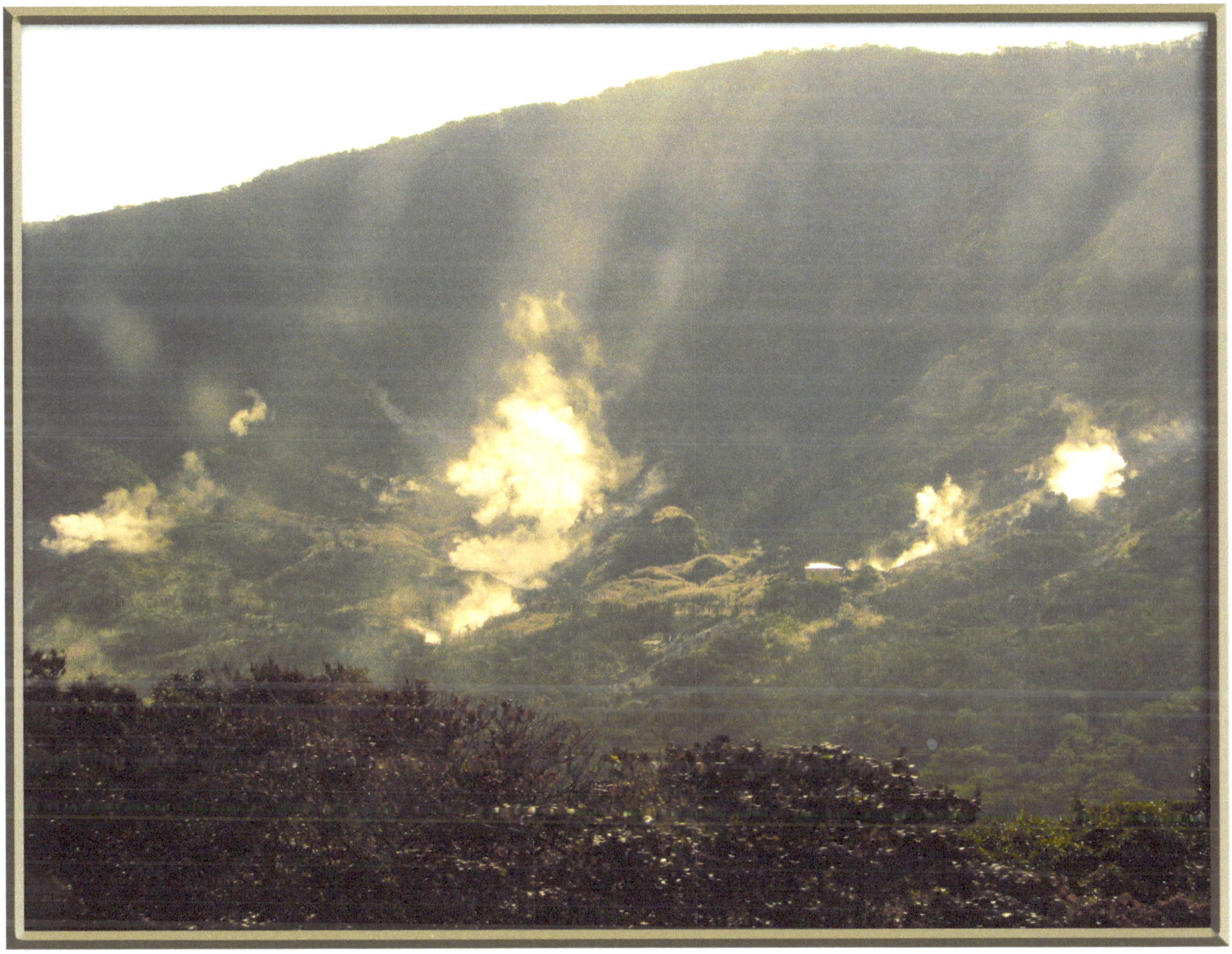

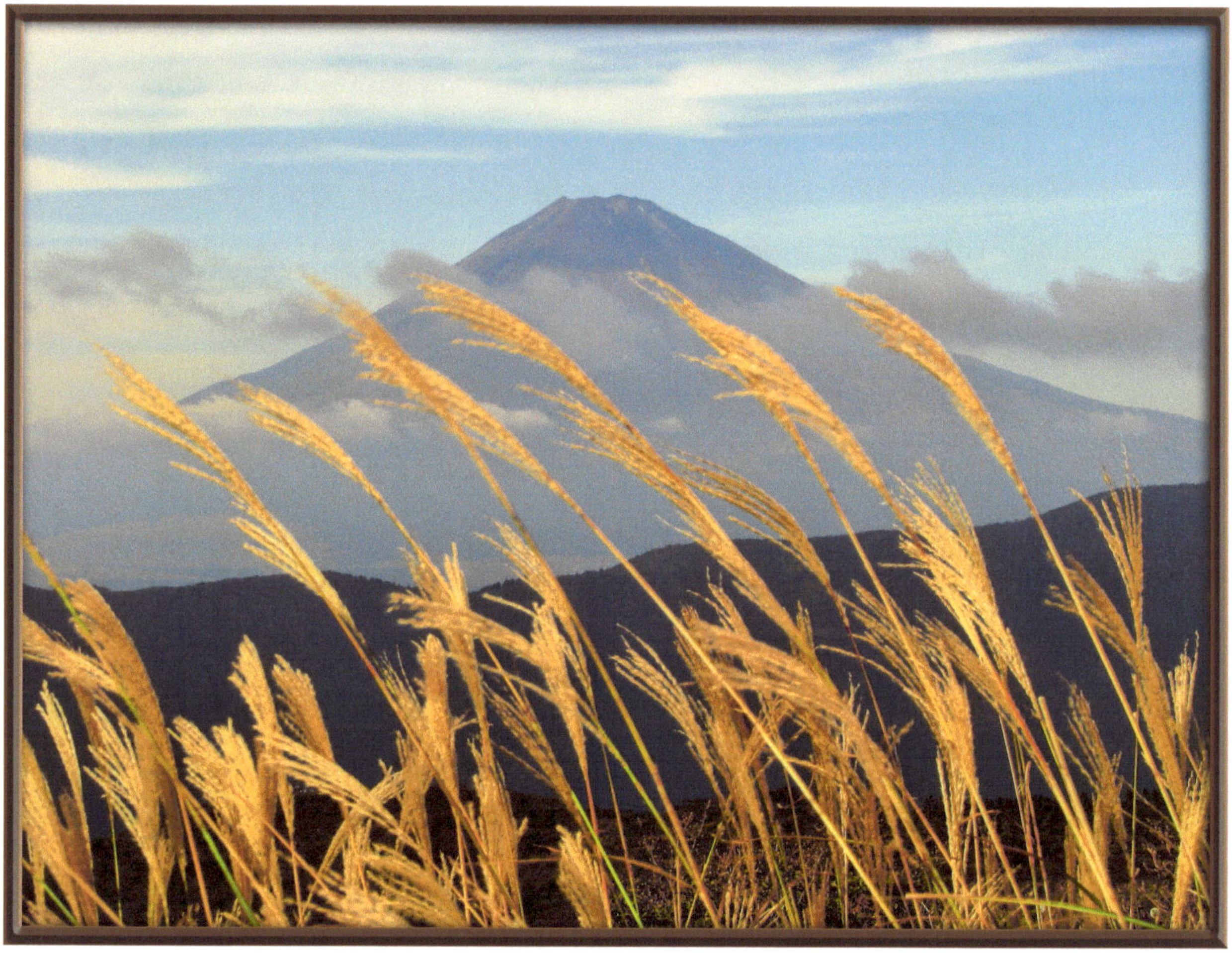

Here, just above, is the final October photo. This was taken from the **Owakudani** parking lot (see page 95 for a spring photo taken here). This is, of course, Mt. Fuji and it was taken through the **Susuki Grass** (***Miscanthus sinensis***) which was growing along the edge of the parking lot here. We went to great efforts to get good depth-of-field for this photo so that everything would be in focus. We shot several images here – looking through various weeds and autumn flowers. We had a choice of looking through Thistle Flowers, Goldenrod Flowers or this Susuki Grass. When we got home and looked at all of them this had the most appealing colors. The ones taken through the bright yellow Goldenrod and the pink Thistle were just too gaudy.

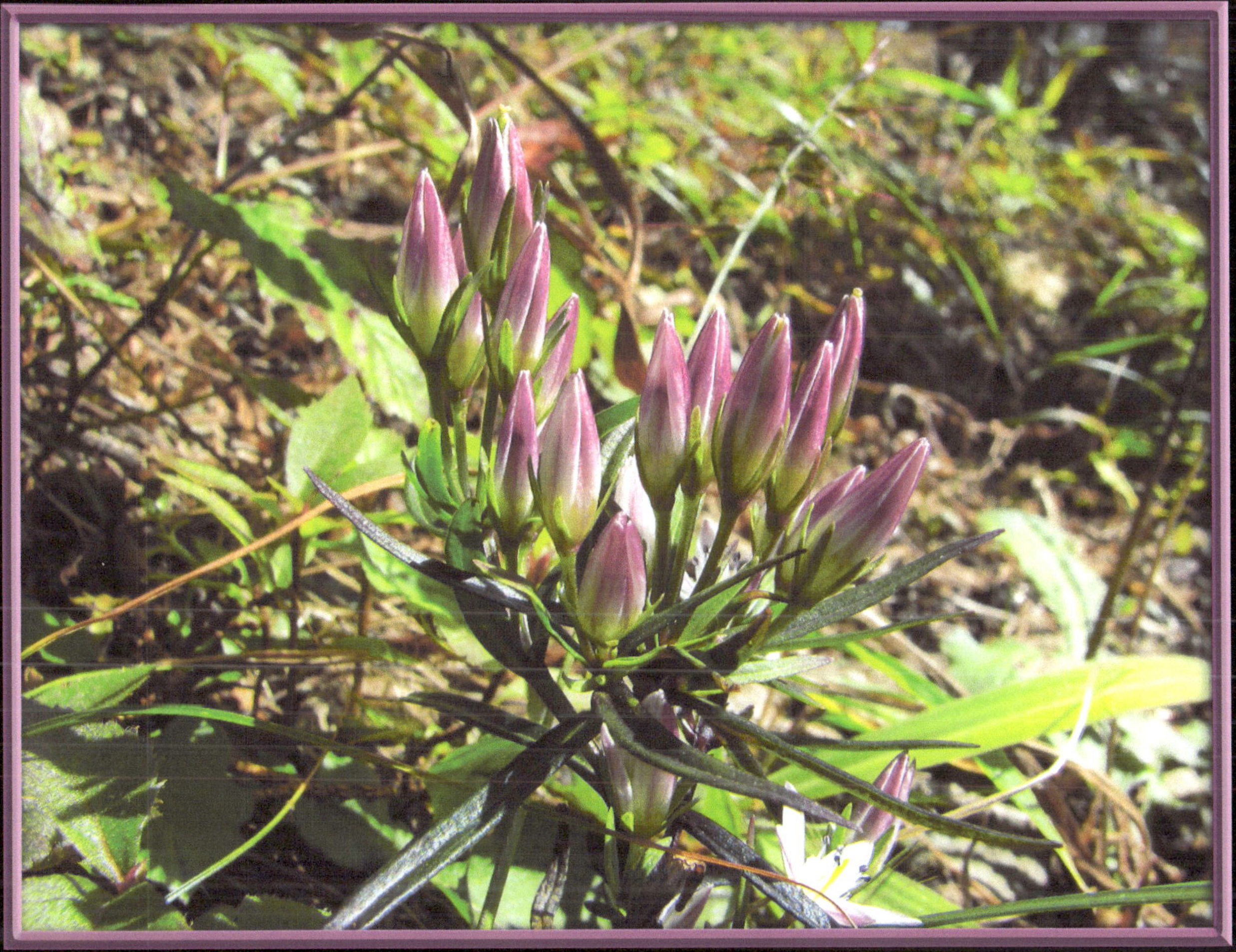

November Photos and Story

Here we begin the photos taken during November. Once again, these photos have been taken over the course of several years.

This cute little plant is ***Swertia japonica*** or ***Senburi*** in Japanese. This is probably just about the very latest blooming flower which we find in the autumn. To get these flower photos we have once again returned to **Mt. Hinode** and **Mt. Mitake** in **Western Tokyo**. We really love finding this flower – it can range from snow white in color to just a bit pink. Of course this photo shows unopened buds. We have noticed that the flower has five petals most of the time, but it is not at all uncommon to find a flower with only four petals.

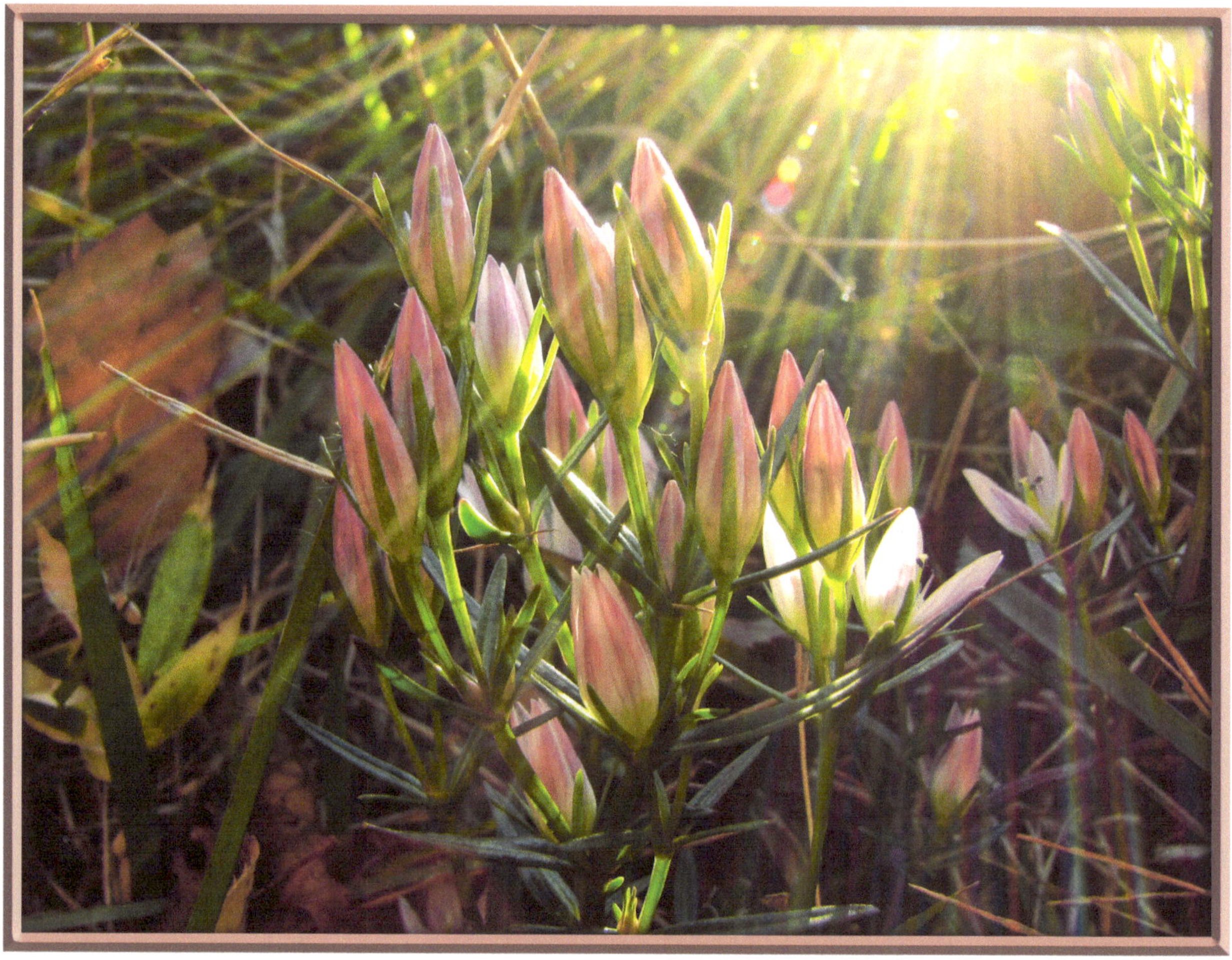

The above photo shows a very interesting lighting effect – the sun was shining through the plant and it was lit in a very photogenic manner. This only lasted a few moments and then the effect was gone and the sun did not help the photo at all.

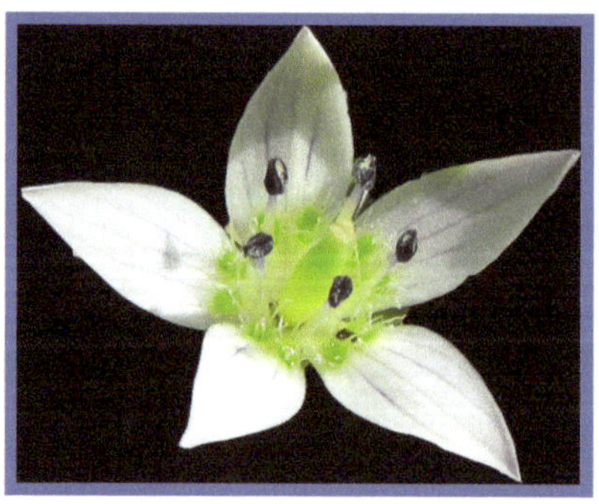

This little insert shows an open flower – one which has five petals.

We always get excited to find this flower in bloom, we are not sure why it should excite us so – possibly it is because that although the weather is getting cold and the first frosts have already happened that something can survive and actually blossom and be beautiful.

The facing page photo was taken along the Mt. Kawanori Trail (pages 11, 12 and 13). It is a pretty good autumn color shot. In November the autumn colors peak around the Tokyo area – you will see several autumn color shots this month.

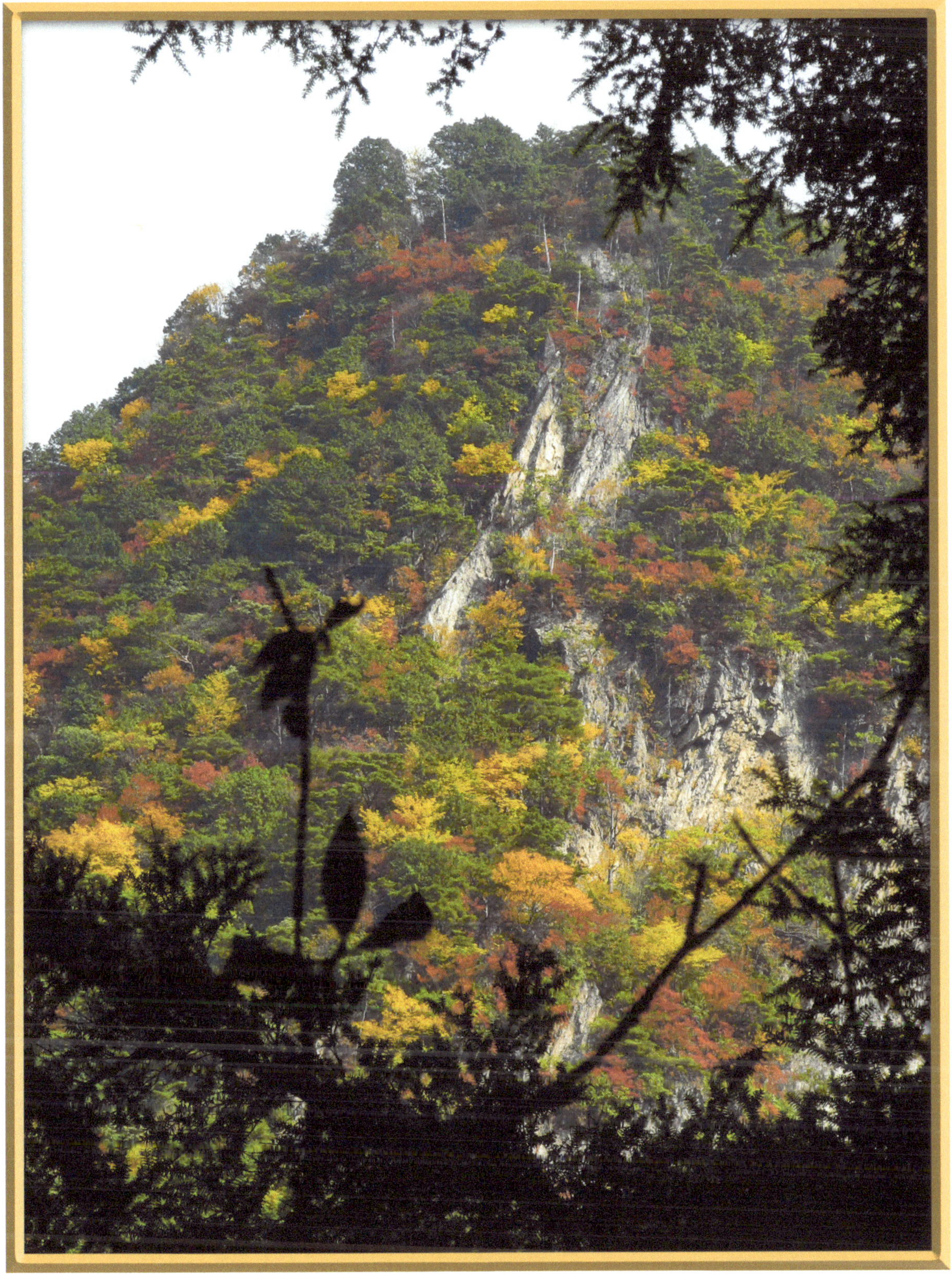

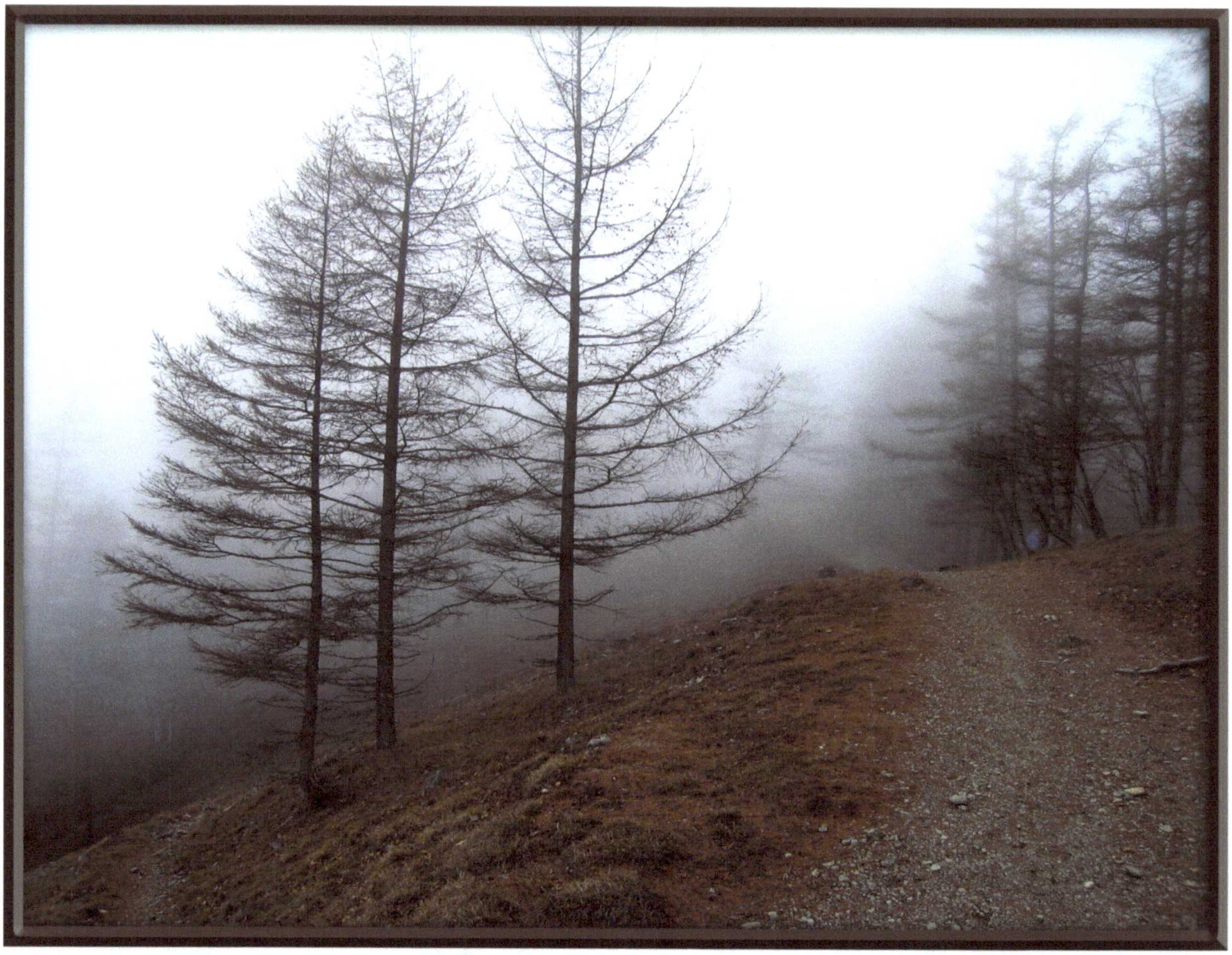

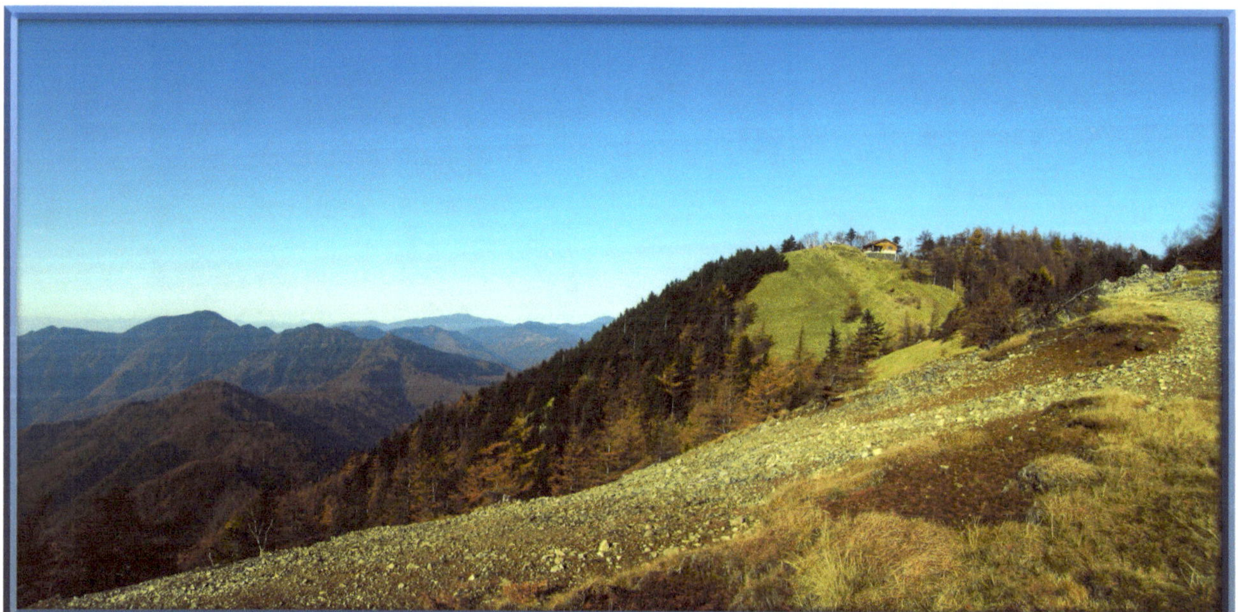

The two photos on the facing page were both taken on **Mt. Kumotori** (pages 64 – 66, 79, 215 – 224). The upper photo shows that on the day which we climbed this peak (2,017.6 meters = 6,619 feet) in November one year that the weather was not very nice.

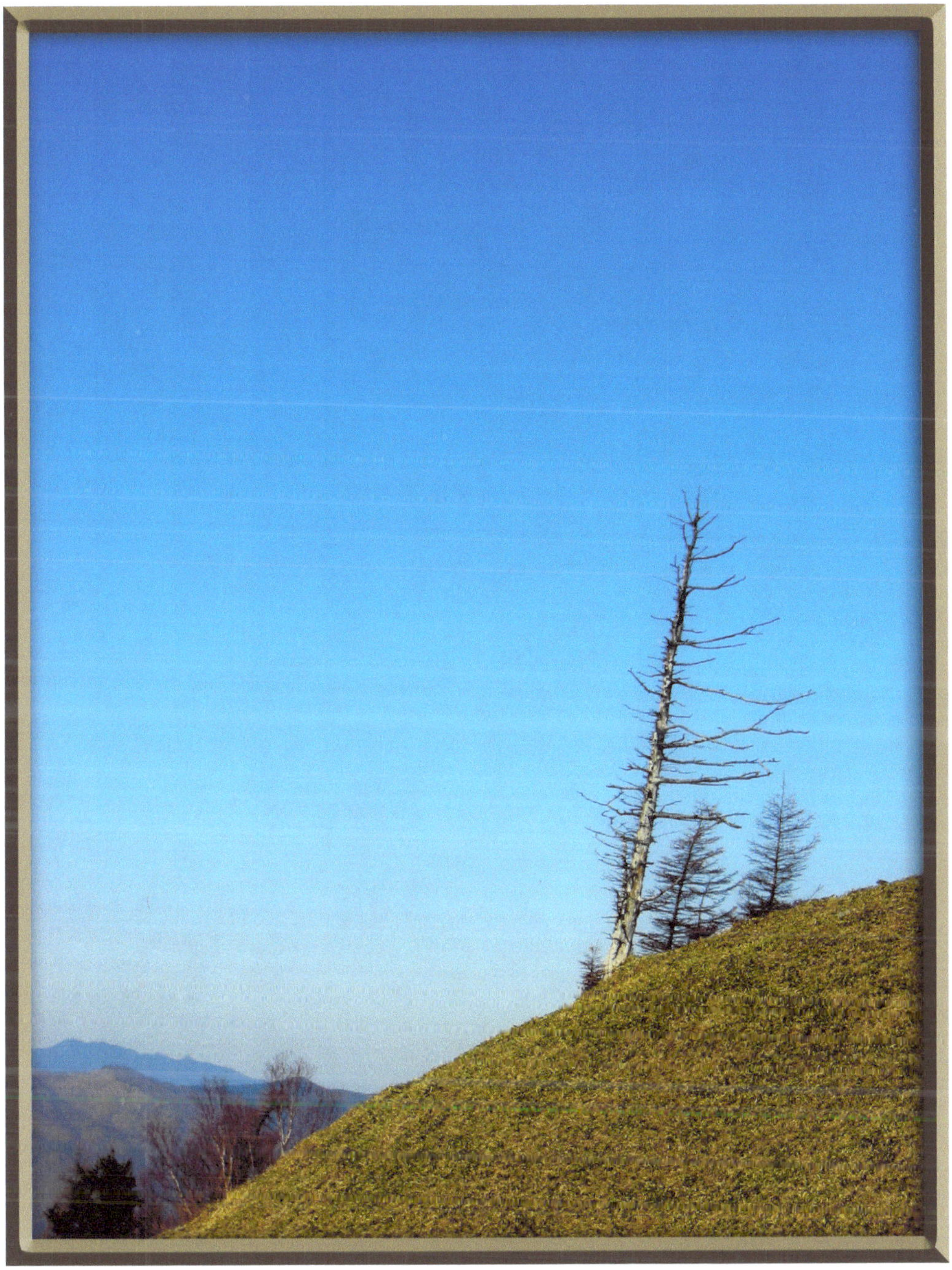

The lower photo, a panorama of the summit which shows the summit hut, also shows that on the next morning the weather had cleared up and it was a beautiful day. In both of these photos you will probably notice that most of the leaves are already gone at this elevation.

The photo on this page shows you the very same snag which we displayed for you back on page 65. That photo showed some sunset colors and this photo shows the beautiful **"big sky"** and bright colors of autumn. This photo was taken at 8:37 AM. This is not far below the summit of **Mt. Kumotori**.

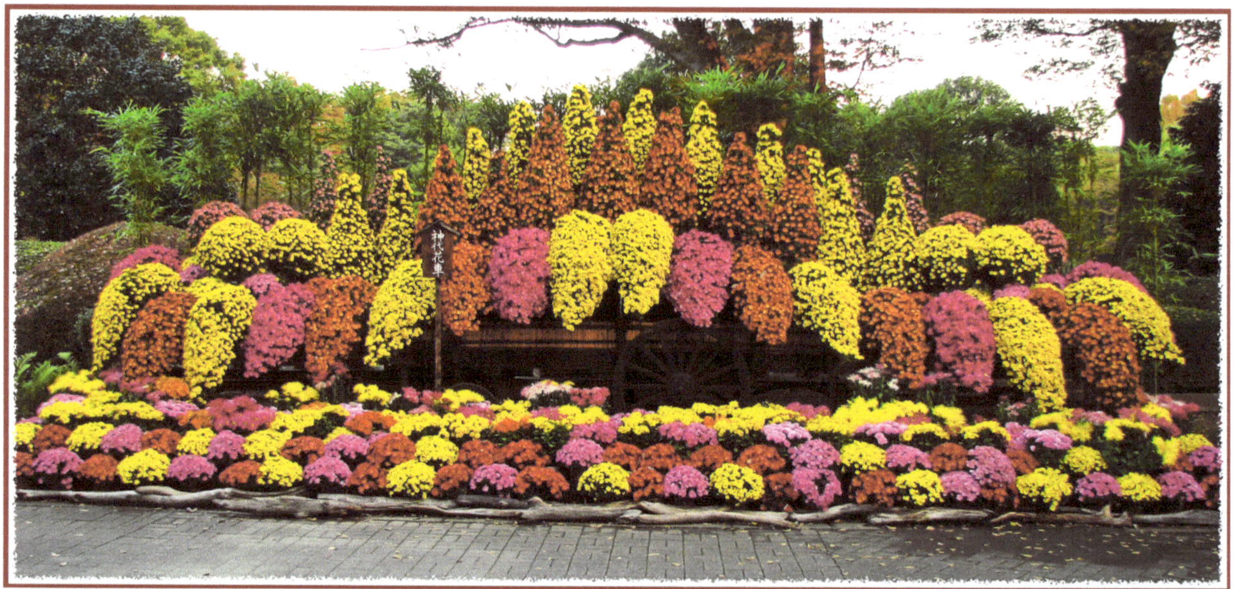

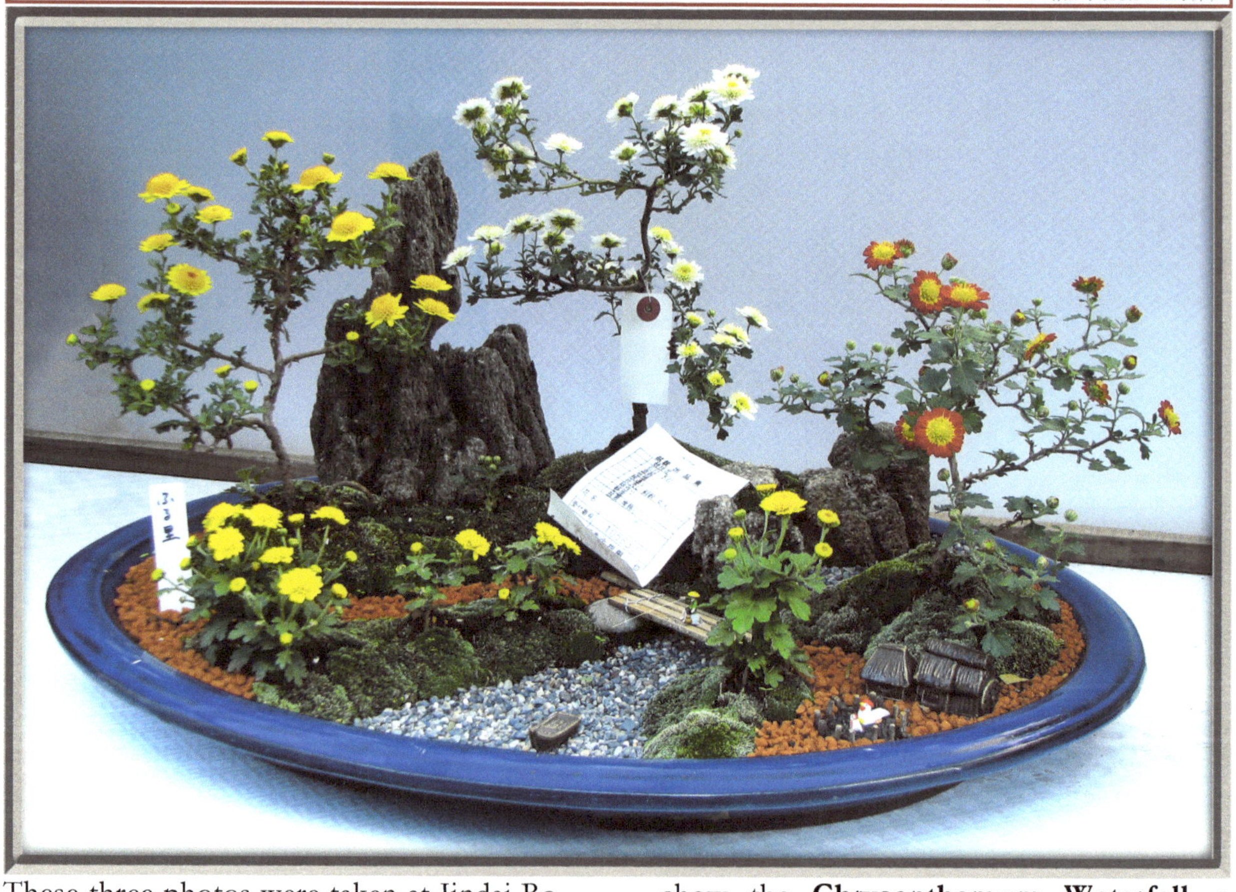

These three photos were taken at Jindai Botanical Garden – in the autumn they have a **Chrysanthemum Fair** – these three photos show the **Chrysanthemum Waterfall**, a **Bonsai Chrysanthemum** and a **"Wagon" Full of Chrysanthemums**.

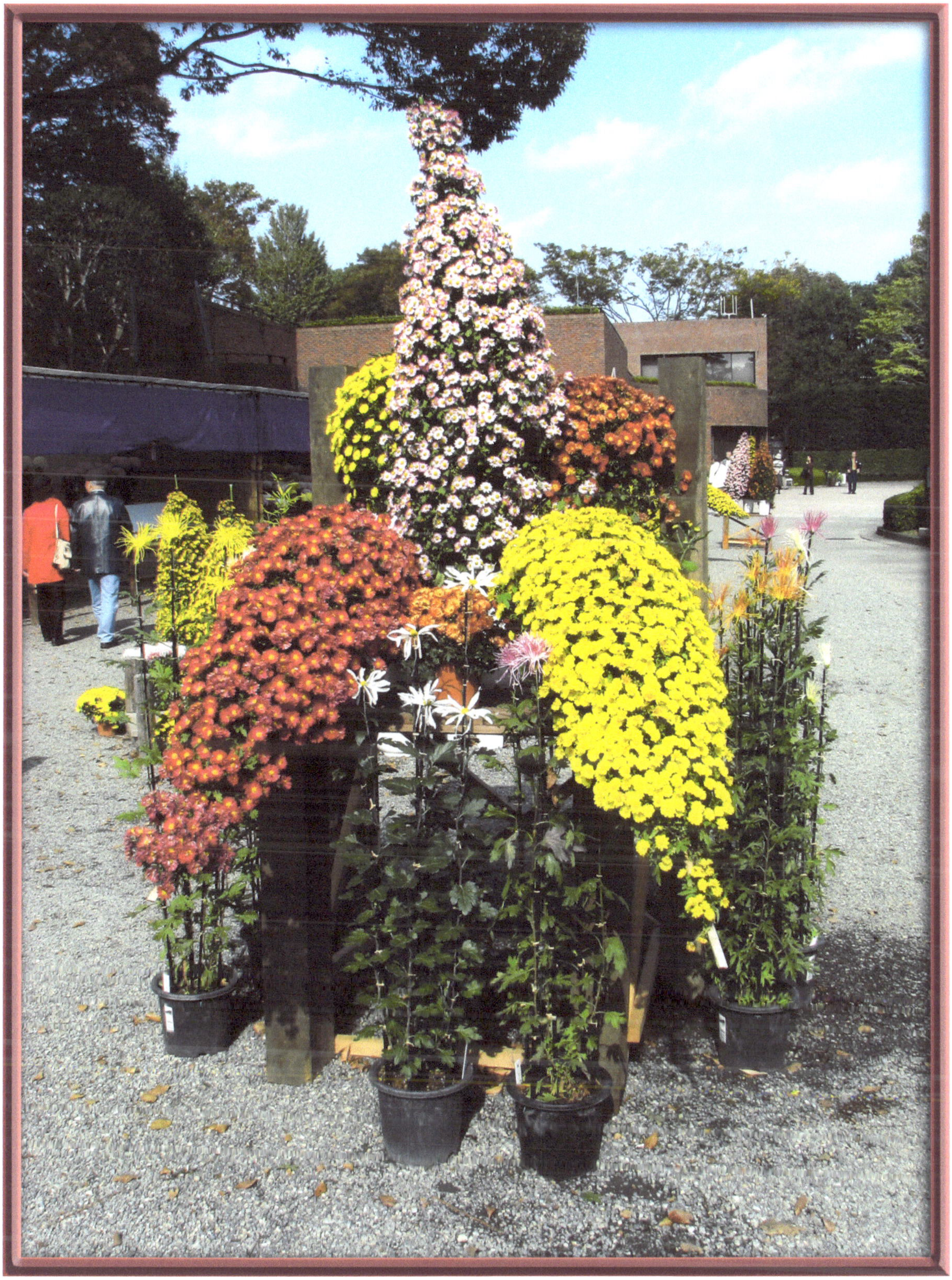

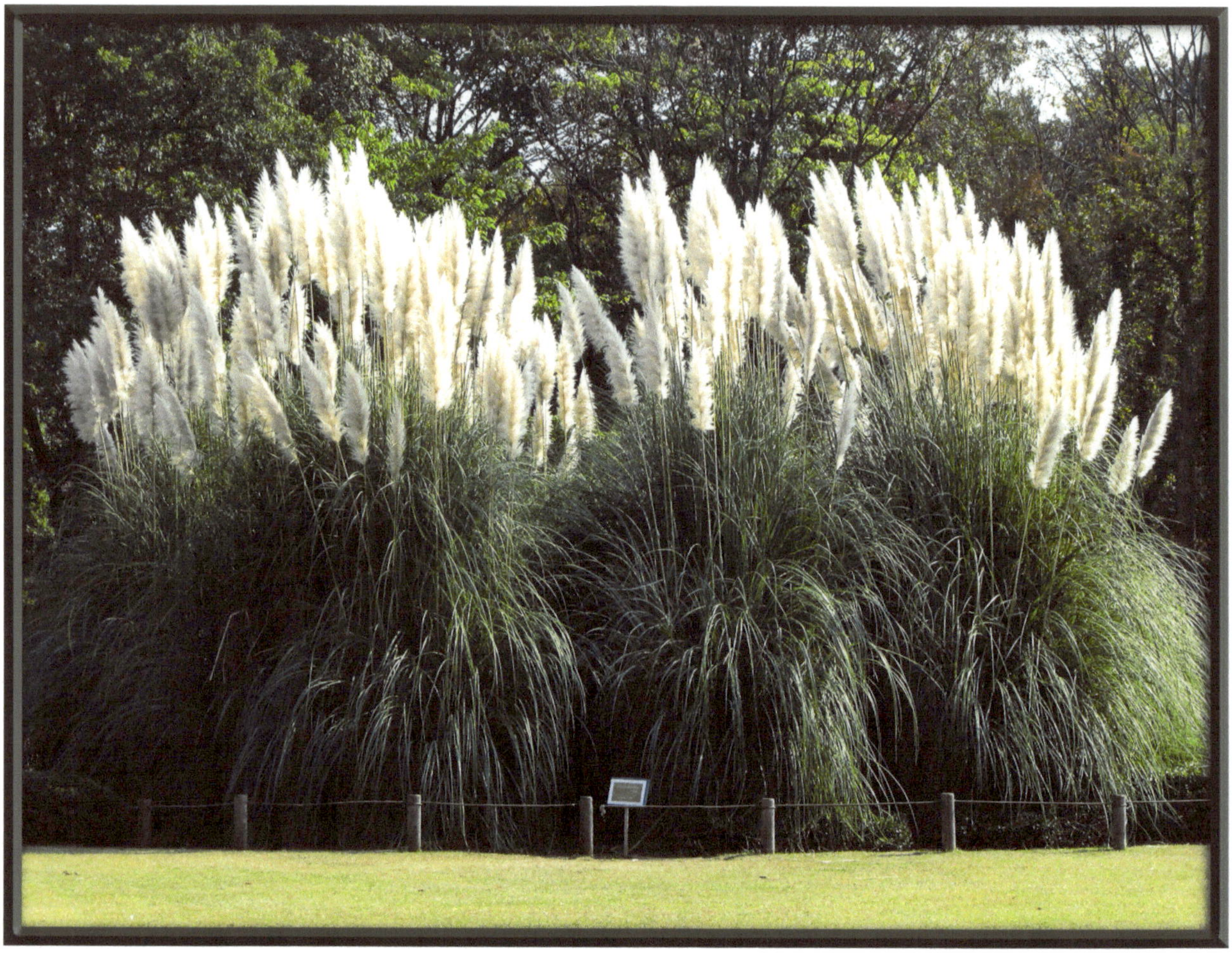

Here is another photo which shows ***Cortaderia selloana*** commonly known as **Pampas Grass**. You saw this same patch of Pampas Grass back on page 226 in Jindai Botanical Garden. That previous photo, taken in September, showed it at its absolute peak, but you could not really see anything for scale. This photo, taken in November, shows a knee-high rope fence for scale and also shows some minor fall colors in the background trees. At this time of the year the seed heads are starting to get just a little bit ragged and they are not quite as beautifully white as they were back in September.

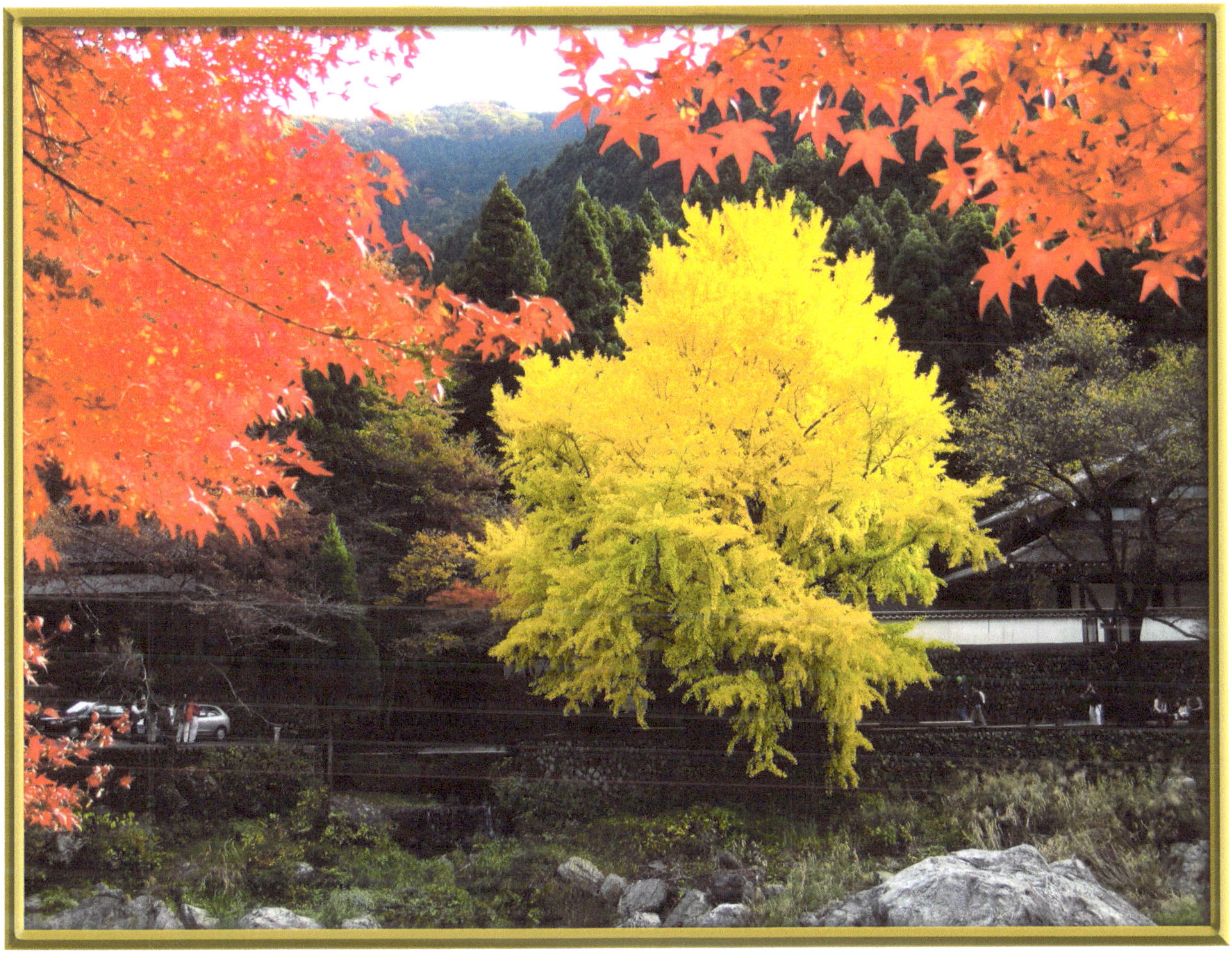

Every year sometime in November we go out to the **Upper-Tama River** at **Mitake** to view the incredible combination of colors shown in this photo. On the near shore of the river are some smaller Red Maple trees which offer the brightest red color that you can imagine. Then, on the far side of the river is an amazingly yellow-leaved **Ginkgo tree** (***Ginkgo biloba***). The building behind the Ginkgo tree and to the right is a restaurant. You can get the most magnificent photos from this spot if you spend a nice sunny day here. The light changes from morning through late afternoon. This particular photo was taken at 2:20 PM. You can even see the top of the mountain ridge in this photo.

Over the next few pages we're going to show you several photos taken from this area through the years. We'll give you the time of each photo, but other than that we won't say too much about the individual photos.

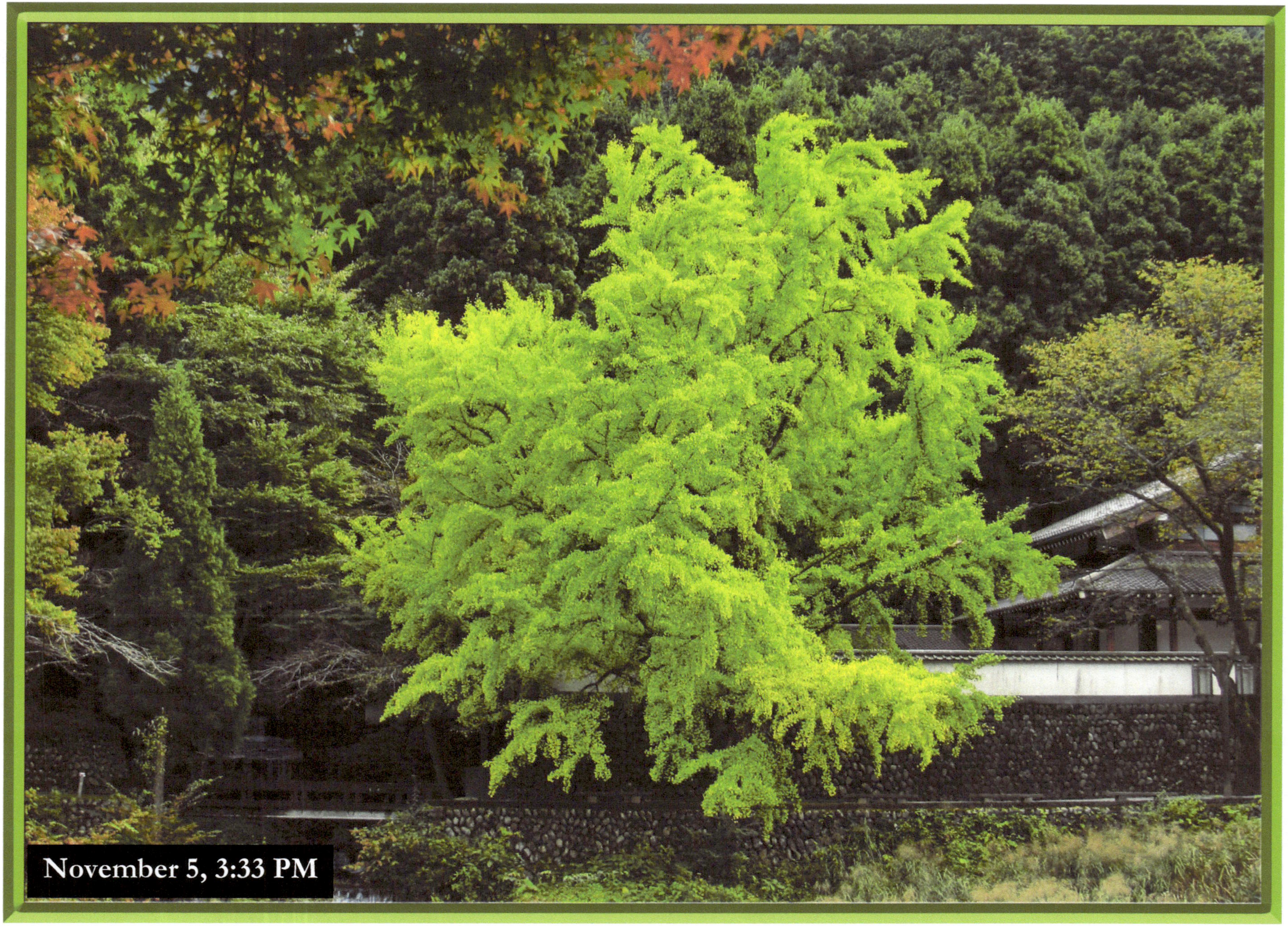
November 5, 3:33 PM

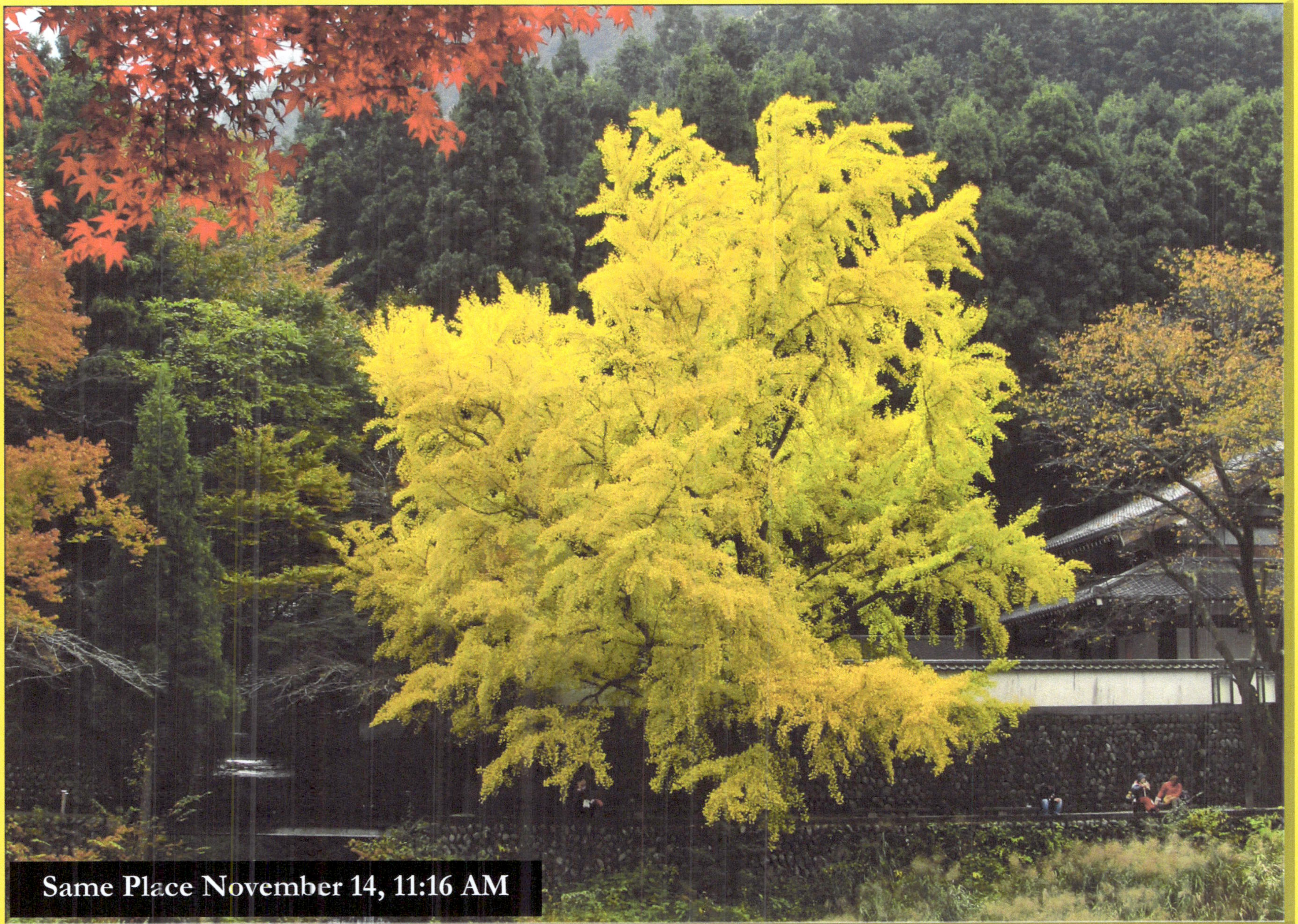
Same Place November 14, 11:16 AM

On the previous two pages we showed you two shots which were taken from the same spot, but separated in time by nine days. They were both taken from approximately the same place as the shot on page 303 and also on this page. This was a challenge – how does a person remember the precise location where one stood and shot a picture when shooting in a place where many people frequent every day? It's not easy. Well, we just relied on our memories and did our best and the result shows that we did a pretty good job of remembering.

The photo on this page was taken in a different year than the ones on pages 304 and 305. It was taken at 1:18 PM and the tree trunk was used to block some undesirable scenery.

The facing page photo shows the Famous Ginkgo Tree and its yellow reflection in the Upper-Tama River.

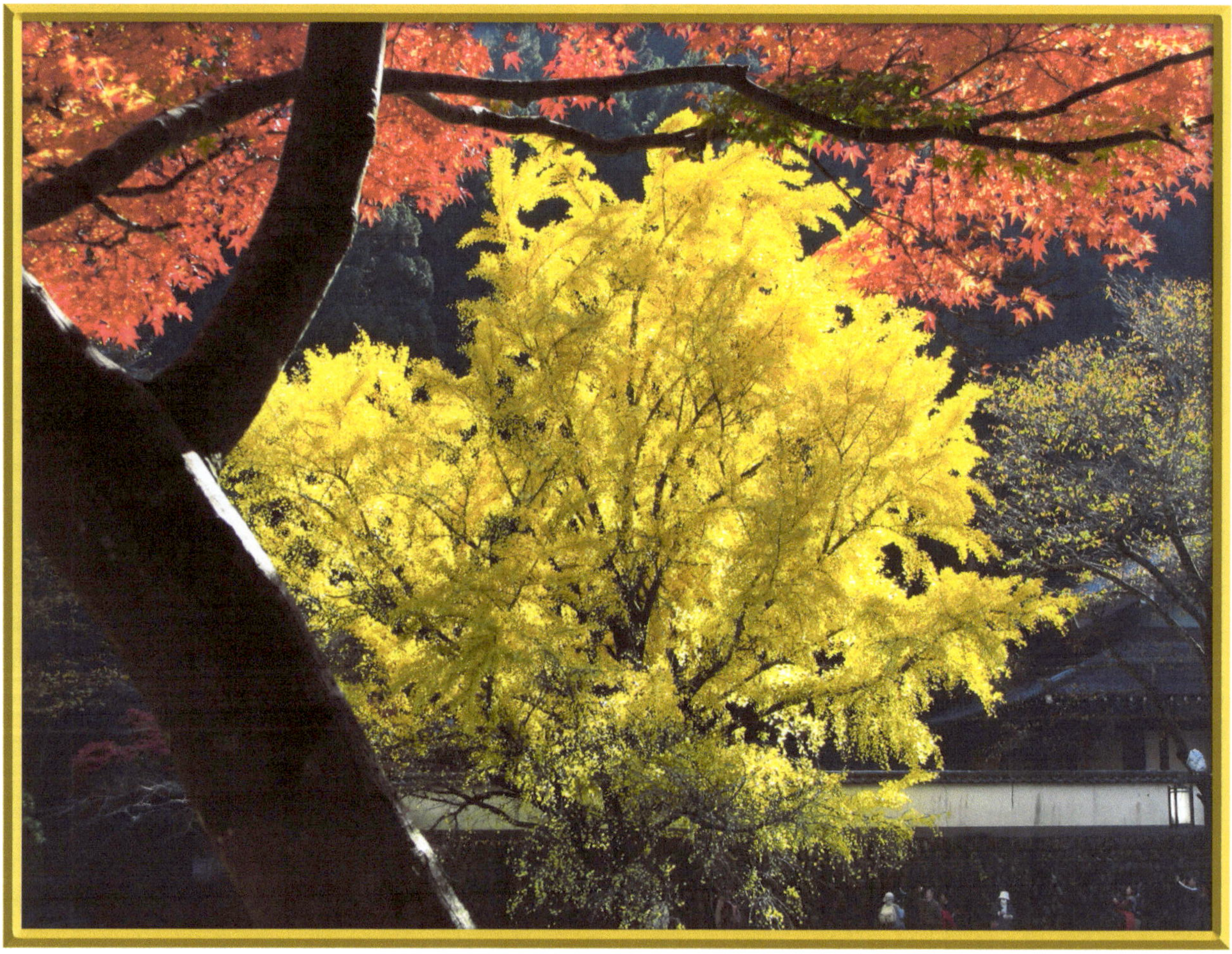

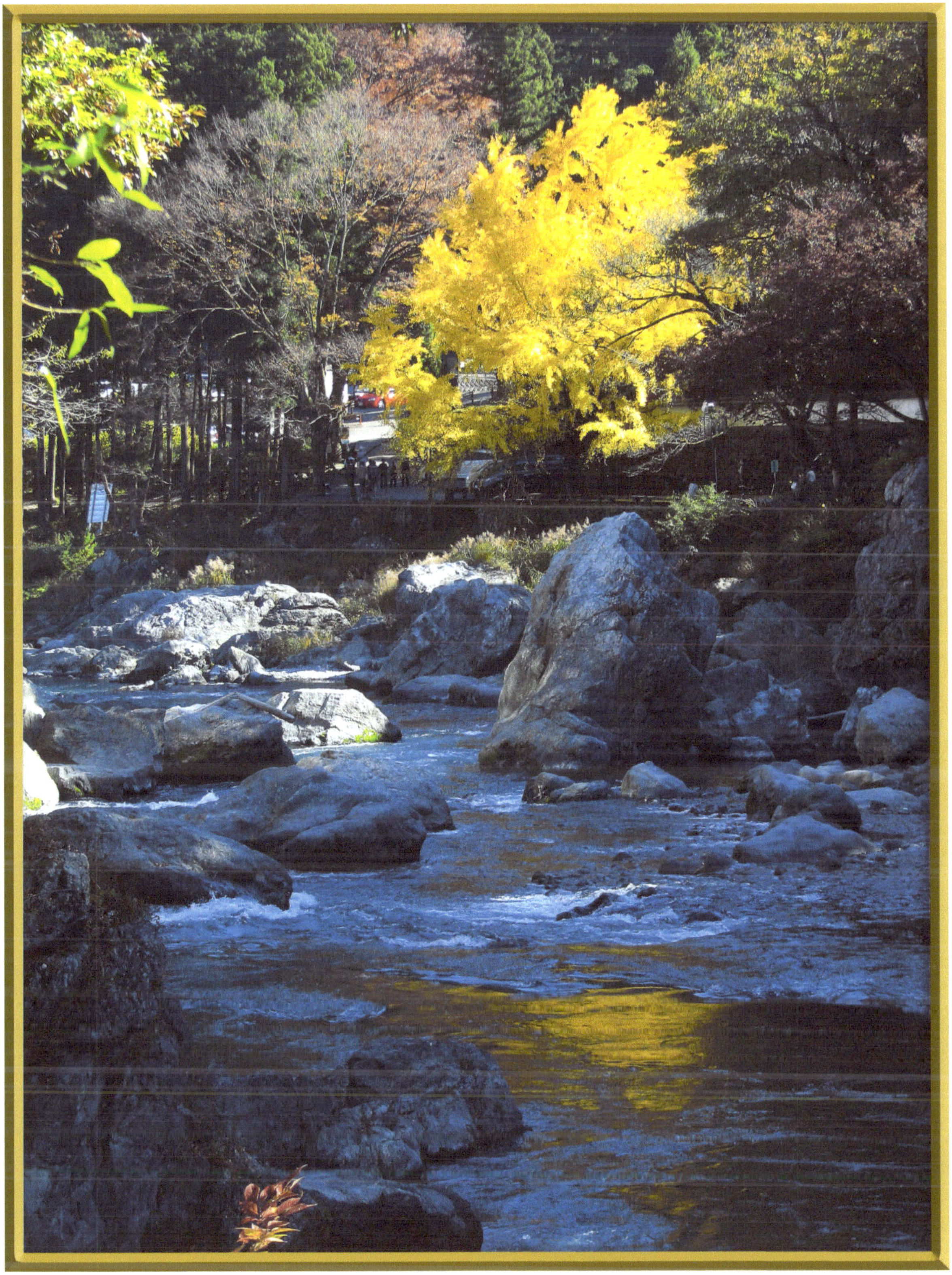

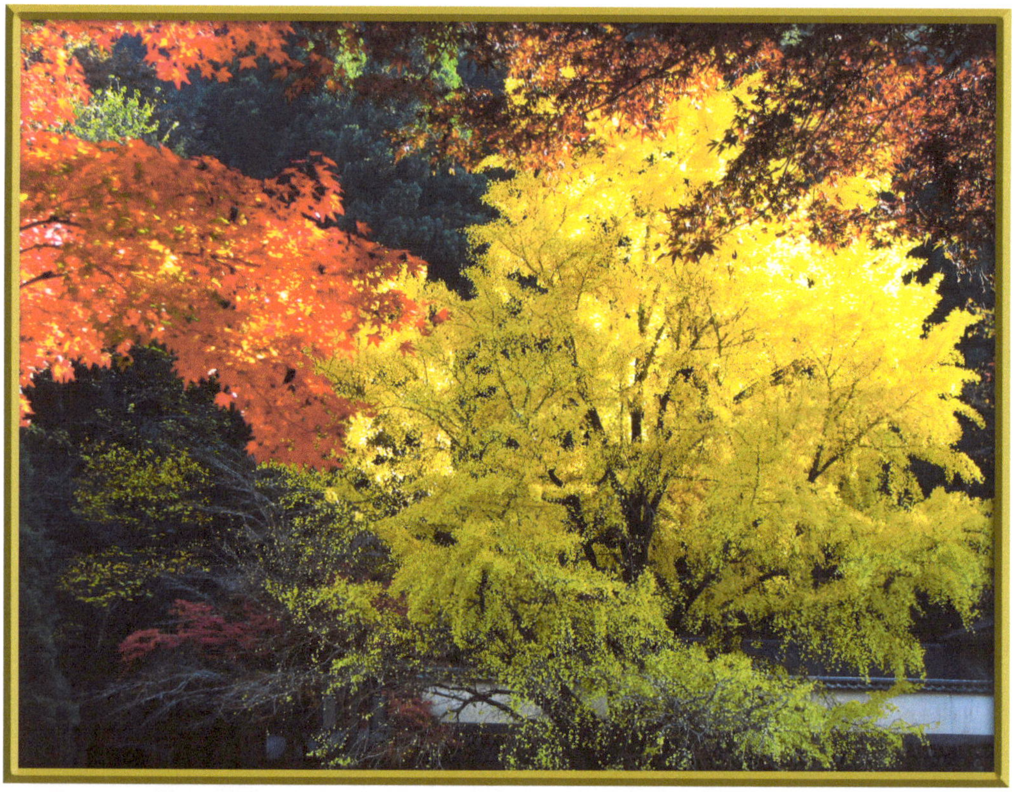

This photo ended up having very vivid colors – we did not do anything to it to increase the saturation or vibrance. This photo was taken at 2:40 PM. It is also zoomed in quite a bit.

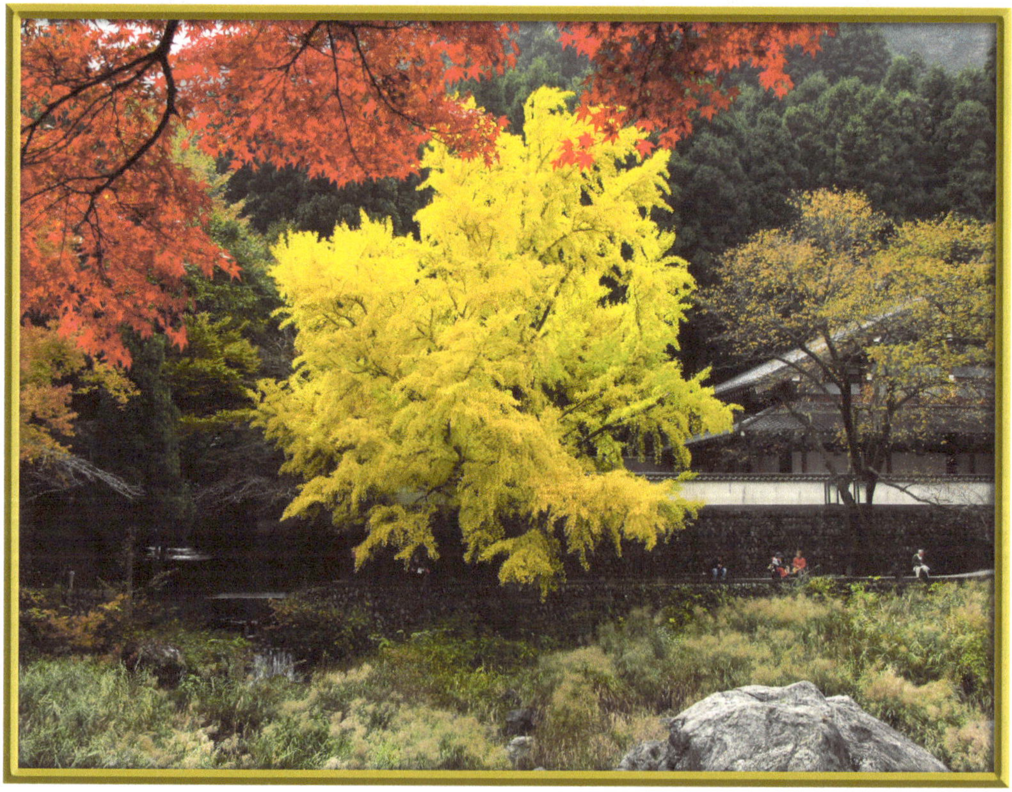

Here is a late morning shot – 11:16 AM. It is quite similar to the photo on page 305, but this one shows quite a bit more **Red Maple** color than that one did.

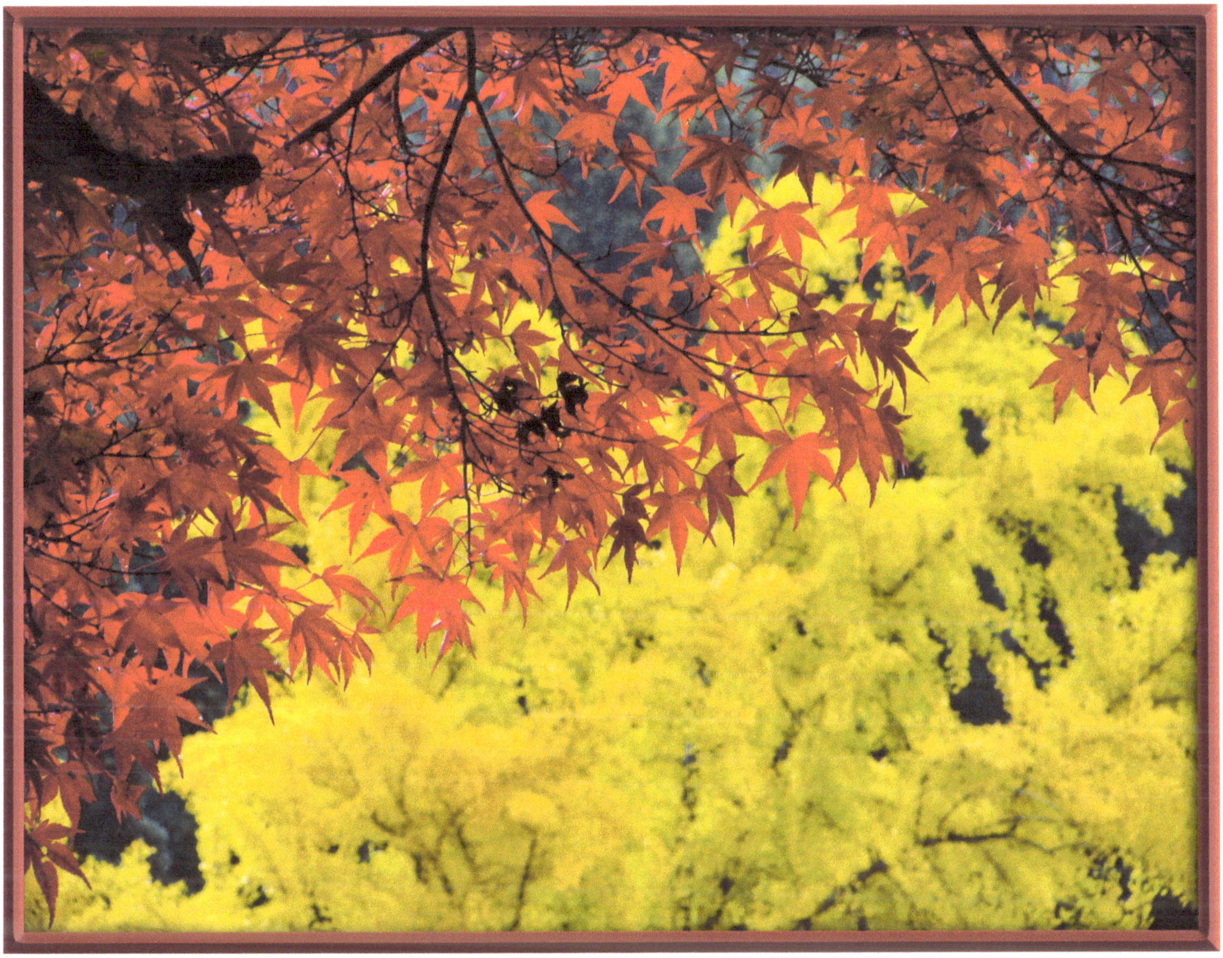

Here is the final shot of the famous ***Ginkgo biloba*** tree at **Mitake** which was taken through the Red Maple trees (there is one more photo, but not taken through the maple leaves). For this shot we focused on the Red Maple leaves and let the yellow Ginkgo leaves remain unfocused. This photo was shot at 3:56 PM.

If you ever find yourself in Tokyo in November it is definitely worth your time and effort to take the **Chuo Line Train** and the **Ome Line Train** out to **Mitake**, walk down to the **Tama River** and check to see if you happen to be here at the right time of the season to be able to see this – you won't be sorry you did it.

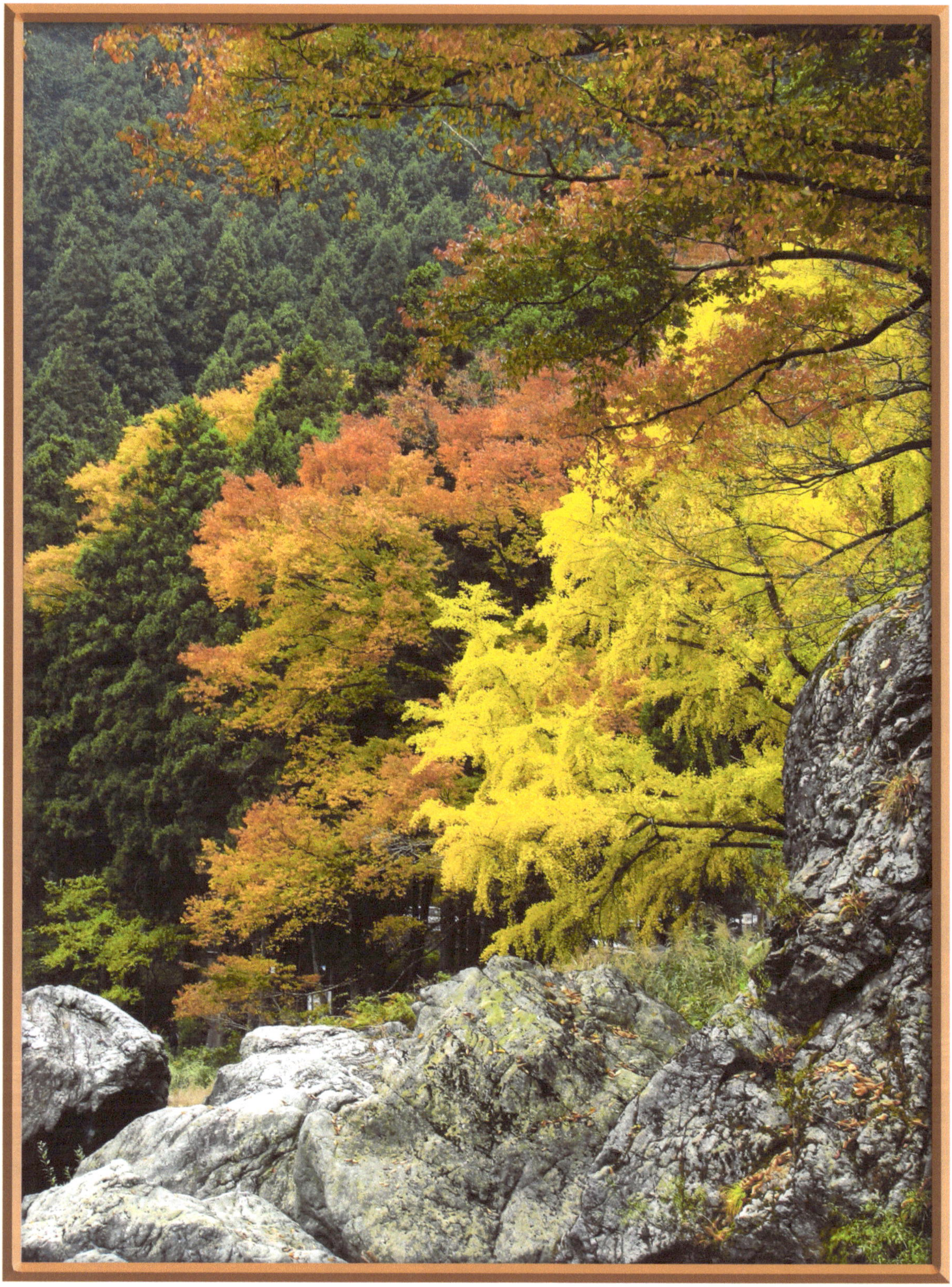

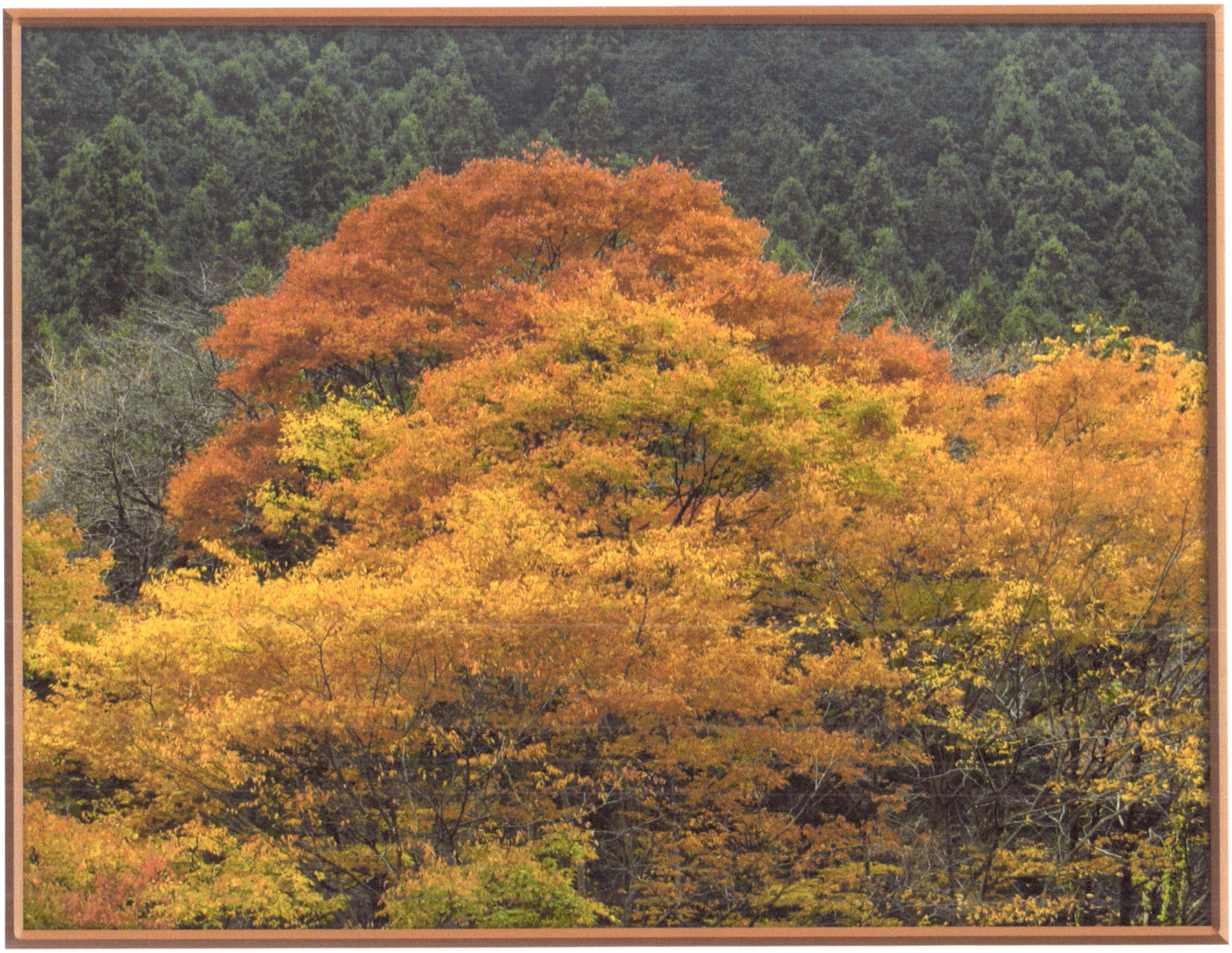

The facing page photo is another (and the final) of the Ginkgo tree at **Mitake**. It was taken somewhat upstream from where the Red Maple trees are. It was also taken on the opposite side of the river – this is the side where the Ginkgo tree actually is. You'll notice the huge rocks along the river. Did you notice that this is the cover photo on this book?

Here is a beautiful autumn color shot of golden-brown colors. This photo was also taken near **Mitake** as we hiked up the river towards **Sawai Station**. The colors are nice against the green of the coniferous forest on the side of the mountain. You can find scenes like this on the same day you can see the beautiful yellow Ginkgo tree shown on the previous few pages.

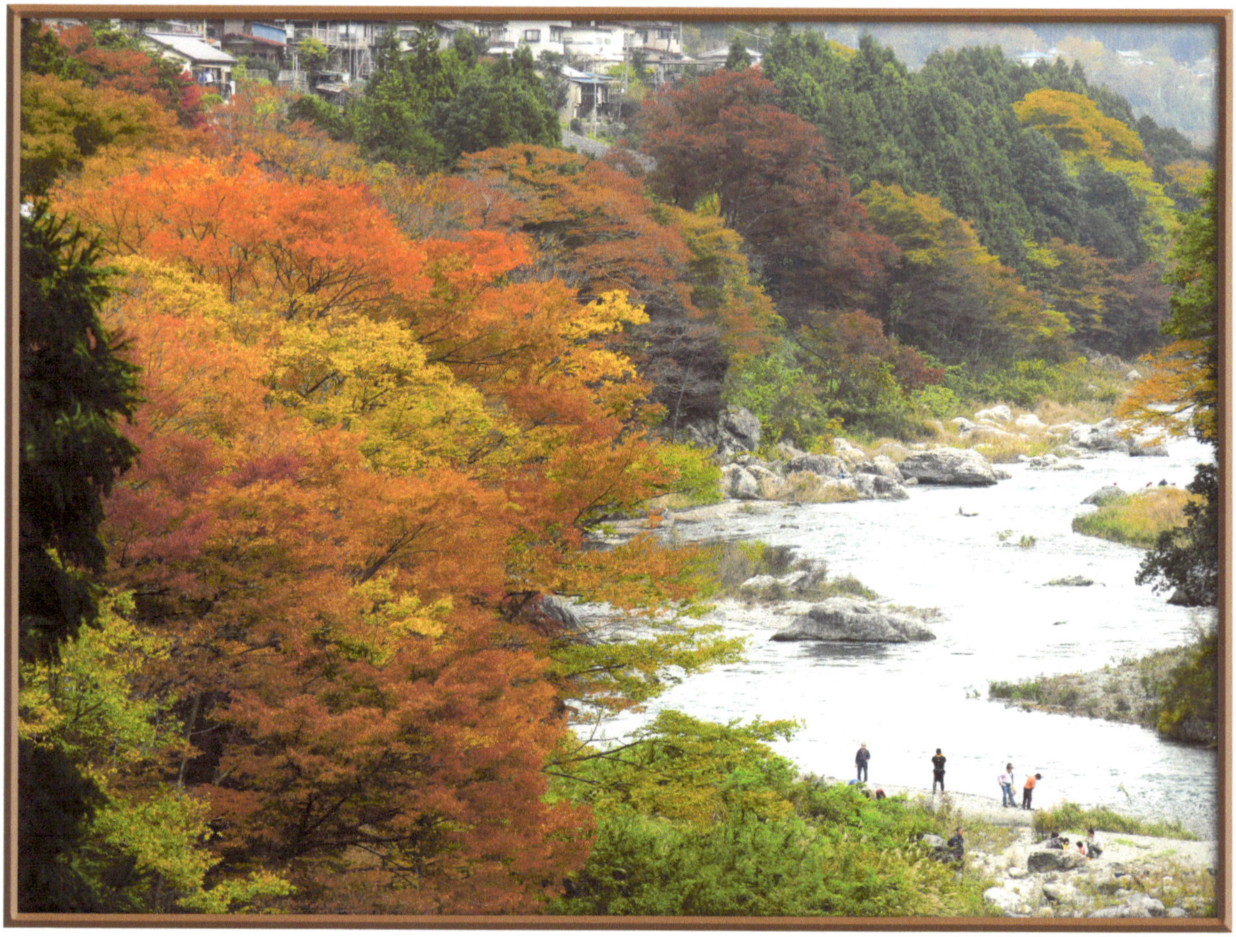

The above photo is actually quite a wide angle shot. It consists of three portrait-mode photos which have been stitched together to create this panorama. These photos were taken from the footbridge at the **Sawanoi Saké Brewery** near **Sawai Station**.

You cannot expect to see colors this wonderful here every year. This happened to be a very good year for autumn colors and we saw more colors than we had ever seen before. The Ginkgo and the Red Maple trees at Mitake are quite marvelous every year, but these golden-browns and oranges are not apparent every year. This had been an extremely hot summer and then there was an early freeze and this was what we attributed these great colors to.

The facing page photo was taken further west from **Mitake** – it was taken along the old road from **Okutama** to **Okutama Lake** – at the end of the **Ome Train Line** in **Western Tokyo**. It is actually an image composed of 3-exposure bracketed photos which have been combined into one image using imaging software. This is what is referred to as an **HDR** (**High Dynamic Range**) image.

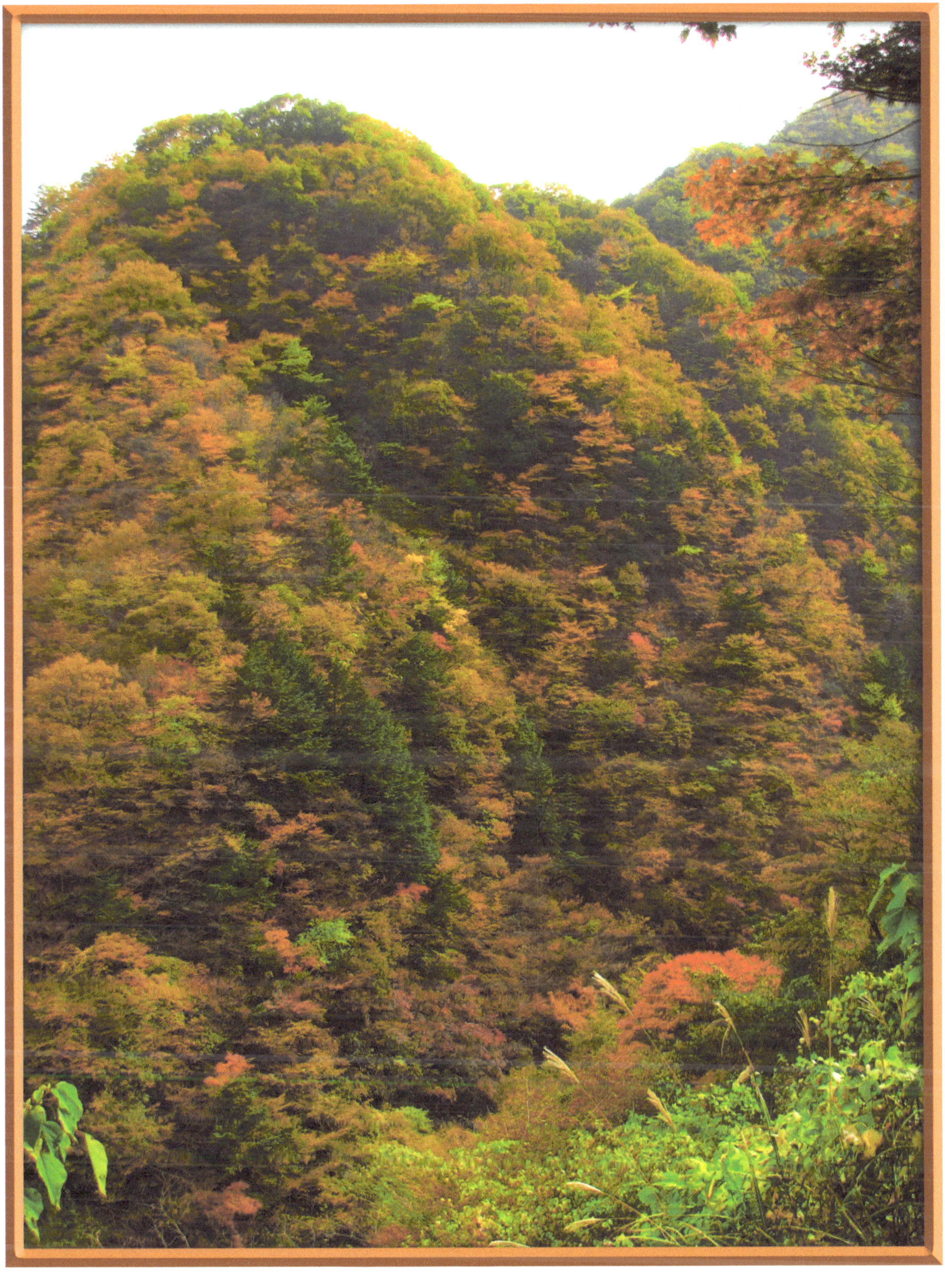

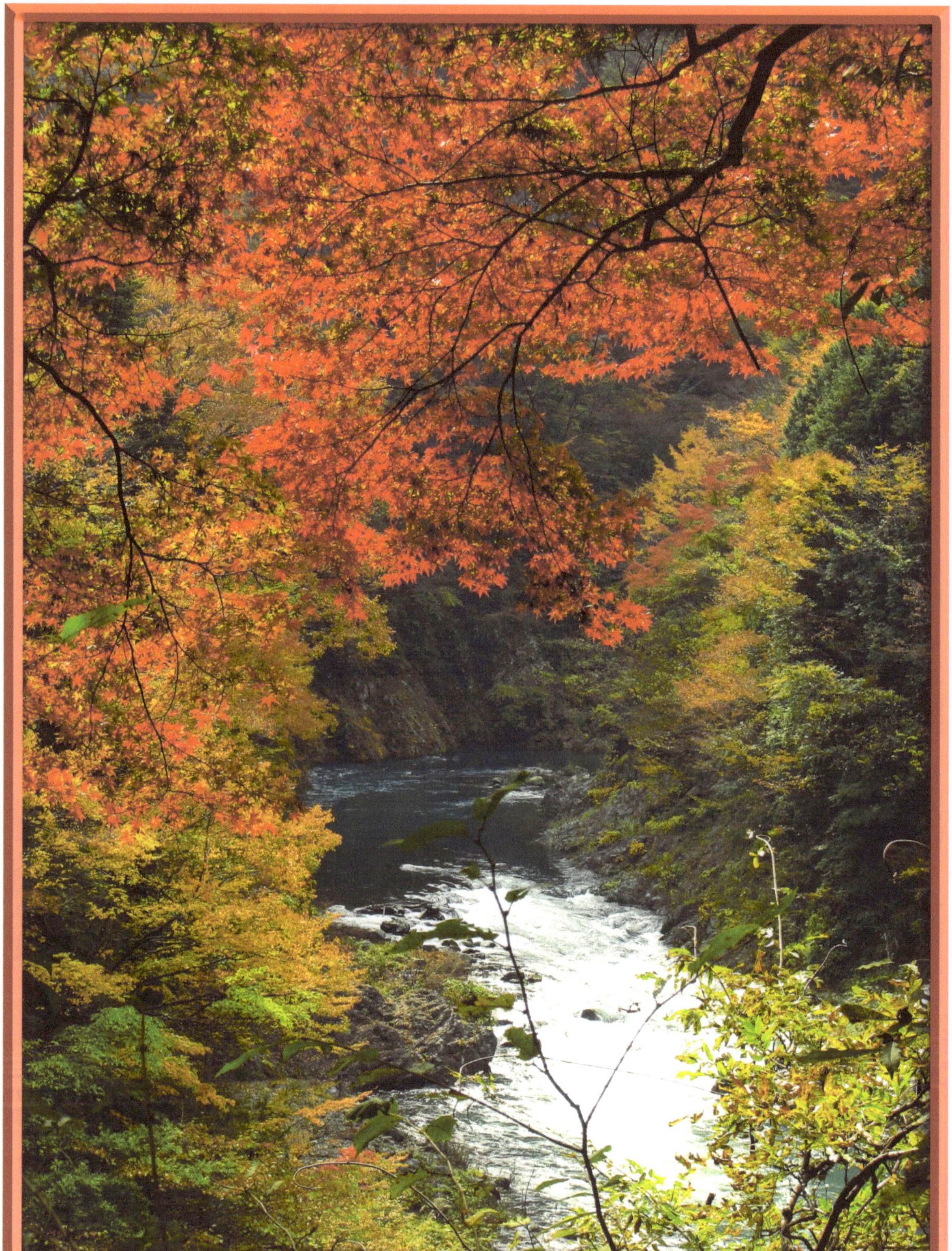

The photo on the facing page was also taken as we hiked the **Okutama Old Road** from **Okutama** to **Okutama Lake**. The river is the **Upper-Tama River** and it is not very far below Okutama Lake. You'll note that this is a very steep area. This maple tree is quite colorful most years.

The below photo was taken at Okutama Lake on a somewhat foggy morning one year. The time was 10:22 AM, so the sun is well up in the sky and offering pretty good light. This photo was zoomed to quite an extent, so we are looking through quite a bit of light fog. The autumn colors show up fairly well.

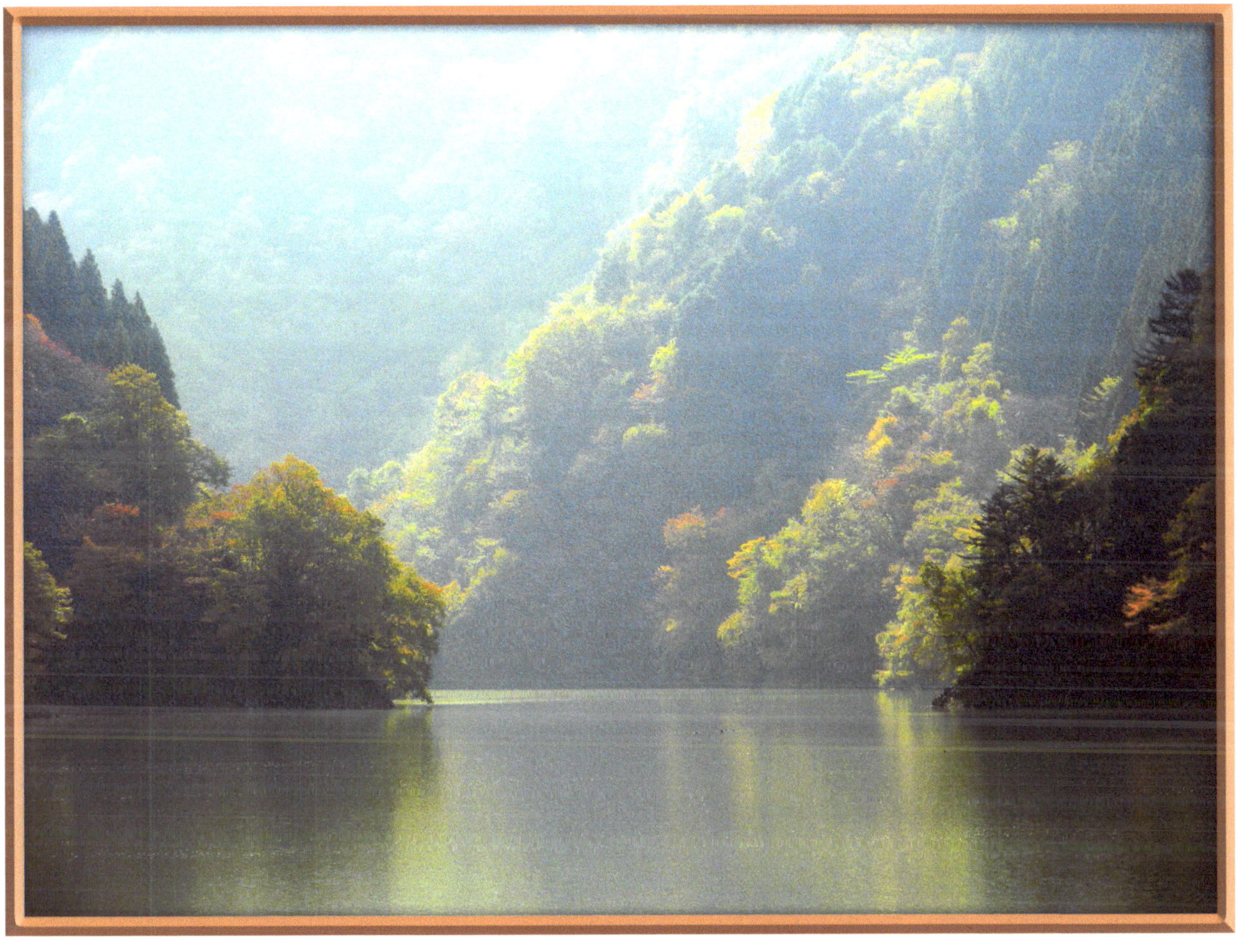

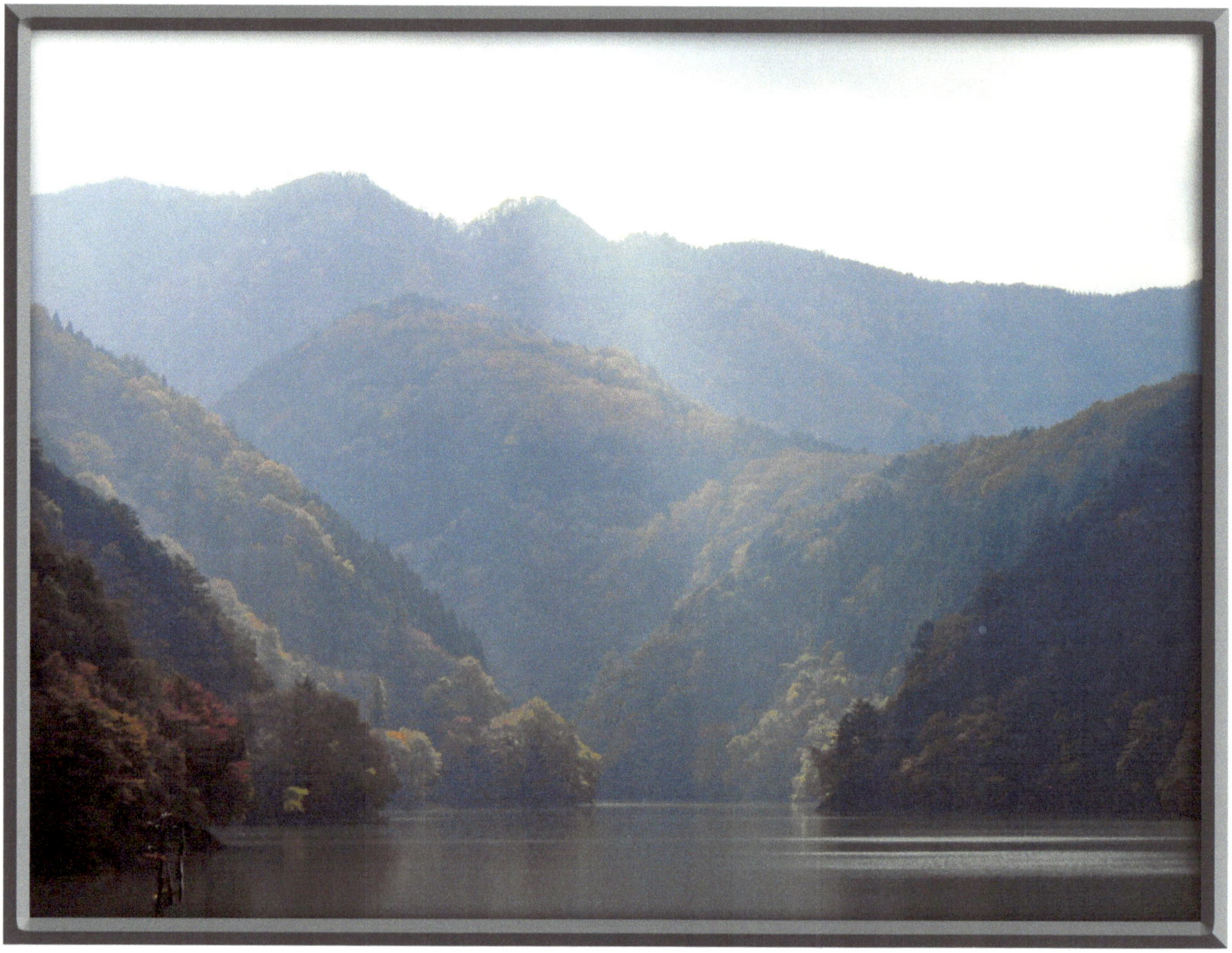

Here, immediately above, is another shot of Okutama Lake. This photo was taken at approximately the same time as the one on the previous page, but, obviously this one was not zoomed as much. The clouds, in combination with the light fog and the sun shining through holes in the clouds make for a very interesting effect. You will also note that the autumn colors are pretty good in this photo. We wondered if this kind of weather was actually nicer than clear blue skies. We certainly would not have been able to get this type of effect if it had been a clear blue sky day. Also, in the autumn and looking across this kind of distance, it is often very hazy.

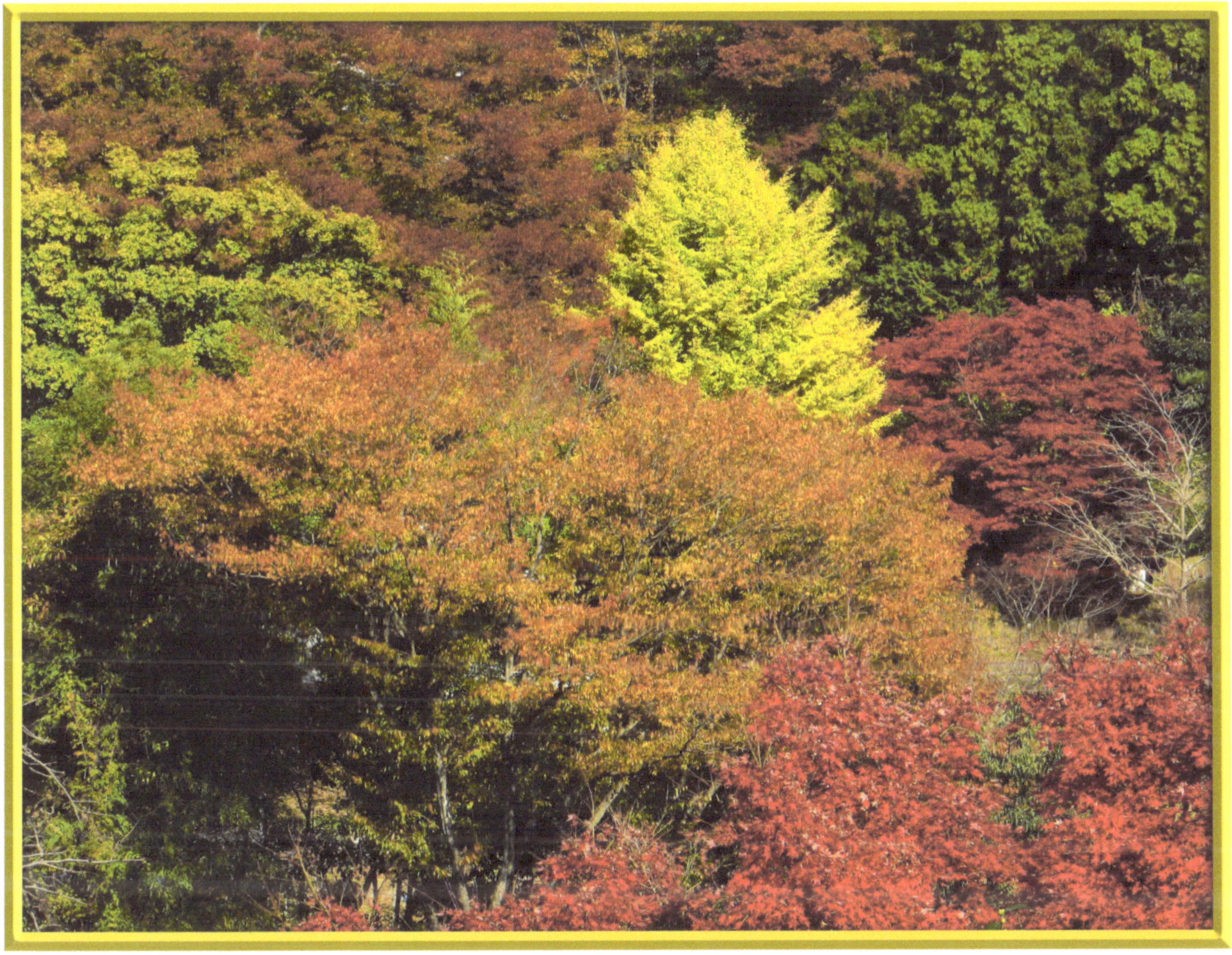

This photo was taken as we hiked towards the west from **Musashi-Itsukaichi Station** at the end of the **Itsukaichi Train Line**. This shows some pretty amazing color. You can get here from Tokyo by taking the **Chuo Train Line** from **Tokyo, Shinjuku** or another station, riding to **Tachikawa** and transferring to the **Ome Train Line** and then riding to **Haijima Station** and transferring to the **Itsukaichi Train Line**. There are city buses which take you west, but then you will be forced to merely take photos from the bus windows, so it's better to walk west during the time of good light and then take a bus back to the station when you get tired.

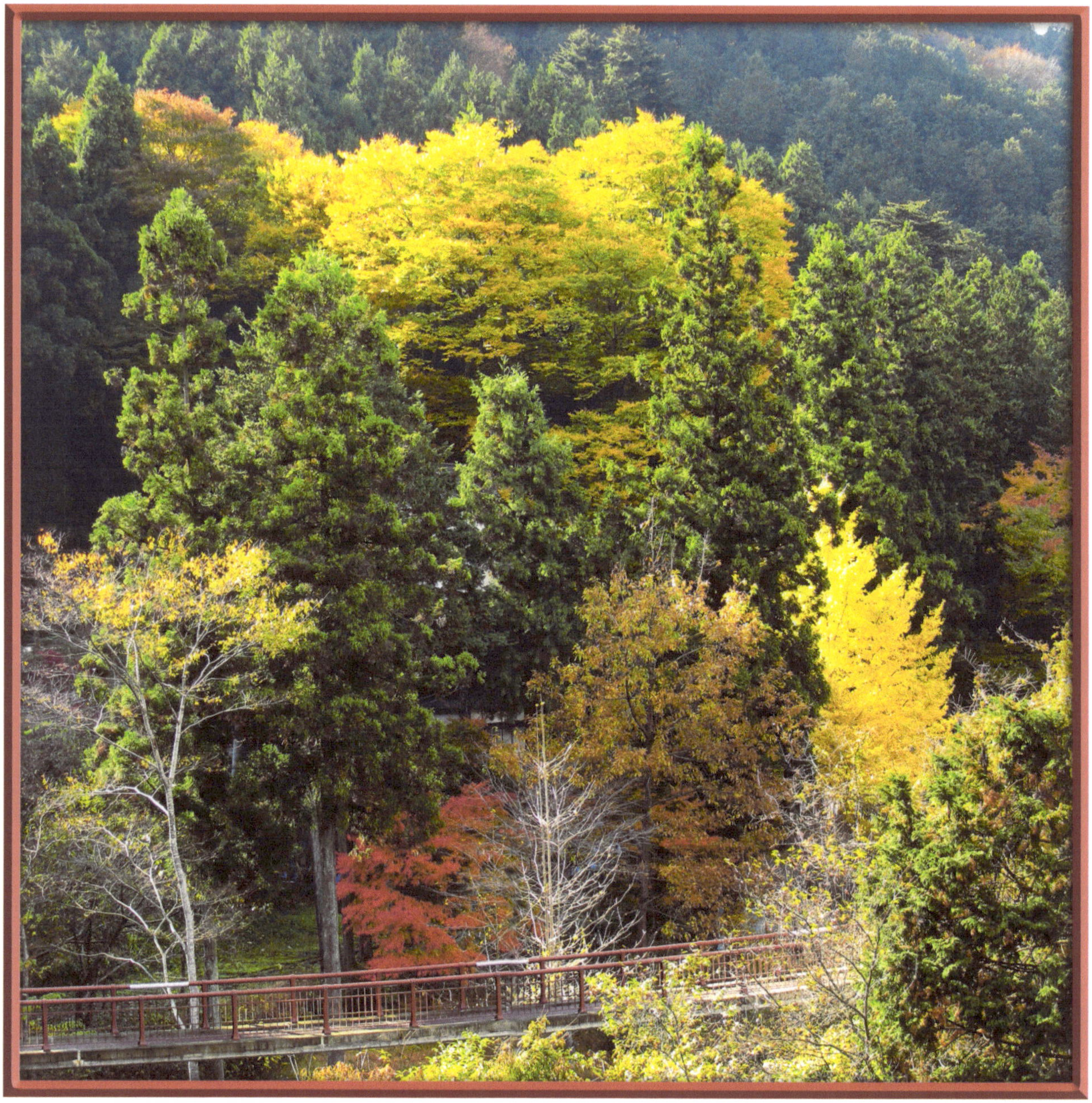

This photo was also taken as we hiked towards the west from **Musashi-Itsukaichi Station** at the end of the **Itsukaichi Train Line**. The footbridge shown in this photo leads to a Hot Spring. The image shown here consists of two portrait-mode photos which have been stitched together to create this panorama.

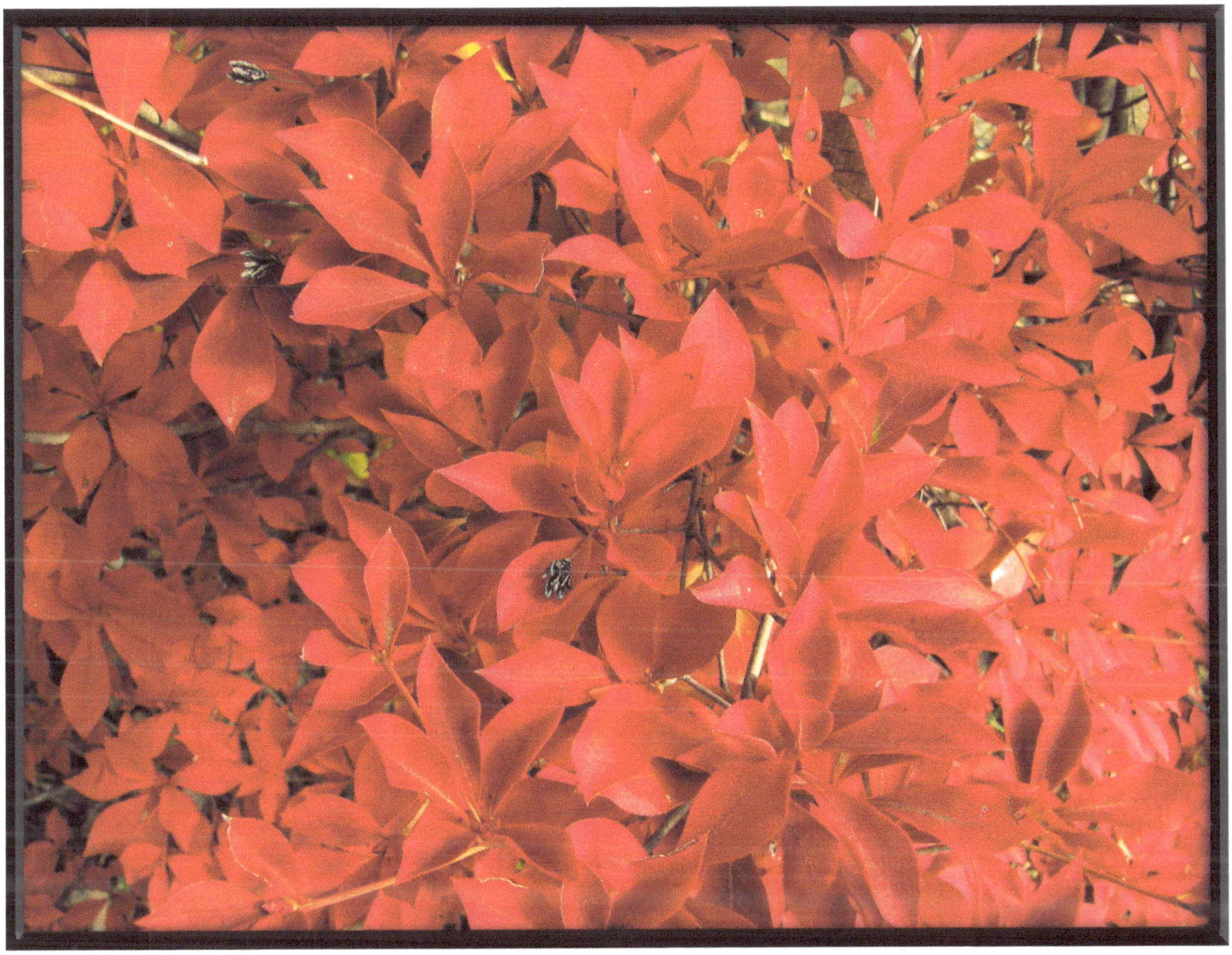

Back on page 282 we showed you a photo of what we called "The Burning Bush", well, that one actually pales in comparison to this one – another **"Burning Bush"**! This was taken very close to home – just a fifteen minute bicycle ride away – in **Nogawa Park**.

It was November 21st and the colors were beginning to peak right here in the Tokyo area. We are not sure what kind of bush this is, but the colors were so brilliant that this photo cannot be left out of any exhibit of autumn colors.

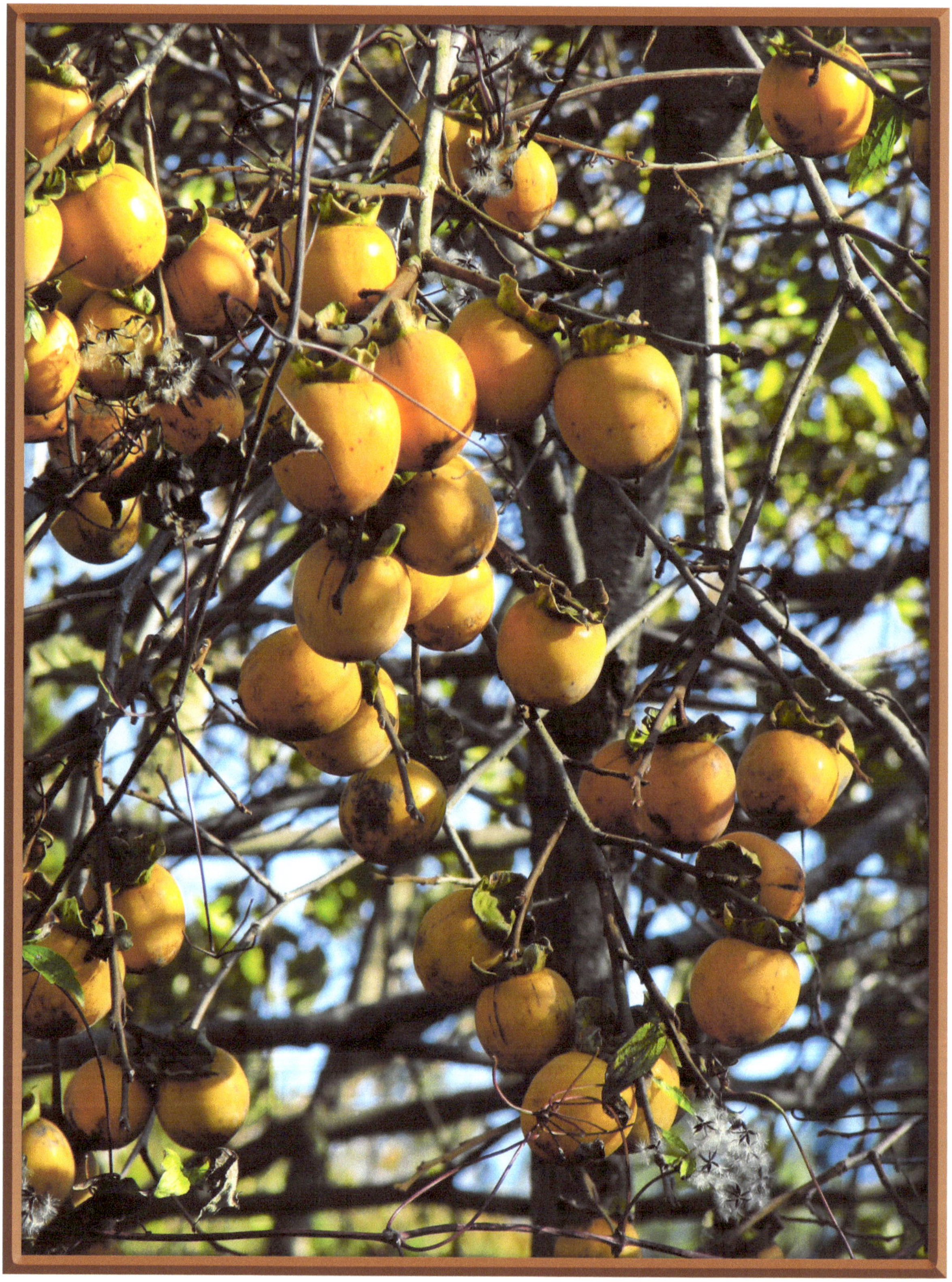

For the facing page photo, of ripe **Persimmon Fruits** (***Diospyros*** **sp.**) we went to **Mt. Kobotoke-Shiro** (670 meters = 2,199 feet), near **Mt. Takao**. Although there are many persimmon trees in Japan, it is so difficult to find one which does not have a house, electric wires or something else unappealing behind it. It is very difficult to find one which is photogenic.

The photo just below on this page highlights a very small branch on a **Red Maple tree**. This small branch just happens to be illuminated by the bright sun at this particular moment in time. Of course just a moment or two later the effect was gone as the sun and the shadows shifted. We were fortunate to have been at this spot at this precise moment in time.

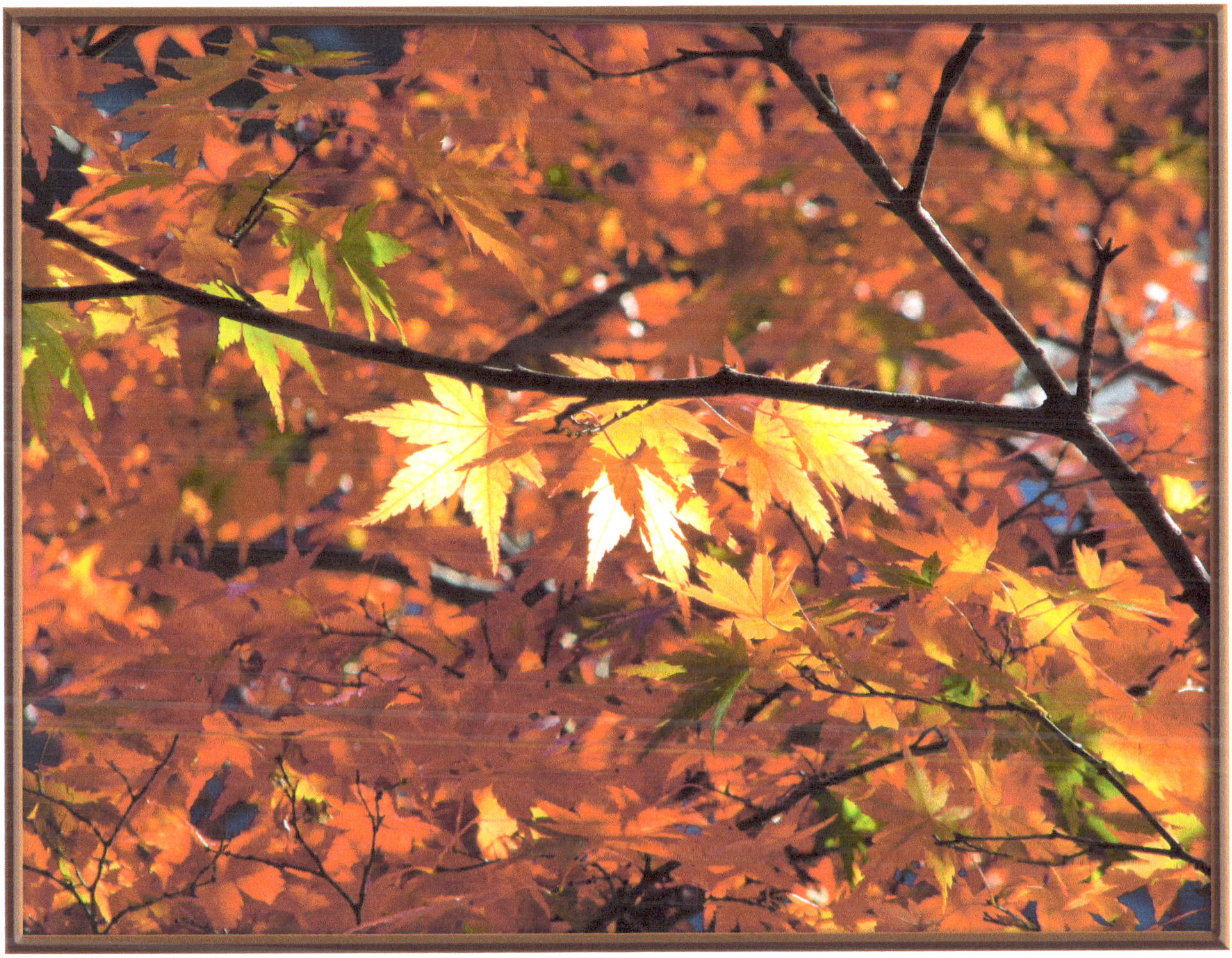

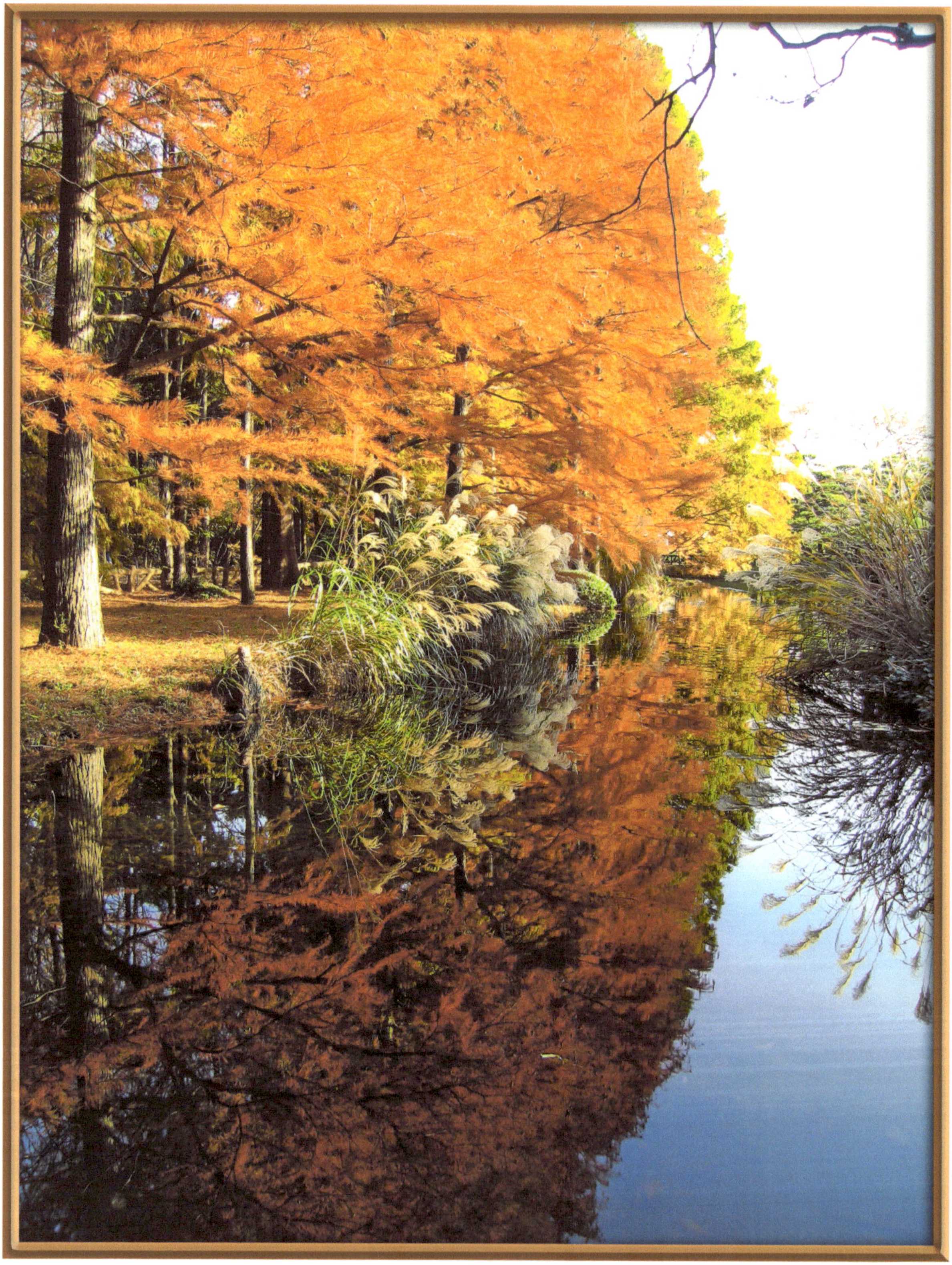

The facing page photo was taken at **Jindai Botanical Garden** in late November and shows the brick-red colors of the **Metasequoia** (***Metasequoia glyptostroboides***) trees and their reflection in the pond. There is also a small patch of **Susuki Grass** (***Miscanthus sinensis***) to add some variety. These trees become brick-red like this every year, but they don't always become this brilliant so as to be practically orange.

The photo on this page is of the same trees, but it was taken in a different year and, obviously, from a different location; it was shot from the right side of the pond shown in the previous shot. The contrast of the green needles of the pine trees and the brick-red of the Metasequoia trees came out very nicely in this photo. You'll note that this year the Metasequoia trees are not as brilliant as they were in the photo on the previous page.

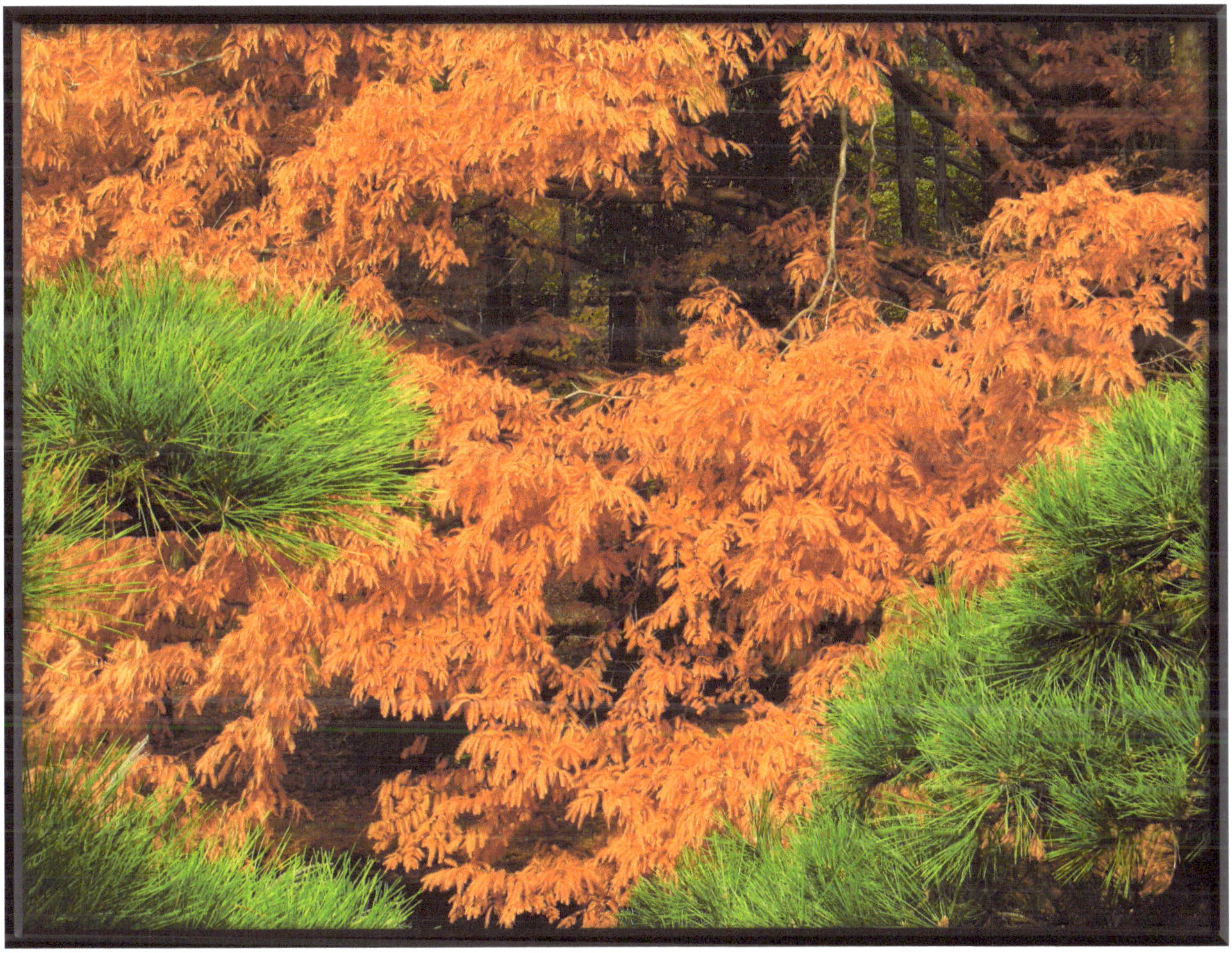

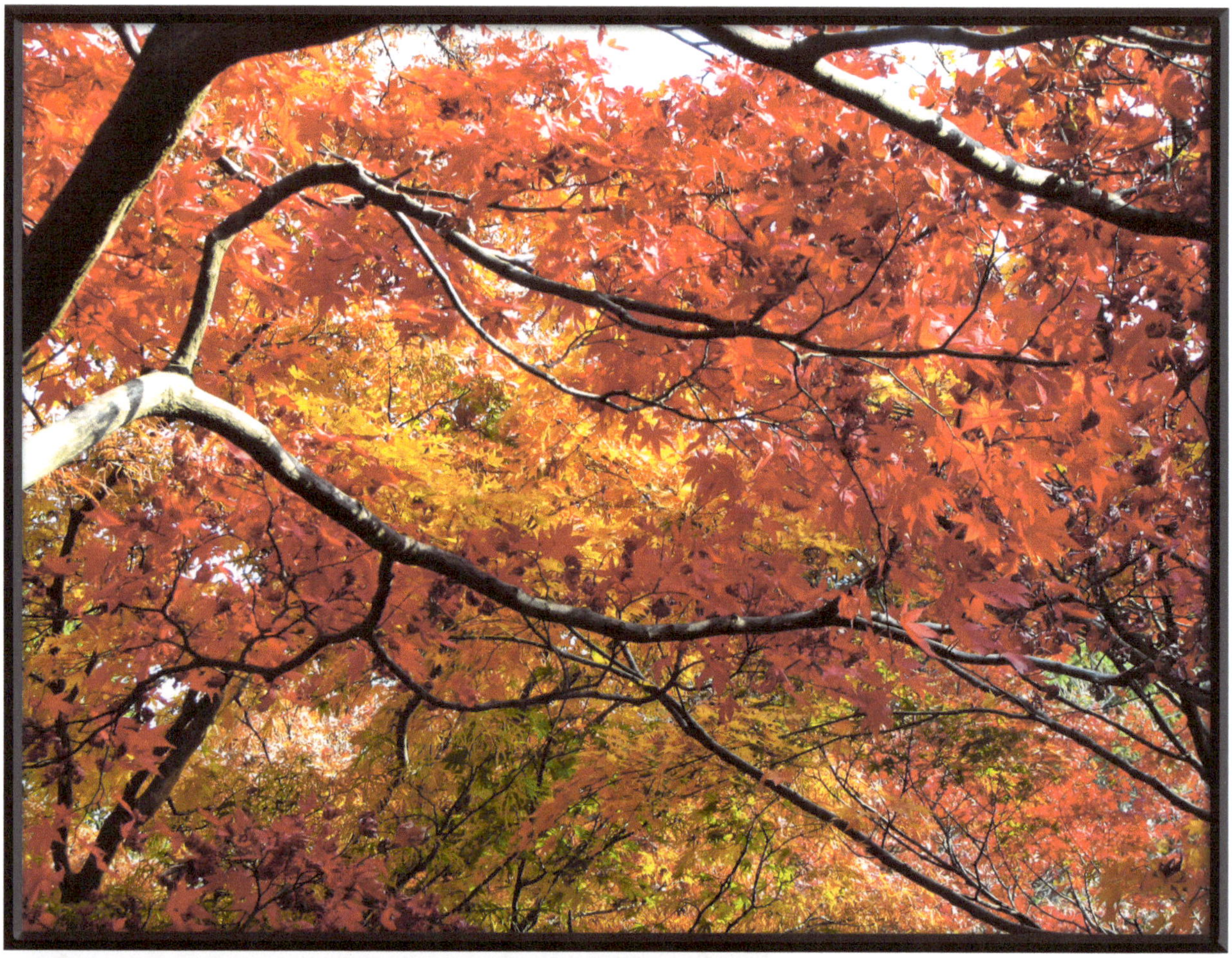

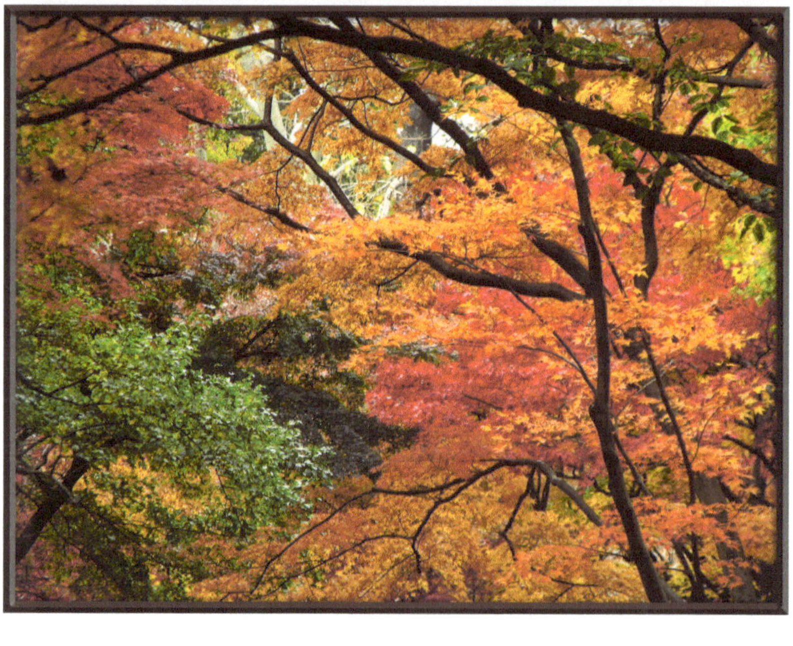

The photos on this page were also taken at **Jindai Botanical Garden** – in their **Maple Garden**. The Maple Garden has many maple trees, as the name implies, and they can range in color from green through brilliant red and orange. Note the green in the lower photo. Virtually every color of the spectrum can be found in this area of the Botanical Garden. It is amazing to see.

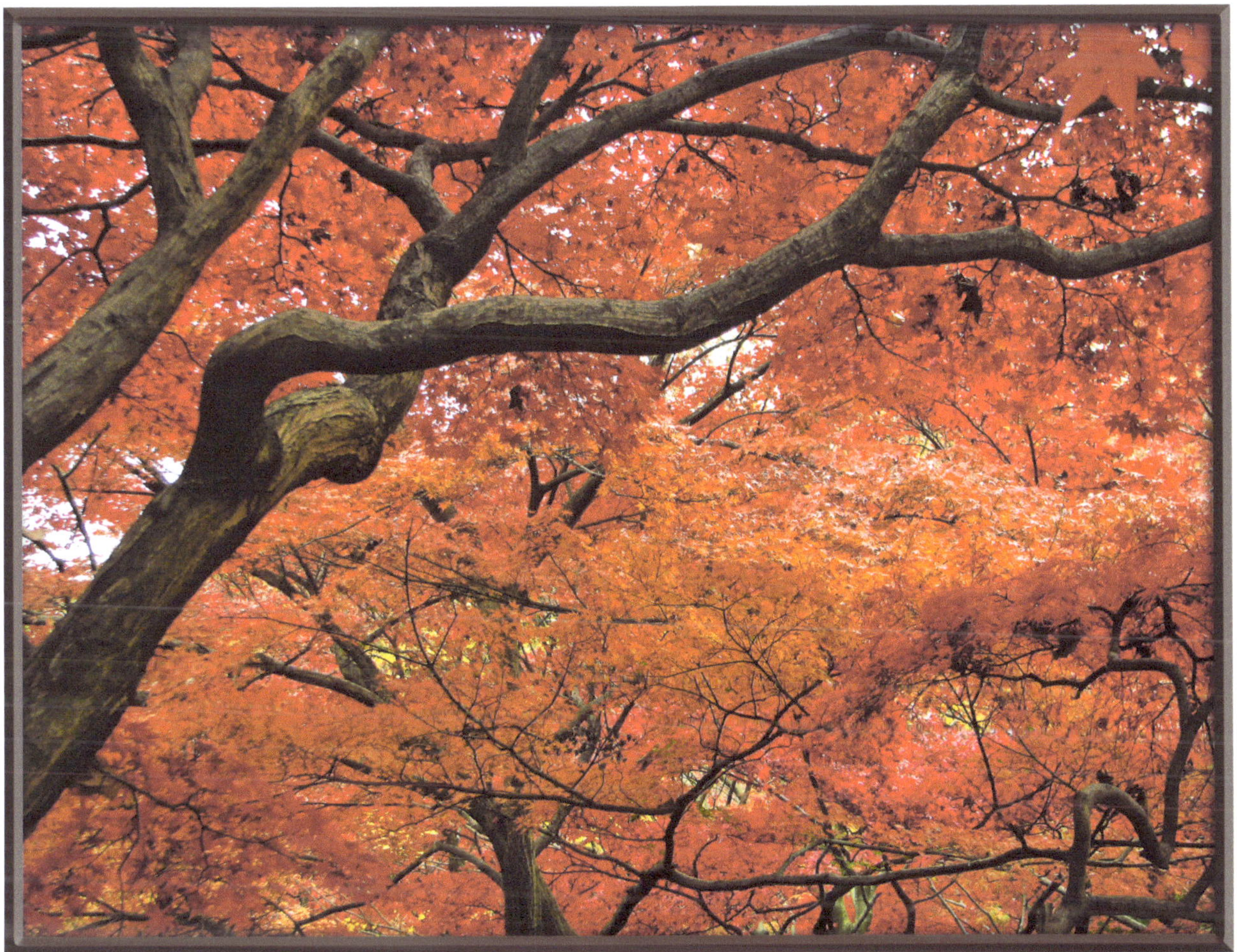

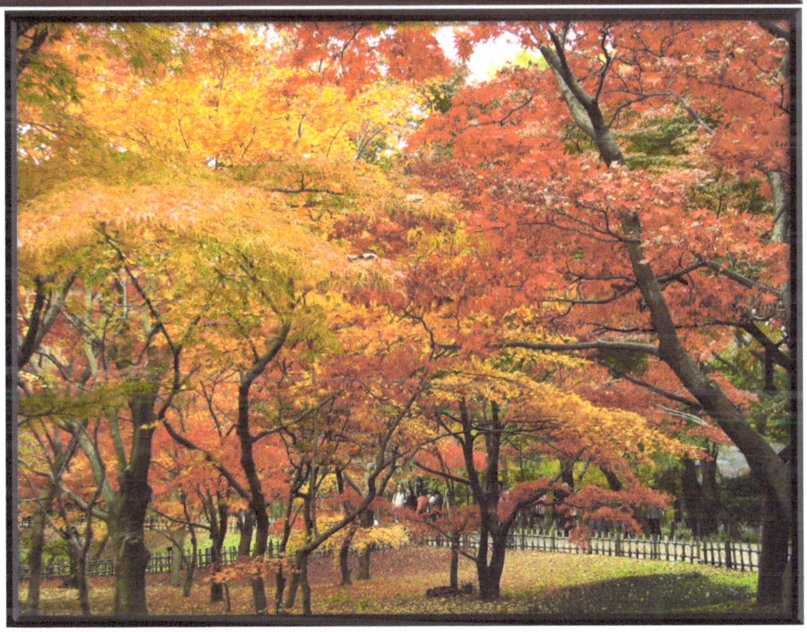

Here are two more photos from the Maple Garden of **Jindai Botanical Garden**. You may be able to tell that the upper photo was taken on a cloudy day, and despite that handicap – the colors are still brilliant.

This lower photo includes some people so that you have something to judge the scale of everything.

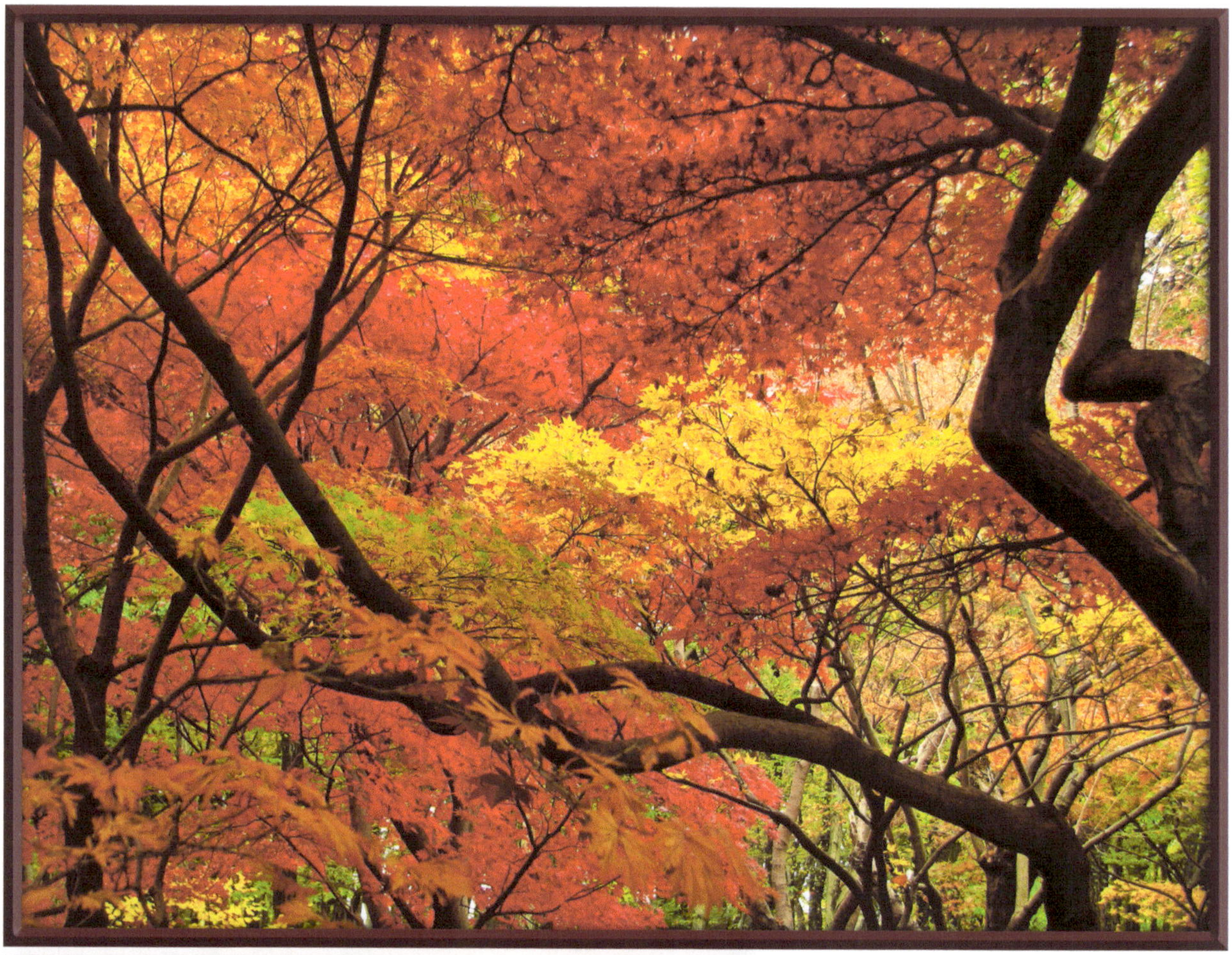

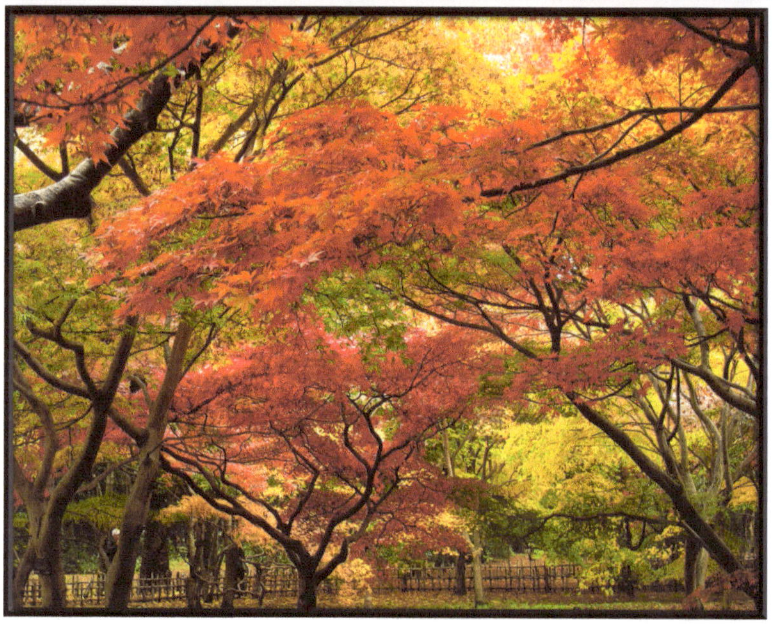

Here are the final two shots taken in the Maple Garden of **Jindai Botanical Garden**. We hope that this convinces you that if you are ever on Tokyo in November that you should search for Jindai Botanical Garden and then proceed to the Maple Garden portion. The earlier in the day you can arrive, the better it will be, as this area gets shady in early afternoon.

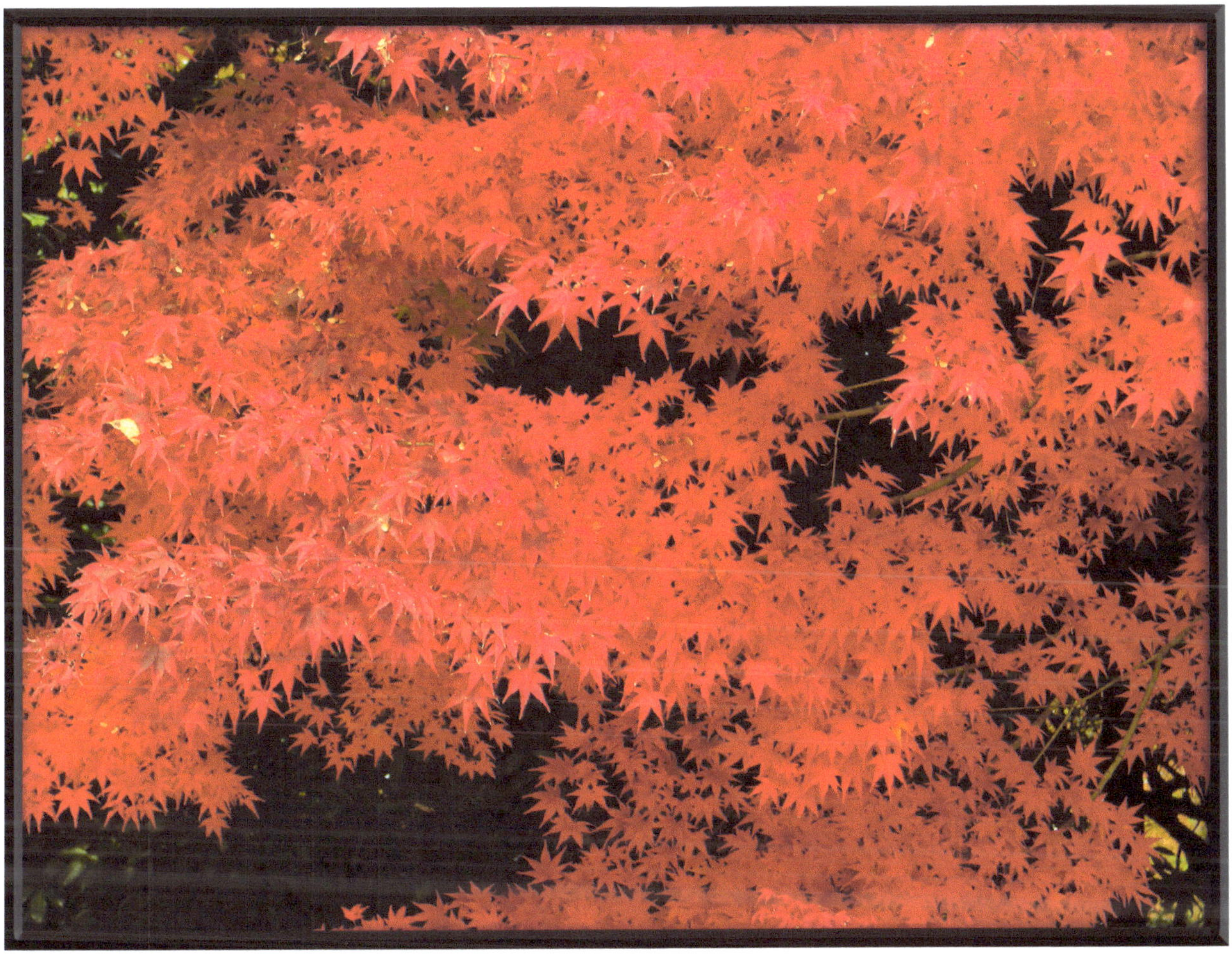

This amazing photo was taken in a very small park in **Chofu City**, on the west side of Tokyo. We could not believe how brilliant of a red color this single tree was. It was just so incredible. We happened to find this on our way to Jindai Botanical Garden via a rather roundabout route, a route which we seldom travel, but for some reason we decided to bicycle this route on this date. We were pleased that we did.

Here are the final two photos from November. The upper one was taken at **Tonogayato Garden** in **Kokubunji**, on the west side of **Tokyo**. It is a goldfish in a pond with a few Red Maple leaves floating around.

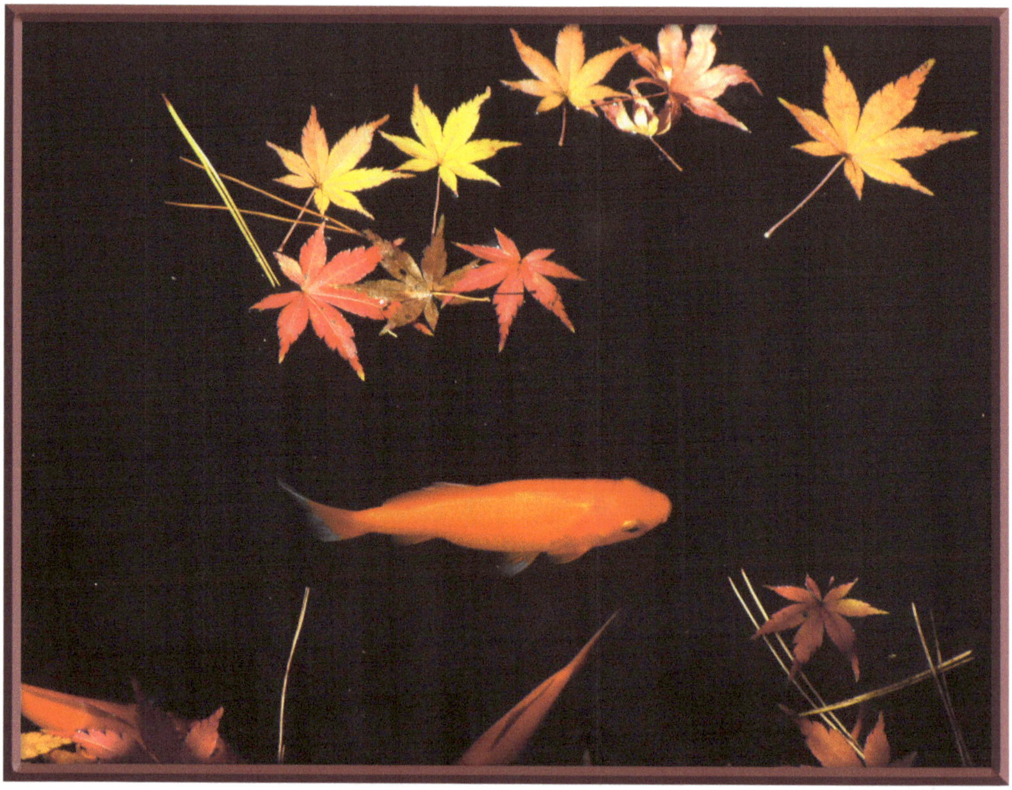

The lower shot was taken near our apartment house and it shows a colorful residential street.

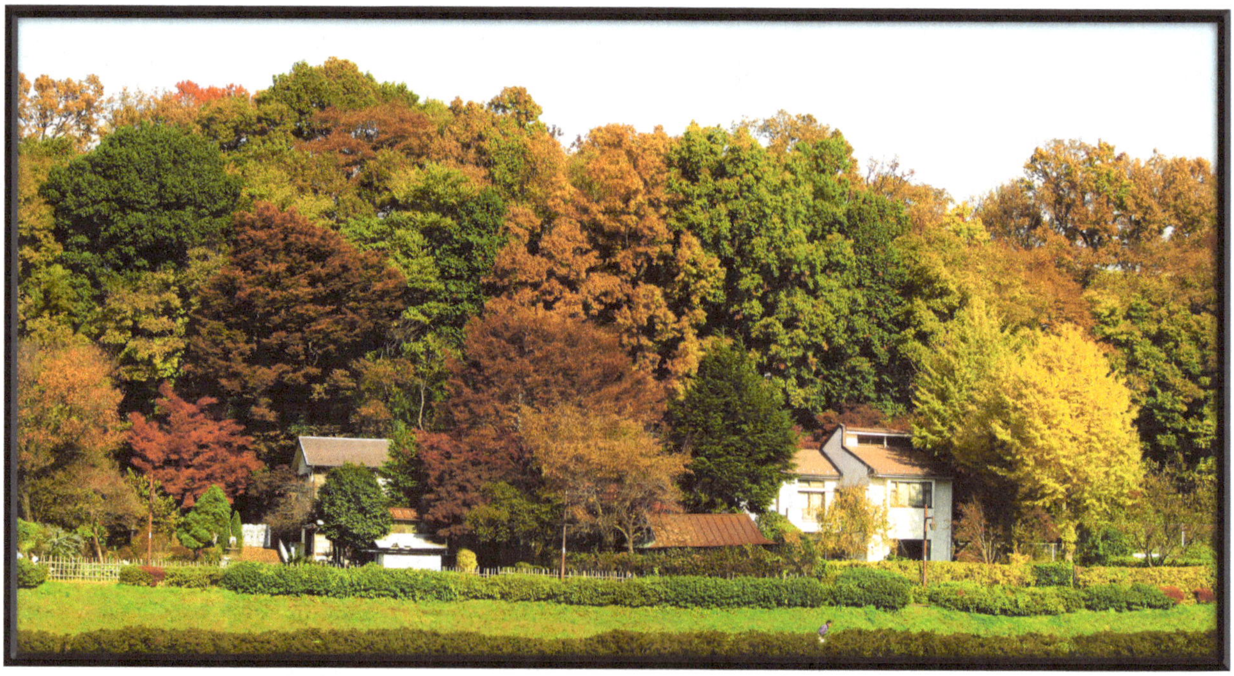

December Photos and Story

Here we enter the final month of the year and we have only selected thirteen photos from December which we have taken through the years that we want to show you, so we will wrap up this month pretty quickly. Virtually all of the photos which we have to show you which were taken during December through the years are of final autumn color. Hopefully you enjoy seeing autumn colors.

This photo immediately below shows a lily seedhead on a bright sunny day. This was taken at **Nogawa Park** – that's the park where we can easily go to on bicycle. We are able to see many seedheads like this one and they are persistent even into very late winter. We have sometimes even collected them and brought them home to use as winter decorations in bud vases.

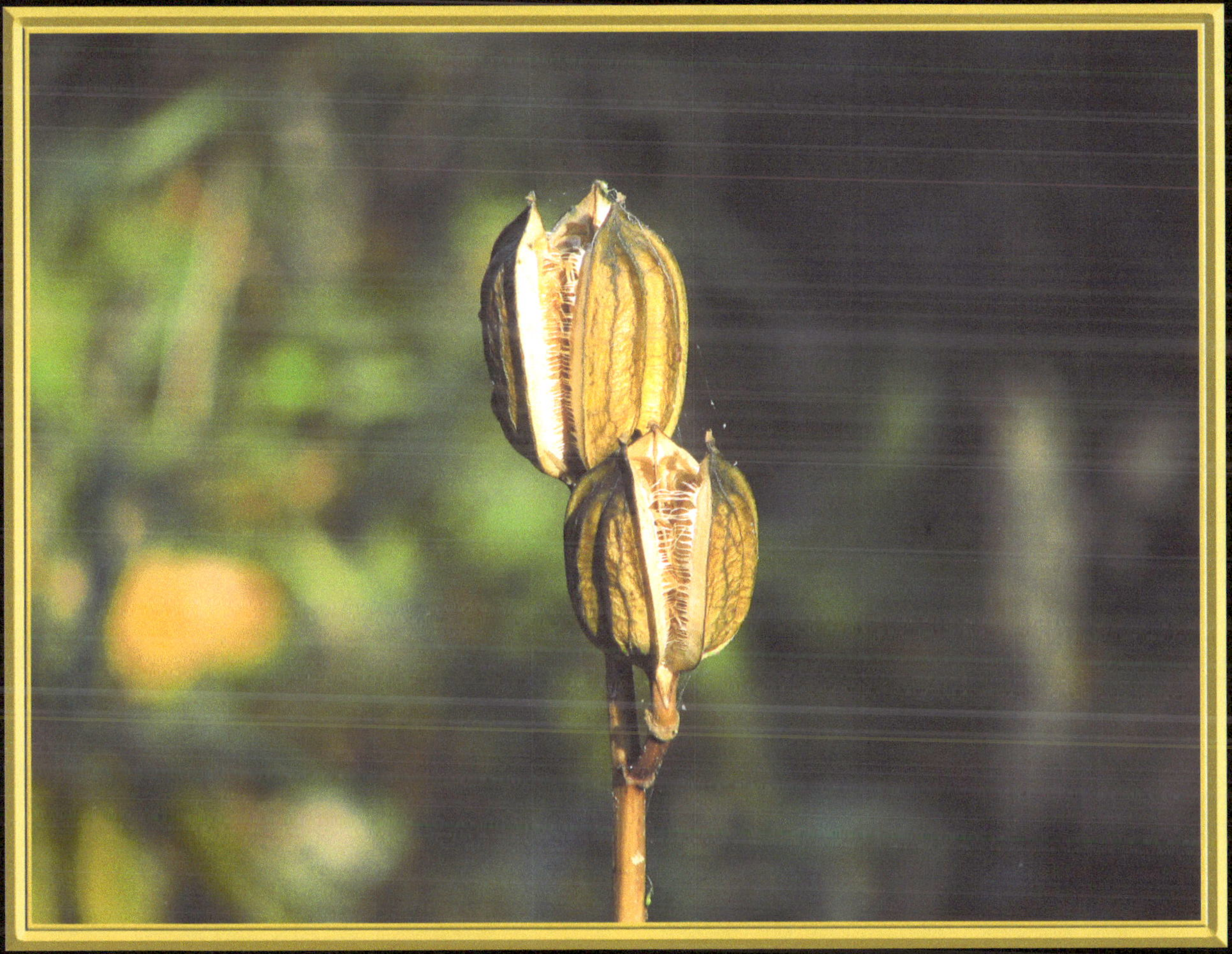

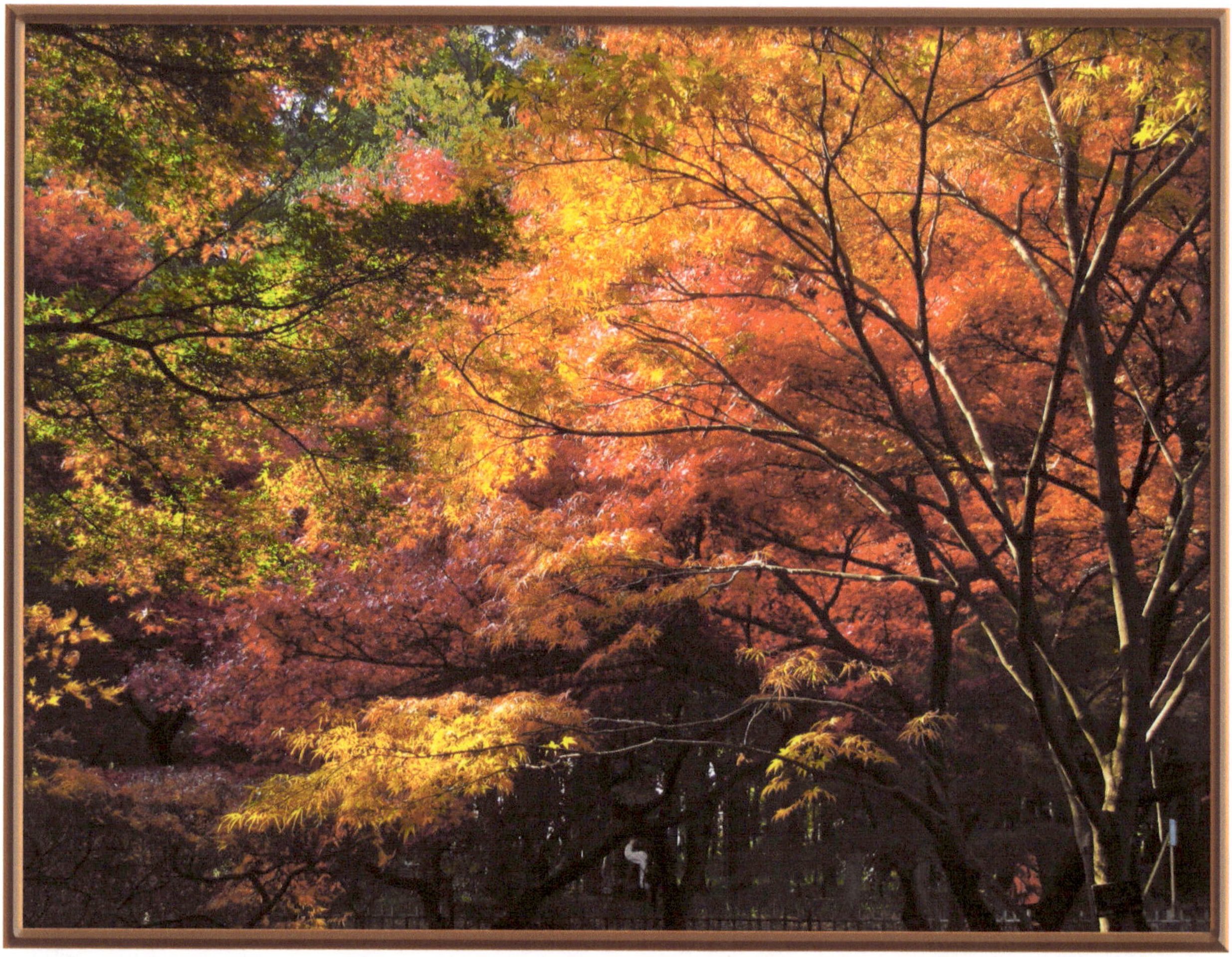

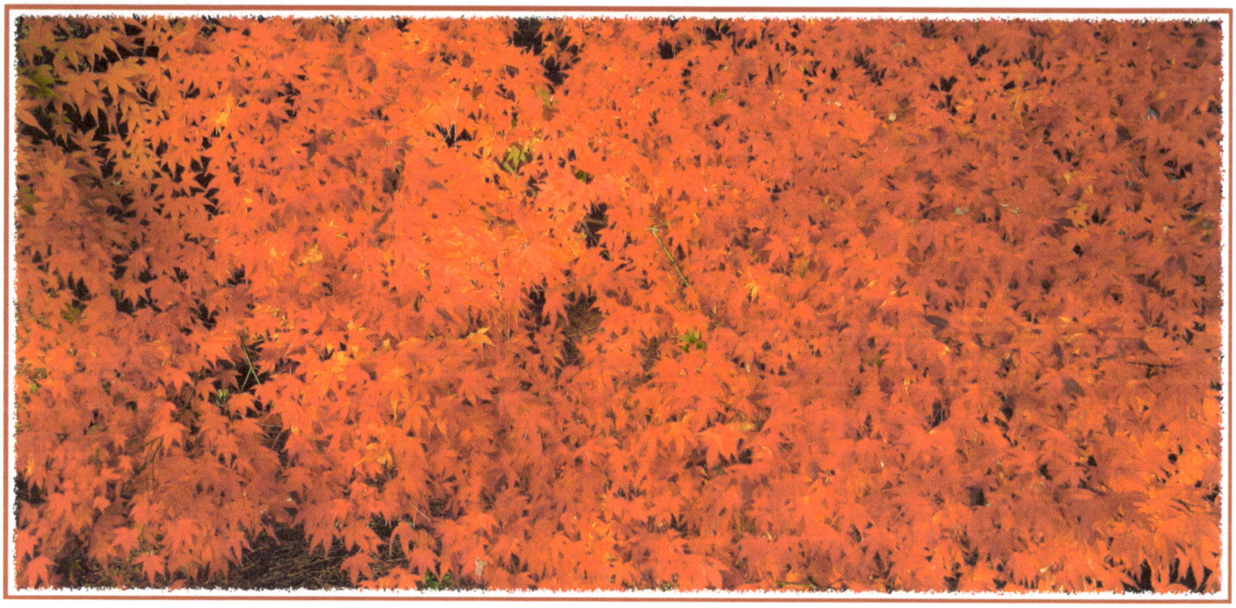

The two photos on the facing page were taken one year at **Jindai Botanical Garden** in the **Maple Garden** in December. Some years the fall colors come later than they do in other years. It all depends on the date of the first good freeze in combination with the photoperiod (hours of daylight). If the first good freeze is too late and the days are already too short then there will not be good colors at all. If the first hard freeze is early then we will most likely have some wonderful autumn colors. We never know what will happen.

The below photo, also taken in **Jindai Botanical Garden** shows some very stunning colors. This was the only year we have ever seen these three trees with good color. So, if you visit Jindai Botanical Garden in November or December and happen to notice these three trees, do not be totally surprised if they do not exhibit colors such as this. This photo was actually taken in 2007 – you can research the weather records for that year if you have the intense interest to do so. Apparently we had a hard frost at precisely the proper time.

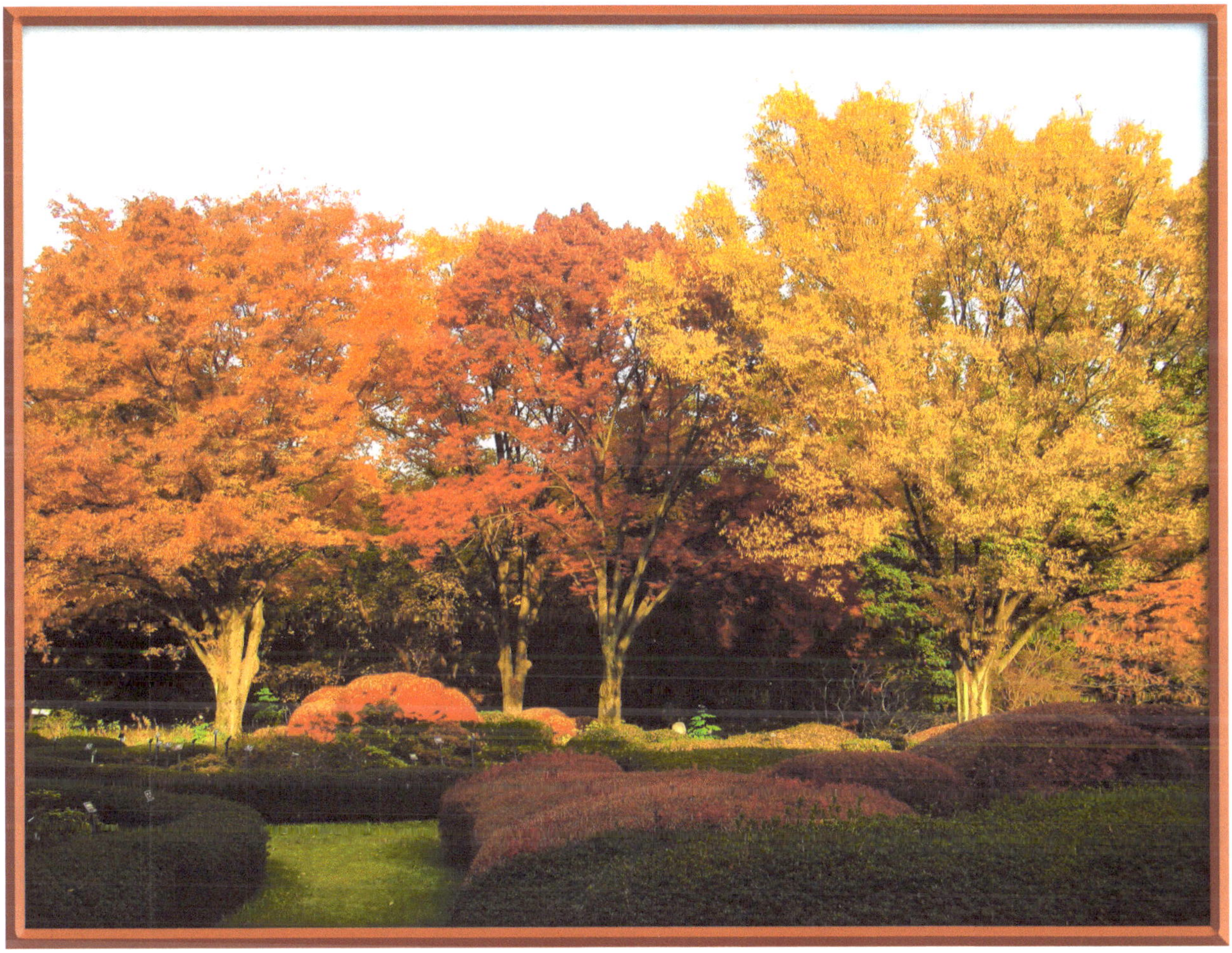

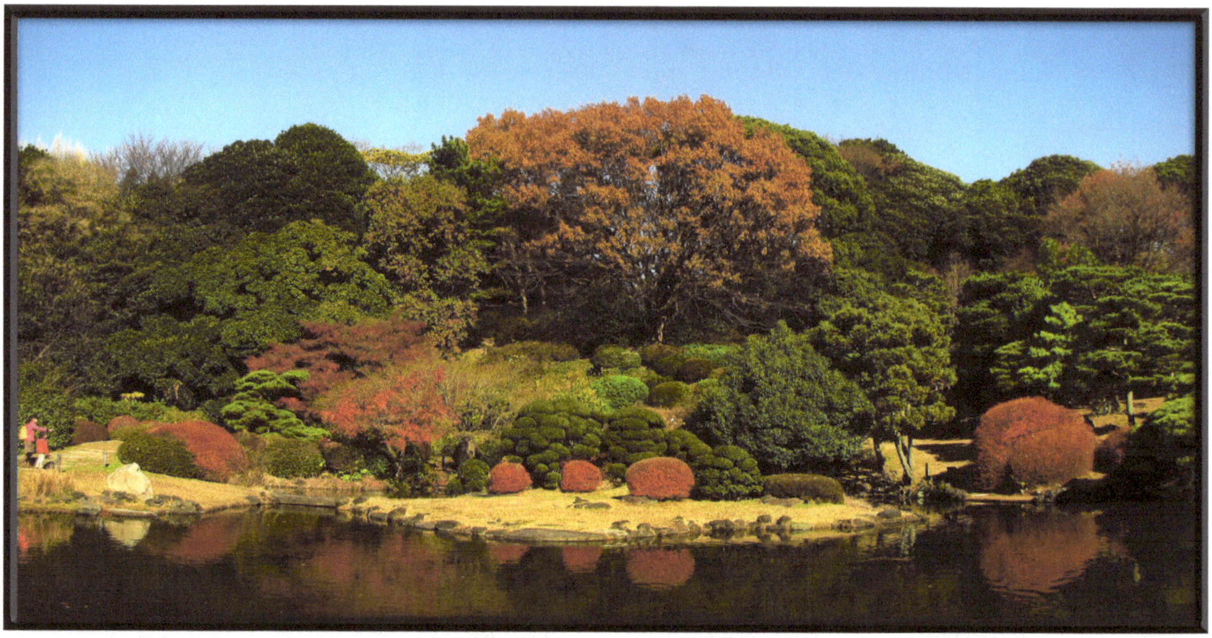

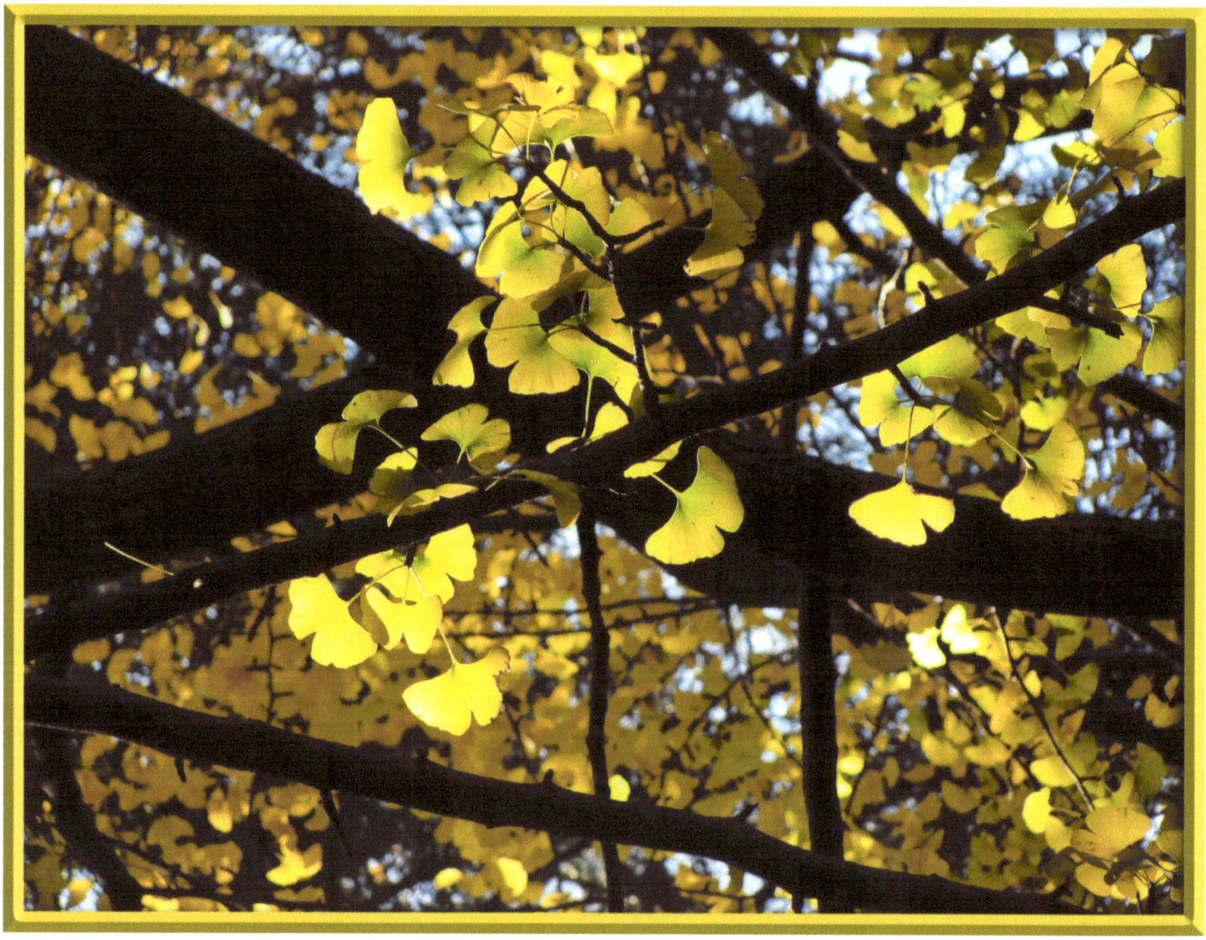

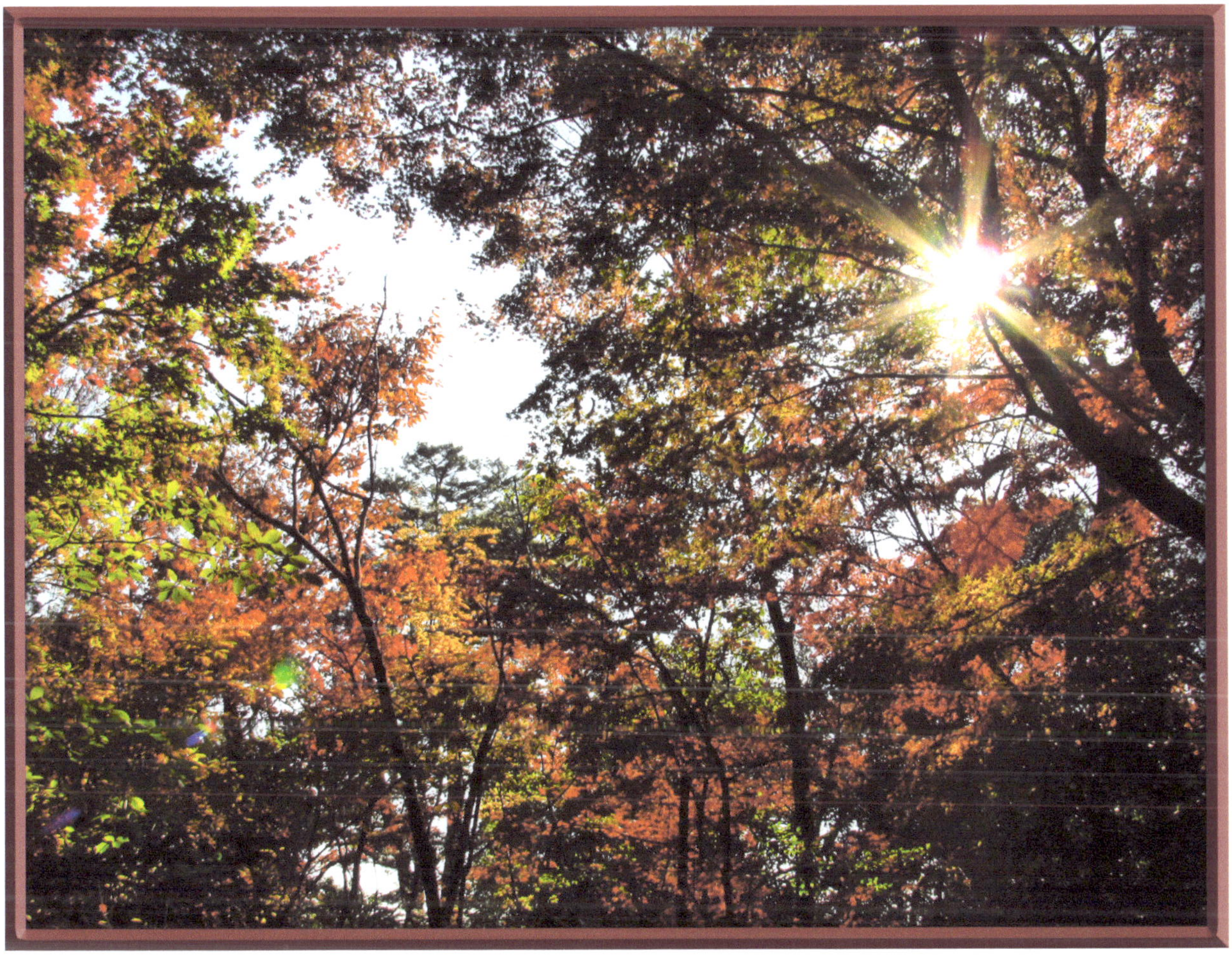

On the facing page in top position is a two shot panorama of the pond area at **Koishikawa Botanical Garden**. This Botanical Garden is run by **Tokyo University** and is quite large. It is a very nice place to go in all seasons – for various flowers in the spring and summer, and then in the autumn for the colors.

In the lower position on the facing page is a nice shot of colorful ***Ginkgo biloba*** leaves which was taken at **Sourousenen** (**Sourousen Garden**) in **Kokubunji**, on the west side of Tokyo.

The photo on this page was taken at the same place – **Sourousenen** (**Sourousen Garden**) and exhibits a beautiful sun phenomenon. We never use any kind of filters or any imaging software to achieve this effect – we always manage to find it naturally. This is not the first time you have seen this star effect in our photos (pages 143 and 212).

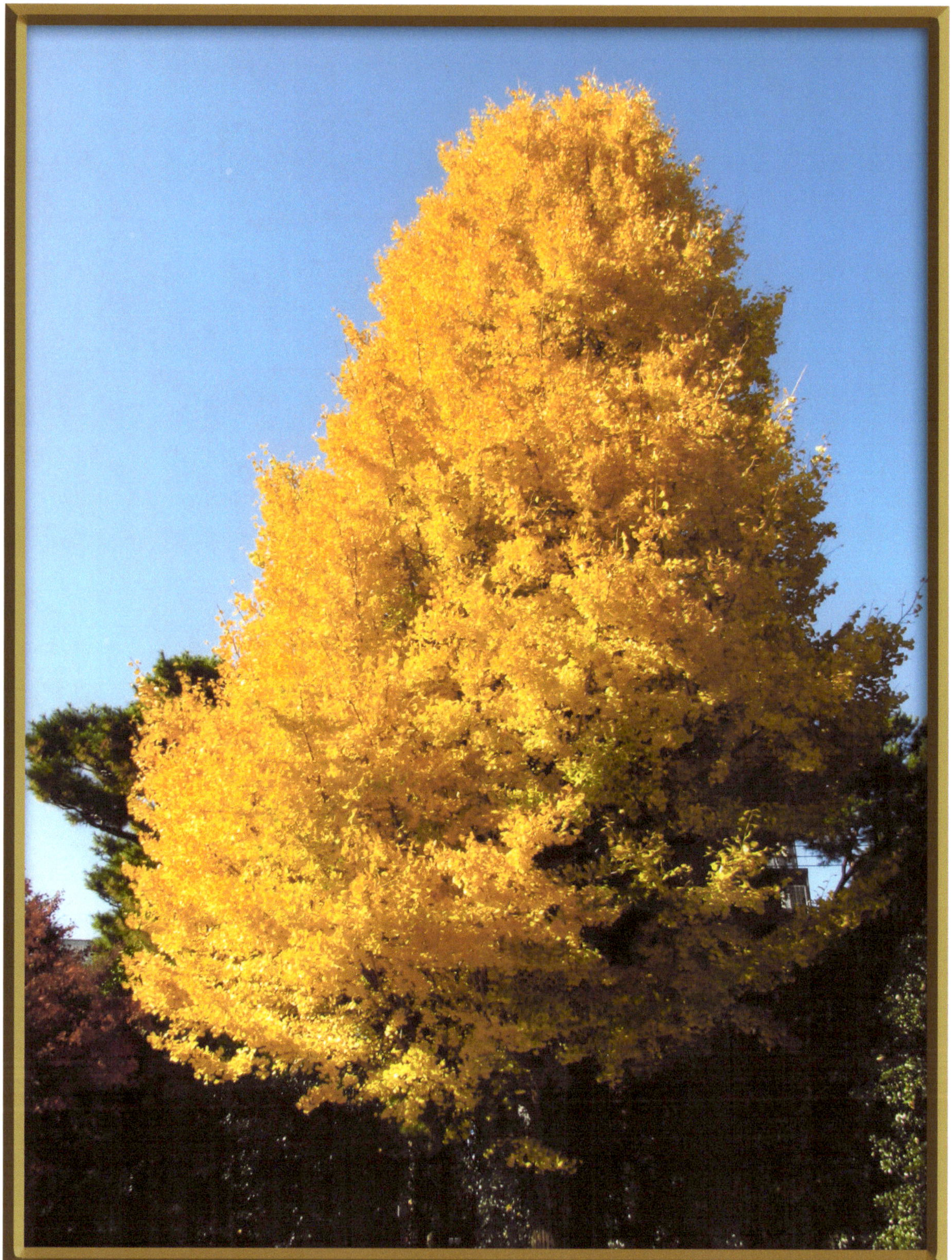

You may be able to guess that the facing page photo is the brilliant yellow of another ***Ginkgo biloba*** tree. This shot was taken at **Tonogayato Garden** in **Kokubunji**. This photo was taken in a different year than the one shown on page 328, which was taken in November.

The right photo on this page was taken at our local **Nogawa Park** – obviously the reflection of brilliant Red Maple leaves on a pond.

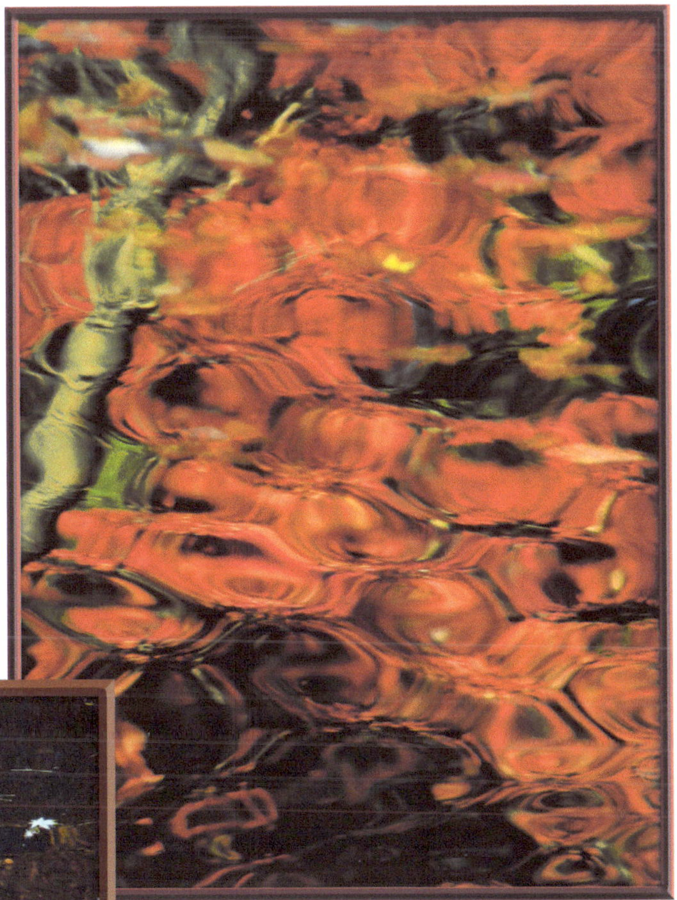

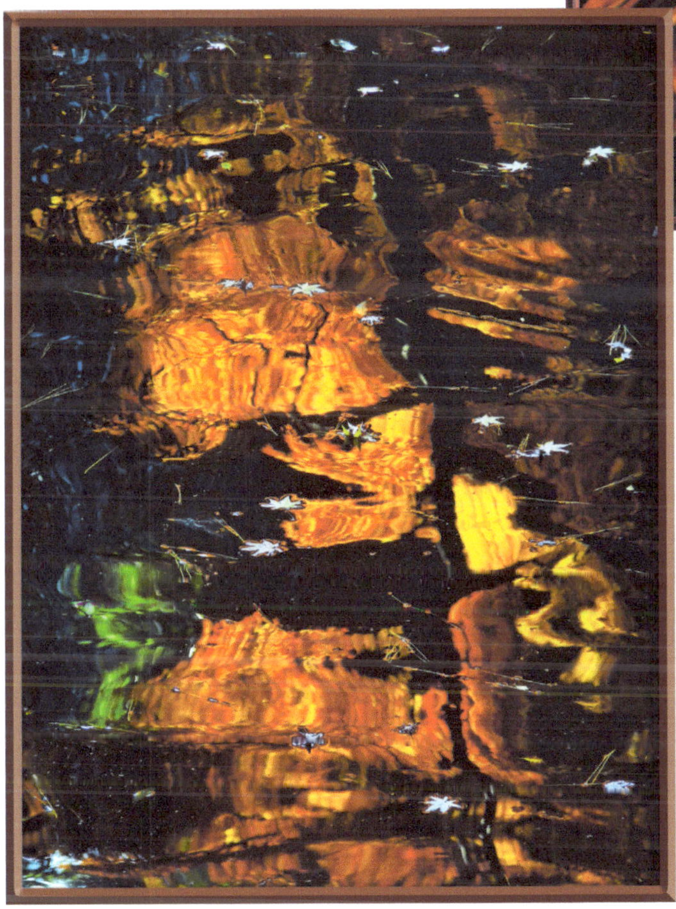

The photo to the left was shot at **Tonogayato Garden** in **Kokubunji**. It is the reflection of an amazingly orange maple tree on the water of a pond. You may notice some weird silver colored leaves floating on the surface of the pond. We are not sure why they appear to be silver in color, it was an accident of lighting, the effect was not achieved with imaging software or anything else.

We very rarely get good results when we try taking these reflection shots. We were quite pleased with these two shots. Hope you enjoy them too.

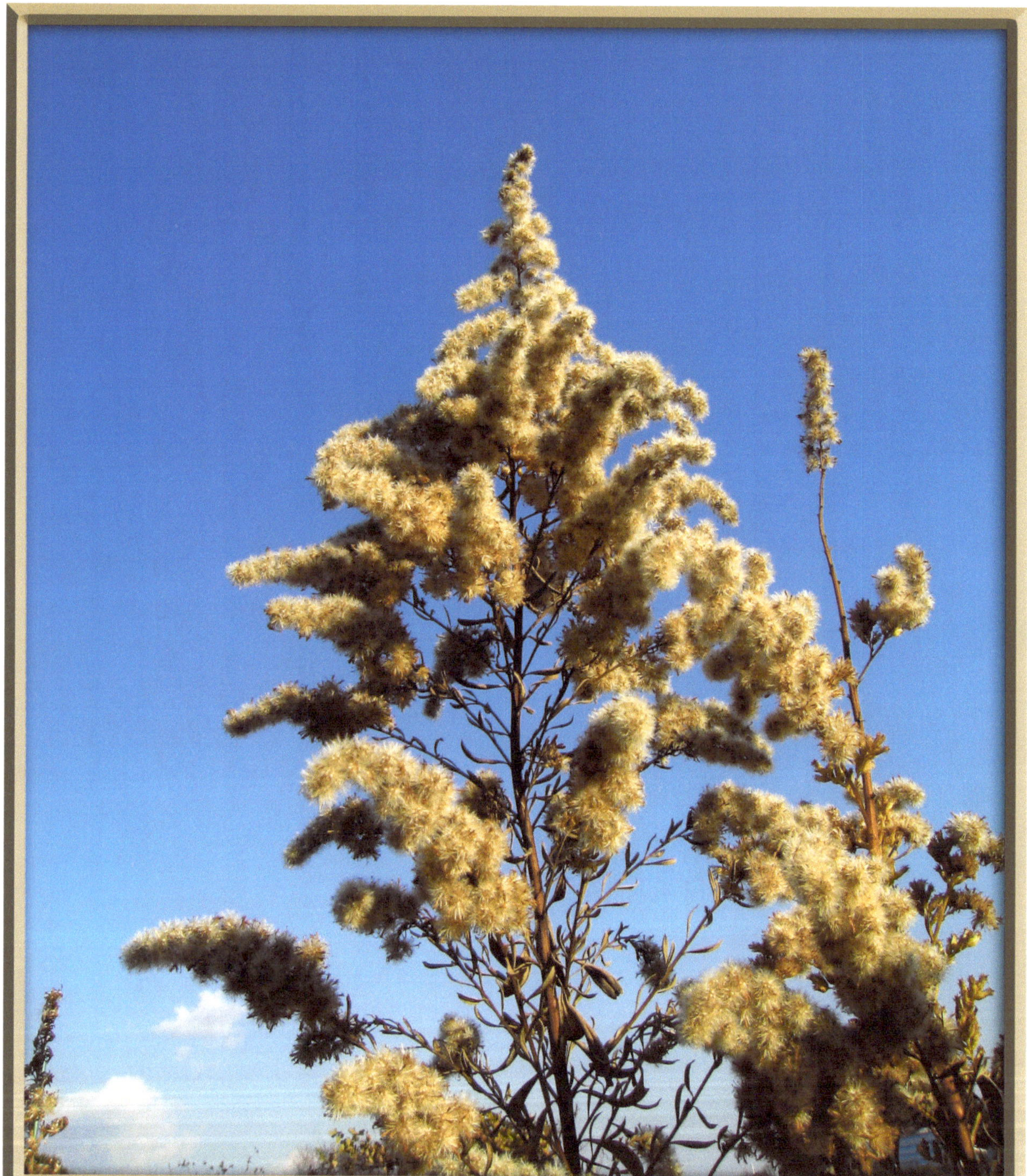

Here is a very late fall **Goldenrod** plant. This was taken along the **Tama River** not far from **Koremasa**, on the **Seibu Tama-gawa Train Line**.

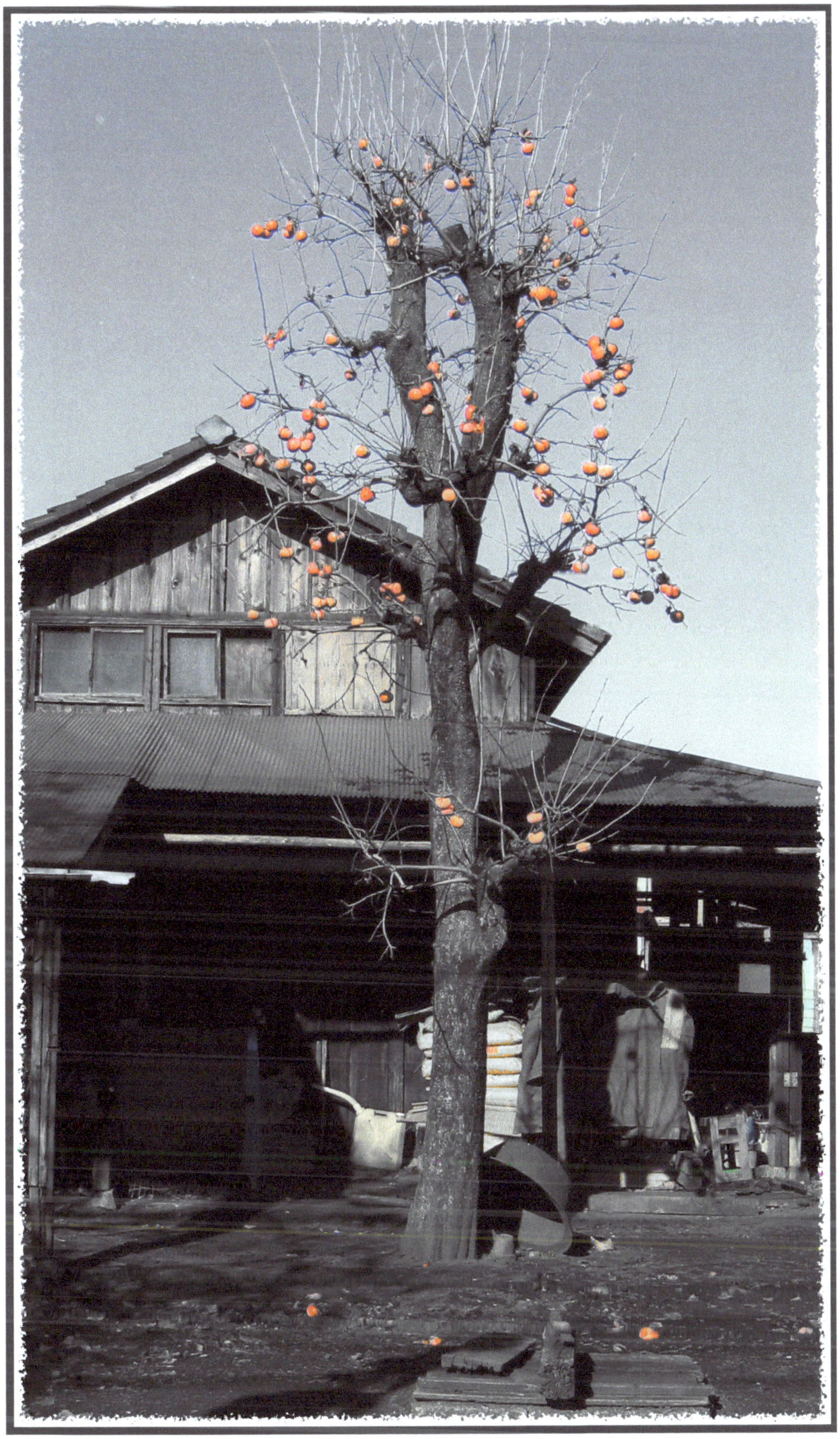

This is a Persimmon Tree (***Diospyros* sp.**) which was found growing in front of a picturesque old house. This was quite near our house. Obviously this photo was manipulated with imaging software to convert everything to grayscale except for the Persimmon fruits.

We are sorry to report that this tree is no longer here, it was cut down a couple of years after this photo was taken. It would not surprise us to see the house disappear one day soon too – to be replaced by something more modern and "plastic".

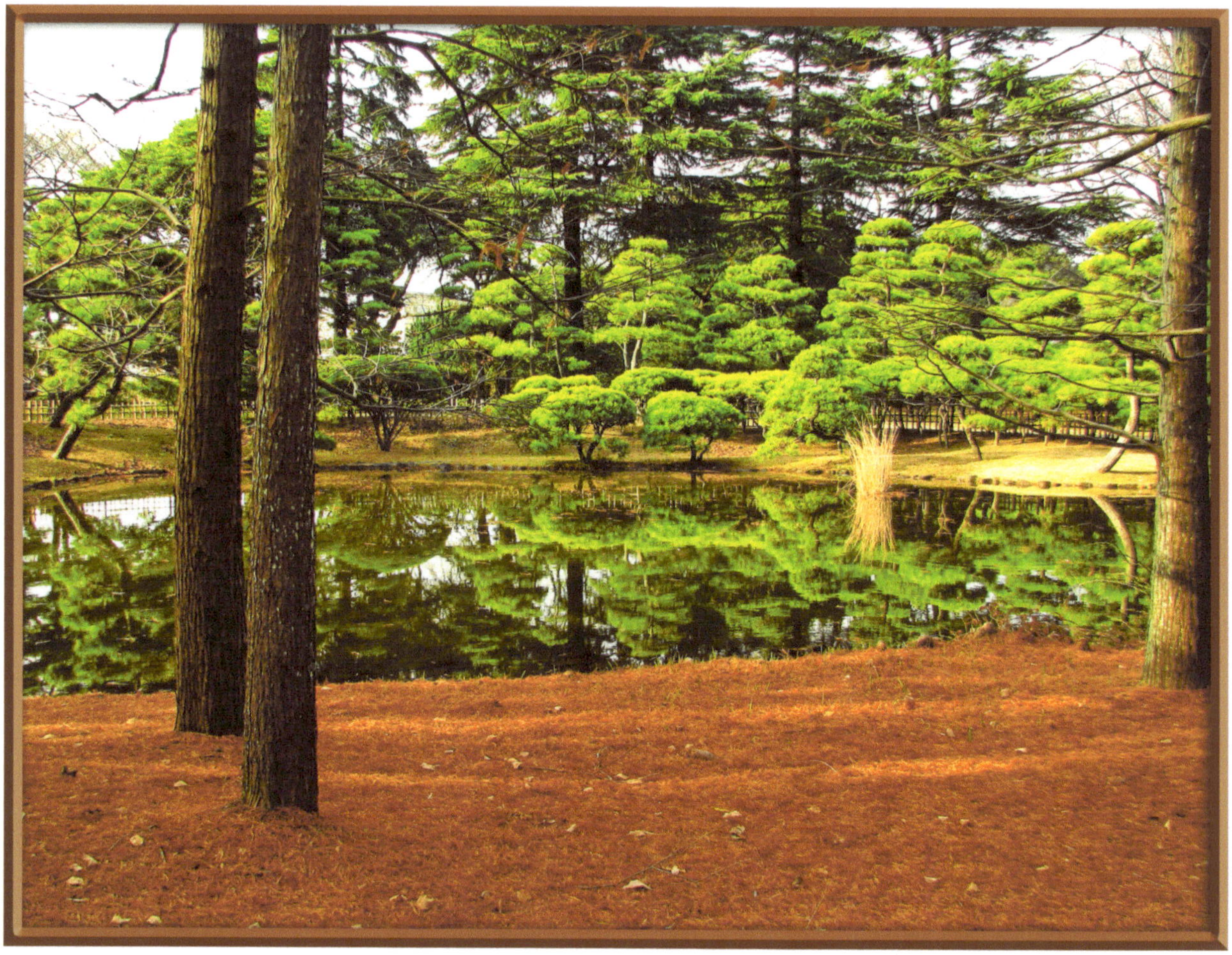

Here is the final photo of autumn – this photo was taken one year on December 19th. It is under the **Metasequoia** (*Metasequoia glyptostroboides*) trees at **Jindai Botanical Garden**. You saw the trees from which these needles fell back on pages 322 and 323. The photos on those two pages were taken from the opposite side of this pond and looking at the trees which you only see the trunks of in this photo. It is amazing that these needles can be so orange or brick-red.

We hope that you have enjoyed your tour of the areas of Japan which we have taken you to in these several pages. For more photos you can take a tour of our respective websites – http://www.danwiz.com is Daniel's website and Kazuya's can be found at:
http://studiesofplantsandwildlife.blogspot.com
or alternately:
http://www2.blogger.com/profile/02622643778290337101. If you are reading this several years after it is published we cannot guarantee that these websites will still exist, but as long as we live we hope to maintain them. You can also contact us through our respective websites. There is an e-mail link on http://www.danwiz.com. You can leave a comment on Kazuya's Blog and ask him to contact you.

AFTERWORD

As this book is having the finishing touches put on it in April, 2011 – just a few short weeks after the **March 11, 2011 "Great Eastern Japan Earthquake"**, we feel that we should include a couple of words about this terrible happening. We are okay and everybody we know came out of the experience okay, but the nuclear problems persist and we wonder if and hope that they will be solved without killing all of us. We hope that the people who lost their homes, family members, fishing boats, businesses and so on can keep fighting to keep going and maintain their hope and courage as their problems are very slowly solved.

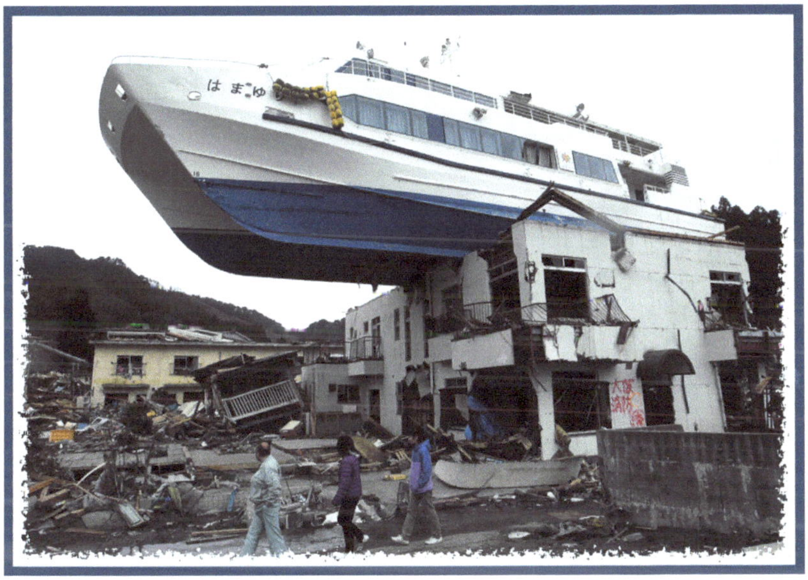

We do not own this photo, but it kind of says it all.

This one says even more – maybe you cannot read the tiny name of the person to whom this image is credited. The name down there in the right corner is Vicente Valentine.

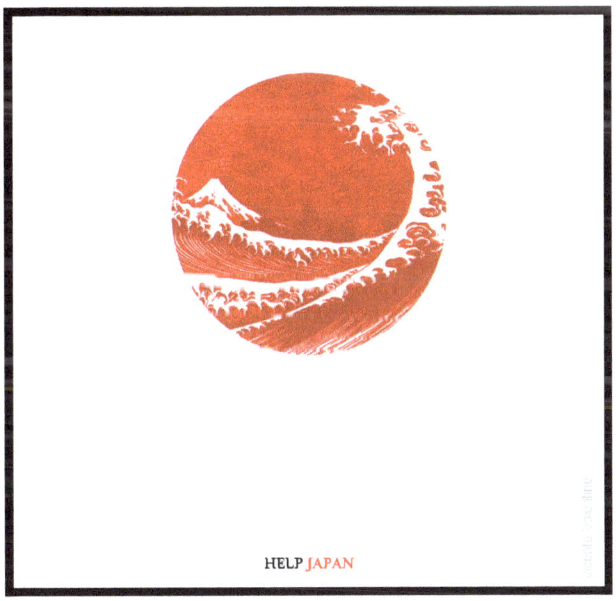

The End

Index

ABOUT THE AUTHORS

Daniel Wieczorek was born in 1947 in Ionia, Michigan. He graduated from the University of Michigan with a B.S. in Forestry in 1969. He moved to Oregon to work in the field of forestry in 1971. That was followed by a move to Alaska in 1975, where he continued his career in forestry. After about a 14 year career in forestry, Daniel decided to do something different and he served as a Peace Corps Volunteer in The Philippines from 1985 – 1987. Upon completion of his Peace Corps service he returned to Alaska, where he attended the University of Alaska – Fairbanks and received an M.B.A. in 1991. This was followed by a move to South Korea in 1992, where Daniel taught English to Korean people wishing to improve their English Language skills. Daniel's next stop was in New York City, where he worked as temporary staff at Deutsche Bank from 1998 – 2001. He left NYC in March 2001 and moved on to his present home in Mitaka City, Tokyo, Japan. He is teaching English in Japan and at this time he's been teaching as a career for about 17 years. He has been hiking, climbing and doing photography since he was about 12 years old.

Kazuya Numazawa was born in 1979 in Shinjo in Yamagata Prefecture, Japan. He was raised in Funagata Town in Yamagata Prefecture. He graduated from Tokyo University in 2005. Since that time he has worked in several fields, but primarily in Cram Schools around the Mitaka Area.

Daniel and Kazuya met in 2001 and they have been hiking, mountain climbing and doing photography together since that time and generally enjoying life being together.

Photo Credits:

Daniel's Photos:

Pages 1 all, 2, 3, 4 all, 5 all, 6 bottom, 7, 8, 9, 10 all, 11, 12, 13, 14, 15, 16, 17 both, 18, 19 all, 20 all, 22 all, 23 all, 25 all, 26, 28 center & bottom, 29 all, 30 all, 31, 32, 33, 35, 36, 37, 38, 40 all, 41 top, 43, 44, 45, 46, 47, 48, 49, 50 all, 51, 52, 53 some smaller photos, 54, 56 bottom, 57 some, 58, 59 bottom, 60, 61 all, 62 all, 63, 64, 65, 66 all, 67 all, 68, 69 all, 70 all, 71, 72, 73, 75, 76, 77, 78 all, 79, 80, 81, 82 top, 88 all, 89, 90 all, 91 all, 92 top, 95 all, 96 all, 97 all, 99, 100 all, 101 all, 102, 103, 104, 105, 106, 107 bottom, 108 all, 109, 110 all, 112 all, 113 all, 114 bottom, 115 some, 116 some, 118 some, 122, 123, 124 top, 127 top, 128, 129, 132 all, 133 all, 136, 137 all, 138 all, 139 top, 140 all, 141, 142, 143, 144, 145, 146, 147, 148, 149 top & bottom, 158, 159 all, 160, 161 all, 162, 163, 164 all, 165 all, 166, 167 all, 168, 169 all, 170, 171, 172 bottom, 173 top, 174 all, 175 left, 178, 179, 181 top, 182, 183, 184 bottom, 185, 186, 187, 188, 189, 190 all, 191 left, 192, 193, 194, 195, 198, 199, 200, 201, 202, 203, 204 all, 206, 207 all, 208, 209, 212 all, 213, 214, 215, 216, 217, 219 all, 220 all, 222, 223, 224, 225, 226, 227, 229, 230, 231 all, 232, 233, 234, 235, 236, 237, 238 all, 239, 240, 241, 242, 243, 244, 245 all, 246, 247, 248, 249 all, 250, 251, 252 all, 253, 254, 255, 256, 257 all, 258, 259, 260, 261, 262, 263, 264, 265, 266, 267, 268 all, 269, 272, 275, 276, 277, 278, 279 all, 281, 282 all, 283, 284, 285 all, 286, 287, 288, 289, 290 all, 292 top, 292 bottom left, 293, 294, 295, 296 all, 297, 298 all, 300 all, 301, 302, 303, 304, 305, 306, 307, 308 all, 310, 311, 312, 313, 314, 315, 317, 318, 319, 320, 321, 322, 323, 324 all, 325 all, 326 all, 327, 328 bottom, 329, 330 all, 331, 332 top, 335 all, 336, 337, 338.

Kazuya's Photos:

Pages 6 top, 21 all, 24, 27 all, 28 top, 34, 39, 41 bottom, 42 all, 53 main photo and some smaller photos, 55, 56 top, 57 some, 59 top, 74, 82 bottom, 83, 84, 85 all, 86, 87 all, 92 bottom, 93, 94, 107 top, 111 all, 114 top, 115 some, 116 some, 117 all, 118 some, 119 all, 120, 121 all, 124 bottom, 125, 126, 127 bottom, 130 all, 131 all, 134, 135, 139 bottom, 149 small inset, 150 all, 151 all, 152 all, 153 all, 154 all, 155 all, 156 all, 172 top, 175 right, 176, 177 all, 180, 181 bottom, 184 top, 191 right, 196 all, 197, 205, 211, 218, 221, 270, 271, 273, 274, 280 all, 291, 292 bottom right, 299, 309, 316, 328 top, 332 bottom, 333, 334.

Unknown:

Pages 173 bottom, 210 all, 341 all.

CPSIA information can be obtained
at www.ICGtesting.com
Printed in the USA
LVHW072339030323
740866LV00013B/1117

9780996216104